THE
ENCYCLOPEDIA OF
WINES

THE
ENCYCLOPEDIA OF
WINES

Descriptions of well known and the less known
Wines from around the world

CHRISTIAN CALLEC

REBO
PRODUCTIONS

© 1999 Rebo International bv Lisse, The Netherlands
www.rebo-publishers.com - info@rebo-publishers.com

2000 published by Rebo International b.v.,
Lisse, The Netherlands

Text and photographs: Christian Callec
Translations: Stephen Challacombe
Editing, production, and coordination: TextCase,
Groningen, The Netherlands
Design and layout: Signia Winschoten, The Netherlands
Cover design: Minkowsky Graphics, Enkhuizen,
The Netherlands
Typesetting: de ZrIJ, Maarsen, The Netherlands
B0365R&B

ISBN 1 84053 119 3

All rights reserved.
No part of this publication may be reproduced by means
of printing, photocopies, automated data files, or any
other means without prior permission in writing from the
publisher.

Contents

Introduction

This encyclopedia results from a truly exciting journey of discovery through more than a thousand of the word's wines. It was a wonderful journey through scores of different wine-growing countries and their cultures.

So much has been written already about wines, so why another encyclopedia? Because the world of wines is changing so rapidly with new countries, new growing areas, and new wines joining the list each year. The market too is changing. In the early 1990's the consumer started to realise that wine is also made in Greece, Bulgaria, Hungary, Rumania, the former Yugoslavia, and the 'New World' countries of California, Chile, Argentina, and Australia in addition to France, Italy, Germany, Spain, and Portugal,.

The current problem is that wine growers have intensively cultivated their land so long that most vines do not root so deeply and are dependant on fertilizer. Some argue for lower output per hectare, for reduction of fertilisation and agrochemicals, and more emphasis on the soil and less on the vine itself. The debate continues and the world of wine is in a constant state of flux.

The best known varieties of grape

Red grapes

CABERNET SAUVIGNON

This grape variety was originally used to produce French Médoc, Graves, and Bordeaux. Today Cabernet Sauvignon is grown in almost every growing region, such as California, Chile, and Australia.

Cabernet Sauvignon delivers wines that are full of tannin and flavour, with distinctive aromas (or nose), that are suitable for long storage in oak barrels. The nose and flavour suggest blackcurrant, violet, cedarwood, and tobacco.

MERLOT

Merlot is known from its association with the Bordeaux wines of St Emilion and Pomerol. Merlot is also grown and used in wine making in various

Left: Alsace: six white grapes and one red one.

Cabernet and Merlot vineyards, Montravel.

Balkan countries, Italy, Chile, California, and Australia.

Merlot is softer, somewhat more rounded in flavour, and above all lower in tannin than Cabernet Sauvignon. For this reason both grapes are often used to supplement each other's qualities. The nose and flavour of a good Merlot conjures up red fruits such as cherry, but sometimes redcurrant.

CABERNET FRANC

Cabernet Franc is often used to blend with the two types of grape previously mentioned but the purest Cabernet Franc wines come from the Loire. Wines from Bourgueil, Chinon, and Saumur-Champigny are often of surprisingly high quality. The wine produced with this grape is often softer and lower in tannin than Cabernet Sauvignon but much fuller than Merlot. Cabernet Franc is particularly distinguished by its fruitiness, with echoes of strawberry, blackcurrant, and aroma of freshly sliced green pepper (paprika).

PINOT NOIR

Pinot Noir above all is the red grape of Burgundy. It is also used to make red Sancerre and Pinot Noir

Pinot Noir, Burgundy.

wines of Alsace. This grape also produces excellent wines in Italy, the Balkans, Hungary, South America, California, and Oregon. Wine from the Pinot Noir grape is generally rather more elegant and generous than it is heavy. It is characterised by earthy undertones, somewhere between stable air and manure. After the initial shock. a second fruity taste is discovered, principally of redcurrant, wild strawberry, and sometimes of cherry.

SYRAH (SHIRAZ)
This is the only grape permitted for the northern Rhône wines (Hermitage, Crozes-Hermitage, St Joseph, Côte Rôtie, Cornas). Syrah largely has characteristics similar to those of southern Rhône growing areas (Chateauneuf de Pape, Gigondas). Syrah grapes (or Shiraz as they are also known) are currently grown in South Africa, Australia, and the USA. Syrah is deeply coloured and fat. The wine is full and strongly flavoured often requiring some maturing in the bottle in certain years. A good Syrah is often easily recognised by its spicy and peppery nose and flavour of sun ripened fruit with almost

Syrah or Shiraz, Hermitage (Rhône).

animal undertones that recall the smell of a hot saddle after a long ride on a horse.

GAMAY
Gamay is world famous through Beaujolais but wines are also widely made with the Gamay grape along the Loire, and in Touraine.

Above all, a Gamay wine should be fruity. Raspberry, wild strawberry, currant, and cherry can be discerned. Floral notes are also detected in the better Beaujolais crus. The more simple the wine, the lighter and brighter, the better the quality, the fuller and more generous it is.

GRENACHE
Grenache grapes are principally known in France (Rhône, Tavelrosé, Languedoc, Roussillon) and Spain (Rioja and above all Navarra). The grape is also occasionally encountered from California. Grenache is mainly substantial and very alcoholic, but is also fruity and supple. The wine is mainly recognised by a combination of peppers, herbs, and fruit.

TEMPRANILLO
Tempranillo is the grape used in the better Rioja wines from Navarra and Riberia del Duero. As the Spanish name suggests, this grape ripens quickly. Although these grapes are often blended with others, Tempranillo on its own can provide surprising results, such as the wines from Navarra. Young Tempranillo wines that are not aged in the cask are light and fruity (strawberry, plum), and soon drinkable.

Matured in oak casks for a period, the wine develops a typical herbal taste with undertones of vanilla and tobacco and hints of prunes or Grandmother's jam.

SANGIOVESE
Sangiovese is the key to the best Tuscan wines, such as Chianti, Vino Nobile di Montepulciano, and Brunello di Montalcino. Good wines from Sangiovese grapes are full of tannin, fat, and fairly full flavoured. The wine often smells and tastes of blackberry, cherry, or plum with hints of herbs and spices. Vanilla and tobacco can also be discerned in good wines.

NEBBIOLO
One of the world's best grapes. Nebbiolo is best known in northern Italy where these grapes are used to produce Barolo, Barbaresco, and Gattinara. These wines are always high in tannin and almost opaque in colour.
The wine definitely needs to mature for some years before it is ready to drink. Good Nebbiolo wines have the nose and taste of laurel or liquorice, stewed plums, truffles, humus, toadstools, and sometimes cocoa or tar.

ZINFANDEL
This variety of grape was taken to USA long ago, probably by an Hungarian immigrant. Zinfandel is produced in California but the number of Zinfandel fans is also growing in Europe. In addition to pleasant rosés (dry or medium sweet) Zinfandel can also produce fat, herbal red wines. Both kinds smell and taste of ripe fruits, such as blackberry, bilberry, and blackcurrant, with herbal undertones and the bite of peppers.

White grapes

SAUVIGNON BLANC
This is the extremely well-known grape that provides top wines in the regions of Bordeaux, the Bergerac, and the Loire. The wines from this grape are known as Blanc Fumé, whilst in America and Mexico they are known as Fumé Blanc. In any event these wines still bear the Sauvignon name on their labels. Good Sauvignon Blanc is available these days almost throughout the world.
The scent and taste characteristics of Sauvignon are dependent on where the grape is harvested. The wines are always fresh, lively, very perfumed and

fruity. Sauvignon's from Bordeaux or Bergerac often have the nose and taste of green (Granny Smith) apples, newly mown grass, or even box, or basil. In professional circles these last two characteristics are irreverently referred to as 'cat's piss'.

With Sancerre and Pouilly Fumé in the Loire region, the taste and scent of green asparagus is also noted, and sometimes fennel or aniseed and a hint of liquorice can be distinguished. The most expressive Sauvignon's originate from New Zealand which treat you to an explosion of tropical fruit, grapefruit, and gooseberry. Sauvignon tastes best when young.

CHARDONNAY

The best known wines of Burgundy and Champagne are produced with the Chardonnay grape which now grows almost everywhere, both because of the quality of the wines but also because they sell well.

Chardonnay is often fresh and pleasant when not aged in oak casks. When matured in such a manner, Chardonnay changes into a fat, creamy wine with characteristic scent and flavour, that mainly evokes thoughts of freshly toasted bread, thickly spread with butter.

Some winemakers do not have the necessary skill to strike the balance between oak and fruit and produce wines in which a sticky, almost sickly vanilla taste of American oak predominates. This is a shame because a well made Chardonnay should have a hearty nose in which exotic fruit, peach, melon, pineapple, and citrus fruit can be distinguished.

The taste and perfume of aged white Burgundies contain hints of nuts, predominantly hazelnuts or walnuts.

SEMILLON

A pure Semillon is surely not to be scorned but the problem is that the grape contains little acid so that other grapes are generally added. In Europe this is generally Sauvignon (Bordeaux and Bergerac) but the white Semillon grape is often blended with Chardonnay in Australia to make a more lush wine, especially if the grapes are affected by the beneficial fungus *Botrytis cinerea*, which shrivels the grapes. This concentrates the perfume, flavour, and sugars. Typical example of wines that benefit from the so-called 'noble rot' are Sauternes, Barsac, Monbazillac, and Saussignac.

A Semillon can be distinguished by its nose and taste of juicy fruit such as peach, apricot, or mango with definite undertones of honey and occasional hint of hot butter.

CHENIN BLANC (PINEAU DE LOIRE)

Chenin Blanc's renown is based on the superb Loire wines of Vouvray, Saumur, Anjou, Bonnezeaux, Châteaux du Layon, and Quart de Chaumes. In South Africa the grape is also known under the name of Steen.

Chenin Blanc has a fresh acidic taste which is not only valued in dry and sparkling wines. Especially in sweet wines the fine acidity provides additional body and balance and extends the wine's life. A Châteaux du Layon of the best vintages can be kept for more than 30 years. Sweet Loire wines need to be laid down for at least ten years before they are at their best. Then you will be treated to a cocktail of honey, peach, apricot, fragrant flowers, hazelnuts, and much more, depending on the soil in which the vine is grown.

Tempranillo, Navarra.

Pinot Blanc or Auxerrois (French Toul).

RIESLING

Enthusiasts of Riesling wines believe the grapes to be among the finest there are. These vines originate from Germany and Alsace but Riesling is now cultivated throughout the world.

Most Riesling wines are fresh and fruity, stirring memories of flowers and herbs. Matured Rieslings develop a very characteristic scent best compared with the smell of old-fashioned paraffin heaters. Young Riesling exhibits hints of fresh apples, citrus fruits, and some times of passion fruit. The scent and taste of older wines tend towards honey and full blown blooms. Riesling is often grown on volcanic or mineral soils in Germany which can be detected in well-made wines.

GEWÜRZTRAMINER

These grapes, renowned in association with Alsace, are known as Traminer in Germany and Italy. Wines from these grapes can be either dry or sweet. There are two types of Gewürztraminer in Alsace: lighter, fairly dry, to drink young, and a more full bodied, heavier type that usually has sugar residues. There are also honey sweet wines from late harvested grapes, sometimes individually selected by hand. This is dealt with more fully when we describe the wines of Alsace.

Some say that Gewürztraminer wines are strongly spicy. Personally, I have not found this to be the case, rather a fat, full, enormously concentrated wine with an overemphatic perfume and taste that readily conjures flowers and overripe fruit. Some wines also have an inexplicable hint of the skins of Muscat grapes.

MUSCAT

One grape that is surely instantly recognisable is Muscat. A well-made Muscat wine both smells and taste of freshly-picked Muscat grapes, and is slightly exotic with floral notes. Muscat wines can be dry (Alsace, Tunisia, Samos, Navarra), sweet (Italy), to very sweet (Navarra, Samos, Beaumes de Venise, Frontignan, Australia). They are always sensual wines with considerable charm.

PINOT BLANC

Well-known from Alsace but also grown in Italy and the Balkans. Pinot Blanc wines from Alsace and Italy are fairly neutral, pleasant, and with little acidity.

Pinot Blanc vines in Slovenia (known as Beli Pino) can produce wines of exceptional style. In the area around Ormoz the grapes are sometimes harvested very late. This imbues the wine with tremendous complexity and the potential to be laid down for some time.

SYLVANER (SILVANER)

These grapes are known as Silvaner in Germany and are best known from vineyards in Germany and Alsace where light and elegant wines are produced with them that have a recognisable but light floral bouquet with a hint of herbs.

VIOGNIER

Who had heard of the Viognier grape 20 years ago? Only enthusiasts for the older wines made around the town of Condrieu and the French Rhône region knew of Viognier. After some young growers blew new life into this almost lost and legendary wine the world was convinced of the grape's quality and new Viognier vines were planted in other places. Result from these in the Languedoc-Roussillon, Ardèche, Australia, the USA, and even Canada are very good. Well-made Viognier is unbelievably rich in the smell and taste of juicy peach and apricot, coupled with a soft delicate bouquet of wild flowers and honey.

MACCABEO/VIURA

These grapes are known as Viura in Rioja and Navarra but elsewhere in Spain and in Catalan parts of France they are known as Maccabeo. Viura generally produces a very vulnerable, light, fresh and fruit wine that does not age well. Although some wholly Viura wines are of reasonable quality, connoisseurs – especially those in Navarra – prefer a blend of about two-thirds Viura to one third Chardonnay. This provides the wine with more of a backbone and makes it rounder.

This list of grapes grown for wine making is not comprehensive. There are countless other varieties that can be encountered on a tour around the world.

Europe

France

For centuries France has been regarded as the leading wine country. It was almost universally considered that only French wines were good. This was unjust because countries such as Italy, Spain, Germany, Hungary, and Greece have long made wine of top quality but the French managed to persuade the world that their wines had something special, that bit of extra quality.

The French have certainly long been lovers of wine, from the red plonk for daily drinking of the vin ordinaire to the great wines from Bordeaux and Burgundy. Life without wine is unthinkable to most of the French. Daily enjoyment of wine, with family or friends, or with a meal, is an essential pause in French life. Wine is the soul of the French and despite countless invasions, the French always managed to save that soul.

The French love their wine.

Some wines come from a single vineyard.

Ideal climate and geology

That France continues to be the best known wine producing country of the world is probably due to the conditions for cultivating vines in its vineyards.

Nowhere else in the world has such ideal circumstances for cultivating grapes as France. Winters are not too severe nor are summers too dry, there is ample rain, and plenty of sun. The tremendous variety of soil types also plays its part in centuries of successful viticulture in France: thick layers of chalk in Champagne, sedimentary layers with lots of shells in the Auxerrois (Chablis), marl, clay, pebbles and gravel in Médoc, blue and grey shale in Muscadet, tufa in Anjou and Saumur, slate slopes in Collioure and Banyuls, warm boulders in southern Rhône.

Furthermore there is sufficient water throughout France, indirectly from the sea or directly from the many rivers and underground reserves.

Chalk creates Champagne's success.

11

The various categories

Vin de table

Basically Vins de table are fairly simple wines for daily consumption with a consistent taste that is usually achieved through blending. Some specific wines are also included in this category. The world famous firm of Chapoutier of Tain-l'Hermitage in the Rhône valley for example offered Les Coufis vin de table from Ardèche that was made with 100 per cent Viognier overripe grapes that were harvested by hand. The superb dessert wine with 14 per cent alcohol was the most expensive table wine of France. The price was far higher than known AOC wines from the region and its quality was superb but it did not live up to expectations in terms of commercial success.

Table wine: Vin de table.

Vins de Pays

The growth in Vin de Pays wines is enormous at the present time and this is not surprising because of the great improvements in quality of this better table wine in recent years.

A Vin de Pays originates from a strictly defined wine-growing area, representing the soul of a specific terroir (growing territory) and is linked to the special characteristics of one or more varieties

Country wine: Vin de pays.

of grapes. Consumers find these wines approachable with clear language on the label.

Some Vins de Pays wines are so well made and demonstrate such love on the part of the wine maker that they outperform characterless AOC wines of anonymous wine merchants in both quality and price. Today's wine drinkers demand quality for their money.

Appellation – Vins Delimité de Qualité Supérieure (VDQS)

The quality of these wines is certainly not lower than AOC wines. The criteria for selection are indeed often more rigid than for most AOC wines. VDQS wines are the only ones which have to be tested annually in order to retain their category.

A VDQS wine is always therefore approved by a panel of experts before the predicate is awarded. For this reason you can rely totally on this category.

Appellation d'Origine Contrôlée (AC)

Wine classed as AOC (usually referred to as AC) originates from a clearly defined area in which the soil, climate, variety of grapes, and various legally-defined requirements (minimum alcohol percentage, maximum yield per hectare, pruning methods,

VDQS wines.

AC (Appellation Contrôlée) wines.

production, and vinification conditions etc.) provide a guarantee that the wine originates from a given place.

This is not, however, a guarantee of quality since these wines are not tested each year and some of them do not deserve a quality predicate. Despite this, AOC wines form the top category of French wines.

Additional information on the label

Here we mean additions such as 'Premiere Cru', or 'Grand Cru' for Bordeaux wines, not such meaningless phrases as 'Vin Supérieure de la cave du patron' or 'Cuvée reservé du sommelier'.
The better Bordeaux were classified in 1855 for a World Exhibition, based on quality criteria of the time (if well known, prices achieved etc.). At that time it related solely to wines of Médoc, Sauternes, and one wine from Graves. This latter category received its own Cru in 1959. Other areas which have a similar Premier and Grand Cru classification include St Emilion (since 1955, reviewed every 10 years, most recently in 1996), and Côtes de Provence (since 1955). Since 1932 the term 'Cru bourgeois' has also been used in Médoc.

In Burgundy terms such as 'Premier Cru' and 'Grand Cru' are part of the official name of origin. These will be dealt with in the appropriate sections on the wine areas.

We start our tour in Champagne.

Champagne: white wine without equal.

Champagne: the secret of a sparkling life

Champagne, the outstanding symbol of festivity, may only be produced in the Champagne region of France. No other wine from wherever else it is made, inside France or elsewhere, may not use the prestigious name of Champagne. Champagne is an unparalleled wine.

The area

The historic heart of Champagne is Reims, about 150 km (93 miles) north-east of Paris. The geographical centre of the Champagne region is at Epernay, slightly south of Reims. Champagne is subdivided into four large areas: the Montagne de Reims (slopes to the south of Reims), the Vallée de la Marne (the Marne valley from Château-Thierry to Châlons-sur-Marne), the Côte des Blancs (hill ridge south of Epernay), and finally the Côte de Bar in the department of Aube, between Bar-sur-Seine and Bar-sur-Aube.

Each of these areas has its own geographic identity resulting from countless variations in position, sun-hours, contour, soil, and finally the different vines. This makes each area unique with its own character and potential.

There are more than 300 different terroirs, here referred to as crus, each equally unique and the subject of countless village interpretations.

We start our tour of France in Champagne. A better place to start can hardly be imagined. From Champagne we tour the French vineyards in a clockwise direction. We will visit the north-east, then Alsace, the Jura, Burgundy, Rhône, Savoie, Provence, Languedoc-Roussillon, the south-west: Bordeaux, the Auvergne, and finally conclude our journey in valley of the Loire.

Undulating hills of chalk.

The soil

The chalk of the gently-sloping hills is covered with a thin layer of loam. The vines send their roots really deep into the chalk rock (sometimes up to 5 metres/ 16 feet deep) in order to derive the required nutrients and water. In addition to their role in regulating water supply, the chalk rocks also help to regulate temperature.

The grapes

Only three varieties of grape are permitted. These three, together with the soil, give Champagne its specific character. Pinot Noir provides the backbone and fullness, Chardonnay is responsible for the elegant acidity and refined taste, and Pinot Meunier imparts the wine with a fresh and lively character.

The various types of Champagne examined

Some labels bear predicates such as 'Grand Cru' or 'Premier Cru'. These descriptions are in no way a guarantee of quality of the Champagne. They merely relate to the quality of the grapes used in the making of the wine.

The best communes of Champagne, from which in theory the best grapes should come are given a quality rating of 100%. The growers will therefore receive the full price established for grapes grown within the specific communes and these communes may bear the predicate Grand Cru. The slightly lower quality Premier Cru communes receive between 99 and 90% of the price set. All other communes can only be paid a maximum of 89% of the price. However, a modest winemaker will only make modest Champagne whatever quality of grapes are used.

EXTRA BRUT/BRUT SAUVAGE/ULTRA BRUT
This wine is very very dry. After dégorgement, extra brut is solely topped up with the same wine and therefore contains virtually no residual sugar (max. 0.6% by volume). Few people appreciate Champagne as dry as chalk.

BRUT (NON VINTAGE)
This is the most widely drunk type of Champagne: dry but not too dry. This main product of the Champagne houses contains a maximum of 1.5% by volume of residual sugar . Brut is made from a blend of the three classic grapes: Chardonnay, Pinot Noir, and Pinot Meunier. As a rule they come from different parts of Champagne and from different years.

A young brut is fresh and boisterous, its colour pale yellow, occasionally with a sparkle of pink. Depending on the blend, a young brut will smell of either white fruit (almond, green apple) or red fruit (grape, raspberry), with the suggestion of hot white

Non vintage Brut Champagne.

Vintage Brut Champagne (millésimé).

bread. It is a perfect aperitif but can also be served with most light starters.

A mature brut (older than three years) will be less fresh but fuller and more herbal in taste. The colour tends towards darker yellow with hints of orange and the smell is reminiscent of ripe apple, dried fruit, spices, and sometimes of black cherry or blackcurrant (lots of Pinot Noir). In terms of both nose and taste it has something of French croissants or brioche. The wine is ideal with fish and poultry. A fully aged brut (older than five years) is less rumbustious in terms of carbon dioxide bubbles but will have acquired a full, complex, and very rich, almost creamy taste. The colour is dark yellow with hints of brown. The smell is reminiscent of roasted nuts and dried fruit with occasional suggestions of the tertiary aromas of coffee and sometimes even of old leather. This wine can be drunk on any occasion.

VINTAGE BRUT (MILLÉSIMÉ)
This brut has the same characteristics as ordinary brut but is only made in years when a vintage is declared.

BRUTS BLANCS DE BLANCS
Champagne Blanc de Blancs is made exclusively from the Chardonnay grape and is hence a white wine from white grapes. It may be either vintage or non vintage. This is normally a fresh, fruity wine with lots of fine acidity.
The colour is pale yellow with a green haze when young, turning increasingly yellow to golden as it ages. A young brut Blancs de Blancs has tempting aromas of citrus fruits, fresh mint, wild flowers, and an also shameless freshness. A mature brut Blancs de

Cuvée Brut Blanc de Blancs Millésimé.

Blancs tends more towards a freshly-picked posy of wild flowers, ripe fruit, and a hint of lime blossom. Although still very fresh, this wine is more rounded and full-bodied than when young. The taste is fuller and more balanced.

A fully-aged brut Blancs de Blancs is a bowl filled with exotic fruits, with suggestions of freshly-ground pepper and spices.

BRUT BLANCS DE NOIRS
This Champagne is extremely rare. This is a robust and very tasty white wine, produced from the blue-black Pinot Noir and Pinot Meunier grapes.

EXTRA DRY/EXTRA SEC
Normally only found on labels intended for the American or British markets. Perhaps the motto is: 'Call them dry but make them sweet' for these Champagnes contain 1.2–2% residual sugar .

SEC
Rather confusing with the same comment as above. This wine is not truly dry and contains between 1.7 and 3.5% residual sugar .

DEMI-SEC
This wine is delightful, slightly sweet, and has 3.3–5% residual sugar .

DOUX
This is the sweetest of all with a minimum of 5% residual sugar.

PINK (ROSÉ)
Pink Champagne of Champagne Rosé is made using still red wine (Cumières, Bouzy) of Champagne, which are added to the Cuvée. Pink Champagne is sold as straight-forward brut, vintage brut, and brut demi-sec.
The colour varies from pale pink, through salmon pink, to even raspberry and cherry red. Pink Champagne truly seduces and is a superb aperitif. Served at table, pink Champagne best accompanies meat dishes and poultry.

Non vintage pink Champagne.

Special cuvée pink Champagne Millésimé.

Other wines from Champagne

In addition to sparkling wines, Champagne also produces a number of still wines.

CÔTEAUX CHAMPENOIS
This wine has been classified AOC since 1974. It is available as white, red, and rosé. These are exceptionally rare wines, remnants of the past. The best known red wine bears the name of its commune or village, Bouzy, Cumières, or Ambonnay. Côteaux Champenois wines are best drunk when young. The red wine is served chilled to (approx. 10°C/50°F).

Côteaux Champenois.   *Rosé des Riceys.*

ROSÉ DES RICEYS
This is extremely rare and undoubtedly one of the best French rosés. The simple Rosé des Riceys is drunk young and chilled. When aged in oak the wine can be kept longer (more than 10 years) and is then served slightly less chilled (10–12°C/50–53.6°F).

The north-east's forgotten vineyards

Lorraine was once a flourishing wine-growing area. In the late nineteenth century the vineyards covered at least 30,000 hectares and the French Moselle wines enjoyed great fame in France and much further afield. The phylloxera disease combined with the economic instability which followed and the destruction of World War I put an end to the aspirations of the local growers. Replanting and re-establishment only started under a new generation of growers after World War II. Their efforts were finally rewarded in 1951 when the government officially recognized the vineyards around Toul and the Moselle.

VINS DE MOSELLE
Small vineyards line the gentle slopes of the valley of the Moselle (upper reaches of the river known in Luxembourg and Germany as the Mosel) on soil enriched by sediments. A total of 19 villages are permitted to produce Moselle wines but most of the

activity is centred on Metz. The volume is small, not least because of the scattered nature of the vineyards.

The wines produced are predominantly fresh tasty, fruity white wines of great finesse made from Pinot Blanc or Auxerrois grapes. The even rarer wines made from the Pinot Gris is of outstanding quality and available for a very reasonable price. The local red wine, made with Pinot Noir and Gamay, is fruity and pleasant but without the finesse of the white wine.

CÔTES DE TOUL

The area of Côtes de Toul is slightly further south than the district from which the Moselle wines originate, to the west of the town of Toul and the banks of a sweeping bend in the Moselle. The vineyards are spread between eight communes on sedimentary deposits, clay, and broken chalk. The good drainage, ideal position for the sun, and mild climate, make this wine area one of the most interesting in France.

Almost the entire production, that is too small for large-scale exports, is drunk locally at home or in the many restaurants of Lorraine. Toul's speciality is undoubtedly the pale, fresh, elegant, rounded, and delightful rosé, Gris de Toul, made with Gamay. In addition to the exceptional rosé, a fresh, pleasant and elegant white wine is made from Auxerrois grapes and a delicious, idiosyncratic red wine made from Pinot Noir. These wines too are available in limited volume.

Côtes de Toul.

Alsace

Although Alsace is fairly northerly in its situation, it

The rolling hills of Alsace.

Alsatian village.

has an exceptionally favourable climate. The Vosges mountains shield the area from the westerly winds and rain. Consequently Colmar has the same level of rain as Perpignan in the furthest south. The summers are hot but the winters are not severely cold. Spring is gentle and moist while the autumn is often warm and dry. Because most vineyards have southerly aspects, conditions are right for high quality wine making.

The seven Alsace grapes

With most French wines the area from which they originate is the most important information on the label. All wines in Alsace are Alsace AOC but they are identified by their grapes. A wine may be ordered in France as a Riesling, Sylvaner, Gewürtztraminer, Pinot Blanc, Pinot Noir, or Pinot Gris/ Tokay but everyone knows immediately that these are Alsace wines.

Only the local place name is indicated on the labels of Muscat wines because there are different types of Muscat wine in France (such as the sweet wines of the south). No other area in France follows this practice.

SYLVANER

Wine from the Sylvaner grape is pleasant, light, fresh, and thirst-quenching.

PINOT BLANC

This is the most widely cultivated grape variety in Alsace. Wine from these grapes is fresh, supple, and usually has no strong taste so that it can be drunk with anything. An offshoot of the Pinot Blanc family is the Auxerrois grape and wines from these are sometimes sold under their own name. The earlier local name for Pinot Blanc of Clevner or Klevner may also be encountered.

Pinot Blanc.

MUSCAT D'ALSACE

Muscat is immediately recognisable by its sensual, heady aroma of Muscat grapes. Muscat is always made as a dry wine in Alsace unlike the southern Muscats. No other wine retains the smell and taste of the fresh grapes like Muscat.

RIESLING

The Riesling is regarded as a noble grape throughout the world. Riesling achieves outstanding quality in Alsace.

The wine is elegant, fresh, and delicate. Depending on the soil it yields hints of fruit, flowers, or even minerals. Better Riesling wines have both a great deal of character and refinement at the same time. It is an ideal wine to serve with meals.

GEWÜRZTRAMINER

Gewürztraminer and Alsace are inextricably associated with each other. Wine from the Gewürztraminer grape has a great deal of character, a full colour, intense and almost exotic perfume of tropical fruits (lychee, grapefruit), native fruit (quince), flowers (acacia, roses), or spices (cinnamon, pepper, clove), and a generous, rounded finish.

PINOT GRIS/TOKAY D'ALSACE

The Pinot Gris of Alsace is worthy of praise. The wine is dark in colour and is possessed of an extremely expressive aroma, in which spices predominate. The taste is like the smell, strong, full and intensely complex.

PINOT NOIR

There is only the one type of red grape but three different types of Pinot Noir wines. First in line are generous, fresh, and friendly rosés. Higher up the scale come next the pale red Pinot Noir wines which most resemble a simple Burgundy. These characteristically have the smell and taste of red fruit (cherry).

Finally, there are the best Pinot Noirs, of which the juice is continuously drained during vinification from the fermentation vats or barrels and poured

Tokay Pinot Gris.   *Pinot Noir.*

again over the grape skins.. This imparts deeper colour, intensifies the flavour, and makes a more full-bodied wine. These Pinot Noirs 'vinifiés en rouge' are usually aged in large oak casks. The best wines come from the oldest vineyards are identified by 'cuvée vielles vignes' on the label.

OTHER GRAPE VARIETIES

In addition to the well-known grapes already mentioned, there are two others that need a mention.

One is Chardonnay, grown in Alsace but reserved solely for sparkling wine, the second is Klevener, an old variety of Alsace grape, better known as Traminer or Savagnin in the neighbouring Jura. These grapes were once widely used but are being replaced by the more aromatic Gewürztraminer. Klevener is fine to drink at table.

French Jura

The area

The department of Jura lies in eastern France, in Franche-Comté between the Burgundian Côte d'Or and Switzerland. This small strip of vineyards in the Jura known as the 'Bon Pays' (the Good Land) or 'Revermont' (hill ridge), stretches for about 100 kilometres (62 miles) in a gentle north-south arc at a height of 250–480 metres (820–1,574 feet) on marl with broken chalk in places. The climate is semi-continental with characteristically hard winters and early, gentle springs, very hot summers, and warm autumns. These are ideal growing conditions for vineyards.

The five grape varieties

Only five varieties of grape are permitted for the production of AOC (guarantee of origin) wines. Chardonnay, imported in the fourteenth century from neighbouring Burgundy, represents about 45% of the vines planted. This is an easily cultivated grape that usually ripens fully without difficulty

Riesling.   *Gewürztraminer.*

Centuries old wine cellars in Arbois.

around mid-September, containing plenty of sugars and therefore potentially a high level of alcohol, that produces very floral, fruity, and generous wines.

The Savagnin (15% of the total) is highly regarded locally. This is a native vine and this local variant of the Traminer produces the finest wines to come from the Jura, the famous vins jaunes. This late-ripening grape is often harvested as late as the end of October.

They makes lots of Savagnin wines here.

The Pinot Noir was also brought from Burgundy, but in the fifteenth century. These grapes ripen quickly and are full of flavour but are virtually never used on their own but in combination with the Poulsard to impart more colour and body.

Trousseau (5%) is also a native variety which thrives well on warm sandy soil in the northern part of the Jura. This vine blossoms fairly late and produces very colourful and concentrated juice. Trousseau wines reach an unprecedented level of maturity after being laid down in a cool cellar for ten years. Unfortunately this wine is extremely rare and little known. If you get the chance to taste it you should certainly do so.

Finally, the Poulsard (20%), a native vine with grapes that impart a fine pale red colour to their wine that contains many fruity and unusual aromas. Poulsard is used to make light red wines but also for rosés such as the famous Pupillin Rosé.

The four regional appellations of origin of the Jura

CHÂTEAU-CHÂLON

The village of Château-Chalon dominates this wine region both literally and figuratively. It is 450 metres (1,476 feet) above sea-level, in the centre of the Jura, and gave birth to the king of all Jura wines, the vin jaune (yellow wine), which is exclusively made from Savagnin grapes.

Vins jaunes may be made throughout the Jura but the best originates from Château-Chalon. This wine is of the utmost highest quality and is not made every year. The preparation for making it in the village is the same as elsewhere for vins jaunes but the level of quality control is far higher.

Vins jaunes, including those of Château-Chalon are put in dumpy 62 cl clavelin bottles, since this is all that remains of a litre of young wine after maturing for six years and three months in a cask. The clavelins of Château-Chalon are the only ones to bear a decorative red seal around their necks.

Château-Châlon.

L'ETOILE

No-one knows precisely why this village got its name (etoile means star in French). It is probably due to the five encircling hills that together form the shape of a star, or the five beautiful castles in the neighbourhood.

Perhaps though the name is derived from shells and star fish remains found in the chalky soil of the vineyards. Very high quality and highly regarded white and sparkling wines are made from about 80 hectares in this village.

ARBOIS

The vineyards surrounding the pleasant small town of Arbois supply the greatest volume of wines from the Jura.

That these 800 hectares can produce exceptional quality wines with their own character is shown by the fact that wine from Arbois was the first in France to be permitted to bear an Appellation d'Origine Contrôlée.

The production is chiefly of white and red wine but some Pupillin rosé is also made.

Arbois red.

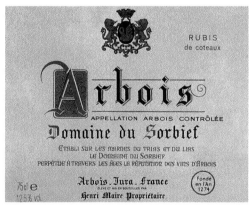

Arbois Pupillin rosé.

Arbois Chardonnay white.

CÔTES DU JURA

A colourful collection of white, red, rosé, and sparkling wines are covered by this appellation. It is astounding that so many different quality wines are made from such a small area.

The wholly Chardonnay white wine is pale yellow and smells of fresh grapes. After two to three years maturing in casks it develops its characteristic flinty smell. Wines made with Chardonnay and Savagnin have an even more clearly pronounced terroir scent and flavour. Those of just Savagnin are above all very delicate and aromatic.

The Poulsard rosé is elegant and subtle. Rosés from this area often have a coral-like colour and are exceptionally juicy and full bodied.

The red wine is quite peculiar. Made from Poulsard, it resembles a rosé but is actually a true red wine. The scent and flavour are reminiscent of mould and wild fruits of the forest.

By contrast, that made from Trousseau is warm, full of tannin, rounded, and full-bodied with the nose of red fruit. It is strongly alcoholic and be kept until quite old.

SPARKLING WINE FROM THE JURA

The Mousseux and Crémant originate mainly from l'Etoile and Vernois. These are available in brut, sec,

Jura Mousseux sparkling wine.

or demi-sec and in white or rosé. They are made by the traditional method with a second fermentation in the bottle.

Burgundy

Throughout Burgundy there are terroirs with chalk, marl, clay, stony ground, and iron in places. The hard winters and hot summers together with the soil ensure individual characters and personality.

The grapes here are Pinot Noir, Chardonnay, Aligoté, and Gamay. Near St-Bris in the Auxerrois they also grow a little Sauvignon Blanc. Burgundy is a complex patchwork of vineyards, referred to here as climat, villages, clos, and crus. There are also four Burgundy-wide appellations.

APPELLATIONS RÉGIONALES
Bourgogne, Bourgogne Aligoté (for white wine), Bourgogne Grand Ordinaire, and Bourgogne Passe-Tout-Grains can be used for the appropriate grapes from throughout the area. The better Burgundies come from specific localities (such as Côtes de Nuits, Côtes de Beaune).

THE 53 APPELLATIONS COMMUNALES
These wines bear the name of the parish or community such as Chablis, Nuits-St-Georges, Vosne-Romanée, or Vougeot).

THE 561 PREMIER CRU APPELLATIONS
In addition to the village or community appellation, these wines are permitted to identify the particular

Premier Cru Burgundy.

piece of land or climat. These climats are of sufficient quality that their wines may be termed premier cru. Examples of these are Chablis 1er Cru Montmains, Chambolle-Musigny Armoureuses, Puligny-Montrachet Folatières, Beaune Clos des Mouches, and Beaune Grèves.

THE 32 GRAND CRUS

These climats have became very famous by their constant quality over the centuries. It is sufficient for these wines just to bear the name of the climat. Examples are Chablis Grand Cru Vaudésir, Echezeaux, Charmes-Chambertin, Clos de Vougeot, Bonnes Mares, Romanée-St-Vivant, Corton, Montrachet.

The different wine areas

Burgundy is divided into nine different areas: Chablis, Auxerrois, Côtes de Nuits, Côtes de Beaune, Côtes Chalonnaise, Mâconnais, Beaujolais-Villages, Beaujolais, and Côteaux du Lyonnais. In reality the last three fall within Beaujolais, and Auxerrois is subsumed in Chablis.

Chablis

PETIT CHABLIS

This light, fruity and fresh tasting wine is drunk young.

CHABLIS

True Chablis can be laid down for maturing but is also very enjoyable in its first year. The wine is fully matured after three years. Chablis is a light golden colour with a green tinge and pronounced fruity and vegetal aromas of grapefruit, coriander, fern, privet, asparagus, and even artichoke. The taste is both literally and figuratively as dry as chalk, but also fruity, with the occasional mineral undertones and sometimes a hint of iodine.

CHABLIS PREMIER CRU

Chablis Premier Cru is at its best after three to five years. It does not contain the depths of the Grand Cru but can be drunk much earlier for those too impatient to wait.
A Premier Cru Chablis is golden with a definite tinge of green. The nose is fruity but above all vegetal : lemon balm, fern, and the suggestion of coriander. The taste is dry and reminiscent of chalk with a touch of iodine. Known Premier Crus are: Mont de

Chablis, Premier Cru and Grand Cru Vaudésir.

Milieu, Montée de Tonnere, Fourchaume, Séchet, Montmains, Vaillons.

CHABLIS GRAND CRU

These wines need to be laid down for at least five years after bottling and can certainly be left for twenty years. These are rare wines, very dry, with a good balance between strength and finesse. The colour is a very clean pale yellow with the minimum of green tinge.

Chablis Grand Cru Les Clos.

The nose tends towards fern and coriander with the occasional suggestion of preserved citrus fruit. The chalk soil is readily discovered in the flavour, with a pronounced undertone of iodine. The preserved citrus fruits put in a further appearance in the aftertaste. There are seven Grand Cru wines: Vaudésir, Les Preuses, Les Clos, Grenouilles, Bougros, Valmur, and Blanchots.

Auxerrois

SAUVIGNON DE ST-BRIS (VDQS)

This is a very fresh and fruity white wine.

IRANCY

This is a fruity red wine that can be high in tannin. There is also a rosé.

CRÉMANT DE BOURGOGNE

Most Crémant de Bourgogne wines are made with grapes from the Auxerrois. This is a very fresh, generous, and enjoyable wine.

Crémant de Bourgogne.

Côtes de Nuits

The Côtes de Nuits is world-famous for its red wines and home to a great assortment of terroirs and styles. The area starts in Marsannay and ends at Corgoloin. The soil is chalky with a lower layer of marl.

MARSANNAY

The red wine is somewhat heavy and rough when young but after several years ageing it becomes gentler, more rounded, and plump, with the aroma of red fruit, in particular cherry, blackcurrant, and redcurrant, with the occasional hint of prune, liquorice, cocoa, or coffee.

The best known wine is the Rosé de Marsannay. This wine is pale pink with some orange. The smell is fresh and pleasant while the taste is reminiscent of red fruit. The white wine is very fresh, full-bodied, and impetuous but more supple and rounded when mature. The wine is intensely coloured, has a characteristic Chardonnay scent with exotic fruit, such as pineapple and grapefruit, and a big taste.

FIXIN

Fixin is best known for its red wines. This is usually a fleshy, powerful wine with quite a lot of tannin when young which enables it to be kept. When young the wine is ruby red and has the nose of cherry, strawberry, and raspberry. When mature the scent is of plum or even leather.

GEVREY-CHAMBERTIN

The wine is an attractive ruby red that is pure and clear. The characteristic aromas are of black cherry, blackberry, and other small fruit, with an occasional hint of liquorice.

It acquires a bouquet of spices, including nutmeg, and leather through maturing in oak which takes on earthy tones, bushes, wet leaves, and toadstools when it has reached a respectable age. The wine is high in tannin but not so that it disturbs the taste, in part because of the fullness of the wine. The taste is very full and fruity. The wine can be kept for 10–20 years after its harvest. The Gevrey-Chambertin Premier Cru Les Cazetiers is highly recommended.

Gevrey-Chambertin.   *Gevrey-Chambertin Combottes.*

CHAMBERTIN GRAND CRU

This is one of the best wines from Burgundy but also one of the most difficult wines to make because of the vagaries of its microclimate. The colour is clear, pure, and intensely dark ruby red.

A young Chambertin smells of black cherry, and sometimes of bitter chocolate. Suggestions of the flavour of liquorice, truffle, and mould can be detected after several years maturation which after a further period of maturity has a tendency towards leather and animal scents, combined with the aromas of preserved fruits. The wine is strong in tannin but this harmonises well with the rounded, full, almost fat taste of the wine and its elegant, refined acidity. The taste is reminiscent of ripe fruit and tends towards black cherry jam with the suggestion of liquorice.

CHAMBERTIN CLOS-DE-BÈZE GRAND CRU

This wine has been famous since the seventh century. It is a superb, and intensely dark red in colour with the scent of raspberry, suggestions of wood, and spices, and occasionally of roasted almonds. The taste is full and powerful, fatty, and well structured. This is certainly a wine to lay down.

LATRICIÈRES-CHAMBERTIN GRAND CRU

This wine is slightly less well structured and full than a Chambertin Clos-de-Bèze. There can be a hint of spiced loaf in the scent with the occasional suggestion of marmalade. This is still though a very elegant wine.

CHAPELLE-CHAMBERTIN GRAND CRU

This wine is full-bodied, complex, and very well structured. Here too there are suggestions of spiced bread and orange. This is a superb wine which remains supple and velvety smooth despite its intrinsic power.

CHARMES-CHAMBERTIN GRAND CRU

This wine has a wonderful colour, seducing perfume of strawberry, black cherry, and raspberry, with the occasional hint of apricot stone, lime blossom, or liquorice. Wood can sometimes dominate too much, especially in the nose of immature wine.

The fruitiness is released when the wine is swirled around the glass for a time. The aftertaste is a true experience: preserved fruits such as cherry, exotic wood, herbs, and spices. This is a classic and complex wine that retains sufficient fruitiness to remain charming. This wine should certainly not be drunk too warm (max. 18°C/64.4°F).

Charmes-Chambertin.   *Griottes-Chambertin.*

GRIOTTE-CHAMBERTIN GRAND CRU

The aromas of Griotte-Chambertin are complex and unusually subtle. Hints of cherry brandy and preserved cherry have been discerned, with suggestions of leather and a pinch of nutmeg. When more mature there are also the aromas of truffle and animal scents. The French describe this smell as 'gamey' because it is reminiscent of well-hung game. Tannin is clearly apparent yet muted, which combined with a high level of alcohol by volume, ensure a velvet soft, almost caressing wine. The sensations of the nose are echoed in the taste although less pronounced and accompanied by the elegant hint of wood. A good Griotte-Chambertin has remarkable style, richness, and complexity.

MAZIS-CHAMBERTIN GRAND CRU

This rare wine from Chambertin is both powerful and supple, well structured, complex, yet elegant and subtle.

MAZOYÈRES-CHAMBERTIN

This is an elegant and charming red wine with average structure, not especially complex or powerful but certainly very fruity. It should not be kept too long.

MOREY-ST-DENIS

Although somewhat overlooked among the great character wines of Chambertin and the delicate seducers of Chambolle-Musigny, the wine of Morey-St-Denis is worthy of greater recognition. It possesses a very clear red colouring, fruity nose (morello cherry) with hints of wood, herbs, spices, fungus, and leather, and has a fulsome, soft as velvet, and very balanced taste. Furthermore this wine is

Morey-St- Denis.

Morey-St- Denis Clos Sorbé.

suitable for keeping for a long time. Specially recommended: the Premier Cru 'Les Ruchots'.

CLOS DE LA ROCHE GRAND CRU

The wine is a very dark ruby colour. The aroma recalls black cherry and sometimes a hint of animal scents such as musk. The suggestion of cedarwood cigar box is almost always present. It is a big but harmonious wine with plenty of tannin yet retains a velvety-soft texture. The wine continues to 'breathe' in the mouth for some time.

CLOS ST-DENIS GRAND CRU

This wine is a fine ruby colour with the suggestion of a tinge of granite. It has a surprising and complex nose in which blackcurrant, blackberry, prune, occasionally musk, herbs, spices, coffee, but also sometimes violets or other flowers can be discerned.

CLOS DES LAMBAYS GRAND CRU

This wine is somewhat modest and overlooked. It is a classic fruity Burgundy with suggestions of black cherry and hints of floral and animal aromas such as leather and musk. This is a full-bodied, rounded wine of some style.

CHAMBOLLE-MUSIGNY

This is a feminine, almost gentle wine of a pure ruby red with a nose filled with fruit (raspberry and cherry) when young, tending towards toadstools, humus, or game undertones when more mature. It is a elegant and refined wine.

The better wines originate from the Premier Cru climats, especially that of Les Amoureuses, a name and a wine to fall in love with. The colour tends

Chambolle Musigny.

Chambolle Musigny Les Amoureuses.

Bonnes Mares.

Musigny.

towards cherry red and the nose varies from raspberry to cherry brandy with hints of truffle, toadstool, or other fungus. Some years the wine has a more distinct animal scent, such as musk. This is a very seductive wine to which many lose their hearts and heads. Do not drink too warm (approx. 17°C/62.6°F).

BONNES MARES GRAND CRU

This is a classic, totally Burgundian Burgundy with a magnificent, very intense, and clear ruby-red colouring. The wine is very aromatic with black cherry, raspberry, tobacco, cherry wood and even truffle and musk when more mature. It is a very pleasing, full-bodied but soft wine with a powerful yet elegant texture. The taste lingers on the palate for some time.

MUSIGNY GRAND CRU

This is one of the pearls of Burgundy. The wine is a very pure ruby colour. When young it develops a nose of violets and cherry pips but after several years ageing in the bottle the bouquet becomes extremely rich and complex: humus, shrubs, autumn leaves, moss, many animal scents such as leather or even large game.

These powerful aromas are accompanied in the more mature wine with an amazingly soft and rounded texture that is velvety, fresh, and elegant. The flavour lingers on the palate. The finish is of cherry pips once more together with exotic wood.

VOUGEOT

Great wine is produced in this tiny village. Although almost exclusively red wine is made, the extremely rare Clos Blanc de Vougeot is well worth mentioning. The Premier Cru Vougeot is an elegant, fruity wine with a strong note of blackcurrant and occasional hint of violet and liquorice.

CLOS DE VOUGEOT GRAND CRU

At least 70 different owners share this vineyard of 50 hectares. The wines enjoy world-wide fame and are relatively expensive although it is questionable if this is appropriate. The vineyard was once symbolically encircled with a wall by Cistercian monks. The superb château of Clos Vougeot also helps this wine's reputation. The château is still the headquarters of the famous wine fraternity of Confrérie des Chevaliers du Tastevin.

Most Clos de Vougeot are of superb quality. The young wine is a superb bright ruby red which later becomes a warmer red with tendency to orange. The aromas also evolve during the wine's life. Initially there is the scent of raspberry and wild cherry, but later the nose is more of fungus, truffle, and preserved fruit. The texture is firm but above all elegant while the taste is fat, generous, and yet at the same time fresh; it is above all well-balanced. The aftertaste is enduring and heavenly.

ECHEZEAUX GRAND CRU

The wine is an intense bright red with nose of fruit such as blackcurrant, blackberry, cherry, and raspberry, together with fruit stones, cocoa, and cedarwood of cigar boxes. It is an extremely juicy wine that is fresh and well-structured, velvet-smooth, with a finish of bitter chocolate. The wine continues to breath for some time.

GRANDS-ECHEZEAUX GRAND CRU

The wine is a very dark but particularly bright and pure granite red. The fruity nose dominates the young wine with hint of burnt cocoa or bitter chocolate. After maturing in the bottle the bouquet takes on the smell of fungus, truffle, and leather, with a hint of cedarwood and tobacco. This is a very elegant, classic Burgundy with refined tannin and velvet soft texture, that is fresh and exceptionally harmonious. The aftertaste lingers very long.

VOSNE-ROMANÉE

The wine is an attractive clear colour with fascinating reflections. There is an intriguing scent of wild cherry, redcurrant, raspberry, cocoa, nutmeg, leather, and various vegetal undertones.

When older the wine often develops the distinctive nose of black truffle. It is a very rich, refined, and complex wine with velvety texture and prolonged aftertaste. Do not drink a Vosne-Romanée before it is 7–8 years old.

Clos de Vougeot.   *Echezeaux.*   *Grands Echezeaux.*   *Vosne-Romanée.*

Premier Cru Vosne-Romanée.

RICHEBOURG GRAND CRU

This wine is an exciting dark ruby red colour, with strong nose of plum or prune, black cherry, red fruit such as redcurrant, and hints of cocoa, burnt vanilla, herbs, and animal scents.

The taste is powerful too, tremendously concentrated, with great potential for laying down for a long time. Truly a wine to keep.

LA ROMANÉE GRAND CRU

This is one of the smallest vineyards of France but one of the best. The wine possesses an intense ruby colouring with fiery reflections. The nose is reminiscent of red fruit, cherry brandy, and preserved fruit. This is an extremely intense wine that is velvety smooth and generous.

LA ROMANÉE-CONTI GRAND CRU

The same applies to this wine as La Romanée, albeit that this wine is perhaps somewhat finer and more elegant with a distinctive expression of its climat. This is a sublime wine for the happy few and one of the most impressive experiences a wine drinker can undergo.

Romanée-St-Vivant.

ROMANÉE-ST-VIVANT GRAND CRU

This wine is an intense, dark ruby colour in common with the other Romanée wines. The youthful nose is of blackberry, raspberry, black cherry, preserved fruit, and fruit liqueurs but this makes way later for a more vegetal bouquet with hints of moss, humus, truffle, and game. The texture is full and firm, the taste is fresh, elegant, and juicy. Ripe fruit and a touch of exotic spices can be discerned in the aftertaste. Allow this wine to rest for at least 10–15 years.

LA GRANDE RUE GRAND CRU

This wine is less well-known and less complex than its companions from Vosne-Romanée. The appellation is relatively recent (1992) and it has yet to prove itself as a gain for the area.

CÔTES DE NUITS-VILLAGES

The wine is perhaps more representative than Côtes de Nuits and the climat is somewhat larger. The

Côtes de Nuits Villages.

colour is a clear bright ruby red and the wine has seductive aromas of cherry, other small red and black woodland fruits, with the suggestion of herbs and spices in both the nose and taste. After a number of years maturing in the bottle, a bouquet develops of toadstools and other fungus. This wine is a little rough and boisterous when young but becomes soft and pliant after a few years. Drink this fine and fairly inexpensive wine between 16–18°C (60.8–64.4°F).

NUITS-ST-GEORGES

The wine is granite red and has an intense yet refined nose of cherry, wood, and spices which, when older, typically changes to suggestions of wild game. The taste is heady, fleshy, juicy, and velvety at the same time. The aftertaste is often filled with a

Nuits-St-Georges.

Nuits-St-Georges Les Boudots.

great concentration of ripe fruit, with the suggestion of spices. Do not drink this wine too young, certainly not before 10 years old, but also not too warm (16–17°C/60.8–62.6°F).

Côtes de Beaune

The Côtes de Beaune, between Ladoix-Serrigny and Maranges is mainly known for white wines.

LADOIX

This is yet another example of a little known wine and yet we are in close proximity to the world-famous vineyards of Corton. The wine is ruby red in colour with a hint of amber. The bouquet is seductive, containing herbs, leather, and humus in the upper notes. The taste is fruity with a lingering aftertaste. Drink Ladoix at about 16°C (60.8°F).

Uncork the wine some time before drinking to allow it to breathe. Some white Ladoix is also made which is dry with a light vegetal nose with hints of hazelnut and other dried fruit. It is a charming and concentrated wine.

ALOXE-CORTON
This is a firm, concentrated wine that travels well. The colour, though strong and deep, is slightly unusual – somewhere between ochre and rust. This

Aloxe-Corton. *Corton.*

results from the strong presence of iron in the soil. All manner of fruit is present in the nose: cherry, plum, raspberry, blackberry, and blackcurrant. This is a superb wine, full and powerful, with suggestions of herbs and wood in the lingering aftertaste.

PERNAND-VERGELESSES
There are both white and red wines from here. The white wines are rarer and less well-known. They are a wonderful golden colour, characteristic of Chardonnay, with a pale tinge of green. The nose is reminiscent of honey, honeysuckle, citrus fruit, and an explosion of tropical fruit in the better years. Early on the wood perhaps dominates too much but this changes after a year's ageing in the bottle. The taste is rich and full, with great tenderness and charm. The red wine is ruby red and has a remarkable nose evoking sloes, Russian fur, hazelnut, blackcurrant, herbs, and chocolate. The wine has a fabulous taste that is full and fatty, velvet soft and powerful simultaneously, with a very prolonged aftertaste.

CORTON GRAND CRU
This is an exceptionally well-known wine, not because it is better than other Burgundies, but because the wine travels well without the quality suffering. The colour is an intense red and there are powerful aromas of preserved fruit, plum, musk, and humus as the wine matures, with a hint of pepper and herbs. This full, strong, fatty wine that is high in tannin needs to mature for some years in the bottle. The taste improves considerably with maturity. The aftertaste is full and very prolonged. This is a wine for winter drinking.

CORTON-CHARLEMAGNE GRAND CRU
The vineyards of this magnificent white wine are reputed to have been established under instructions from Charlemagne. He was renowned for both sloth and a love of red wine. He spilt so much wine on his fine white beard though that he was forced, reluctantly, to switch to white wine which had to be a good one and hence his orders. This is a very pure, clear white wine with the characteristic nose of a Chardonnay in which hot butter, toast, roasted almond, hazelnut with occasional suggestion of honey and minerals are discerned. This is a very full,

Corton-Charlemagne. *Savigny-lès-Beaune.*

almost plump wine that is a perfect ambassador for the good Burgundian life. Do not drink this wine too cold (12–14°C/53.6–57.2°F).

SAVIGNY-LÉS-BEAUNE
This is a fine white wine with a wide assortment of fruity, floral, and even mineral aromas. The wine is full and elegant and sometimes has a generous undertone. It is exceptionally full in taste with hints of white fruit such as apple, pear, or peach, and suggestions of freshly-toasted bread with melted butter.

Perhaps the red Savigny wine is better known. It is an attractive ruby colour and has a nose suggesting wild fruit and a touch of pepper that are characteristic of this area. It is a delightful, delicate, and supple wine.

CHOREY-LÉS-BEAUNE
This is an wonderful wine to look at with its pure, clear, and attractive cherry red colour. It has an intense bouquet predominated by fruit (raspberry, pomegranate, blackberry, and cherry) which later change to the classic nose of preserved

Chorey-lès-Beaune.

fruit, humus, and game. This is not a truly complex wine but the texture is good and the taste is full, supple, and above all velvet smooth.

BEAUNE

The very ancient vineyards around Beaune produce countless fine red wines. The strength of this district is to be found in the Premier Cru parcels of land of which Les Gravières is the best known. The wine is richly coloured, dark, and clear. The youthful aromas of red fruit and herbs with occasional undertones of blackcurrant quickly gives way to

Beaune Grèves.

Beaune Clos des Mouches white.

stronger scents which are often reminiscent of smoke and tobacco. This is a very concentrated wine, strong and complex, that mellows after several years ageing in the bottle.

The white wines are pale golden in colour and very clear. The bouquet is reminiscent of butter, honey, almond, lemon balm, and later of hazelnut and roasted dried fruit. Do not serve this wine too chilled (13–14°C/55.4–57.2°F).

Beaune Clos des Mouches red.

Côtes de Beaune Villages.

The red Clos des Mouches is a pale ruby red with a nose of ripe cherry, herbs, and a suggestion of smoke.

It is a full, elegant but powerful wine. Do not serve too warm (16–18°C/60.8–64.4°F).

CÔTES DE BEAUNE

This is a fairly rare red wine that is generally high in tannin.

CÔTES DE BEAUNE VILLAGES

Originates from vineyards in approximately sixteen communes. It is an excellent red wine that the locals prefer to drink when young – within three to five years of the harvest. Drink this wine at about 17°C (62.6°F).

POMMARD

Without doubt the best-known Burgundy in the

Pommard.

Pommard Epenots.

world. The name resonates just like the wine's taste – of a thunderclap on a hot autumn evening. The colour is an exciting red and the bouquet (black cherry, herbs, leather) and taste are both strong. This is a full, fatty wine that is both powerful and harmonious. A more classic traditional Burgundy is not to be found.

VOLNAY

This red wine is strangely better known with painters, sculptors, and writers than gastronomes. Perhaps this is because of its almost artistic, tender,

Volnay, Volnay Chevrít, and Volnay Santenots.

28

and feminine qualities. Volnay is certainly not a macho wine. It has a very pure and clear red red colour and the nose suggests violets and blackcurrant or sloes when young, which later develop into a complex bouquet with an assortment of fruits, flowers, herbs, and toadstools. It is a rounded, velvety wine that above all is sensual.

The better wines originate from the Premier Cru climats. This wine merits serving with fine food.

MONTHÉLIE

It is impossible to explain why Monthélie has not yet been truly discovered. Exceptionally pleasant white and red wine is made here which is certainly not inferior to neighbouring Volnay. It is a wine then for the astute who want quality at a lower price. The red wines are better than the whites which are classic Burgundian Chardonnay with lots of butter (sometimes too much) and wood in the nose with a mild but full taste. The best Monthélie whites also contain hints of toast, white flowers, and honey with the occasional suggestion of Virginian tobacco.

The red Monthélie wine is a seductive clear, and cheerful red colour. Its nose is fruity when young (blackberry, bilberry, blackcurrant) with occasional floral notes (violets). When more mature this changes to the classic fungal aromas while the fruitiness reminds of home-made jam. It is a rich, lithe, generous, and friendly wine which is at its best after several years maturing in the bottle.

AUXEY-DURESSES

The same hill has two very different sides to it. Red wine is made from one side and white wine from the other. White Auxey-Duresses is pale yellow, very aromatic (fruity and minerals) with the occasional suggestion of exotic fruit such as mango. The taste is warm, open, and generous. Red Auxey-Duresses steels the show. Do not drink it too young when it is still rather rough. The colour often tends towards granite red and the aromas evoke ripe fruit. It is a warm, full wine with a considerable structure.

ST-ROMAIN

Although a very acceptable red is also made, it is the white wine from here that is of greatest interest.

It is a very typical Chardonnay, pale golden, sometimes tinged with green, that has refined aromas of white flowers and white fruit such as pear, mirabelle plum, and peach. The nose and taste often contain strong notes of butter, hazelnut, almond, and occasionally of baked dried fruit. It is a rich and complex wine.

MEURSAULT

Wine from Meursault is celebrated throughout the world for its wonderful golden colour, intense bouquet of butter, honey, hazelnut, and lime blossom in which surprising suggestions can be detected of may blossom and spiced bread. It is a silken soft, full, and generous with an aftertaste that lingers on the palate. Enjoy a young Meursault as an

Meursalt.

Meursalt-Charmes.

aperitif or with a light starter. Do not drink any cooler than 12°C (53.6°F).

There is also a red Meursault, which is fruity and pleasant but never truly convincing.

PULIGNY-MONTRACHET

The 'ordinary' Puligny-Montrachat is a perfect example of refinement and complexity. It is a pale golden colour with nose of white flowers and fruit, sometimes combined with honey, roasted dried fruit, almond, and quince. In the better years the bouquet develops hints of tropical fruit. It is a really fine wine, fresh and silken, with a tremendous

Puligny-Montrachet.

Puligny-Montrachet Les Folatières.

assortment of flowers and fruit in the taste and a prolonged aftertaste. The Premier Cru (e.g. Folatières, Clos de la Garenne) has a more complex bouquet. The nose is reminiscent of new-mown hay, honey, fresh almond, dried fruit, and herbs. This wine needs to be kept for at least five years in order to fully enjoy its quality. Do not chill too much (approx. 13°C/55.4°F).

MONTRACHET GRAND CRU

This wine is one of the pillars on which the reputation of Burgundy is built both within France and abroad. It is a fabulous pale golden colour. It takes a number of years for scents captured in the wine to develop themselves fully. Those who drink this wine too young will be disappointed because the bouquet fails to open out. Remain patient for after five years it develops an unimaginable bouquet in which young exotic fruit are combined with the nose of exotic wood, citrus fruit, herbs, lily-of-the-valley, peach, and almond. Wines from certain climats also possess a light mineral undertone.

The wine is simultaneously fresh and rounded, full and elegant, refined and seductive, and the aftertaste lingers almost for ever. Drink this rare and expensive wine at 14–15°C (57.2–59°F).

CHEVALIER-MONTRACHET GRAND CRU
Has a golden colour and very seductive bouquet containing butter, toast, and vegetal undertones with occasional hint of mineral. It is a full, warm, generous, and juicy wine with a very aromatic taste.

BÂTARD-MONTRACHET GRAND CRU
This other member of the Montrachet family needs to be laid down for some years before it can be fully enjoyed. Then the colour is clear, pure golden yellow and the heady bouquet is readily released from the glass. It has a nose of exotic fruit, croissants with butter, exotic wood, almond, and honey. The taste is fresh and silken with a hint of tannin and a prolonged aftertaste. Drink this wine at about 13°C (55.4°F).

BIENVENUES-BTARD-MONTRACHET GRAND CRU
The wine is golden yellow with a green tinge. It has a very fruity bouquet together with hints of toast, butter, citrus fruit, and sometimes a characteristic flinty undertone.

CRIOTS-BTARD-MONTRACHET GRAND CRU
This is a very rare white wine that in many respects resembles the Bienvenues-Bâtard-Montrachet, certainly sharing its flinty smell and taste.

CHASSAGNE-MONTRACHET
Once only red wines were made here, today the reds and whites are of equal importance. White

Montrachet.

Bienvenues-B,tard-Montrachet.

Chassagne-Montrachet is a pale golden colour and it possesses a very intense nose in which buttered croissants, flowers, lemons, and later roasted almond and herbs can be recognised. Some wine also has a noticeable mineral scent and taste. The white Chassagne-Montrachet is generally a fresh, juicy, and very refined wine of great character.

Red Chassagne-Montrachet is dark red and has a bouquet of ripe cherry, blackcurrant, and other woodland fruit, with a hint of liquorice. Most it is well structured, full, and fatty.

Chassagne-Montrachet white.

Premier Cru Chassagne-Montrachet white.

Chassagne-Montrachet red.

ST-AUBIN
Red wine is also made here but the reputation is mainly due to the white wines. The colour is pale golden yellow and the nose recalls acacia blossom, yellow plum, and almond. This later develops into dried fruit and honey. This is a fine, fresh, and generous wine, with sometimes a tendency to plumpness and mineral undertones. The taste and aftertaste are very aromatic.

SANTENAY
This is a ruby red wine with aromas of red fruit and fruits of the forest such as blackberry and bilberry. The wine can be somewhat harsh in tannin when young but this changes after several years ageing in the bottle. Once fully mature a good Santenay develops a very exciting bouquet incorporating wild fungi including truffle.

The white wine is generally not among the best whites but choose one from a Premier Cru vineyard for these are well worth drinking. It is a fulsome and fruity wine with clearly recognisable Chardonnay characteristics: butter, croissants, toast, hazelnuts. citrus fruit, and white flowers.

Santenay.

Premier Cru Santenay.

White Burgundy.

Red Burgundy.

MARANGES

This is less well-known wine-growing area which produces both red and white wines. For the white wines choose for preference from a Premier Cru vineyard. It should then be fruity (apricot and almond), fresh, and have a somewhat fatty taste but be full of tenderness and elegance.

Premier Cru Maranges.

Red Maranges (certainly the premier cru wines) are of outstanding quality. The best have a very intense colour, nose, and taste. The wine is very aromatic with suggestions of ripe red fruit and black cherry, liquorice, and herbs.

Generic Burgundy

Before we continue our journey south let us consider a few of the generic wines of Burgundy.

BOURGOGNE

White Bourgogne AC (Chardonnay) is an aromatic, fresh white wine. Drink it at about 11°C (51.8°F) and preferably within two years of the harvest.

Red Bourgogne AC (Pinot Noir) is ruby red and has a nose of red fruit and woodland fruit (raspberry, blackcurrant, blackberry, and redcurrant). It is a lithe, generous, and friendly wine. Drink at about 16°C (60.8°F) within five years of the harvest.

BOURGOGNE PASSE-TOUT-GRAIN

The red wine is made with a minimum of one third Pinot Noir to which Gamay grapes are added. The better wines though contain more Pinot Noir. It is a light, cheerful, and generous wine that should be drunk when young. For completeness, there is also a rosé variant.

Burgundy Aligoté.

BOURGOGNE GRAND ORDINAIRE

This appellation is rarely seen these days because it sounds too 'ordinary' for a Burgundy yet very acceptable whites, reds, and rosés are to be found at a very reasonable price in this category.

BOURGOGNE ALIGOTÉ

This white wine is very popular in Burgundy and much further afield. This very fresh wine is often strongly acidic and has a bouquet of green apple, lemon, and may blossom with the occasional hint of flint.

Côte Châlonnaise

The Côtes Châlonnaise between Chagny, Montagny and Couches will probably surprise many a visitor.

BOURGOGNE CÔTE CHÂLONNAISE

This is a fairly recent appellation (1990) for white but especially red wines, spread through 44 communes.

The white wine is a light, floral and fruity Chardonnay (citrus and exotic fruit) with a lithe, fatty, and balanced taste. The very fruity cherry red wine is light, friendly, warm, and generous.

RULLY

These white and red wines acquire an aromatic finesse through their chalk soils. The white Rully is a very pure and clear golden white with very seductive bouquet containing broom, almond, and citrus fruit with a fresh and elegant taste that has undertones of fruit and flowers.

The ruby red Rully has a nose when young of red fruit such as blackberry, blackcurrant, and redcurrant. Late this evolves into a riper fruit bouquet with suggestions of tobacco and moist autumn soil.

The taste is typical of a Burgundy, fat and fresh, with elegant tannin and much fruitiness, especially in the aftertaste.

MERCUREY

Most white Mercurey wines are a light, friendly, and above all uncomplicated aperitif wine. The red

Rully white.   *Mercurey.*

Mercurey is an attractive ruby red colour and fruity aromas of blackcurrant, redcurrant, and cherry, often with a pinch of herbs.

GIVRY

Like its neighbours from Montagny, wine from Givry is an entirely under regarded Chardonnay white. Consequently it is modestly priced for the quality offered.

There are a couple of whites from Givry that have gorgeous bouquets of acacia and may blossom, apple, almond, and sometimes also lime blossom and lilac. These full, fatty whites can be found in the totally reliable Guide Hachette. Drink this wine with freshwater fish.

Red Givry is very colourful with an intensely aromatic nose of redcurrant and blackcurrant. When older there are herbal undertones. This is a fleshy wine with considerable finesse and a pleasant fruity taste.

MONTAGNY

The best Montagny wine has a pale and unimposing colour but with an exceptional array of scents: apple, citrus fruit, fresh almonds, fern, hazelnut, and butter.
The taste is lithe, elegant, fresh, and rounded.

BOURGOGNE ALIGOTÉ DE BOUZERON

This wine is better than the general Aligoté AC. It is an exceptionally pleasing fresh wine with a seductive nose of roses, peony, and white fruit, sometimes accompanied by cinnamon.

Mâconnais

The Mâconnais, between Sennecey-le-grand and St-Vérand, is the home of the quick charmers.

MCON
MCON SUPÉRIEUR
MCON VILLAGES

With a few exceptions, the ordinary white Mâcon is an uncomplicated and excellent wine which can be

drunk without a long wait.
The red compatriots are of better quality and are made from Pinot Noir and Gamay grapes. The greater the proportion of Gamay the more approachable, generous and often more fruity is the wine. Some Mâcons with lots of Pinot Noir can be more powerful and high in tannin, with plenty of structure, particularly when aged in oak.

Mâcon-Villages white.

The better white wines from the Mâconnais have their own appellation.

POUILLY-FUISSÉ

Chardonnay is always most at home on chalk and that is apparent in the wine. This wine is a very clear and pale golden colour with a bouquet of fresh grapes and almonds, with a juicy and fresh taste of great elegance. When the wine is aged in oak casks it develops a characteristic nose of vanilla, toast, hazelnuts, and roasted almonds.

Pouilly-Fuissé (négociant).   *Pouilly-Fuissé (estate).*

POUILLY-VINZELLES
POUILLY-LOCHÉ

These wines are less well-known and generally lighter than Pouilly-Fuissé.

They are usually elegant, very aromatic wines with a bouquet of butter, lemon, flowers, and grapefruit.

St-Véran.

ST-VÉRAN

This is an exceptional wine from the borders with Beaujolais. (note the name of the wine is written without the final 'd' of the village of St-Vérand).

Beaujolais

Although Beaujolais is officially within Burgundy, it is usually treated as an independent wine area. We do this because Beaujolais wine has its own identity which is further strengthened by the considerable publicity that surrounds this individually-minded Burgundian brother. The most famous Beaujolais is the new wine or Nouveau, which is introduced each year with much ado. There is much more though to discover in the Beaujolais, with at least twelve different appellations.

The area

Beaujolais starts about 10 kilometres (6 miles) south of Mâcon, in the department of Rhône. It is a relatively small area about 60 km long by 12 km (37 miles by 7¹/₂ miles) wide that spreads itself across a ridge of hills that border the valley of the Saône. The area is subdivided into two sub-regions: in the north Haut-Beaujolais where the best wines are made, the 10 crus, and Beaujolais Villages. The soil is predominantly granite and quartz fragments on a bed of slate.

The southern part or Bas-Beaujolais has soil that is a mixture of clay and chalk. The everyday white, rosé, and red Beaujolais are produced from these vineyards.

The vineyards

Only about 2% of the vineyards are planted with Chardonnay. The extremely rare white Beaujolais is made from these grapes. The remainder of the vineyards are planted with the Gamay grape. Some rosé but mainly reds are made from Gamay.

The preparation of Beaujolais

In recent decades the growers of Beaujolais have realised that improvement and above all greater environmental awareness in the protection of their vineyards, combined with better equipment and hygiene in

Classic Beaujolais 50 clële potí bottle.

the wine cellar improves the quality of the wine. Consequently far less sulphate fertiliser is now used and wine-makers control temperature far better during vinification. This protects the characteristics of the soil, climate, and grape far better. Unfortunately there are still growers in Beaujolais who want to make a profit as quickly and as cheaply as possible – a scandal for those hard-working growers who seek to improve the quality of their wine.

Carbonic maceration

The general wine-making method in Beaujolais is carbonic maceration. The Gamay grapes are tipped into large vats of timber, concrete or stainless steel as soon as possible after they are picked.

The entire bunch including stems is left intact. The weight of the grapes themselves gently presses the grapes at the bottom and the juice from these (10–30% of the total volume) begins to ferment slowly. The sugars in the juice are converted to alcohol and carbon dioxide through fermentation. The pressure of carbon dioxide increases and forces the 'cap' or grapes upwards. The soaking in carbonic acid gas causes the alcohol to break down natural colourants and tannin and these are absorbed in the subsequent fermentation.

The pressure of carbonic acid gas is highest at the top of the vat and the pressure causes metabolism within the grapes. These start to ferment internally, with alcohol being produced and the level of malic acid significantly reduced. Just as important though and a characteristic of this method of wine-making is that the presence of oxygen ensures the retention of outstanding fruitiness in the aroma and taste. After the carbonic acid has soaked the grapes in a process that takes four to ten days, depending on the type of wine to be produced, the naturally pressed juice or 'vin de goutte' is drawn off. The remaining grape matter is then pressed gently and added to the initial tapping. Some cuvées may make wine consisting solely of the initially tapped natural pressing and these wines can usually be spotted by their 'heavenly' names on the label of 'Paradis'as the French call this sweet, very fruity, and aromatic wine.

When this initial fermentation is completed a second fermentation occurs in which the harsh malic acids are converted to more gentle lactic acid. The young wine is then ready to drink at once as Beaujolais Nouveau or undergoes further handling to become Beaujolais, Beaujolais Villages, or Crus du Beaujolais.

BEAUJOLAIS NOUVEAU

This young, extremely fruity wine is sold according to tradition from the third Thursday of November. Clacking tongues suggest that the early sale of these wines is a marketing stunt to reduce wine stocks. It is not surprising that Beaujolais Nouveau is nicknamed 'the third river of Lyon'. Others wax lyrical about the outstanding fruitiness of the new season's Beaujolais. Experienced wine drinkers regard this young wine as heralding the results of that vintage and do not make such a fuss. They consider the arrival of Beaujolais Nouveau more as a custom than a passing fad. It is up to you whether to buy them or not. In any event try to avoid the cheaper examples. Always drink the better Beaujolais Nouveau such as a Beaujolais Villages Nouveau chilled at about 10°C (50°F).

BEAUJOLAIS

The basic Beaujolais is produced as a white, rosé, and red. Light, fruity wines are made on more than 10,000 hectares of predominantly chalky soil. Drink these wines at approx. 11°C (51.8°F).

Since the most southerly white Burgundy appellation of St-Véran came into existence the

Beaujolais.

Beaujolais white.

Beaujolais Villages.

production of white Beaujolais has been significantly reduced. Beaujolais Blanc is made with Chardonnay grapes (and occasionally a little Aligoté). The wine is fresh and fruity in taste and nose. Experienced wine drinkers may detect a hint of hazelnut, mint, butter and sometimes green vegetal such as green pepper (paprika).

BEAUJOLAIS VILLAGES

There are 39 communes which are permitted to call themselves AC Beaujolais Villages.

The wine is soft and generous with a delightful cherry red colour and considerable scent and taste of fruit such as blackcurrant and strawberry. Drink at 11–12°C (51.8–53.6°F).

The ten Crus

Local experts say that an Easter must pass before these wines are at their best. 'Les Crus du Beaujolais doivent faire leurs Pâques.' The wine is rarely to be found in shops earlier than this in any case. The wines of the ten Crus only fully develop after being allowed to rest for a few months.

CÔTES DE BROUILLY

Two of the ten Crus of Beaujolais are located on the slopes of the 485 metre high Mont Brouilly, on granite and slate soils. The 300 hectare of vineyards of Côtes de Brouilly are found on the sunny side of the extinct volcano.

The wine is purple to mauve with a very refined and elegant bouquet of fresh grapes and irises. Leave a Côtes de Brouilly wine to rest for a time before opening. Drink it at approx. 13°C (55.4°F).

Côtes-de-Brouilly.   Brouilly.

BROUILLY

The vineyards are somewhat more extensive here, covering approx. 1,200 hectares. The soil is mainly granite and sand. The wine is ruby red in colour and has a fruity nose in which red fruits such as plum, and occasionally peach are clearly discernible. The better Brouilly wines also have a hint of mineral in them. This is a full, darker wine with a firm taste. Drink it at about 12°C (53.6°F).

RÉGNIÉ

The 520 hectares of this vineyard were only recognised as Cru du Beaujolais in 1988. The ground is gently undulating and relatively high (average 350 metres/1,148 feet). A fairly supple wine is made here which is both elegant and seductive. The colour is pure cherry red and the nose reminds of red fruit

Régnié.

(raspberry, redcurrant, and blackberry) with occasional floral note. Régnié is at its tastiest when fruity and young, within two years of the harvest. Serve at approx. 12°C (53.6°F).

CHIROUBLES

The vineyards surrounding the village of Chiroubles are on granite soil at a height of about 400 metres (1,312 feet).

Only the vine thrives on such an acidic and poor soil with no other plants being able to compete. The subtle, refined, pale coloured wine is very seductive, almost feminine. The nose evokes a complex bouquet of wild flowers in which violets, peony, and lilies-of-the-valley predominate. Drink this wine at about 12°C (53.6°F).

Chiroubles.   Morgon.

MORGON

The local wine archives show Morgon has been known of since the tenth century. The Morgon vineyards cover 1,100 hectares of granite and slate shale soils.

Morgon is a pungent, powerful, and generous wine which can be kept for some time. It possesses a great assortment of aromas which evoke fruit with stones such as cherry, peach, apricot, and plum. Those that reach a respectable age often acquire an undertone of kirsch and start to resemble a Burgundy. Drink this wine at about 13°C (55.4°F).

FLEURIE

The most fruity, and as the name suggests, most floral Crus of Beaujolais are produced from 800 hectares of vineyards at the foot of the Black Madonna. Ferruginous soil and blocks of granite provide Fleurie with something special, a rare refinement and feminine charm but above all tremendous strength of aromas such as iris, violet, and rose perfumes.

Fleurie.

The colour is a pure ruby red with wonderful reflections and the taste is both velvet smooth and fleshy.

Good Fleurie from the best vintages can be kept for ten years or more. Drink Fleurie at about 13°C (55.4°F).

MOULIN-À-VENT

This Cru derives its name from the recently and perfectly restored windmill in Romanèche-Thorins. The soil of the 650 hectares of vineyards comprises pink granite and manganese. This imparts a darker, more highly concentrated ruby red colour to the wine in which purple and dark red are also present when young.

The nose is mainly reminiscent of flowers such as roses with a hint of raspberry. The taste is powerful and reasonably full of tannin. This firm texture enables Moulin-à-Vent to be kept for some time (up to 15 years). When mature this wine resembles Burgundy. Allow this wine to rest for a couple of years before serving at about 14°C (57.2°F).

Moulin-à-Vent (not cask matured).   Chénas.

CHÈNAS

This wine is almost unknown outside the area but this is not at all just. A very elegant wine is made with refined bouquet of peony and roses with occasional hint of wood and herbs on 260 hectares of granite soil. The taste is soft, generous, and friendly. Serve this wine at about 14°C (57.2°F). This wine too can be kept for quite a few years.

JULIÉNAS

This is the most northerly Cru of Beaujolais, bordering on the Mâconnais. Deeply ruby red coloured wine is produced from 580 hectares of stony soil with layers of clay and

Juliénas.

sediments. The wine has a powerful full taste and the bouquet is dominated by fruity (wild strawberry, redcurrant, and raspberry) scents with floral undertones (peony and roses).

Good Juliénas can be kept for a few years. Drink this wine at about 13°C (55.4°F).

ST-AMOUR

This is the last of these northerly Crus. The vineyards extend for 280 hectares and border the chalky Mâconnais (Chardonnay) and granite hills of Beaujolais (Gamay). The soil is a mixture of clay, boulders, granite, and sandstone. The wine possesses a wonderful ruby red colour and very aromatic nose of peony, raspberry, redcurrant, apricot, and also sometimes a suggestion of kirsch. The taste is

St-Amour.

seductive, velvet soft, and full, with hints of herbs. Serve this wine at about 13°C (55.4°F).

The Beaujolais 'satellites'

Although they do not officially fall under the Beaujolais classification, the following three wine regions produce wines that closely resemble Beaujolais in both character and taste. All three of the red wines are made with the Gamay grape.

CÔTEAUX DU LYONNAIS

This ancient vineyard is a victim of the expansion of Lyon.

It is a friendly, light, but generous wine with pronounced fruity nose. Drink this wine chilled to about 12°C (53.6°F). Chardonnay and Aligoté whites are also produced here.

CÔTE ROANNAISE

This is a very clear, ruby red coloured wine that is strong on fruit and has a light, pleasing taste. Chill this wine to about 12°C (53.6°F).

CÔTES DU FOREZ

These are light, friendly wines that are very fruity. The rosé is ideal to serve with informal lunches and picnics.

The red wine is ideal for warm summer evenings,

Côteaux-du-Lyonnais.

Côtes du Forez.

Côtes du Forez.

A fresh breeze

The wine from the district around Uzès in the department of Gard enjoyed so much fame in the seventeenth century that it was readily imitated. To protect its origins and quality it was officially recognised in 1650 and its area of origin strictly defined. After a further battle lasting more than a century the Appellation Côtes du Rhône Contrôlée eventually became a fact in 1937. In 1956 the feared winter mistral blew at speeds of more than 100 km/62 miles per hour for three weeks and the thermometer remained stuck at about minus 15°C (59°F). Disastrously this killed all the olive trees but since the vines had survived these conditions the ruined farmers decided to switch to wine-growing. This was the start of the enormous growth of Côtes du Rhône.

for instance with a cold buffet. Serve both wines at about 12°C (53.6°F).

The Rhône Valley

Wine has been made for more than 2,000 years between Vienne and Avignon in the valley of the Rhône river. The basis of arguably the best known wine-growing region of France – Côtes du Rhône was established by the Celts, Greeks, and Romans. This very extensive wine region with its many different terroirs and microclimates eventually became established as a distinctive entity.

23 types of grape

There are at least 23 different varieties of grape permitted to be used in the wine-growing region of Côtes du Rhone plus the Muscat Petit Grain that is used for the naturally sweet Beaumes-de-Venise.

In the northern part of the Rhône Valley red wine is exclusively made with Syrah but white wines are produced from Viognier, Roussanne, and Marsanne. In the south they use some Grenache, Mourvèdre, Cinsault, and Carignan grapes in addition to Syrah

Terraced vineyards in Rhône (Hermitage).

for their reds with the Grenache Blanc, Clairette and Bourboulenc for the white wines.

The appellations

Rhône wines are divided into four categories: the generic Appellation Côtes du Rhône Régionale, the better Côtes du Rhône Villages, the Crus, and the satellites that are geographically related but have their own identities (Clairette de Die, Crémant de Die, Vins du Diois, Côteaux du Tricastin, Côtes du Ventoux en Costières de Nîmes).

CÔTES DU RHÔNE AC

About 80 per cent of the generic Côtes du Rhône produced are very good. Because this category represents such a wide diversity of terroirs, microclimates. and winemakers, the wine has an equally diverse range of aromatic properties. Generally these are comforting and friendly wines. The red is well structured, full of aroma and taste

Côtes du Rhône red.

Côtes du Rhône rosé.

Côtes du Rhône white.

and very rounded. It can be drunk when still young but can also be left for a while. The rosé wines come from the south of the region and they range from raspberry colour to salmon pink. These rosés are always fruity and yielding. The white wine is dry, well-balanced, well structured, very aromatic, and thirst-quenching.

CÔTES DU RHÔNE-VILLAGES AC

There are 77 communes in the southern Rhône Valley which are permitted to use Côtes du Rhône Villages on the label of their wines and of these sixteen may also use the village name on the label.

The stipulations about the planting, care of the vines, yield, and wine-making for these white, rosé, and red wines are more rigid. Certain of the best known Côtes du Rhône Villages are Beaumes-de-Venise (red and rosé), Cairanne (red, rosé, and white), Chusclan (red and rosé), Laudun (red, rosé, and white), Rasteau (red, rosé, and white), Rochegude (red, rosé, and white), Séguret red, rosé, and white), Valréas (red, rosé, and white), Vinsobres (red, rosé, and white) and Visan (red, rosé, and white). These wines are ideal for drinking with Provençal dishes. Drink the red wine at approx. 16°C (60.8°F), the rosé at approx. 14°C (57.2°F), and the white at about 12°C (53.6°F).

The Côtes du Rhône Crus

Each of these thirteen great wines has a character of its own. Often the wine is legendary one that offers the drinker the chance to become acquainted with the region, the soil, the variety of grape, and to meet the wine-maker in person.

The climate is a mild continental one on the steep, rough slopes around Tain-L'Hermitage with granite beneath the soil. In the southern part of the Rhône the soil is chalky, overlain with sediments in places and the climate is warmer and drier in proximity with the Mediterranean.

CÔTE RÔTIE

Côte Rôtie is solely red wine and comes from two very steep granite hills, the Côte Blonde and the Côte Brune. According to legend the domain of the estate owner Maugiron was divided in the Middle-Ages between his two daughters: one was blonde, the other brunette. This is said to be how the hills got their names. Côte Rôtie is dark red and has a bouquet in which raspberry, herbs, and a suggestion of violets can be discerned. When older, the upper notes are of vanilla, and apricot or peach stones. The wine is fairly full-bodied with plenty of tannin but well-rounded with a tremendous experience of taste and prolonged aftertaste. Open the bottle in advance of drinking.

CONDRIEU

This white wine originates from steep granite slopes which cannot be cultivated other than by hand. The

Côte Rôtie.

Condrieu.

grape used is Viognier and the wine is a pale golden colour and possesses a powerful nose of wild flowers, irises, violets, and apricot. The wine has considerable strength and is well-rounded. Since 1990 the rare Condrieu Vendanges Tardives Cuvée les Eguets has reappeared, made with sympathy by Yves Cuilleron.

CHÀTEAU-GRILLET
This minuscule vineyard of only 3.3 hectares and 10,000 bottles per year is one of the smallest appellations and also one of the best white wines of France.

The wine will have to be tried locally. The colour is a clear yellow and tends towards straw colouring when older. The bouquet is somewhat closed and only develops after a time. Once again apricot and white peach are discovered in the upper notes. The taste is a full one, fatty, very rich and complex. Remember to open the bottle a few hours before drinking.

St-Joseph red.   *St-Joseph white.*

ST-JOSEPH
This fine, harmonious and elegant dark red wine, with a subtle perfume of blackcurrant and raspberry, later develops suggestions of leather and liquorice. Drink slightly chilled at approx. 15°C (59°F). The white wine is a sunny yellow with a green tinge and its nose suggests wild flowers, acacia blossom, and honey. This is a fresh wine with great depths. Drink chilled at approx. 12°C (53.6°F).

CROZES-HERMITAGE
In terms of volume, this is the largest of the northern Crus. Although not of the same quality as its cousin, Crozes-Hermitage does come close to Hermitage in terms of its characteristic bouquet and taste. The white wine is a clear yellow with very floral nose and full, fatty taste. Drink chilled at approx. 12°C (53.6°F).

The red wine is dark red and very intense. The bouquet recalls red fruit, leather, and herbs. The taste is elegant despite the discreet presence of tannin. Drink slightly chilled at approx. 15°C (59 °F).

Crozes-Hermitage red.   *Crozes-Hermitage white.*

Hermitages red.   *Hermitages white.*

HERMITAGE
Red Hermitage is somewhat harsh when young and requires some years rest; depending on the quality, this can be 5, 10, or even 20 years. Those with sufficient patience are rewarded with a very great wine with a sensual bouquet in which leather, red and white fruit, and wild flowers are present in the upper notes. The taste is largely of preserved fruit. Serve at 16–18°C 60.8–64.4°F). The white wine is ready for drinking much earlier than the red but can also be kept for some time. Its smell is reminiscent of a sea of flowers with suggestions of vanilla and

Hermitage Vin de Paille.   *Cornas.*

roasted almonds. It is a powerful, rounded wine with considerable aromatic potential. Drink at approx. 12°C (53.6°F).

CORNAS
This red wine is dark coloured and has an exciting bouquet in which red fruit, freshly-ground pepper, sweetwood, preserved fruit, and even truffles are present. The undertones are almost animalistic.

ST-PERAY
This is the only appellation which also makes sparkling wine. It is more of an amusing wine than an exciting one that is best drunk when young.

GIGONDAS
Gigondas is made from Grenache, supplemented with mainly Syrah and Mourvèdre. The red wine is a wonderful colour and has a bouquet filled with fresh red fruit through to animal undertones and when older some fungal notes. It is a full, powerful, and well-balanced wine that is a little harsh when young. The wine needs keeping for a few years.
The rosés are fresh, cheerful wines with a great deal of extract. Drink these when young.

VACQUEYRAS
The whites and rosés are drunk when young for any occasion. The red wine with its characteristic scent

Châteauneuf-du-Pape white.

Lirac.

white wine while still young. The white wine is very aromatic and rounded with a nose that has floral undertones such as camphor oil and narcissus. True estate bottled Châteauneuf-du-Pape bears the arms of Avignon on the bottles: the papal crown and cross-keys of St Peter.

LIRAC
Lirac is growing in popularity. These are good wines at a relatively low price.

TAVEL
Tavel is one of the finest rosés of France. The pink

Gigondas.

Châteauneuf-du-Pape red.

of ripe red fruit such as cherry, and hint of sweetwood, has more power. Drink it at approx. 17°C (62.6°F).

CHÂTEAUNEUF-DU-PAPE
Although 13 different varieties of grape are permitted, the red wine is generally made from Grenache, Cinsault, Mourvèdre, Syrah, Muscardin and Counoise, while the whites use Clairette and Bourboulenc.

The red wine has a very complex bouquet containing red fruit, leather, anise, sweetwood, and herbs, and equally complex taste that is rounded, unctuous, with a prolonged aftertaste. Wait for five years after harvest before drinking the red but consume the

Tavel (négociant).

Tavel (estate).

colour tends towards terracotta tiles or even orange. Hints of apricot, peach, and roasted almond can be detected in the bouquet.

Drink this wine at approx. 13°C (55.4°F).

The Rhône satellites

These are wine-growing areas that are geographically part of the Rhône but have their own identities: Clairette de Die, Crémant de Die, Vins du Diois, Côteaux du Tricastin, Côtes du Ventoux and Costières de Nîmes.

Steeply sloping Die vineyards.

CLAIRETTE DE DIE

Clairette de Die is an ancient wine that was known by the Romans (Plinus the Elder 77 BC). At that time the wine was called Aigleucos and was made by the local Celts. They dipped the vats in which the wine had just started to ferment into the ice-cold mountain streams. This brought an early end to the fermentation process so that the bubbles were retained. Up to World War II Clairette was only ever intended to be drunk as a young, still fermenting wine, drawn from the barrel. This situation changed radically in 1950 when the Cave Coopérative Clairette de Die was established. The vineyards were extended and the technique of wine-making was enormously improved. With respect for tradition, a new élan was given to this almost lost traditional local drink. Clairette de Die is made from Muscat and Clairette grapes. The wine is bottled before the fermentation is complete without any other additives. The carbonic acid gas that is produced during the fermentation is therefore trapped in the bottles as naturally-occurring bubbles. This ancient method is officially known under the name 'Méthode Dioise Ancestrale'. The taste of this traditionally made Clairette de Die is exceptionally fruity (the Muscat grapes), gentle, and seductive. The low alcoholic content (7%) makes it a sensual aperitif but it can also be served with chicken or rabbit casserole to which a generous amount of this wine has been added.

Crémant de Die.

Clairette de Die.

Châtillon Gamay.

CRÉMANT DE DIE
The dry (brut) version of this wine, made exclusively with Clairette grapes and by the Méthode Traditionnelle, has been known as Crémant de Die since 1993. The nose is reminiscent of apples and other white and green fruit. When older these are supplemented by suggestions of dried fruit and almonds.

CHÂTILLON-EN-DIOIS
This small area of appellation is found at the foot of the first outcrops of the Alps. Châtillon Gamay, red or rosé, is a fruity and yielding wine with a rich bouquet. Drink these wines young except for the special cuvée that is aged in oak, which can be kept for a time before drinking. Châtillon Aligoté is an elegant, fresh dry white wine with a bouquet of wild herbs. It needs to be drunk when young, for instance as an aperitif. Châtillon Chardonnay is a fuller, more serious white wine, which improves with a year's

Châtillon Chardonnay.

Côteaux du Tricastin.

maturing in the bottle. In addition to these generic wines there are also various domain wines of superb quality. Be quick off the mark though because the demand exceeds the supply.

CÔTEAUX DU TRICASTIN
This wine is little different from Côtes du Rhône. For some obscure reason it is not included within

the elite Rhône wines. White, rosé, and red wines are produced here on the same types of vine, and similar soils.

CÔTES DU VENTOUX
The climate is somewhat cooler here than in the

Côtes du Ventoux.

Côtes du Luberon.

Rhône Valley. The wine is therefore less alcoholic than other Rhône wines. Red wine predominates and this is fresh, elegant, and needs to be drunk while still relatively young.

CÔTES DU LUBÉRON
This appellation has only existed for white, rosé, and red wine since 1988. The climate here is also cooler which explains a predominance of white wine. Generally speaking these are quite inexpensive but good quality wines which are becoming increasingly popular. It is expected that this area will develop further in the twenty-first century. Keep an eye on these wines. In terms of taste there is little difference with Rhône wines, except perhaps that Lubéron is slightly less full-bodied and structured. Finally, a mention for a good VDQS wine: the Côtes du Vivarais.

CÔTES DU VIVARAIS
Red wine is mainly made here from the Grenache

Muscat de Beaumes-de-Venise (négociant).

Muscat de Beaumes-de-Venise (estate).

and Syrah grapes. There is also a local fresh-tasting rosé that is particularly pleasing.

NATURALLY SWEET WINES

Two communes in the Rhône Valley region make high quality sweet desert wines using Muscat grapes. A full-bodied. strong white wine with enormous aromatic potential is made in a natural manner in Beaumes-de-Venise. This white wine both smells and tastes of the Muscat grape, together with peach, apricots, and occasionally also of freshly-picked wild flowers. Drink this wine well chilled (5–8°C/41–42.8°F). By contrast, a fortified red wine is made in Rasteau. Fermentation is stopped by adding pure wine alcohol to the wine juice. The wine produced is very sweet, very fruity, and somewhat resembles Port. Drink slightly below room temperature.

Savoie

The vineyards of Savoie only amount to about 2,000 hectares but these are spread across a large area. From Lake Geneva in the north, the wine country spreads itself out to the foot of the Alps in the east and the as far south as the valley of the Isère, south of Chambery, about 100 km (62 miles) south of Lake Geneva. It is a shame that wine from Savoie is not better known. The predominant white wine is fresh and full of flavour. The scattered vineyards and hilly terrain make both wine-growing and making difficult so that these wines are not cheap. Savoie wines are subtle, elegant, and characteristic of their terroir like no other wine.

Vins de Savoie (Savoy wines).

The region

The vineyards of Savoie resemble a long ribbon of small areas in a half moon facing south-east. The climate is continental in nature but is moderated by the large lakes and rivers. To the west the vineyards are protected from the rain-bearing westerly winds by the Jura mountains and other hills. The high level of annual sun hours (1,600 per annum) are an important factor.

The vineyards are sited between 300 and 400 metres (984–1,312 feet) above sea level. The soil is a mixture of chalk, marl, and debris from Alpine glaciers.

Wine-making

The most important appellation is Vin de Savoie (still, sparkling, and slightly sparkling). There are 18 Crus which are permitted to use their name on the label.

The Roussette de Savoie appellation (which uses solely the local Altesse grape) has an additional 4 Crus. Savoie is a wine region well-worth making a detour to visit, if only to discover the four unique native grape varieties: the white Jacquère, Altesse or Roussette, Gringet and red Mondeuse. In addition to these native grapes, Aligoté, Chasselas, Chardonnay and Molette are grown for white wines and Gamay, Persan, Joubertin and Pinot Noir for the red and rosé wines.

VINS DE SAVOIE BLANC
ABYMES
APREMONT
CHIGNIN
JONGIEUX
CHAUTAGNE
CRUET
MONTMÉLIAN
ST-JOIRE-PRIEURÉ

These white wines are all made from the Jacquère grape. These are fresh, very aromatic wines. The colour varies from barely yellow to pale yellow depending on the terroir and from light and comforting with floral undertones such as honey-

Abymes.

Apremont

Montmélian.

Chignin.

St-Joire-Prieuré.

Jongieux.

suckle that lightly prick the tongue to fully-flavoured and fruity. Chill this wine to 8°C (46.4°F). and drink when still young.

MARIN
MARIGNAN
RIPAILLE
CRÉPY

The Chasselas grape (known from the best Swiss wines) typifies the white wine. The colour is pale yellow and the nose reminds of ripe fruit, sometimes even of dried fruit. There is a full and fresh taste.

Ripaille.

Chautagne.

Crépy.

Certain wines such as Crépy in particular prick the tongue. Locally they say of a good Crépy: 'Le Crépy crépite,' or in other words it crackles.

CHIGNIN-BERGERON
This superb white wine made with Roussane grapes is worth a mention of its own. It is a very complex wine with suggestions of roasted nuts, toast, dried fruit, and occasional hint of anise or fennel. It is surprisingly fresh with a full flavoured taste, with a prolonged development of the bouquet. Do not drink too cold (approx. 12°C/53.6°F).

ROUSSETTE DE SAVOIE

Chignin-Bergeron.

Roussette-de-Savoie Frangy.

FRANGY
MARESTEL
MONTHOUX
MONTERMINOD
SEYSSEL
The white wines (Roussette de Savoie and Seyssel) are made with the Altesse (Roussette) grape. This ancient variety of vine is reputed to have been brought back from the crusades by a princess from Cyprus. The colour of the wine is pale yellow and somewhat pearl-like when young but this disappears in due course.

The scent is reminiscent of a large bunch of wild flowers such as violets and irises with a hint of almonds. The taste is a full one and rounded. The wine sometimes also contains sugar remnants which makes it even more pleasant.

Roussette-de-Savoie Monthoux.

Roussette-de-Savoie Monterminod.

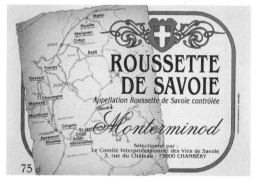

VINS DE SAVOIE ROUGE
ARBIN
CHAUTAGNE
JONGIEUX
ST-JEAN-DE-LA-PORTE
CHIGNIN
CRUET
ST-JOIRE-PRIEURÉ
There are three different types of wine here. The Gamay is fairly typical and characteristic of its terroir. It colour is cheerful and bright while the aromatic taste is correspondingly fresh. Drink

chilled to approx. 12°C (53.6°F). The Mondeuse is much darker in colour with purple tinges. The bouquet and taste are more complex than that of the Gamay. You can smell and taste a mixture of red fruit, pepper, and spices. The tannin present can be somewhat harsh when the wine is young but this softens later. Good Mondeuse can be kept for a long time. Serve at 14°C (57.2°F). The Pinot Noir is somewhat rarer. It is ruby red and has a complex bouquet and taste. Serve lightly chilled at 14°C (57.2°F).

Arbin.

St-Jean-de-la-Porte.

Red Gamay Savoy wine.

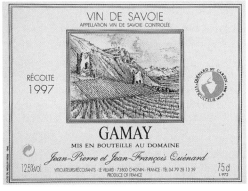

Red Mondeuse Savoy wine.

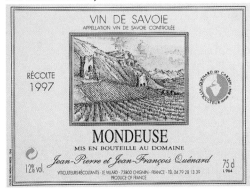

Red Pinot Noir Savoy wine.

PÉTILLANT & VINS MOUSSEUX DE SAVOIE
AYZE
SEYSSEL

Ayze is made with the Gringet grape, while Seyssel derives its charm from the Molette and Altesse grapes. Both are excellent lightly sparkling white wines of great elegance. Drink at 10°C (50°F).

VINS DU BUGEY

The vineyards of Bugey lie to the west of Savoie in the department of Ain. This VDQS wine is relatively unknown and often also unloved because of its fresh

Ayze.

Seyssel.

acidity. The Bugey wine-growing district was once more extensive but today the small vineyards are scattered over a large area, mainly on land with broken chalk soils.

Although there are a number of acceptable red and white still wines produced in Bugey, the sparkling Cerdon is the most interesting to mention. This wine is constantly improving its quality.

Provence

The region

The wine-growing region of Provence covers a large territory from Nice to Arles. It is no surprise therefore that Provençal wines vary so greatly in their colour, bouquet, and taste. The vineyards are

The best wines come from independent estates.

often widely scattered which makes working them more difficult. Most growers therefore belong to a co-operative to keep their costs down. The best wines generally come from smaller independent estates, which bottle their own wines. The price of these wines is naturally dearer than those from co-operatives but the difference in quality justifies the extra cost.

The grape varieties

In common with much of the rest of the south of France, a wide assortment of grape varieties are grown in Provence. There are 20 different types in total. Most wines are made by blending more than one grape variety.

For red and rosé wines the choice is from Carignan, Cinsault, Grenache, Mourvèdre, Cabernet Sauvignon, Syrah and the less well-known Tibouren, Calitor, Braquet, Folle Noire (Fuella) and Barberoux. For the white wines Ugni Blanc, Clairette, Rolle and Semillon are used, sometimes supplemented with Chardonnay, White Grenache, Picpoul, Sauvignon Blanc and Muscat.

The wines

There are eight AC areas in Provence. We start with the most Northerly and then travel via Nice and along the coast to Arles.

CÔTES DE PROVENCE

This is the largest appellation of Provence wines in terms of volume. The area is subdivided into five terroirs: Les collines du Haut Pays, La vallée intérieure, La bordure maritime, Le bassin du Beausset and La Ste-Victoire.

CÔTES DE PROVENCE ROSÉ

The colour of the rosé depends on the wine-making method used and the length of time that the juice remained in contact with the grape skins. The longer this is, the darker is the wine. Provençal rosé is dry, fruity, and elegant. The colour is always clear and sparkling. Drink at approx. 10°C (50°F).

One of the most popular rosé wines.

CÔTES DE PROVENCE ROUGE

This is an excellent wine made by traditional methods but with the help of modern technology. The wide differences in colour, bouquet, and taste result from the different terroirs, grapes used, and vinification method. Some wines are light and fruity with floral notes, others are mainly aged in wood, stronger, and fuller. These wines need to be kept for a few years before drinking them.

Drink the lighter coloured fruity types slightly chilled at 14°C (57.2°F) while the heavier types are better served slightly warmer at approx. 16°C (60.8°F).

Côtes de Provence red.   *Côtes de Provence (estate).*

CÔTES DE PROVENCE BLANC
This is a very rare wine of high quality and always made with just white grapes: Blancs de Blancs. The choice of grapes and the terroir determine the character of the wine – from fresh and lithe to full-bodied and rounded.
This wine is worth discovering. Drink it chilled at approx. 10–12°C (50–53.6°F).

Côteaux Varois rosé.

BANDOL
The vineyards of Bandol are planted in terraces or restanques on poor, calciferous gravels, protected by the amphitheatre of the wooded mountains (Massif de Ste-Beaume, 1,147 metres/3,763 feet).

The sun shines here for at least 3,000 hours per year. Fortunately the easterly and south-easterly winds bring showers and the southerly winds from the Mediterranean mitigate the heat.

CÔTEAUX VAROIS
Côteaux Varois has only been recognised with an AC appellation since 1993. Pleasing, fruity, and full-bodied wines are made in the centre of the department of Var, around the picturesque little Provençal town of Brignoles.

Of these, 60% are rosé, 35% red, and a mere 5% white wines. The wine is similar to the Côtes de Provence.

Côteaux Varois red.

Generations of hard-working wine-growers built and maintain the restanques by hand. It is a constant battle over the course of centuries on this dry soil and steep slopes to prevent erosion. There is never a quiet time in these vineyards. Every job has to be done by hand because machines cannot work these terraces. This has its effect on the price of a good Bandol wine. An important factor in the price is the profit per hectare.

The legally prescribed maximum yield of 40 hectolitres per hectare is almost impossible to achieve here. The average is around 35 hectolitre per hectare. The total area in cultivation amounts to slightly more than 1,000 hectares. The local winemakers are perfectionists who constantly seek the best sites, the best grapes, the best vats etc. Their results mirror their efforts. Bandol belongs to the elite club of great French wines.

BANDOL ROUGE
Red Bandol must contain at least 50 per cent Mourvèdre, which can be made up to 90 per cent of the volume with Grenache and/or Cinsault. The remaining 10 per cent may be Syrah and Carignan. The character of red Bandol is determined therefore by the Mourvèdre grape.

Where other grape varieties provide almost baked aromas to the wine because of the great number of hours of sun, Mourvèdre retains its fruity bouquet, making it an ideal choice for the Bandol vineyards. Bandol red is very full of tannin when young so that it needs to be aged for at least 18 months in oak. Many find Bandol red too expensive and the wine too harsh. These are people who do not have the patience to lay the wine down for at least six but preferably ten years before drinking. Only then is Bandol at its best.

The bouquet is a sublime combination of red and black fruit (wild cherry), peony, humus, and heliotrope. When the wine is older (more than ten years), classic aromas of truffle, pepper, vanilla, liquorice, cinnamon, and musk come to the top. A good vintage Bandol red can be kept for at least 20 years. Do not drink Bandol red then when young

Bandol red.   *Bandol rosé.*

but at a mature age and serve at approx. 16–18°C (60.8–64.4°F).

BANDOL ROSÉ
The same strict proportions of grapes apply to this wine also. A Bandol Rosé combines the essential elements of Mourvèdre (wild cherry, red and black fruit, peony, heliotrope, and pepper) with its own charm, power, freshness, and depth. Serve Bandol Rosé at approx. 10–12°C (50–53.6°F).

BANDOL BLANC
This white wine is exceptionally fresh, full-bodied, and impertinent. The wine is made with Clairette, Ugni Blanc and Bourboulenc. Grapefruit and lemon together with floral notes can be detected in the bouquet. The taste is full of flavour, fleshy, and whimsical. Do not serve Bandol Blanc to cool (approx. 10–12°C/50–53.6°F).

CASSIS
This much-loved wine has nothing whatever to do with the popular blackcurrant soft drink. Cassis is the name of an idyllic harbour town on the Mediterranean.

The harbour is encircled by imposing cliffs which protect the vineyards of one of France's most delightful white wines. Of the 175 hectares of

Cassis Blanc de Blancs.

vineyards, 123 hectares are devoted to white wines. Rosé and red Cassis are also produced. Both are surprisingly fruity, lithe, and pleasant.

CASSIS BLANC
A good Cassis Blanc is not readily found outside its locality because local demand exceeds the supply. The wine smells of beeswax, honey, ripe fruit, cedarwood, may and lilac blossom, almond, and hazelnut.
The taste is very fresh and full-bodied. The acidity that is clearly present provides a good structure to the wine. Drink white Cassis at 10–12°C (50–53.6°F).

Côteaux d'Aix-en-Provence

This extensive area lies to the south of Durance, stretching to the Mediterranean in the south and the Rhône in the west. The soil is chalky and the changeable landscape is characterised by small mountains and alluvial valleys. The mountains run parallel to the coast and are covered with scrub, wild herbs (maquis), and coniferous woodland. The valleys have a subsoil of broken rock and gravel, interspersed with calciferous sandstone and shale, mixed with sand, gravel, and alluvium. The wine-growing area is fairly large, covering approx. 3,500 hectares.

Côteaux d'Aix-en-Provence.   *Côteaux d'Aix-en-Provence rosé.*

CÔTEAUX D'AIX-EN-PROVENCE ROSÉ
This wine is light, fruity, and very pleasant. The better Côteaux d'Aix-en-Provence rosé is full-bodied and powerful, with dominant floral notes. Drink this wine young at approx. 10–12°C (50–53.6°F).

CÔTEAUX D'AIX-EN-PROVENCE ROUGE
This is an exciting wine that can be somewhat rustic. The wine is none too elegant and lacks finesse but is characteristic of its terroir, with fruitiness, power, and sultry notes of leather, pepper, spices, and herbs.
The tannin is muted, so that the wine can be drunk while young. The better wine is however at its best

Côteaux d'Aix-en-Provence red.

after about three years. Drink it at about 14–16°C (57.2–60.8°F).

CÔTEAUX D'AIX-EN-PROVENCE BLANC

This fairly rare white wine made with Grenache Blanc, Bourboulenc, Clairette, Grolle, Sauvignon and Ugni Blanc is often full-bodied, charming, and at the same time elegant. It smells of blossom such as may and/or shrubs such as privet and box. The taste is fresh, full, very romantic, and very characteristic. Serve it about 10–12°C (50–53.6).

Les Baux-de-Provence

This area is actually part of the Côteaux d'Aix-en-Provence, but gained its own AC in 1995. The landscape here is dominated by the rugged and picturesque Alpilles hills that are interspersed with vineyards and olive groves.

The area gained its own AC because of its local microclimate and enforcement of stricter production criteria. Only the red and rosé wines from a designated 300 hectares surrounding the town of Les Baux-de-Provence are permitted to bear this appellation.

LES BAUX-DE-PROVENCE ROSÉ

The colour is the first thing that strikes one. It is a superb salmon-pink, while the nose is reminiscent of redcurrant, strawberry, and other red fruit. The taste is fresh, fruity (grapefruit and cherry), and very pleasant. This is a rosé that can charm most people. Drink it chilled at 10–12°C (50–53.6°F).

LES BAUX-DE-PROVENCE ROUGE

The colour of this wine is a fairly dark ruby red. The nose is complex and strong with hints of wood, vanilla, liquorice, plum jam, caramel, coffee, humus, and occasionally of cherry brandy. The taste is fairly coarse in the first five years because of the strong youthful tannin but after some years in the bottle the taste becomes more rounded, fuller, and more powerful. Drink at 16–18°C (60.8–64.4°F).

Corsica

Two faces

The grapes used for the first eight AC wines listed are the traditional varieties of Niellucciu, Sciacarello and Vermentinu, whilst Vermentinu, Nielluccio, Sciaccarello and Grenache are used for the generic Vins de Corse AC. The Vins de Pays wines are dominated by Cabernet, Merlot and Chardonnay. Corsica is divided in two areas in terms of its terroir. In the north (Bastia, Calvi, Corte, and Alèria) have complex soils of clay and chalk around Bastia (Patrimonio AC) and blue shale on the east coast, while the south (Porto, Ajaccio, Sartène, Bonifacio en Porto-Vecchio) consist entirely of igneous rock and granite. This dividing line is only a guide of course since there are countless mini-terroirs and microclimates to discover on the island.

Grape varieties

The three 'native' varieties of grape on Corsica are not actually entirely native. The names may be different but in reality two of the three are well-known from elsewhere.

VERMENTINU

The white Vermentinu grape, also known as Corsican Malvoisie, is a typical Mediterranean grape which is also cultivated in Italy, Spain, and Portugal, where it produces white wines of quality.
The wine are very floral, usually strong in alcohol, full-bodied, and with abundant taste but definite aftertaste of bitter almond and apple. In common with the Italian practice this grape is also often added to red grapes to make a fine rosé, but also to enhance the flavour of red wine.

NIELLUCCIU

This is a world-famous grape that is better-known under the name of 'Jupiter's Blood' or Tuscan Sangiovese. The wine from this Niellucciu can be recognised by its nose of red fruit, violets, herbs, and sometimes apricot. When it is older it develops characteristic flavours of game, fur, and liquorice. The taste is worldly, fatty, and lithe. Niellucciu is particularly used to produce Patrimonio wines.

SCIACCARELLO

Sciaccarello is also known locally as Sciaccarellu, which has a meaning akin to 'crackling'. These vines thrive extremely well on granite soil, such as around Ajaccio. Sciaccarello wines are very refined and recognisable above all by the characteristic pepper taste and aroma.

The nine AC wines

CÔTEAUX DU CAP CORSE

This is a minuscule wine-growing appellation area with a mere 30 hectares, situated on mountainous slopes to the north of Bastia. Red, rosé, but chiefly white wines are made here. The white, based on the Vermentinu grape, is excellent and very refined.

MUSCAT DU CAP CORSE

This wine is produced in the same mountainous areas as the Côteaux du Cap Corse and also in the Patrimonio area. This appellation was officially recognised in 1993, although the local Muscat wines have enjoyed international fame for centuries. It is fine and very aromatic.

The best Muscat is made from grapes that are picked very late, ripened and dried under the sun in small boxes. This makes a full-flavoured, very aromatic wine, that is fatty and strong. It can be readily laid down and should be drunk chilled to approx. 8°C (46.4°F).

PATRIMONIO

This is one of the best known and often also best wines of Corsica. Red and rosé wines are produced from the Niellucciu group and the Vermentinu grape here produces a superb white.

PATRIMONIO BLANC

This is a pale yellow wine that is tinged with green, It has floral notes (may blossom and white flowers), a fresh and fruity taste and it is full-bodied and rounded, sometimes causing a light tingling of the tongue. Drink this elegant wine at approx. 10°C (50°F).

PATRIMONIO ROSÉ

This wine has a pale, clear pink colour and aromas of red fruit (cherry, redcurrant), and sometimes also of exotic fruit. Drink this fresh and fruity rosé at approx. 10°C (50°F).

PATRIMONIO ROUGE

Two different types of Patrimonio red are made: a lighter one and the traditional more robust wine. The lighter Patrimonio is generally ruby red, very fruity (blackcurrant, blackberry), velvet soft in spite of the presence of tannin, and very well balanced. When it is older the fruity nose develops earthly notes such as humus. Drink this wine at approx. 16°C (60.8°F) with red meat, game, casseroles, and hard cheeses. The more robust, traditional Patrimonio is darker in colour and has more tannin

Patrimonio white, rosé, and red.

than the lighter version. When older its fruity bouquet develops into a complex nose of overripe preserved fruit, leather, and liquorice. Drink this 'strong man' of a wine between 16–18°C (60.8–64.4°F). Both wines are best decanted several hours before a meal.

VIN DE CORSE CALVI

Here very fruity red wines, fascinating, refined, and aromatic rosés, and almost colourless, comforting, and approachable white wines are produced on very changeable soils of coarse stones, boulders, and gravel using Niellucciu, Grenache, Cinsault, Sciaccarellu, and Vermentinu grapes.

Vin de Corse Calvi.

Ajaccio

This wine area lies on rough, rocky hills. Ajaccio is proud of its permanent resident – the Sciaccarellu grape –with which the greatest wines from this area develop a nose that evokes roasted almond and red fruit such as raspberry.

This traditional wine is good for laying down. The white Malvoisie (Vermentinu) is also worth laying down.

Ajaccio white and rosé.   *Ajaccio red.*

Vin de Corse Sartènais

The Sciaccarellu, Grenache and Cinsault vines cultivated on these steep hills produce a full-bodied red wine and fresh rosé. These wines are mainly consumed by the local populace and are rarely seen outside the island.

VIN DE CORSE FIGARI
The most southerly wine-growing area of France, just north of the town of Bonifacio. Sturdy red, rosé, and white wines are produced.

VIN DE CORSE PORTO VECCHIO
An elegant, full-bodied, and rounded red wine and fresh, refined, and very aromatic rosé are made in the south-east of the island using the Niellucciu and Sciaccarellu grapes, together with Grenache. A very dry white wine that is intensely fruity is made here with Vermentinu grapes.

VIN DE CORSE
In Corsican terms the vineyards around Alèria and close to Bastia are immense at 1,550 hectares. This is a relatively new appellation but the early results are promising.

After centuries of neglect the vineyards have been re-established in places where the Greeks and Romans made their best wines, at the foot of 1,200 metres (3,937 feet) high rocky walls. All the types of wine are produced here, including Vin de Pays. There are both very traditional winemakers and ultra-modern co-operatives which are gaining an increasing reputation in France and abroad for their less traditional but well-made wines. Even the Vin de Pays here is of quality. The demand for this AC is increasing as is also the case for the Vins de Pays and vins de cépages. Fewer inferior wines are now being produced on Corsica with the growers having decided to improve their image.

Languedoc-Roussillon

A third of all French wines originate from Languedoc-Roussillon. Most of this wine though falls below the category of Vins de Pays or even Vins de Table. This region produces at least 75 per cent of French Vins de Pays, slightly better than the ordinary table wine but generally not of the standard of a well-made AC wine. There are of course many exceptions. Many of these Vins de Pays are sold under the variety of grape as vins de cépages.

Between Rhône and Languedoc

COSTIÈRES DE NÎMES
This area lies between the Rhône and Languedoc-Roussillon but is not accepted as part of either. You may often encounter Costières de Nîmes as the odd-man-out among the wines of Languedoc. Costières de Nîmes is produced as white, rosé. and red wines

Vin de Pays díOc with Mediterranean delicacies.

Costières de Nîmes. *Costières de Nîmes.*

within the very picturesque area between Nîmes and the Camargue. The area of the appellation has grown enormously in recent decades but it set to grow further (currently 10,000 hectares). The vineyards of Costières de Nîmes are in hilly countryside on soils that are full of gravel and boulders.

The white wine is often made with the latest technology and is fresh, very aromatic (floral notes, exotic fruit, peach) and very pleasing. Drink it chilled at approx. 10°C (50°F).
The rosé is dry, full-bodied, and very fruity (red fruit and peach). The taste is fresh and rounded with a good balance between acidity and roundness. Drink it chilled at 10–12°C (50–53.6°F).
The red wine is fruity, full of flavour, and full-bodied. The nose is reminiscent of freshly picked blackberry, redcurrant, and blackcurrant, with a suggestion of vanilla, wood, and tobacco. Drink it at approx. 14–16°C (57.2–60.8°F).

Languedoc

Much effort has been devoted in recent decades to achieve a comeback, with the key words being quality and diversity. With its 30,000 hectares of vineyards categorised as AC, Languedoc is the third largest wine region of France. The Languedoc developed in less than 20 years as the newest large wine-growing area of France. The former short-sighted mass production has given way to quality and consistency with a respect for tradition but with the help of the latest technology.

Perfect conditions

The success of the comeback is largely due to the work of the wine-growers and the government, who had the courage to start afresh. Mother nature has played her part though. The Languedoc is an extensive region of great variety: wide sandy beaches on the Mediterranean coast, countless lakes, the steep hills of the Cévennes, chalk soils, shales, gravel, boulders and a real mosaic of different terroirs and vineyards. The vineyards of Languedoc have been entirely renewed in the past 20 years with an emphasis given to planting vines of the Mediterranean varieties of Grenache, Mourvèdre and Syrah.
Additionally research was carried out into the restoration and improvement of various native grapes. The grapes of this region are generally vinified individually per variety and blended after fermentation.

The appellations from east to west

CÔTEAUX DU LANGUEDOC

Various white, rosé, and red wines are produced from 8,255 hectares of vineyards between Nîmes and Narbonne. Certain of these wines (St-Chinian and Faugères reds and the white Clairette du Languedoc) are permitted to bear their own AC label.

The other wines carry the Côteaux du Languedoc AC combined with the name of their terroir or just plain Côteaux du Languedoc AC.

Each terroir has its own added value and character but it is characteristic of all Côteaux du Languedoc

Côteaux du Languedoc/Vins de Pays de l'Hérault.

Côteaux du Languedoc. *Unfiltered wine.*

wines to be fresh, lithe, pleasing, and friendly in their taste.

The terroirs:

CÔTEAUX DE ST-CHRISTOL
CÔTEAUX DE VÉRARGUES
ST-DREZERY
PIC ST-LOUP
CÔTEAUX DE LA MÉJANELLE
ST-GEORGES-D'ORQUES
(All north of Lunel and Montpellier)

ST-SATURNIN
MONTPEYROUX
(North of Clermont-l'Hérault)

CABRIÈRES
PICPOUL DE PINET (BLANC)
(North of Sète)

LA CLAPE (ROUGE & BLANC)
QUATOURZE
(South of Narbonne)

Try them all: each wine has something different to impart of sea, herbs, shrubs, the soil, the lakes, and the sun.

The red wines are dominated by Syrah, either on its own or in company with Grenache, Cinsault, Carignan and (increasingly) Mourvèdre.

The whites are made with Marsanne, Roussanne, Grenache Blanc, Rolle, Bourboulenc, Clairette and Picpoul. This last grape variety gives its name to the well-known Picpoul de Pinet.

Drinking temperature: white wines 10°C (50°F), rosé 12°C (53.6°F), and red at 14–16°C (57.2–60.8°F).

Picpoul de Pinet.   *La Clape.*

MUSCAT DE LUNEL

This is a relatively small appellation area (307 hectares) which produces an exceptionally fruity Muscat wine that is a vin doux naturel. The ground is strewn with boulders with a subsoil of red clay. The vineyards are situated on a ridge of hills around the town of Lunel, between Nîmes and Montpellier. Only the very scented Muscat Petit Grains grapes are used to make this wine. The characteristic nose

Rare late harvested organic wine.

of a Muscat de Lunel is of citrus fruit and floral scents, completed with notes of honey, preserved fruit, and raisins. The best Muscat de Lunel wines sometimes also have a pleasing bitter and peppery aftertaste. Drinking temperature: 6°C (42.8°F).

CLAIRETTE DU LANGUEDOC

The white Clairette grape is one of the oldest varieties and Clairette de Languedoc is one of the oldest and smallest appellations of Languedoc. The vineyards are situated on the hills of the Hérault valley, south of Lodève, approx. 30 km (19 miles) from the sea. Drinking temperature: 10–12°C (50–53.6°F).

MUSCAT DE MIREVAL

This is a vin doux naturel from Mireval, between Montpellier and Sète. The vineyards are on the southern slopes of the Gardiole mountain which dominates the Vic lake. The ground is chalky with alluvium here and there and also rocks. This wine is also made using the Muscat Petit Grains. It is a comforting, fruity wine that is almost like a liqueur. The charm of Muscat de Mireval is in its refined floral and fruity aromas of jasmine, lime blossom, citrus fruit, and raisins. Drinking temperature: 6°C (42.8°F).

MUSCAT DE FRONTIGNAN

The Frontignan vineyards are slightly more southerly than those of Mireval, immediately north of Sète. This Muscat wine is stronger than the previous two and is even more like a liqueur. The bouquet is somewhat less aromatic than the other Muscat wines and generally somewhat coarser, though there are exceptions. The nose does contain recognisable notes of citrus fruit, overripe Muscat grapes or even of raisins. The best Muscat de Frontignan wines develop a superb nose of exotic fruit such as passion fruit, and peach, and are very elegant. Drinking temperature: 6°C (42.8°F)

FAUGÈRES

The vineyards of Faugères are slightly to the north of Béziers, situated on a gently rolling ridge of hills of shale. The area is off-the-beaten track, hilly, but both inviting and intimate. A lithe and silken red

Muscat de Frontignan.

Faugères red.

St-Chinian.

Minervois.

wine is produced in the small villages that both smells and taste of ripe fruit and liquorice. After several years of maturing the wine tends towards spicier aromas and notes of leather. Drinking temperature: 14–16°C (57.2–60.8°F). Faugères also produces a little rosé which combines the velvet smooth and fruity character of the red wine with a mellow freshness. Drinking temperature: 12°C (53.6°F).

Faugères red.

ST CHINIAN
Red and rosé St Chinian wines are produced at the foot of the Montagne Noire, north-east of Béziers. There are two different types of St Chinian: a light, playful wine that is lithe and comforting, with much fruitiness and a heavier, more powerful wine with nose of ripe fruit, bay laurel, and flint. The first type is drunk when young, preferable chilled (12–14°C/53.6–57.2°F) while the latter is better left a few years before drinking at 14–16°C (53.6–57.2°F). Drink the St Chinian rosé at 12°C (53.6°F).

MUSCAT DE ST-JEAN DE MINERVOIS
The vineyards of St-Jean de Minervois lie amid the maquis and wild Provençal herbs at a height of 200 metres (656 feet). The soil is a mixture of chalk and shale on a base of red clay. Here too the grape used

is exclusively Muscat Petit Grains. A superb, very aromatic wine is produced in this very small area of 159 hectares. Intense aromas of citrus fruit, fresh Muscat grapes, exotic fruit, and menthol are characteristic of Muscat de St-Jean de Minervois. In spite of its liqueur-like properties, this Muscat is still exceptionally fresh-tasting. Drinking temperature: 6°C (42.8°F).

MINERVOIS
The vineyards of Minervois, which are largely arranged on terraces, are situated in a triangle formed by Carcassonne, Narbonne and Béziers. The production is mainly of red wine but if you search you will also find rosé or even the rarer white Minervois. The red wine is fruity, refined, elegant, and well-balanced. There are as many different types of Minervois as there are different terroirs. In the Minervois the wine gives you a free lesson in geology with gneiss, chalk, shale, lignite, and alluvial deposits mixed together in the soil to give the Minervois its own character. Drink the rosé chilled (12°C/53.6°F) and the red wine at 14–16°C (57.2–60.8°F).

CABARDÈS
Excellent rosé and red wines are produced from 331 hectares to the north of the fine Medieval town of Carcassonne. Drinking temperature: 14–16°C (57.2–60.8°F).

Cabardès VDQS.

MALEPÈRE
This is the most westerly wine-growing area of the Languedoc, located in the triangle formed by Carcassonne, Limoux, and Castelnaudary. Malepère is in the process of achieving Appellation Contrôlée status. The rosé and red wines from here are fairly light and fruity. Drinking temperature: rosé 12°C (53.6°F), red 14–16°C (57.2–60.8°F).

Limoux

Still and sparkling white wines are produced in the 41 communes around Limoux. The climate in this area is clearly influenced by the Mediterranean, moderated by the influence of the Atlantic. It is much greener here than elsewhere in the Languedoc but from this apparent cool the local wines are somewhat tempestuous. Various Roman authors extolled the quality of the still wine of Limoux around the start of the first millennium. The natural conversion of still wine into sparkling was not discovered by a Benedictine monk until 1531. The first brut was produced at St-Hilaire, close to Limoux.

BLANQUETTE DE LIMOUX

This fresh sparkling wine must be produced with a minimum of 90 per cent of Mauzac grapes. The only grapes permitted to be supplemented are Chardonnay and Chenin Blanc. After the initial fermentation and acquisition of the basic wine, tirage de liqueur is added to the wine. This causes a second fermentation in the bottle which adds bubbles to the wine.

The residues from the fermentation are removed after at least nine months in the process of dégorgement. Depending on the desired taste (brut or demi-sec) either none, a little, or more liqueur is added. Blanquette de Limoux is pale yellow tinged with green, is lightly but enduringly sparkling and has a fine nose of green apple and spring blossom together with a floral, fresh, and fruity taste. Drinking temperature: 6–8°C (42.8–46.4°F).

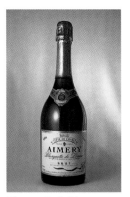

Blanquette de Limoux.

Crémant de Limoux from a co-operative.

CRÉMANT DE LIMOUX

This wine is actually closely related to the Blanquette. The differences are in the proportion of grapes used: a minimum of 60 per cent Mauzac (instead of 90) and a maximum of 20 per cent Chardonnay and 20 per cent Chenin Blanc together with a minimum maturation of 12 months instead of nine. The colour is pale golden, while the nose is very aromatic with suggestions of white flowers and

toast, the taste is complex, light, and fresh. This Crémant is always characterised by its gentle, more delicate bubbles that make this a very subtle and elegant wine. Drinking temperature: 6–8°C (42.8–46.4°F). There are special luxury cuvées of both the Blanquette and the Crémant. These do not perhaps possess the same finesse at top Champagnes but they do benefit from the warmth and generosity of the Mediterranean and the South of France. The price is exceptionally reasonable.

BLANQUETTE DE LIMOUX MÉTHODE ANCESTRALE

This Blanquette is made according to an ancient method in which the wine from 100 per cent Mauzac grapes ferment until there is only 100 grams of sugar per litre remaining. The fermentation is stopped by tapping the must and filtering it. The wine that is not fully fermented is then bottled and through

Crémant de Limoux Cuvée from a co-operative.

warmth a second fermentation occurs in the bottle. When the right balance between alcohol (5–7%), sugars (approx. 70 grams per litre), and the pressure in the bottle is achieved, the fermentation is abruptly

Antech's Crémant de Limoux Luxe Cuvée.

Blanquette de Limoux, méthode ancestrale.

Limoux Terroir Méditerrannéen.

Limoux Terroir Haut-Vallée.

Pays d'Ocë7 sisters' Sauvignon and Chardonnay.

halted by chilling the bottle. The colour of the wine is straw yellow and not always clear. Since this is an ancient traditional method with little modern technology the wine can contain sediments of unfermented sugars and dead yeast cells. The scent is similar to a ripe Goudreinet apple. The taste is fresh due to the 4.5 grams per litre of acidity and the presence of the carbonic acid gas combined with fruitiness and softness imparted by the sugar residues. This wine is low in alcohol (7%). Drinking temperature: 6°C (42.8°F).

LIMOUX

In addition to the better-known sparkling wines, excellent white wines are also produced here. These must contain a minimum 15 per cent of Mauzac grapes but may be supplemented with Chardonnay and Chenin Blanc. The local Cave des Sieurs d'Arques manages to achieve sublime heights with this still Limoux wine, of which four different types, each with its own terroir are made.

The Terroir Méditerranée is a rounded, harmonious and lithe wine with much fruitiness. Drinking temperature: 12°C (53.6°F).

The Terroir Océanique is somewhat lighter coloured than the others. It has wonderful scents of citrus fruits that are fine and elegant.

The taste is fruity with a hint of iodine. This wine is

Cabernet rosé and Merlot red.

Pays d'Oc Cabernet Sauvignon.

very fresh and elegant. Drinking temperature: 12–14°C (53.6–57.2°F).

The Terroir d'Autan is yellow with golden tinges. It has intense aromas with a finish of preserved fruit, and is broad, rounded, and fruity in flavour. Drinking temperature: 12–14°C (53.6–57.2°F).

The Terroir Haute Vallée is yellow with golden tinges and has delicate scents of white flowers combined with a very harmonious taste that is

Limoux Terroir Océanique.

Limoux Terroir d'Autan.

Pays d'Oc Grenache.

Pays d'Oc Syrah.

rounded, fresh, and both subtle and complex. Drinking temperature: 12–14°C (53.6–57.2°F).

The Cave Coopérative des Sieurs d'Arques also produces pleasing Vins de Pays and vins de cépage.

Corbières

The Corbières landscape is so hilly and sometime so inhospitable that not other form of agriculture than viticulture is possible. The vineyards, spread over 23,000 hectares, lie between countless silent witnesses to a tempestuous history. The strong wind blows eerily through the ruins of the old Catholic establishments and shake them to their foundations. Higher up in Corbières the ground is chalk and slate. With the exception of the odd proud cypress that is forced to bend its head to the wild wind, there are few trees to be seen. The more mellow coastal strip of Sigean consists of chalk hills, while central Corbières is predominantly gravel and stone. The Corbières region is a veritable patchwork, consisting of diverse soil types and microclimates, divided into 11 terroirs: Sigean, Durban, Quéribus, Termenès, St-Victor, Fontfroide, Lagrasse, Serviès, Montagne d'Alaric, Lézignan and Boutenac. It is therefore almost impossible to give generalised characteristics for the wines of Corbières. The white wines are fine and fresh with floral aromas. The acidity and roundness are in perfect balance. The wine from Lagrasse smells of exotic fruits, wood, and of something smoky, while those of Quéribus have the scent of pears and pineapples with a finish of white flowers. The bouquet of Lézignan is reminiscent of anise or fennel. Drinking temperature: 10–12°C (50–53.6°F).

The rosé is fresh and very pleasing, sometimes light and fruity (Durban), can be full-bodied and velvety (Alaric), but generally very aromatic with refined bouquet of fruits, flowers, and herbs. Drinking temperature: 12°C (53.6°F). The red wine is intense, broad and rounded with aromas typically of red fruit, herbs and peppers. There is tannin present, though muted so that the wine can be kept for several years. The Mourvèdre in Sigean imparts the

Corbières white and rosé.   *Corbières red.*

wine with greater elegance, while this role is taken in Serviès by the Syrah. The velvet, full-bodied, and complex wine of Quéribus often develops notes of cocoa, coffee, or other roasted aromas. Those of Alaric are very fruity (wild berries) with vegetal or herbal undertones. The wine of Termenès develops the classic humus and truffle aromas as it ages. Those of Lézignan are intensely fruity (of overripe or even preserved fruits) with suggestions reminiscent of the maquis and very aromatic wild herbs of the Provençal landscape. There may even be a hint of clove to be detected. The wine of Boutenac immediately invokes thoughts of the Provençal wild thyme, rosemary, bay laurel, and also sometimes has notes of liquorice and vanilla. There is always

Corbières red.   *Fitou.*

something else to discover in Corbières. Drinking temperature: 14–16°C (57.2–60.8°F).

Fitou

This is the oldest established red wine AC of the Languedoc. There is a clear differentiation between Fitou that is made from the coastal strip and that produced inland. A superb full-bodied, and powerful red wine is produced from approx. 2,500 hectares between Narbonne and Perpignan. The bouquet and the taste of the best Fitou have overwhelming influences of Provençal herbs such as bay laurel, thyme, and rosemary, sometimes with a touch of clove, and flint. The best Fitou benefits from lengthy maturing in oak and can certainly be laid down. The wine is extremely popular with the French and English. Drinking temperature: 16°C (60.8°F).

Roussillon

The vineyards of Roussillon are situated south of Corbières, at the foot of the Pyrenees, on part of Catalonia that has been French since 1642. The vineyards stretch themselves out, beneath the hot and drying Mediterranean sun, across a variety of different types of soil and landscape, from the coast to deep inland. The coastal strip south of Fitou to Argelès-sur-Mer is an oasis of calm for both nature lovers and sun-worshippers. From Argelès to the Spanish border the landscape is more rugged and hilly, with the only haven being the picturesque bay of Collioure.

Maury

Once of France's finest wines – the red vin doux naturel – is produced in the country around the small town of Maury. The blue vines of Grenache that are kept pruned low produce very low yields of grapes but they are high in juice in the sun-baked rocky soil. Young Maury is granite red while more mature ones tend to the colour of mahogany. A good Maury is very aromatic: when young is develops above all fruity aromas (red fruit), later suggestions of cocoa coffee, and preserved fruits dominate. Although the cheaper Maury wines can be pleasant, it is better to choose the best ones for these are better value. One estate is worthy of particular recommendation for its velvet soft wine with an unparalleled and fascinating bouquet of spiced

Vintage Maury.

Maury.

bread, liquorice, plums, and cocoa: Domaine du Mas Amiel. Drinking temperature: 16–18°C (60.8–64.4°F).

Rivesaltes

This is the largest appellation for vin doux naturels at 10,821 hectares. Moderately sweet wines used to be made here once from both red and white Grenache grapes. There has been a change under way here though since 1996. The areas cultivated have been significantly reduced, with the yield per hectare lowered as the growers seem to have become aware of the potential quality of their wine. Various grape varieties are used to make these vin doux naturels: red and white Grenache, Macabeu, Malvoisie, and Muscat. There are two types of Rivesaltes: the amber-coloured wine produced with white grapes, and the roof-tile red wine of

at least 50 per cent Grenache Noir. The better cuvées (Rivesaltes hors d' âge) should be kept for at least five years. The young ordinary Rivesaltes should be drunk at approx. 12°C (53.6°F), while the better ones are best at 14–16°C (57.2–60.8°F).

MUSCAT DE RIVESALTES

Amidst the vineyards of Maury, Rivesaltes, and Banyuls, 4,540 hectares *Muscat de Rivesaltes.*
are planted with Muscat of Alexandria and Muscat Petits Grains. The Muscat of Alexandria imparts breadth to the Muscat de Rivesaltes in addition to aromas of ripe fruits, raisins, and roses, while the Muscat Petits Grains is responsible for the heady bouquet of exotic citrus fruit and suggestion of menthol. This Muscat de Rivesaltes is at its fruitiest when still very young. Drink it at 8–10°C (46.4–50°F).

Côtes du Roussillon

The soils of the vineyards of Roussillon are very complex and variable: chalk, clay, shale, gneis, granite, and alluvial deposits, causing great variety in the types and tastes of these wines. The climate is extremely hot in summer and mild in winter but rain does not fall evenly throughout the year. An entire vineyard can be destroyed by a cloudburst. Wine-making in Roussillon in the past decades has changed greatly with significant improvement of the regulation of temperature before and during fermentation. The white wine is light, fresh, and fruity: drink it at 10–12°C (50–53.6°F). The rosé is produced by the saignée methode, meaning that the red wine is drawn off early and then vinified as white wine. Because the wine is drawn off so quickly, the grape skins have had just enough time to impart their wonderful red colour without adding tannin

Côtes du Roussillon white

Côtes du Roussillon Taïchat white

Côtes du Roussillon rosé.

Côtes du Roussillon red.

Côtes du Roussillon Villages Latour de France.

Côtes du Roussillon Villages Caramany.

Cask-aged Côtes du Roussillon red.

Côtes du Roussillon Villages Tautavel.

to the wine. This rosé is very fruity. Drink it at 12°C (53.6°F). There are two different types of red wine. A light wine is often produced by steeping in carbonic acid gas (macération carbonique), which is fruity, slightly spicy, and particularly pleasing. Drink it at 12–14°C (53.6–57.2°F).

The traditionally made red wine is stronger and more rounded. The bouquet tends towards red cherry, plums, preserved fruit, and spices. The wine can be kept for some time because it is aged in wood. Drink it at 14–16°C (57.2–60.8°F).

Côtes du Roussillon Villages

The difference of this red wine from the other Côtes du Roussillon wines is its specific terroirs, which mainly consist of the sides of hills or terraces of shale, chalk, and granite. The grapes used are the same as ordinary Côtes du Roussillon but the output per hectare is much lower. The appellation Côtes du Roussillon Villages may be used by 32 communes in the north of the department on vineyards extending to 2,000 hectares. These wines are stronger, more powerful, and more complex than Côtes du Roussillon, and can be kept longer. Drink at 16°C (60.8°F).

Among the 32 communes of Côtes du Roussillon Villages, there are four which are permitted to bear their name on the label, in recognition of their higher quality.

Collioure

This fairly small appellation of 330 hectares is spread across four communes: Collioure, Port-Vendres, Banyuls-sur-Mer, and Cerbère. Collioure is produced as rosé, red, and white, and is made with Grenache, Mourvèdre, and Syrah. The red wines are very harmonious, full, warm, and fleshy, with aromas of ripe fruits, minerals, and exotic notes such as pepper, vanilla, and oriental spices.

There are also special cuvées, produced from ancient vineyards of which the ground is rocky, including igneous types. These Cuvées Vignes Rocheuses are highly concentrated. Red Collioure can be drunk in two manners: young and cool (12°C/53.6°F), or mature and at cellar temperature (16°C/60.8°F). Collioure red is one of France's top wines.

The rather rarer rosé is fresh, full-bodied, and extremely rich. Drink at approx. 12°C (53.8°F).

Côtes du Roussillon Villages.

Côtes du Roussillon Villages, traditional vinification.

Collioure.

Collioure Vignes
Rocheuses.

Banyuls

The vineyards of this vin doux naturel are situated along the coast on terraces of shale. The vines grown on the 1,460 hectares of this appellation are mainly Grenache Noir, with some Carignan, Cinsault, Syrah and Mourvèdre. The rich, warm, and powerful character of Banyuls comes from 50 to 75 per cent Grenache Noir. The soil here is extremely poor and rocky with a thin layer of earth that is washed away by each heavy thunderstorm. The work here is hard and much has to be done manually. The grapes ripen ideally in the strong sun so that they are extremely high in sugar when harvested.

The addition of alcohol to the must or mutage often occurs very early in the process, even before the grapes have been pressed. In common with Maury, the oxidation of the wine is the secret of Banyuls. The oxidation is encouraged by only partially filling the barrels or by leaving the wine in the sun in large wicker-covered bottles to partially evaporate.

Countless different cuvées are blended by the wine-maker according to the type of wine desired. Some Banyuls (rimages) are not exposed to oxidation. Instead they are vinified to retain their fruity aromas. Depending on the type, Banyuls can be very fruity (red fruit, cherry), or possess aromas of roasted cocoa or coffee, and preserved and dried fruit

(raisins, almond, other nuts, prune, fig). Young fruity Banyuls (rimages) are drunk as an aperitif at approx. 12°C. Mature to very mature hors d' âge is better drunk slightly warmer at between 14–18°C (57.2–64.4°F).

BANYULS GRAND CRU
These superb jewels are only made in the years of the best vintages. They encompass and sublimate all the wonderful characteristics of Banyuls. A sip of this rich, intense wine is to sample paradise.

The south-west: between Bordeaux and Languedoc-Roussillon

The French sud-ouest is a large area that accounts for almost a quarter of France. The boundaries of the wine territories are not so easily defined. Certain wine-growing areas that are geographically in the south-west prefer for socio-economic reasons to align themselves with their better-known compatriots of Bordeaux.

Consequently, areas such as Bergerac and Côtes de Duras are located in the south-west but are closer socially to the provincial capital of Aquitaine (Bordeaux) than the principal city of the south-west (Toulouse). The alignment is reinforced by the fact that these areas grow the same varieties of grape as Bordeaux. To make matters more simple we stick to listing by geographical region, with Duras and Bergerac added to Aquitaine.

The vineyards of Aveyron

ENTRAYGUES ET LE FEL VDQS
This minuscule area in the heart of the valley of the Lot, between Rouergue and Auvergne, is one of the most picturesque wine-growing areas of France. The vineyards are situated on steep hills surrounding the town of Entraygues and the village of Le Fel, and total about 20 hectares. Around Entraygues the soil consists of broken granite, while it is brown shale at

Banyuls (négociant).

Traditional Banyuls.

Banyuls Hors d'Âge.

Banyuls Hors d'Âge,
Special Reserve.

Le Fel. Both soil types ensure good drainage and temperature regulation by means of the stony ground in this cold wine-growing area. The wines from Entraygues, Le Fel, and nearby Marcillac were once famous and highly regarded in France. It took until the 1960s before this area started to re-establish itself following the phylloxera epidemic and the emptying of the French countryside.

The white wine is made using the old Chenin grape, which produces a fresh wine full of aromas of flowers, citrus fruit, and box. It is a full-bodied wine to be drunk at 10°C (50°F).

The rosé is fresh and somewhat acidic. Drink it at 12°C (53.6°F).

The red wine in common with the rosé is aromatic and fresh-tasting. It possesses a fuller, more rounded taste though. This wine from the Fer Servadou grape (Mansoi) and Cabernet Franc appears to have been made for the regional dishes of the Auvergne and Aveyron, where Montignac appears to remain unheard of. Drinking temperature: 16°C (60.8°F).

MARCILLAC

This area around the town of Rodez was one of the classic French wines prior to the phylloxera epidemic. The 135 hectares of vineyards are typically on soil of red clay at the foot of high chalk plateaux.

The dominant grape for this AC, which was recognised in 1990, is the Mansoi (the local name for the Fer Servadou). The individual character of both Marcillac rosé and red wines, which is somewhere between rustic and modern fruitiness, is imparted by the combination of the Mansoi grape and the soil.

The better Marcillacs are true discoveries for those who like some bite to

Marcillac.

Vins d'Entraygues et du Fel rosé.

Vins d'Entraygues et du Fel rosé.

their wine. The terroir can be tasted in the wine which has aromas of raspberry, blackcurrant, bilberry, and blackberry, together with vegetal notes of green pepper (paprika) and green chillies.

There are often also suggestions of cocoa which ensure an extremely complex finish. Spicy and rounded tannin strengthens the individualistic nature of this wine which is best drunk at 16°C (60.8°F).

Cahors

The vineyards of Cahors are among the oldest in France, enjoying great fame as early as the fifth century. The wine could be shipped throughout the world without loss of quality because it was robust, complex, and highly concentrated. Consequently wine from Cahors was much prized in America but especially in Tsarist Russia.

Nothing happened around Cahors for many years after the phylloxera epidemic of the late nineteenth century, with the vineyards falling into neglect and little more than 'plonk' for daily consumption being produced. A halt was called to this neglect after World War II.

Ideal circumstances

The vineyards lie between the 44th and 45th parallel. This latitude guarantees a fine, full-bodied wine in the northern hemisphere.

Other important influences on the success of the vineyards is their position midway between the Atlantic Ocean and the Mediterranean. This protects them from the moist influence of the westerly winds and from the generally rainy autumn weather of the Mediterranean climate, so that the grapes can ripen fully. There are two different soil types for Cahors: the valley of the Lot has underlying chalk with a topsoil of alluvium with outcrops of boulders and scree; and the chalk uplands or Causses with a fairly shallow upper layer of stones and marl.

The grapes

Only red wine is produced in Cahors. The basic grape variety is the Auxerrois, which is also known elsewhere as Cot Noir. This must be a minimum 70 per cent of the vines in order to qualify for AC Cahors status. The Auxerrois imparts the backbone to the wine, the strong tannin, its colour, and its potential for ageing.

Traditional Cahors red is made using solely Auxerrois or this grape combined with Tannat (known from Madiran and Irouléguy) which has many of the characteristics of Auxerrois. The more modern style of wine often contains a substantial amount of Merlot, which makes the wine more rounded, more comforting, and more aromatic.

Red Cahors from the
Auxerrois grape.

Quality wine from a top
Cahors estate.

The wines

The modern style Cahors is best drunk while young.
Its tannin makes it the perfect accompaniment for
goose and duck. Drink it at 14°C (57.2°F).

The tradition-style Cahors is much broader and
complex. If drunk while young it is dominated by
tannin so it is better to wait five to ten years with
better wines. These are rounder, velvet soft, full-
bodied, and powerful. The bouquet is much finer
when more mature. Drink the wine at 16°C (60.8°F).

Gaillac

Gaillac wine was already known in the fifth century,
particularly in ecclesiastical circles. With the arrival
of the Benedictine monks in the tenth century
Gaillac became known as one of the best wine-
growing areas of France. The vineyards cover 2,500
hectares on either side of the river Tarn, stretching
from the town of Albi, north of Toulouse. The soil
on the left bank of the Tarn is poor, consisting of
stone and gravel, which is ideal for red wine. The
right bank of the Tarn is more complex and diverse
with granite, chalk, and sandstone predominant.
White, rosé, and red wines are produced, with the
current production of Gaillac consisting for 60 per
cent of red wine.

The white Gaillac is made
with Mauzac grapes,
which are also found in
Languedoc (Limoux) and
in various small south-
western wine-growing
areas. Mauzac is
supplemented here with
the Len de l'el grape for
its finesse and aromatic
strength. The Len de l'el
grape is also grown in
both French and Spanish
Catalonia. Wine from the
right bank is well-
balanced and possesses

Gaillac red.

rich fruitiness, floral bouquets, and is very fresh. The
modern-style white wines are slightly less broad,
lithe, and lingering in their aftertaste than the
traditional Mauzac and Len de l'el wines. The wines
produced on the left bank are fruity, juicy, and
warm. Drink Gaillac white at 10°C, and the sweet
white at 8°C.

There is also sparkling white Gaillac, available in
two types: the méthode artisanale is achieved
without the addition of liqueur. The gas bubbles are
created by the fermentation of the sugars already
present in the wine. This Gaillac méthode artisanale
is very fruity and full of character. Gaillac méthode
traditionnelle is produced with a second
fermentation in the bottle after a dose of liqueur has
been added to the wine. This sparkling wine is
perhaps somewhat fresher but less complex and
above all less fruity. Drink it as an aperitif at about
8°C.

Gaillac rosé is generally made by modern means
using the saignée method (early drawing off during
the steeping of the wine of a little red and
subsequent vinification as white wine). This is a
friendly, fairly light, and easily drinkable rosé.
Drinking temperature: 10–12°C (50–53.6°F).

Gaillac red is made with the Duras grape, an old
variety that made a comeback about twenty years
ago, to which the native Braucol or Brocol (local
names for the Fer Servadou or Mansoi) is added.
Duras imparts colour, backbone, and refinement to
the wine while Braucol gives it fleshiness and rustic
charm together with superb aromas of blackcurrant
and raspberry. The red wine made by modern
methods from grapes grown on chalky soils are light,
aromatic, and easy to drink. The wine has much in
common with the Gaillac rosé. A warm, stronger,
but more lithe red with plenty of fruit aromas
(preserved fruit, redcurrant and blackcurrant)
originates from the granite soil of the hills. This wine
can be readily laid down. The red wine from the left
bank is darker in colour and more richly flavoured,
with bouquet of preserved fruit, spices, and
blackcurrant. This wine, which is robust and rich in
tannin, needs to be aged in the bottle for some years.
Drink the modern-style Gaillac at 14–16°C
(57.2–60.8°F), and the traditional and robust red at
16°C (60.8°F).

Côtes du Frontonnais

Present-day Frontonnais is a combination of two
older wine-growing areas close to Toulouse:
Fronton and Villaudric. The Côtes du Frontonnais,
between Toulouse and Montauban, is about 2,000
hectares and the soil here is fairly poor and dry, with
lots of stone and gravel, which imparts fruity aromas
to the wines. The area under cultivation by vines
will increase in the near future by about one third.
A peculiar characteristic of the Côtes du
Frontonnais wines (only rosé and red) is the use of
the ancient native Négrette grape, which accounts

Red and rosé Côtes du Frontonnais.

Traditional Côtes du Frontonnais red.

for 50–70 per cent of the vines planted. This grape provides the wine's characteristic refinement and highly fruity nature. In addition to the Négrette they also grow Cabernet Franc, Cabernet Sauvignon, Syrah, Fer Servadou, Cot (known locally as Merille) and to a lesser extent Gamay and Cinsault.

The Frontonnais rosé is fairly pale in colour and very aromatic. It is quite dry with a fine taste. Drink it at about 10°C (50°F).

The Frontonnais red is found in two types. The modern wine is light, elegant, lithe, fruity, and often smells of blackcurrant and plum. Drink it at approx. 14°C (57.2°F).

The traditional Frontonnais red is more complex, more robust, and fuller. Its bouquet is somewhat less boisterous and the taste is often deeper. Drink it at 16°C (60.8°F).

Buzet

The vineyards of Buzet cover about 1,700 hectares in the heart of Gascony, south of the town of Buzet, on the left bank of the Garonne. Almost the entire production is controlled by the local co-operative known as Vignerons du Buzet. The vineyards of Buzet are ancient and existed before the start of the first millennium. Buzet is an exception in south-west

France in being the only area that was not driven out of wine-making for many years following the phylloxera epidemic. In fact the areas cultivated during those difficult times were actually larger. Buzet attained VSQS status in 1953 but with the individual style and sympathetic effort of the united growers they achieved AC status in 1973.

The area is divided into two different soil types. The wine produced from the stony and sandy soil of the terraces is elegant and delicate. That made from vines growing in the richer ground of clay, and alluvial deposits with outcrops of sandstone is fuller, heavier, and more aromatic. Buzet produces predominantly red wines which are made by combining Merlot, Cabernet Franc and Cabernet Sauvignon. The wine is a ruby red and the bouquet is reminiscent of red fruit, vanilla, and preserved fruit.

Drinking temperature: 12–14°C (53.6–57.2°F).

The better Buzet wines (chàteaux or estates) are more full-bodied and richer in tannin. These can be kept for 10 to 15 years and have a more complex bouquet that tends towards humus, strawberry jam, tobacco, cedarwood, and the nose of wild game. Drinking temperature: 14–17°C (57.2–62.6°F).

Côtes du Marmandais

The Côtes du Marmandais AC vineyards cover 1,800 hectares on the right bank of the Garonne on gently undulating hills with soil of gravel and pebbles, interspersed with calciferous sandstone, and chalk-bearing clay.

White Côtes du Marmandais, made with the Sémillon, Sauvignon, Muscadelle and Ugni Blanc, are fine dry wines that are fresh and fruity with a bouquet of white flowers and sometimes a note of almond. Drinking temperature: 10–12°C. (50–53.6°F)

The rosé is fresh, fruity, and pale. Drink it at 12°C (53.6°F).

Côtes du Marmandais red is produced with the Bordeaux grapes of Cabernet Sauvignon, Cabernet Franc, Merlot and Malbec, supplemented with the local Abouriou and Fer Servadou, and when

White, rosé and red Buzet.

Traditional Buzet red.

Nectar like Déesse rosé from Marmande.

Traditional Marmande red.

necessary with a little Gamay and Syrah. It is better value to buy the slightly more expensive cuvées such as Richard Premier, Tap de Perbos, or La Vieille Eglise. Drinking temperature: 14–16°C (57.2–60.8°F).

Côtes de St-Mont VDQS

The Côtes de St-Mont were admitted to VDQS status in 1981. The red and rosé wines are made using Tannat and Fer Servadou, supplemented when necessary with Cabernet Sauvignon and Cabernet Franc to provide greater roundness and finesse. The white wine is blended from typical local varieties such as Gros Manseng, Arrufiac, Petit Manseng and Petit Courbu, with occasional use of a little Clairette. The red wine area is on the eastern and southern facing hills which have two soil types. The stony ground provides a light red wine made by modern methods which is pleasing, comforting but unpretentious to drink well chilled at approx. 12°C (53.6°F). The heavier clay soil produces rounder, more fleshy wines which can be readily kept. Drink these at 12–14°C (53.6–57.2°F) when young and at 16°C (60.8°F)when mature.

The rosé is soft, very pleasing, and aromatic. The taste is fruity and fresh. Drink it at 12°C (53.8°F).

The western hills with their soil of chalk and clay deliver very subtle, elegant white wines. The aromatic properties of the young wine quickly changes to a complex bouquet. Drink it at 10–12°C (50–53.6°F).

In addition to the VDQS wines listed here there are also some good wines known as vins de pays des Côtes de Gascogne, which have justifiably established themselves in the past decade.

Tursan VDQS

The vineyards of Tursan are situated on the borders of Les Landes, an extensive area that these days is covered with pines but was once marsh and sand dunes. The other neighbours are Gascony and Béarn. The soil of the 500 hectares of vineyards here is a mixture of clay and sand with some chalk and sandstone. The best vineyards are situated on hills of broken chalk. Approximately half the production is of white wine with the rest being rosé and red.

Tursan white is made with the Baroque grape, supplemented with a maximum of 10 per cent of Gros Manseng and Sauvignon. The wine is fresh, fruity, and very aromatic with a very pleasing taste. Drinking temperature: 8–10°C (46.4–50°F).

The rosé is pale, fresh, dry, and very delicious. It is made using Cabernet Sauvignon and Cabernet Franc. Drinking temperature: 10–12°C (50–53.6°F). The red wine is made with a minimum 60 per cent Cabernet Sauvignon and Cabernet Franc supplemented with a maximum 40% Tannat. This wine is full-bodied, rounded, and comforting with great finesse, charm, and great aromatic properties. Drink it at 16°C (60.8°F).

Modern-style white, rosé and red Tursan.

Traditional Tursan red.

Madiran

Madiran was certainly known a century before the birth of Christ.

Here too the success of the local wine results from the input of Benedictine monks.

Château Montus vineyards, Madiran.

Côtes de St-Mont red.

Côtes de Gascogne vins de pays.

Château Montus cellars, Madiran.

Young Madiran is strongly tannic.

Alain Brumont

After an extremely dark period during which Madiran seemed to have been wiped from the wine menu, a saviour appeared in the form of Alain Brumont, a modest, stubborn, ambitious, but charming and friendly son of a local winegrower. He bought the abandoned Montus estate, and replanted it with the traditional Tannat grapes, that once imparted their charm to Madiran wines. The quality of the vineyards and the vines was the foremost issue with high quality standards and low yields. The true Madiran was reborn. In less than 15 years this shiny knight of the Madiran ensured that it had become one of the best known red wines of France. This is a huge achievement.

Wine-growing in Madiran

The 1,100 hectares of vineyards of Madiran are sited on calciferous clay interspersed with areas of poorer and stony soil.

Madiran wine is produced with Tannat, possibly supplemented with Fer Servadou, Cabernet Sauvignon and Cabernet Franc, which mellow the harshness of the Tannat. Madiran wine is full of tannin which needs at least 2–4 years maturing in the bottle (and at least 10 years for the best wines) in order to develop its full charm.

The best Madiran can certainly be kept for 20–30 years. Madiran is the stereotype for masculine wine: sturdy, full-bodied, substantial, sensual, and fleshy. When drunk young (after at least two years) a Madiran is very fruity but the tannin will dominate. Drinking temperature: 14°C (57.2°F).
Older Madiran has a bouquet of toast, coffee, cocoa, herbs, vanilla,

Château Montus, Madiran.

preserved fruit, liquorice, and much more. Drink it at 16°C (60.8°F).

Pacherenc du Vic-Bilh

The Vic-Bilh wine-growing area is the same one that produces Madiran. This area produces the red Madiran wine and dry, medium sweet, and sweet white wines as Pacherenc du Vic-Bilh. Pacherenc is derived from the Basque or Gascon word for little berry or grape.

The ideal soil for this white wine is a mixture of clay and sandstone. The grapes used are the native Arrufiac, Petit Manseng, Gros Manseng, and Courbu, with a little Sauvignon Blanc and Semillon being used for the modern type of wine.
Dry Pacherenc du Vic-Bilh is very aromatic with floral notes and hints of citrus fruit combined with a full taste of ripe and preserved fruits. Drinking temperature: 10–12°C (50–53.6°F).
The medium-sweet or sweet Pacherenc du Vic-Bilh shares the aromatic properties of the dry wine (citrus fruit, preserved fruit, dried fruit, and flowers) with the addition of a little honey, toast, and exotic fruit. The texture and taste are fuller, fatter, more fleshy, and juicy. Drinking temperature: 8–10°C (46.4–50°F).

Very aromatic Pacherenc du Vic-Bilh.

Pacherenc du Vic-Bilh has ideal soil.

Late picked sweet Pacherenc du Vic-Bilh.

Slightly sweet Jurançon.

Your attention is drawn to the excellent quality of the local vins de pays des Côtes de Gascogne and the many vins de cépages. The vins de pays des Côtes de Gascogne of Colombard, Gros Manseng, and Sauvignon (white wines) and reds of Egiodola, Tannat and Cabernet Sauvignon, together with those from Jurançon are worth a separate mention.

Top quality dry Pacherenc du Vic-Bilh.

Jurançon

This wine-growing area, south of Pau and close to the French Pyrenees, is slightly less ancient than its predecessors. The first signs of wine-growing date back only to the tenth century. Jurançon was one of the first AC status wines in 1936 and Jurançon Sec acquired its own recognition in 1975.

The wine-growing

The area is barely larger than 600 hectares with the vineyards being dispersed throughout the district. They can be found strung out along a 40 km (25 miles) stretch like small islands amidst the other greenery. The better wines are produced on hills of about 300 metres (984 feet) high with soil of clay, sandstone, and boulders.

The climate is a mixture of high and regular rainfall from the Atlantic combined with the harsh winters of the Pyrenees. The area does though appear always to be blessed with warm autumns and dry southerly winds that make it possible for the grapes to be left to overripen in order to make a great sweet wine. The grapes used for Jurançon are the native Gros Manseng, Petit Manseng, Courbu, Camaralet, and Lauzet. Jurançon Sec is truly dry with fresh acidity, with floral notes (broom and acacia) and fruity aromas (passion fruit, white peach, and citrus fruit). As the wine matures it develops a more complex bouquet with almond and other nuts, dried fruit, and sometimes a marked suggestion of truffle. Drinking temperature: 8–10°C (46.4–50°F).
Either Jurançon Doux or Moelleux are little gems. The colour drifts between gold and amber, the bouquet is fine and complex, varying from honey, vanilla, toast and preserved fruit to the subtlest hints of white flowers, lime blossom, camomile, pineapple, and citrus fruit. The taste is full and rounded. The high sugar content is perfectly balanced with fresh acidity. This sweet wine can be kept for a very long time. Drinking temperature: 10–12°C (50–53.6°F).

Béarn-Bellocq

Béarn is fairly hilly, lying at the foot of the Pyrenees where it enjoys an ideal microclimate that combines Atlantic moisture with a harsher mountain climate. Béarn white is quite rare and is produced in the vicinity of Bellocq. This white wine made with Raffiat and Manseng grapes is fresh and fruity with an undertone of floral notes (broom, acacia). Drinking temperature: 10–12°C (50–53.6°F).
The more widely available Rosé de Béarn owes its charm to the combination of Tannat with Cabernet Sauvignon and Cabernet Franc (better known in this locality as Bouchy). This is a wonderful rosé that is velvet smooth, full-bodied, rounded, and very fruity. Drinking temperature: 10–12°C (50–53.6°F).

The more straightforward Béarn red is lightweight but comforting and easily consumed. The taste and scent tend more towards Cabernet Franc than Tannat. Drinking temperature: 12°C (53.6°F).

The better Béarn-Bellocq red by contrast is sturdier, fuller, more full-bodied, and fleshier. Tannin clearly has the upper hand in this wine. Drinking temperature: 14–16°C (57.2–60.8°F).

Béarn-Bellocq.

Irouléguy

This wine region lies in the heart of the French Basque country and was known already at the time of Charlemagne. The village of Irouléguy was then a trading centre for these Basque wines. Wine-growing fell into decline following the phylloxera epidemic until a number of growers decided in the 1950s to establish a co-operative. The vineyards of the once famous Irouléguy were restored or replanted. Enormous investment was made to improve the quality of the wine and in the 1980s further great efforts were undertaken to reach greater heights. New vineyards were planted, mainly on terraces. In addition to the efforts of the local co-operative venture, various private initiatives were also undertaken such as those of Etienne Brana, whose business has become world famous. In recent decades the wine-growing and making in Irouléguy is so improved that it can be fairly described as one of France's premier wine-growing areas.

The wine-growing

The vineyards around Irouléguy are situated in the neighbourhood of St-Jean Pied de Port and St-Etienne de Baïgorry. They are mainly sited in terraces with soil of red sandstone, clay, and shale, interspersed with some chalk. The green of the vineyards set against the red-oxide sandstone makes for a picturesque scene.

The climate is set between moderate oceanic weather and the extremes of the mountains and continent. The winter is fairly mild with plenty of rain and snow. The spring is wet with occasional harmful periods of frost. Summer is hot and dry. The greatest risk lies in thunderstorms which can cause destruction, when combined with hailstorms.

The autumn is often hot and dry, which is ideal for harvesting and ripening of healthy grapes. These circumstances combined with the difficulty of access to many of the vineyards means that the output is fairly low here.

The wines

About two thirds of the production from Irouléguy is of red wine. The wine's character is derived from the Tannat (maximum 50%), Cabernet Franc (Axeria) and Cabernet Sauvignon. There are three categories of red wine: ordinary Irouléguy, the cuvées and the estate bottled wines in escalating levels of quality. The simplest Irouléguy is sturdy, high in tannin, fruity (blackberry) and spices. The better cuvées are more full-bodied, are aged longer in oak, and benefit from several years ageing in the bottle. The top estates (Brana, Ilarria, Iturritxe and Mignaberry) make outstanding wines with powerful bouquets of spices and black fruit (blackberry and plum) with a hint of vanilla. The taste is complex, full, and rounded with a perfect balance between the fresh acidity, fruitiness, alcohol, body, and strong but rounded tannin. Enthusiasts never stop talking about the aftertaste.

Just as with Collioure, ordinary Irouléguy red can be drunk when young with grilled fish, if chilled, especially if they are garnished with baked peppers. Drinking temperature: 14–16°C (57.2–60.8°F).

The cuvées and estate wines can be drunk at 16–18°C (60.8–64.4°F).

The rosé is fresh and quite dry. It was this wine that originally established the good name of Irouléguy. Here too there is a combination of Tannat with Cabernet Franc and Cabernet Sauvignon. The colour resembles redcurrant and the delicate nose is fruity too with redcurrant and cherry, while the taste is both fresh and fruity. Drinking temperature: 10–12°C (50–53.6°F).

The rare Irouléguy white made with Xuri Ixiriota (Manseng) and Xuri Cerrabia (Petit Courbu) is

Top estate Brana's Irouléguy red.

Top estate Brana's Irouléguy white.

richer and fuller than its cousins of Béarn. This white wine of great class has a bouquet containing white flowers, white peach, citrus fruit, butter, hazelnut, and almond underscored with a hint of vanilla and a mineral undertone. Drinking temperature: 9–10°C (48.2–50°F).

Aquitaine: the wines of the Dordogne and Garonne

In the part of this book dealing with wines of South-west France it was explained that the wines of Duras and Bergerac have their own entity alongside the wines of Bordeaux and those that are truly of the south-west.

To avoid dispute and confusion and not to take sides, both wine-growing areas are listed separately here. Both have closer social and economic affinity with the capital of Aquitaine (Bordeaux) than that of the south-west (Toulouse). The daily trade and business of Bordeaux in the daily business of both areas and the economic importance of Duras and Bergerac all play an important role.

Côtes de Duras

The wine-growing area of Duras appears to be wedged between the vineyards of Bordeaux to the west, those of Bergerac to the north, and south-west vineyards of Pais Marmandais. Duras is not a large wine region with about 2,000 hectares. Centuries of experience makes this area special and the wine superb. Although the folk of Duras are proud of their wines you will find little fuss about it in the local media. The people prefer to work quietly away at improving their vines and their wines. Duras (AC since 1937) is aimed more at the connoisseur rather than those attracted to a wine by its label. Only those prepared to make the effort to seek out quality and the simple pleasure of wine without a fuss will experience the delight of the superb Duras wines.

The vineyards of Duras are sited at the tops of the gently undulating hills (white wines) and the southern slopes (red wine). The subsoil is extremely varied but the tops of the hills consists of a calciferous sandstone while the slopes are a mixture of compacted clay and chalk with many fossilised shells. The climate is similar to that of Bored, except that it is generally hotter and drier in Duras. The predominant white wine grapes are Sauvignon, Sémillon, and Muscadelle (with the odd trace of Ugni Blanc, Mauzac, Ondenc, and Chenin Blanc) while Merlot, Cabernet Sauvignon, Cabernet Franc, and a small amount of Cot (Malbec) is used for the rosé and red wines. The majority of the production is of red wine (54%) and dry white (42%), with sweet white accounting for (2.5%), and rosé (1.5%).

Côtes de Duras Sec is a light, fresh, elegant, and fruity dry wine with a wonderful pale yellow colour that is tinged with green. This wine, which is dominated by the Sauvignon Blanc, is certainly one of the best Sauvignon wines from Aquitaine. Drinking temperature: 8–10°C (46.4–50°F).

Côtes de Duras Moelleux is a rare sweet white wine dominated by Sémillon. It is a harmonious, wholly sweet wine with a nose of honey, vanilla, toast, apricot, peach, preserved fruit, almond, walnut, hazelnut, and figs. The texture is fatty, almost unctuous, and the taste lingers long on the palate.

Côtes de Duras dry white.

Top estate Bergerac wine.

Bergerac red.

The French enjoy this wine as an aperitif with goose and duck liver paté. Drinking temperature: 6–8°C (42.8–46.4°F).

Côtes de Duras rosé, created by the saignée (early drawing) method, is fresh, fruity and very aromatic (blackcurrant and acid drops). It is an ideal wine to drink with summer dishes. Drinking temperature: 10–12°C (50–53.6°F).

Côtes de Duras red can be a very pleasant, lithe, elegant, and fruity wine, made by steeping in carbonic acid gas (macération carbonique). Today though most wine is vinified by traditional methods which produce a fuller, fleshier wine with loss of the fruity character. Always drink the first type chilled when young (12°C/53.6°F)). The traditional wine can be kept for five to ten years. Drinking temperature: 14–16°C (57.2–60.8°F).

Bergerac

Wine-growing

Bergerac is full of surprises and presents every visitor with the beauty of the natural surroundings, the zeal and passion of the winegrowers, the eternally sought after truffles, other fungi, paté de foie gras, and wild boar of the Périgord, and the emotions that are unleashed with each sip of wine.

The delight of Bergerac.

The soil of this area is chiefly a mixture of loam and chalk, loam and granite sand on the plateaux, granite sand in the Périgord and river-washed sediments and pebbles.

There are terraces with poor soil and a top layer of sediment on the right bank of the Dordogne. The south-facing slopes are covered with stones. The soil on the left bank is very chalky, especially on the slopes of the hills, interspersed with some loam. Everything is present here, just as in the bordering Bordelais, to guarantee high quality wines: plenty of sun, enough rain, harsh winters are not common (the exceptions being 1956, 1985, and 1987). The humidity is fairly high through the proximity with the Atlantic Ocean and the abundance of water in the Dordogne and its many tributaries.

However good a terroir is it does not actually make the wine. Vines have been grown in Bergerac for 2,000 years. Wine-making has almost been elevated to art through the input and experience of generations of wine-makers here. Currently most of the younger wine-growers seek to retain much of the centuries old tradition while adapting to the latest vinifcation techniques.

With the different combinations of varying terroirs and grapes, there is a wide range of types of wine from just 11,000 hectares (12 AC wines).
The grapes used for red wine are Cabernet

Montravel's secret is calcareous soil.

Sauvignon (sturdiness, tannin, colour, bouquet (blackcurrant and cedarwood), Cabernet Franc (prolific bouquet of strawberry and freshly-sliced green pepper, with high alcoholic content), and Merlot (bouquet: cherry, red berries, plum, juicy with a velvet smooth texture).

White wines are made with Semillon (sensitivity for noble rot; bouquet: honey, apricot, peach, or mango, with good balance between sweetness and acidity), Sauvignon Blanc (finesse and bouquet of green apple, new-mown grass) and Muscadelle (intense aroma of honeysuckle and acacia).

The wines

BERGERAC ROUGE
This red wine mainly originates from the slopes and high plateaux. It is predominantly fine fruity wine with nose and aromas of strawberry, blackcurrant, and other small red fruit. This wine is enjoyable when drunk young. Drinking temperature: 12–14°C (53.6–57.2°F).

CÔTES DE BERGERAC ROUGE
It is mainly the better Bergerac reds that fall under this name. These are wines with an intense colour, more structure, greater complexity, that have a bouquet of preserved fruit like plum and prune. These wines are invariably high in both alcohol and tannin. Drinking temperature: 14–16°C (57.2–60.8°F).

PÉCHARMANT
The vineyards of the quality red wine of Pécharmant are favourably sited in an amphitheatre of hills. The soil determines the quality of the wine.

Sand and gravel that have been deposited from the erosion of granite have been washed frequently in the course of the centuries by the sea and rivers. It is this hard top layer, that is impermeable by water, which gives the wine its typical terroir derived taste. Wine from Pécharmant is generally dark in colour and very concentrated, being high in tannin, and

Extremely rare Rosette.   *Monbazillac liquid gold.*

therefore bitter and undrinkable when young. It can certainly be laid down and when more mature it is fuller and has a broad assortment in its nose and taste. Drinking temperature: 16–17°C (60.8–62.6°F).

BERGERAC ROSÉ
Bergerac Rosé is generally quite pleasing but a fairly simple wine. It is produced by the saignée method. Following the short macération it is always a fresh, companionable wine that is salmon pink and possesses broad aromas of fruit. Drink it at 12°C (53.6°F).

BERGERAC BLANC SEC
The vineyards of Bergerac Blanc Sec are sited on both banks of the Dordogne, principally on the hills and plateaux.
The increasingly widely used modern method of vinification such as macération pelliculaire imparts greater richness in both taste and aroma than the wine otherwise would possess naturally. Drinking temperature: 10–12°C (50–53.6°F).

MONTRAVEL
The superb dry white Montravel is produced in the extreme west of the Dordogne. Here too modern wine-making methods produce a wine that is very aromatic, and also velvet smooth in the mouth. Ordinary Montravel can be drunk young as a fruity wine but can also be kept a couple of years. Better quality Montravel, which is first aged in oak, needs to be kept somewhat longer. Drinking temperature: 10–12°C (50–53.6°F).

CÔTES DE MONTRAVEL
The slightly sweet Côtes de Montravel white provides a subtle change between the dry white Montravel and the sweeter white Haut-

Côtes de Bergerac red.   *Pécharmant.*   *Montravel.*

Montravel. Drinking temperature: 10–12°C (50–53.6°F).

HAUT-MONTRAVEL
Haut-Montravel originates mainly from the banks of the river. It is generally a smooth wine that is high in sugar but it has sufficient acidity to provide balance and enable the wine to be kept. Drinking temperature: 8–10°C (46.4–50°F).

CÔTES DE BERGERAC
Côtes de Bergerac Moelleux, which is mainly produced with Sémillon, can originate from throughout the area. It is darker in colour than the companion dry wines and it often has a greater bouquet, more finesse, and more body. The quality of the wine is partially determined by the soil, but also by the grape variety and method of vinification. This wine is ready to drink after four or five years but it can also be kept much longer. Drinking temperature: 8–10°C (46.4–50°F).

ROSETTE
Rosette Moelleux, comes from the sunny slopes north of the town of Bergerac but is rarely encountered outside the district. This is a pity because a good Rosette is always a masterpiece, pale straw yellow with an overwhelming bouquet of flowers and fruit.
The elegant civility of the wine and its fine acidity are in perfect balance. Drinking temperature: 9–10°C (48.2–50°F).

SAUSSIGNAC
Saussignac is very small area, consisting of a small valley between the vineyards of Monbazillac and the first vineyards of the Bordelais. The wine from this district is mainly produced from old vineyards.

Saussignac Moelleux is well balanced, lithe, and has a subtle aroma of honey, lime blossom, and grapefruit. Drinking temperature: 10–12°C (50–53.6°F). Saussignac Liquoreux are comforting, rounded wines that are broad and fat, with aromas of acacia and peach.

Rosette   Monbazillac

Both wines need to lay for a minimum of five to ten years before they are drunk. They are then absolute gems to be drunk at 9–10°C (48.2–50°F).

MONBAZILLAC
The honey sweet, liqueur like Monbazillac Liquoreux comes from the south bank of the Dordogne. The vineyards are on the northern slopes at a height of 50–180 metres (164–590 feet), opposite the town of Bergerac. The good position and microclimate ensure plenty of moisture and warmth in the vineyard in autumn which enables Botrytis cinerea to develop, which is essential for the creation of truly great liqueur type wines.
Monbazillac should certainly not be drunk too cold, say 6–8°C (42.8–46.4°F) for the lighter types but 10–12°C (50–53.6°F) for the richer wines. This enables the sumptuous scent of acacia and honey to develop fully and the broad range in the taste also has the chance to be fully appreciated.

Bordeaux

No other name of wine is so well known throughout the world, nor does any other area deliver so many top class wines year on year as Bordeaux. The names of Mouton-Rothschild, Lafite-Rothschild, Pétrus,

Château de Monbazillac.

Haut-Montravel   Côtes de Bergerac
                 Moelleux.

and Yquem resound around the world like the intangible dreams of children. The top-quality Bordeaux wines enjoy a status all of their own. This stands out far above the other wines but is also sometimes more elevated than the reality. Whether this is truly deserved is open to question.

Bordeaux wine-growing

The vineyards of Bordeaux are sited in the French department of the Gironde, that derives its name from the estuaries of the Garonne and Dordogne rivers. The wine-growing area does not extend to the entire department, although this is officially permitted. Not every piece of land is suitable for cultivating vines (woodland, urban areas, and arable land for maize, and tobacco). The climate of Bordeaux is very mild thanks to the presence of water in the rivers, the Gironde, and the Atlantic Ocean. Bordeaux winters are generally mild, spring comes early with abundant rain, summer is hot and mainly dry, while autumn is often calm and sunny. This means that the vines get the right amounts of water and sun. That such perfection does not always occur is shown by the 1956 winter that was exceptionally cold, when almost all the vines were killed by frost, and also by the frequent flooding of the Garonne and Dordogne rivers.

The generic AC appellations

Our journey begins on the borders of Bergerac and Duras but before we look at the local or communal appellations, first let is consider the generic appellations. These wines may be produced anywhere within the defined area of Bordeaux wines.

BORDEAUX BLANC SEC
It may surprise many people but two centuries ago ten times as much white Bordeaux wine was produced as red wine. The quality of dry white Bordeaux is in the mean time significantly improved. This is partially due to the complete replacement of most wine-making equipment, even by the co-operatives which produce the largest volumes. Dry

white Bordeaux is made with Sauvignon Blanc, Sémillon, and Muscadelle. The better quality wines are aged in oak to make them fuller and more elegant. Generally, Bordeaux Blanc Sec is very scented: grass, box, acacia, lemon, peach, and grapefruit. The taste is fresh and delicate. Drinking temperature: 9–10°C (48.2–50°F).

BORDEAUX ROSÉ/BORDEAUX CLAIRET
The difference between Bordeaux Rosé and Bordeaux Clairet is simple: the grape skins are allowed to steep longer to produce Bordeaux Clairet than for Rosé (24 to 36 hours instead of 12 to 18 hours). This gives the Rosé a pale pink colour while Clairet is dark pinkish red. In other respects both wines are produced after steeping in the same way as white wine. Both wines are made with Cabernet Sauvignon, Cabernet Franc. and Merlot. They are light and very fruity wines (raspberry, redcurrant, cherry, and strawberry) with suggestions of flowers such as irises and violets. Drinking temperature: 10°C (50°F).

BORDEAUX ROUGE/BORDEAUX SUPÉRIEUR ROUGE
Welcome to the largest wine-growing area of France (60,000 hectares). Bordeaux and Bordeaux Supérieur together account for more than half the total production of the Bordeaux region. Bordeaux and Bordeaux Supérieur have managed to win over both French and foreign consumers by profiting on the good name of the leading wines of Médoc, St-Emilion, Pomerol, and Sauternes. Important reasons for this success in addition to the wide awareness of the name is also due the excellent relationship between price, quality, and pleasure of these wines. It is difficult to give an overall profile of these wines because they are produced by so many different people (individual growers, co-operatives, and negociants or trading houses), and also come from completely different types of soil. When the influences of the countless microclimates and different proportions of the grapes used is considered it is apparent that with Bordeaux one is faced with an enormous variety of different wines and tastes.

BORDEAUX ROUGE
This wine is produced using the well-known Cabernet Sauvignon, Cabernet Franc and Merlot grapes. The wine area for Bordeaux red is about 38,000 hectares. The wine is an attractive colour and possesses a delightful range of aromas such as wood, vanilla, violets, blackcurrant, cherry, and peppermint. The structure of the wine is rich and smooth with a full taste. The strength of the wines depends according to the vintage. Drinking temperature: 14–15°C (57.2–59°F)for wines from the lesser years and 16°C (60.8°F) for the greater ones.

BORDEAUX SUPÉRIEUR ROUGE
The wine area for the Bordeaux Supérieur red is

Bordeaux AC dry white.

Bordeaux AC rosé.

Bordeaux Supérieur.　　　*Bordeaux Blanc Moelleux.*

much smaller than for the 'ordinary' Bordeaux red at approximately 8,000 hectares. Bordeaux Supérieur is slightly higher in alcohol, has a lower output per hectare, and may not be sold until it is a year old. Most of these wines are characteristic of the region and generally keep well. Drinking temperature: 16°C (60.8°F).

BORDEAUX BLANC SUPÉRIEUR/BORDEAUX BLANC MOELLEUX

These wines are always medium sweet (doux meaning soft and moelleux meaning mellow). They are made in modest volume (only accounting for about 2% of sales) yet surprising quantities of this wine can be found on supermarket shelves. Genuine Bordeaux Blanc Moelleux is a wonderful, almost unctuous wine, having a bouquet with floral notes, and of peach, apricot, and pineapple. Drinking temperature: 8°C (46.4°F).

CRÉMANT DE BORDEAUX

The excellent Crémants de Bordeaux are made by the traditional method. The combination of typical Bordeaux grape varieties and Champagne-style vinification have exceptional results. The white and rosé Crémants de Bordeaux are known especially for their freshness, elegant mousse or foam, and their pleasing fruitiness. Drinking temperature: 6–8°C (42.8–46.4°F).

Graves

The area formerly all known as Graves extends from below the village of St-Pierre de Mons to Blanquefort south-west of Bordeaux. It is subdivided into three large wine-growing areas: Graves itself (Graves Rouge, Graves Blanc Sec, Graves Supérieures Moelleux and Liquoreux), Pessac-Léognan (Rouge and Blanc Sec), and the sweet wine enclaves Sauternes, Barsac and Cérons. The area stretches for about 50 km (31 miles) and comprises 43 different communes. Graves is the only French wine to carry the bedrock or soil of its terroir in its appellation on the label. The name 'Graves' is French for gravel, the ground on which vines best thrived during the occupation of Aquitaine by the English. Médoc then was still swampland that was later drained and reclaimed by the Dutch. The name Graves became forever linked to its wines because of the favourable nature of the ground for wine-making. Wines from Graves contributed to establishing the great name of Bordeaux rather than those of Médoc which only came into being in the second half of the eighteenth century, when they profited from the fame of Graves.

The wine-growing

With Graves too what is instantly apparent is the great diversity of different terroirs. Generally the soil consists of terraces of clay and sand with gravel and plenty of boulders. The quality of the soil here ultimately determines the quality of the wine. The Graves vineyards came under tremendous pressure in the twentieth century. The expansion of the city of Bordeaux caused about 7,000 hectares of land to be lost and this process was exacerbated by the economic crisis that preceded World War II, by that war, and the severe frosts of 1956. The vineyards close to the suburbs of Bordeaux suffered most in these times. For foreigners it is quite surprising to see that top châteaux such as Haut-Brion and La Mission Haut-Brion are almost permanently bathed in the smoke from Bordeaux.

In the 3,000 hectares of Graves, 53% red wine and 47% white wine is produced. The better wines (including all the Graves grand crus) have had their own appellation of Pessac-Léognan since 1987.
Red wine throughout the area is made using Merlot, Cabernet Franc, and Cabernet Sauvignon, sometimes supplemented with Malbec and Petit-Verdot. White wine is made using Sémillon, Sauvignon Blanc, and Muscadelle.

GRAVES ROUGE

Historically the red Graves were the great Bordeaux wines. The vineyards were planted by the Romans and the wine was highly desired by the Roman emperors. The wine became world famous thanks to the English but the French kings were also extremely

Graves red.　　　*Pessac-Léognan Grand Cru Classé white.*

fond of the wine. Recognition with an AC was granted in 1937.

Depending on its terroir Graves red can either be light and elegant or full, fatty, fleshy, and full of tannin. The latter type in particular keeps well. A characteristic of the Graves red is the slight smoky undertone in both the bouquet and taste. This taste is derived from the soil. Other characteristic aromas are vanilla, ripe fruit such as strawberry, blackcurrant, orange peel, toast, green pepper (paprika), and a little cinnamon, coffee, cocoa, and humus as the wine matures. Drinking temperature: 16°C (60.8°F).

GRAVES BLANC SEC

The dry white Graves is always fresh, fruity, and very aromatic with scents of box, laurel, peach, apricot, citrus fruit, ivy, mint, vanilla, toast, and almond. If drunk when young the acidity of Graves Blanc Sec is rather sharp. Drinking temperature: 10–12°C (50–53.6°F).

GRAVES SUPÉRIEURES

Genuine Graves Supérieures are superb but you will not find them among the cheaper wines. Expect to pay about double the price of the special offer wines. These sweet (moelleux) to liquorous wines are very aromatic with suggestions of hazelnut, vanilla, toast, honey, peach, and apricot, and they are velvet smooth. The presence of fresh acidity provides the wine with balance. Drinking temperature: 6–8°C (42.8–46.4°F).

PESSAC-LÉOGNAN

Since 1987, the communes of Cadaujac, Canéjean, Gradignan, Léognan, Martillac, Mérignac, Pessac, St-Médard d'Eyrans, Talence, and Villenave d'Ornon have borne the appellation of Pessac-Léognan. All the grand crus of the former Graves (1959) fall within this appellation, including Château Haut-Brion. There are a total of 55 estates and châteaux that bear the Pessac-Léognan AC. The wine produced from these is generally of higher quality than the rest of Graves. This is partly due to the poor soil of Pessac-Léognan, to the hilly

Pessac-Léognan Grand Cru Classé red.

landscape, ideal situation of the vineyards, good drainage, and adequate water in the lower strata. The total production area of Pessac-Léognan amounts to 950 hectares of which almost half has been replanted since 1970. At that time the vineyards of Pessac-Léognan were threatened with suffocation from the smoke of the expanding city of Bordeaux. The survival plans of the remaining growers (almost all owners of grand crus)

Premier Grand Cru Classé Châteaux Haut-Brion.

resulted in their own AC recognition in 1987. Since that time the vineyards have been well protected against further expansion of Bordeaux. The wines belong in the top category but remain affordable.

Pessac-Léognan Blanc is always a dry wine. Sauvignon Blanc dominates here with the possible supplement of Sémillon. The colour is a clear pale yellow to straw and the nose is particularly seductive: vanilla, toast, lime blossom, broom, grapefruit, apricot, peach, quince, mango, lychee, butter, and almond. The taste is fresh, fruity, fatty, and rounded. Drinking temperature: 12°C (53.6°F).

Pessac-Léognan Rouge is of exceptional quality. The colour is intense and exciting dark purple to carmine. When young there is a bouquet of ripe fruit such as blackcurrant and plum, together with vanilla, toast, almond, and a characteristic smokiness. These change as the wine matures to humus, prune, game, and truffle. Most wines use Cabernet Sauvignon as their principal grape with some Merlot and Cabernet Franc. The wine consequently keeps well. Drinking temperature: 16–17°C (60.8–62.6°F).

Sauternes, Barsac en Cérons

Late harvesting of grapes is a practice that is carried on throughout Europe. The practice was already used by the Greeks and Romans, long before a single drop of Sauterne was made. Botrytis was probably already present in the area before the first wines were made. The process is a natural one that can only occur where the climate is warm and humid. Botrytis is a stubborn, unreliable fungus though, that cannot be relied upon to appear in the same way in the same place each year. Sometimes it does not occur at all. Producing really fine sweet wines is very labour intensive and painstaking work that also requires a great deal of good luck. Wine-growers consider themselves blessed if the overripe grapes become infected by botrytis. The water in the grape is eviscerated by the fungus and evaporates in the warm air. The concentration of aromatic substances and sugars increases as the grape shrivels. Wine derived from such grapes is very aromatic, full, comforting, powerful, and very alcoholic.

SAUTERNES
The vineyards of Sauternes extend to slightly more than 1,600 hectares. The soil is very varied but predominantly chalk, calciferous clay, and gravel-bearing clay.

Premier Cru Classé Sauternes.

To make this nectar of the gods 70–80% Semillon is used with 20–30 Sauvignon Blanc and sometimes a little Muscadelle. Semillon provides the wine with its charm, luxuriousness, comforting nature, and wonderful scents of honey, apricot, peach, quince, oranges, mandarin, pineapple etc. Sauvignon provides freshness and balance. A good Sauternes is comforting, fatty, and velvet smooth but also fresh, refined, and elegant. Sauternes can be drunk while young (only the cheaper types) provided it is well chilled (6–8°C/42.8–46.4°F) as an original and refined aperitif with canapés with duck and goose liver. Young Sauternes also combines superbly with Salmon for example.

A great Sauternes (Yquem, Rieussec, Sigalas-Rabaud, Clos Haut-Peyraguey, Doisy-Daëne, Doisy-Védrines, Fargues, Guiraud, Lafaurie-Peyraguey, Lagnet La Carriére, Les Justices, Malle, Rayne-Vigneau, Roumieu, Suduiraut) is not drunk as an aperitif and certainly not young. The combination of dew and honey should be allowed to mature for a few years. Top quality Sauternes can be kept for 20–30 years. A fascinating and luxuriant bouquet develops in the bottle as the wine matures, containing honey, quince, preserved fruit, orange marmalade, and hazelnut as the upper notes. Drinking temperature: 8–9°C (46.4–48.2°F).

Cérons.

BARSAC
The wine produced in the commune of Barsac has an ideal dilemma. The wine is permitted to be sold as either its own name of Barsac but also as Sauternes. The difference between Barsac and Sauternes is perhaps that the Barsac is somewhat lighter and less liquorous than the other wines of Sauternes. Apart from this they are like two peas in a pod. Barsac is often more attractively priced though. Drinking temperature: 8–9°C (46.4–48.2°F).

CÉRONS
Cérons are perhaps slightly lighter than both Barsac and Sauternes. They form a golden middle path between the better liquorous wines and the best sweet wines of Graves Supérieures. Cérons is an extremely fine wine in its own right though with a bouquet of flowers, honey, and fruit such as peach and apricot. The taste is full, rounded, harmonious, and juicy. The wine is attractively priced for it quality and ability to please. Drinking temperature: 9–10°C (48.2–50°F).

Entre-deux-mers: between Garonne and Dordogne

We leave the left bank of the Garonne and journey on to a triangle of land 'between-the-two-seas', meaning in fact the rivers Garonne and Dordogne. Anyone who has witness a flood of these rivers can understand what is meant by 'Entre-Deux-Mers'. The wine-growing area of Entre-Deux-Mers is a huge plateau, criss-crossed by countless small valleys and streams that wind their way through the softly undulating hills. It is a fairly large area from which the main output is of the dry white Entre-Deux-Mers AC. The other appellations are Côtes de Bordeaux St-Macaire, Ste-Croix-du-Mont, Loupiac, and Cadillac (all of which are sweet liquorous white wines), Graves de Vayres (red, dry and sweet white), Premières Côtes de Bordeaux, and Ste-Foy Bordeaux (both red and sweet liquorous whites) In addition to the wines listed above the entire area of Entre-Deux-Mers also produces a great deal of Bordeaux and Bordeaux Supérieur (red, rosé, dry and sweet white).

The Eldorado of sweet white wines

Another golden challenger exists in terms of sweet liquorous white wines to Sauternes, Barsac and Cerons.

CÔTES DE BORDEAUX ST-MACAIRE
The Côtes de Bordeaux St-Macaire, that are officially the Premières Côtes de Bordeaux, was once famous for its superb sweet white wines. Because consumers are drinking less white wine and the competition of their neighbours is murderous, this area increasingly is switching to producing red wine that is sold as Bordeaux or Bordeaux

Supérieur. Only 60 hectares still produces sweet white wine that may be called Côtes de Bordeaux St-Macaire AC. Drinking temperature: 8–9°C (46.4–48.2°F).

STE-CROIX-DU-MONT

Unfortunately for the growers, the fine wines of Ste-Croix-du-Mont are not as well known as their excellent quality deserves. The vineyards of Ste-Croix-du-Mont are directly opposite those of Sauternes on an ideal bed of chalk and gravel. The microclimate in Ste-Croix-du-Mont is also ideal for botrytis to do its work. In short, the same grapes, a superb terroir, the same beneficial microclimate, the same method of wine-making, virtually the same quality, but a much lower price.

You can drink this rich, full-flavoured, and fatty wine with its bouquet of honey, citrus fruit, peach, quince, preserved fruit, spices and spiced bread, white flowers, etc., in the same way as Sauternes. Drinking temperature: 8–9°C (46.4–48.2°F).

St-Croix-du-Mont.

Loupiac

The wine of Ste-Croix-du-Mont generally tends towards the liquorous while those of Loupiac to the north-west are more open. Loupiac is an ancient wine-growing area that was famous as early as the thirteenth century. The wines of Loupiac in comparison with those of Ste-Croix-du-Mont are perhaps fresher, certainly in terms of their aromas of oranges, peach, acacia, broom, quince with honey, preserved fruit, and almonds.

Loupiac.

The wine is juicy, fatty, rich, and powerful, with a good balance between the considerable sweet-

A top estate Loupiac.

ness and fresh acidity. Drinking temperature: 8–9°C (46.4–48.2°F).

Cadillac

The name of the American car maker from Detroit is probably derived from the village of Cadillac in the Gironde. It is not known for certain if the name of the village was given to the wine in honour of the local Marquis de Cadillac or the name of the wine for the luxury American car. What is certain is that

Cadillac.

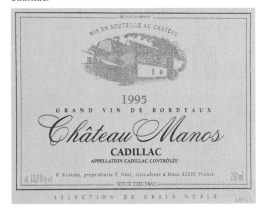

the sweet wine of Cadillac is of exceptional quality, but only gained AC status in 1980. The best Cadillac wines are full, fatty, and well-balanced. They tend more towards soft than liquorous. The nose is luxurious with aromas of preserved citrus fruit, toast, almonds, peach, honey, and occasional hint of beeswax. The taste is fully-flavoured with a good balance between sweet and sour. Drinking temperature: 8–9°C (46.4–48.2°F).

Premières Côtes de Bordeaux

The wine-growing area on the right bank of the Garonne is about 60 km (37 miles) long and runs from the suburbs of Bordeaux to the border with the Côtes de Bordeaux St-Macaire. The landscape is hilly and there are magnificent views across the river and the vineyards of Graves. The underlying beds are varied but chiefly chalk and gravel on the hills and alluvial deposits closer to the Garonne. Production is mainly of red wines but some smooth to liquorous white wines are made in the south-eastern tip close to Cadillac, Loupiac, and Ste-Croix-du-Mont. A great deal of white wine disappears almost anonymously into the great mass of sweet Bordeaux.

The rare sweet white Premières Côtes de Bordeaux are generally of outstanding quality: fairly complex, fatty, broad, and soft, but also possess a certain finesse and elegance. The rich aromas of honey, toast, oranges, preserved fruit, spiced bread, and overripe grapes (with or without botrytis) will seduce many. Drinking temperature: 8–10°C (46.4–50°F).

The majority of the wine is red. Premières Côtes de Bordeaux Rouge always ensures a pleasant surprise and much satisfaction. The colour is deep, the wine is quite full-bodied, and filled with strong aromas of ripe red fruit, plum, toast, vanilla, spices, and occasional hint of coffee roasting and leather. The tannin is quite clearly apparent in the young wine but this becomes rounder and softer with time. Drinking temperature: 16°C (60.8°F).

Premières Côtes de Bordeaux.

Entre-Deux-Mers.

Entre-Deux-Mers

Entre-Deux-Mers AC does not extend to the entire area of Entre-Deux-Mers. Although Entre-Deux-Mers was once known for its sweet white wines, the present AC is solely for dry whites. The wine, made chiefly with Sauvignon Blanc, is bitingly fresh (certainly when young) and very aromatic with notes such as citrus fruit, almonds, and exotic fruit. The best wines though are made with Sémillon, Sauvignon, and Muscadelle, and these are somewhat fuller and broader. These have additional floral notes and aromas of white peach. Drinking temperature: 10–12°C (50–53.6°F).

Graves de Vayres

The small wine area of Graves de Vayres (approx. 525 hectares) is located to the south of the Dordogne and the town of Libourne. The production here is predominantly red but with smaller volumes of dry white wine but most Graves de Vayres that reaches the shops is white. The white wine was the original strength of this district but with the change in drinking habits increasing numbers of red varieties of vine are being planted. Most of the production is sold as plain Bordeaux or Bordeaux Supérieur with only the best wine bearing the Graves de Vayres AC.

The dry white wine is fresh and fruity with aromas of citrus fruit and sometimes also terroir-derived suggestion of flint. Drinking temperature: 10–12°C (50–53.6°F).

The red wine is sometimes full of tannin and rather rough when young, but is always pleasingly fruity (blackberry, raspberry, blackcurrant, cherry, plum). The taste is soft, full, lithe, rounded, and fruity, with a spicy finish. Drinking temperature: 16°C (60.8°F).

Ste-Foy-Bordeaux

This wine area is situated to the south of Bergerac. The small town of Ste-Foy appears to consist of two parts. Port-Ste-Foy is on the right bank of the Dordogne, hence in the Bergeracois, while Ste-Foy-la-Grande is in the Bordelais on the left bank. The soil of Ste-Foy varies from clay bearing alluvial deposits for the reds to chalk bearing strata on which the whites are grown. The underlying strata are gravel, sand, and calciferous clay. This explains the difference in types and taste of the Ste-Foy wines. A remarkable and positive fact regarding this wine-growing district is their quality charter that is signed by the communal winegrowers.

The red wine is the most widely produced, using Merlot, Cabernet Sauvignon, and Cabernet Franc. Most of these are fairly dark, very fruity, with a bouquet of red fruit and vanilla, which merge into more complex aromas such as leather, fungus, coffee, and spices, when mature. Drinking temperature: 16°C (60.8°F).

Dry white Ste-Foy is fresh and very lively. It is mainly made with Sauvignon Blanc, sometimes supplemented with a little Semillon and Muscadelle, and is very aromatic with scents of exotic fruit, flowers, white and yellow fruit, vanilla (when aged in oak). Drinking temperature: 10–12°C (50–53.6°F). The sweet white Ste-Foy Bordeaux is an classic wine of good quality, It is only made in the top vintage years. It is light, fresh, fruity, with typical Semillon aromas of honey, ripe Muscat grapes, lime blossom, beeswax, and apricot. When the overripe Semillon grapes are also 'visited' by botrytis, the wine is full, rich, and especially powerful. Drinking temperature: 8–9°C (46.4–48.2°F).

Libournais, home of the Merlot grape

The vineyards of the Libournais surround the town of Libourne on the right bank of the Dordogne. This is the home of the well-known names such as St-Emilion, Pomerol, Canon-Fronsac, and Fronsac. Although this wine area is not far from Bordeaux, the landscape is totally different. These are not large, bleak estates such as the Médoc, but much smaller, sociable little domains with similarly blessed fine houses. While the Cabernets rule the roost in the Médoc, the Merlot grape dominates here. The wines of the Libournais are therefore not able to be kept as long as the distant relatives of the Médoc, but they are accessible much sooner. The less harsh character of this wine fits more readily with your culinary wishes.

Côtes de Castillon

Wine from the Côtes de Castillon has been entitled to bear this AC name on its label since 1989. Previously it formed part of the anonymous family of Bordeaux and Bordeaux Supérieurs. Analytically this Côtes de Castillon varies little from ordinary Bordeaux. The difference is to be found in the lower output and therefore the higher level of complexity and concentration of the wine. The bouquet is representative of the whole of Bordeaux with cherry, blackcurrant, plum, toast, vanilla, pepper, menthol, spices, and when more mature also game, cocoa, coffee, cinnamon, and dried fruit. Depending on the style imparted by the wine-maker this wine is either elegant and feminine or powerful, fleshy, full-bodied, and masculine. The wine is especially recommended for its excellent value for money for the quality and enjoyment it brings. Drinking temperature: 16–17°C (60.8–62.6°F).

Bordeaux Côtes de Franc

Very acceptable red and white wines are produced from about 490 hectares between St-Emilion and the Bergeracois. The Côtes are relatively high hills of marl and chalk-bearing clay. The dry white which is made from Sauvignon Blanc, Sémillon, and Muscadelle, is refined, sensual, and very aromatic with floral notes plus vanilla, dried fruit, almond, and ripe white and yellow fruit (peach). This luxuriance of aromas and the fattiness of Semillon is kept in good balance by the freshness of Sauvignon. Drinking temperature: 10–12°C (50–53.6°F).

The red Côtes de Franc is dark in colour and possess rich aromas of red fruit (raspberry, cherry, and blackcurrant), vanilla, and somewhat earthy notes such as Russian fur, leather, and wood. It is full and broad in flavour, fatty, and powerful. Most wine is somewhat coarse in the first years following maturing in oak but this changes after two or three years in the bottle. Drinking temperature: 16°C (60.8°F).

St-Emilion

The vineyards of St-Emilion surround the picturesque village of that name. The ancient Romans were certain of the quality of the local vineyards, as witnessed by the famous poet and consul Ausonius. The vineyards surrounding St-Emilion are situated on a plateau of calciferous soil and on hills of chalk-bearing loam or clay soils. West of St-Emilion the underlying ground is gravel. This is the area of the great wines. Most St-Emilion wines though originate from sandy-sediments and ferruginous sandstone beds which reach to the Dordogne.

The dominant grape variety here is the Merlot with some Cabernet Franc (sometimes known locally as Bouchet), Cabernet Sauvignon, and Malbec or Cot. The fairly recent classification, which is rigidly enforced and also reviewed every ten years, is interesting, serious, and original. This provides an additional stimulus to keep an eye on quality since it is the wine over a period of a decade that is checked for quality, rather than the terroir or grower. The system of promotion or demotion keeps everyone on their toes and the consumer is therefore the winner. Little needs to be said about the quality of the wines. Most St-Emilion wine is of outstanding quality. The dark red wines are accommodating, rounded, and quickly accessible. Their aromatic palette usually contains ripe fruit (blackberry, cherry, strawberry), dried fruit (apricots), herbs (bay laurel), spices (cinnamon), floral notes (ivy), leather, and earthy touches (wood, humus, and truffle). The better wines contain the

St-Emilion AC.

necessary tannin and require several years ageing in the bottle. The structure is broad and supple despite the presence of tannin. A good St-Emilion gives the taster a warm, sensual, and juicy impression which endures in the mouth and the memory. Drinking temperature: 14–16°C (57.2–60.8°F).

ST-EMILION (PREMIER) GRAND CRU CLASSÉ
The classified (Classé) wines of St-Emilion are perhaps slightly better than the others and usually originate from the better wine-growing soils. Most Crus Classé wines are concentrated in the direct area around St-Emilion itself and the conditions for their quality, yield, and minimum price are strictly controlled.

Generally this results in slightly more strength, backbone, tannin, and therefore potential for laying down, and clearly greater complexity. Drinking temperature: 16–17°C (60.8–62.6°F).

St-Emilion Grand Cru.   St-Emilion Grand Cru.

Ch. St-Georges St-Emilion.   Montagne St-Emilion.

THE ST-EMILION SATELLITES
North of the main St-Emilion area there are four communes which can append their own name to the appellation of St-Emilion though it is more like borrowing the St-Emilion name for their own purposes.

The wines from these four communes are generally more rustic and less refined in texture and taste than their compatriots from St-Emilion, but they are certainly worth considering. Furthermore they are attractively priced for their quality. The names are:

ST-GEORGES ST-EMILION
This is a sturdy wine.

MONTAGNE ST-EMILION
This is a full-bodied, sturdy, and rich wine.

PUISSEGUIN ST-EMILION
This wine is perhaps less elegant than its neighbours.

LUSSAC ST-EMILION
This is the most gentle wine of the four and perhaps the most feminine but looks can deceive.

Pomerol

This is a very big name for such a small wine-growing area of only 800 hectares. Wine-growing here takes place on a small area with a ferruginous soil. The soil varies greatly: it is sandy in the vicinity of Libourne, gravel-bearing sand and clay to the west, gravel-bearing clay in the centre, and gravel-bearing sand to the north. Despite this variety of soils the wines of Pomerol are clearly all offspring of the same family.

Pomerol is at the same time full, powerful, and supple, and very fruity with blackberry, cherry, raspberry, and plum dominant, sometimes tending towards preserved or dried fruit in the best years. Other recognisable aromas in top Pomerols include violet, iris, vanilla, spices, toast, game, leather,

Pomerol AC.   Pomerol.

tobacco, cocoa, coffee, liquorice, and sometimes also cinnamon (Pétrus), and truffle.

Pomerol is exceptionally sensual, creamy fat, fleshy and rounded, often with a mineral undertone in the aftertaste. Never drink it too young and certainly never before its fourth or fifth year for an ordinary Pomerol, and not before the sixth or seventh year for the better ones. Drinking temperature: 16–17°C (60.8–62.6°F).

Lalande de Pomerol

North of the Pomerol area is the territory of Lalande de Pomerol. This wine-growing area is far larger than Pomerol. Only red wine is produced under this AC and in common with its grander cousins of Pomerol it is rich in aromas, full-bodied, powerful, fleshy, and fatty.

There are discernible notes in the nose of plum, liquorice, ripe fruit, vanilla, spices (such as nutmeg), cocoa and coffee, and occasional suggestion of menthol. The top estates of Lalande de Pomerol can easily hold their own with the wines of Pomerol and St-Emilion. Drinking temperature: 16–17°C (60.8–62.6°F).

Fronsac en Canon-Fronsac

This area of the Libournais is characterised by fairly steep hills reaching the astronomical height of about 75 metres (246 feet), providing wonderful views of the surrounding countryside. The underlying strata of this wine area that extends to more than 1,100 hectares is calciferous clay. The hills contain more chalk; wine from these may bear the AC Canon-Fronsac.

Both wines are red, elegant and refined but also full-flavoured and full-bodied. The bouquet contains clearly recognisable suggestions of ripe red fruit (cherry), vanilla, toast, leather, roasted almond and hazelnut, humus, and occasional hints of spices, menthol, coffee, or cocoa. Fronsac wines can also contain floral notes of iris and violet and sometimes develop a smoky aura. Drinking temperature: 16–17°C (60.8–62.6°F).

Gironde. Red wines are produced in the south of this area and dry white wines in the north.

CÔTES DE BOURG

This 3,600 hectares wine region is often called the 'Switzerland' of Bordeaux, because of the many rolling green hills. Both red and white wines are produced here.

The white wines are extremely rare and to be honest best ignored as they offer nothing special in terms of quality. This Sauvignon white wine is extremely fresh tasting and pleasing but best drunk as an aperitif. Drinking temperature: 9–10°C (48.2–50°F). The red wine is deeply and attractively coloured and fairly aromatic. When young it is quite rough but after several years ageing in the bottle the harsh tannin mellows. The taste is then rounded, full, and sometimes even seductive. The better quality wines possess class, refinement, and elegance. Drinking temperature: 16°C (60.8°F).

CÔTES DE BLAYE

This white wine was once intended for use in making Cognac. Currently more acidic and moderate quality wines from this region are used as the basis for Fine de Bordeaux, the local distilled spirit, that otherwise is very tasty.

The better quality wines bear the appellation Côtes de Blaye and are dry. The wine is quite aromatic (citrus fruit and pineapple), fresh, broad, and quite dry. Drinking temperature: 10–12°C (50–53.6°F).

PREMIÈRES CÔTES DE BLAYE

Most of the wines are red but a small quantity of dry white wine is also produced. The white wine is fresh, elegant, and has a typical Sauvignon Blanc nose

Lalande de Pomerol.   Canon-Fronsac.   Côtes de Bourg.   Côtes de Blaye.

Blayais and Bourgeais

Two Bordeaux wine areas are situated south of Charentes Maritime (the area famous for distilling Cognac): the larger Côtes de Blaye (including the Premieres Côtes de Blaye) and the smaller Côtes de Bourg.

Both lie on the right bank of the mouth of the

with citrus fruit (predominantly grapefruit), and plant undertones (box and broom). It is an excellent aperitif or with fresh oysters. Drinking temperature: 10–12°C (50–53.6°F).

The Premières Côtes de Blaye reds are mainly thinly textured but the better ones are fuller and more complex. In general, Premières Côtes de Blaye reds are fruity wines with plant undertones. It is best to choose a top estate as these represent better value for money. These better wines are often surprisingly powerful, with an almost typical nose of game and leather without being 'rustic'. Drink the simple wine when young and slightly chilled (14°C/57.2°F) and the fuller wines at 16–17°C (60.8–62.6°F).

Médoc

We leave the right bank behind and complete our journey through the wine region of Bordeaux in the Médoc, on the left bank of the Gironde. Médoc is more or less a peninsula with vineyards, bordered by the waters of the Gironde in the north, the Atlantic Ocean to the north-west, and the city of Bordeaux to the south-west, with the extensive forest of Les Landes to the south.

Soil and climate

The sand and gravel-bearing strip of land of about 5–10 km (3–6 miles) wide provides a broad assortment of terroirs and microclimates. What is locally known as 'graves' is actually a complex mixture of clay, gravel stone, and sand. The stones have been deposited by the Garonne and some come from the Pyrenees (quartz and eroded material from glaciers). Some material is of volcanic origin from the Massif Central (quartz, flint, sandstone, igneous rock, sand, and clay) which has been carried first by the Cère and then the Dordogne. Here and there calciferous clay breaks through the gravel. The plateau of the Médoc is criss-crossed by countless small valleys, which not only provide a pleasing change in the landscape but also ensure excellent drainage. This all provides excellent ground on which to grow vines. The ground is so poor that the vines have to struggle to gain their nutrients and water but this improves the quality of the grapes produced. It is therefore not surprising that the most famous wine in France originates from this soil. The climate is fairly mild, influenced by the favourable position on the 45th line of latitude, the presence of the Atlantic Ocean, and the waters of the Gironde, Garonne, and Dordogne. This means that the vineyards receive sufficient warmth, sunlight, and moisture. The vines are reasonably protected from spring frosts and against fungal infections by the westerly winds. Although this situation in principal is ideal for wine-growing, this does not guarantee constant quality and quantity of the harvest. No great wines will be made in years with cool, wet summers. The fickleness of the Médoc's climate is part of the excitement for lovers of wine.

Grape varieties

Actually all the grape varieties here originate from the ancient Biticura (Biture, Vidure) according to the well-informed specialists of the Conseil des Vins du Médoc, which were brought to the area by the

Médoc.

Romans. All present-day varieties in the Médoc are derived from this origin. Names such as Cabernet, Malbec, and Verdot first appeared in the eighteenth century and Merlot a century later. What is surprising is the almost total disappearance of an exceptionally interesting variety of grape: the Carmenière, which was the foundation on which the Médoc's success and quality was founded. You will only find this variety in the Médoc after a long search and then only in tiny quantities. The wines produced from these grapes is of outstanding quality. The yield though is so low in comparison with the other Médoc grapes that growers have switched in large numbers to the Cabernet Franc, which is a genetic offspring of the Carmenière. The Cabernet Franc though is not a Médoc grape by origin, coming as it does from the western Loire where it is locally known as Breton.

The Cabernet Sauvignon is the real discovery of the Médoc. No other type of vine has been as widely exported as the Cabernet Sauvignon. It is to be found in South Africa, California, Australia, in the Balkans, Spain, Italy, and Greece. People were so convinced by the quality (and probably also the price) of Bordeaux wines that Cabernet Sauvignon and Merlot were planted in the hope that imitation Bordeaux wines could soon be produced that could be sold at lower prices. This did not succeed though because although the variety of grape is important, the terroir is also important. And the terroir is less easily imported or imitated.

In addition to the Cabernet Sauvignon, which provides the wine with its backbone and fruity aromas, there are Merlot (which matures more quickly and makes wine accessible sooner by mellowing the Cabernet Sauvignon) Cabernet Franc (superb bouquet), Petit Verdot (colour, power, and body), and Malbec (tannin, colour, finesse, and aromas).

MÉDOC AC

Although the entire geographical region of the Médoc has the right to use the Médoc appellation (including the Haut-Médoc and the six communes appellations) most Médocs AC wines originate from the north of the 'peninsula', particularly from the areas between the villages of St Vivien de Médoc and St-Germain d'Esteuil. The vineyards of the northern Médoc are generally of newer origin than those of Haut-Médoc. There are older vineyards here and there but they are in a minority.

The wine domains of the Médoc AC are mainly small in area. Many of these have joined together in cooperatives to increase efficiency and in order to survive. The underlying ground is typical of the Médoc, with various gravel-bearing strata and sporadic calciferous clay.

The Médoc AC is very variable in style and taste because of the great difference in terroirs and because of the many small domains. Two main types can be recognised though:
– light, elegant, refined, subtle, and seductive aromatic wines which can be drunk when young. Drinking temperature: 14–16°C (57.2°F).
– full-bodied, stronger, and tannin-rich wines that benefits from a number of years ageing in the bottle. Drinking temperature: 16–17°C (60.8–62.6°F).

HAUT-MÉDOC AC

The southern Médoc or Haut-Médoc ('Haut' refers to the higher situation along the river from its source and has nothing to do with contours) extending for

Haut-Médoc Cru Bourgeois.

St-Estèphe Cru Bourgeois.

about 60 km (37 miles), from the village of St-Seurin de Cadourne to Blanquefort. The division between northern and southern Médoc officially dates from 1935, but was in practice by the start of the nineteenth century. Many growers in the south of Haut-Médoc are confronted with the expansion of the city of Bordeaux, so that many vineyards (and also some estates) have disappeared for good. People are fighting in every way they know to call a halt to this process but the battle is tough.

Here too the great variety of terroirs causes great diversity in taste and types of Haut-Médoc wines. All the wines from this large family though have much in common: Haut-Médoc produces wines of deep colouring that are fresh, elegant, rich but not too powerful, with superb bouquets of ripe fruit (plum, raspberry, blackcurrant, and cherry), vanilla, toast, cedarwood (cigar boxes), and sometimes a little menthol, spices, tobacco, coffee, or cocoa. These wines deserve to be kept for a few years to enable their nose to develop more fully. Drinking temperature: 16–17°C (60.8–62.6°F).

ST-ESTÈPHE

St-Estèphe Grand Cru.

This is the most northerly of the six communes appellations. The vineyards of St-Estèphe extend to about 1,245 hectares around the village and commune of the same name. This wine differentiates itself from the others of Haut-Médoc through its northern situation and relatively higher position (the dizzy heights of 40 metres/131 feet), and the greater amount of gravel in the sandy and clay soils. The wine is darker in colour, more robust in structure, the bouquet and taste are more characteristic of their specific terroir, and the tannin is very pronounced. This makes wines from St-Estèphe perfect for laying down. The youthful freshness and fruitiness are retained for surprisingly long periods of time. Characteristic St-Estèphe aromas are: red fruit, vanilla, wood, toast, smoke, spices, cocoa, humus, and liquorice. Drinking temperature: 17–18°C (62.6–64.4°F).

PAUILLAC

The vineyards of Pauillac lie to the west of the town, parallel with the Gironde. The northern vineyards are slightly higher on more noticeable slopes than those of the south. Both areas have infertile soil that is very stony. In the south the gravel stones are generally larger than in the north, forming pebbles. The entire area is bedded in strata than ensure good drainage.

The wine of Pauillac is strongly influenced by its

terroir. It is rich in colour (purple or granite red) strong, powerful, with substantial backbone and tannin, but also juicy, very refined, and elegant. It is worth leaving for at least five years but far better ten before opening.

Some of the characteristic aromas are blackcurrant, cherry, plum, strawberry, raspberry, violet, rose, iris, cedarwood (of cigar boxes), vanilla, menthol, spices, cocoa, coffee, liquorice, leather, and toast. This robust wine with a great deal of finesse and elegance is just as delicious with a simple but wonderful roast leg of lamb, served with mushrooms as it is with a tournedos Rossini (with real goose liver and truffle).

In view of the price of most of these wines the preference might be for one of the very exclusive first growth wines, but the Cru Bourgeois can be greatly enjoyed, especially with local dishes. Drinking temperature: 17–18°C (62.6–64.4°F).

Pauillac Grand Cru Classé.   *St-Julien Grand Cru Classé.*

ST JULIEN

The vineyards of St Julien are to be found slightly to the south of Pauillac, concentrated around the twin centres of St Julien and Beychevelle. There are few small estates here. Almost all chateaux are owned by big companies. The area of St -Julien lies more or less in the heart of the Haut-Médoc and is subdivided into two smaller areas: that of St Julien Beychevelle in the north, and the other of Beychevelle in the south. Both areas have soils that are predominantly gravel with some pebbles. The main differences between the terroirs of St Julien are related to the distance from the river. The closer to the river, the more mild is the microclimate. The vineyards of St Julien are well-protected from flooding of the Gironde by the main hill ridges.
The wines of St Julien are somewhat less robust and powerful than those of its northern neighbour St Estèphe. It is a wonderful ruby red colour, very aromatic, juicy, well-balanced, full and rounded, rich and elegant. In short it has much charm which is widely prized throughout the world. Unfortunately this has a big influence on the price and these appear to climb continuously. Certain characteristic aromas are: cherry, blackcurrant,

pepper, freshly-sliced peppers (paprika), spices, animal overtones, leather, vanilla, toast, hazelnut, and menthol. Drinking temperature: 17–18°C (62.6–64.4°F).

MARGAUX

Everyone has heard of Château Margaux of course, the showpiece from this appellation. The AC Margaux includes the communes of Margaux, Arsac, Cantenac, Labarde, and Soussans.

The underlying soil of Margaux is extremely poor gravel with some larger stones. The microclimate is somewhat different to the other areas. Firstly Margaux is more southerly than the other Grand Cru vineyards which means more warmth and quicker ripening of the grapes. Equally important though is the role that the islands and sand banks play for Margaux. These protect the area against the

Margaux.

cold northerly winds, creating ideal conditions for producing great wine.
The wines of Margaux are excellent for laying down of course but their charm is rather more in the finesse and elegance than in their tannin. Margaux is perhaps the most feminine wine of the Médoc, being soft, delicate, subtle, sensual, and seductive.

Certain characteristic aromas include red ripe fruit, cherry, plum, spices, resin, vanilla, toast, gingerbread, coffee, and hot rolls. Drinking temperature: 17–18°C (62.6–64.4°F).

LISTRAC-MÉDOC

The small area with its own appellation does not have any first growth (Grand Cru) class appellations but it is still distinguished by the quality of its wines. Listrac is the 'roof' of the Médoc with its hills of 43 metres (141 feet) high! The underlying ground here consists of a combination of gravel and chalk-bearing strata, which ensure good drainage. The grapes ripen less quickly here than in the previously mention areas, due to the presence of countless woods and the chill northerly winds. The wine is full, rounded, fleshy, velvet smooth, and broad. Its tannin enables it to be kept for some time. Drinking temperature: 17–18°C (62.6–64.4°F).

MOULIS

The vineyards of Moulis are about half-way between Margaux and St Julien, in the interior of the Haut-Médoc, on a mixture of gravel and calciferous soil. Anyone who has drunk a top quality Moulis probably feels inclined to revise the Grand Cru classifications of 1855. The wine is a dark ruby red colour with an amazing assortment of aromas, and a very full taste that is complex and powerful. The level of tannin enables Moulis to be laid down for some time. The relationship between quality, price, and pleasure is highly gratifying. Drinking temperature: 17–18°C (62.6–64.4°F).

The valley of the Loire

France's longest river, the Loire, (approx. 1,012 km/632 long) has its source in the Ardèche. The wild mountain stream first flows northwards towards Orléans where it turns with a broad sweeping bend to the left into a majestic river as it then calmly proceeds towards the sea.

The valley of the Loire displays a constantly changing face. The vineyards are spread out from the flat land near the banks and on gently undulating hills alongside forests and every type of agriculture. Its nickname of 'Le jardin de la France' (the garden of France) comes from the colourful fields of flowers.

Listrac-Médoc.

Moulis.

The Loire: country of gardens and châteaux.

Wine-growing

The vineyards of the Loire are spread out in differing concentrations along the entire valley. The vineyards are sometimes up to 80 km (50 miles) away from the river itself. There are more than 100 different types of wine produced from the Loire valley.

These are divided into four main regions of which only the area around Nantes, Anjou-Saumur, and the Touraine form clearly defined geographical areas. The fourth region known as the 'central' region is a collection of smaller areas which do not fall within the other three larger ones. Here you will find the Sancerre wines of the Sancerrois, but also those of the Auvergne. The vineyards of the Côte Roannaise and the Côte de Forez also belong to the Loire wines but because of their character and geographical origins they have been dealt with in the section on Beaujolais.

PAYS NANTAIS

The area around the town of Nantes is mainly known for Muscadet, which is of exceptional quality. Depending on their position, Muscadets are categorised within four different appellations: Muscadet, Muscadet Côteaux de la Loire, Muscadet Côtes de Grand-Lieu, and Muscadet de Sèvre et Maine. The underlying strata through the Muscadet growing area is principally blue or grey slate, gneis, and primeval alluvial deposits, with some strata of volcanic origin. The bedrock of igneous rock and granite is criss-crossed by countless small valleys

which ensure good drainage. This is also very necessary because of the proximity to the Atlantic Ocean. The climate here is a moderate maritime one with mild winters and often damp summers.

MUSCADET

This wine may come from anywhere within the defined area but usually excludes wines from the three more specific appellations (see below).

MUSCADET CÔTEAUX DE LA LOIRE

This wine is produced from vineyards around the small town of Ancenis, on the banks of the Loire.

MUSCADET CÔTES DE GRAND-LIEU

This quality wine originates from the hills surrounding the small lake of Grand-Lieu, south of Nantes. This appellation has only been permitted since 1994.

MUSCADET DE SÈVRE ET MAINE

This wine accounts for 80–85% of the production and this is where the best Muscadets originate. These vineyards are distributed through 23 communes on the banks of the rivers Sèvre Nantaise and Petite Maine, from which the name is derived. The landscape is hillier than the rest of the Muscadet-growing area. This appellation has been recognised since 1936. All Muscadets are made exclusively with the unique Muscadet grape, also known originally as Melon de Bourgogne. This variety has been entirely forgotten in Burgundy from

Muscadet is an outstanding wine area.

Muscadet de Sèvre et Maine sur Lie.

A good Rosé d'Anjou is superb.

Charentes as the basis for distilling Cognac.In the area around Nantes these grapes produce a very searing wine, high in acidity, and generally a somewhat rustic character. Gros Plant du Pays Nantais is always very dry and harsh and is therefore not to everyone's taste.
Drinking temperature: 8–9°C (46.4–48.2°F).

which it originated but here they are lionised. The better
Muscadet is vinified and bottled off its sediment or lees mise en bouteille sur lie. This traditional method guarantees great freshness and enhances the fine taste and aroma of the wine but unfortunately it also increases the price. Muscadet is dry and has a fine fresh bouquet. Drinking temperature: 7–10°C (44.6–50°F).

GROS PLANT DU PAYS NANTAIS VDQS.
Gros Plant is de local name of the Folle Blanche grape variety from Charentes. Wine from the Folle Blanche is tart and very acidic and is used in

ANJOU-SAUMUR
Great wines were made here more than fifteen centuries ago. With its 27 appellations the area around Anjou and Saumur has something for everyone. It is a true journey of discovery from which newcomers to wine drinking and connoisseurs will both experience pleasure.
The underlying ground is extremely complex around Anjou. Crudely speaking there are two main types: the 'blue' of Anjou which is blue slate and eroded igneous rocks from the Massif Central, and the 'white' Anjou of Saumur, Vouvray, and Montlouis with underlying beds of chalk and tufa.
The most widely grown variety of grape is Chenin Blanc (Pineau de la Loire) for white wines and both Cabernets for reds. You will also encounter some

Domaines de Fesles vineyards in Anjou.

Chardonnay and Sauvignon Blanc for white wines here and there and some Gamay for red wines.

ANJOU BLANC
This wine is generally dry, sometimes medium dry. It is made using Chenin, sometimes with the addition of a little Chardonnay and Sauvignon. Certain characteristic aromas are: apple, pear, grapefruit, pineapple, and exotic fruit. Drinking temperature: 9–10°C (48.2–50°F).

ANJOU GAMAY
This red wine is fairly simple, fresh, and light. Drunk while young, the wine is characterised by an attractive purple colour with a gentle bouquet and soft taste with a hint or redcurrant and other red fruit. Drinking temperature: 12–14°C (53.6–57.2°F).

ANJOU ROUGE/ANJOU VILLAGES
Produced using both of the Cabernets this wine presents an opulence of aromas such as raspberry and blackcurrant.
The occasional hint can also be detected of freshly-sliced green pepper (paprika) and something smoky. This is generally a fairly light wine that must be drunk while young. Anjou-Villages can be kept a little longer and is also served slightly less chilled. Drinking temperature: 14–15°C (57.2–59°F).

ROSÉ D'ANJOU/CABERNET D'ANJOU
Both rosés are semi-sweet. The Rosé d'Anjou, made with the Grolleau, Cabernet Franc, and Gamay, is generally light and very biddable. It is best drunk while young and very fruity. In contrast, the Cabernet d'Anjou has more backbone and in the better years shows a remarkable capability for laying down. It is generally more elegant and fuller than the ordinary Rosé d'Anjou. Drinking temperature: 10–12°C (50–53.6°F).

ROSÉ DE LOIRE
This wine is made with Cabernet, Gamay, and Grolleau. It is a dry rosé wine though that is fresh, welcoming, and very pleasing. It is best drunk young and chilled. Drinking temperature: 10–12°C (50–53.6°F).

CÔTEAUX DE L'AUBANCE
This is a semi-sweet or sweet white wine that truly is for keeping, made with the Chenin Blanc. It is very aromatic with mineral undertones. Drinking temperature: 9–10°C (48.2–50°F).

ANJOU CÔTEAUX DE LA LOIRE
This semi-sweet white wine made with the Pineau de la Loire is golden-coloured with superb aromas of overripe fruit and a feisty character. It is characterised by its great refinement, freshness, and elegance. Drinking temperature: 9–10°C (48.2–50°F).

SAVENNIÈRES
This dry, sturdy wine is one of the best French white wines. The Chenin Blanc thrives at its best here in part due to the terroir of steep, rocky hills that are interspersed with slate and sand. The south to south-east siting is also ideal. Two exceptional vineyards are permitted to carry their own name on the label: these are the Grand Crus of Savennières-la-Coulée-de-Serrant and Savennières-la-Roche-aux-Moines. The first is special in being owned by just one person, Nicolas Joly, the guru of organic wine-growing in France. Savennières wines are a perfect accompaniment to lobster, crab, crayfish, freshwater fish, or other shellfish. Drinking temperature: 10–12°C (50–53.6°F).

CÔTEAUX DU LAYON
This is a truly sweet wine that is ideal for laying down. It is very fruity and delicate, developing its very complex but subtle aromas after a number of years. Drinking temperature: 8–10°C (46.4–50°F).

BONNEZEAUX
This sweet liquorous wine is a true classic. Harvested when overripe it gives the Chenin Blanc an unusually full taste and scent of currants, apricots, mango, lemon, pineapple, and grapefruit, together with floral notes of may and acacia blossom. It really is an experience. Drinking temperature: 9–11°C (48.2–51.8°F).

QUARTS DE CHAUME
A 'better' Côteaux du Layon is made with overripe

Anjou rosé.

Côteaux de l'Aubance.

Savennières.

Savennières/Roche aux Moines/Coulée de Serrant.

Côteaux du Layon. *Bonnezeaux.*

grapes. This golden-coloured wine has an over-whelming nose of honey, spices, and ripe fruits. Drinking temperature: 8–10°C (46.4–50°F).

CRÉMANT DE LOIRE

Whether white or rosé, Crémants de Loire are excellent sparkling wines that are fresh and very aromatic. Drinking temperature: 8–10°C (46.4–50°F).

SAUMUR BRUT

The Saumurois is second only to Champagne as a producer of sparkling wines. The white or rosé Saumur Bruts are very fine, elegant sparkling wines that are produced by the traditional method. They

are also available as demi-sec.
Drinking temperature: 8–10°C (46.4–50°F).

SAUMUR BLANC

This is a dry white wine produced with Chenin Blanc grapes, both with and without the addition of Chardonnay and Sauvignon. Served chilled, this subtle and fruity wine is best as an accompaniment to lobster, crayfish, and freshwater fish. Drinking temperature: 8–10°C (46.4–50°F). For

Excellent quality Saumur white.

those who do not want to spend endless time searching for a white Saumur then the best to try is to be found at Souzay-Champigny. Very traditional style Saumur Blanc Sec is made here at the Château de Villeuneuve. So much power and grandeur is not to be found elsewhere along the Loire (and perhaps difficult to improve upon throughout France).

SAUMUR ROUGE

This very aromatic and approachable wine is made with Cabernet Franc and/or Cabernet Sauvignon. When young it is full of tannin and should be chilled for drinking. Drinking temperature: 12–14°C

Quarts-de-Chaume ageing in the cask.

(53.6–57.2°F). After the wine has aged for a few years the Saumur red can be served a little less cool. The wine is then fuller in taste and more fleshy. Drinking temperature: 15°C (59°F).

CABERNET DE SAUMUR

This is an extremely small appellation of dry rosé that is produced from Cabernet Franc grown on chalky soil. The colour is a wonderful salmon pink and the wine is very fresh tasting with great fruitiness (raspberry and redcurrant). Drinking temperature: 10–12°C (50–53.6°F).

CÔTEAUX DE SAUMUR

This is a delightful full-bodied sweet white wine from the Chenin Blanc grown on a bed of tufa. This wine with its rich full taste and surfeit of fruity (pear and citrus fruit) and floral aromas together with the suggestion of toast and hot croissants can be drunk just for the pleasure. Drinking temperature: 8–10°C (46.4–50°F).

SAUMUR CHAMPIGNY

It is the underlying chalk that distinguishes this wine. Both Cabernet grapes here develop rich aromas of red fruit and spices. The wine achieves its full promise after maturing for a number of years. Drinking temperature: 12°C (53.6°F) when young and 15°C (59°F) when mature. A classic example of a traditional old-fashioned and powerful Saumur-Champigny can be found at the Château de Villeneuve (Souzay-Champigny) from the friendly Chevallier family. A less classical wine but superb and very seductive Saumur-Champigny is the wonderful Château du Hureau (Dampierre-sur-Loire) from the Vatan family.

The finest Saumur-Champigny wine.

Sauvignon de Touraine.

Touraine

There are nine appellations around the picturesque town of Tours. The wines are made from the same grapes as those of Anjou-Saumur. The climate here is very mild and moderate. The underlying strata are mainly tufa but calciferous clay and flint are found in some valleys.

TOURAINE

The dry white Touraine is perhaps the most interesting of the wines from these parts. It is fresh and fruity, with a pronounced nose and abundant character. In contrast to most of the wines from the area, this one is made with Sauvignon Blanc. Drinking temperature: 9–10°C (48.2–50°F).

The red Gamay (Pineau d'Aunis) wine is light, lithe, and fresh. It is suitable to be drunk with any meal. Drinking temperature: 12–14°C (53.6–57.2°F).

There is also a dry, fresh rosé which is very tasty with meat and grilled fish. Drinking temperature: 8–12°C (46.4–53.6°F).

For the sake of completeness, we must mentioned the sparkling Touraine, that can be vinified as mousseux or pétillant. This wine is produced by the traditional method as both white and rosé. Drinking temperature: 8–10°C (46.4–50°F).

TOURAINE AMBOISE

These white, rosé, and red wines are of higher quality. The best of them can be laid down. A white Touraine Amboise is best with casseroles and fish, eel, or chicken stews. Drinking temperature: 8–10°C (46.4–50°F). A rosé Touraine Amboise tastes best at 10–12°C (50–53.6 (46.4–50°F).

TOURAINE AZAY-LE-RIDEAU

This is a superb white wine with fresh acidity. Drinking temperature: 8–10°C (46.4–50).

There is also a fresh-tasting rosé for lunch-time drinking. Drinking temperature: 10–12°C (50–43.6 (46.4–50°F).

TOURAINE MESLAND

These wines are produced as white, rosé, and red. They are fresh, fruity wines that must be drunk young. Touraine Mesland red can be served with any meat dish, especially if some of the wine is incorporated in the sauce. Drinking temperature: 12–14°C (53.6–57.2°F). Touraine Mesland white is best with freshwater fish. Drinking temperature: 8–10°C (46.4–50°F). Touraine Mesland rosé can be drunk at any time, but especially with meat. Drinking temperature: 10–12°C (50–53.6°F).

BOURGUEIL

There are two different types of Bourgueil red wine. That which comes from lighter soils is also light in structure and is best drunk while fruity and young. The other, which comes from a heavier soil has a greater potential for ageing. Generally this latter type has more body and is more rounded. Certain characteristic aromas include freshly-sliced green pepper (paprika), wild strawberry, raspberry, and blackcurrant. Drink the lighter Bourgueil at 12–14°C (53.6–57.2°F) and the mature one at 14–16°C (57.2–60.8°F). There is also a light, fresh and fruity Bourgueil Rosé. Drinking temperature: 10–12°C (50–53.6°F).

ST-NICOLAS-DE BOURGUEIL

The lighter red wine is a lot like the related

Bourgueil.   *Good to best Chinon.*

Bourgueil. Drinking temperature: 12–14°C (53.6–57.2°F).

CHINON
Cabernet Franc here produces a full-bodied wine with aromas of red fruit (redcurrant, wild strawberry, and raspberry), freshly-sliced green pepper (paprika), and violets. Chinon must either be drunk very young (within a year) or after three to five years. In the interim period of two or three years the wine often has less taste and does not release its bouquet. Drinking temperature: 12–14°C (53.6–57.2°F). Chinon rosé is very fresh and fruity and delicious with meat, paté, terrine, and especially pork and veal. Drinking temperature: 10–12°C

Dry to fairly sweet Montlouis.

(50–53.6°F). Chinon white is extremely rare. It is a fresh and pleasant wine. Drinking temperature: 10–12°C (50–53.6°F).

MONTLOUIS
This sparkling wine is usually produced semi-sweet. In the really best years a full sweet Montlouis can be made. There is also a dry Montlouis. The better Montlouis wines can be laid down for some time. Non sparkling Montlouis is elegant, refined, and fruity. Drink a dry (sec) at 8–10°C (46.4–50°F), the semi or sweet Montlouis (moelleux) at 8–10°C

Still and sparkling Montlouis wines.

(46.4–50°F). There are two different sparkling Montlouis wines: Mousseux and Pétillant. Both make excellent aperitifs. The Pétillant is lower in carbonic acid gas. Drinking temperature: 8–10°C (46.4–50°F).

VOUVRAY
Perhaps the best-known wine from Vouvray is the semi-sweet (demi-sec) sparkling wine made by the traditional method.

Dry and sweet Vouvray.

The wines from Vouvray are recognised by a great assortment of ripe fruit aromas (plum and quince) and also by honey. Both sweet and dry Vouvray whites are also sometimes made and a first class Vouvray can be kept and better enjoyed when really old. Drinking temperature: 8–10°C (46.4–50°F). Demi-sec or moelleux Vouvray is also drunk at 8–10°C (46.4–50°F). The dry sparkling (Mousseux Brut) is a first class aperitif. Drinking temperature: 7–9°C (44.6–48.2°F). Its demi-sec kin can also be served as an aperitif but is more of a wine to serve with food.

CÔTEAUX DU LOIR
This is not a spelling mistake! The river known as Le Loir combines with the rivers Mayenne, Oudon, and Sarthe to join the river known as La Loire south of

Angers. The hills on both banks of the Loir produce white, rosé, and red wines. The white wine is made exclusively from Chenin Blanc (Pineau Blanc de la Loire) and is very fruity (apricot, peach, and exotic fruit) plus a suggestion sometimes of something smoky. It is a fine and well-balanced wine. Drinking temperature: 8–10°C (46.4–50°F).

The rosé from here is fresh and fruity with characteristic spicy aroma. Drinking temperature: 10–12°C (50–53.6°F). The red Côteaux du Loir is produced from Pineau d'Aunis, Gamay, or Cabernet Franc. It is a light, fruity wine with a hint of spice. Drinking temperature: 12–14°C (53.6–57.2°F).

JASNIÈRES

This wine-growing area is only 4 km (2 ¹/₂ miles) long and several hundred metres/yards wide, along the hills of the Loir, north of the vineyards of Vouvray and Montlouis. Small volumes are produced here on a bed of tufa of a consequently rare white wine that is considered to be among France's best. The wine is made from the Pineau de la Loire (Chenin Blanc) and it is distinguished by its finesse. The characteristic aromas are citrus fruit, almond, quince, apricot, peach, and sometimes also floral notes like rose or herbs such as thyme and mint. Depending on the season and the maker's preferences, the wine can be either dry or semi-sweet. Drinking temperature: 10–12°C (50–53.6°F).

CHEVERNY

Cheverny has held its own appellation since 1993. Currently there are about 400 hectares of vineyards cultivated but it would be surprising if this is not soon expanded. White, rosé, and red wines are produced here. White Cheverny is made with Sauvignon Blanc, sometimes supplemented with Chardonnay. The wine is fresh, elegant, and possesses wonderful floral perfumes. Fruity hints of gooseberry and exotic fruits can be detected in the taste. Drinking temperature: 10–12°C (50–53.6°F).

Cheverny red is mainly produced from Gamay and Pinot Noir grapes and is fairly fresh and fruity when young. After several years maturing in the bottle Pinot Noir takes the upper hand and the bouquet contains animal or gamey aromas. Drinking temperature: 14°C (57.2°F).

COUR-CHEVERNY

This is an extremely rare white wine from immediately around Chambord that is only permitted to use the old native grape variety of Romorantin in its making. Romorantin charac-teristically has a powerful nose of both honey and acacia. The Cour-Cheverny AC has been permitted on labels since 1993. Drinking temperature: 10–12°C (50–53.6°F).

HAUT-POITOU VDQS

This wine is undoubtedly part of the Loire wine area but as it seems not to be connected in any way it is given a separate listing. This is quite an honour for an area that was only a few years ago on the verges of bankruptcy. The take-over by the enterprising Georges Duboeuf of the failing local cooperative not only meant rescue from certain death but the start of a second life, more dynamic than ever. The Neuville-de-Poitou cooperative now backs some 85% of the production of Haut-Poitou.

The underlying beds of chalk and marl are exceptionally well-suited in particular for growing the white wine grapes of Sauvignon Blanc and Chardonnay. The Chardonnay whites wine are elegant and subtle with aromas characteristically of white fruit and citrus fruit. The taste is fresh and harmonious and the wine makes an excellent aperitif. The better cuvées such as La Surprenante are more complex and contain seductive bouquets reminiscent of privet, acacia, vanilla, toast, and hazelnut. Drinking temperature: 10–12°C (50–53.6°F). The Sauvignon whites are fresh and elegant, with suggestion of flint in the nose. Drink as an aperitif or with seafood. Drinking temperature: 8–10°C (46.4–50°F). The red wine can be made from a variety of different grapes. The best originate from Cabernet Franc and Cabernet Sauvignon vineyards with chalk or flint-bearing clay. These have a characteristic nose of red fruit and violets with a hint of tufa. Drinking temperature: 12–14°C (53.6–57.2°F).

Cheverny.

Haut-Poitou.

Surprising Chardonnay from Haut-Poitou.

Haut-Poitou red.

The centre

The wine area in the centre of France has three isolated areas of vineyards: the Sancerrrois (Gien, Sancerre, Bourges, and Vierzon), Chàteaumeillant (above Montluçon) and the Haute-Auvergne (between St-Pourçain and Roanne).

Sancerrois

The appellations of the Sancerrois are Pouilly sur Loire, Pouilly Fumé, Sancerre, Menetou-Salon, Quincy en Reuilly, and Côteaux du Giennois VDQS.

CÔTEAUX DU GIENNOIS
The vineyards of the Côteaux du Giennois are situated on the best gravel and chalk-bearing hills along both banks of the Loire between Gien to slightly north of Pouilly-sur-Loire. The traditional grape varieties are grown here: Sauvignon Blanc for white wines with Gamay and Pinot Noir for both rosé and red wines.
Côteaux du Giennois white is a fresh and easily consumed wine with generous nose of citrus fruit, white fruits, gooseberry, blackcurrant, quince, pineapple, white flowers, and light vegetal notes. Drinking temperature: 8–10°C (46.4–50°F).
Côteaux du Giennois rosé is light and fresh, fruity, and lithe. Drinking temperature: 10–12°C (50–53.6°F).
Côteaux du Giennois red combines the finesse in its bouquet of Pinot Noir with the playful generosity of Gamay. The scent is seductive with aromas of fresh fruits such as cherry, blackberry, strawberry, and bilberry, while the taste is quite mild. Drinking temperature: 12–14°C (53.6–57.2°F).

POUILLY SUR LOIRE
Pouilly sur Loire is a town on the Loire, to the east of the well-known Sancerre vineyards. Two wines originate from here: the famous Pouilly Fumé (see below) and the Pouilly sur Loire. Both wines are exclusively white and they originate from similar chalk-bearing soil. The different between the wines is the grapes used. Pouilly Fumé is made solely with Sauvignon Blanc while Pouilly sur Loire uses Chasselas grapes. Anyone who regards the Chasselas grape as less worthy should visit Pouilly sur Loire in order to sample the local wine.
Pouilly sur Loire is very fresh and aromatic with characteristic nose in which hazelnut, dried fruit, white flowers, citrus fruit, exotic fruit, and sometimes also a hint of menthol or anise can be detected. The wine leaves a pleasing fresh impression in the mouth which is reminiscent of ripe oranges. Drinking temperature as aperitif: 8–9°C (46.4–48.2°F), or 10°C (50°F) with food.

POUILLY FUMÉ
The description 'fumé' or smoked does not refer to smoky undertones in the wine as many people think but to the ashen grey film that is commonly seen on

Pouilly-Fumé.

the grapes here so that they appear to have a deposit upon them.
This white wine from the Sauvignon grape is very fresh and aromatic. Hints of green asparagus, box, blackcurrant, broom, white roses, acacia, white peach, and aniseed can be detected in its nose. In short this is a truly wonderful wine with a rich and powerful taste. Drinking temperature: 8–10°C (46.4–50°F).

Sancerre

Sancerre is one of the best-known Loire wine-growing areas and also one of the best-known wines of France. Since its early beginnings as an AC wine in 1936 Sancerre white has made the area part of the French wine-growing elite.

Sancerre rosé and red only gained their recognition in 1959. The vineyards for white, rosé, and red Sancerre (approx. 2,400 hectares) are located within 11 communes, of which Sancerre, Chavignol, and

Sancerre from the village of Chavignol.

Sancerre from Bué.

Château Sancerre
(Marnier-Lapostelle).

Menetou Salon.

Quincy.

Bué are the best known. The area is noted for its attractive landscape of gently undulating hills with chalk or gravel-bearing soils. The grapes used here are Sauvignon Blanc for the white and Pinot Noir for both the rosé and red wines. Sancerre white is fresh, lively, and very aromatic. Certain of the characteristic aromas in its bouquet include citrus fruit, white peach, broom, acacia, jasmine, exotic fruits, white flowers, green ferns, green asparagus, and newly sawn timber. The taste is also fresh but rich and full of flavour. Drinking temperature: 10–12°C (50–53.6°F). Sancerre rosé is delightful, generous, and subtle with fruity aromas of apricot, red berries, or even grapefruit and there can be a suggestion of peppermint. Drinking temperature: 10–12°C (50–53.6°F).

Sancerre red is definitely and characteristically Pinot Noir. In years of a good vintage, the red Sancerre is of outstanding quality. In lesser years it is best ignored because the relationship between quality and price is then out of balance. The best Sancerre Rouge (such as from Paul Prieur & Fils or, Sylvain Bailly) is light, delicate, and very aromatic (cherry, blackberry, and liquorice). In exceptional years the wine is fuller and rounder. Drinking temperature: (a young Sancerre with fish) 12°C (53.6°F), otherwise 14–16°C (57.2–60.8°F).

MENETOU SALON

These wines are simply wholly undervalued. There are white, rosé, and red wines from this area. Menetou Salon is situated close to the town of Bourges on chalk and alluvial deposits. The entire area of the appellation amounts to barely 330 hectares. The white wine made with the Sauvignon grape is fresh and fruity with bouquet containing recognisable notes of citrus fruit, box, peppermint, and white flowers with a subtle hint of nutmeg. The taste is full of flavour, rounded, lithe, and friendly. Drinking temperature: 9–10°C (48.2–50°F).

Menetou Salon Rosé is made with Pinot Noir. This wine is usually fresh and fruity with delicate scents of white and red fruits. Drinking temperature: 10–12°C (50–53.6°F). Menetou Salon red surprises the taster with its superb ruby red colour and great

fruitiness with suggestions of plum and cherry. Drinking temperature: 12°C (53.6°F) with fish, otherwise 14°C (57.2°F).

Quincy

On the other side of Bourges, in the direction of Vierzon, you will find the small wine area of Quincy. The Quincy AC was recognised way back in 1936. The wines of Quincy have been among the elite of French viticulture for more than 60 years but they are hardly ever to be found outside their own area. This wine area in the centre of France, west of the Loire, and on the left bank of the Cher, had acquired a reputation by the Middle Ages. The wine-growing area comprises just two communes: Brinay and Quincy, totalling about 180 hectares. The terraces on which the vines grow are covered with a mixture of sand and ancient gravel. The underlying strata consists of chalk-bearing clay. The Sauvignon Blanc grapes thrive particularly well on this poor soil. Quincy resembles the better Sancerre Blanc. It is fresh and surprisingly aromatic: with suggestions of white flowers, citrus fruit (orange and lemon), and vegetal undertones including box, broom, or green asparagus. The taste is fresh, elegant, juicy, and exceptionally pleasing. Drinking temperature: 9–10°C (48.2–50°F).

REUILLY

People confuse Reuilly and Rully too readily with each other. Rully is also white but is a Burgundy. Similar confusion exists between Pouilly Fumé (Loire) and Pouilly Fuissé (Bourgogne Mâconnais). The 130 hectares of the Reuilly appellation vineyards are slightly to the west of Quincy. The vines grow on gently undulating hills of calciferous marl and terraces of chalk-bearing sand. Unlike neighbouring Quincy Reuilly produces white, rosé, and red wines. Reuilly white, from Sauvignon Blanc, is a perfect example of Sauvignon from the Loire. You will probably wax bucolically lyrical about the bouquet that is reminiscent of asparagus beds, still not fully emerged from beneath their blanket of

Reuilly, most bucolic
French wine.

Châteaumeillant Gris.

rosés are strawberry, raspberry, white peach, and peppermint. Drinking temperature: 10–12°C (50–53.6°F).

Reuilly red is made with Pinot Noir and it is colourful but very light in body and taste. This wine is a veritable explosion of fruity aromas in which cherry, plum, blackberry, wild strawberry, redcurrant, and blackcurrant can be distinguished. This can be extended with typical Pinot Noir aromas such as leather, game, and peppers in the finish. Drinking temperature: 14°C (57.2°F).

CHÀTEAUMEILLANT VDQS

The wine from this wine-growing area of 80 hectares has been permitted to carry the predicate VDQS since 1965. The wine has quickly become well respected among the knowledgeable and by local barkeepers and restaurateurs. The secret of the area is the special rosé or vin gris made from Gamay grape which represents exceptional value for money. Châteaumeillant has a complex soil that is gravel-bearing sand and clay. The grapes used here are Pinot Noir, Pinot Gris, and Gamay.

The Vin Gris de Chàteaumeillant is fresh, lively, and very seductive. It possesses rich aromas of white fruit such as peach, with spicy undertones and occasional floral notes. The taste is equally fresh but also supple and generous. Drinking temperature: 10–12°C (50–53.6°F).

Chàteaumeillant red is less well-known but can be surprisingly good. The wine is very fruity with aromas of ripe red fruit, especially blackcurrant, and suggestions of menthol and liquorice. Drinking temperature: 12–14°C (53.6–57.2°F).

morning dew, woken gently by the first morning rays of sunshine. The nose recalls white wild flowers of the meadow, grass, clover, and white fruit, with suggestions of menthol, lemon or lime. The taste is fresh, fruity, and very expressive. Drinking temperature: 10–12°C (50–53.6°F).

Reuilly Rosé is always exceptionally fruity and fresh. In the best years (with plenty of sun) the better wines can be more robust and fuller. Most rosés are made with Pinot Noir but there are subtle traditional rosés to be found here and there that are made with Pinot Gris. Certain characteristics aromas of Pinot Noir

Châteaumeillant red.

Vins d'Auvergne

Finally in France we make a short visit to the Auvergne. We leave the upper reaches of the Loire and drop down towards its tributary, the Allier. There are two wines growing areas here: St-Pourçain and the Côtes d'Auvergne.

Although the neighbouring wine districts of Côtes de Forez and Côtes du Roannais are officially part of the Upper Loire, they have been dealt with under the section on Beaujolais, which they more nearly resemble.

St-Pourçain

South east of the town of Moulins is the small town of St-Pourçain-sur-Sioule, situated on the Sioule river. There are nineteen communes in the wine area of St-Pourçain that between them have about 500 hectares of vines under cultivation. The vineyards are on the hills and level areas with chalk and or gravel soils. The local Tressaillier grape once enjoyed great fame but the red grapes of Gamay and Pinot Noir are now more common. Attempts though by the local cooperative to replant with the traditional white variety arc proving successful. The

St-Pourçain.

wine-growers of St-Pourçain now offer the full range of white, rosé, and red wines of excellent quality. The quality hereabouts left much to be desired in the past but the younger generation of hardworking

Ficelle is the nicest St-Porçain red.

and passionate growers now deserve your full trust. St-Pourçain white is made by blending Tressaillier, Chardonnay, and Sauvignon Blanc. The combination of calciferous clay or sand, favourable position with regard to the sun, and these three grape varieties leads to an exceptional wine. The wine has different characters depending on the percentage of Tressaillier, Sauvignon, and Chardonnay it contains. Those in which Tressaillier and Chardonnay dominate are good to lay down, while Tressaillier-Sauvignon types are fresh and fruity but better suited for early consumption. Where Chardonnay dominates, the wine combines Chardonnay's rich finesse with the freshness of Sauvignon. There is also a fatty and highly aromatic wine made combining Chardonnay, Tressaillier, Sauvignon, and Aligoté. Hence there is something for everyone. Drinking temperature: 8°C (46.4°F) for Sauvignon-Tressaillier) and 12°C (53.6°F) for the Chardonnay types. St-Pourçain rosé and Vin Gris are made with 100% Gamay. These are fresh, elegant and fruity wines. Drinking temperature: 10–12°C (50–53.6°F). Finally the red St-Pourçain is made with Gamay and Pinot Noir. Depending on the percentage of grape varieties used and style of wine making these wines can be fresh, fruity, and easily consumed (100% Gamay), fuller and more complex (80% Gamay, 20% Pinot Noir), or harmonious, complex, rich, and delicate (50% of each). The terroir also determines the eventual richness and complexity of the wine. Those reds from chalk soils are generally more elegant and complex than those sited on gravel-bearing sand. These are fuller and richer tasting though. Drinking temperature: 12–14°C (53.6–57.2°F).

Côtes d'Auvergne VDQS

Vines have been growing on the sides of the old volcanoes of the Auvergne for more than two thousand years. Wine-growing started to flourish again in the Auvergne recently after a long period of disasters and troubles stretching back to the phylloxera epidemic, World War I, the economic crisis of 1929, and World War II that followed. A new generation of quality-seeking wine-growers and makers is re-establishing a reputation for quality that had been lost by a previous generation that was more concerned with volume production. These new young growers are not only better educated and more professional, they are also proud of their business, their terroir, and of their wine and you can tell this by drinking their wines.
The soil of the Côtes d'Auvergne is very varied. Around the town of Clermont-Ferrand two different types can be found: volcanic strata and chalk-bearing marl. Both originate geologically from enormous volcanic eruptions during the Quaternary. The landscape around here is extremely hilly, making a visit of great interest. The wine-growing area is about 500 hectares, stretching from north of Riom to south of Issoire. The vineyards are

situated at a height of 300–500 metres (984–1,640 feet), between the ancient volcanoes of the Chaine des Puys and the river Allier. Rainfall is similar to that of the Sancerrois. About 90% of the vines planted are Gamay. The remaining 10% consist of Pinot Noir and Chardonnay. The Côtes d'Auvergne appellation mainly consists of generic wines but there have been five recognised crus since 1977 that each has its own personality. The generic white, rosé, and red wines may come from throughout the area. White Côtes d'Auvergne are made with Chardonnay and they are very fruity, elegant, and fresh. The best of these are aged in oak and can be laid down and kept for ten years. Drinking temperature: 9–12°C (48.2–53.6°F).

Côtes d'Auvergne rosé is made from Gamay grapes and it is fresh, very fruity, generous, and easily consumed. Drinking temperature: 10–12°C (50–53.6°F). Côtes d'Auvergne red can be made with Gamay, Pinot Noir, or a blend of both. This wine is surprisingly fruity and fresh, while at the same time supple and fresh. Drinking temperature: 12–14°C (53.6–57.2°F).

From north to south the crus are: Madargue (above Riom) both rosé and red wines. Both characterised by deep colour, seductive fruitiness (raspberry and redcurrant), full and rounded flavour with muted tannin. Drinking temperature: 14–16°C (57.2–57.2°F). Chateaugay (between Riom and Clermont-Ferrand) where white, rosé, and red wines are made. The most interesting is the dark ruby red with characteristic spicy bouquet including cinnamon and nutmeg and an elegant and well-balanced taste. Drinking temperature: 14–15°C (57.2–59°F). Chanturgue (above Clermont-Ferrand) produces only red wine. This is dark ruby coloured and very aromatic with red fruit such as raspberry

Cru d'Auvergne Châteaugay.

Corent is one of the nicest French rosé wines.

and cherry. The taste is fresh and fruity. Drinking temperature: 13–15°C (55.4–59°F). Corent (between Clermont-Ferrand and Issoire) is the rosé domain. This wonderful rosé will silence all sceptics immediately with its superb bouquet containing citrus fruit, hazelnut, cherry, apricot, peony, and fresh butter. The wine is full-bodied, broad, and almost fleshy and has a very lingering aftertaste. Discover this fantastic wine during a visit to the Auvergne. Choose the best of them such as those of Jean Pierre and Marc Pradier. Drinking temperature: 10–12°C (50–53.6°F). (Good white and red wines are also made in Corent, but less special than the rosé). Boudes (below Issoire) produces white, rosé, and red wines. The lower quality Boudes wines are interesting and well made but not exciting. The top quality wines by contrast are veritable jewels. Consider the white and red wines of Claude and Annie Sauvat, who perform miracles in this small wine area. The Chardonnay white can easily compete with the best white Burgundy The red Gamay is deeply coloured with wonderful bouquet containing raspberry, redcurrant, spices, vanilla, and pepper. The Pinot Noir wines exude scents of plum, cherry, leather, liquorice, wood, coffee, and toast. Do not anticipate a light-footed feminine wine. These red Boudes are sturdy but with yielding tannin and have a full, fatty, and complex taste. Drinking temperature: 14–16°C (57.2–60.8°F).

Spain

Wine-growing

The total area of Spanish vineyards is in the region of 1.2 million hectares. That is enormous and about 300,000 hectares larger than either the French or Italian wine-growing areas.

Yet less wine is produced than in either of the other two countries, at approximately 35.5 million hectolitres, a vast 20 million hectolitres less than France or Italy.

The difference in production volumes is partly accounted for by the large proportion of Denominación de Origen wine. Spain produces relatively smaller volumes of vino de mesa, vino comarcal (table wine) and vino de la tierra (country wine or vin de pays) than France or Italy.

The majority of Spanish wines originates from Catalonia, Valencia, and La Mancha. Regions such as La Rioja, Aragon, Levante, and Andalucía produce quality wine in much lower volume. The lower yield can also be explained by the extremely hot and arid climate of southern Spain. The vines have to be kept low because of the extremes of weather so that the yield is little more than a few bunches per vine.

Champagne and Cava

It is a shame that almost everything with bubbles in gets called Champagne. There are top quality Cavas made by the traditional method that are far better in quality than the most lowly of Champagnes. Calling these wines Champagne is to undervalue them. Not only is it incorrect but in common with other sparkling wines, the Spanish Cavas have their own story to tell about the grape varieties used, the soil on which they are grown, and the weather conditions that are quite different to those of Champagne. This Spanish wine has been made by the same méthode traditionnelle as French sparkling wines since the end of the nineteenth century.

Cava came into being in the province of Barcelona in 1872 because the local innkeepers and hoteliers could not meet the increasing demand for good sparkling wine. The Catalans decided to make their own sparkling wine instead of always having to import either expensive Champagne or cheap Blanquette de Limoux. This wine was made in precisely the same way as the other méthode-traditionnelle wines, but the Cavas have their own taste and character. This is determined by the use of different grapes and other ideas about how a good sparkling wine should taste.

Cava vinification

In Spain too, the grapes intended for production of Cava are carefully selected and harvested. The best grapes for making Cava are grown on very chalky soil at a height of between 200–450 metres (656–1,476 feet).

The vineyards of the Spanish interior are lower than in the province of Barcelona. The hot Mediterranean climate is moderated by the altitude of the vineyards which ensure a certain cooling from winds at this height. The best Cava vineyards surround the small community of St Sadurni d'Anoia in Barcelona province.

The following grapes are used for the base wine: Macabeo (fruit and freshness), Parellada (floral perfumes) and Xarel-lo (acidity and alcohol). Sometimes a little Chardonnay is also added. For Cava Rosado the grapes used are Cariñena, Garnacha Tinto (Grenache Noir), Tempranillo, and Monastrell. Inland Cavas are usually made from Viura (Macabeo) grapes. Because it can become extremely hot in Spain the grapes for Cava are usually picked early in the morning. The grapes are pressed as soon as they are brought in from the vineyards.

The juices are transferred to stainless steel tanks where fermentation takes place at a constantly controlled low temperature. After fermentation the wine is rested for a while before being sampled by the cellar master. The best cuvées are selected and blending takes place in great secrecy. The wine is then bottled and held in enormous cellars for a minimum of nine months but often for longer.

During this period a second fermentation takes place in the bottle. Just as with Champagne, Saumur, or Limoux lots of tiny bubbles form. The bottles, which are stored on racks or rotating pallets, are manually or mechanically shaken to get the floating remnants of unfermented sugars and dead yeast cells to fall to the neck of the bottle. Here too the neck of the bottle is dipped into a special salt solution to freeze the sediment. When the bottle is opened the plug of sediment is forced out of the bottle by the pressure. The wine, which is now clear, is topped up with a liqueur (see main section on sparkling wines) and provided with a cork and retaining wires and cap. The wine is now ready to be shipped to the customers.

The taste of Cava

More than 90% of all Cava originates from Catalonia, particularly from Penedes. Two major companies control about 90% of the market. Freixenet (which also owns Segura Viudas and Castell Blanch) is the undoubted leader of the export market.

The true market leader though in Spain is Codorniu. Cavas are generally somewhat less dry than French sparkling wines. They have that little bit of Spanish temperament. The price of the top quality Cavas is exceptionally low for their quality but one needs to be careful. Corners are sometimes cut, especially with the nine month's period of maturing in the bottle. There have been cases for many years against brands which do not stick to the minimum nine months and whose wine is therefore not permitted to be termed Cava. There are officially only two different types of Cava: white and pink. The white Cava though is subdivided into a variety of different taste types.

CAVA ROSADO BRUT
This is an exceptionally elegant pink Cava with a sparkling colour. It has wonderful floral and fruity aromas and is full-flavoured, dry, and fruity. It makes an excellent aperitif.

CAVA EXTRA BRUT
This is the driest (least sweet) of all Cavas. This type contains less than 6 grams of sugar per litre.

Cava Rosado (rosé)   *Cava Extra Brut.*

CAVA BRUT
This wine is slightly less dry than the previous one. Although quite a dry wine it is much less so than a French Champagne for example.
Cava Brut is by far the most favourite Cava with non Spanish drinkers. It has 6–15 grams per litre of sugar.

CAVA EXTRA SECO
This wine has sugar content of 12–20 grams per litre.

CAVA SECO
Although termed 'dry' this is really a semi-sweet Cava but still fairly fresh and pleasing with sugar content of 17–35 grams per litre.

CAVA SEMI-SECO
This Cava starts to taste really sweet but not yet too sweet. The Spanish still prefer this sweeter sparkling wine to the Extra Seco or Brut. It has a sugar content of 33–50 grams pr litre.

CAVA DULCE
This wine is for those who like a truly sweet wine. Its sugar content is greater than 50 grams per litre.

ESPUMOSOS
In addition to Cava there are a number of other sparkling wines made in Spain which are not permitted to be termed Cava DO.

MÉTODO TRADICIONAL
This sparkling wine is made by the same method as Cava but from areas which are not permitted to be Cava DO. The quality is generally nothing special although some are very pleasant. These wines are seldom encountered outside their area of origin.

GRANVÁS
Granvás is the Spanish name for the méthode charmat or méthode cuve close.
The principle is simple: the second fermentation takes place in a huge tank (grandes envases) that is hermetically sealed instead of in the bottle. The wine is clarified and bottled after the second fermentation. The taste with this type of wine is also determined by the sugar content.

The gradations from dry to sweet are:
– Extra Brut (less than 6 g/l sugar)
– Brut (0–15 g/l)
– Extra Seco (12–20 g/l)
– Seco (17–35 g/l)
– Semi-Seco (33–50 g/l)
– Dulce (more than 50 g/l)

Cava Brut.

The north west

The following autonomies or areas are found in north-western Spain: Galicia, the País Vasco, Castilla y León, Asturias, and Cantabria.
The latter two of these autonomies only produce vinos de mesa. The other areas can be split into their DO wine-growing areas.

Conditions

The climate of north west Spain is clearly influenced by the Bay of Biscay and the Atlantic Ocean.
The weather is much cooler, wetter, and more windy than the rest of the country. Daily life is clearly marked by the sea and fishing.
This part of Spain is less typically Spanish, having more Celtic and Basque characteristics with little sign of the Castilian and Moorish invasion. The local dishes are inspired by the sea's harvest: fish and other seafood.
The local wine is generally white, dry, fresh, and light, with the exception of a few red wines.

Galicia

It seems as though Galicia first appeared on the Spanish wine map about ten years ago. The excellent wine was reserved for local hostelries that sold it from the barrel and for restaurants. Few tourists were to be seen in green Galicia, the forgotten corner above Portugal, although thousands of pilgrims visit annually on their way to the famous shrine of Santiago de Compostella. Because this area has remained isolated for so long, the local wine-growers had great riches of old varieties of grapes which give the Galician wine its charm.
Who had ever heard of Albariño, Godello, or Treixadura fifteen years ago? The Galician wines were said to be too low in alcohol, too thin, to acidic, too rustic, and to oxidise far too readily. Many growers were so hurt by the criticism that they planted more readily marketable non-native varieties of grapes.

The wine from these though was of such poor quality that a new generation of growers have brought honour once more to the original varieties. Less wine is made but the quality is better.

The best combinations of grape variety, micro-climate, and soil type were sought out. The results are apparent. Galician wine is tremendously popular, the quality is excellent, and the recognition of these jewels is quickly becoming known around the world.
Galicia, as the name implies, has a definite Celtic or Gallic or Gaelic background.

Present day culture is largely Portuguese in influence. Both influences can be found in the names given to the wine areas and their wines.

Rías Baixas

This is certainly the best known but not the only quality DO of Galicia. The white wine of the Albariño grape is deservedly famous. Galicia has an attractive coastline with large inlets or estuaries here and there known as rías baixas or 'low rivers'. These are slightly reminiscent of the Scandinavian fjords. The rest of the country consists of green valleys in which the coolest and moistest vineyards of Spain are to be found.
There are three different soil types in Rías Baixas: bedrock of granite covered with alluvium, alluvial deposits, or a bedrock of granite with a covering of sand. The average height at which the vineyards are situated is about 450 metres (1,476 feet). The wine is mainly white and made from 90% Albariño grapes. These Albariño grapes are said to be a twin of the Riesling. These are said to have been brought to Santiago de Compostella as gifts by German monks. Some wine is also made with Treixadura and/or Loureira Blanca, and also an extremely rare red produced from Brancellao and Caiño.

The white Albariño must be made exclusively with this variety of grape. It is a taut, fresh and crackling wine with much class and a delicate taste in which the upper notes are floral and fruity. Drinking temperature: 8–10°C (46.4–50°F).

Rias Baixas from Galicia.

Ribeiro

Ribeiro is inland from elongated Rías Baixas in the province of Orense. Ribeiro was once a famous centre for the export of Galician wine. When the rest of Europe improved its methods of wine-making, Ribeiro did not keep up and became somewhat overlooked. The quality of the wine produced here left much to be desired and was certainly not up to the standards of Rías Baixas. Much has changed though since both domestic and foreign investment has been attracted to the area. The wine-making equipment is greatly improved and large Spanish-style bodegas have been built to cope with the planned development. Ribeiro is in the ascendancy at the moment. The white and red wines from Ribeiro are first class wines for daily consumption but a few superb ones can be discovered among them.

The white wine made with Treixadura grapes, sometimes supplemented with grapes such as Palomino, Torrontés, Albariño, Loureira, Godello, or Macabeo. The better quality wines tend to be made with Albariño. Drinking temperature: 8–10°C (46.4–50°F).

Most red wine is made with Caiño grapes , supplemented with others such as Garnacha and Mencía, and is light but fairly high in tannin. The better wines are made with Garnacha and are somewhat more full-bodied. Drinking temperature:

Good table wine is made in León.

12–15°C (53.6–59°F) depending on the quality. Do not chill if possible . The rosé wine is fresh, fruity, and light. Drinking temperature: 10–12°C (50–53.6°F).

RIBEIRA SACRA

The vineyards of this area lie on terraces in the picturesque landscape of the provinces of Lugo and Orense. The white wines here are made from Albariño, Treixadura, Godello, Loureira, Torrontés, and Palomino, and are very similar to those of Ribeiro, but often with less freshness to them. The reds made with grapes such as Mencía, Alicante, Caiño, Sousón, and Garnacha are of acceptable quality. Much has been invested here too in replacement or renewal of the vineyards, wine-making equipment, and storage areas so that quality is likely to improve rapidly. Drinking temperature: 8–10°C (46.4–50°F) for white wine and 12–14°C (53.6–57.2°F) for red wine.

MONTERREI

This DO still has to establish itself. The quality is moderate to acceptable. Despite this the area has gained its own DO nomination. The wines here are principally made from the white Palomino, Godello (also known as Verdelho here) and Doña Blanca grapes, and the red Alicante and Mencía grapes. The best whites and reds are fresh and fruity. The wines have a relatively low alcoholic content.

Valdeorras

This wine area lies mainly inland on the border with Castilla y León. Most of the vineyards are in the valley of the Sil. Until recently a heavy dark wine was made here that disappeared anonymously on draught through the local bars. The grape varieties of Godello (white) and Mencía (red) are gradually being restored to their true position of honour and increasing amounts of quality wine are now being made. The wine-making installations are greatly improved and the wine-making itself is now far more hygienic.

The white wine is typically Galician: light, fresh, and crackling dry. Drinking temperature: 10–12°C (50–53.6°F). The red wine is much rarer than the white but well worth the trouble of finding. Most of them are light and fruity but the better Crianza red possesses a wonderful nose of blackberry, plum, and liquorice, a superb cherry red colour, and a smooth, rich, and very pleasing taste. Drinking temperature:12–14°C (53.6–57.2°F).

Castilla y León

Castilla y León is an enormous wine-growing area in which a great deal of excellent quality table and country wine (equivalent to vin de table and vin de pays) is made such as Cebreros, Valdevimbre-Los Oteros, Fermoselle-Arribes del Duero, and Tierra del Vino de Zamora, plus superb DO wine from the localities of Bierzo, Cigales, Ribera del Duero, Toro, and Rueda. The last four of these are located around the town of Valladolid and the Duero and are dealt with in the following section. The DO Bierzo is the odd one out, located in the extreme north west of Castilla y León. In terms of its climate, Bierzo (León) has more in common with the other wines in this section than its four neighbours from Castilla.

Bierzo

This DO has officially existed since 1989 but it is only since 1991 that only grapes from within the designated area were permitted to be used. This last measure in particular has led to an improvement in quality of Bierzo wines.

Wine-growing now covers some 5,500 hectares. Bierzo is the only Castilla y León DO not directly situated on the river Duero. Instead it lies against the border with Galicia. Bierzo is regarded as a transition zone between the wine-making of Galicia, particularly nearby Valdeorras, and the area of the Duero valley. The Bierzo area lies in a valley surrounded by the mountains of the Cordillera Cantábrica and the Montes de León, which protect the valley from extremes of weather. The climate is influenced by the Atlantic Ocean (moisture and wind), but gets more hours of sunshine than Galicia. The vineyards are on the sloping sides of the hills, which are composed of granite and clay. They produce good white wine from the Doña Blanca and Godello, rosé and red wine from the Mencía with some use of Garnacha. Unfortunately white wines are also still encountered from the lower quality Palomino grape.

The white wine is less pronounced in its taste than those of Galicia. The tasty, light, and fresh dry wine is very enjoyable as an aperitif. Drinking temperature: 8–10°C (46.4–50°F).

The rosé made with Garnacha is of excellent quality, especially when it is aged in oak when it is fully-flavoured, aromatic, and powerful. Drinking temperature: 10–12°C (50–53.6°F).

I consider the red wine from Bierzo to be the best from this area. Most wine here is made to be drunk when young. They are light, fresh, and fruity, with floral undertones. The better wines are aged in oak and are sold as Reserva. These are more full-bodied, robust, and grown-up. Finally there are Gran Reservas, which promise much for the future. Most red Bierzo wines have a distinctive nose of red fruit, plum, dates, or sultanas, occasionally with a hint of liquorice and celery or fennel. Drinking temperature: 12–16°C (53.6–60.8°F); but 16°C (60.8°F) for the Gran Reservas.

País Vasco

The Basque country has three faces: the picturesque coastline with endless countless beaches and fishing harbours, the large industrial towns, and the interior. The Basques have their own culture and own language that is possibly the original European language, and above all their own character. The Spanish part of the Basque country still has close ties with the French part (Pays Basque and Gascony or Gascogne). In this section we restrict ourselves to the north of the País Vasco, and in particular the areas of Bizkaya (Vizcaya) and Getaria (Guetaria). We use the Basque spellings with the Castilian spelling in brackets.

GETARIAKO TXAKOLINA (CHACOLÍ DE GUETARIA)

You will be unlikely to encounter Txakolí (pronounced schakoli) outside the Basque country. This is a pity because it is an extremely delicious wine to drink with shellfish and other seafood. This white wine and a small amount of red is produced from 40 hectares around the towns of Zarautz, Getaria, and Aia. No great finesse can be anticipated from these wines because of the heavy soil, consisting of clay and alluvial deposits, and the severe, cold, wet, and windy climate. The native white Hondarrabi Zuri and blue Hondarrabi Beltza grapes never ripen fully under these conditions. Yet the white, rosé, and red Txalolí wines are pleasingly fresh, often with a tingle of carbonic acid on the tip of the tongue. In general the quality is not very high. Drinking temperature: 8–10°C (46.4–50°F) (white/blanco), 10–12°C (50–53.6°F) (rosado/rosé), and 12–13°C (53–55.4°F) (red/tinto).

BIZKAIAKO TXAKOLINA (CHACOLÍ DE VIZCAYA)

This is the newest addition to the Txakolí family. The vineyards of Bizkaiako Txakolina are situated around Bilbao on about 60 hectares of clay soil and alluvial deposits. The climate here is windy, cold, and wet, all far from ideal for wine-growing. The grapes used for these Txakolí wines are the same as Getariako Txakolina: Hondarrabi Zuri for white and Hondarrabi Beltza for the red and rosé wines. Drinking temperature: 8–10°C/46.4–50°F (white/blanco), 10–12°C/50–53.6°F (rosé/rosado), and 10–12°C/50–53.6°F (red/tinto).

The high Ebro valley

The high Ebro valley encompasses the south of the País Vasco, Navarra, La Rioja and Aragón, which are all areas producing DO wines, except La Rioja which is the only DOC area in Spain. Rioja is also permitted to be produced in parts of Navarra and the southern part of the Basque country (País Vasco).

Conditions

The climate in the high valley of the Ebro is a good deal warmer than in north west Spain, where the moderating influence of the Atlantic Ocean and Bay of Biscay is apparent. The Ebro valley is protected by a long chain of mountains (about 900 metres/

2,952 feet high) and Aragón to the west is not higher than 300 metres (984 feet). The climate is largely of the continental type although southern parts of the Basque country are still partially influenced by the cold and moist air from the Atlantic. The winters are cold and the summers are hot high up in the Ebro valley, while spring and autumn are mild and moist. Navarra and La Rioja have directed themselves for many years at the French market and consequently close links have been established, for instance, between Bordeaux and both of the Spanish areas. One example of this to be found in Rioja is the bodega of Enrique Forner (Marqués de Caceres), which has become very well known in Bordeaux under the name Henri Forner. It is not surprising therefore that the style of the wine is influenced by their northern neighbours. Many of these wines are less characteristically Spanish, being more French or even European, and this does not harm their quality. The traditional white wine of the Ebro valley was often heavy and robust to act as a foil for Basque cooking (specialities are freshwater and sea fish). The traditional red wine was also robust and was ideal with many meat dishes (lamb and beef), that are often locally grilled over a fire or spit-roasted. Nowadays far more modern-style wines are being made. The white wine is fresher and lighter, and the red wine is more scented, more fruity, and has a more delicate taste.

For the sake of clarity, Rioja wines are given by their denomination and not their area of origin.

Rioja DOC

Rioja is made in three different areas as previously indicated: the southern Basque country, Navarra, and La Rioja. (note only the area around Longroño has the definite article before the name, not the wine itself.) The area of La Rioja and Rioja wine derive their name from the small river Oja, hence Rio Oja. The river flows into the Ebro near Haro. The Rioja wine region is subdivided into three areas: the highlands of Rioja Alta in the north west, the most northerly vineyards of Rioja Alavesa in Alava Province, and the lowlands of Rioja Baja in Navarra and La Rioja. The entire area is protected from the cold north winds by the mountains of the Sierra Cantábrica. The river Ebro rises in the Cantabrian mountains and flows towards the Mediterranean. Wine has been produced in La Rioja for more than two thousand years, but the breakthrough for present Rioja wines occurred in the late nineteenth century.

Considerable numbers of vines of the Tempranillo variety were grown in the area. Some of the well-heeled nobility though grew Cabernet and Merlot because of the fashion of the day to plant French varieties. When the French vineyards were destroyed by the combination of first fungal disease and then Phylloxera, French wine-makers were forced to travel to Spain to buy young Cabernet Sauvignon and Merlot wines. They discovered the charm of the Tempranillo and helped the Spanish to improve their method of vinification. This did not go smoothly at first because the local wine-growers did not at first appreciate the superior know-all manner of their northern neighbours. Furthermore most of the Spanish could see no point in the expensive equipment or of hygiene. Fortunately there were some with foresight for the future, such as the famous Marqués de Riscal. Thanks to these people the area of La Rioja developed into one of the most famous wine-growing areas in the world. The first Rioja wine that became known was made from 100% Cabernet Sauvignon. Although Rioja was granted its first DO in 1926, it was a long time before it appeared under its own name in the European market. The British continued to call Rioja 'Spanish claret' or 'Spanish Burgundy', while the French shipped immense volumes of Rioja to France to support the ailing Bordeaux. The good name of Bordeaux therefore owes a great deal to Spain, although the wine experts of the French capital city of wine prefer not to be reminded of this. Today the name of Rioja is associated throughout the world with quality in the same breath as Bordeaux and Burgundy.

Soil and climate

The underlying ground of La Rioja consists largely of a mixture of calciferous and ferruginous clay.

White Rioja Blanco.

There are also alluvial deposits along the banks of the Ebro, while in Rioja Baja there is also sand. The best vineyards are situated at a height of 300–600 metres (984–1,968 feet), particularly in the north-western part of Rioja Alavesa (País Vasco) and Rioja Alta (La Rioja and a small enclave of the province of Burgos). With its heavier soil and lower altitude (a maximum of 300 metres), which does not provide as much cooling for the grapes, the wine from Rioja Baja is less refined than from the other two Rioja areas. Consequently the wines from this latter area are ready to drink earlier, therefore more quickly consumed, helped by a relatively cheaper price.

In the highlands of Alavesa and Rioja Alta the remnants of the westerly winds from the Atlantic cool the vineyards. The harsh winds from the north are filtered by the Pyrenees and by the Cantabrian mountains. The result is a cold winter, mild and sunny spring, hot summers, and mild autumns with cooling night-time breezes. Although the highlands have a typical continental type of climate, a more Mediterranean climate rules in Rioja Baja with hot, dry summers with many hours of sunshine.

The wines from Rioja are white, rosé, and red. The Viura grape is mainly used for the white wine (known elsewhere as Macabeo or Macabeu), which imparts the wine with delicate acidity. This grape is supplemented with some Malvasía. This latter variety is responsible for the fresh bouquet and fine acidity. Finally, some Garnacha Blanca is also added to impart greater roundness to the wine and increase the level of alcohol. Rosé wines are made with the Garnacha, with or without the addition of some Tempranillo and even the white Viura. Modern-style rosés (Rosado) though are increasingly being made with Tempranillo grapes. Red wines are mainly produced with Tempranillo, often mixed with Garnacha, Mazuelo and/or Graciano. The once so popular Cabernet Sauvignon is not planted any more and is disappearing from present-day cuvées. Rioja wines are distinguished by their vintage and the extent to which they have matured. This information is contained on the label, the label on the back of the bottle, or sometimes on the neck seal. Plain 'Rioja' indicates that the wine is bottled in its first year (vino joven) and must be drunk young. The indication 'Crianza' says that the wine has been aged in oak for at least one year (for red wines) and six months (for whites), in small barricas, and has then been bottled. This wine is not permitted to leave the bodega before its second year (for white and rosé) and even the third year for red wine. The term 'Reserva' is used for red wine that has been aged for at least one year in oak barricas and then has spent at least a further year in the bottle. For white and rosé wines this term means they must have been aged in oak for at least six months and may not leave the bodega before they are three years old. Gran Reserva wines are exceptional and are only made in the better years.

Rioja Blanco Reserva.

Rosé Rioja Rosado.

Red Rioja Tinto Reserva.

Old style red Rioja.

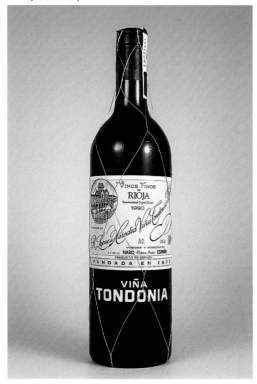

These wines must be aged in barricas for at least two years and then further aged in the bottle for at least three years. These wines (that are mainly reds) may not leave the bodega before they are six years old. White Rioja (joven) is excellent, fresh, and fruity. Drinking temperature: 8–10°C (46.4–50°F)

White Rioja Crianza/Reserva/Gran Reserva is often rounded, full-bodied, and juicy wine with extensive bouquet ranging from citrus fruit to white fruit, floral and wild herbal notes. Depending on the style of the maker, the wine can be very fresh or rather ponderous. Old-fashioned white Riojas are often dominated by oak, while the more modern wines have more of an impression of fruitiness, and in particular of the Viura grape. Drinking temperature: 10–12°C (50–53.6°F). Rosé that has not been aged in wooden casks is fresh and fruity. Drinking temperature: 10–12°C (50–53.6°F). Red Rioja that has not been cask-aged (joven) is mainly made with Tempranillo. It is best to drink this wine when young while still fresh and seductively fruity. Drinking temperature: 12–14°C (53.6–57.2°F). The better Rioja Tinto Reserva or Gran Reserva are full-bodied, elegant, and refined with a clear suggestion of oak which is reminiscent of vanilla. Traditional Riojas often possess both the scent and taste of citrus fruit, together with fine acidity. Old-fashioned ponderous Rioja is still to be found for sale but fortunately these are less commonly made now. The best modern Riojas can readily compete with the best French and Italian wines, especially in terms of price. Drinking temperature: 16–18°C (60.8–64.4°F).

Navarra

There are two denominated wines that originate from Navarra: Navarra DO and Rioja DOC. Since we dealt with Rioja wines together above we will deal here solely with the Navarra DO wines. The landscape of Navarra is extremely hilly. The northern border with France is formed by the Pyrenees and the Ebro divides Navarra from La Rioja in the south. The western and eastern neighbours are the Basque country and Aragón. The entire area of Navarra is rich in history. The kingdom of Navarra once extended to Bordeaux. Memories of this former period of glory and the former ruler, King Sancho the Elder (1005–1035) are to be found throughout Navarra.

Soil and climate

The ground of northern Navarra (Valdizarbe, Tierra Estella, Baja Montaña, and Ribera Alta) consists of permeable layers of chalk and gravel covered with a brown loam-like soil, while in the extreme south (Ribera Baja) there is an arid sandy soil. The altitude generally varies between 240 and 540 metres (787–1,771 feet).

There are great differences in Navarra's climate between north and south. The influence of the Pyrenees is very apparent in the north (Valdizarbe,

Chivite wine cellars.

Baja Montaña, and Tierra Estella) and the climate here is semi-continental with hot summers, harsh winters, and little precipitation. The further south one travels the hotter and drier becomes the climate. The scene in Ribera Baja is almost desert like. There is some vestige of a maritime climate in western

Navarra (Estella) with slightly more precipitation, and cooling westerly breezes near the Ebro. The climate in Ribera Alta is more Mediterranean in nature.

The wines

Navarra uses an age classification in common with other Spanish wine-growing areas. The ordinary Navarra or vino joven is not aged in oak and is intended to be drunk when young. Wine that is aged for at least six months in barricas and then further matured in the bottle is known as Crianza. This wine is not permitted to leave the bodega before it is three years old. Reserva has to be aged for at least one year in barricas and at least a further year in the bottle. This wine must not leave the bodega before its fourth year. Finally, Gran Reserva must be kept in oak barricas for at least two years and at least three years in the bottle. This wine may not be sold before it is six years old. Navarra also produces some white wine from the Viura grape, supplemented with 30% Chardonnay. Wines that are made solely from Viura grapes are very harshly acidic and do not possess the roundness of the Viura/Chardonnay blends. Only a few 100% Viura wines are of acceptable quality. One that can be recommended is Gran Feudo Blanco of Chivite. Drinking temperature: 9–10°C (48.2–50°F).

The better and rarer Chardonnay whites can be surprisingly good, as in the case of the excellent Coleccion 125, made wholly of Chardonnay by the same Chivite house. Drinking temperature: 12°C

The vineyards of Chivites: Señorio de Arienza.

Top quality Chardonnay.   *Navarra rosé.*

One of Spain's best rosés.   *Superior quality Tinto Crianza.*

(53.6°F). The dry wines made with the Muscatel grape are in a class of their own but very rare. Drinking temperature: 10–12°C (50–53.6°F).

The rosé wines are generally made with the Garnacha grape, and are among the best Spanish rosé wines, if not among the world's best. Drink this wine while young when it tastes best. Most of the rosé wines are fully-flavoured, rounded, spicy, fruity (redcurrant), and often very alcoholic. Drinking temperature: 10–12°C (50–53.6°F).

The ordinary red (tinto) vino joven from Navarra can be drunk at 12–14°C (53.6–57.2°F). The Tinto Crianza is a better choice than the younger reds

because of its maturation in oak barrels. Both the bouquet and taste are dominated by red fruit but a hint of vanilla can also be detected. Drinking temperature: 14°C (57.2°F).

The Tinto Reserva and Gran Reserva are little gems but it is important to differentiate between the cheaper wines from the cooperative bodegas and those of the top houses such as Chivite, Magaña, Ochoa, Guelbenzu, and Virgen Blanca. The last of these houses makes more traditional wine which possess higher levels of tannin when young than those of the cooperatives. This wine also has a better taste and greater power, more finesse, and greater

Gran Reserva red.

Top quality Güelbenzu Eva from Navarra.

107

breadth. The wine is characterised by the broad range of its taste and nose, with vanilla (wood), blackcurrant, redcurrant, cherry, herbs (bay), and liquorice. Drinking temperature: 15–17°C (59–62.6°F) but 17°C (62.6°F) for the Gran Reservas. Finally an additional mention of the superb sweet Muscatel from Navarra. The old-fashioned, dark-brown syrupy Muscatel can be left for the connoisseurs but the modern-style fresh, fruity, and tremendously seductive Muscatels such as the sublime Capricho de Goya from the bodega of Camilo Casilla or the Vino Dulce de Moscatel of Ochoa or Chivite, must be among the finest Muscatel wines from anywhere. Drinking temperature: 8–10°C (46.4–50°F).

Aragón

The autonomous region of Aragón is situated between Navarra and Cataluña, covering a large area from the foot of the Pyrenees through to the Sierra de Javalambre, about 50 km (31 miles) north-west of Valencia. The major towns of Aragón are Zaragoza, Huesca, and Teruel. Three of the four wine-growing areas of Aragón are situated close to each other near the town of Zaragoza; Campo de Borja lies to the west and Cariñena en Calatayud to the south-west in the province of Zaragoza. The fourth wine area of Somontano is situated at greater altitude and further to the east, on the eastern side of the town of Huesca, almost bordering Cataluña. Here too it is astounding how these four areas, especially Somontano, have adapted to the demands of modern wine-making. Aragón was once notorious for its heavy and highly alcoholic wines that were intended to fortify the weaker ones.

Until not so long ago the wine from this area was almost exclusively sold in bulk. The DO wines are gaining the upper hand as the bodegas themselves are being modernised and through better management and control of the vineyards. It is important that all four of these wine-growing areas have managed to retain their own identities. Unfortunately the quality of these wines is rarely discovered, even within Spain, where the locals still swear by Rioja and Ribera del Duero. It is a pity, for the wines of Somontano must surely have a great future ahead of them.

Campo de Borja

The wine-growing area of Campo de Borja borders in its north with the southern tip of Navarra and follows the southern bank of the Ebro in the east. The Sierra de Moncayo forms the western boundary and is also the highest point of the region. The vineyards are concentrated around the three towns of Ainzón, Albeta, and Borja. The area was only granted DO status in 1980 since when the growers have worked steadily but surely to improve both the quality and image of their wines. Campo de Borja's soil chiefly consists of underlying beds of chalk with

scattered ironstone which ensures good drainage, overlaid with brown alluvial sand. The vineyards at the foot of the Moncayo mountain are sited higher at (600 metres/1,968 feet) than the others which are at about (300 metres/984 feet). The climate is purely continental with very hot and dry summers and harsh, windy winters. The white wine is made from Viura grapes (Macabeo), while the rosé and red wines use Garnacha and Cencibel (the local name for the Tempranillo grape), which may be supplemented with a little Mazuela or Cabernet Sauvignon.

Campo de Burja Blanco (white) is fresh, spicy, and fairly simple. Drinking temperature:8–10°C (46.4–50°F). Campo de Burja Rosado (rosé) is mainly intended for drinking when young. Rosados made with Garnacha grapes that are harvested in hot climates often produce strong and highly alcoholic wines. The Campo de Burja though is surprisingly fruity and fresh. Drinking temperature: 10–12°C (50–53.6°F).

The young (vino joven) Campo de Burja Tinto (red) is also intended to be drunk while still young. It is mainly fresh and fruity, rounded, and quite alcoholic. Drinking temperature: 12–14°C (53.6–57.2°F). Campo de Burja Tinto Crianza (that must be kept at least six months in barricas, and ageing in the bottle for the remainder of the minimum period of three years) is somewhat more grown up than its younger compatriots. This is a fruity wine but with a sturdy body and considerable level of alcohol (13–14%). Seek pleasure from these wines rather than finesse. Drinking temperature: 14°C (57.2°F). Campo de Burja Tinto Reserva and Gran Reserva (the former being aged for at least one year in barricas and one more in the bottle, the latter for one year and a further three in the bottle) are better value for money.

The longer ageing in both barrel and bottle impart greater profundity and roundness that compensates somewhat for the high level of alcohol (13–14%). Drinking temperature: 16–17°C (60.8–62.6°F). Some sweet liqueur wines are also produced in this region. These are made with the Muscatel Romano grape, and with Garnacha and Mazuela. These strongly alcoholic wines (at least 17.5%, maximum 22%) are often somewhat ponderous.

If you are attracted by the alcohol and sweetness then drink this Muscatel in the shade and not too quickly! Drinking temperature: 6–8°C (42.8–46.4°F).

Cariñena

Slightly to the south east of Campo de Borja lies the wine area of Cariñena, the oldest DO of Aragón. The recognition was granted as long ago as 1960. The vineyards surround the town of Cariñena in the province of Zaragoza, chiefly in the area between the Sierra de la Virgen and the river Ebro. In common with Campo de Borja, wine-growing originated during the Roman occupation. The present-day town of Cariñena, which derives its name from the Roman settlement of Carae, has been an important centre for both wine-growing and the wine trade since ancient times. The well-known Cariñena grape (known in French as Carignan) gets its name from the town and has spread from its home town via Cataluña to French Catalonia and even to the Rhône valley. The soil of Cariñena resembles Campo de Borja with underlying chalk and broken rock topped with brown alluvial sand. However close to the river the underlying rock is slate with a greater coverage of alluvium. In common with Campo de Borja a continental climate rules with hot summers and harsh winters. There are frequent frosts in spring. The major grape varieties of Cariñena are Garnacha and Cencibel (Tempranillo), supplemented with some Cariñena, Mazuela, and Cabernet Sauvignon for red wines and Viura for white wines, either with or without the addition of Garnacha Blanca or Parellada.

Cariñena was once renowned for the high alcoholic content of its wines. For that reason they are often now avoided. Today's consumers prefer lighter, more elegant wines than heavy, very alcoholic ones. This is a major problem for an area that is bathed in hot sunshine. Yet despite this a new generation of wine-makers are managing to make very acceptable wines. It is impossible for Cariñena to make a wine that is truly light in characteristics because of the extreme heat of summer and the nature of the soil –

Red CariÒena Tinto.

Monte Ducay

which is a blessing for connoisseurs of a wine full of character and strength. Most of the red wines are 12.5–13%, significantly lower than the 15% or even 18% for which Cariñena was famous not so long ago. Cariñena Blanco is fresh and reasonably dry. The high acidity of the Viura grape (Macabeo) makes the wine pleasing to drink but do not expect to find any outstanding wines among them. Drinking temperature: 8–10°C (46.4–50°F). Cariñena Rosado is like that of Campo de Borja, but with a stronger taste and often with greater alcohol. Drinking temperature: 10–12°C (50–53.6°F). The red wine has the same age classification as all other Aragonese wines. The ordinary Cariñena Vino Joven is not aged in oak and is meant to be drunk when young. The Crianza has been kept in oak for at least six months and then further in the bottle before being released for sale, while Reserva wines are kept in the barricas for at least two years and a further three years in the bottle. Generally the vinos jovenes are chiefly made with Garnacha, while the matured wines are produced with Tempranillo. Drink the vinos jovenes at 12–14°C (53.6–57.2°F). Drink crianza, reserva and gran reserva at 14–16°C (57.2–60.8°F). Cariñena also has a long tradition of making matured sweet wines that are intentionally exposed to the air and later oxygenated in large vats. These rancio wines are similar to those found at Maury and Banyuls in southern France but they lack the finesse of the French wines. If you encounter one of these rancio wines take a careful sip first to ensure you really do wish to continue drinking. Some of the wines are of very indifferent quality. The drinking temperature according to preference can be either well-chilled at about 8°C or at room temperature (approx. 18°C/64.4°F).

Calatayud

This DO is certainly the least well-known of the four Aragonese wine-growing regions. This is unjust for although the wines of Campo de Borja and Cariñena are full and powerful, those of Calatayud exhibit greater finesse and elegance. Because the area is protected in the east by the Cordillera Ibérica and in the north by the Sierra de la Virgen, the climate is more moderate than the previous two areas. The wines therefore have a better balance between acidity and alcohol.

The region's name may prove a greater obstacle to successful marketing than the quality of the wine. Catalayud is derived from the Moorish castle of Qalat that was built by the ruler Ayub. Qalat-ayub became distorted to Calatayud. Wine-growing was started here by the Celts, long before the arrival of the Romans. The great improvement in quality though is of very recent origin. The soil of Calatayud consists of chalk on marl with a top layer of sand and loam in the north and of slate and gypsum in the south. The more elevated vineyards at the foot of the Sierra del Virgen are situated at almost 900

White Calatayud.

Red Calatayud.

Pinot Noir does well in Somontano.

First class wine from Gewürztraminer.

metres (2,952 feet), while the average height of the vineyards in the Jalón valley is about 450 metres (1,476 feet). The entire area has a continental climate with hot summers and harsh winters. The elevated position of the vineyards and presence of cooling mountain winds keeps the vineyards cooler than in Campo de Borja and Cariñena. It would be a mistake to assume that with such favourable circumstances the local growers concentrate on making quality wines. Fortunately there are some younger growers who now seem set to achieve the area's potential. There first results are very promising. These modern wine-makers are succeeding through the replacement of hopelessly decrepit equipment but also by forging a better link between terroir, climate, and grape variety to create wines with bouquets of individual character rather than the former concentration on alcohol and volume.

The wines are produced with Viura (Macabeo) and Malvasía grapes, sometimes supplemented with a little Garnacha Blanca and the native Juan Ibáñez. Drink this wine at 8–10°C (53.6–50°F). The rosados are somewhat better in quality, full-bodied and fresh, but also very fruity. They are chiefly made with Garnacha Tinto. A warning though: read the label carefully to see the level of alcohol! There are Rosados de Catalayud that are 14% alcohol. Drinking temperature: 10–12°C (50–53.6°F).

The reds (Tinto) are predominantly vinos jovenes. Drinking temperature: 12–14°C (53.6–57.2°F).

The rarer Crianzas, Reservas, and Gran Reservas of Garnacha, Mazuela, Tempranillo, and Cabernet Sauvignon are certainly worth seeking out. They offer a warm, full flavour, combined with a certain freshness and elegance. Drinking temperature: 16–17°C (60.8–62.6°F).

Somontano

Somontano is the most surprising part of Aragón for connoisseurs. The vineyards of Somontano are barely 50 km (31 miles) from the Pyrenees in the province of Huesca. Wines have been made here for

many years for creative French wine traders. No-one had heard of Somontano thirty years ago but today the wines are to be found everywhere with quality ranging from honest and pleasing to superb. The wine-growers of Somontano are not held back by old-fashioned and stifling traditions in wine-making so that they try all manner of experiments. The terroir and climate of Somontano offer excellent prospects for the persistent among the wine-growers. The best results are achieved with a combination of traditional grape varieties and methods with newer varieties and modern vinification techniques.

The quality of wine from such daring combinations as Tempranillo and Cabernet Sauvignon, Moristel and Cabernet Sauvignon, Macabeo (Viura) and Chardonnay, or even Macabeo and Alcañon is quite astonishing. Even imported varieties such as Gewürztraminer and Pinot Noir seem to make good wine in Somontano. Not only does Somontano make some fine wines, its landscape is also extremely attractive with plenty of green, countless picturesque villages, historical churches, orchards, and terraced vineyards. These vineyards are sited on the slopes of small mountains at a height between 300 and 600 metres (984 and 1,968 feet). The soil consists of a mixture of heavy clay and sandstone in the higher vineyards, with alluvial soil in the Ebro valley. The soil is generally rich in minerals and trace elements, which are a blessing for wine-growing. The climate is continental, with hot summers and cold winters.

The presence of the Pyrenees, which shelter the vineyards from the cold northerly winds is also pretty advantageous. The native grape varieties of Somontano, the white Alcañon and the blue Moristel (not to be confused with Monastrell) co-exist alongside more Spanish varieties like Viura (Macabeo) and Garnacha. There is a great deal of experimentation though with countless new varieties such as Tempranillo, Cabernet Sauvignon, Merlot, and Pinot Noir for the blue grapes and Chenin Blanc, Chardonnay, Riesling, and Gewürztraminer for white wines. Traditional style white Somontano is made with Viura and Alcañon.

This wine is fresh, light, and dry for drinking when young. The modern-style whites is a carefully blended combination of Viura, Alcañon and Chardonnay or Chenin Blanc, and is much fuller and surprisingly pleasing. There are also several very interesting wines made solely from Riesling or Gewürztraminer.

Drinking temperature 8–10°C (46.4–50°F) for the traditional wines and 10–12°C (50–53.6°F) for the modern types. The rosados from Somontano have a very pleasing taste and also possess both finesse and elegance comparable with the best wines together with the warmth and power of the south. Drinking temperature is 10–12°C (50–53.6°F). The common or garden vinos jovenes tinto or young reds of Somontano are pleasant light wines of Moristel and Garnacha. Drinking temperature is 12–14°C (53.6–57.2°F).

One of Spain's finest wines.

The crianzas, reservas, and gran reservas contain less Moristel and Garnacha, but more Tempranillo and/or Cabernet Sauvignon. The maturation in the barrel imparts this robust wine with great roundness and balance between alcohol and body. Drinking temperature is 16–17°C (60.8–62.6°F).

Catalonia and the Balearics

Ampurdán-Costa Brava

This is the most northerly DO of Catalonia, situated at the foot of the Pyrenees, bordering directly with France. The Catalans call this Empordà-Costa Brava. The area is delineated to the north and west by the Pyrenees and to the east and south east by the Mediterranean. Empordà-Costa Brava once produced sweet, syrupy and heavily oxidised wine such as Penedès. Because of dwindling demand for such wines a major changeover started about 25 years ago. Today Ampurdán-Costa Brava produces excellent, modern, light, and above all fresh wines, which are eagerly bought by the holiday-makers that visit the beaches of Costa Brava, but are also increasingly finding their way to wine lovers abroad. The area has held DO status since 1975.

The soil of Ampurdan-Costa Brava consists chiefly of the chalky foothills of the Pyrenees. Most of the area has a thin top covering of fertile soil. Although the wine-growing area reaches as far as the sea, the better vineyards are inland, particularly on the hills and in sheltered valleys on the sides of the western range of hills (at a height of about 200 metres/656

feet). The climate is clearly Mediterranean with hot summers and mild winters. Proximity to the Pyrenees ensures the area is kept cooler. Ample cooling winds regulate both the temperature and humidity and one of these winds is the notorious Tramontana (Tramontagne on the other side of the mountains) that is feared for the great destruction it frequently causes. The Vines are well fastened to poles to prevent such damage. The most widely planted variety of grape if Mazuelo (local name for the Cariñena), principally used for the many rosados, closely followed by Garnatxa (Garnacha), and the white Xarel-lo, Macabeo, and Garnacha Blanca. Several 'new' varieties have been tested here for some years with varying results: Cabernet Sauvignon, Ull de Llebre (Tempranillo), Merlot, Syrah, and white varieties of Parellada, Chardonnay, Riesling, Gewürztraminer, Muscat, and Chenin Blanc.

The majority of wines from Ampurdan-Costa Brava are still rosados made with Garnatxa, frequently supplemented with Cariñena. In addition, both white and red wines are made here and some excellent Cavas. The largest local producers, the Perelada Group (Cavas del Ampurdan and Castillo de Perelada) have advanced and established the Ampurdan-Costa Brava DO over the years. It is due to this group that this DO has become an established name throughout the world. If you visit the region then in any event visit Castillo de Perelada in the

Top quality Castillo de Perelada Cava.

Delicious rosé.

Rare Cabernet Sauvignon rosé.

Dry white Empurdá.

Rare Empurdá Chardonnay.

small Medieval town of Perelada, in the centre of the Ampurdan region. The castle of Perelada is the historical and commercial heart of Perelada and it contains very impressive wine cellars that are centuries old, together with a superb glass and wine museum, to view by appointment.

The Cavas of Castillo Perelada are excellent and exceptionally good value for their price. There are a number of types to choose from ranked here by ascending quality. Drink the Cava Extra Brut, Brut Reserva, or Chardonnay as aperitif, Brut Rosado as aperitif or with fish dishes, and the sublime Gran Claustro for festive occasions. The Marc de Cava of Castillo Perelada is an exceptionally pleasing surprise. The rosados of Garnatxa or Garnatxa and Cariñena, with or without a little Ull de Llebre (Tempranillo), are outstanding. These are dry wines that are lithe and fruity with characteristic elegant cherry red colour. The lightly sparkling Cresta Rosa of Cavas del Ampurdan is a delicious surprise with their gentle fruity rosé wines that are lightly sparkling through natural fermentation by the cuve close method. Drinking temperature is 10–12°C (50–53.6°F).

Look out for the rare Cabernet Sauvignon rosados, which are of a different calibre to the other rosé wines with their pale strawberry red colouring, rich and fresh fruitiness combined with elegance, refined structure, and Mediterranean warmth. Drinking temperature is 10–12°C (50–53.6°F).

Ampurdan-Costa Brava whites vary from bodega to bodega, depending on the varieties of grapes used, the method of vinification, and the wine-maker. Most of the wine is of the traditional Garnatxa Blanca and Macabeo grape, sometimes supplemented with juice from Garnatxa Tinta for additional body, Xarel-lo, or even Chardonnay for greater roundness. All these wines are fresh, fruity and modern wines for drinking when young. A very special wine and also one of the best selling wines of Spain is the lightly sparkling Blanc Pescador of Cavas del Ampurdan. This Vino de aguja natural is produced by natural fermentation by the sealed tank method. Drinking temperature is 10–12°C (50–53.6°F).

Look out for the rare wines made wholly of Chardonnay that are still in the experimental stages, but are extremely delicious. This wine retains its attractive colour and characteristic Chardonnay bouquet by being kept in barrels of French oak for a short time.

This adds the slightest hint of vanilla that is detectable in the background. This is a light and elegant wine that resembles a good Chardonnay from the French Catalan Limoux. Drinking temperature is 12°C (53.6°F).

Red Tinto Crianza.

Excellent Reserva.

Empurdá Cabernet Sauvignon.

The red wines are usually blends of Garnatxa and Cariñena. Most of this wine is sold as vinos jovenes, for drinking while still young. Drinking temperature is 12–14°C (53.6–57.2°F).

Recently better quality Ampurdan-Costa Brava wines have been produced intended for export. If you look carefully you may find excellent Crianza and Reserva wines (such as those of Castillo de Perelada).

The Crianza wines are generally aged in barrels of American oak, which impart a definite sweet and vanilla-like scent and taste. This taste is intense and pleasing. Drinking temperature is 14–16°C (57.2°F60.8°F).

The superb Reserva Tinto (first 12 months in American oak and then further in French oak before a further two years in the bottle before being sold) promises much from this area.

The traditional varieties of Garnatxa and Cariñena are used in its making, supplemented with a minimum of 40% Cabernet Sauvignon and 20% Mazuela (Tempranillo). This produces a dark red wine with amber nuances that is full-bodied, elegant, with a warm taste in which the oak supplements rather than dominates the fruitiness. This is an excellent wine for a reasonable price. Drinking temperature is 16–17°C (60.8–62.6°F).

The same Castillo de Perelada also produces a rare wine that is wholly Cabernet Sauvignon, which is aged first for 18 months in American oak and then in barrels of French oak before being bottled for a further period of several years ageing in the cellar. This wine is full-bodied, rather high in tannin but well-balanced (alcohol/tannin/acidity). Drinking temperature is 17°C (62.6°F).

Also extremely rare is the traditional Gran Reserva of 80% Cariñena and 20% Garnatxa which can be found for tasting at Cellers Santamaria. This is a fine, full-bodied and warm wine which is best drunk in combination with asados. Drinking temperature is 16°C (60.8°F).

Finally a further mention of the old-fashioned rancio produced from Garnatxa d'Ampurdan. This wine is very sweet, syrupy, and has distinct aromas of roasted coffee and cocoa.

Drinking temperature according to taste from 8–16°C (46.4–60.8°F).

Alella

Alella is a relatively small wine-growing area surrounding the town of the same name, slightly north of Barcelona. The area was threatened for many years by expansion of the Catalan capital city. It was only in 1989 that government called a halt to this threat. The wines of Alella had been granted DO status in 1956 but the area's history as a wine-growing area date back to the time of the Roman occupation and even earlier. The original wine-growing area surrounded Alella at a height of about 90 metres (295 feet). The soil of these ancient vineyards is mainly sand on underlying granite. The vineyards of Vallès has been officially part of Alella since 1989. These vineyards are situated much higher at the foot of the Cordillera Catalana, up to 255 metres (836 feet), and the soil is sand underlain with chalk. These higher situated vineyards are kept cooler than those surrounding Alella in spite of the Mediterranean climate. The vineyards that are sighted at lower altitudes though are mainly well sheltered. Alella produces, white, rosé, and red wines. Alello whites are chiefly made with the Pansá Blanca (local name for Xarel-lo) and Garnacha Blanca, which may or may not be experimentally supplemented with Macabeo or even partly replaced by the 'foreign' varieties of Chenin Blanc and Chardonnay. A characteristic of the traditional Alello wines is their surprising freshness and fruitiness. Drink these light dry wines as an aperitif or with the renowned Mediterranean seafood dishes. Drinking temperature is 8–10°C (46.4–50°F). The rare wines made wholly from Chardonnay are still in the course of development but promise much. The Chardonnay grape seems to thrive in the stony upper layer to be found in all the vineyards of Alella. These Chardonnays are elegant, full-bodied, fresh, fruity, and rounded. Drinking temperature is 12°C (53.6°F).

Alella rosados and tintos are produced with the unique Pansá rosada, Ull de Llebre (Tempranillo), and Garnatxa (Tinta and Peluda). Although these wines are generally of acceptable quality they are rarely to be found imported elsewhere. Drinking temperature for rosé wines is 10–12°C (50–53.6°F) and 12–14°C (53.6°F57.2°F) for red wines.

Penedès

Position, soil, and climate

Penedès is situated to the south of Barcelona, divided between the provinces of Barcelona and Tarragona. While the centre for Cava production and trade is San Sadurní d'Anoia, the main centre for still wines is Vilafranca del Penedès. The

Jean Leon Cabernet Sauvignon from Penedès.

Torres Fransola.

vineyards are sited between the coastal strip of the Mediterranean and the central plateau, the Meseta. In practice Penedès is subdivided into three large sub-regions. The vineyards of Baix Penedès lie along the coast at a height of 250 metres (820 feet). This is the hottest area and the wines produced here are for daily consumption.

The vineyards of Medio Penedès are sited slightly higher (250–500 metres/820–1,640 feet) and are responsible for the bulk of the quality wines. Higher still are the vineyards of Alt Penedès (500–800 metres/1,640–2,624 feet) that are much cooler. Here, on the edge of the Meseta, the best grapes are produced for the best quality wines. Although generally speaking the lowest vineyards are the hottest and the highest the coolest, there are so many microclimates in this area of 5,000 hectares, that the most discerning wine-makers can enjoy the challenge of finding the best combination of grape variety, soil, and micro-climate. The soil varies far less than the climate. The

coastal strip has a more sandy top layer while the higher ground comprises more clay. The underlying rock beneath throughout is chalk and is rich in trace elements, which are beneficial for growth and the health of the vines.

The wines

The whites from Penedès vary widely. Most are a blend of local varieties and 'foreign' varieties. The basic grapes for Cava (Parellada, Macabeo and Xarel-lo) are frequently mixed with Chardonnay or

Gran Viña Sol uses Chardonnay.

Top quality Torres white.

Surprising wine of Gewürtraminer and other grapes

Sauvignon Blanc, which leads to countless different types and varying tastes.

Generally the ordinary Penedès whites are dry, fresh, and fruity wines which are mainly for drinking when young. Drinking temperature is 8–10°C (46.4–50°F).

The better white wines are produced from one or at most two varieties of grape. Dry white wines can be found that are 100% Chardonnay, Parellada, and Riesling, or 85% Sauvignon Blanc and 15% Parellada, or 85% Chardonnay and 15% Parellada. These wines are certainly all worth discovering.

Drinking temperature is 10–12°C (50–53.6°F).

The best Penedès wine is undoubtedly the Crianza made wholly from Chardonnay (such as Milmanda of Miguel Torres or the Jean Leon Chardonnay). These wines are powerful, abundantly scented and rich in taste, fresh, and refined, with ideal acidity. There are suggestions of vanilla, roasted hazelnut, butter, toast, and cocoa in both the nose and taste of the Jean Leon Chardonnay, or of fresh melon and exotic fruits, butter, toast, vanilla, and truffle with the Torres Milmanda. Drinking temperature for both is 12°C (53.6°F).

The semi-sweet wine from Penedès is also very surprising. The gentle sweetness of the Muscat and Gewürztraminer is specially exciting, with rich aromas of spices, floral notes, and fruit (lavender, aniseed, rose, orange blossom, peach, and sweet apples). Many experienced wine tasters will be pleasantly surprised too by the wine made with Parellada grapes. This has the unusual nose of quince, ripe bananas, sweet grapes, honey, and acacia. Drinking temperature is 8–10°C (46.4–50°F). Penedès dry rosado wines are chiefly made with Garnatxa and Cariñena and are fresh and fruity (cherry and plum) with floral notes (iris and mimosa). Drinking temperature is 10–12°C (50–53.6°F). The reds of Penedès come in every style and form.

You may encounter Spanish-type wines, chiefly from Tempranillo and Garnatxa grapes, but also more European-style wines of Cabernet Sauvignon, Pinot Noir, Merlot, and Cabernet Franc, many of which, but by no means all, may be blended with Tempranillo. Penedès also makes a few sweet wines. The Muscatel is produced from Muscat (Grano Menudo and/or Alexandria) and it is exceptionally aromatic with suggestions of orange blossom, honey, preserved orange peel, lemon peel, currant, rose, geranium, lily, tobacco, and spices. Choose a known and trusted label for these Muscatels because not all the wines are of the same quality or refinement.

Those that can be recommended include Moscatel d'Oro of Torres and Moscatel of Vallformosa. Drinking temperature is 6–8°C (42.8–46.4°F).

Renowned Torres rosé.

Full-bodied warm Penedès.

Undoubtedly the best Penedès red.

Seductive sweet and fresh Muscatel.

You may also still find some old-fashioned type rancio wines made with Garnatxa. Those dessert wines that are produced from Garnatxa and Cariñena in stainless steel tanks and then aged in American oak are the better types. It is possible to discern date, plum, red fruit preserve, spices, and vanilla in these wines. Drinking temperature is 8–12°C (46.4–53.6°F).

Tarragona

The vineyards of Tarragona were already in existence in Roman times. In those times loads of full-bodied, strong, and sweet fortified Tarragona wines were shipped to Rome. The trade was later taken over by the French at which point Tarragona flourished in the sale of wine in bulk volume. This heavy wine was very suitable for 'cutting' various so-called French wines, and trade flourished, especially after Algeria, which was the former main supplier, gained its independence. A small amount of Tarragona Classico is still produced today but in common with the rest of Penedès the emphasis has now increasingly been placed on quality wines. Much has changed since the 1960s but to a less spectacular extent than in Penedès.

Tarragona is that largest DO of Cataluña. The wine-growing region extends from the boundary with Penedès, but is hemmed in between the Mediterranean on one side and the Cordilleras Corstero Catalanas on the other. In the south-west the area abuts the vineyards of Terra Alta. There is the Priorato enclave renowned for its heavy red wines in the south-west of Tarragona. Trade in Tarragona is concentrated around the capital town of the same name and the small town of Reus. The small town of Falset is the centre of the Tarragona Classico trade in the west of the region.

Tarragona is subdivided into two sub-regions. The vineyards of El Camp de Tarragona (approx. 70% of the DO) are situated at a height varying between 40 metres (131 feet) near the coast and 195 metres (639 feet) at the foot of the Cordilleras. The soil chiefly consists of an upper layer of loam and chalk with a sub-layer of alluvial deposits. The south-western part, below the enclave of Priorato, from the small town of Falset to the vineyards of Terra Alta, is situated somewhat higher. Around Falset itself the vineyards reach up to 450 metres (1,476 feet), but in the west, in the Ebro valley their height is about 105 metres (344 feet). The soil of Comarca de Falset consists of underlying granite with a covering layer of loam and chalk around Falset and of alluvial deposits in the Ebro valley. The climate is predominantly Mediterranean but the higher vineyards are cooler in summer. The necessary rainfall comes mainly in the spring and autumn, while the summers are hot, dry, and of long duration. The winters are mild in the valley but harsher higher up where an almost continental climate rules. The major white grapes of Tarragona are the white Macabeo, Xarel-lo, Parellada, and Garnacha Blanca, with blue Garnacha, Mazuelo (Cariñena), and Ull de Llebre (Tempranillo). Tarragona too is busy experimenting with new varieties such as Cabernet Sauvignon, Merlot, and Chardonnay. The vineyards of Comarca de Falset are restricted exclusively to Cariñena and Garnacha. Six different types of wine are made here. El Camp Blanco and Rosado are dry, fruity wines for every day consumption and these have little to offer except when they are young. El Camp Tintos are chiefly produced from Garnatxa, perhaps with addition of or even replacement by other permitted blue grapes. Drinking temperature is 8–10°C (46.4–50°F) for whites, 10–12°C (50–53.6°F) for rosé and 12–14°C (53.6–57.2°F) for red vino joven wines. The better El Camp red wines contain a higher amount of Tempranillo (sometimes 100%). These are very suitable for maturing in oak. Tarragona maintains the maturing levels of Crianza, Reserva, and Gran Reserva for its wines. Although these are of very acceptable quality you are unlikely to encounter them outside the area. Drinking temperature is 14–16°C (57.2–60.8°F).

The red Falset Tinto is a full-bodied and heavy wine that is at least 13% alcohol by volume. This wine too is unlikely to be found outside the area. Drinking temperature is 14–16°C (57.2–60.8°F).

Tarragona Classico (also written Clásico) is the old-fashioned type liqueur wine of Tarragona. It is mainly made from just Garnacha grapes and must be at least 13% alcohol by volume and have been aged for a minimum of twelve years in oak barrels. This is a real museum piece of a wine that is well worth discovering. Drinking temperature is according to taste from 8°C (46.4°F) to room temperature (for those with a sweet tooth).

Finally, the old-fashioned Tarragona Rancio which is more than 17% alcohol by volume. This wine is left exposed to the sun for a time in glass carboys to mature. The taste is somewhat similar to dry Madeira wine but with less finesse. Drinking temperature is 8–10°C (46.4–50°F).

Priorat/Priorato

Priorat, or Priorato as it is called in Catalan, is one of the oldest wine-growing areas of Cataluña. The landscape of Priorat is reflected in the wine, with the strength of the mountains, the warmth of the sun, the gentle embrace of the valleys, the blissful scents which are spread by the mountain winds, the ruggedness of the granite beneath the feet of the vines, and the sparkle of mica in the sun. Few wines in the world reveal so much of themselves as the wines of Priorat. A Carthusian monastery (priorat) was built on the site where about 1,000 years ago a shepherd saw an angel climbing to heaven on a hidden staircase. Only ruins now remain of the monastery but the village of Scala Dei (staircase to God) that was built around the monastery now flourishes as a wine centre.

Priorat has been known for centuries for its powerful, warm, and very alcoholic red wines.

Traditional Priorat wine from Scala Dei.

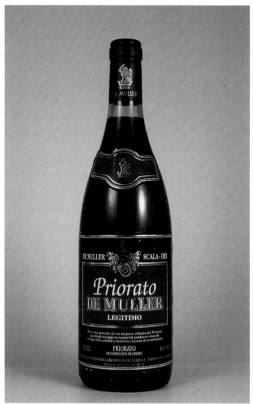

Traditional Priorat wine from Scala Dei.

Whilst most fermentation exhausts itself at around 14.5–15% alcohol, the fermentation of Priorat wines continues to even 18% alcohol, which is unique. The high level of alcohol and strength of this wine enables it to be kept well and transported without problems.

Although increasing amounts of blanco and rosado are now being produced in Priorat, there remains a loyal following for the exceptional Priorat red wine. This is not a clumsy, syrupy wine but one which is unique and which despite the high level of alcohol has sufficient strength, body, finesse, and refined acidity to be regarded as an excellent wine. Everyone should try at least one glass of the true classic Priorat at least once in their lives. It is an experience never to be forgotten. Remember though that this wine is among the most expensive of Spanish wines and that a cheap Priorat is not a true Priorat.

The landscape of Priorat is very hilly. The hills of Montsant reach up to an altitude of almost 1,200 metres (3,937 feet) and they are crossed by deep river valleys. The vineyards are sited between 100–600 metres (91–548 feet), on very unusual ground, known as the 'licorella', which looks like a tiger skin when viewed from afar.

The ground is as unique as the wine produced here. The underlying strata are volcanic in origin and are banded alternately with reddish quartzite and black slate. The fertile upper layer is formed of broken pieces of mica and weathered slate. The steep vineyards on the hills of Montsant are reminiscent of the Douro valley in Portugal. The vineyards are frequently terraced, because of the steepness of the slopes, to prevent the vines from being washed out of the ground. Naturally such terrain does not make mechanisation possible.

The climate of Priorat is also different from elsewhere. The heat of a continental climate is moderated by the south-easterly mistral, while the cold and usually wet northerly winds are able to penetrate the valley. The winters are generally fairly cold but not extreme, while the summers are long, hot, and dry.

The most widely used variety of grape in Priorat is the Garnacha (both Tinta and Peluda), often supplemented with Mazuelo (Cariñena). Garnacha Blanca, Macabeo, and a small amount of Pedro Ximénez are used for the rarer white wines and liqueur wines.

Recently growers have been trying out other varieties such as Chenin Blanc, Pinot Noir, Syrah, and Cabernet Sauvignon. Most of these trials are being carried out on the less hilly and lower area around Gratallops. The trials are seeking to discover how these 'foreign' varieties adapt here and whether they can be grown on their own or should be used in combination with other (native) varieties. The initial results are very promising. The higher siting of the area around Scala Dei will however continue solely to produce the traditional wines.

Whether experimental or not, the vinos jovenes blanco, rosado or tinto are generally fresh, pleasant wines for every day use. They are made for drinking when young. Drinking temperature is 8–10°C (46.4–50°F) for white wines, 10–12°C (50–53.6°F) for rosés, and 12–14°C (53.6–57.2°F) for the red vino joven.

The famous Priorat red is also available as Crianza (minimum one year in oak and not for sale before three years old), Reserva (minimum one year in barrel and at least two in the bottle) and Gran Reserva (minimum two years in oak and at least four in the bottle).

Depending on the age of the wine it is more or less black in colour, intense in bouquet (blackberry), and very powerful with alcohol varying between at least 13.5 and 18%.

Most of the wines do not exceed 16% alcohol, although this is very high. One of the best and most spectacular Priorats is made by the famous Spanish wine expert José Luis Pérez: the Martinet Bru. This is an impressive monument of a wine, while the more modern Clos Martinet is a harbinger of what Priorat may become in the 21st century: lower in alcohol and more fruity. Maximum drinking temperature is 16°C/60.8°F (lower is acceptable but not below 14°C/57.2°F.)

Priorat also makes excellent Rancio, which is matured under the hot sun in glass carboys. The wine is exposed to the air which causes it to oxidise. The Priorat Rancio is somewhat similar to a Madeira, with the strength of a Maury or Banyuls, and the taste of terroir of a top-class port. Drink chilled as aperitif at 8–12°C (46.4–53.6) or at room temperature after food (16–18°C/60.8–64.4°F).

Finally, there are also liqueur wines, liquorosos or generosos, made of Garnacha and Pedro Ximénez. In the best cases they resemble good oloroso sherry. Drinking temperature is 8–12°C (46.4–53.6°F).

Terra Alta

The region of Terra Alta is unfortunately mainly known for the production of wine in bulk. The area seems comparable with Tarragona and the circumstances for wine-growing of Terra Alta are particular suitable for wine-growing. The soil in this fairly inaccessible mountainous area consists of underlying chalk and clay with a deep top layer of poor soil. The vineyards are situated at an average height of 400 metres (1,312 feet), on ground which is porous and well drained. The climate is continental with slight Mediterranean influences: long hot summers and cold to very cold winters. While the rest of Cataluña is experimenting with new ways and achieving greater awareness of its wines abroad, Terra Alta appears to lag behind. Perhaps the difficult access and remoteness from Barcelona is the cause. Whatever the reason, a substantial start has recently been made to remedy the situation.

The traditional wine of Terra Alta is rancio, which is a heavily oxidised with a dwindling number of customers. More interesting are the new developments in terms of more modern, light, and fresh white, rosé, and red wines. Terra Alta Blanco covers a range of qualities, from fresh, light, dry vinos jovenes to full-bodied, rounded Reservas (aged in wood for a minimum of 6 months and not less than 3 years old), but also semi-sweet liquorous wines (generosos). Drink the vinos jovenes (Macabeo, Garnacha Blanca) at 8–10°C, Reserva at 10–12°C and the semi-sweet or even liquorous wines at 8–9°C (46.4–48.2°F). Terra Alta Rosados are principally vinos jovenes, made with Garnacha and intended to be drunk while young. These are fresh, light, and very pleasant rosados. Drinking temperature is 10–12°C (50–53.6°F).

The Terra Alta reds can be young, fresh, and light, of the vinos jovenes type, but also mature, full-bodied, and well-balanced, such as their Crianza (6 months in oak and at least 3 years old) Reserva (at least 1 year in oak and 4 years old) and Gran Reserva (at least 2 year in oak and 6 years old). This sturdy wine generally has alcohol of 13–13.5%. Drinking temperature is 14°C(57.2°F) for Crianza and 16°C (60.8°F) for Reserva and Gran Reserva.

Conca de Barberá

This wine region is wedged between those of Tarragona and Costers del Segre. The name 'Conca' in this case does not mean shell but combe or cwm, a valley surrounded by mountains. Conca de Barberá and its capital of Montblanc are bordered and protected by three mountain spines: Tallat in the north, Prades to the east, and Montsant to the south. Conca de Barberá's soil is ideal for the production of the basic grapes for Cava. In recent years more money and time has been invested in producing both rosé and red wines. The more modern bodegas have extended or wholly renewed their wine-making installations. New varieties such as Cabernet Sauvignon and Merlot have been introduced alongside the native Trepat (possibly a variety of Garnacha), Garnacha, and Ull de Llebre (Tempranillo).

The initial results are very promising. The vineyards are situated relatively low in valleys at about 200–400 metres (656–1,312 feet). The underlying ground is predominantly chalk with an upper layer of alluvial deposits interspersed with chalk. The climate is definitely Mediterranean but moderated and cooled somewhat by the sheltered position of the Conca. Summers are hot and the winters are cold but not severe.

There are five types of Conca de Barberá wines.

The blancos made with Parellada and Macabeo are fresh and fruity for early consumption. Drinking temperature is 8–10°C (46.4–50°F). The blancos made with the Chardonnay grapes being tested are very interesting. Drinking temperature is 10–12°C (50–53.6°F).

The blancos that are wholly made with Parellada are very popular at the present time. These are very fresh, light, dry and aromatic wines which are certainly pleasing as an aperitif. Drinking temperature is 8–10°C (46.4–50°F). The rosados are also fresh, light, and very fruity. They are chiefly made using Garnacha grapes sometimes supplemented with Trepat. Drinking temperature is 10–12°C (50–53.6°F). The tintos are increasingly made from blends of Garnacha and Ull de Llebre (Tempranillo). The vinos jovenes are very pleasant and can be drunk on any occasion when young.

Conca de Barbera Chardonnay.

Conca de Barbera Merlot.

Drinking temperature is 12–14°C (53.6–57.2°F). The early Crianza and Reserva wines that have been made with blends of Garnacha and Ull de Llebre promise much, but there are also rarer versions made with Cabernet Sauvignon and Ull de Llebre. These latter wines are better than the former, being more 'European' in character while the former are more Spanish in character. Drinking temperature is 16–17°C (60.8–62.6°F).

Costers del Segre

The river Segre is a tributary of the Ebro which flows from the Pyrenees through the province of Lleida. The four sub-areas of the Costers del Segre DO are situated on both banks of this river. They are Artesa to the north east of the town of Lleida, Vall de Riu Corb and Les Garrigues, east of Lleida, and the smaller area of Raimat around the village of Raimat, to the west of Lleida. The ground of Costers del Segre consists almost entirely of a sandy soil with underlying chalk. The climate is continental with hot summers and cold winters.

Costers del Segre has a long history of supplying wine from the town of Lleida. The attitude to wine-making used to be quantity first and hopefully a good taste. About 30 years ago a small group of innovative bodegas started to try out different varieties of grapes and different methods of vinification.

One name is synonymous with Costers del Segre, that of Raimat. This enormous estate of approx. 3,000 hectares of which 1,000 are vineyards belonged for many years to the Raventós of Codorníu Cava and today it is one of the most high-tech bodegas of all Spain. This bodega was the powerhouse that led to great renovation in Costers del Segre. Increasing numbers of growers have seen the advantage of turning their backs on mediocre wine-making to direct their attention towards a more lucrative future. It is still possible to find old-fashioned white, rosé, and red wines in the region but these are intended for drinking when young and are mainly found in the bars of Lleida.

The modern style wines, especially those from Raimat, are of an entirely different calibre. While the traditional wine-makers stick to Macabeo, Parellada, and Xarel-lo for white wines (the basic grapes for Cava) and Garnacha, supplemented with Ull de Llebre (Tempranillo) for their reds, the modern wine-makers make other choices. The white varieties include Garnacha Blanca and especially Chardonnay with Cabernet Sauvignon, Merlot, Pinot Noir, Monastrell, Trepat, and Mazuela (Cariñena) for the red wines. The best results are generally achieved by blending Cabernet Sauvignon, Tempranillo, and Merlot or Cabernet Sauvignon and Merlot.

The modern-style whites are made mainly wholly of Chardonnay or by blending Chardonnay, Macabeo, and Xarel-lo. The best Chardonnay wines are briefly aged in oak barrels to impart extra body and

Raimat Cabernet Sauvignon.   Raimat Abadia Reserva.

roundness. Drinking temperature is 10–12°C (50–53.6°F).

The modern-style rosado wines are certainly drinkable and even very pleasant but they do not yet achieve the standard of either the whites or reds from Costers del Segre. The best results to date have been achieved with 100% Merlot (Castell del Remei), but it is impossible to tell when drinking this wine if it originates from the south of France, Italy, or Spain. Drinking temperature is 10–12°C (50–53.6°F).

The red Crianza through to Reserva wines are certainly worthy of consideration, particularly in view of their reasonable prices. The Raimat Abadia Reserva and Raimat Cabernet Sauvignon Reserva are typical examples of an intelligent and caring approach to high-technology wine-making with a respect for tradition. These superb wines have already achieved such a high quality that even the most pessimistic expectations of ten years ago are likely to be great improved upon. Drinking temperature is 16°C (60.8°F).

Binissalem

Binissalem is relatively small DO area of just 312 hectares on the island of Majorca (Mallorca) in the Balearics, making it the first of DO to gain recognition in the Balearic Islands and moreover the first Spanish DO outside the mainland. Wine-growers have made wine for local consumption in the Balearic Islands for many years. Once these islands became home to the package holidays and Club Med in the 1960s the local wine trade went into top gear. Most of the bodegas are happy with this situation with just a few far-sighted growers believing better results were possible. Their struggle for better quality was rewarded in 1991 with the award of the highly coveted DO status.

The vineyards of Binissalem are situated on Majorca's high plateau above Palma. The soil consists of chalk with some clay but is well drained. The Balearic climate is typically Mediterranean with warm moist summers and mild winters. The choice of grape varieties is very interesting. The native Manto Negro, Callet (red) and Moll (white), are blended as required with Spanish varieties such as Ull de Llebre (Tempranillo) or Monastrell (both red) and Macabeo and Perellada (both white).

The blanco and rosado wines are fresh and light and need to be drunk while young. A few bodegas are trying out maturing their white wine in oak barrels, with varying degrees of success. Drinking temperature is 10–12°C (50–53.6°F).

The tintos are certainly more alcoholic than the blancos and rosados. Try the typical Crianza and Reserva of Jose L. Ferrer (Bodega Franja Roja) or the Crianza of Herederos de Hermanos Ribas. It will be necessary to visit Majorca to try these wines because only small amounts are made and non is exported. Drinking temperature is 16°C/60.8°F (or lower by choice to 14°C/57.2°F.)

The Duero valley

We have already dealt with one of the DO regions of Castilla y León with Bierzo. Bierzo is officially one of the five wine areas that form Castilla-León. This book has separated Bierzo (León) from the other areas for both geographical and climatalogical reasons.

The other areas are all situated in Castilla. These remaining four DO areas are sited on the banks of the Duero river (which is known in Portugal as the Douro). The Toro and Rueda DO areas are situated south of Valladolid in a rectangle formed by the towns of Zamora, Salamanca, Segovia, and Valladolid. The Cigales and Ribera del Duero DO areas are found to the north and north east of Valladolid.

Toro

Toro has developed as a real gain for the top division of Spanish wines since its DO recognition in 1987. The area only covers 2,500 hectares of vineyards and a mere seven bottling bodegas. The area is very arid and has a definite continental climate with little precipitation.

The two main business centres of the region are the towns of Toro and Morales. Because of the extreme heat and drought conditions here the emphasis used to be on almost syrup-like very alcoholic red wines but thanks to radical replacement of the wine-making equipment and different attitudes, the local bodegas have succeeded in making a wine like the Toro red the best wine Spain has to offer.

In the north of Toro the ground consists of a top layer of sand with a solid layer of underlying chalk. The soil is more fertile with a top layer of alluvial deposits near the Duero and Guareña rivers. Most vineyards are sited at a height of between 600–750 metres (1,968–2,460 feet).

The climate is truly continental with long hot summers and short but extremely cold winters. The

White Toro Blanco.   *Red Toro Tinto.*

location at height of the vineyards ensures some degree of cooling in the summer nights and by the gentle westerly breezes.

The most important grape varieties for Toro wines are the Tinta de Toro (related to Tempranillo) for red wines, and Malvasía for white wines. The blue Garnacha and white Verdejo grapes are also used in making these wines..

Toro white made with Malvasía, with or without the addition of Verdejo, is fresh, gentle, soft, elegant, and above all very floral in both nose and taste, with a hint of fruit. Drink this wine young at 8–10°C (46.4–50°F).

Toro Rosado is fresh, full-bodied, rounded, and somewhat reminiscent of the rosés from Navarra. It is simultaneously fruity and warm with alcohol up to 14% alcohol by volume. Drinking temperature is 10–12°C (50–53.6°F).

Toro Tinto Jovenes is fresh, fruity, and very pleasing. All red wines from Toro must contain at least 75% Tinta de Toro. The climate produces warm wines with a great deal of body. Alcoholic percentages around the 14 or even 15% are not unusual.

It is remarkable though that despite this high level of alcohol Toro is more well-balanced than other wines from hot climates. This is particularly due to the fine acidity present in the wine. Even the simplest Toro Tintos are a pleasant surprise. Drink the ordinary Tinto Joven while it is still fruity at 12–14°C (53.6–57.2°F).

The famous Marqués de Riscal Rueda.

Wines from Rueda and Castilla y León.

Toro Crianza, Reserva, and Gran Reserva are all outstanding wines. They possess a great deal of body. roundness, power, and warmth and yet retain the freshness for which Toro is renowned. Drinking temperature is 16–17°C (60.8–62.6°F).

Rueda

Rueda has a similar name for white wines to that established by Toro for its reds. The area of 5,700 hectares has become famous since 1980 for its superb white wines. The area is situated between Valladolid, Seville, and Avila.

The climate here is very continental with treacherous frosts which naturally reduce the output of the vines.

Modern dry white wholly Sauvignon Rueda.

The ground is very infertile chalky soil and the vineyards are sited at heights of between 700–800

Modern blend of Viura and Sauvignon.

metres (2,296–2,624 feet). Excellent wine has been made here for centuries but the arrival of the famous Rioja house of Marqués de Riscal has caused Rueda to make a breakthrough in the international wine market.

Rueda produces five types of wine: the simple Rueda (minimum 50% Verdejo, supplemented with Palomino or Viura), Rueda Superior (minimum 85% Verdejo, mainly supplemented with Viura), Rueda Sparkling (minimum 85% Verdejo) and the much rarer Pálido Rueda and Dorado Rueda liqueur wines.

Rueda wines are mainly bottled when young but can also be aged in the cask. This latter category of wine is increasingly being produced from Sauvignon Blanc grapes, which are new to the area. Drinking temperature is 8–10°C (46.4–50°F).

Rueda Superior has greater character than the simple Rueda. Although it may be bottled young, the best wines are cask aged for six months or more. These wines smell of fresh grass, hay, herbs, aniseed, or wild fennel. Drinking temperature is 12°C (53.6°F).

Rueda Espumoso is made by the traditional method and will lay in its sediment in the bottle for at least nine months (in common with Cava). Some Rueda Espumosos can be very alcoholic at around 13%, but most are nearer 12%. Drinking temperature is 6–8°C (42.8–46.4°F).

The old-fashioned sherry-like Pálido Rueda liqueur wine is a vino de flor, like its distant cousins of Jerez de la Frontera. In other words a film is formed on the wine during fermentation that protects it against further oxidisation. The wine has to be cask aged in oak for at least three years before it may be sold. Drinking temperature is 10–12°C (50–53.6°F), although some connoisseurs prefer to drink it at room temperature.

Dorada Rueda, which is probably of much earlier origins, is similar to rancio, in that it has been exposed to oxidisation and the sun while maturing. This wine may only be sold following at least three years maturing in oak casks with a minimum alcohol of 15% by volume.

Drinking temperature is 6–8°C (42.8–46.4°F) although some prefer room temperature of approx. 18°C (64.4°F).

Cigales

Only 15 bodegas bottle Cigales. The area is situated on both sides of the Pisuerga river, between Valladolid in the south and Burgos in the north, with vineyards extending to a mere 2,700 hectares. Cigales has a long history as a supplier of fine rosado wines which were served at the Castilian court in the thirteenth century but it has only enjoyed DO status since 1991. Nowadays there are also excellent red wines from Cigales.

The climate of Cigales is continental, but there is some influence from maritime winds which result in greater rainfall than the other wine areas of Castilla. The vineyards are sited both in the valley and on the slopes, at a height of 700–800 metres (2,296–2,624 feet).

It is hot everywhere here in summer but the vineyards are cooled at night so that conditions are ideal for making the best wines. In recent decades much effort has gone into renewing the equipment of the bodegas and once completed the name of Cigales will become well known. The ground in Cigales consists mainly of chalk with a covering of fertile soil interspersed with stone which aids drainage.

Most Cigales wine is rosado (75%), which is considered the best rosé of Spain. These rosé wines must contain at least 50% Tempranillo (known locally as Tinto del País) in order to bear the DO on its label. The rest may be supplemented with blue grapes such as Garnacha or even white grapes like Verdejo, Albillo, or Viura. It is customary here to make rosé wine that is a mixture of blue and white grapes, which are vinified together. This gives the wine the power of the blue grapes and the freshness and bouquet of the white grapes. The fairly recently introduced Cigales Nuevo is a vino joven made with at least 60% Tinto del País and not less than 20% white grapes. The combination of freshness and fruit, coupled with reduced alcohol makes this wine ideal for newcomers to wine drinking. Drinking temperature is 10–11°C (50–51.8°F).

The true Cigales Rosado (without Nuevo on the label) are made with the same proportions of grapes but are more full-bodied, fleshy, and alcoholic. This wine has a fine and elegant bouquet in which the freshness and fruit dominate. This is a wine with true character that even succeeds in seducing those who proclaim to detest rosé wines. Drinking temperature is 10–12°C (50–53.6°F).

The best rosados are cask aged and sold as Crianza. This wine is mainly produced from red grapes with a minimum of 60 % Tinto del País and not less than 20% of either Garnacha or Viura. These rosados are aged in oak casks for at least six months. Drinking temperature is 12°C (53.6°F).

Cigales Rosado Nuevo.   *Cigales red.*

Finally the Cigales Tinto, made with at least 85% Tinto del País, supplemented with Garnacha and/or Cabernet Sauvignon. This wine is making great advances.

The first Tinto Crianza and even Reserva wines have already arrived and are superb. This red wine has a remarkable combination of seductive fruitiness with very masculine power and body. Drinking temperature is 12°C (53.6°F) for the Tinto, 14°C (57.2°F) for the Crianza, and 16°C (60.8°F) for the Reserva.

Ribera del Duero

This wine region of 11,500 hectares, situated at the centre of a square formed by Burgos, Madrid, Valladolid, and Soria, makes the best and most expensive wine of Spain. Many will have heard of Vega Sicilia, but just as in France there is both Mouton and Lafite Rothschild, there are also countless superb bodegas to discover in this region. Ribera del Duero is ideally suited for the making of quality wines, with its favourable soil, climate, and use of the best grapes. The economic strength of the region has also played its part for it is far easier to find people ready to invest in a wealthy area than a poor one and there is then also a more ready market at hand for more expensive wines.

The best vineyards are sited at heights of between 750 and 900 metres (2,460 and 2,952 feet) which is somewhat high both for Spain and elsewhere in Europe. The remainder of the wine-growing is sited in the valleys and at the foot of the hills.

The soil consists of chalk-bearing strata with alluvial

Ribera del Duero Crianza.

covering close to the river, calciferous clay at the foot of the hills, and gypsum, and chalk that is rich in trace elements in the more elevated vineyards.

The climate is a mixture of severe continental and moderating maritime influences. The difference between the heat of the day and cooler evenings is very important for wine-making for this causes optimum growth.

This is important in view of the height of the best vineyards, for the summers are consequently of short duration and frosts at night in autumn are not unusual. Late blossoming of the vines or retarded growth can have dire consequences.

The varieties grown in addition to the classic Tinto del País (Tempranillo, and also known as Tinto Fino), are Cabernet Sauvignon, Malbec, Merlot, and Garnacha. Although the bulk of Ribera del Duero wine is red, some excellent rosé wines are also produced.

Ribera del Duero rosados are mainly made from Garnacha (sometimes called Tinto Aragonés), sometimes softened with a little white Albillo. The ordinary vinos jovenes are very pleasing rosados, which should be drunk when young. The Crianza

Many top wines from Ribera del Duero.

Ribera del Duero Reserva.

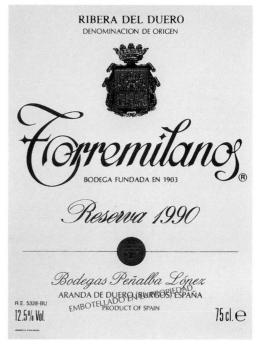

Ribera del Duero Reserva.

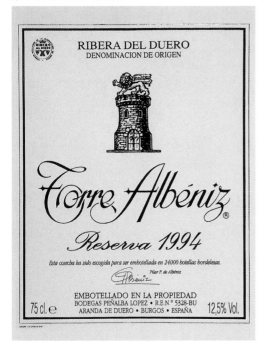

Rosado wines are cask aged and are hence more full-bodied and mature. Drinking temperature is 10–12°C (50–53.6°F).

Ribera del Duero Gran Reserva.

The ordinary vinos jovenes reds should also be drunk young. These are fresh, fruity wines redolent of blackberry. Drinking temperature is 12–14°C (53.6–57.2°F).

The Crianza is aged for at least 12 months in oak casks and is stronger in taste. It may not be sold before three years old. This wine is still very fruity, broad, and elegant. Drinking temperature is 14°C (57.2°F).

The powerful Reservas are aged for at least one year in oak barricas and then been bottled for at least a further year. Drinking temperature is 14–16°C (57.2–60.8°F).

The Gran Reservas are the best wines, but these are laid down by few people, not just because of their high price but also because this wine is made in small volume and most finds its way to the Royal and governmental tables, plus some of the best restaurants. Do not hesitate if you get the chance to buy a Gran Reserva of Ribera del Duero. If you do not the bottle will quickly be sold to someone else. Drinking temperature is 17°C (62.6°F).

The high Meseta plateau

The high Meseta plateau is enormous, and with the exception of a few small hills, is a vast plain. The wine-growing areas include the DO territories of Vinos de Madrid and Mentrida (below Madrid), La Mancha and Valdepeñas (between Madrid, Ciudad Real and Albacete), and the brand new DO of

Ribera del Guadiana in Extremadura, close to the border with Portugal.

The Meseta is a high plateau with an average height of 600 metres (1,968 feet) where the climate is continental with very hot summers and extremely cold winters. Anyone who wishes to make good wine here needs nerves of steel, considerable enthusiasm, and above all the very best of basic materials.

Not every variety of grape will thrive in such extreme circumstances. For this reason the region is therefore best known for great volumes of cheap and sometimes delicious wines from La Mancha, Valdepeñas and Extremadura.

Vinos de Madrid

Madrid, the capital city of Spain, has been better known for centuries as a large consumer of wine than as producer. The Vinos de Madrid only made their appearance on the market in 1990. This wine is produced close to the city, at Alcorcón, Móstoles, Leganès, and Getafe in the west, Arganda and Aranjuez in the south-east, and a very small area of Alcalá de Henares between Guadalajara en Madrid. Because of the large market on the doorstep no attempt has yet been made to export these wines. For this reason you are unlikely to encounter these wines of the Meseta.

Wines were being made for local consumption before Madrid was established as the capital in 1561. The award of DO status is intended to encourage the wine-growers to achieve higher quality. Admittedly there are wines that scarcely deserve the DO predicate but some excellent wine is also made, such as that from Arganda. The 5,000 hectares of the Vinos de Madrid area is subdivided into three sub-areas of Arganda, Navalcarnero, and San Martín de Valdeiglesias. The soil of each area imparts its own character on the wines. In San Martín de Valdeiglesias there is an overlying brown top soil with underlying granite; in Navalcarnero the top layer is light sandy soil over sand and clay, while Arganda is overlaid with marl and clay with underlying granite interspersed with chalk. Each of these soil types is poor for general agriculture but ideal for wine-growing, except perhaps in the case of Navalcarnero which is less free draining and therefore can become more sodden than Arganda and San Martín.

The climate is typically continental with hot summers and very cold winters. Any precipitation is mainly carried on the south-westerly winds in the spring and autumn. The red wine hereabouts is produced from Garnacha and Tinto Fino (Tempranillo), while the whites use Malvar, Albillo, and Airén. It is remarkable that each of these sub-areas has its own preferences in terms of grape varieties. Arganda uses Tinto Fino for red wines and Malvar plus Airén for whites, Navalcarnero chooses Garnacha for reds, Malvar for whites, while San Martín prefers Garnacha for its red wines and Albillo for white wines.

The blanco, rosado, and tinto vinos jovenes of Madrid are generally pleasing light and fresh wines so far as the whites and rosés are concerned but more robust and full-bodied reds. Drinking temperature for blanco is 8–10°C (46.4–50°F), rosado 10–12°C (50–53.6°F) and 12–14°C (53.6–57.2°F) for tinto.

Crianza wines wholly made of Tinto Fino (Tempranillo) or 85% Tinto Fino and 15% Garnacha are rare but well worth while in view of their modest price. At present it is best not to expect too much of them.

The rustic power and character of the vinos jovenes is somewhat tamed and harmonised by the short period of cask maturing. Drinking temperature is 14–16°C (57.2–60.8°F).

Mentrida

This area to the south-west of Madrid (close to the small towns of Mentrida and Torrijos) was also renowned for its cheap but heavy and highly alcoholic wine which sold readily through bars and cafés in Madrid. Even after the authorities gave a quandary to the apathetic growers, who had little ambition, with DO recognition in 1960, little appeared to change among the local bodegas. It was only after nearby Madrid gained its own DO and threatened Mentrida's market that the growers in Mentrida woke up. Since 1991 the wine making equipment has been replaced at a vigorous tempo or at least greatly improved. The wine has been somewhat amended to meet the wishes of today's wine drinker with a lighter structure and less alcohol but above all more refinement in taste.

Mentrida's vineyards are situated at heights of between 200 and 500 metres (656 and 1,640 feet) on soil that is underlain with calciferous clay topped with sand. The climate here is continental with hot summers and pretty cold winters. Most of the rain falls in the autumn and winter. Mentrida wines are either red or rosé. Most of the vines are Tinto Aragonés (Garnacha), with some Tinto de Madrid, Tinto Basto, and Cencibel (Tempranillo). Government advisors are recommending replanting the Tinto de Madrid and some of the Garnacha with Cencibel, which is better suited to the soil and climate of Méntrida.

The rosados and tintos vinos jovenes are light, fresh, pleasing, and fruity. The Crianzas are more full-bodied and with greater taste and these promise much for the future from this area. Drinking temperature is 10–12°C (50–53.6°F) for rosado, 12–14°C (53.6–57.2°F) vinos jovenes tinto, and 14–16°C (57.2–60.8°F) for the Crianza wines.

La Mancha

In terms of area this is by far the largest DO of Spain at 194,864 hectares. In this immense area of La Mancha, where once the legendary Don Quixote tilted at windmills, the wine-growers fought against what they regarded as arbitrary rules laid down by

La Mancha white.   *La Mancha red.*

the European Community. Even today not every-body in La Mancha accepts that there is a vast lake of surplus wine in Europe. Fortunately more and more bodegas are addressing themselves to the demands of the market and improving the bad name associated with La Mancha wine. These bodegas have substantially replaced their equipment and directed themselves towards making quality wines. Thanks to the effort of these innovative houses the name of La Mancha has increasingly been linked to quality wines, that can be trusted, at a reasonable price. In the latter 1990s the sales of these wines increased significantly. Wine from La Mancha in bottles is being sold in greater volume both within Spain and abroad while the bulk sale of wine is drastically reduced. The growing demand in the home market for La Mancha has exceeded the volume of exports.

La Mancha's vineyards are situated at heights varying between 490 and 645 metres (1,607 and 2,116 feet). Generally the soil is clay topped with brown sand. The better vineyards have underlying clay and chalk with a top layer of loam and calciferous red or brown sand. The ruling climate is continental with very cold winters and very hot summers. The mountains surrounding the area shelter the vineyards from moist maritime winds. White, rosé, and red wines are made here. The whites can be seco (dry) semi-seco (medium dry), abocado (slightly sweet) or dulce (sweet). The grapes used for white wine are Airén, Macabeo, and Pardilla, while Cencibel (related to Tempranillo), Garnacha, Moravia, Cabernet Sauvignon, and Merlot are used for red wines. Because La Mancha is the biggest wine producer of Spain and one of the world's largest, its most widely planted variety of grape, the Airén is the most planted variety of grape in the world. The government is advising the growers however to replant this variety with Cencibel (Tempranillo).

Thanks to modern wine-making technology, including chilled vinification, the white wine made from the Airén grapes is very fresh and fruity with surprising aromas of celery, and newly mown grass. Because there is a surfeit of these grapes the price of this wine is extremely low. In addition to drinking it as an aperitif it goes well with both freshwater and sea fish. Drinking temperature is 8–10°C (46.4–50°F).

The rosados are made wholly with Moravia grapes or with a blend of various blue grapes almost always including Garnacha and sometimes also white grapes. Drink this fresh, young rosé with salads for instance at 10–12°C (50–53.6°F).

La Mancha's red vinos jovenes are light and fruity and can be drunk on many occasions. Drinking temperature is 12–14°C (53.6–57.2°F).

The better La Mancha reds are aged in oak casks (usually American oak). Those of 100% Cencibel (Tempranillo) are surprisingly good for their relatively low price. Those blended from Cencibel, Cabernet Sauvignon, and sometimes Merlot are also excellent. Some bodegas also make very fine Crianza wines that are 100% Cabernet Sauvignon but these lack any Spanish character. Drinking temperature is 14–16°C (57.2–60.8°F).

Valdepeñas

A quick glance at a wine map of Spain will reveal that Valdepeñas is actually an enclave in the southern part of La Mancha. The traditional trading centre of Valdepeñas lies at the heart of the wine-growing area that bears its name.

Valdepeñas is situated somewhat lower than the rest of the Meseta in a broad valley encircled by small

Valdepeñas red.

Valdepeñas Tinto Gran Reserva.

hills on the boundary between the Meseta en Andalucía.

The wine from Valdepeñas, in common with much of the Meseta, was thick, sticky, and very alcoholic. It was as if time had stood still with the same type of wine being produced at the start of the nineteenth century that had been made in Roman times. The wine was stored in huge earthenware jugs or tinajas, often covered by nothing more than a couple of straw mats. When the railway reached Valdepeñas in 1861 it was decided to improve the quality of the wines. Less wine was made but of better quality and it was sold to wealthy consumers in Madrid, on the coast, and even as far afield as the Americas and the Philippines.

When the vineyards of Valdepeñas were destroyed by phylloxera this policy proved its value because there was sufficient wine in store to carry them through until the next harvest three years after new vines were planted on American rootstocks. The growers also saw the value of strict quality control and a common wine-growing policy. Due to this early foresight, Valdepeñas is highly respected and regarded today as a forward-looking wine-growing area. With today's technology, including computer-controlled temperature regulation during vinification, Valdepeñas produces fresh and fruity wines alongside the robust reds on which the area's fame has been established.

The soil of Valdepeñas is like the name itself ('valley of the rocks'), extremely stony. The underlying strata are chalk which often reaches to within 25 cm of the surface while the thin yellow-red top layer is a mixture of crumbled chalk and alluvial clay. Most vineyards are sited at a height of 600–700 metres (1,968–2,296 feet).

The climate is strictly continental with very hot summers and very cold winters. The encircling hills protect Valdepeñas so that there is little precipitation. Some parts are almost like desert. When the rain does fall though it usually pours down in cloudbursts. These heavy thunderstorms have in the recent past caused severe flooding. Although a great deal of the Airén variety of grape is grown too in Valdepeñas, these are gradually being replaced on government advice with Cencibel (Tempranillo).

the white jovenes of Airén are very fresh and fruity with vegetal nose of celery and newly mown grass. This wine is made for early consumption and every day use. Drinking temperature is 8–10°C (46.4–50°F).

The rosados are mainly also vinos jovenes for drinking within a year of the grapes being picked. These are also fresh, light, and cheerful rosé wines made with Cencibel (Tempranillo), often supplemented with the white Airén. Drinking temperature is 10–12°C (50–53.6°F).

Valdepeñas red vinos jovenes of Cencibel are pleasing thirst quenchers just like the rosés. Drinking temperature is 12–14°C (53.6–57.2°F).

The Crianza, Reserva, and Gran Reserva wines from Valdepeñas that are wholly made with Cencibel are certainly worth considering. Not only are these very pleasing wines with great fruitiness derived from Cencibel but there is also a sweet vanilla-like quality imparted by the American oak and to cap it all an unbelievably low price.

The Gran Reservas are velvet smooth, rounded, full-bodied, and usually with far less tannin than a Navarra, Rioja, or Ribera del Duero. Drinking temperature is 16°C (60.8°F) for a Crianzas and 17°C (62.6°F) for both Reservas and Gran Reservas.

Ribera del Guadiana

This is the newest DO of Spain (1997) located in Extremadura, the region which borders on Portugal, in the extreme west of central Spain. Wine had already been exported from this area for some years under the name of the Tierra de Barros sub-region of Ribera del Guadiana.

Renewal has also won the day in Extremadura. It had seemed as though Extremadura would forever remained linked with past glories of towns such as Badajoz, Cáceres, and Trujillo, renowned from the past history of the sixteenth and seventeenth century conquistadors. The landscape here is attractive, hilly, soft, and green, but there are also high plateaux which are the domain of agriculture and cattle breeders. The economy of Extremadura once relied on the income from cork and the output of the olive

trees but with drastic renovation of the wine-growing hopes for a better economic future have also grown.

Things are going well in Extremadura, the 'furthest land on the other side of the Duero'. The climate of Ribera del Guadiana is continental, but is moderated by the nearby Atlantic Ocean. The two rivers, the Guadiana and Tajo, ensure ample moisture in the soil and humidity. The summers are very hot and winters are exceptionally mild. The growers here do not need to fear frosts. The soil chiefly consists of a mixture of clay and reddish brown sand interspersed with broken chalk.

At the time of publication the recognition of a provisional DO for Ribera del Guadiana was a fairly unique occurrence for the Spanish wine industry. This all hinges on the better wines of Tierra de Barros, which account for 80% of the DO wine production. Only 3,433 hectares of a total 87,450 hectares of vineyards are permitted to bear the DO predicate. There were fewer than 30 bodegas in 1998 that could meet the strict criteria of the DO. This number will grow appreciably in future as more bodegas replace outdated tinajas with more modern installations and their own bottling plants. It is expected that the old bulk wine culture of Extremadura will have been totally replaced within fifteen years. In addition to Tierra de Barros the provisional Ribera del Guadiana DO, the 52nd Spanish DO consists of the other sub-regions: Cañamero and Montanchez in the Cáceres province, Matanegra, Ribera alta del Guadiana, and Ribera Baja del Guadiana in Badajoz province.

Tierra de Barros received its provisional DO in 1979. The area of Tierra de Barros (55,000 hectares) borders Portugal and is cut across by the Guadiana river. The vineyards lie along both banks of the river which flows towards Portugal. They are situated at a height of 300–350 m. The area derives its name from the 'barros', or clay-like soil which covers the land here.

Matanegra

Matanegra surrounds the small town of Zafra, approximately 30 km (19 miles) south of Almendrajelo. The production of wines in this area with 8,000 hectares of vines in cultivation is mainly in the hands of family businesses.

Ribera Baja del Guadiano (the lower loop of the Guadiana, that extends to 7,000 hectares) is situated just to the west of Badajoz.

Ribera Alta del Guadiano (upper loop of the Guadiana, that extends to 8,500 hectares) is found around the towns of Don Benito and Villanueva de la Serena, about 120 km (75 miles) upstream of Badajoz.

Montanchez is a small territory of 4,000 hectares, situated surrounding the small town of the same name, about 70 km (44 miles) north-east of Badajoz. This area is known for its ancient vines and olive trees.

It is a picturesque region with lots of gently undulating hills and hospitable valleys.

Finally, Cañamero is an even smaller area of approx. 1,200 hectares in the Sierra de Guadalupe, about half-way between Badajoz and Toledo. The small town of Cañamero is the production centre for the area bearing its name. The vineyards are situated on the shoulders of the mountains at heights of 600–800 metres (1,968–2,624 feet). The soil consists of slate. The vineyards in the valleys are sited on alluvial soil. The production of this small district is chiefly in the hands of small, long-established family bodegas.

While Tierra de Barros may bear DO on its label, the other areas officially remain Vinos de la Tierra. The DO predicate may only be added to the label after each bodega has been approved according to criteria established.

The wines

This area is mainly known for its young, fresh, and lively wines which at present are very inexpensive. Most of the vineyards are planted with native white varieties such as Pardina,

Full-bodied Ribera del Guadiana red.

Cayetana Blanca, Montœa, Eva, Alarije, and Cigüentes.

The Pardina grapes in particular produce excellent results with the present technology. Drinking temperature is 8–10°C (46.4–50°F).

The rosé and red wines are chiefly made with Cencibel (Tempranillo) and Garnacha.

Drinking temperature is 10–12°C (50–53.6°F) for rosado and 12–14°C (53.6–57.2°F) for red jovenes.

The red Crianza, Reserva, and Gran Reserva, especially those produced with Cencibel, are very promising and offer a great deal for their price. Drinking temperature is 14–16°C (57.2–60.8°F).

The Levante

The area of Castilla-La Mancha is so large that it is dealt with in two parts. In the previous section that dealt with the high plateau of the Meseta we travelled through the western part of Castilla-La Mancha (Vinos de Madrid, La Mancha, Mentrida, and Valdepeñas). It is now time to visit the eastern part of Almansa.

Almansa is situated on the high plateau of the Levante, close to the autonomías of Valencia (Alicante, Utiel-Requena, and Valencia) and Murcia (Bullas, Jumilla, and Yecla). Although Levante is the Spanish name for the east coast and therefore strictly only applies to Murcia, Almansa's position and isolation justifies our dealing with this enclave of La Mancha within our section on the Levante.

The climate in this eastern part of Spain varies between a distinctly Mediterranean one on the coast to a semi-continental one with Mediterranean influences in Almansa. The weather is much like that of Cataluña here although it is both hotter and wetter. Foreign investment and large scale exports have occurred for many years in the Levante. The attitude here was also one of ready acceptance of all manner of viticultural and scientific experimentation. The wine from Levante in general terms has little to offer in terms of quality with a few exceptions. It is generally good but inexpensive wine.

Almansa

The wine-growing area of Almansa is situated in the eastern part of Castilla-La Mancha, in the province of Albacete. We leave the dull and endless Meseta behind here as we enter the high plateau of the Levante. Everything here seems different than in the rest of Castilla-La Mancha. The landscape is gently undulating, the vineyards are low lying on more or less level ground, the grapes are different, and the wines too. The only thing in common between Almansa and La Mancha is the climate, which is continental, arid, with a great range in temperature

Utiel-Requena Tinto Reserva.

between hot summers and cold winters. It rains rarely here but when it does, especially in the autumn and spring, it rains very heavily and often with destructive hail stones. The soil of this red wine territory is chiefly underlying chalk with a fertile top soil. Around the two towns of Almansa in the east and Chinchilla de Monte-Aragón in the west, the red Monastrell, Garnacha, and Cencibel (Tempranillo) grapes are harvested, together with a small quantity of white Merseguera. The strength of the area though lies in its red wines made from the Monastrell grape, which can produce excellent results here as they also do in Alicante, Jumilla, and Yecla Not every bodega is as well equipped but the results with this grape are very promising.

The Almansa Blanco is a light, fresh, modern-style wine intended for early consumption. You can drink it as an aperitif, thirst quencher, or with any type of sea-food. Drinking temperature is 8–10°C (46.4–50°F).

Almansa Rosado is a fresh, fruity, and pleasant rosé without much pretension. Drink it with fish, other sea-food, or with cold paella. Drinking temperature is 10–12°C (50–53.6°F).

Almansa Tinto is available as vinos jovenes or Crianza. Drink the vinos jovenes, which are often ponderous and very alcoholic, with light meat dishes at 12–14°C (53.6–57.2°F).

The better Almansa Tinto Crianza, Reserva, and Gran Reserva of Bodegas Piqueras are well worth seeking out at their very reasonable prices. Drink these well-balanced and pleasing wines of Tempranillo and Monastrell with the tastiest roasted pork dishes. Drinking temperature is 14–16°C (57.2–60.8°F).

Valencia

Valencia is one of Spain's major cities and its largest wine-shipping port. The province surrounding the city is also called Valencia, together with the autonomía region of Valencia as provincial capital. As if that is not complicated enough, Valencia is also the name given to a DO wine area. There are two other DO territories: Utiel-Requena in Valencia province and Alicante, the province bearing its name.

The growers of Valencia would prefer that there should be one large DO area of Valencia with three sub-regions which would be permitted to bear their own name on the label. This would enable them to use grapes harvested throughout the region so that reasonable quality could be ensured in poor years. In the best years the sub-regions would make their own wines in their own ways. The fact that this would cause monumental confusion among their consumers does not appear to have dawned on these creative Valencianos, but they continue to try to bring their plans to fruition. The growers of Utiel-Requena and Alicante of course have no time for these plans which only serve the interests of the Valencianos.

Valencia still produces an enormous lake of vino comœn or vin ordinaire or plonk in the English vernacular, to the great concern of the agriculture commissioner of the European Community who is trying to reduce the enormous wine lake.

UTIEL-REQUENA

This is a DO of the autonomía of Valencia which is situated furthest from the coast. In common with the other two DO areas of Valencia, Utiel-Requena also specialised for centuries in producing bulk wine for the trade. Vast quantities of wine disappeared anonymously into Switzerland, Russia, or central Africa. The wine of Utiel-Requena (especially the famous Doble Pasta) was sturdy and alcoholic. It was of great service in giving other rather thin European wines some strength and body. Because there is far less interest now throughout the world for this type of wine (and because the controls are becoming much tighter), Utiel-Requena has been experiencing harsh times. The rescue has to be a complete about face but whether it will come in time to save the bodegas is very much in question.

The vineyards of Utiel-Requena are situated around the two towns of Utiel and Requena, at heights of 600–900 metres (1,968–2,952 feet). The ground in the south consists of marl and clay underlain with sandstone, with alluvial soil in the Magro valley. The climate is continental with great differences in temperature between the hot summers and cold winters but also between day and night (up to 30°C/86°F). The most widely planted variety of grape is the native blue Bobal, but more territory is being won over by Tempranillo and Garnacha. The most important white grape is Macabeo followed by Merseguera.

Utiel-Requena Blancos are fine wines but they have little of their own character. They are light, fresh, and fruity. Drinking temperature is 8–10°C (46.4–50°F).

Utiel-Requena Rosados are worth considering. They are mainly produced with Bobal and Garnacha and they are full-bodied, fleshy, and powerful. These are definitely rosés to drink with a meal. The choice is from ordinary rosado (Garnacha and Bobal) or for the fuller and heavier Rosado Superior (100% Bobal). Drinking temperature is 10–12°C (50–53.6°F).

Utiel-Requena Tintos exist both as vinos jovenes and as Crianza types. Drink the light, fresh, and fruity young wines at parties. Drinking temperature is 12–14°C (53.6–57.2°F).

For serious use it is best to choose the better Crianza wines, usually made from Garnacha and Tempranillo. The curious climate and height of the vineyards causes the grapes to ripen here much quicker than elsewhere in Spain so that little of the older Crianza wines is to be found in Utiel-Requena. It is not customary to produce Reserva or Gran Reserva wines but a few bodegas achieve good results from blending Tempranillo and Cabernet Sauvignon. Drinking temperature is 14–16°C (57.2–60.8°F).

Valencia white.

VALENCIA

Valencia DO is mainly dependent on export of its wines, chiefly in bulk. The trade is dominated by huge concerns which have specialised in this trade. Medium-sized and small businesses are not important in either their numbers or their volume. Yet a change in affairs seems on the hand now that increasing numbers of bottles of Valencia wine are to be found on the shelves of Spanish supermarkets. This will probably never change the export-led attitude of the big Valencian wine producers, to the sorrow of both the Spanish government and European authorities. There is still far too much mediocre wine produced in Valencia.

The region is subdivided into four sub-areas: Alto Turia (in the north-west of Valencia province), Clariano (in the south of Valencia province), Moscatel de Valencia (in the centre), and Valentino (also in the centre). So far as the geology of the four sub-areas, this is dependent on the contours on which they stand. Alto Turia is the highest and most hilly of the four and its vineyards are situated between 400 and 700 metres (1,312 and 2,296 feet). In Clariano the vineyards are planted in terraces at height between 160 and 650 metres (524 and 2,132 feet), in Moscatel and Valentino this is 100–400 metres (328–1,312 feet). Generally there is underlying chalk with a top covering of a red-brown loam with alluvial deposits in the river valleys. The top soil in Alto Turia is more sandy, while in

Valencia red.

wholly with Mersequera. Valencia and Valentino Blancos are produced from a mixture of Merseguera, Planta Fina, Pedro Ximénez, and Malvasía and are available in seco (dry), semi-seco (medium dry) and dulce (sweet) forms. Clariano Blanco Seco is produced from Merseguera, Tortosí and Malvasía. Drink the dry wines as an aperitif or with fish and shellfish. The slightly sweeter wine can be drunk as an aperitif if you like that kind of thing. The sweet types are best avoided, or if this is not possible then serve with a fresh fruit salad. Drinking temperature is 8–10°C (46.4–50°F) for seco/semi-seco and 6–8°C (42.8–46.4°F) for dulce wines. Valencia, Valentino and Clariano Rosados are fresh and light and have little to say for themselves. These rosados main contribution to a meal is their discretion. Drinking temperature is 10–12°C (50–53.6°F).

Valentino and Clariano Tintos are as discrete as the white and rosé wines so that they can be served at almost any time, with paella and fish and with any type of lightly-flavoured meat dish. Drinking temperature is 12–14°C (53.6–57.2°F).

Tintos Crianza that are wholly made from Monastrell, Tempranillo, or Garnacha are the most interesting table wines from the area (the term table wine here differentiates from the various sweet liquorous wines of Valencia). Secretive trials are being carried out with Cabernet Sauvignon, particularly in combination with Tempranillo, which have delivered first class results. The combination of Monastrell and Garnacha, with and without a little Tempranillo, are also very promising. The best results are coming from bodegas that have rid themselves of the old-fashioned vinification techniques (epoxy or concrete vats without temperature control) and switched to the latest techniques which yield greater finesse and greater aromatic properties. Drinking temperature is 14–16°C (57.2–60.8°F).

Valencia DO also makes lots of old-fashioned mistelas (must distilled with wine alcohol) but prefer to call them vinos de licor. Some of these are excellent but most are really not worth mentioning. Drinking temperature is 6–8°C (42.8–46.4°F).

Rancio Valencia and Rancio Valentino are heavy, sweet, very alcoholic, and wholly oxidised wines which can be served as an aperitif or with hors d'oeuvres. Drinking temperature is 6–8°C (42.8–46.4°F) or if preferred up to room temperature (17°C/62.6°F). Vino de Moscatel Dulce and Vino de Licor Moscatel are undoubtedly the best sweet wines from this area. Do not expect any explosion of fresh aromas since most bodegas still produce old-fashioned syrupy, unctuous, and almost stupefying Muscatel.

Valentino the top soil is perhaps both looser and thicker. The climate is clearly Mediterranean though with continental influences in Alto Turia, where the summers are hotter, the winters colder, and where there is less rainfall than in the sub-areas closer to the coast. There are also localised microclimates which mainly result in greater warmth from the sun. It is remarkable that there are such marked differences between daytime and night-time temperatures throughout the Levante.

There are twelve varieties of grapes that may be used in the Valencia DO. Some are recommended, others merely tolerated. Highly recommended are the white Macabeo, Malvasía, Merseguera, Moscatel de Alejandría, Pedro Ximénez, and Planta Fina de Pedralba and the blue Garnacha, Monastrell, Tempranillo, and Tintorera. Equally permissible are the white Planta Nova and Tortosí and blue Forcayat. Valencia produces countless different wines with local names and the descriptions of blanco, rosado, tinto, espumoso, licoroso, rancio, moscatel dulce, and moscatel licoroso. Most of these wines are of the vinos jovenes type, but you will find some Crianzas. It is a shame to realise that Valencia probably possesses the most advanced wine-making equipment and laboratories for analysing wine but that customers generally prefer the cheapest and most simple of wines. This is an enormous brake on the movement towards better quality.

Alto Turia Blancos are fresh, light wines made

Alicante

Alicante is the most southerly of the Valencian DO areas. The area under cultivation by vines comprises a fairly large tract of land from the Mediterranean to the foot of the central hills of the Meseta. This region is further subdivided into two sub-areas of La Marina, around Cabo de la Nao inland from Benidorm, and Alicante, around and to he north-west of the town of the same name. The famous beaches such as Benidorm and Villajoyosa are to be found between these two sub-areas. Oddly enough almost everyone in the world has probably heard of Benidorm but few will have heard of Alicante wine. Here in Alicante like elsewhere the local growers have been engaged for centuries in the production of wine to trade in bulk, such as the doble pasta wine, a heavy double concentration wine for 'cutting' with other wines. Alicante was once famous for its rancio wine, which sold readily. When the market for heavy, oxidised wines collapsed, its was recognised that something must happen in the region, and that it was essential to invest in the future. With the help of modern equipment and the most advanced technology Alicante is now able to make up for lost time. Today good white and red wines are made of which perhaps the finest is the Muscatel of Spain. A local curiosity though is the very rare Fondillón, a fortified wine that is wholly made from Monastrell grapes and aged by the solera method (see the main entry concerning sherry). In the sub-area of La Marina a definite Mediterranean climate holds sway, with high humidity, hot summers, and mild winters. The vineyards are at sea level or just above on alluvial soil. Near Alicante the vineyards are more elevated, reaching upwards to almost 400 metres (1,312 feet) and the soil there is chalk overlaid with a loose brown top soil. Inland the climate is more continental in nature with hot summers and cold winters and it is also drier than La Marina. Red wine and rosé is made throughout the area from Monastrell, Garnacha, Tempranillo, and Bobal. The grapes chosen for white wines are Merseguera, Macabeo, and Planta Fina, with Moscatel Romano for the sweet wines. Although doble pasta is still made it is difficult to find it in its original form these days. This heavy wine is solely intended for 'cutting' with weaker wines.

Alicante Blancos are mainly made from Merseguera, Macabeo, Planta Fina and (much less these days) Moscatel Romano. These can be dry (seco), medium dry (semi-seco) or sweet (dulce). These vinos jovenes are light, fresh, and above all cheap. Alicante's future will probably lie in the white wines currently being developed that are made with Chardonnay but most of all from Riesling. The initial results, in particular those with Riesling, are astonishing. Drink these white Alicante wines as an aperitif. Drinking temperature is 8–10°C (46.4–50°F). Alicante Rosados are made from Monastrell, Bobal, and Tempranillo. Most of them are seco, but you may also encounter the odd semi-seco rosado. Their combination of freshness coupled with fruitiness and roundness makes them ideal with all fish dishes. Drinking temperature is 10–12°C (50–53.6°F). Alicante Tinto wines are available as vinos jovenes and Crianza. The first of these are light, fresh, and fruity wines for everyday consumption. The best Alicante Tintos are naturally

Crianza types (aged in oak for at least six months and a minimum of two years old). These are more full-bodied and richer tasting than the vinos jovenes. Developments are underway at the moment with Cabernet Sauvignon, both with and without Tempranillo. The results of these trials are also very promising. Drink these Crianzas and the very rare Reservas for instance with red meat, lamb, and smaller game at 14–16°C (57.2–60.8°F).

Alicante Moscatel Vino de Licor is a superb wine, especially when vinified by modern techniques. Then the colour is golden yellow, clear and overwhelming and there are powerful aromas of fruit and musk. The taste is soft, luxuriant, juicy, and very broad, with an after taste in which the Muscatel grape endures. Drink this superbly successful liqueur wine for itself or at most with a slice of sharp tasting lemon cake. Drinking temperature is 6–8°C (42.8–46.4°F).

Alicante Fondillón is also a vino de licor, but stored according to the solera method, as in Jerez de la Frontera (see by sherry). The principle is simple: a little of the oldest wine is bottled each year and the space left is filled with a wine one year younger, which in its turn is replaced with a younger wine. In this way the young wines pass through several levels of barrels (20 or more) and the final wine remains of constant quality. The result is an amber golden coloured wine with hints of mahogany and the scent of vanilla, croissant, cake, tobacco, and sometimes cocoa and coffee. The wine is well balanced. elegant, light, juicy, and taste wonderful. Drink this very rare wine as an aperitif or after eating on a winter's day. Drinking temperature is to taste: 10–12°C (50–53.6°F) or at room temperature up to 18°C (64.4°F).

Murcia

The autonomía of Murcia is trying to forget its past. Here too heavy and very alcoholic wine was produced for cutting with lighter wines and here too the trade specialised for centuries in the sale of wine in bulk. In recent years however there has been a definite change in direction by a number of the serious and forward-looking bodegas. Wine is only one of the local agricultural produces and certainly not the easiest or most financially rewarding. Times change and today's market has no demand for the heavy, alcoholic, and heady wines of Murcia. The bodegas of Jumilla DO and to a lesser extent Yecla are taking action to react to this change in the market. It was only much later that the third DO of Murcia, Bullas jumped aboard the departing train.

Jumilla

Before La Rioja became recognised as a wine-growing area, Jumilla was already a respected wine territory. Admittedly the wine from Jumilla does not achieve the level of the best Rioja wines, but it has

Jumilla white.

Jumilla Tinto Reserva (red).

won a place for itself in both the Spanish and export market. This is justified because the quality of Jumilla wine is always reliable, whether it be the old-fashioned rancio wines or the more modern wines. Jumilla has character, which is often missing in Valencian wine, regardless of whether it is made by modern or old-fashioned methods. Of course they also make doble-pasta here too, even with 100% Monastrell. The future of Jumilla though lies in the better table wines and not in these 'cutting wines' or in rancio wines. Jumilla's vineyards are situated around the town of Jumilla and to its west. These are relatively new vines because the vineyards of Jumilla were replanted at the end of the 1980s as a consequence of a late attack of phylloxera. This happened about 100 years later than in the rest of Spain. Turning adversity to good fortune, the Jumilian wine-growers were able to choose the most appropriate grape varieties for replanting and chose Monastrell, Garnacha, and Cencibel (Tempranillo) for the blue grapes and Mersequera, Airén, and Pedro Ximénez for their white grapes. About 80% of the vines are Monastrell. The vineyards in Jumilla are sited fairly high, some even above 700 metres (2,296 feet) which gives some protection from the withering effects of the sun. The ground is underlying chalk with a top layer of crumbly and reddish-brown sandy soil. The climate is truly continental with extremely hot summers and exceptionally cold winters with much frost.

Jumilla blancos are mainly made from Merseguera, but Airén grapes are beginning to be more widely used because their resulting wines are preferred by foreign buyers. The best of these whites are fresh, fruity (green apples), juicy, and very pleasant but there is little more that can be said. These are certainly not the best wines from this area. Drink these whites as an alfresco aperitif or with fish at 8–10°C (50°F). Jumilla rosados, in common with their tintos, must contain at least 50% Monastrell. Usually this is more, even 100%. The colour of this wine varies from salmon pink to raspberry and its nose is intense (raspberry and strawberry), with floral notes. The taste is fresh, juicy, and fruity. Drink these very pleasant rosados for example with paella. Drinking temperature is 10–12°C (50–53.6°F). The tintos make up the majority of Jumilla's production of wines. Many of these reds contain 100% Monastrell, but there are also blends of Monastrell and Cencibel (Tempranillo). The vinos jovenes are fresh, fruity (black cherry, date, currant) juicy, and exceptionally pleasant. The Crianza, Reserva, and Gran Reserva wines are clearly cask aged but the wood does not dominate. The striking feature is the balance between alcohol, acidity, body, and taste. The future of Jumilla lies in such wines without any shadow of doubt. Drinking temperature is 14–16°C (57.2–60.8°F).

Finally, there is also a local speciality made wholly with Monastrell. This is a sweet rancio wine that

Jumilla Tinto Crianza (red).

may have been cask aged for five to six years, and which is very aromatic. The wine can be drunk as an aperitif or after dinner in the evening. Drinking temperature is 10–12°C (50–53.6°F) or if preferred to room temperature (17–18°C/62.6–64.4°F).

Yecla

Yecla is a relatively small DO surrounding the town of the same name but it is actually an enclave in the much larger area of Jumilla. The smaller bodegas have been busy now for several decades with a policy of change and radical renewal.

The lack of success is not due to either the soil or the climate for these are comparable with neighbouring Valdepeñas: chalk with underlying clay and thick surface layer plus the same continental climate with hot summers and cold winters with large temperature range between night and day. The blue grapes used are Monastrell (80%) and Garnacha. Trials are also being carried out with Tempranillo, Cabernet Sauvignon, and Merlot.

For the white wines the grapes used are Merseguera, Verdil, Airén, and Macabeo. The vineyards are situated on a high plateau around the town of Yecla, at heights ranging from 400–700 metres (1,312–2,296 feet) and they are protected by the undulating hills and small mountains. The wine area is subdivided into Yecla and Yecla Campo Arriba – the low-lying land – in which only Monastrell is

planted and from which the wine is much more full-bodied than the rest of the DO. Yecla currently makes several acceptable fresh, fruity light wines without much character, perhaps because of an absence of acidity. Drink these wines mainly as an aperitif or thirst quencher. Drinking temperature is 8–10°C (46.4–50°F).

The better Yecla Blanco is the Crianza (Viña Las Gruesas Crianza or Castaño Barrica of Bodega Castaño, Yecla). These wines have powerful aromas with a hint of vanilla (the wood), a fine fruity scent and taste, and greater body. Unfortunately this wine also lacks in acidity and therefore lacks overall balance. This will surely come too for a great deal is being invested in Yecla and in the techniques of wine-making. Drinking temperature is 10–12°C (50–53.6°F). Yecla's rosado, which are generally a mixture of Monastrell and Garnacha, are reasonable. They a very fruity and juicy. Drink these pleasing rosé wines for instance with embutidos (meat products). Drinking temperature is 10–12°C (50–53.6°F). Many ordinary Yecla reds are offered as vinos jovenes. These are largely produced by the macération carbonique or method of steeping in carbonic acid and they are fresh, light, and very fruity. Drinking temperature is 12–14°C (53.6–57.2°F). Yecla too has its better Crianza and Reserva wines (such as Pozuelo Crianza and the Reserva of Bodega Castaño, Yecla). These wines are blends of Monastrell, Garnacha, Cencibel (Tempranillo), Cabernet Sauvignon, and Merlot for the Crianza, and Monastrell and Garnacha for the Reserva. Both wines are fairly dark in colour and possess wonderful fruity bouquets with clear hints of vanilla. The taste if fully-flavoured, juicy, with mild tannin, and not too much alcohol. Drinking temperature is 14–16°C (57.2–60.8°F).

Bullas

Bullas stood waiting at the door for nomination to the elite of Spanish wine-growing as long ago as 1982. Final recognition as a DO territory was not granted though until 1994. The story in Bullas is the same as the rest of the Levante: the demand for good but cheap wine within Spain and abroad was so great that no-one felt much need to try harder. Surpluses were not a problem until the consumer turn increasingly towards quality and away from quantity. Bullas too found times very hard but the crisis now seems to be slowly receding and at least one large bodega is now engaged in the production of wine of acceptable quality.

The vineyards of Bullas are spread out over a fairly large area, mainly in the river valleys, but there are also terraced vineyards in the encircling hills. The height of these vineyards varies from 500 metres (1,640 feet) to slightly higher than 700 metres (2,296 feet). They are sited on either sandy or alluvial soils. Despite the short distance to the Mediterranean, the climate in Bullas is more continental than maritime with very hot summers and cold winters. The grapes here are the blue Monastrell and Tempranillo with white Airén and Macabeo.

Bullas mainly produces white and rosé wines yet it is the red which is of greatest interest. Most of the reds are sold as vinos jovenes but this is most certainly no light wine, rather a very fruity, full-bodied wine with a good balance between acidity, alcohol, and fruit. Drink this very pleasant wine with lightly-flavoured meat dishes or poultry. Drinking temperature is 12–14°C (53.6–57.2°F). The better wines are cask aged in wood and the initial results from these are exceptionally promising. This new DO needs to be followed closely for the future.

Andalucía and the Canary Islands

Our journey through Spain ends in the extreme south of the Iberian Peninsula and on the Canary Islands which lie off the Atlantic coast of Morocco. As wine territories Andalucía and the Canary Islands have two entirely different stories to tell. While the Canary Islands are mainly known for their white, rosé, and red dessert wines, Andalucía almost exclusively produces fortified wines (Jerez de la Frontera, Sanlœcar de Barrameda, Huelva, Montilla-Moriles, and en Málaga). The climate in both Andalucía and on the Canary Islands is clearly influenced by water. The eastern and southern coast of Andalucía is typically Mediterranean and the western coast and the Canary Islands have both maritime and almost sub-tropical climates.

It is perhaps surprising in these areas, which have long had contact with piracy and conquest by sea, that there are clear indications of the early contacts with the ancient civilisations of the Greeks, Phoenicians, and Carthaginians. The long-term rule by the invading Moors has also left its marks. With their extensive contacts with the outside world, both Andalucía and the Canary Islands are very export-orientated. Indeed they are dependant on exports. Because much of the diet of Andalucía is fish, there was a demand long ago for drier and lighter wines in addition to the famous sweet wines of Málaga, Huelva, Montila-Moriles, and Jerez de la Frontera, resulting in Manzanilla de Sanlœcar de Barrameda and Fino de Jerez for example. Almost everything grows on the Canary Islands and there is an abundance of both meat and fish. The demand for different wines was prompted in part by the flourishing tourist industry resulting in various types of white, rosé, and red from very dry to sweet as honey. With its mild climate and volcanic soil, the Canaries can readily fulfil these demands (see also page 142).

Andalucía

Many books claim that wine-growing and making in the Iberian Peninsula started in Andalucía but this is entirely wrong and does a disservice to the early Celtic people of northern Spain, who made wine long before the visitors from over the sea. But Andalucía did have an established and properly organised wine industry after the arrival of the Phoenicians and Greeks, who established vineyards close by each of their anchorages. This contrasts with the Celts who at first gathered the wild berries in the woods and later grew vines haphazardly around their villages. The vineyards of the Phoenicians and later Carthaginians and Greeks were well maintained. This also happened with the founding of the town of Cádiz in about 1,100 BC. The Phoenicians quickly discovered that the climate and soil were ideally suited for wine-growing and they planted further vineyards further inland, in the neighbourhood of present-day Montilla, Huelva, and Málaga. The vineyards around Cádiz probably produce one of the oldest-established quality wines of the world, namely sherry. The local wine growers were more or less left alone to continue their occupation even during the occupation by the Moors. After the Reconquista the harbour of Cádiz became one of Spain's most important trading ports. The wine trade here flourished more than anywhere else in the entire world. The relative riches of the region were further reinforced during the twentieth century by the tourist industry. Wine is made in the west of Andalucía but chiefly drunk by the many tourists on the eastern coast.

Condado de Huelva

This is the most westerly DO of Andalucía. The wine from this area was sold for generations as 'sherry' to unsuspecting supermarket customers but since January 1996 only wines from Jerez de la Frontera and Manzanilla de Sanlúcar de Barrameda DO regions may use the term 'sherry' both at home and abroad. Since then the bodegas of Condado de Huelva DO have been forced to take action to get their area better known. The county or condado of Huelva is situated in the province of the same name to the east of Portugal. The area under cultivation by vines comprises the land between the Atlantic coast and the town of Huelva. The vineyards are sited quite low, less than 30 metres (98 feet) above sea-level, on a bed of chalk and alluvial deposits topped with red-brown sand.

The climate has much in common with the Mediterranean despite the westerly position on the Atlantic. The summers are hot and the winters are mild and wet. The most widely planted grape variety remains the Zalema. This is a troublesome grape for traditional wine-growing but ideal for making sherry-type wines because it produces a light wine which oxidises quickly. A long way behind the Zalema are the other grape varieties of Listán (local name for Palomino), Pedro Ximénez, Garrido, and Moscatel.

In recent years a fresh, fruity and dry white wine has also been made with Zalema grapes, known as vinos jovenes afrutados. Drink this wine with its distinct vegetal nose (including grass) as an aperitif if you do not like the sherry type of wine or with fish and shellfish at 8–10°C (46.4–50°F).

In addition to these modern afrutados there is a second type of wine, the old-fashioned corrientes. The difference with these wines starts during harvesting. The grapes intended for afrutados are gathered earlier and these have a higher proportion of acid with lower sugar content. The grapes for corrientes are harvested much later and contain more sugar and less acid. The young wine is fortified with wine alcohol to 15.5% or 17–23%, depending on the style of wine intended.

The wines which are lower in alcohol (15.5–17%) usually acquire a film from fermentation known as the flor (meaning the bloom of the wine). This film or bloom prevents air from coming into contact with the wine so that it retains its original light colour. The wine does acquire many typical yeast aromas from the fermentation. This type of wine is dry and is also known as fino in Huelva because of the refined and delicate bouquet and taste. This name is only used locally. For export the wine must officially bear the name ondado pálido. This type of wine has undergone the solera process (see Jerez de la Frontera and Sanlœcar de Barrameda DO entries). The characteristic aromas and taste are of yeast, slightly bitter, salty, and nutty. This is a typical aperitif (although somewhat heavier than the superb Fino of Jerez or Manzanilla de Sanlœcar de Barrameda). Drinking temperature 8–10°C (46.4–50°F). The more greatly fortified wines (17–23% alcohol), do no develop flor because the yeast cells are killed off by the greater concentration of alcohol. Because there is no protective film, the wine quickly oxidises in contact with hot, moist air and this results in the darker colouring and stronger nose. This wine is still known as oloroso or fragrant because of the sultry aromas. For export the name is restricted to ondado viejo. This type of wine is also aged by the solera method. The characteristic nose and taste for this wine is of freshly basked croissants, toast, wood, vanilla, and alcohol. Enthusiasts of this wine drink it as a winter aperitif but it is better suited for consumption after dinner, with cheese for instance or with nuts and dried fruit. Drinking temperature is 6–8°C (42.8–46.4°F) or up to room temperature if preferred.

All manner of rarities can also be discovered hereabouts such as the light sweet Pálido, very sweet 'cream' (usually intended for the British market) or honey sweet, powerful, and balmy 100% P.X. (Pedro Ximénez). These wines though are much overtaken by the earlier wines that form the majority of local production.

Jerez – Xérès – Sherry

The Greeks called the town Zera (the dry land), the Romans, Ceritium, the Western Goths, Ceret, the Arabs Sheriz or Sherish, the French Xérès, the British and the Dutch call it Sherry, and the Spanish call it Jerez, pronounced 'Heref'.

Fino de Jerez sherry.

Ideal conditions

The unparalleled success of sherry is largely due to the perfect conditions for making fortified wine. Vineyards soak up the sun from early morning until late evening (3,000 sun hours or 290 sun days per year) within the triangle formed by Sanlœcar de Barrameda, Jerez de la Frontera and El Puerto de Santa María, between the rivers Guadalquivir and Guadalete.

The only cooling comes from a little early morning shade and some gentle sea breezes. The climate is wholly Mediterranean in nature, with hot summers and mild winters. The soil appears to be ideal for making sherry type wines. The large but undulating albariza hills of white organic marl, high in chalk, clay, and silica dioxide, absorb water during the short rainy seasons in winter and spring. During the hot summer and autumn these minerals form a hard white crust on the surface which reflects sunlight while the water absorbed in the ground remains trapped so that the vines are prevented from drying out. This mineral mixture known locally as albariza is only found in this particular triangle of towns, forming the area known as Jerez Superior.

Beyond El Puerto de Santa María, to the east, is another zona, or area with less ideal clay (barros) and sandy soil (arenas), which produces wine of lesser quality.

The classic grape variety of the Jerez area is the

Oloroso Seco sherry.

Palamino Fino or Listán. The Palomino is an old traditional grape variety which has been grown since the start of viniculture in this area and which is perfectly adapted to the climate conditions it encounters and it thrives on albariza. The second grape variety that is important for sherry making (especially of sweet Oloroso) is Pedro Ximénez, often abbreviated to PX. This variety has also been here for as long as anyone can remember. The experts consider that both varieties of grape vine originated in the region around the Caspian Sea. It is probable that they were brought here by the Phoenicians.

The final variety of grape permitted here is the Moscatel de Alejandro (Muscat of Alexandria), which was brought from Egypt to Spain by either the Phoenicians or ancient Greeks.

Special vinification

The grape harvest begins each year around 10 September. The grapes are picked by hand because the vines are pruned low to the ground and also because the grapes need careful handling in view of the extreme heat. The pickers therefore use small plastic crates that can each hold 18 kg to bring the grapes undamaged to the press. Some bodegas still use the traditional arroba baskets that hold only 11.5 kg. Pedro Ximénez and Muscatel grapes are use for the sweet wines.

In order to increase the sugar content of these grapes, they are lain on mats of esparto grass and exposed to the sun to ripen further for at least two days (being covered at night to protect them from evening dew). In Jerez the wine presses are usually sited in the vineyards themselves or close by, just outside the towns. The bunches are removed from their stalks and then pressed in a pneumatic press. This pressing produces 70 litres of must per 100 kg of grapes. Only the must from this first pressing is permitted to be used in making sherry.

Immediately after pressing the must is transferred to stainless steel tanks that contain 40,000 litres. Fermentation takes place under fully automatic temperature control. Fermentation (the conversion of grape sugars into ethyl alcohol and carbonic acid gas) is started by wild yeast cells (*Saccharomyces apiculatus*) and continued by the true wine yeast cells (*Saccharomyces ellipsoideus*). Initially fermentation is very turbulent (it looks as though the fermenting must is boiling), but this becomes more gentle after about three days. Fermentation lasts about seven days in total. The young wine spends a long period in a vat to come to rest following fermentation, when it can develop its special characteristics.

The young wine is tested and classified from vat to vat and given a mark using the ancient raya system in which one stripe or raya is given for the finest wine with pure aromas (basic wine for Fino, Manzanilla, and Amontillado), one stripe with one dot after it for wine that is full of character and body (for Oloroso), two stripes for wine that does not possess the character or body for Oloroso, nor the pure aroma for a fino, and finally three stripes for wine that is rejected for use only in distilling.

The wine with one stripe is fortified with wine alcohol to 15–15.5%. It is then sent to the maturing cellars or criaderas for Fino, Manzanilla, and Amontillado.

In contrast with the maturing of most wines where contact with the air is kept to a minimum, the barrels here are left open. The wine does not oxidise in the case of Fino, Manzanilla, and Amontillado because a film of yeast cells or flor forms to prevent oxygen from coming into contact with the wine. These yeast cells feed on alcohol during the maturing process and gives the sherry its characteristic bouquet. These yeast cells are living organisms which are more active in summer and weaker or even die off during the winter. Consequently the flor film is thinner in winter than in summer, when old yeast cells are replaced by new ones.

The wine marked with one stripe and one dot is fortified to a minimum 17.5% alcohol. This kills off the yeast cells and hence no film of flor is formed on the wine. This young wine is sent to the criadera for Oloroso, where maturing in full contact with air takes place.

In short, the fine and delicate wine which forms a film of flor does not oxidise and is known as Fino. This wine retains its light colouring.

Rich Cream sherry.

The more powerful wine of character which does not form a film of flor because of the higher level of alcohol develops a characteristic oxidisation bouquet. This sherry is known as Oloroso, meaning sweet smelling and fragrant. This wine is darker in colour.

The wine matures slowly in the cellars or criaderas. The wines are aged in casks of American oak which each hold 600 litres. These casks are not filled to the top (only to about 5/6 of their capacity) to permit the flor to form in the case of Fino, Manzanilla, and Amontillado or to permit the surface of the wine to come in contact with the air for Oloroso. The wines from Jerez were once indicated by the year of their vintage but because the demand for sherry became so great (particularly from the United Kingdom) a new system was needed that would guarantee the quality of sherry from year to year. The solera system was adopted in the criaderas in about 1830.

Solera system

The system is simplicity itself: three rows of casks are piled up on top of each other in each criadera. The name solera is derived from suelo for the wine in the bottom row, which is the oldest of the three. The top row houses the youngest wine.

As wine is drawn of for bottling this is done from the lowest casks and the space created is then filled by wine from a cask that is one row higher. The space created in this cask is then filled by wine from the next row above.

Some bodegas have solera consisting of numerous rows of casks on top of each other so that some Fino and Manzanilla sherries may pass through fourteen stages in three years. After the wine has passed through the solera system it is tested and marked once more.

The marking system of palms or staves is principally intended for the cellar master and the buyers so we will not delve into this matter which is not of direct interest to the consumer. Just remember that the purest wines are sold as Fino while those Fino wines which eventually have developed more of the character of an Oloroso without the strength of this type of sherry, are known as Cortado. After the wine has aged it is decanted to clarify it and if necessary gently filtered.

Types of sherry

It may be possible to find a sherry at the very best wine merchants that originates from one defined year. These superb quality sherries are usually very expensive and represent such a small percentage of the whole that they are not dealt with here separately. In this book we observe the Spanish grading system.

FINO

This is a straw yellow wine that is always dry and fresh with the characteristic bouquet and taste of almond and walnut, wood and flor; alcohol 15.5%. It makes a first class aperitif to drink at 10°C (50°F).

AMONTILLADO

The name is derived from nearby Montilla. The style of this wine is similar to the wines of Montilla and this name approximates to 'in the Montilian style'. This wine is darker in colour than other Fino sherries and has cask aged for longer than most Finos (ten to fifteen years instead of a minimum of three years). The bouquet and taste is fresh and redolent of hazelnuts; alcohol 17.5%. A first class winter aperitif to drink at 12–14°C (53.6–57.2°F).

OLOROSO

This fragrant sherry, which has been allowed to oxidise fully, is much darker coloured than Fino sherry, ranging from amber to mahogany. The taste and texture of this naturally dry sherry can be full and powerful with clear suggestions of walnut. To prevent confusion with Oloroso dulce (or cream sherry) this sherry is often labelled as Oloroso seco. This wine smells sweet but is dry with a alcoholic finish which is a little like a caress; alcohol 18%. Drinking temperature is 12–14°C (53.6–57.2°F) for young Olorosos, 14–16°C (57.2–60.8°F) for more mature ones.

PALO CORTADO

The colour of this sherry tends towards mahogany, it has a dry but well-balanced taste which is reminiscent of hazelnuts. It is fairly rare sherry that has the soft rounded taste of an amontillado combined with the fullness and character of an Oloroso; alcohol: 18%. Drinking temperature is 14–16°C (57.2–60.8°F).

PALE CREAM
This smooth pale sherry that resembles a fino in appearance, is actually slightly sweet with a refined and delicate taste; alcohol 17.5%; this sherry is surprisingly good combined with paté and fresh fruit to drink at 8–10°C (46.4–50°F).

RICH CREAM
This type of sherry also goes under the names of cream or oloroso dulce. This type of sherry is made using an Oloroso so that it is full-bodied and with much character.
The basic wine is Pedro Ximénez, sometimes supplemented with Moscatel, and this sherry can be from five to fifteen years old. The taste is sweet, full, powerful, and yet smooth; alcohol 17.5%. This sherry is mainly served as a dessert sherry at 12–14°C (53.6–57.2°F).

PEDRO XIMÉNEZ
This dark (mahogany coloured) sherry that is also known as PX, is quite rare. Its nose and taste is of raisins with suggestions of roasted coffee or cocoa. This sherry is made using sun-dried Pedro-Ximénez grapes; alcohol 17%. This sherry is often served with sweet pastries and cakes. Drinking temperature is 16–18°C/60.8–64.4°F. (Some prefer to drink this sherry chilled. Try it yourself or choose your own temperature)

The indications 'dry' or 'medium dry' sherry, are somewhat imaginative and not very reliable. Their origin is among English sherry shippers who might wish to mask the dubious origins of their 'sherries'. Hence slightly sweet sherry-type wines are termed 'dry' and honey sweet ones as 'medium dry'. The terms 'pale', 'pale dry', and 'dry' should relate to Fino sherries and 'medium dry' relate to Pale Cream or Oloroso Semi-dulce. In practice this is not adhered to. There has been stricter control since 1996 but some houses still live by the motto 'Make it sweet and call it dry.'

MANZANILLA DE SANLÚCAR DE BARRAMEDA
Manzanilla fino type sherry wine may only be produced in the harbour town of Sanlúcar de Barrameda. The wine is somewhat lighter but is often more elegant than other finos. This wine derives a character all of its own thanks to the position of the bodegas close to the sea so that cooling sea breezes waft into the storage cellars. Manzanilla from Sanlúcar de Barrameda recently acquired its own DO and is likely now to be increasingly differentiated from sherry from Jerez de la Frontera or El Puerto de Santa María. This is a reaction to the situation that is unsatisfactory for

Pedro Ximénez sherry.

the producers of Manzanilla whereby almost all the promotional budget for sherry is used to promote fino.
Although Manzanilla is certainly of no lesser quality, they are often seen by promotional activity to be lesser wines than finos. The Manzanilla producers have now taken the initiative themselves with promotional activity led by houses such as the well-known Barbadillo bodega.
The colour is pale to straw yellow, the nose is fresh and vegetal with distinct hint of flor. The taste is somewhat saltier and above all drier than a fino sherry with a pleasing bitter note in the finish; alcohol 15.5%. It is an outstanding aperitif. Drinking temperature is 10°C (50°F).

Málaga

The Málaga DO is situated in the province of the same name and consists of two zones: the western one on the coast near Estepona and a northern one around the town of Málaga as far as the borders with the provinces of Granada en Córdoba. Only this latter area is of any interest. Although Málaga officially makes seco (dry) and abocado (medium sweet) wines, the area is better known for the honey sweet Málaga Dulce. The wine came to fame through British visitors during the Victorian era.
The soil constituency of the two areas differs slightly.

Montilla-Moriles

Like Jerez, this is one of the oldest wine-growing areas of Spain. The history of Montilla-Moriles is similar to that of Jerez. The Montilla wines were adored by both the Greeks and Romans but what has become known as the characteristic Montilla style was only developed in Medieval times. Despite its reputation, Montilla has always remained in the shadow of sherry. In an ironic situation, the growers of Jerez have named one of their best sherries after the old-style Montilla wine: Amontillado.

The wine-growing area of Montilla-Moriles is situated around the towns from which the name is derived in the province of Córdoba.

The best soil is located in the centre of the area and is known as the Superior wine territory. The soil here is also albariza in common with Jerez (which the locals here sometimes call alberos); soil that is high in chalk that stores water so that the vineyards do not dry out in the hot summers. In the rest of Montilla-Moriles the soil is sandy, which is termed arenas in Jerez but ruedos in these parts. The vineyards are sited at an elevation of between 300 and 700 metres (984 and 2,296 feet).

The climate is Mediterranean verging on sub-tropical in the south around Moriles, with some continental influences on the high inland country around Montilla. The Pedro Ximénez grape accounts for 75% of all the vines here followed by Moscatel and some Airén (known here as Layrén or Lairén), Torrontés and Baladi in some of the newer vineyards for modern wines still under development. These newly developed wines, vinos jovenes afrutados, are at their best light fruity and fresh wines – which is quite an achievement in such a hot climate where normally only heavy sweet wines are made – and make a fine aperitif. Drinking temperature is 8–10°C (46.4–50°F).

The Vinos de Crianza are not fortified, must contain at least 13% alcohol naturally, and have been cask aged or at least one year. These wines are available as seco/dry, semi-seco/medium dry, and dulce/cream. To create the sweeter versions of these naturally dry wines sweet syrup (dulces) or vinos de licor is added.

Vinos generosos naturally have alcoholic strength above 15%. These wines pass through a solera system (see Solera and Sherry) to arrive at a homogeneous quality. This wine is available as

Fino seco: dry, pale wine with fine but full-bodied bouquet and taste. It is reminiscent of Provençal herbs. Alcohol: 14–17.5%.

Amontillado: dry, golden or amber-coloured, strong nose and taste of hazelnut, smooth and full-bodied. Alcohol: 16–18%.

Oloroso: oxidised (no flor), mahogany coloured, very aromatic, velvet smooth, dry or slightly sweet. Alcohol: 16–18% for young wine and up to 22% for mature wine.

Palo cortado: oxidised, mahogany coloured, very aromatic, half-way between Oloroso and an Amontillado. Alcohol: 16–18%.

There is underlying chalk bedrock virtually throughout the area with chalk-bearing upper layers but on the coast there is rather more ferruginous clay interspersed with mica and quartz. The climate is definitely Mediterranean on the coast but slightly more continental inland. Only two varieties of grape are recognised in Málaga: Moscatel along the coast and Pedro Ximénez, which thrives inland.

Málaga Dulce is made from overripe grapes that have been sun dried. The juices acquired from such grapes are very concentrated and sweet. During fermentation the wine is fortified with wine alcohol to about 18% alcohol by volume. A thick sweet syrup or arrope is also added to the wine. Only the lágrima or 'tears' (juices acquired without any pressing from the weight of the grapes pressing on each other) and first pressing or pisa may be used for this wine. Málaga Dulce Lágrima is only made with the initial juices before the pressing proper begins. This is somewhat more refined in taste than the ordinary dulce. Málaga Dulce of any quality is cask aged by the solera method as with sherry (see Solara System). Good Málaga Dulce is very fruity, sweet, and juicy with a powerful bouquet containing wood, raisins, caramel, and roasted coffee and cocoa. Drink this wine after dinner with cheese and nuts. Drinking temperature is to taste, either chilled 8–10°C (46.4–50°F), slightly chilled 12–14°C (53.6–57.2°F) or at room temperature 16–17°C (60.8–62.6°F).

Pedro Ximénez: probably the best Montilla-Moriles wine. Made wholly from overripe grapes which are then sun dried. This wine cannot fully ferment naturally because of the high concentration of sugar. Hence distillate of wine aguardiente is added to the honey sweet wine. This results in a very dark wine with sugar content in excess of 272 grams per litre. The serving temperatures are similar to the sherries of Jerez (q.v.).

Canary Islands

The Canary Islands lie off the south-western coast of Morocco, to the south of the Portuguese island of Madeira. The seven large islands and six small ones form two offshore Spanish provinces named after their capital cities: Las Palmas de Gran Canaria (the eastern islands of Gran Canaria, Fuerteventura, and Lanzarote) and Santa Cruz de Tenerife (the western islands of Tenerife, La Palma, Gomera, and Hierro). The largest island is Tenerife and Hierro is the smallest.

The islands are volcanic in origin and the volcanoes on Tenerife, La Palma, and Lanzarote are still active. The most recent eruption was on La Palma in 1971. The landscape is mountainous with the highest point being Pico de Teide (3,718 metres/12,198 feet) on Tenerife.

The climate on the islands varies with the most rainfall in the mountains carried on northerly winds. There is eight to fifteen times more rain on Tenerife, Hierro, Gomera, and La Palma each year as that which falls on Fuerteventura and Lanzarote. The eastern islands are often affected by hot Sirocco winds from the Sahara. The average temperature is certainly mild and apart from in the mountains frost is virtually unknown.

Wine growing in the Canary Islands has a rich past, largely due to the fondness in Britain for Malvasian wine. This was a full-bodied and sweet wine that steered a middle course between a Madeira and a Spanish Oloroso sherry. It is very difficult to find a good Malvasia any more because of the extensive development in the direction of table wines during the 1980s and away from rancio, generoso, and such-like wines. This is partly due to the explosive development of tourism on the islands. The old vineyards were replanted with suitable native varieties to meet the demand for wine from tourists. The varieties chosen were Negramoll or Listán Negro.

The wine-making equipment was fully renewed and a good trade was created for local wines. The first area to achieve DO status was Tacoronte-Acentejo quickly followed by La Palma, El Hierro, Valle de la Orotava, Ycoden-Daute-Isora, Valle de Güimar, Abona, and Lanzarote).

The Canarian wines are mainly sold to local restaurants and shops, with the remainder going to the duty-free shops. Consequently few Canarian wines will ever be encountered outside the islands.

Because of this exceptional position the growers and cooperative bodegas can demand relatively high prices (in Spanish terms) for their wines. The DO territories from north-west to east are as follows.

La Palma

Granted DO status since 1994, there are three sub-areas of Hoyo de Mazo (south-eastern hills of Santa Cruz de La Palma through to Mazo), Fuencaliente-Las Manchas (south-western hills of Tazacorte to Fuencaliente), and the northern area of Tijarafe to Puntallana.

The vineyards are sited on black volcanic soil at heights of between 200 and almost 1,000 metres (328 and 3,280 feet). Because of the strong winds, the vines are each planted individually inside a shelter of a stone wall in a slight depression in the ground. The climate is sub-tropical but with strong maritime influences (La Palma is the most westerly island of the Canaries).

The Malvasía from the grape of the same name is available as seco, semi-dulce, or dulce.

The more modern Seco (dry) is very elegant and full-bodied and possesses much character. It often smells of hay, herbs, wild mint, and flowers. Alcohol: 14–16%. Drink this wine as an aperitif at 10–12°C (50–53.6°F).

The traditional Semi-Dulce or Dulce Malvasía is darker coloured and reminiscent of apples, wild mint, and hay. It can be drunk as an aperitif at 14–16°C or at room temperature.

The Moscatel of La Palma is excellent. This sweet wine with alcohol of 15–22% is very fruity and has a fine balance between sweet and sharp taste. Drinking temperature 8–10°C (46.4–50°F).

Currently modern-style rosé and red wines are also being made from a wide variety and quality of grapes. Ignore the cheaper ones and choose instead one of the better ones. The reds of Negramoll are generally the better wines. Drink them in local restaurants if you are visiting.

One local curiosity is the Vino de Tea which is similar to a Greek retsina. This wine is available as white, rosé, and red and is actually a Crianza wine that has been cask aged for six months in Canarian pine which gives the wine an individual, elegant, and fresh resinous taste.

El Hierro

This Canarian DO is in the hands of just one cooperative bodega which has certainly finished with the less glorious past history of wine-making on the island.

Through the modernisation and replacement of their wine-making equipment and improved methods of vinification an end has been brought here to dirty, non-sterile, and heavily oxidised wine.

Now they make fine whites, rosés, and reds for local consumption. Traditional wine is still blended from a variety of grapes (white: Listán Blanco (Palomino), Vermejuela, or Bermejuela and Vijariego; rosé and red: Listán Negro or Negramoll. The more modern wines though are made from a single variety or at most from two. The choice is from the varieties listed above but also includes Pedro Ximénez, Verdello, Breval, Diego, Gual, Malvasía, and Moscatel. Many of the grape varieties used have long since disappeared from the Spanish mainland but they thrive on the volcanic soil.

The vineyards of El Hierro are situated on terraces on the volcanic slopes at heights of 200–700 metres (656–2,296 feet). The climate here is mild and very dry, except higher in the mountains.

El Hierro Blanco is a light fruity wine with vegetal undertones. Drink this juicy wine as an aperitif or with seafood. Drinking temperature is 8–10°C (46.4–50°F).

El Hierro Rosado is a fine, pleasant, fresh and fruity rosé without too many pretensions. Drink it with fish, preferably grilled or barbecued. Drinking temperature is 10–12°C (50–53.6°F).

El Hierro Tinto is usually cask aged for at least six months, normally in American oak. The taste is fresh and fruity with a hint of the volcanic soil. Drinking temperature is 12–14°C (53.6–57.2°F).

Tacoronte-Acentejo

This was the first official DO of the Canary Islands. The territory is situated on the north-western slopes of the extinct volcano of Mount Teide or Pico de Teide (3,718 metres/12,198 feet), where the vineyards are sited on terraces at heights of 200–800 metres (656–2,624 feet).

The climate is sub-tropical but with strong maritime influences. The vineyards in this area received much more water relative to other parts of the Canaries. The soil consists of underlying volcanic layers covered with a red loam interspersed with some chalk.

Tacoronte-Acentejo is best known for its red wines but some white and rosé is also produced. The local bodegas have modernised in rapid tempo in recent years and the wines are improving as a result.

The whites. mainly produced with Listán Blanco sometimes mixed with Gual or Malvasía, are fresh, honest wines with character. Drink them as an aperitif or with seafood. Drinking temperature is 8–10°C (46.4–50°F).

The rosé wines of Listán Negro are extremely fresh and fruity (raspberries), dry, and intensely flavoured. Drinking temperature is 10–12°C (50–53.6°F).

The reds are generally of the vino joven type for early consumption by tourists. These are fresh, fruity, and easily drunk, with lightly-flavoured meat dishes for example. Drinking temperature is 12–14°C (53.6–57.2°F).

The best red wine is cask aged in American oak which imparts more roundness, finesse, and herbal nose, with a hint of humus, to the wines that are usually made from Negramoll and Listán Negro. This is an ideal wine for more robust meat dishes. Drinking temperature is 14–16°C (57.2–60.8).

Lanzarote

The territory of the Lanzarote DO includes the majority of that island. Lanzarote was promoted to DO status in 1994. The soil here in the vineyards too is black and volcanic in origin, known locally as picón.

Each vine is planted separately in a small depression which is protected by a low circular stone wall. This is necessary to prevent damage by the strong winds, especially the Sirocco from the Sahara, that can be devastating. The depressions surrounded by their little walls give the landscape a somewhat surrealistic appearance from a distance. The vines are planted at 400–500 per hectare. For a decade now there have been good white, rosé, and red wines made for the tourists. Although these wines are well worth tasting, the true strength of the island lies in the superb Muscatel and Malvasía wines. The Muscatel is available as dulce and licoroso.

DULCE

The sweet dulce wine is very fruity and has an excellent balance between acidity and sugars. The taste of the fresh Muscatel grapes lingers long on the palate. Drinking temperature is 8–10°C (46.4–50°F).

LICOROSO

The liquorous licoroso has an unusually pleasant scent and taste of overripe Muscat grapes and it is velvet smooth, sweet as honey, but well-balanced thanks to the presence of delicate acidity. There is a slight bitterness to the finish and the aftertaste is both prolonged and almost soporific. Drinking temperature is 6–8°C (42.8–46.4°F).

MALVASIA

Malvasía wine is made in various types ranging from dry to honey sweet.

Malvasía seco is an outstanding aperitif that is dry, full-bodied, with considerable character. Its characteristic nose contains notes of hay, wild mint, and flowers. Drinking temperature is 10°C (50°F).

Malvasía semi-dulce is very powerful and aromatic (hay, mint, apple) with a broad taste. The balance between alcohol, acidity, sugar, and slightly bitterness is good. Drinking temperature is 10–12°C (50–53.6°F).

Malvasía dulce is more concentrated than the semi-dulce possesses an exciting bouquet of roasted mocha coffee or cocoa. Drink it after dinner or at the end of a meal. Drinking temperature is 16°C (60.8°F) to room temperature, although some prefer it chilled.

Portugal

Portugal, the exciting discovery

Portugal's climate is generally moderate without extremes of temperature. The winters are mild and the summers are warm but definitely not too hot. The north of the country is warmed by the gulf stream of the North Atlantic and the ocean ensures ample moisture. The centre of the country is hotter and drier, especially in summer. The winters there are mild and short. The south has the hottest and driest weather with a moderate Mediterranean climate. Countless wines of distinction originate from this idyllic land, which have been popular with European consumers for a long time. There are other wines that are waiting to be discovered that are of no less quality.

We will deal with the various wine areas of Portugal from north to south and then continue onwards to Madeira and the Azores. The enormous technical backwardness of the Portuguese wine industry has been almost totally done away with in recent decades. There are small places still to be found where wine is still made as it was 100 years ago but that is in stark contract with the high-tech adegas or independent quintas where everything is computer-controlled. The best quintas (independent wine companies) choose a perfect middle road with respect for tradition with the hygienic methodology and certainty of the latest technology.

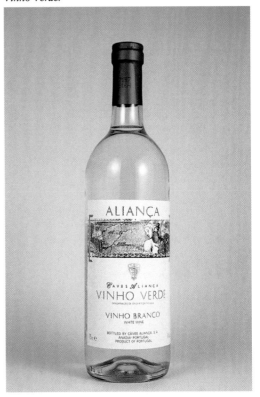

Vinhos Verdes

The wine territory of the Vinhos Verdes is situated in the north west of Portugal, just below Spanish Galicia and north of the town of Porto. The area extends between the de Minho river which forms a natural border with Spain and the Douro river in the south, between the coast and the foot of the eastern mountains. The area has the appearance of a natural amphitheatre in which the vines and wine-growers play the leading roles in a mythological play.

Wine-growing in the Vinhos Verde can be traced back to Roman times but it is probable that the Celts made wine here long before that as they did in neighbouring Galicia. The wine-growing strength of this region lies in the combination of an ideally suitable microclimate, the suitable soil (granite overlaid with sand and humus), the gentle contours of the landscape, and the excellent traditional and ancient grape varieties.

The vineyards of the Vinhos Verde comprise about 10% of the total area of vines in cultivation on the Portuguese mainland. The biggest producing areas are Viana de Castelo, Porto, and Braga. The manner in which the vines are cultivated in the Vinhos Verdes is very striking for instead of pruning to keep

them low, the vines are trained upwards to more than 2 metres high (6 feet). This is done to prevent the grape from rotting in the humid climate that rules in these parts.

The vines are trained along trellis, pergolas, or even cruciform concrete structures and they are usually harvest from below by standing on a trailer drawn behind a tractor.

The Vinhos Verdes (literally 'green wines') get their name from the attractive green countryside and not as some suggest because of the acidity of the wines. It is also quite wrong to believe that Vinhos Verdes are only white wines, since more red wine is actually produced but this is consumed locally by the inhabitants and many tourists. The relatively low alcoholic content of these wines (8.5% or more) makes them especially popular for it is possible to enjoy drinking them in greater volume. These Vinhos Verdes should ideally be consumed within one year and not more than two of their harvest. The only exception to this is wine from the sub-region of Monçao, made entirely from Alvarinho grapes. These Vinhos Verdes Alvarinho are undoubtedly the best of their type and can also be kept longer.

The grape varieties used for the ordinary Vinhos Verde include Alvarinho, Avesso, Loureiro, Pederná, and Trajadura for whites and Azal Tinto, Borraçal, Brancelho, Padeiro de Basto, and Pedral for red wines.

The Vinhos Verdes Brancos are ideal aperitifs with their slight carbonic acid sparkle. The fine bubbles are formed naturally by quickly bottling the wine following a second fermentation (malolactic fermentation). Carbonic acid gas is given off during this second fermentation and by quick bottling at this stage the tiny bubbles are captured in the bottle. The bubbles give the wine additional freshness in its taste. This wine is about 10% alcohol, making them tasty thirst-quenchers. Drinking temperature is 8–10°C (46.4–50°F).

The Vinhos Verdes Alvarinho are better quality and are slightly more alcoholic. Drinking temperature is 10–12°C (50–53.6°F).

Vinhos Verdes Tinto are just as light and refreshing as the white wines but have perhaps slightly more body. Drink this wine with lunch. Drinking temperature is 10–12°C (50–53.6°F).

Douro

The Rio Douro (golden river) lends its name to the north-eastern part of Portugal. This wine-growing territory has been known for its wines for more than 2,000 years, especially for the very special vinho do Porto, which is better known as port or port wine. Whilst port has been made here for centuries it seems as if far more table wines are now also being made in the Douro valley. In recent years indeed there has been more unfortified wine produced than port. The vineyards of the Upper Douro start about 100 km (62 miles) inland of the harbour town of Porto. The majority of them are sited on hills of basalt and granite. The climate is fairly dry of the semi-continental type with fairly big temperature ranges between the hot summers and cold winters. Good quality red and white wines are produced here, varying in style depending on the variety of grapes used and the wishes of the wine-maker. The choice for white wines is made from Malvasia Fina, Rabigato, Viosinho, Donzelinho, Verdelho, and many others. The red wine grapes are Bastardo, Mourisco Tinto, Tinta Roriz, Tinta Francisca, Touriga Nacional, and Tinto Cão. Although the different types of Douro wine vary widely there has been an enormous leap forward in their quality in recent decades. Douro Branco is a fresh lively and sometimes very aromatic wine with a delicate and refined taste. It is certainly not a heavy wine. This wine must be at least 11% alcohol and it is required to have aged for at least nine months in the bottle before being sold. Drinking temperature is 10–12°C (50–53.6°F).

Douro Tinto exists in many styles. Some of them are young, fruity, almost playful, while others are intentionally more robust and powerful. This depends on the grapes used, method of vinification, and length of cask maturing that has been undergone. All Douro reds must be at least eighteen months old before they may be sold and contain at least 11% alcohol. Whichever Douro you may

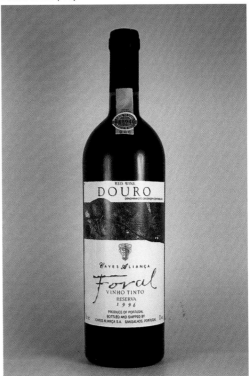

Douro Tinto (red).

choose, they are always surprisingly good value for money. The modern style wines are very colourful and fruity. They are velvet smooth, juicy, and very tasty. The traditional style wines are fairly dark, very aromatic, often somewhat rustic with hints of terroir including granite. Drinking temperature is 12–14°C (53.6–57.2°F) for the modern-style wines and 14–17°C (57.2–62.6°F) for the traditional ones.

Port

Although the Douro region is one of the most Portuguese of the wine territories, the famous port or port wine as it was once called from the Douro valley is almost entirely due to the inventiveness of the English.

Port or porto derives its name from the harbour town of Porto, the second city of Portugal. Porto is situated close to Vila Nova de Gaia where most port is stored, bottled, and traded.

Ideal circumstances

The valley of the Alto-Douro is probably the most picturesque wine area anywhere in the world. The vineyards start about 80 km (50 miles) to the east of Porto and Vila Nova de Gaia and they are protected by the 1,400 metre high Marao mountain against the worst influences of a maritime climate.

The soil is chiefly comprised of shale and folds of

crumbled basalt which force the vines to send down long roots in search of nutrients and water. The summers are extremely warm and dry with bitingly cold and very wet winters. To prevent erosion and make it easier to tend the vines, the area is widely terraced. Despite this everything is hard manual work. That these working conditions are difficult is underscored by the fact that only 40,000 hectares of the permitted 250,000 hectares are actually planted with vines. The traditional varieties of grape for making white port are Arinto, Boal Cachudo, Cercial, Malvasia Fina, Samarrinho, and Verdelho. Red port is made from a choice that includes Bastardo, Malvasia, Tinto Mourisco, Touriga Francesa, Tinta Roriz, Touriga Nacional, Periquita, and Tinta Barroca. This wide variety helps in part explain the wide differences between different ports. The same exciting ritual takes place in about mid September of each year. Long lines of grape-pickers enter the quintas or vineyards to pick the ripe grapes, terrace by terrace.

After picking, the grapes are collected in huge baskets to be brought to the press some tens of kilometres away. Today most port-making companies use pneumatic presses but some of the smaller companies still utilise the traditional huge but low granite tubs or lagares, in which the family, pickers, and friends press the grapes with their bare feet or with special shoes. This scene out of folklore is often done to music and attracts scores of tourists.

During vinification, which nowadays happens in stainless steel tanks, wine alcohol is added during fermentation at the rate of 10 litres per 45 litres of fermenting must. The new port is then transferred to wooden casks and left to rest for several months. After this the casks are transferred to Vila Nova de Gaia, where they are stored to mature in enormous cellars or lodges (armazéns).

More recently some port is now also left in the Douro valley to mature. The maturing process takes a minimum of two years. During the maturing in the huge 550 litre casks known as pipas the wine changes colour from purple/red to tan and the immature wine acquires specific character and bouquet.

PORT

Port is one of the drinks that is most imitated but nowhere else has succeeded in making such wine of the same quality. Port is sun in a bottle but it is also inseparable from its early origins, the soil of shale and basalt. These factors ensure the difference between true port an its imitators.

WHITE PORT/PORTO BRANCO

For centuries, port was only a red wine but since 1935 white port has also been made in the same manner as red port. The only difference is the use of white grape varieties such as Malvasia. White port can be sweet, dry, or very dry.

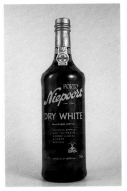

Dry white port.   *Sweet white port.*

RUBY/TINTO ALOIRADO

Ruby port derives its name from the wonderful ruby red colour of the immature port. A ruby port is aged for at least three years in wooden casks and then immediately bottled. The taste is full, rounded, and above all fruity.

VINTAGE CHARACTER

This is a blend of different vintages of about four years old and more. The colour is intense, the taste very full in flavour, and very complex. The quality is always superb and often approaches that of the best vintage ports. The price though for the quality is relatively low.

Ruby port.

TAWNY/ALOIRADO

This type of port acquires its tawny colouring through a long period of cask maturing at least five years). The taste is full and smooth with herbal and nutty undertones.

It is worth remembering that good tawny port cannot be cheap and that cheap ones are therefore blends of cheaper ruby and white ports.

AGED TAWNY

Some high quality tawny ports are cask aged for longer periods. These can be recognised by the

Tawny port.   *Ten year-old port.*

147

indication of age on the label: 10 years old, 20 years old, 30 years old, over 40 years old. The age given is the average age of the ports use in creating the blend which is then bottled immediately after blending.

COLHEITA

Colheita (pronounced kol-yé-ta) means harvest in Portuguese. Colheita relates to tawny ports and indicates that in contrast to other tawny ports, which are a blend of several vintages, this type is a single vintage port.

The port must be cask aged for at least seven years and the year of the vintage is indicated on the bottle.

LATE BOTTLED VINTAGE (L.B.V.)

This wine has been aged in casks for five or six years and is more full bodied and complex than most ruby ports, though it does not achieve the quality of vintage ports.

This port has two advantages; unlike vintage port this type can be drunk immediately and the price is much less than for a vintage port.

CRUSTED PORT

This port, which is blended from several vintages, is bottled without filtration. The wine must have been bottled for at least four years before being sold. The wine sediments form a crust on the inside of the bottle of this wine, which is dark, rich, full-bodied and requires to be decanted before drinking.

Colheita port.

Late bottled vintage port.

VINTAGE PORT

The better ruby ports from an exceptional year are bottled after two years maturing in the cask.

The capture of the young fruity taste and superb ruby colouring is thereby guaranteed.

A vintage port needs at least ten years to develop fully but can happily be kept for decades. A true vintage port should not be opened in under 30 years.

There is a clear difference between the so-called Portuguese vintage port (Ramos-Pinto, Royal Oporto, Rainha Santa) and English vintage port (Croft, Offley, Taylor, Osborne, Sandeman, Graham, Warres, Dow). Portuguese vintage port seems generally more readily accessible than English vintage port.

Vintage port.

SINGLE QUINTA VINTAGE PORT

In those years in which not all wine can be declared a vintage, wines from a single vineyard may still be declared a vintage year.

This wine is always of exceptional quality. Some houses also make single quinta vintage port in years when an overall vintage is declared.

Bairrada

The vineyards of Bairrada are not far from the coast, north of the town of Coimbra and south of the Vinho Verde territory. The area is bordered by the Atlantic to the west and the Dão region to the east. Bairrada's climate is clearly influenced by the Atlantic Ocean. The name Bairrada is derived from the Portuguese word for clay loam of bairro or barro. In common with the Spanish Tierra de Barros this says everything about the local soil. Excellent wine is made here full of extract and colour. The wine-growers of Bairrada are quite fanatical in their perfectionism. The beauty of some wines reflects the magnificent landscape, hospitality, and conviviality of the inhabitants. The Bairrada wines are seductive charmers that are available as red, white, or rosé. Little white wine is produced, comprising about 10% of the total and the grapes use include Bical and Rabo de Ovelha (which is also known as Rabigato), a similar 10% is rosé with the remaining 80% being red wines. Both reds and rosés use grapes such as Baga and Rufete. A very acceptable sparkling wine made by the traditional method is also available from Bairrada. Most of the production is in the hands of the adega's coöperativas and a few independent quintas. Bairrada Branco is a fairly rare wine but well worth finding, especially those which undergo a short period of maturing in casks, which are surprisingly delicious. This fresh but refined wine can be drunk early but it can also be kept for a few years. Drinking temperature is 8–10°C (46.4–50°F).

Bairrada Rosado is more full-bodied than the whites but less so than the Bairrada red. Drinking temperature is 10–12°C (50–53.6°F). Bairrada Tinto has a strikingly intense bouquet with broad, full taste. This is a powerful wine of much character and a prolonged after taste. Drinking temperature is 12–14°C (53.6–57.2°F) for the younger wines and 14–17°C (57.2–62.6°F) for more mature examples.

Bairrada Branco (white).

Bairrada Tinto (red).

Dão Branco (red).

Dão

The wine-growing area of Dão can be found just beneath that of Douro on the map. Wine-growing here was protected in law as long ago as the fourteenth century but the area's history of wine-making is much older, probably going back to before Roman times. The area is situated in the centre of Portugal, between the Spanish border and the wine area of Bairrada. Dão is encircled by a ring of mountains which shelter the vineyards from the moist winds off the Atlantic Ocean and also protect the area from the extreme inland cold climate of the continent. The north and central parts of the area are underlain with hard granite, with slate and shale to the south. The vineyards are sited on terraces on the steep slopes on the sides of the mountains, just as in the Douro valley. The climate is fairly moderate with generally warm and dry summers and cool autumns. Blue grapes thrive best on the granite while white varieties do best on slate and shale. The traditional varieties of Dão include Alfrochero Preto, Tinta Pinheiro, Tinta Roriz, Jaen, Rufete, and Touriga Nacional for red wines and the ancient Barcelo, Bical, Cercial, Encruzado, Malvasia Fina, Rabigato, and Uva Cão for white wines. Most wine from Dão is red but the increasing demand for white wine is leading to an increase in white wine production. All Dão wines must contain at least

11% alcohol. The role of the cooperatives is essential because of the small areas of each vineyard and their widely dispersed distribution. Despite this there are increasing numbers of estates or quintas that are maturing and bottling their own wines. This bodes well for the future of this area. Dão Branco has to be aged for at least six months before being sold. Some of these wines are aged in wooden casks. Modernisation has led to outstanding dry, fresh, and fruity Dão white wines being produced. Drinking temperature is 8–10°C (46.4–50°F). Dão Tinto has to be aged just like the white wines but for at least eighteen months. When young these reds are ruby-coloured and quite stiff and full-bodied. After several years of ageing they develop a velvet smooth texture and very characteristic taste with exceedingly complex bouquet. Some aged wines are sold as Reserva or Garrafeira. Drinking Dão Tinto is good for the digestion. Drinking temperature is 12–14°C (53.6–57.2°F) but 14–17°C (57.2–62.6°F) for Reserva/Garrafeira.

Alentejo

Alentejo is not really a wine region, more a collection of countless small wine-growing areas: Portalegre, Borba, Redondo, Evora, Reguengos, Granja/Amareleja, Vidigueira, and Moura. These territories are scattered along the border with Spain to the east and south east of Lisbon. Alentejo covers a fairly large slice of country in which olive oil has

Dão Tinto (red).

been produced for as long as anyone can remember. There are still a few olive trees in the vineyards to right and left as in Tuscany in Italy but most of the vineyards today are separated from the olive groves. Much good quality wine is made in Alentejo, thanks in part to the investment in modern equipment. Most of the wine production is in the hands of huge cooperatives (adega's coöperativas. Red wine making dominates, except perhaps in the Vidigueira district, but the increasing demand for white wines will probably see an increase in growing white grapes here too. This large area of vineyards (13,000 hectares) is on level ground that is mainly dry and rocky.

The climate is Mediterranean with some influence from the Atlantic. Summers here are very hot and dry. Some 20 varieties of grape are grown here, of which six are the main varieties. These are the white varieties of Roupeiro (lemon colour and refined aromas), Rabo de Ovelha (volume and colour), and Antão Vaz (specific aromas), and the red sorts of Periquita (fruity, subtle perfumes), Trincadeira (alcohol and freshness), and Aragonez (darker colour and body). Each wine district in Alentejo has its own character so we will take a look at them individually.

Portalegre

This is the most northerly district, close to the hills of São Mamede, in a densely wooded area. The hills and contours combine to create Portalegre's microclimate. The soil is chiefly granite interspersed with slate, shale, or quartzite. The reds here are mainly made from Aragonez, Grand Noir, Periquita, and Trincadeira while the grapes used for white wines are Arinto Galego, Roupeiro (known as Alva locally), Assario, Manteœdo, and Fernão Pires.

Borba

Borba is equally well-known for its wines and attractive marble. The ground here is crystalline chalk and some red shale. The red wines are made by blending from Aragonez, Periquita, or Trincadeira as the main grapes with supplements of Alfrocheiro, Alicante Bouschet, Grand Noir, and Moreto. White wines use Perrum, Rabo de Ovelha, Roupeiro, and Tamarez.

Redondo

Redondo is bounded by the Ossa chain of mountains to the north and by the waters of the Vigia dam in the south. The underlying rock is chiefly granite and shale.

The main grape varieties here are Periquita, Aragonez, Trincadeira, and Moreto for the red wines and Roupeiro, Fernão pires, Tamarez, and Rabo de Ovelha for the white wines.

Evora

Evora was once a famous wine-making area but for reasons that are not entirely clear it looked almost set to disappear from a wine map of Portugal in the near future. Now following drastic replanting with varieties such as Periquita, Trincadeira, Aragonez, and Tinta Caiada for red wine and Arinto, Rabo de Ovelha, Roupeiro, and Tamarez for white wine, Evora is enjoying a renaissance. Although Evora is officially part of the 'Denominação de Origem Controlada' of Alentejo, the area of Evora itself does not yet have full official recognition. The labels bear 'Indicação de Provenencia Regulamentada', which precedes a full DOC recognition.

Reguengos

The underlying ground of Reguengos consists chiefly of granite and some shale. The climate here is continental with cold, dry winters and hot, dry summers. There are about 3,000 sun hours per annum. Reguengos wines are recognised for their high quality. The reds are made with Periquita, Trincadeira, Aragonez, and Moreto grapes while Roupeiro, Rabo de Ovelha, Mantecœdo, and Perrum are used for the whites.

Granja/Amareleja

Granja/Amareleja is not yet entitled to the Alentejo DOC. At present the wine from this district falls within the IPR classification (see Evora). The district lies in the south west of Alentejo on the border with Spain. The climate is continental with sub-tropical influences, with a large temperature range between hot summers and cold winters. Granja/Amareleja only makes red wines with a great deal of body and seductive bouquet. The grape varieties used are Moreto, Periquita, and Trincadeira.

Vidigueira

This is probably the oldest wine-growing area of Portugal. The area is bounded to the north by the Portel hills. The climate is continental with sub-tropical characteristics but with a large range in temperature between summer and winter. The underlying ground varies from the rest of Alentejo in being volcanic in origin. Red wines are made using Alfrocheiro, Moreto, Periquita, Tinta Grossa, and Trincadeira grapes with the choice from Antão Vaz, Mantecœdo, Perrum, Rabo de Ovelha, and Roupeiro for white wines.

Moura

This is the most southerly of all the small districts and it has an underlying bed of chalk. The climate here is virtually sub-tropical.

Alentejo Tinto (red).

Red wine grapes are Alfrocheiro, Moreto, Periquita, and Trincadeira, with Antão Vaz, Fernão Pires, Rabo de Ovelha, and Roupeiro for white wines.

Alentejo wines

In addition to Alentejo wines from the DOC districts and IPR area wines, there are also generic Alentejo DOC wines which may be produced anywhere within the area described above.

Alentejo Branco (generic or from a defined territory) is generally fresh with mellow fruitiness but intense bouquet. This wine must contain at least 11% alcohol. Drink it by preference when young at 8–10°C (46.4–50°F).

Alentejo Tinto is fruity and fresh with a rich bouquet, and smooth and fleshy taste. Drinking temperature is 12–14°C (53.6–57.2°F) for young wine and 14–17°C (57.2–62.6°F) for more mature examples.

Algarve

The Algarve is in the extreme south of Portugal and runs from the Atlantic Ocean to the Spanish border.

Torres Vedras.

The climate here is sub-tropical and the soil is chiefly sandy.

The white wine has low acidity and is fine and delicate but fairly high in alcohol (up to 13%). Drinking temperature is 8–10°C (46.4–50°F).

The red wine is mellow and velvet smooth with relatively high alcohol but rather less body and acidity. Drinking temperature is 14–16°C (57.2–60.8°F).

Madeira

The island of Madeira was discovered relatively late in 1418. Wine-growing was established here quite soon after the island's discovery. The island was almost totally devastated by a volcanic eruption in 1470 with everything being covered with a thick layer of ash which enriched the island's soil. This ideal geology and exceptional climate circumstances make Madeira exceptionally suitable for growing vines. Madeira quickly achieved great fame, in particular in Great Britain and among its colonies. The trade in sweet Madeira wine reached its zenith in the eighteenth century. The island was beset with phylloxera at the end of the nineteenth century in common with elsewhere in Europe. The area of vineyards was reduced by half and Madeira never again achieved the level of success it had enjoyed in the eighteenth and nineteenth centuries,

despite the growth in tourism in the twentieth century.

The island is about 1,000 km (625 miles) south west of Portugal in the Atlantic Ocean and only about 600 km (375 feet) west of the coast of Africa. Madeira has a moderate climate that is fairly moist. The landscape is dominated by green forests and countless flowers. The neighbouring island of Porto Santo is in direct contrast with Madeira for the climate is exceptionally hot and dry with almost desert-like landscape.

The surface area of Madeira (capital is Funchal) is approximately 730 sq. km (281 sq. miles), measuring 53 km (33 feet) long from west to east and 23 km (14 miles) wide from north to south. The island is dominated by a 2,000 metre (6,561 feet) high volcano. The vineyards are situated at the foot and on the lower southern slopes of this mountain. The vines have to be trained off the ground along lathes or poios because of the high humidity in the air and ground. Together with the very hilly nature of the terrain this makes working on the vines extremely onerous.

Madeira is a fortified wine like port. The type and taste of the wine is entirely dependent on the choice of grapes. The variety of grapes is indicated on the label. The alcoholic content of Madeira is between 18 and 20%. Once Madeira made a long sea voyage during which it crossed the equator twice but these days the maturing occurs in large casks kept in areas

Periquita.

Moscatel de Set'bal muscatel.

Madeira Boal.

MALVASIA
Malvasia makes the sweetest Madeira which is very dark in colour, heavy, almost syrupy, but with a surprisingly elegant bouquet and wonderful broad taste. Drinking temperature is to personal preference between 8 and 14°C (46.4–57.2°F) depending on the occasion, the company, and the season (the wine may be drunk slightly warmer in winter but never at room temperature). Whether the choice is Sercial, Verdelho, Boal, or Malvasia a glass of Madeira is always beneficial for the digestion.

The Azores

Wine is made on these Portuguese islands but you are unlikely to ever encounter it outside of these islands. Should you chance to visit the islands, the wines to seek out are Biscoitos, Graciosa, and Pico.

PORTUGUESE ROSÉ
These once so notorious rosés with their idiosyncratic bottles have grown up but few of them are equal in quality to the best Spanish rosados. Portuguese rosé wines still provide a dry, delicious, and thirst-quenching accompaniment to a summer lunch or beach barbecue. Drinking temperature is 10–12°C (50–53.6°F).

known as estufas that are naturally warmed by the sun which causes the wine to oxidise so that it acquires the characteristic 'port-type' bouquet and taste. The process is known as 'Maderisation'. The better wines are further aged in above-ground storage areas known as canteiros which are also heated by the sun.
Madeira is usually a blend of several years though there are exceptions.

SERCIAL
The Sercial grape produces a pale, dry, light wine with fine acidity, very pleasing bouquet, and lively taste. This wine makes an excellent aperitif. Drinking temperature 10–12°C (50–53.6°F).

VERDELHO
Verdelho is darker in colour than Sercial, less dry, and less refined, but has a seductive bouquet and taste in which fresh grapes, honey, and something slightly smoky can be detected. Drinking temperature is 10–13°C (50–55.4°F).

BOAL
The Boal-Cachudo grape produces a full-bodied, rich, and velvet smooth sweet wine. This wine is less suitable as an aperitif and better for an informal evening with friends.
Drinking temperature is 10–14°C (50–57.2°F) or to taste.

Portuguese rosé.

Italy

The Italian wine industry

Italy is a long and narrow peninsula in the form of a thigh-high wading boot. The island of Sicily that is shaped like a bunch of grapes lies off the toe of the boot with the larger island of Sardinia above it. Italian wine-growing has clearly defined areas in the same way as France and Spain. Wine-growing takes place throughout the peninsula except in the highest mountains. In the north of the country the Alps run from west to east. while the Apennines run down the country from the centre to the south from north to south. The mountains, which form the backbone of the country, do account though for about 40% of the area cultivated by vines. Vineyards can be found in every sheltered valley. Between the two areas of mountains is the fertile Po valley. Although there are countless microclimates throughout Italian vineyards, in general terms the north has a continental climate while the south enjoys a Mediterranean climate. The vineyards are never far from the sea so that extremes of temperature are moderated. In broad terms, the geology of the north is chalk bearing while the south and Sicily is of volcanic origin.

Grape varieties and types of wine

Italy is a veritable labyrinth of vineyards from which the enthusiastic wine connoisseur can discover more than 2,000 different types of grape. Most of these grapes have been growing in the peninsula for almost 3,000 years. There are ancient native grapes but also vines that were introduced by the Greeks and then more modern varieties, which mainly originate from France. Italy has a total of about 14 DOCG wine denominations, 270 DOC denominations, and 115 IGT wines. When you consider that most production areas make white, rosé, and red wines and that some denominated areas may use 20 different varieties of grapes it becomes obvious that it is impossible to give a complete survey of all Italian wines. This book will concentrate on the most popular wines and where possible mention the others.

Virtually every type of wine that exists is to be found in Italy from superb dry sparkling wines (spumante), made in the same traditional way as in Champagne, or by the charmat/cuve-close (sealed tank) method; or seductive sweet sparkling Moscato wine; dry white wine that is fresh, light and fruity or full-bodied white wine that is cask aged in small French barriques; semi-sweet (abbocato) or sweet (dolce) white wine and rosé; light and fruity or full-bodied and powerful red wines; and finally a number of different late harvested grape wines (passito), such as the sweet Recioto and Vin Santo or the dry Recioto Amarone. Whatever you want, Italy has it.

Introduction to the Italian wine areas

We start our journey in the north-west of Italy and at first we follow the line of the Alps from west to east before heading south to deal with the areas on either side of the Apennines. Finally we look at the islands of Sicily and Sardinia.

Piemonte (Piedmont)

The name describes the position of the area: 'at the foot of the mountains', in this case being the Alps which bound Italy with France and Switzerland in a graceful arc. Countless rivers, of which the Po is the best known, flow from these mountains to form wonderful valleys in the lower lying areas. The principal city of Piedmont is Turin (Torino), famous for its heavy industry, although the rest of the area remains in traditional agricultural. The valleys of Piedmont make a welcome contrast with the massive mountain ridges of the Alps. The southern part of Piedmont has something of the nature of Tuscany's rolling hills. Piedmont is rich in tradition, mainly derived from successful generations of farmers. The local cuisine is best known for sturdy dishes in which herbs and spices are strong. No-one gives a second thought here to a mere couple of cloves of garlic. It is therefore no surprise to discover that the red wine from these parts is also powerful

Moscato d'Asti DOCG.

and full-bodied, especially those made with the ubiquitous Nebbiolo grape. For as long as anyone can recall wine has been made in Piedmont, witnessed by many references in both Greek and Roman literature. Today Piedmont, together with Tuscany, is a temple to the art of Italian wine making.

ASTI SPUMANTE DOCG AND MOSCATO D'ASTI DOCG

The sparkling Asti Spumante is made by a natural second fermentation in the bottle (in the case of the best), or in closed fermentation tanks. The colour is clear, ranging from straw yellow to golden and the nose is reminiscent of the seductive Muscat grapes which form the basis of this wine. The taste is mellow, delicate, fruity, and sweet, with a good balance between acidity and sweetness. Women often prefer this wine slightly chilled as an aperitif. The drinking temperature should be 6–8°C (42.8–46.4°F). The light bubbles of Moscato d'Asti, also made with Muscat (or Moscato) grapes, is clear straw yellow in colour with an intense bouquet of Muscat grapes. The taste is aromatic and sweet but the presence of fine acidity leaves a fresh impression on the palate. A genuine Moscato d'Asti is certainly not cheap. The drinking temperature should be 8–10°C (46.4–50°F).

BARBARESCO DOCG

This red wine made with Nebbiolo derives its name from the Barbaresco district of the province of Cuneo. It is an exceptionally fine wine, with a full, deep red colouring with an orange tinge. The nose is very aromatic (herbs such as bay) and the flavour is very full, rich, and quite dry. The wine can be extremely harsh when young but this disappears after a few years laying down. A fully mature Barbaresco will be velvety smooth. Ordinary Barbaresco need to be aged for at least two years, Riserva wines are aged for four years. The drinking temperature when young should be 13–15°C (55.4–59°F) but 16–17°C (60.8–62.6°F) when fully mature.

BAROLO DOCG

This is probably the best-known wine from Piedmont. Barolo is also made with Nebbiolo and like the Barbaresco it originates from Cuneo. The cradle of Barolo is situated in Langhe, close to the small town of Barolo. This top Italian wine is a very deep and dark granite red that has a very intense and aromatic bouquet (containing herbal notes such as bay, rosemary, and alcohol), is very full-bodied, powerful, and quite alcoholic at a minimum of 13%. A young Barolo is barely drinkable because of the harshness of its tannin so leave it for at least five years. Ordinary Barolo has to be at least three years old before it may be sold (but that does not mean it is ready to drink), while a Riserva must be at least five years old. Do not buy any cheap Barolo for it is commercial wine without character. The drinking temperature should be 16–18°C (60.8–64.4°F).

Barolo DOCG.

Gattinara DOCG

The Nebblio grape is also the basis for Gattinara. This red wine originates from around Gattinara in the province of Vercelli. Gattinara has enjoyed great fame for centuries, despite its low levels of production.

The wine's colour is dark granite red with an orange tinge. The bouquet is finer than that of either Barolo or Barbaresco and tends towards floral notes, such as violets. The taste is less pronounced than the two tough brethren from Piedmont but it remains very much a masculine wine that is full, well-balanced, and rich. In particular Gattinara has a characteristic bitter note in its finish that makes it a perfect companion for roast beef or game.

An ordinary Gattinara must be at least three years old and contains at least 12.5% alcohol, a Riserva is at least four years old and contains 13% alcohol. In the best vintage years (with ample sun) a Gattinara will leave a Barolo far behind. Drinking temperature 14–16°C (57.2–60.8°F).

Gattinara DOCG.

Dolcetto di Dogliani.

BARBERA DOC

There are three types of wine produced with the Barbera grape. All three are ruby red when young and granite red when mature. This wine is not suitable for drinking when young because it is so high in tannin. With a few years ageing in the bottle the wine becomes more full-bodied and more amenable. Choose the slightly more alcoholic Superiore version which is more balanced. Barbera d'Alba is only made with Barbera grapes but Barbera d'Asti and Barbera del Monferrato are permitted a maximum of 15% Freisa, Grignolino, or Dolcetto. In contrast with the other two, Barbera del Monferrato sometimes has a slight sweetness and a little carbonic acid to tingle the tongue. Drinking temperature 13–15°C (55.4–59°F).

DOLCETTO DOC

Of all the wines made with Dolcetto grapes the best known is the Alba, although it is not necessarily the best. Dolcetto d'Alba is reddish purple and has a pleasant fruity nose and full flavour with a slight bitterness that is reminiscent of bay leaves. It is possible with most Dolcetto wines to choose a Superiore version, that has slightly higher alcohol. Drink this wine with any main dish of red meat, poultry, or roasted pork. Drinking temperature is 12–15°C (53.6–59°F).

The range of Dolcetto wines are: Dolcetto d'Acqui, Dolcetto d'Alba, Dolcetto d'Asti, Dolcetto delle Langhe Monregalesi, Dolcetto di Diano d'Alba, Dolcetto di Dogliani, and Dolcetto d'Ovada.

FREISA DOC

Freisa is a long established grape of Piedmont. The name coincidentally resembles the word *fraise* for strawberry (*fragole* in Italian) but this special red wine often tastes of strawberries and raspberries, with a hint too of roses. There are two Freisa DOC wines: those of Asti and the other from Chieri. Both are available as dry (secco) or sweet (amabile), still, lightly sparkling (frizzante), or naturally sparkling (spumante naturale). This relic of the past must be tried if visiting Piedmont. Choose the better rather than cheaper varieties which are often unstable and continue to ferment in the bottle. Drinking temperature for dry Freisa is 10–12°C (50–53.6°F), and 6–8°C (42.8–46.4°F) for sweet and sparkling types.

GAVI/CORTESE DI GAVI DOC

These are a pair of the few white wines from Piedmont. The popularity of Gavi or Cortese di Gavi surpasses its actual quality, although it is a good, fresh, delicate, and quite dry, available as frizzante and spumante with the Gavi label. These are excellent wines for drinking with fish. Drinking temperature 8–10°C (46.4–50°F).

GHEMME DOC

This is one of the best red from northern Italy for quality and price. It does not achieve the standard of top Nebbiolo wines such as Barolo, Barbaresco,

Gavi.

or Gattinara, but a good Ghemme costs significantly less and offers a great deal of pleasure in its drinking. The colour is deep granite red, the bouquet is intense and very pleasing and refined, with floral notes including violets. The wine is full of flavour, rounded, with a lightly bitterness in its finish. A good Ghemme needs to mature for at least four years before being sold. You are unlikely to be disappointed if you buy a Ghemme. Drinking temperature 14–16°C (57.2–60.8°F).

MALVASIA DOC

Two DOC wines are made from Malvasia in Piedmont: Malvasia di Casorzo d'Asti and Malvasia di Castelnuovo Don Bosco. Although from different varieties of Malvasia, the wines are similar. Both sweet red wines have a fruity nose and taste and often possess a light tingle of carbonic acid. They are especially popular for their relatively low alcohol content of 11–12%. Drink at 8–10°C (46.4–50°F).

Nebbiolo d'Alba DOC

The name implies this wine is made with Nebbiolo grapes from the area of Alba. What it does not say is that Nebbiolo d'Alba tastes great, with a full rounded and velvet smooth flavour with a long finish. Check the label before opening for in addition to this delicious dry wine there is also a sweet amabile version which can be extremely sweet.

Sizzano.

Ghemme.

There is also a spumante. The dry wine is worth the necessary additional maturing in before opening. If you buy a top year's vintage this wine can almost achieve the levels of a good Barbaresco or Gattinara. Drink at 13–15°C (55.4–59°F) dry or 6–9°C (42.8–48.2°F) for sweet or sparkling.

Sizzano DOC

Once again this is an excellent red wine made from Nebbiolo from the hills around Sizzano. This wine is less full and powerful than a Barolo or Barbaresco but resembles a more delicate and smoother Gattinara with floral undertones of violets instead of the Italian culinary herbs that characterise a Barolo or Barbaresco. This wine requires at least three years maturing before it can be sold. Drinking temperature 14–16°C (57.2–60.8°F).

Other recommended DOC wines from Piedmont

Boca (violet, pomegranate), Bramaterra, Colli Tortonesi Barbera, Fara (violets),Gabiano and Lessona, Roero Rosso, Rubino di Cantavenna, Ruché di Castagnole Monferrato, Verduno Pelaverga, Piemonte, Langhe, Colline Novaresi, Carema DOC, Erbaluce di Caluso/Caluso DOC, Grignolino DOC, Loazzolo DOC, Cortese dell' Alto Monferrato, Anghe (Favorita, Arneis), Monferrato (Casalese Cortese), Piemonte (Pinot Bianco, Pinot

Colli Tortonesi.

Grigio, Cortese, Moscato, Moscato Passito and spumante), and Oero (Arneis).

Valle d'Aosta

The picturesque valley of Aosta is in the north of Piedmont, at the foot of the mighty Mont Blanc and the Matterhorn. The Aosta valley owes more in terms of culture to the Francophone Swiss and the French from Savoie than to the rest of Italy. This can be seen in both the local place names and the names of the wines such as Donnaz, Enfer d'Arvier, Blanc de Morgex et de La Salle. You are unlikely though to encounter the wines from the Valle d'Aosta elsewhere for production is quite limited and the local inhabitants and passing tourists can happily consume it all.

BLANC DE MORGEX ET DE LA SALLE
This is an exceptionally delicious gentle dry white wine that is delicate with a distinctive bouquet of mountain herbs and grass and a fresh taste due to the presence of carbonic acid. This wine is often drunk with the local cheese fondue of Toma and Fontina. Drinking temperature 8–10°C (46.4–50°F).

DONNAZ DOC
This elegant dry red includes Nebbiolo grapes. The

wine is an attractive red, delicate and aromatic in taste and nose (almond and other nuts). With a discernible bitter note in the aftertaste. Drink at 13–15°C (55.4–59°F).

ENFER D'ARVIER DOC
There is nothing infernal about this wine beyond its fiery granite red. It is mild and delicate in taste and nose with a velvet soft texture and slight bitter finish. Drink at 12–14°C (53.6–57.2°F).

NUS DOC
Nus Rouge (rosso) is a dry and soft as velvet red wine with unusual vegetal nose, perhaps of new-mown grass. This wine can be served throughout a meal. Drinking temperature 12–14°C (53.6–57.2°F). Nus Malvoisie is made from Pinot Gris and is a full-bodied and very aromatic dry white wine. Drinking temperature 10–12°C (50–53.6°F). Nus Malvoisie Flétri (passito) is sweet and very aromatic with hints of resin, wood, and nuts, including chestnuts). Drinking temperature 10–12°C (50–53.6°F) or slightly more chilled in summer.

VALLE D'AOSTA DOC
Valle d'Aosta produces many generic wines in white (blanc/bianco), red (rouge/rosso) or rosé (rosato), and single grape (mono-cépages) from Müller-Thurgau, Pinot Gris, Pinot Noir (white wine from black grapes), Chardonnay, and Petite Arvine for whites, and Gamay, Pinot Noir, Premetta, Fumin, and Petit Rouge for the reds. Most whites are dry, fruity, and fresh, the reds are light, fruity, and often high in tannin. Drink the whites at 10–12°C (50–53.6°F), and the reds at 12–14°C (53.6–57.2°F).

OTHER WINES
– Arnad-Montjovet
– Torette
– Chambave DOC

Liguria

Liguria is one of Italy's smallest regions but is also one of its most beautiful. Liguria is sheltered to the north by the foothills of the Apennines, which make a small paradise of the area. Most vineyards are sited on the lower slopes facing south and towards the Mediterranean. It will be difficult to find any Ligurian wines outside Italy although some Cinqueterres are exported.

CINQUETERRE/CINQUETERRE
SCIACCHETRÀ DOC
This is the best wine from Liguria. It is the colour of straw and made using Vermentino, Bosco, and Albarola grapes. It has a subtle perfume and a fresh pleasing dry taste. Drink at 10–12°C (50–53.6°F). Cinqueterre Schiacchetrà is a sweet Cinqueterre made with partially dried grapes. The taste is deeper than the ordinary Cinqueterre, but can vary between almost dry and very sweet. The minimum alcohol

level is 17%! Drink at 10–12°C (50–53.6°F) for the almost dry examples, 8–10°C (46.4–50°F) for the sweeter ones, although cooler is also possible.

OTHER WINES FROM LIGURIA

Vermentino, Iviera Ligure di Ponente, Olli di Luni, Olli di Levanto Rosso, Igato, Ossese Iviera Ligure di Ponente, Osesse di Dolceacqua (also known as Olceacqua).

Lombardia (Lombardy)

Lombardy (Lombardia) lies right in the centre of northern Italy running from the foot of the Alps to the Po valley. Various tributaries of the River Po flow from the Alps, of which the best known is the Ticino. The area is characterised by water and it is home to four huge lakes: Lago Maggiore, Lago Como, Lago Iseo, and Lago Garda (Lake Garda etc. in English).

Lombardy is a fairly large area with a number of famous cities and towns including Milan (Milano), Como, Bergamo, Pavia, Cremona, Brescia, and Mantua (Mantova). This is a land of great contrasts such as that between the bustle of commercial life in the big cities and the quiet rural life in the picturesque mountain villages.

Lombardy's wine-growing is fairly concentrated, especially in Valtellina (north east of Milan), around Lake Garda and in the Oltrepò Pavese (around Pavia, in the south).The Lombardian attitude to wine is 'small but fine'. It is surprising that the inhabitants of the big towns and cities seem to prefer wines from other regions to their own. You will search in vain in Milan for a bottle of local wine but this is no problem for the wine industry for rural consumption is almost equal to the production. Little wine is available for export.

Oltrepò Pavese DOC

This area is typical of the small zones referred to in the introduction to Italian wines. The small nominated area produces about 20 different types of wine from a similar number of grape varieties. The name indicates that this area of some 40 small communities lies 'over the Po, in Pavia'. The vines grow on gently sloping hills in the south of the province. Oltrepò Pavese wines can be white, rosé, red, and sparkling.

OLTREPÒ PAVESE ROSSO

This ruby red wine is highly aromatic, full bodied, and sometimes high in tannin. In youth it often has a hint of carbonic acid to tingle the tongue. Made with Barbera, Croatina, and several other types of grape, including Pinot Nero. Drink at 10–14°C (50–57.2°F).

Riserva has a hint of orange colour and is higher in alcohol with greater depth. Drink at 14–16°C (57.2–60.8°F).

OLTREPÒ PAVESE ROSATO

From the same grapes as the red, this wine has an attractive pale cherry colour, mild taste but slight tingle. Drink at 10–14°C (50–53.6°F).

OLTREPÒ PAVESE BUTTAFUOCO

Also from the same grapes as the red, it is dry, full in flavour and rounded a slight tingle. There is also a lightly sparkling (frizzante). Drink at 10–14°C (50–57.2°F).

OLTREPÒ PAVESE SANGUE DI GIUDA

A ruby red from the same grapes as the ordinary rosso but slightly sweet and with a post-fermentation tingle. The taste is full of flavour and pleasant. Drink at 10–12°C (50–53.6°F).

OLTREPÒ PAVESE SPUMANTE

Bianco or rosato, the best of these is made by the metodo classico using at least 70% Pinot Nero, (minimum 70%), and a maximum of 30% Chardonnay, Pinot Grigio, and Pinot Bianco. A very fresh and juicy wine with much fruit that is elegant. Drink at 6–8°C (42.8–46.4°F).

San Colombano DOC

North east of Pavia is a small wine territory with a great name. The history dates back to the seventh

are numerous types of Valtellina depending on the combinations of grapes used yet despite this Valtellina wines can usually be characterised by their typical bright red colour, the subtle bouquet that is characteristic of the area, and a dry taste that may be strongly tannic. Drinking temperature is 14–16°C (57.2–60.8°F).

VALTELLINA SFURSAT
This is a special wine from grapes that have been partially dried. This almost orange coloured, powerful sweet wine (minimum alcohol 14.5%), is best with an appropriate dessert. Drink at 6–8 (42.8–46.4°F) or 10–12°C (50–53.6°F) according to taste.

VALTELLINA SUPERIORE
Only 5% of other grapes may be added to the Chiavennasca (see Valtellina DOC). The colour is ruby to granite red, the nose is strong when young but more subtle with age. The taste is very strong in tannin and acidity in the early years but this mellows and become broader and rounder with maturity. The ordinary wine may not be sold before two years old and the rare Riserva only after four years. Drink at 12–14°C (53.6–57.2°F) when young up to 14–16°C (57.2–60.8°F) when mature.

VALTELLINA SUPERIORE SASSELLA
VALTELLINA SUPERIORE INFERNO
VALTELLINA SUPERIORE GRUMELLO
VALTELLINA SUPERIORE VALGELLA
These four wines are all 'crus' of the Valtellina Superiore, meaning they come from rigidly defined areas (Sassella, Inferno, Grumello, and Valgella). These are slightly better than the straightforward Valtellina Superiore, especially the Sassella which is excellent. Drink at 14–16°C (57.2–60.8°F).

Valcalepio DOC

This area is situated on both sides of Lago d'Iseo, near Bergamo. To the east of Bergamo the soil is a mixture of clay and chalk, while in the north it consists of shingle, shale, and slate. The wines are made from ancient native grapes (Moscato di Scanzo, Merera, and Incrocio Terzi) and more modern varieties (Pinot Bianco, Pinot Grigio, Chardonnay, Merlot, Cabernet Sauvignon, and Cabernet Franc). These wines are sold under the name of either Valcalepio Rosso (red) or Valcalepio Bianco (white). Both types of wine are the realisation of a successful combination of tradition and modern methods. Valcalepio Rosso is chiefly made with Cabernet Sauvignon and Merlot to which the wine-maker adds various supplementary grapes. The colour is usually ruby red with tinges of granite red. The bouquet is pleasing, vinous, and aromatic. The taste is dry and typical of the grapes used (blackcurrant, pepper, and cherry). Riserva wines must be aged for at least three years and contain at least 12.5% alcohol. Drink at 14–16°C (57.2–60.8°F).

century, when an Irish monk moved from Lorraine in France to northern Italy. He converted the local population by teaching them how to make wine. Thirteen centuries later, wine from San Colombano is a by-word despite its rarity. The vines, which are mainly Croatina and Barbera, grow on hills of chalk and sand that are high in minerals and trace elements. This soil imparts the wine with special character. San Colombano wines are reds that are available as either still or vivace (with a light tingling sparkle). They possess considerable body and are well rounded. Drink at 12–14°C (53.6–57.2°F).

Valtellina DOC

The Valtellina valley is a real wine-lover's paradise and an unforgettable experience for those who enjoy activity and nature. The vines here grow on steep rocky hills that hang over the Adda river. The local wine has to adhere to very stringent rules regarding the origin of the grapes, their cultivation, and vinification. The wines must be wholly vinified and aged within the denominated zone.

VALTELLINA
This red wine is made from Chiavennasca, which is the local name for Nebbiolo, which may if required be supplemented with some Pinot Nero, Merlot, Rossola, Pignola Valtellinese, or Brugnola. There

Valcalepio Bianco is usually made with Pinot Bianco, Chardonnay, and Pinot Grigio, in a variety of blends within these grapes. Each wine is unique but the best are intensely straw yellow and have a refined bouquet and a well-balanced and characteristic taste. Drink at 10–12°C (50–53.6°F). Finally there is also the old-fashioned style Oscato Passito, which is of outstanding quality. Remember though that this is a sweet red wine that is ruby to cherry red, with hints of granite red. The nose is typical of red Moscato in its intensity and characteristic sensuality. The taste is sweet, but well-balanced thanks to its fine acidity. Bitter notes of almond can be detected in the finish. This wine must be aged for at least eighteen months and contain at least 17% alcohol. Drinking temperature is 8–12°C (46.4–53.6°F) depending on season and personal preference.

Brescia wines

Brescia is not a DOC wine but a wine area around the town of the same name and the famous Lake Garda. The region of Brescia encompasses the following denominated (DOC) wines: Botticino, Capriano del Colle, Cellatica, Garda, Garda Bresciano, Garda Classico, Franciacorta, Lugana, and San Martino della Battaglia. From this it is apparent that this region produces a large number of different types of wine so that it is impossible to describe them all. Below are some pointers for each denomination to make choosing a little easier.

Botticino DOC

This is a geographical area that has the village of this name at its epicentre. The vines grow on the rocky hills around Brescia on soil that is clay, marble, and chalk. The wines are made using Barbera, Marzemino, Sangiovese, and the many varieties of Schiava grapes. The Botticino wines are generally ruby red with hints of granite red, and are warm in bouquet and taste and extremely pleasing. Drinking temperature is 13–15°C (55.4–59°F).

Garda DOC

Because most Garda DOC wines are made in the province of Veneto, I described them there.

Riviera del Garda Bresciano/Garda Bresciano DOC

This wine is only made on the Brescian side of Lake Garda and this DOC has existed for thirty years. The vineyards receive ample sun and moisture and the surroundings here are always green. The geology though is complex, without one definite soil type. White, red, pale red, rosé, and spumante wines are produced here under this DOC label. Garda

Bresciano Bianco is made with Riesling Italico and/or Riesling Renano supplemented with up to 20% of other grapes. The wine is pale golden yellow tinged with green. The nose is aromatic and slightly herbal while the taste is soft on the palate and almost velvet, with a clear bitter note and hint of salt. Drinking temperature is 10–12°C (50–53.6°F). Garda Bresciano Rosso is made with Gentile, Santo Stefano, Mocasina, Sangiovese, Marzemino, and Barbera. Single varietal wines can also be found but others contain two or more types of grape. Consequently the range of possible taste for these wines run into thousands. A ruby red colouring and bitter note in the finish are characteristic of the area though. Drinking temperature is 12–16°C (53.6–60.8°F), depending on the individual type of wine. Garda Bresciano Chiaretto is a pale red wine (claret, clarete, clairet), made using the same grapes as the Garda Bresciano Rosso. The colour is usually cherry red and the taste is normally very smooth and rounded with a bitter almond finish. Drink at 10–14°C (50–57.2°F). Garda Bresciano Groppello is a ruby red wine made with Gentile, Groppellone, and varieties of Groppello grapes. This too is fully flavoured, smooth and rounded, and has a pleasing bitter aftertaste. The better wines are sold as Superiore. Drink at 12–14°C (53.6–57.2°F). The spumante rosato/rosé made with Groppello is a much rarer wine. This is deliciously full of flavour while remaining fresh tasting. Drinking temperature is 6–10°C (42.8–50°F).

Franciacorta DOCG

The wine region of Franciacorta lies between Brescia and Bergamo, on the banks of Lago d'Iseo. Good wine is made here in a mild but windy climate. The fame of Franciacorta has been established chiefly by its sparkling wines. The Franciacorta Crémant is made with Chardonnay and/or Pinot Bianco, Franciacorta rosé uses Pinot Nero (minimum 15%) and Chardonnay and/or Pinot Bianco. The best Franciacorta Spumantes are white wines made with Chardonnay, Pinot Bianco, and/or Pinot Nero (without skins). The wine has a superb colour that is deep golden yellow with a tinge of green and a sparkle of pure gold. The nose is fresh and heady while the taste is juicy, and both fresh and refined. Drinking temperature is 6–9°C (42.8–48.2°F). Franciacorta also produce a number of pleasant red and white still wines. The reds are made with Cabernet Sauvignon, Cabernet Franc, Merlot, Barbera, and Nebbiolo. These are well worth discovering. These are sold as either bianco or rosso Terre di Franciacorta DOC.

Lugana DOC

Lugana originates from the south of Lake Garda where both still and sparkling wines are made with the Trebbiano grape. A slight saltiness is typical of

Vini Mantovani

Garda DOC wines are also made to the south of the lake, which falls within the province of Mantua (Mantova). These wines vary little from the other Garda wines. Single varietal wines include Pinot Bianco, Pinot Grigio, Pinot Nero, Chardonnay, Tocai, Sauvignon Blanc, Cabernet Sauvignon, Cabernet Franc, and Merlot. Good frizzante wines are also produced here, usually with Pinot Bianco, Chardonnay, and Riesling. Colli Morenici Mantovani del Garda DOC is worth a special mention. This wine from the south of Lake Garda originates from the most favourably placed hills (Colli) above Mantua. This wine is slightly better than the other Lake Garda wines. The basic grapes are Pinot Bianco and Garganega for the whites (bianco) and Rondinella, Rossanella, Negrara, Sangiovese, and Merlot for the rosés and reds (rosato and rosso). The vineyards of Lambrusco Mantovano DOC are south of Mantua. This wine contains quite high levels of carbonic acid created by fermentation. At least four different varieties of Lambrusco type grapes may be used in this wine, which can be supplemented with Ancellotta, Fortana, or Uva d'Oro. The wine is ruby red in colour and tastes fresh and juicy. Both dry and sweet versions are available. Drinking temperature is 10–12°C (50–53.6°F). There is also a lighter rosato version of this wine.

Lugana.

these wines, derived from the minerals in the soil here. The colour varies from pale greenish yellow when young to golden yellow after a few years maturing. The bouquet is fresh and pleasant, the taste is fresh, smooth, and dry, with good balance between acidity, body, and alcohol. Drink the sparkling wine as an aperitif and the still wine with freshwater fish. Drinking temperature is 8–10°C (46.4–50°F).

San Martino della Battaglia DOC

This area is less well-known but has much in common with Lugana (q.v.) in terms of climate and mineral soil. San Martino della Battaglia is made using Tocai Friulano (note: not Pinot Grigio but Welsch Riesling. The colour is lemon yellow and the nose is very inviting and intensely aromatic, while the taste is filled with flavour, dry, and with a slight bitterness in the finish. Drinking temperature is 10–12°C (50–53.6°F). There is also a San Martino della Battaglia Liquoroso, which is much darker in colour (golden yellow), very fruity and seductive. The taste is filled with flavour, smooth, and pleasantly sweet.

The wine is well balanced with minimum alcohol of 16%. Drinking temperature is 6–10°C (42.–50°F) depending on personal preference.

Trentino-Alto Adige

Alto-Adige Müller-Thurgau.

Trentino-Alto Adige, also known as Südtirol, is bounded to the west by Lombardy, Veneto to the south, and Switzerland and Austria to the north. The principal towns of Trentino are Trente (Trento) Alto Adige (German speaking), and Bolzano. The area is bisected by the river Adige, the second longest river in Italy. In the north of the region the climate is continental while in the south it is less severe and warmer. Trentino-Alto Adige is somewhat of a transitional zone between Austria in the north and Italy in the south. The Swiss and Austrian influences can be see in the German names for both wines and places. Hence you will find both Santa Maddalena and Sankt Magdalener alongside each other and Caldaro Kalterersee, Alto Adige and Südtirol. The grapes here also have two names and because they are generally exported to Austria, Switzerland, and Germany the German names are generally found on the labels.

The wines

Due to the position at the foot of the mountains or even in the mountains, white wines are the general order of the day here. Because the local gastronomy runs towards fatty, the fresh acidity of these wines is seen as a benefit. The enormous temperature range between night and day during harvest imparts these wines with an aromatic nose which makes them worth considering. The reds too, mainly from more southerly Trentino, have a charm of their own. The fresh rosato, made in the north of the region, is much appreciated.

ALTO ADIGE DOC

The vineyards are sited in terraces on the mountain slopes, which makes their cultivation and management extremely difficult. For this reason Alto Adige is therefore never a cheap wine, but certainly an exceptionally delicious one. Just as in Alsace, this region uses a generic name of Alto Adige for countless single grape varietal wines (sometimes supplemented with up to 15% of a different grape). The best-known wines are the Moscato Giallo (Goldenmuskateller or Goldmuskateller), Pinot Bianco (Weissburgunder), Pinot Grigio (Ruländer), Chardonnay, Riesling Italico (Welsch Riesling), Riesling Renano (Rhine Riesling), Riesling x Sylvaner (Müller-Thurgau), Sylvaner (Silvaner), Sauvignon Blanc, Traminer Aromatico (Gewürztraminer), Moscato Rosa (Rosenmuskateller), and Lagrein Rosato (Lagrein kretzer).

LAGREIN SCURO (LAGREIN DUNKEL)

This is the big brother of Lagrein Rosato. It is a deep ruby red with tinge of granite and pleasant nose of fresh grapes and velvet smooth taste. Riserva examples must be at least two years old. Drink at 10–14°C (50–57.2°F), depending on age. Merlot Rosato (Merlot rosé/Merlot kretzer), Merlot, Cabernet-Cabernet Franc-Cabernet Sauvignon, and

Alto-Adige Müller-Thurgau.

Cabernet-Lagrein are also well-known wines from this area.

CABERNET-MERLOT

There are also excellent wines from either Cabernet and Lagrein or Cabernet and Merlot. If kept for an additional two years to age these wines may also bear the title Riserva on their label.

PINOT NERO (BLAUBURGUNDER)

There is also a sparkling white wine, Alto Adige Pinot Nero Spumante plus Pinot Nero Rosato (rosé), Blauburgunder Kretzer, Blauburgunder rosé, Malvasia (Malvasier), Schiava (Vernatsch), and Schiava Grigia (Grauvernatsch).

SPUMANTE

This is sparkling white with Pinot Bianco and/or Chardonnay, (sometimes with a maximum of 30% Pinot Nero and/or Pinot Grigio). There are dry (extra-brut) and less dry (brut) versions. An ideal aperitif. Drink at 6–8°C (42.8–46.4°F).

The Alto Adige 'crus'

In addition to the previously mentioned generic wines, Alto Adige also produces wines from strictly defined areas or 'crus'.

The quality of these wines is often higher than the ordinary Alto Adige. All the wines named have their own DOC denomination.

COLLI DI BOLZANO (BOZNER LEITEN)

This wine area near Bolzano makes red wine at least 90% Schiava grapes, supplemented as needed with Pinot Nero or Lagrein. The colour is ruby red, with intensity and shade depending on vinification and proportion of grapes. Both nose and taste are mellow and fruity. A delicious but unpretentious wine. Drink at 12–14°C (53.6–57.2°F).

MERANESE DI COLLINA/MERANESE (MERANER HÜGEL/MERANER)

This wine is made in the hills that jut out above the small town of Merano. The red is chiefly made with Schiava grapes is ruby colour, mellow and fruity scented and juicy and pleasant in taste. This is an unpretentious wine that is suitable for all occasions. Drinking temperature is 12–14°C (53.6–57.2°F).

SANTA MADDALENA (SANKT MAGDALENER)

The vineyards of this wonderful wine can be found in the hills around Bolzano. The vines are the Schiava grape, although these may be supplemented with no more than 10% Pinot Nero and/or Lagrein, which contribute their own character. The colour is ruby to intense granite red, the nose subtle and seductive with a hint of wild violets and the taste is mellow and smooth, rounded, juicy, with light bitter almond aftertaste. This gorgeous wine keeps well. Drinking temperature is 14–16°C (57.2–60.8°F).

TERLANO (TERLANER)

The Terlano vineyards run parallel to the Adige river in the province of Bolzano. This white wine is made with Pinot Bianco (Weißburgunder), Chardonnay, Riesling Italico (Welsch Riesling), Riesling Renano (Rheinriesling), Sylvaner (Silvaner), Riesling x Sylvaner (Müller-Thurgau), or Sauvignon Blanc. These grapes can be used to make single grape wines comprising no less than 90% of them, or ordinary bianco with different proportions, which must be indicated. All of these wines are green-yellow when young, becoming more yellow with age. They have fresh acidity and are very aromatic in both nose and taste. Drink at 8–10°C (46.4–50°F) except the Chardonnay varietals which are better at 10–12°C (50–53.6°F). There are also dry (extra brut) or less dry (brut) Spumante versions that are fresh, fruity, aromatic, and elegant. These make an excellent aperitif. Drink at 6–8°C (42.8–46.4°F). Those wines that originate from the heart of the Terlano area are permitted to add Classico to their name.

VALLE ISARCO (SÜDTIROL-EISACKTALER)

The vineyards of this denominated wine are sited relatively high, some of them above 600 metres (1,968 feet), which demands additional input from the growers. The area is situated close to Bolzano in the Isarco valley.

Alto-Adige Pinot Grigio.   *Alto-Adige Chardonnay.*

Mainly white wines are produced here using grapes such as Pinot Grigio (Ruländer), Sylvaner (Silvaner), Veltliner, Riesling x Sylvaner (Müller-Thurgau), Kerner, and Traminer Aromatico (Gewürztraminer), and a small amount of red wine from Schiava, Lausner, and Leitacher grapes. The white wine has a green tinge and is fresh, subtle, fruity, and juicy. Pinot Grigio and Traminer Aromatico generally make wines with a bigger taste than the other wines. Drinking temperature is 8–10°C (46.4–50°F) for Sylvaner, Veltliner, and Kerner and 10–12°C (50–53.6°F) for the others.

The Klausner Leitacher is ruby red in colour, has a mild nose with freshly acidic and fulsome flavour. Drink it with red meat at 12–14°C (53.6–57.2°F).

VALLE VENOSTA (VINSCHGAU)

This is a very traditional wine area that mainly produces whites using Chardonnay, Kerner, Riesling x Sylvaner (Müller-Thurgau), Pinot Bianco (Weißburgunder), Pinot Grigio (Ruländer), Riesling, and Traminer Aromatico (Gewürztraminer). A small amount of red is made from Schiava (Vernatsch) and Pinot Nero (Blauburgunder). The whites have a green tinge, fresh nose and taste, and are fruity and aromatic. Drink at 8–10°C (46.4–50°F) for Pinot Bianco and Kerner, 10–12°C (50–53.6°F) for Chardonnay, Pinot Grigio, Traminer Aromatico, and Müller-Thurgau. The Schiava reds are ruby coloured, taste and smell delicious and fruity, and are suitable for serving throughout a meal. Drinking temperature is 12–14°C (53.6–57.2°F).Pinot Nero reds are also ruby hued with a trace of orange and their characteristic nose has both vegetal and animal notes. The taste is filled with flavour but is mellow and well-balanced. There is a discernible bitterness in the aftertaste. Drink at 12–14°C (53.6–57.2°F).

CALDARO/LAGO DI CALDARO (KALTERER/KALTERERSEE)

This is another well-known quality wine from the Alto Adige. As indicated in the name, the vineyards are close to Lake Caldaro. Superb reds are produced here using various types of Schiava grape, sometimes supplemented with Pinot Nero or Lagrein. The colour varies between bright ruby and dark red while bouquet and taste are mellow, fruity, and elegant. A hint of bitter almond can be detected in the aftertaste. There are also Classico, and Classico Superiore from the heart of the area. The superior wine has 1% more alcohol than the ordinary Caldaro and Caldaro Classico. Drink at 12–14°C (53.6–57.2°F).

Trentino wines

The southern part of Trentino-Alto Adige also makes fine white wines of course but generally produces better and more red wines than the northern (Alto Adige) part of the region. Most of the vineyards are sited in the hills in the valleys of the Adige, Cembra, Lagarina, or the slopes above Lake Garda. The only exception are the vineyards of the Rotaliana valley where they are on the valley floor. The giant trellis along which the vines are trained is a typical scene in Trentino. The trellis keeps the vines off the ground so that fewer leaves are formed, enabling the sun to penetrate better in order to ripen the grapes. This also allows air to circulate freely through the vines to reduce the risk of autumn night frosts. Considerable development work is underway in this area, not just in the field of wine-making itself but also in respect of cultivation and pruning techniques and the introduction of experimental grape varieties. Large scale trials are underway with the Rebo grape, which is a cross between Merlot and Marzemino. Most Trentino wines are single varietals made with just one sort of grape. For the whites the most popular is the Chardonnay (50% of the white grapes and 15% of total production). Chardonnay is used for making both Chardonnay Trentino DOC and the excellent Spumante Trento Classico. An exceptional white grape can be found amid the others here which is a native of Trentino: the Nosiola. This highly aromatic grape imparts its Nosiola-Trentino wine with a delicate and fruity character but even more so in the magnificent Vino Santo Trentino DOC. Schiava holds sway here as the leading red wine grape. accounting for at least 30% of all the vines planted. For those who like Grappa (eaux-de-vie), Trentino perhaps makes the finest in all Italy.

CASTELLER DOC

These are reds and rosés from Schiava grapes, possible supplemented to a maximum 20% with some Lambrusco, Merlot, Lagrein, or Teroldego. These wines are either ruby red or pink, very light in texture, and extremely mellow in taste. They are available as dry (Asciutto) or slightly sweet to sweet (Amabile). These wines keep well. Serve slightly chilled at 12–14°C (53.6–57.2°F) but cooler for the sweeter wines (8–10°C/46.4–50°F).

SORNI DOC

There are two types of Sorni: whites from Nosiola grapes, possibly supplemented with Müller-Thurgau, Pinot Bianco, and Sylvaner, and reds made with Schiava, Teroldego, and possibly Lagrein. Sorni Bianco is pale golden yellow with a green cast and barely noticeable bouquet or taste. It is refreshing though and can be served on any occasion. Drinking temperature is 8–10°C (46.4–50°F).

Sorni Rosso has a more expressive nose and taste than its counterpart. It is an elegant, aromatic wine that is delicious throughout a meal. Choose a Scelto (auslese) for these are slightly higher in alcohol and more rounded. Drink at 12–14°C (53.6–57.2°F).

TEROLDEGO ROTALIANO DOC

This wine from the Teroldego grape that is native to Trentino is virtually unique. The grapes prefer the flat land in the Rotaliana valley, to the north of Trent (Trento). These grapes only develop fully with such great finesse in this one location. Wherever else these grapes are grown in Italy the results are moderate to atrocious. The Teroldego Rotaliano Rosso is very intensely coloured (ruby with glints of purple when young) and its characteristic nose is of violet and raspberry. A hint of bitter almond can be detected in the finish. In common with red Loire wines, Teroldego Rosso is best drunk when young or not before eight to ten years after the harvest. In the intervening years this wine often suffers from evaporation and becomes closed, revealing nothing of itself. Drinking temperature is 10–12°C (50–53.6°F) when young and 14–16°C (57.2–60.8°F) when mature. Teroldego Rotaliano Rosso Superiore has more body and is higher in alcohol and this is equally true of Riserva wines which must have at least two more years maturing before sale. Drinking temperature is 14–16°C (57.2–60.8°F). There is also a Rosato (Kretzer) made from Teroldego which is an attractive pink to pale granite red colour, with an intriguing floral and fruity nose and delicate taste that is juicy and rounded. This wine also has a discernible finish of bitter almond. Drinking temperature is 10–12°C (50–53.6°F).

TRENTINO DOC

This is generic area wine. It is difficult to give an overview because each of the growers and wine-makers uses their own blends and methods. The Trentino Bianco is made from Chardonnay and Pinot Bianco. It is pale golden yellow and a pleasant but unobtrusive. Drink at 8–10°C (46.4–50°F). The better whites are of the single grape variety with their name alongside Trentino DOC on the label. The best are usually the Chardonnay Trentino wines but there are also some excellent wines made with Pinot Bianco, Pinot Grigio, Riesling Italico, Riesling Renano, Traminer Aromatico, and Müller-Thurgau. Drink Pinot Grigio, Traminer, Müller-Thurgau, and Chardonnay at 10–12°C (50–53.6°F) and 8–10°C (46.4–50°F) for the rest. The subtle wine from the native Nosiola is worth considering though do not expect great miracles, rather the discovering of a very different grape. The wine is fine and delicate, pleasingly fruity in bouquet and taste with a slight bitterness in finish. Drink at 8–10°C (46.4–50°F). Finally there is an excellent sweet white wine made with Moscato Giallo. There is also a liquorous version of this wine, identified by the name Liquoroso. This is a first class after-dinner liqueur if well chilled to around 6–8°C (42.8–46.4°F). First class sparkling wines are made with Chardonnay and Pinot Bianco. This Spumante is a remarkably fine aperitif. Drink at 8–10°C (46.4–50°F). Trentino Rosso DOC is made from Cabernet and Merlot and is almost always cask aged. Depending on the wine's origins it may be light and approachable or full-bodied and powerful. The full bodied type keeps well. Drink the light and amenable type while it is still fruity at about 12°C (53.6°F) and the fuller version at 14–16°C (57.2–60.8°F). The other type of Trentino red is made from one or two types of grape and is very characteristic of its grape and terroir. You will encounter wines made with the Cabernets (Cabernet Sauvignon and/or Cabernet Franc), Merlot, Marzemino, Pinot Nero, and Lagrein. These are all excellent but the best are the Riservas, which had at least two year's additional maturing. Drink at 14–16°C (57.2–60.8°F). There is also a full-bodied Spumante made with Pinot Nero. Drink at 10–12°C (50–53.6°F).

VALDADIGE DOC (ETSCHTALER)
These are generic whites, rosés, and reds and varietal wines made from one or more types of grape. The variety indicated on the label must account for no

Trentino Pinot Grigio.

less than 85% of the wine. The ordinary Valdadige Bianco is permitted a wide variety of grapes including Pinot Bianco, Pinot Grigio, Riesling Italico, Müller-Thurgau, Chardonnay, Bianchetta Trevigiana, Trebbiano Toscano, Nosiola, Vernaccia, and Garganega. No one example of Valdadige Bianco is representative. In general these are pale golden yellow, pleasingly fresh, fragrant, but not all dry for some examples may contain sugar residues. Drink at 8–12°C (46.4–53.6°F) depending on the style. There are also countless variations with the ordinary Valdadige Rosso. The choice of grape is from three varieties of Schiava, Lambrusco, Merlot, Pinot Nero, Lagrein, Teroldego, or Negrara. Depending on the style and type of wine Valdadige Rosso can vary from light red to the deepest dark red. The bouquet is reminiscent of fresh grapes and herbs and is always a delight. The wines are not all dry and you may find some slightly sweeter examples among them. Drink at 12–16°C (53.6–60.8°F) depending type. The Rosatos are made with the same choice of grapes as the Rosso and the colour varies widely. The nose and taste are fresh and fruity with a hint of old-fashioned pear drops that can be accompanied with a slight sweetness. This is a surprisingly delicious wine without pretensions. Drink at 10–12°C (50–53.6°F). The other varietal wines, usually made from a single grape, are characteristic of the grape and terroir from which they originate. Generally these whites are a light golden yellow colour and fresh, juicy, and can be slightly sweet with Pinot Grigio examples. Drink at 8–10°C (46.4–50°F) for Pinot Bianco and 10–12°C (50–53.6°F) in the case of Pinot Grigio and Chardonnay. The reds are made with one of three varieties of Schiava grapes (Gentile, Rossa, and Grigia), which may be supplemented with other non-aromatic grapes. This wine is ruby to granite red, slightly aromatic, freshly tart yet mellow and may also be slightly sweet. Drink at 14–16°C (57.2–60.8°F).

Veneto

The region of Veneto is a veritable paradise for lovers of nature, history and gastronomy. The area has been successful in agriculture for centuries. Stretching from the Dolomites in the north to the fertile Po valley and from Lake Garda to the Venetian coast, everything seems filled with the joy of living. The landscape is gently undulating, green and inviting. The climate is ideal, moderated and mildly continental in the north and Mediterranean in the south.

BARDOLINO DOC
The vineyards of this famous denomination are situated on alluvial soil deposited in the distant ice age between the right shore of Lake Garda and the city of Verona. Wine has been made here since before the time of the Roman empire. Bardolino is permitted to use the Corvina Veronese, Rondinella, Molinara, and Negrara (not less than 85%),

supplemented if required to a maximum of 15% with Rossignola, Barbera, Sangiovese, and Garganega. Bardolino is a ruby red wine that sometimes has a touch of cherry red in its colour. As it ages the colour darkens towards granite red. The wine smells fresh and fruity (cherry), sometimes with a touch of herbs, and it has a pleasant taste that is mellow and fruity with a discernible slightly bitter finish. The young wine can be a little sharp but this mellows quickly with age. Drink at 10–12°C (50–53.6°F) when young to 12–14°C (53.6–57.2°F) when mature. The Bardolino which originates from the historical heart of this region carries Classico on its label. Wines with a slightly higher level of alcohol (at least 11.5%) may be called Superiore. You may well encounter lighter coloured Bardolino wines (mainly in Italy). These are made with the short steeping method and are called Chiaretto. This type of wine is lighter in body than the normal Bardolino, but it is more full-bodied than most rosé wines. Finally there are also red Bardolino Spumante wines, with and without the addition of Classico and/or Superiore. This dark pink to pale red wine has a fine sparkle, a fairly muted bouquet, and a pleasant taste that is filled with juicy flavour. These wines have a slight bitter note in their finish. Drink at 10–12°C (50–53.6°F).

VALPOLICELLA DOC

The wines of Valpolicella enjoyed great fame in the time of the Roman empire. The poet Virgil had great enthusiasm for it. Valpolicella's fame has grown rather than lessened since then. The wine is made from Corvina Veronese, Rondinella, and Molinara grapes (not less than 85% of the total), supplemented with not more than 15% Rossignola, Negrara, Trentina, Barbera, or Sangiovese. Like its neighbour in Bardolino, Valpolicella is light ruby in colour, tending towards an intense granite red as it ages. The bouquet is fresh and fruity, sometimes with herbal notes. The taste is smooth, fruity, with a touch of spice, and dry, with a touch of roasted bitter almond in the finish. There are also Classico and Superiore versions (the latter has 1% more alcohol and has been aged for an additional year). Drinking temperature is 12–14°C (53.6–57.2°F).

RECIOTO DELLA VALPOLICELLA DOC

The Italian for 'ears' is 'orecchi' and its diminutive is 'recie' which is the name also given to the top of a bunch of grapes, or in other words the part of the bunch that receives most sun. Recioto wine is made from selected grapes. The bunch is cut in two with the lower part of the bunch being used to

Valpolicella.

Bardolino.

make ordinary Valpolicella and the upper part – the recie or 'little ears'– are kept separate for further ripening in the sun. The liquid in the grapes partially evaporates so that the concentration of sugars, aromatic, and flavour substances is increased. The result is a deeply-coloured dark red wine with seductive and powerful fruity bouquet that suggest conserved fruit, prunes, figs, and raisins etc.), that is filled with extract. The taste is full of flavour, sensual, very warm (minimum alcohol 14%), and overwhelmingly sweet. Drink at between 10 and 16°C, (50 and 60.8°F) according to preference.

RECIOTO DELLA VALPOLICELLA SPUMANTE DOC

This is a dark red sparkling wine with an intense bouquet (see above), filled with extract. This wine has minimum alcohol of 14% and is for those who enjoy sensation, or for a strong and sweet sparkler to accompany a dessert that is far less sweet. Drinking temperature is 6–8°C (42.8–46.4°F).

RECIOTO DELLA VALPOLICELLA AMARONE DOC

This wine is made in the same way as the sweet Recioto della Valpolicella, but this is a dry version with minimum alcohol of 14% alcohol and an additional two years maturing before sale. Not everyone will enjoy this strong macho wine but for those who have the opportunity to eat wild boar that

Recioto della Valpolicella Amarone.

has been slowly roasted (in the oven or on the spit) this wine will contribute to an unforgettable evening. Drink at 16–18°C (60.8–64.4°F).

BIANCO DI CUSTOZA DOC
This wine from the area around Lake Garda is relatively unknown. The many tourists who have drunk this wine and found it enjoyable have somewhat flattered its status. Whether all Bianco di Custoza is of the same quality is another question entirely. The wine can be made from a very broad range of grapes, resulting in many different types of wine that vary in taste different. The wine-makers can choose from Trebbiano Toscano, Garganega, Tocai Friulano (Welsch Riesling), Cortese, Malvasia, Pinot Bianco, Chardonnay, and Riesling Italico, either as single grape or all blended together. At its best this produces a fulsome and aromatic wine with plenty of juice, body, and freshness that has a slight bitter note in its finish.

At its worst it creates an extraordinarily poor and tasteless wine. Hopefully you will be lucky. Drinking temperature is 8–12°C (46.4– 53.6°F) depending on the type and taste. There is also a Bianco di Custozza Spumante, made with the same grapes and hence with the same caution about quality.

SOAVE DOC
The vineyards of Soave, like those of Bardolino and Valpolicella, are situated between the eastern shore of Lake Garda and the city of Verona. The vines of the Gargane grape, which form the lion's share of this famous white wine (minimum 85%), can be seen growing around the medieval town of Soave. The Gargane is permitted to be supplemented with grapes such as Pinot Bianco, Chardonnay, Trebbiano di Soave, or Trebbiano di Toscana. Although the European market is often flooded with many lesser Soave-type wines, a true Soave is truly delicious. The colour is usually fairly pale, ranging from green to pale yellow, the nose is not unduly striking, but the taste is dry, mellow, and pleasing, with a touch of bitter almond. The ordinary Soave is generally light in body. Soave Classico originates from the historical centre of the area, while the Superiore is somewhat higher in alcohol and must be rested for at least five months before sale. The best Soave is undoubtedly the superb Soave Classico Superiore. Drinking temperature is 8–10°C (46.4 -50°F) for the ordinary Soave and 10–12°C (50–53.6°F)for the better Soave Classico Superiore.

RECIOTO DI SOAVE DOC
Just as with other Recioto wines such as the Reciota della Valpolicella (see Valpolicella), the grapes are selected and partially dried. The result is a full-bodied and very aromatic white wine that has a golden colour. The taste is fulsome and fruity, ranging from slightly to very sweet. Do not forget if

Bianco di Custoza.

Soave Classico.

attracted by the seductive excellence of this wine that it contains 14% alcohol. Drinkat 10–12°C (50–53.6°F).

SOAVE SPUMANTE DOC/RECIOTO DI SOAVE SPUMANTE DOC

Pale and fragrant sparkling versions are made of both wines that are not so full-bodied but fresh and pleasing. These wines generally have a characteristic bitter almond note in their taste. Both dry (extra brut) and medium dry (brut) versions are available of Soave Spumante but only a sweet and highly alcoholic (at least 14%) version of the Recioto di Soave Spumante is available. Drink at 8–10°C (46.4–50°F).

GAMBELLARA DOC

Gambellara is a pleasing white wine made from the Garganega grape, supplemented as required with other non aromatic white grapes to a maximum of 20%. The vineyards of Gambellara are sited on the hills that surround the small town of that name in south-western Vicenza. This white wine is usually pale gold to golden yellow and is characterised by its very pleasant nose of freshly-picked grapes. The taste is normally dry (but there are exceptions) and freshly acidic but quite mellow, not harsh or heavy. There is a slight bitterness in the finish. The heart of the Gambellara area is permitted to add the term Classico to the label. Drinking temperature is 10–12°C (50–53.6°F).

GAMBELLARA RECIOTO DOC

The same grapes are used for the Recioto as for ordinary Gambellara, except that for this wine the grapes are first partially sun dried. This concentrates the sugars, flavour, and aromatic substances and produces a wine that is golden yellow with a strong nose of overripe grapes or raisins. The taste varies from sweet to very sweet and some of these wines may have a slight natural sparkle to them. Drink this wine at 6–10°C/42.8–50°F (the sweeter, the colder). There are also Gambellara Recioto Spumante and Gambellara Recioto Classico versions.

GAMBELLARA VIN SANTO DOC

This is a superlative form of the Recioto. It is dark golden in colour and has an impressive bouquet of sweet raisins and these can also be discovered in the velvet smooth taste. This wine contains at least 14% alcohol. Drink at 6-8°C (42.8–46.4°F) or 8–10°C (46.4–50°F) for connoisseurs.

PROSECCO DI CONEGLIANO-VALDOBBIADENE/
PROSECCO DI CONEGLIANO/
PROSECCO DI VALDOBBIADENE DOC

These three wines originate from the north of a triangle formed by the towns of Padua, Vincenza, and Treviso. All three wines are made from Prosecco grapes, supplemented where required with not more than 15% Pinot Bianco, Pinot Grigio, or Chardonnay. There are two main types of Prosecco, Prosecco Frizzante is slightly sparkling, pale gold, very fruity, juicy, and particularly pleasing. The Prosecco Spumante is much more lively, fresh, fruity, and filled with flavour. Both wines are available as secco (dry, light, elegant, with a hint of bitter almond), amabile (slightly sweet and very fruity), and dolce (fully sweet and fruity). You may also encounter a Prosecco Superiore di Cartizze. This wine originates from a strictly defined area of Cartizze (near San Pietro di Barbozza in Valdobbiadene). The taste is virtually identical to the other Prosecco wines. Drink at 6–8°C (42.8–46.4°F) for sweet wines and 8–10°C (46.4–50°F) for dry Prosecco.

VINI DEL PIAVE DOC

You must have seen the large two litre bottles of wine that are served by the glass in most Italian restaurants. These almost certainly originate from the Piave region. Tocai del Piave is used for the white wines and Merlot del Piave for the reds. Generally these wines are very drinkable but certainly not representative of the entire area.
The region of Piave, which runs along both banks of the Piave river, also makes good wine. There are excellent Cabernet and Cabernet Sauvignons with just sufficient vegetal undertones and tannin to compete with a good French wine (though much cheaper). Merlot and Pinot Nero here are just a little smoother than elsewhere, even sometimes bordering on the sweet. The best wines are cask aged and are entitled to be called Riserva. Try a typical Italian

wine, the Aboso del Piave. This is ruby to granite red with a seductive nose of wild violets and other pleasant woodland aromas. The taste is dry, robust, masculine, freshly acidic, sometimes high in tannin, but always true to character and juicy. Drink at 12–14°C (53.6–57.2°F) to 16°C (60.8°F) for the Riserva. The choice with white wines is simpler. The golden yellow but unobtrusive Tocai Italiano is known to most. It goes well with a pizza. Provide it is sufficiently chilled and drunk in moderation it can do little harm. Almost the same is true of the Pinot Bianco and the Chardonnay, although the latter is certainly no advertisement for such a world famous grape. Of much greater interest are the sultry and aromatic Pinots Grigio del Piave or elegant, characteristic and exceptionally pleasant Erduzzo del Piave. Drink at 8–10°C (46.6–50°F), but 10–12°C (50–53.6°F) for the Verduzzo and Pinot Grigio. Efosco dal Pedonculo Rosso is a pleasing and authentic wine. The unusual grape is known as Mondeuse in the French Savoie. Here it produces a wine that is intensely red, slightly tannic with a bitter finish but one that is rounded and filled with flavour. Drinking temperature is 12–14°C (53.6–57.2°F).

Other wines from Veneto include Colli Berici DOC, Colli Euganei DOC, Montello/Colli Asolani DOC, Breganze DOC, Bagnoli di Sopra/Bagnoli DOC, Lison-Pramaggiore DOC, and Lessini Durello DOC.

GARDA DOC

Wine from Veneto bears the denomination of Garda Orientale DOC, that from Lombardy just carries Garda DOC. The wine must be made from not less than 85% of the grapes indicated on the label. These are the well-known Pinot Bianco, Pinot Grigio, Chardonnay, Riesling Italico, Riesling Renano, and Sauvignon Blanc. These are all excellent wines. Drinking temperature is 8–10°C (46.4–50°F) for Sauvignon Blanc, Pinot Bianco, and Rieslings and 10–12°C (50–53.6°F) for Chardonnay and Pinot Grigio wines. Much more interesting to discover though are the Garganega, Trebbianello, and Cortese white wines. All three can be either dry or medium dry and they are fairly aromatic and filled with flavour. Drink at 10–12°C (50–53.6°F). With the red wines there are the essential Cabernets, Merlots, and Pinots Nero wines, which are just as good and as bad as elsewhere in the world. You may also encounter the authentic Marzemino and Corvina wines. These are both fresh, delightful, and fragrant. Drink at 12–14°C (53.6–57.2°F).

Finally there are also white Frizzante wines that are dry or medium dry and always fruity. Drinking temperature is 6–8°C (42.8–46.4°F).

Friuli-Venezia Giulia

The area is partially mountainous but the vineyards are concentrated in the green river valleys (Tagliamento and Isonzo) and on the sunny slopes. The climate is a favourable combination of mild maritime (the Adriatic) and harsh continental (the

Isonzo Chardonnay/Isonzo Pinot Nero.

Alps). The soil is mainly scree carried in the last ice age. Just as in Alsace and certain other northern Italian wine areas, Friuli is used as a generic name followed by the dominant grape used in its production.

COLLI ORIENTALI DEL FRIULI DOC

These wines are made north of Udine. Sauvignon Blanc and Chardonnay will quickly be encountered among the white wines. These are pleasant wines but not especially exciting. They make a fine aperitif or for drinking with fish and the same is true to a lesser extent of the widely available Pinot Bianco, Pinot Grigio, and Riesling Renano. These fresh and fruity wines, with a hint of spice in the case of the Pinot Grigio, are better with a meal than as aperitif. The Traminer Aromatico is very aromatic, extremely sensual, slightly harsh, and full bodied.

This wine is not suitable for drinking with fish, better with poultry, pork, or veal. The earlier wines are drunk at 8–10°C (46.4–50°F), the later ones at 10–12°C (50–53.6°F). The Tocai Friulano, Verduzzo Friulano, Ribolla Gialla, and Malvasia Istriana are far more exciting propositions than those previously mentioned. Drink them at 10–12°C (50–53.6°F). The fruity, sometimes dry, sometimes sweet Verduzzo Friulano is firm and can be slightly tannic. Drink at 10–12°C (50–53.6°F). The fresh and harmonious Ribolla Gialla is always dry. Drink at 10–12°C

(50–53.6°F). The sultry, spicy, aromatic, and full-bodied Malvasia Istriana demands substantial fish. Drink at 10–12°C (50–53.6°F). Ramondolo is made from Verduzzo and it is a delightful and intense golden colour. This wine is fruity and fulsome, sometimes with tannin and body. This wine is always slightly sweet to sweet and its minimum alcohol is 14%. Wines from the centre of the region may add Classico to the name. Drink at 8–10°C (46.4–50°F) for slightly sweet and 6–8°C (42.8–46.4°F) for sweet ones. Wines that are interesting and characteristic of Udine are Malvasia Istriana (pale golden tinged with green, attractive bouquet, dry and fine taste, drink at 10–12°C/50–53.6°F), Tocai Friulano (golden to lemon yellow, seductive nose, sultry, refined and elegant taste, drink at 10–12°C/50–53.6°F), and Verduzzo Friulano (golden, sensual bouquet and taste of fresh grapes, can be tannic, dry, slightly sweet to sweet, drink at 10–12°C/50–53.6°F for dry wines and 6–10°C/42.8–50°F for sweet ones with the colder range for the sweetest wines).

There are also excellent Frizzante and Spumante whites, usually made from Chardonnay and/or Pinot Bianco. There are both brut and semi-secco versions of these. Drink at 6–8°C (42.8–46.4°F).

The more or less mandatory Merlot, Cabernet Franc, and Cabernet Sauvignon can be found among the reds (the latter being a first class wine with vegetal

undertones and lots of fruit). The most enjoyable wine is the Refosco dal Peduncolo Rosso, which ismore representative. This is a full-bodied, elegant, fruity wine with distinctive but pleasing bitter note. Drink at 12–14°C (53.6–57.2°F) but a slightly warmer 14–16°C (57.2–60.8°F) for mature Riserva examples.

COLLI ORIENTALI DEL FRIULI DOC

These wines originate from the province of Udine where you find varietal wines of a specific grape. There are first class Pinot Bianco, Pinot Grigio, Sauvignon, Chardonnay, and Riesling Renano wines and excellent Traminer Aromatico, which is full-bodied, sultry, and has a very intense bouquet and taste. Drink at 8–10°C (46.4–50°F) except the Chardonnay, Pinot Grigio, and Traminer Aromatico (10–12°C/50–53.6°F).

The following wines are very typical of the region. Tocai Friulano: golden to lemon yellow, refined bouquet, fulsome and warm taste with discernible bitter almond note. Drink at 10–12°C (50–53.6°F). Verduzzo Friulano: golden with fulsome and very fruity taste of fresh grapes, can be slightly tannic, dry to medium dry or sweet. Drink at 10–12°C (50–53.6°F) for dry wines and 6–10°C (42.8–50°F) for the sweeter ones (chill the sweeter wines most). Ribolla Gialla: clear golden colour with a tinge of green, refined and elegant taste that is fresh and dry. Drink at 10–12°C (50–53.6°F). Malvasia Istriana: golden, herbal, with intriguing aromatic nose and taste. A full-bodied, rounded, and dry wine. Drink at 10–12°C (50–53.6°F). Ramandolo: an excellent Verduzzo Friulano wine that is intensely golden, very fruity, aromatic in bouquet and taste, fulsome but slightly tannic, but velvet smooth and luxuriantly sweet. It has at least 14% alcohol. Drink at 6–10°C (42.8–50°F) according to taste. Picolit: sweet to very sweet white wines from the native Picolit grape. These are refined, warm, and full-bodied wines. Drink at 6–8°C (42.8–46.4°F).The Rosato wines made from Merlot are particularly pleasant and delicious. Drink at 10–12°C (50–53.6°F). There are excellent Cabernet Sauvignon, Cabernet Franc, Cabernet (Franc and Sauvignon), Merlot, and Pinot Nero to choose from but for greater authenticity choose a Schippettino or Refosco dal Peduncolo Rosso. Both are wines from which much pleasure can be derived, that are high in fruit and of great character. They are full-bodied, warm, and smooth as velvet. The Refosco has a discernible bitter note. Drink at 12–14°C (53.6–57.2°F) but 14–16°C (57.2–60.8°F) for the older Riserva examples.

GRAVE DEL FRIULI DOC

There are many different varietal wines here from a specific grape and a few generic wines. These are made along the banks of the Tagliamento river in the province of Udine. Wines like the Colli Orientali Friulani (see that entry) are also to be found here. The white wines are made from Chardonnay, Pinot Bianco, Riesling Renano, Sauvignon Blanc, Pinot Grigio, Tocai Friulano, Traminer Aromatico, and

Verduzzo Friulano. The last four of these are usually the better wines. The Spumante versions of these wines are also of excellent quality. The Rosato is fresh, fruity, and unforced (and also available as a Frizzante). The red wine is made from either or both of the two Cabernets, Merlot, Pinot Nero, and Refosco dal Peduncolo Rosso.

COLLIO GORIZIANO/COLLIO DOC

This is unquestionably one of the best wine areas of Italy for white wines but the red too is of exceptionally high quality. The vineyards are sited on the hills (Collio) on the eastern side of the Judrio river, close to Gorizia. The ordinary Bianco is made from Ribolla Gialla, Malvasia Istriana, and Tocai Friulano, supplemented to a maximum of 20% as required with other local grapes. This wine is golden in colour, slightly aromatic, dry, refined, delicate, and harmonious. It makes an excellent aperitif. Drink at 8–10°C (46.4–50°F). The Pinot Bianco is pale gold in colour, slightly aromatic, and has a mild fresh taste with a hint of sweet almonds. Drink at 8–10°C (46.4–50°F). The Pinot Grigio is often golden but can have a coppery sheen. It has a very intense bouquet with very full juicy taste. Drink at 10–12°C (50–53.6°F). The Ribolla Gialla is intensely golden with a touch of green. The bouquet is excitingly simultaneously floral and fruity. This is a full-bodied dry wine that is lively and fresh. Drink at 10–12°C (50–53.6°F). The Sauvignon Blanc is paler in colour and has the most pronounced bouquet and taste. The experienced taster can detect vegetal undertones such as grass with a pinch of nutmeg, acacia honey, white blossom, and some herbal notes. The Collio Sauvignon Blanc is of excellent quality and very characteristic of both the grape and its terroir. Drink at 8–10°C (46.4–50°F). The Tocai Friulano is pure golden to golden yellow in colour with the odd hint of lemon yellow. The nose is very characteristic, delicate, and pleasant, the taste is herbal, and can include notes of bitter almond and other nuts. Drink at 10–12°C (50–53.6°F). The Traminer Aromatico here produces a golden yellow wine that is very aromatic with intense flavour. These wines improve with a few years ageing. Drinking temperature is 10–12°C (50–53.6°F). The Riesling Renano is golden to golden yellow with age. It has a very intense nose and taste that is refined and delicate. Drink at 10–12°C (50–53.6°F). The Riesling Italico is pale gold with a hint of green. This is an elegant, subtle wine. Drink at 10–12°C (50–53.6°F).

The Malvasia Istriana is pale gold, has a very fine and subtle nose, is smooth tasting and rounded with slight vegetal undertones. Drinking temperature is 10–12°C (50–53.6°F). The Collio Chardonnay is generally better than most other northern Italian Chardonnays. It is pale gold in colour, delicate, dry, full-bodied, has light floral notes, is smooth and very pleasant. Drink at 10–12°C (50–53.6°F).

The Müller-Thurgau is surprisingly delicious. Its colour is a fairly dark yellow with glints of green. The bouquet is characteristic (green apple and floral

notes) and the taste is dry, smooth and fulsome. Drinking temperature is 10–12°C (50–53.6°F).

The Collio Picolit is the rarest sweet wine from Italy and is perhaps unique among world wines. Picolit grapes grow in a peculiar manner. Natural section takes place among the growing grapes in an unusual way with few grapes achieving maturity. Most grapes fall off early or remain small and hard. The grapes that do develop contain extremely high concentrations of extract, aromatic and flavour substances. These grapes are then also harvested late so that the sun shrivels them to a certain extent, thereby further increasing the concentration of extract, sugars, aromatic and flavour substances. This Picolit bears some relationship to a Trockenbeerauslese from Germany or Austria. The colour is a deep rich golden yellow and the bouquet is seductive, sultry, and overwhelming. The taste is powerfully full and fruity, being strongly reminiscent of ripe fruit and ether (substantial alcohol), with the mellowness of honey and a prolonged aftertaste. Its strange manner of growth means that the Picolit grape produces very little wine and the late harvest reduces this further. Understandably the price of this nectar is not low should you ever have the chance to try it, which you should certainly do. Drink at 8–10°C (46.4–50°F).

The Collio Rosso wines are usually made from one of the Cabernets or Merlot. These are ruby-coloured wines with vegetal bouquet and smooth but lively taste. Drink at 12–14°C (53.6–57.2°F) but 14–16°C

Extremely rare Picolit.

(57.2–60.8°F) for Riserva wines. The other red wines are made from Cabernet Franc, Cabernet Sauvignon, Merlot, and Pinot Nero. The first three have their characteristic vegetal undertones which clearly differentiate them from a Bordeaux. The taste is fulsome and powerful but dry and harmonious. The Merlot from here often has a slightly increased bitter note in its finish. The Pinot Nero has a very smooth taste that is filled with flavour. Drinking temperature is 14–16°C (57.2–60.8°F).

ISONZO/ISONZO DEL FRIULI DOC
Here too we can talk about exceptional white wines and excellent reds. The wine growing area is on the banks of the Isonzo river close to Gorizia. The vineyards extend as far as the border with Slovenia. The difference in taste between the previous Collio wines and these from Isonzo is not very great and the wines are similar. The area produces a generic Bianco from Tocai Friulano, Malvasia Istriana, Pinot Bianco, and Chardonnay. These whites can be dry to slightly sweet but are always remarkably fresh and often are slightly tannic. The other white wines are made using Pinot Bianco, Pinot Grigio, Tocai Friulano, Verduzzo Friulano, Traminer Aromatico, Riesling Renano, Riesling Italico, plus of course Sauvignon Blanc and Chardonnay. There is also a sublime Spumante made from Pinot Bianco supplemented with Pinot Nero and Chardonnay. Drink at generally 8–10°C (46.4–50°F) but 10–12°C (50–53.6°F) for the Chardonnay, Traminer, Tocai, Verduzzo, and Pinot Grigio. The ordinary Rosso is made from Merlot, Cabernet Franc, and Cabernet Sauvignon, supplemented with some Pinot Nero or Refosco. There are numerous styles and taste for these Isonzo Rosso wines.

The best local red wines are made from the popular French Cabernets (Sauvignon and Franc), Merlot, and Pinot Nero. These wines are excellent. The Cabernet wines have slight vegetal undertones and there is a substantial bitter note to the Pinot Nero. Drinking temperature is 14–16°C (57.2–60.8°F).

The most surprising wines are the young and fruity and very aromatic Franconia, and the full-bodied and powerful Refosco dal Peduncolo Rosso. Drink at 14–16°C (57.2–60.8°F) for the Franconia and

Isonzo wines.

Isonzo Merlot/Isonzo Pinot Grigio.

16–17°C (60.8–62.6°F) for the Refosco. The local Passito is an excellent choice for an authentic wine.

FRIULI AQUILEIA DOC
This is the southernmost Friuli wine area. The vineyards stretch from the Adriatic coast to the border with Isonzo. Very worthy white wines are made here from Pinot Bianco, Tocai Friulano, Chardonnay, Pinot Grigio, Riesling Renano, Traminer, Sauvignon Blanc, and Verduzzo Friulano; fresh and fruity Rosato wines from Merlot, the Cabernets, and Refosco, plus excellent reds from Merlot, Cabernet Franc, and Cabernet Sauvignon. The Refosco dal Peduncolo Rosso is the most exciting and authentic of the wines (see also Collio and Isonzo).

Emiglia-Romagna

Italy resembles a boot with a wide open thigh piece. We are now leaving the upper part of that boot and moving towards its middle. Emilia-Romagna is south of Lombardy and Veneto, extending from Liguria to the Adriatic. Emilia-Romagna is separated from Tuscany and the Marche in the south by the Apennines. For Italy, this region is remarkably flat and this gives the local wines a character all of their own among Italian wines. The name of Emilia-Romagna probably says little to most people about the region of origin of these wines but the individual vineyards are readily pin-pointed. These lie between Piacenza and Parma, around Reggio and Modena, and surrounding Bologna, and finally in the triangle formed by Ravenna, Forli, and Rimini. The main city of Emilia-Romagna is Bologna, so famed in culinary terms.

COLLI PIACENTINI DOC
The wines from the southern area of Piacenza have enjoyed fame for a long time. White and red wines of excellent quality are produced here with a clear authenticity that make them the finest wines of Italy. The most interesting white wines from here are not the acceptable Sauvignon Blanc, Chardonnay, and

Isonzo white and rosé.

Sublime Spumante.

Passito from Collio/Isonzo.

fresh in taste and also comes in still, slightly sparkling, and sparkling versions. Drinking temperature is 10°C (50°F) for the dry wines, to 6–8°C (42.8–46.4°F) for the sweet ones.

ORTRUGO
These surprising wines contain a minimum of 85% Ortrugo grapes and they are golden with glints of green. The nose is subtle and fairly characteristic while the taste is juicy but dry with clearly discernible bitter almond in the finish. These wines are available as still, slightly sparkling, and sparkling versions. Drinking temperature is 10°C (50°F). There are a number of well-made generic Rosso wines among the reds as well as outstanding ones of Cabernet Sauvignon and Pinot Nero. These wines though are equally tasty as other wines of these grapes and are therefore not representative of the area. The following wines are far more interesting.

BARBERA
A ruby-coloured wine that is quite characteristic and quite aromatic in nose and taste. It is juicy, dry, slightly tannic, and quite unruly through carbonic acid when young. Drinking temperature is 14–16°C (57.2–60.8°F).

BONARDA
This wine is made from at least 85% Bonarda Piemontse grapes. It too is ruby red with a very aromatic bouquet and slightly tannic taste. It is dry,

Aquileia.

Pinot Grigio wines. The pale golden Sauvignon is delicate, intense, and fairly characteristic. Its taste is freshly acidic, harmonious, with a slight sparkle to tingle the tongue. Drink this Sauvignon young at 8–10°C (46.4–50°F). The equally pale golden Chardonnay often has a glint of green. Its bouquet is fruity and refined and the taste is fulsome, fresh, harmonious, and dry. This wine too often has a slight tingle of a sparkle. Drink at 10–12°C (50–53.6°F). The Pinot Grigio is also golden but can have pink glints and its distinctively aromatic nose is refined. The taste is fulsome, harmonious, and dry and here too there may be a hint of bubbles. A true Spumante version is also available. Drink at 10–12°C (50–53.6°F). The following white wines from this area are far more interesting.

TREBBIANINO VAL TREBBIA
This wine is made from Ortrugo grapes, supplemented with Trebbiano and/or Sauvignon Blanc (better choice is the Ortrugo-Trebbiano). This pleasing golden wine has a relatively modest nose. There is a diversity of styles and tastes from dry to sweet and from still, through hint of bubbles, to truly sparkling. Drink at 8–12°C (46.4–53.6°F) with the cooler range for the sweeter wines.

MALVASIA
This is a very characteristic and intensely aromatic wine which can be dry, medium dry, or sweet. It is

medium dry, or sweet and may be still or slightly sparkling. Drinking temperature is 14–16°C (57.2–60.8°F) for the dry examples, otherwise 10–12°C (50–53.6°F) for the sweet ones.

COLLI DI PARMA DOC

The vineyards here are in the relatively low hills (below 400 metres/1,312 feet) that surround Parma. Although none of the wines from here are truly outstanding they enjoy a fairly well-developed reputation. There are four different types of wine from here.

COLLI DI PARMA ROSSO

This wine is made from at least 60% Barbera grapes supplemented with Bonarda Piemontese and/or Croatina. The colour is ruby and the wine has a pleasing fresh and fruity nose, a dry and harmonious taste that may be accompanied by a little touch of carbonic acid. Drinking temperature is around 14–16°C (57.2–60.8°F).

COLLI DI PARMA SAUVIGNON

This is a very acceptable Sauvignon Blanc that is delicate, refined, and aromatic. The taste is dry with fresh acidity but harmonious with a slight bitter note and occasionally a slight hint of a sparkle. Drinking temperature is 8–10°C (46.4–50°F).

COLLI DI PARMA MALVASIA ASCIUTTO/SECCO

The best Malvasia wines are wholly made from Malvasia di Candia Aromatica but there are less refined types in which the Malvasia is supplemented to a maximum of 15% with Moscato grapes. Depending on the style of wine it may be pale to intense golden in colour.

The nose is very aromatic and characteristic of Malvasia grapes. The taste is also characteristic, fresh, and harmonious. Some of these wines are offered with a touch of carbonic acid gas or even as a Frizzante. There is also a Spumante of this Malvasia. Drinking temperature is 10–12°C (50–53.6°F).

COLLI DI PARMA MALVASIA AMABILE

This wine shares characteristics with the Malvasia Asciutto except that this one is sweet. There are also Frizzante and Spumante versions of this wine. Drinking temperature is 6–8°C (42.8–46.4°F) for the sparkling wines and 8–10°C (46.4–50°F) for the still wines.

LAMBRUSCO REGGIANO DOC

This wine is made from Lambrusco Salamino, Lambrusco Montericco, Lambrusco Marani, and Lambrusco Maestri grapes with a maximum 15% Ancelotta. The wine is pink to ruby red and has a fine but persistent sparkle. The nose is fruity and vegetal and quite characteristic. The taste may be dry or sweet but is fresh and very light. These Lambrusco wines are best drunk while still young. Drinking temperature is 10–12°C (50–53.6°F).

BIANCO DI SCANDIANO DOC

Within the Lambrusco Reggiano wine district there is an enclave of white wine around the village of Scandiano. These slightly sparkling to sparkling white wines are made from Sauvignon Blanc. This is a very surprising wine which is very aromatic, fresh and fulsome.

There are dry (secco), medium dry (semi-secco), and sweet (amabile) versions. Drink the secco as an aperitif or with cold dishes. The semi-secco combines well with creamy sauces with fish or with white meat in fruity sauces.

The amabile is best reserved for serving with fruit desserts. Drinking temperature is 9–10°C (48.2–50°F) for the secco/semi-secco or 6–8°C (42.8–46.4°F) for the amabile.

LAMBRUSCO MODENESI DOC

The area around Modena makes three types of DOC wines.

LAMBRUSCO SALAMINTO DI SANTA CROCE

This wine is made from no less than 90% Lambrusco Salamino and the other Lambruschi from the area north of Modena. This wine is an attractive ruby red and has a lively and rumbustious sparkle.

The bouquet and taste are very characteristic and especially pleasant. There are both dry and sweet variants of this wine. Both are very fresh and harmonious. Drinking temperature is 12–14°C (53.6–57.2°F) for the dry wines and 10–12°C (50–53.6°F) for the sweet ones.

LAMBRUSCO DI SORBARA

Perhaps the best-known of all the Lambruschi, but certainly not always the best. It is still possible to encounter gassy wines that have more to do with lemonade than a true Lambrusco. The better wines are made with 60% Lambrusco di Sorbara and 40% Lambrusco Salamino. These are ruby red and have a sparkle fighting to get out of the bottle. The nose is very pleasing and in the true wines is reminiscent of wild violets.

The taste may be dry (asciutto) or sweet (amabile), but is always fresh and fulsome. According to the Italians the correct temperature is 14–16°C (57.2–60.8°F) but northern Europeans generally prefer 12–14°C (53.6–57.2°F), especially for the sweet wines.

LAMBRUSCO GRASPAROSSA DI CASTELVETRO

This Lambrusco originates from the south and east of Modena. It is made using 85% Lambrusco Grasparossa supplemented with other Lambruschi. The ruby red colour is broken by glints of purple. The fine bubbles are very lively.

The bouquet is very aromatic and the taste is dry to sweet but always fresh and fulsome. Drinking temperature is 14–16°C (57.2–60.8°F) for the dry wines and 10–12°C (50–53.6°F) for the sweet ones.

Colli Bolognesi DOC

As the name indicates, these wines come from the gently undulating hills to the south and west of Bologna. Drink at 8–10°C (46.4–50°F). The local Sauvignon makes a fine aperitif. It is fresh, dry, slightly aromatic, with a fulsome flavour. Drinking temperature is 8–10°C (46.4–50°F). The Pinot Bianco is delicate and refined, fresh, warm, and harmonious. This is a very successful wine from the usually so neutral Pinot Bianco. Drink at 10–12°C (50–53.6°F). The Chardonnay is very acceptable yet not entirely convincing. Drinking temperature is 10–12°C (50–53.6°F). The Riesling Italico is far more exciting than the Chardonnay, possessing a much finer bouquet and a fresher, fuller, and warmer taste. Drinking temperature is 8–10°C (46.4–50°F). The Pignoletto made from grapes of this name is quite a different type of wine of pale colouring, often tinged with green and with a fine and delicate nose and fresh, warm, and harmonious taste that may be either dry or sweet. This type of wine is available as either a still or slightly sparkling (Frizzante) version. Drinking temperature is 6–8°C (42.8–46.4°F) for the sweet wine and 9–11°C (48.2–51.8°F) for the dry still and sparkling wines.

For red wines there is a choice from light, vegetal Merlot (dry, juicy and harmonious), full-bodied and harsh Barbera, or the equally vegetal Cabernet Sauvignon. There are also Riserva versions of the Barbera and Cabernet Sauvignon wines of high quality. Drinking temperature is 14–16°C (57.2–60.8°F) for a Merlot, young Barbera, or Cabernet Sauvignon and 16–17°C (60.8–62.6°F) for the Riserva wines.

Bosco Eliceo DOC

This wine region lies on the Adriatic coast to the north of Ravenna. There are two types of white wine and two types of red made here.

The ordinary Bianco is made from at least 70% Trebbiano Romagnolo together with Sauvignon Blanc or Malvasia Bianca di Candia. This pale

Colli Bolognesi Merlot.

Pignoletto Superiore Colli Bolognesi.

Pignoletto Frizzante Colli Bolognesi.

golden wine has a light and mellow nose and pleasant mellow taste. It is available as dry or slightly sweet and as a still or lightly sparkling wine. It is certainly not a wine for laying down. Drinking temperature is 8–10°C (46.4–50°F). The Sauvignon wine (not less than 85%) is supplemented with Trebbiano Romagnolo. This wine has a fairly modest bouquet and taste but is warm, velvet smooth, and harmonious in either dry or slightly sweet variants. It makes an excellent aperitif. Drinking temperature is 8–10°C (46.4–50°F). The first of the types of red wine is made from Merlot. This produces an acceptable wine with typical vegetal undertones that is dry, juicy, harmonious, and fresh. Drinking temperature is 14–16°C (57.2–60.8°F). The other red wine is made from Fortana grapes and bears this name. It is a fairly sturdy wine that is quite high in tannin but juicy and fresh. It is very much a wine to be drunk while young. Drinking temperature is 10–12°C (50–53.6°F).

Vini di Romagna DOCG/DOC

This is another generic wine denomination that produces several very special wines: three white wines and two reds. The area is in the extreme south of Emilia-Romagna and extends from south of Bologna by way of Forli to the famous seaside resort of Rimini.

ALBANA DI ROMAGNA DOCG

This is the only DOCG wine of Emilia-Romagna. The wine is made from the Albana grape and may be made in the provinces of Bologna, Forli, or even Ravenna (a small enclave within Bosco Eliceo). In its DOCG form these wines are available as dry (secco), slightly sweet (amabile), sweet (dolce), and liquorous (passito) variants. The secco is a pale golden colour with a light yet sublime bouquet and fresh, warm, and harmonious taste with a little tannin. Drinking temperature is 8–10°C (46.4–50°F). The amabile and dolce wines are somewhat darker in colour to golden yellow with age. Here too the nose is rather more subtle and elegant than powerful. The taste is very high in fruit and is luxuriant. Drink at 6–8°C (42.8–46.4°F).

The passito is darker still, ranging from golden yellow to amber and the bouquet is more intense, intriguing, and stunning. The taste is extremely fulsome, velvet smooth, and more or less sweet, depending on the maker, the year, and the type. Drinking temperature is 6–8°C (42.8–46.4°F). There is also a Romagna Albana Spumante of good quality but this wine only bears the DOC predicate.

Trebbiano di Romagna DOC

This wine also derives its name from the Trebbiano grape which is the majority grape used in its making. The wine is produced in the area around Bologna, Ravenna, and Forli.

The colour of these wines is pale golden to a slightly more intense gold and the nose is fresh and pleasing. The taste is dry and harmonious. There are still, Frizzante, and Spumante versions of these wines. Drinking temperature is 8–10°C (46.4–50°F).

PAGADEBIT DI ROMAGNA DOC

This is a very exciting wine made from not less than 85% Bombino Bianco grapes in the area around Forli and Ravenna. The pale golden colour is hardly striking but in contrast the nose is a strong feature of this wine and is reminiscent of may blossom. It is soft, subtle, and very seductive.

The wine can be dry to slightly sweet but either type is well-balanced by the fine acidity. The taste is refined and extremely pleasant with clear vegetal undertones. There is also a Frizzante version. Drinking temperature is 6–8°C (42.8–46.4°F) for the slightly sweet and 8–10°C (46.4–50°F) for the dry wines.

SANGIOVESE DI ROMAGNA DOC

This red is made from Sangiovese grapes in the vicinity of Forli, Bologna, and Ravenna. The ruby red colour also has traces of purple. The bouquet is very subtle and reminiscent of wild violets. The taste is truly dry and well balanced with a characteristic slight bitter note in its finish. Drink this wine within four years of its harvest. There are also Superiore (at least 12% alcohol) and Riserva (at least a further two years ageing) versions. Drinking temperature is

14–16°C (57.2–60.8°F) but 16–17°C (60.8–62.6°F) for the Riserva wines.

CAGNINA DI ROMAGNA DOC

This is another exciting wine made from the Refosco grape that is known in these parts as Terrano. These wines are produced in the area around Forli and Ravenna.

The colour is mauve to purple and there is a characteristic intense bouquet combined with a fulsome sweet and sour taste that is velvet smooth even with the often strong presence of tannin. Drinking temperature is 6–8°C (42.8–46.4°F).

Toscane (Tuscany)

Tuscan wine making

The vineyards of Tuscany are spread throughout the area, extending from north of Pisa to Florence (Firenze), from Sienna to Montalcino and Montepulciano, from south of Livorno to the border with Latium and Umbria, and finally to the island of Elba. In addition to the famous wines (Chianti, Brunello, and Vino Nobile) there are countless less well-known wines waiting to be discovered. With the prices of some of the best known Tuscan wines going through the roof it is well worth searching in relatively unknown areas. The wines from the area around the little town of Lucca are reasonably

Sangiovese di Romagna.

177

priced for their quality. A search through Tuscan wines is rewarded by authenticity and character in the wines. Our journey through Tuscany starts in the north and we gradually travel southwards.

COLLINE LUCCHESI DOC

The vineyards of this area are sited on the hills between Lucca and Montecarlo. The area around Lucca is well-known for the superb olive oil and excellent white and red wines. Unfortunately these wines are only available in limited quantities and the demand is huge.

The Bianco delle Colline Lucchesi (also known as Colline Lucchesi Bianco) is made from 50–70% Trebbiano Toscano, 5–15% Greco or Grecchetto, 5–15% Vermentino Bianco, and not more than 5% Malvasia grapes. This Bianco is a pale golden colour and its nose is very subtle and elegant. The taste is quite dry, fulsome, and harmonious. The better wine houses also produce a few crus bearing the names of their estates. These top wines are extremely rare and of unparalleled quality. Serve the ordinary Bianco as an aperitif. The better crus should be reserved for the very best fish dishes.

There are also very typical wines made from Vermentino grapes but these bear an IGT (controlled name of origin) rather than a DOC nomination. The quality of this wine is certainly not of lesser standard. Drinking temperature is 10–12°C (50–53.6°F). The Rosso delle Colline Lucchesi (Colline Lucchesi Rosso) is a full-bodied ruby to granite red wine with a fairly subtle but very pleasing

nose. The taste is mellow, fulsome, well-balanced, and rounded.

Most of the wines, like the white, have a fairly high level of alcohol, around 12.5–13%. The better cru wines are only produced in limited volume. They differentiate themselves from the others with their wonderful bouquets (such as iris) and their fuller taste. Drink at 14–16°C (57.2–60.8°F) to 16–17°C (60.8–62.6°F) for the crus. There are of course some 'super Tuscan' wines made here that are of excellent quality but which do not meet the required legal proportions for the grapes they contain. These wines are 'downgraded' to IGT wines but for a long time they were only permitted to call themselves table wine (vino da tavola).

A new IGT classification was introduced in 1992 and the first wines with this category on their label are just reaching the market, while the older ones continue to be called vino da tavola. A typical example of one of these new super Tuscan wines from the area of Lucca is the I Pampini of Fattoria Fubbiano. The same wine house also produces the extremely rare super Tuscan white Del Boschetto Bianco.

CARMIGNANO DOCG

This wine was once part of the top Chiantis. After many years of relentless lobbying and continuing above all to make excellent wine, the inhabitants of the small town of Carmignano managed first to see their pampered child elevated to its own DOC in

Colline Lucchesi Bianco (white).

Colline Lucchesi Rosso (red).

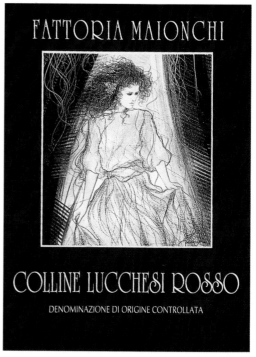

grape and today these contain 75-100% of this variety. The local Vin Santo also enjoys great fame in Italy. The fresh Bianco Pisano has a very subtle taste. Drinking temperature is 8–10°C (46.4–50°F). The Vin Santo is amber coloured, aromatic, fulsome, mellow, and sweet. Drinking temperature is 6–8°C (42.8–46.4°F).

CHIANTI DOCG
Chianti and Tuscany have been inseparable from each other for centuries. Chianti was promoted to DOCG status in 1996 but not every 'Chianti' is permitted to promote itself as such and must first prove itself.

Only the better wines are permitted to bear the DOCG predicate while the others may use Colli dell' Etruria Centrale DOC on the label. Chianti DOCG only originates from seven defined areas: the central zone where they make Classico and the six hills around known as Colli: Arezzo, Florence, Pisa, Sienna, Montalbano, and Rufina. There is also a separate area in the neighbourhood of Empoli, but unlike the other areas, this one does not bear its locality name on the label. The wines from the central zone are also permitted to use the famous black cockerel emblem on the neck of the bottle in addition to the term Classico. This wine is only allowed to be harvested and made in the local authority areas of Greve in Chianti, Radda in

Carmignano DOCG.

1975 and then eventually in 1990 to join the elite ranks of DOCG wines. The charm of this famous wine is probably created by the combination of the noble French Cabernet grapes and the mischievous and unruly Italian grapes.

The Carmignano uses 45–70% Sangiovese, 10–20 Canaiolo Nero, and 6–15% Cabernet Franc and Cabernet Sauvignon. Just as with Chianti, a very small amount of white grapes may also be added. These are a maximum 10% of Trebbiano Toscano, Canaiolo Bianco, and Malvasia. A further important factor in the quality of these wines is the fairly low yield (in Italian terms). The wine is a very intense and clear ruby red which takes on touches of granite red with age. The bouquet is wonderful, intense yet subtle, with a hint of wild violets, and very seductive. The taste too is intense and fulsome, smooth, and very elegant.

The ordinary Carmignano (marked annata and the year) must be at least two years old, the Riserva at least three. The minimum alcohol content is 12.5%. Carmignano is a perfect wine for keeping. Drinking temperature is 14–16°C (57.2–60.8°F) for the Annata and 16–17°C (60.8°F 62.6°F) for a Riserva.

BIANCO PISANO DI SAN TORPÈ DOC
This wine has been a DOC since 1980. The area is to the south east of Pisa. Outstanding white wines have been made for centuries from the Trebbiano

Chianti, Gaiole in Chianti, Castellina in Chianti, and parts of Barberino Val d'Elsa, Castelnuovo Berardenga, Poggibonsi, San Casciano Val di Pesa, and Tavarnelle Val di Pesa.

Chianti Classico.

CHIANTI (CLASSICO) DOCG
The basic grape for this famous wine is the Sangiovese grape (75-90%), supplemented with Canaiolo (5-10%), and the white Trebbiano Toscano, and Malvasia (5-10%). Only 5% of white grapes may be added to Chianti Classico. The white grapes are used to slightly reduce the harsh tannin that can be associated with the Sangiovese grape. A good Chianti is a very intense and clear ruby red colour. With age this tends towards granite red. The nose is very pleasing, full, and delicate. Connoisseurs can detect subtle notes of violets in it. Other typical characteristics include cherry, blackberry, red fruit, pepper, herbs, liquorice, and vanilla. The taste is certainly dry, fresh, and juicy. This wine is often somewhat tannic in its early years but with age of a few years the taste mellows and becomes fuller and more rounded. Chianti wines can vary widely depending on where they come from and how they are made.

The light, cheerful, and unforced Chiantis are best drunk young when they are at their best. More traditional style Chiantis are more full-bodied and require some rest. The superb Riservas are at least three years old before being sold and can happily be left to age further. Drink a modern-style young Chianti during a meal at 12–14°C (53.6–57.2°F) and the others at 16–17°C (60.8–62.6°F).

VIN SANTO DEL CHIANTI CLASSICO DOC
This denomination for just one sweet wine is unique in Italy. This Vin Santo has a long and interesting history like its fellow wines. Only the very best grapes are selected to make Vin Santo and these are spread out to dry on straw mats or in small containers and left either out of doors or in well-ventilated attics for a period of one year. Following this the grapes are pressed and the young wine is then left to mature in small casks or caratelli.
The basic grapes for white Vin Santo are Trebbiano Toscano and Malvasia. For the Rosato Vin Santo del Chianti Classico Occhio di Pernice (Occhio di Pernice is 'partridge eyes', referring to the colour of the wine) the principal grape is Sangiovese. Both wines can be either more or less dry or sweet. These are astonishingly good wines that are mellow, full-bodied, aromatic, and all sharing the same characteristics. Drinking temperature is 10–12°C (50–53.6°F) for dry wines and 6–8°C (42.8–46.4°F) for sweet ones.

COLLI DELL' ETRURIA CENTRALE DOC
Many wines that do not reach the required standard for Chianti DOCG may be classified as Colli dell' Etruria Centrale DOC. It would be an injustice though to merely dismiss this recently created DOC as a receptacle for poor Chianti wines. There are great wines made within this DOC that do not meet the stipulated proportions of grapes. Just as with Colli Lucchesi some wine makers steadfastly refuse to choose solely from the four mandatory grape varieties. They believe that the combination of Sangiovese with the Cabernets (Sauvignon and Franc) delivers much better results. This was absolutely not permitted and hence until recently the 'super Tuscan' wines were downgraded to vino da tavola or table wine. This was unfair for wines that are far above average in terms of their quality. Now the growers and makers can choose to use the denomination of Colli dell' Etruria Centrale DOC for which a higher price can more easily be attained. That said, not all wines from this DOC are 'super Tuscans'.
The Colli dell' Etruria Centrale Bianco is made from not less than 50% Trebbiano Toscano, supplemented with no more than 50% Chardonnay, Pinot Bianco, Pinot Grigio, Vernaccia di San Gimignano, Malvasia, or Sauvignon. These whites are generally fresh, fruity, juicy, and very light. Drinking temperature is 8–10°C (46.4–50°F).
The Rosato and Rosso wines may be made from a minimum 50% Sangiovese, and not more than 50% Cabernet Sauvignon, Cabernet Franc, Merlot, Pinot Nero, Ciliegiolo, and Canaiolo. These allows the wine maker full room for personal expression from light wine to macho bully boy wines. All these wines contain substantial fruit and freshness. Drinking

temperature is 10–12°C (50–53.6°F) for a Rosato, 12-14°C (53.6–57.2°F) for a Rosso, and 16–17°C (60.8–62.6°F) for a 'super Tuscan'.

The same area also produces an intensely aromatic and wonderful Vin Santo. Drinking temperature is 6–8°C (42.8–46.4°F) through to 10–12°C (50–53.6°F) according to personal preference.

VERNACCIA DI SAN GIMIGNANO DOCG

This is another top Italian wine. Superb wines have been made with the Vernaccia grape for centuries in Tuscany and the makers of this Vernaccia wine have not rested on their laurels since being granted DOCG recognition. Constant efforts are made to develop and improve the quality both in the vineyard and with the wine making equipment. San Gimignano is outside the Classico zone for Chianti. The wine is quite pale when young but deepens towards golden with age. The bouquet is persistent, elegant, fresh, yet subtle. The taste is certainly dry, fresh, well-balanced, and astonishingly charming. A slight bitter note can be discerned in the finish. There are also Riserva quality wines that must be aged for an additional years. This wine makes an exceptionally tasting and chic aperitif. Drinking temperature is 10–12°C (50–53.6°F).

VINO NOBILE DI MONTEPULCIANO DOCG

This Vino Nobile is one of the top three denominated wines of Tuscany, and one of Italy's best-known wines. The vineyards are situated to the south west of Sienna, around the small community of Montepulciano, at heights ranging from 250 to 600 metres (656 to 1,968 feet). Montepulciano's soil consists chiefly of sedimentary layers. This 'noble' wine from Montepulciano has a long and rich history although the name was in danger of being pushed into the shadows by the success and popularity of Chianti. Steps to ensure the revival and survival of Vino Nobile were only taken with recent decades. Considerable money and time has been spent on renovating both the vineyards and wine making equipment. This was rewarded in 1980 with Italy's top DOCG denomination. The basis for this sublime red wine is 60–80% Sangiovese grapes (known locally as Prugnolo) and 10–20% Canaiolo Nero. A maximum of 10% of other blue or even white grapes such as Trebbiano Toscano can be added to these two base grapes. Vino Nobile's strength does not merely lie in the grapes used and the soil but also in the relatively low yield (in Italian terms). Vino Nobile wine is usually granite red, sometimes but not always intense, with occasional orange glints as the wine ages. The aroma of the wine is intense, sublime, yet subtle, evoking whole bunches of violets. The taste is fulsome, rounded, and can be quite tannic when young. This is never a light wine since the minimum alcohol must 12.5% and this is considerably exceeded. The wine is best decanted into a broad carafe or port decanter a quarter of an hour before drinking. This permits the wine to breathe and to develop its bouquet. Drinking temperature is 15–16°C (59–60.8°F) when

Vino Nobile di Montepulciano DOCG.

young (if you must) but better when mature at 16–18°C (60.8–64.4°F).

ROSSO DI MONTEPULCIANO DOC

This wine is kin to the Vino Nobile di Montepulciano. The name is somewhat confusing especially if one bears in mind other wines with similar sounding names such as Brunello di Montalcino and Rosso di Montalcino. The difference between the DOC and DOCG wines will be apparent though once tasted. This Rosso di Montepulciano originates from the same wine area as the Vino Nobile. The grapes used are also the same 60–80% Sangiovese (Prugnolo) with other blue grapes and addition of some white. The difference is in the yield per hectare from the vines. The younger and vigorous vines produce grapes used for the Rosso di Montepulciano while the older or less prolific vines are reserved for Vino Nobile.

The Rosso di Montepulciano therefore does not have the same concentration and power as its relative. This can even be seen in the colour difference for this wine is a moderately intense ruby red. The bouquet is almost as seductive as that of Vino Nobile and the suggestion of violets is there too. The taste is dry, well-balanced, and often slightly tannic. This less concentrated wine is also lower in alcohol. Drinking temperature is 14–16°C (57.2–60.8°F).

BRUNELLO DI MONTALCINO DOCG

Yet another giant of a wine from Tuscany, and perhaps the best DOCG wine of Italy. The little town of Montalcino is situated to the south west of Montepulciano. The geology here too consists chiefly of sedimentary layers. The history of Brunello is much more recent than the other great Tuscan wines. The great honour and first official DOCG recognition came in 1980. The soul of this wine is the Sangiovese Grosso grape that is known locally as Brunello. The vines are deliberately pruned short to reduced the yield. A Brunello may not be sold before its fifth year and a Riserva not before its sixth year following the relevant vintage. This guarantees impeccable quality. The wine is intensely ruby red and clear but tends towards granite red with age. The bouquet is very intense, aromatic, and is reminiscent of ripe red fruit with a hint of spice and wood (vanilla). The Riserva wines also have aromas of roasted coffee or cocoa and liquorice. The taste is a full one that is powerful yet mellow and warm. The minimum alcohol is 12.5% but most wines are more like 13.5%. The 'ordinary' Brunello is fruitier than a Riserva while these more mature wines are more spicy. It is well worth decanting this wine at least an hour before it is to be drunk into a broad-necked carafe. Drinking temperature is 16–18°C (60.8–64.4°F).

ROSSO DI MONTALCINO DOC

This lesser kin of the Brunello was granted DOC status in 1983. Since that time things have continued to look up for Rosso di Montalcino. The wines originate from the same vineyards as the Brunello and from the same types of grapes. Here too the wine uses 100% Brunello grapes (Sangiovese Grosso) but the yield per hectare is slightly higher with the Rosso di Montalcino than with the Brunello and there is no mandatory four to five years ageing before sale.

Hence you may encounter some young wines of this type for sale but the better wines (such as those from the famous house of Banfi) are aged in casks of French oak for at least one year. Rosso di Montalcino is certainly not a light wine. This ruby red wine, with its subtle nose of red fruit has a powerful taste that is fulsome, rounded, and warm (more than 13% alcohol). The best wines often have an undertone of herbs and spices and are very high in tannin when young. Drinking temperature is 16–17°C (60.8–62.6°F).

BOLGHERI DOC

This area is close to the Mediterranean coast in the west of Tuscany, between Montescudaio and Massa Marittima. It was famous for many years for its sublime rosé wines but this was overtaken about fifteen years ago by the 'super Tuscan' Sassicaia, which is one of the best and the most expensive wines of Italy.

Because of the stifling bureaucracy of the Italian wine laws, this wine was formerly merely classified as vino da tavola. Now it may be sold as Bolgheri

Brunello di Montalcino DOCG.

Sassicaia DOC, because Sassicaia has been recognised as a sub zone within the area of the Bolgheri denomination. The Bolgheri Bianco is made from 10–70% of Trebbiano Toscano, Vermentino or Sauvignon Blanc. The wide proportional tolerance of these three wines means that countless different variations are available of these wines. Wines in which one of these grapes forms more than 85% of the total are permitted to use the name of the relevant grape on the label in addition to Bolgheri. All these wines are fresh and dry, juicy, and elegant. Drinking temperature is 8–10°C (46.4–50°F).

The Bolgheri Rosato is still the most delicious rosé of not only Italy but the entire Mediterranean region. Today this wine is made using Cabernet Sauvignon, Merlot, and Sangiovese grapes which result in some very exciting blends. Drinking temperature is 10–12°C (50–53.6°F). In addition to this Rosato a Vin Santo Occhio di Perdice (partridge eye Vin Santo rosé) is also produced using Sangiovese and Malvasia Nera. This wine has a very intense taste and is remarkably aromatic. The Bolgheri Rosso, like the Rosato, is made from 10–80% Cabernet Sauvignon, a maximum 70% Merlot, and not more than 70% Sangiovese. This leaves a wide choice of different blends open to the wine maker so that discovering these wines can be exciting. Drinking temperature is 14–16°C (57.2–60.8°F).

The Bolgheri Sassicaia is a totally different story. This top class wine must contain at least 80% Cabernet Sauvignon. The remaining grapes may be Merlot and/or Sangiovese. The yield per hectare permitted for the Sassicaia wine is considerably lower than for an ordinary Bolgheri Rosso. This ensures a powerful, full-bodied wine with lots of extract and great potential for ageing. It is good to know that these Sassicaia wines must be cask aged in oak for at least two years and then spend at least a further five years after bottling before they can be drunk. It goes without saying that this wine, which is probably Italy's best red, is somewhat expensive but it is well worth it. This wine combines hot-blooded Italian temperament with the civilised elegance of a grand cru from the Médoc. The colour is a deep ruby red and the nose is very aromatic with a hint of herbs. The taste is intense, fulsome, rounded, velvet smooth, warm, and tremendously sensual. Every true lover of wine should try this wine at least once in their life. Decant the wine in plenty of time before drinking into a broad-necked carafe. Drinking temperature is 18°C (64.4°F).

ELBA DOC

This is the final Tuscan denomination and certainly not the worst. Excellent white, rosé, and red wines are made on the island of Elba off the coast of Tuscany. It is surprising to discover here such authentic wines still made with native grapes. The island is perhaps best known as the place to which Napoleon was first exiled. The French and the Tuscans introduced grape vines to the island and these provide an exciting array of different types and tastes. The fresh, light, and elegant Elba Bianco uses 80–100% Trebbiano Toscano (known here as Procanico). Drinking temperature is 8–10°C (46.4–50°F). The fuller-bodied and more intense Ansonica white made from not less than 85% Ansonica grapes is much more interesting and authentic in style though. This wine can range from dry to slightly sweet. Drinking temperature is 10–12°C (50–53.6°F). A fine Passito wine is also made from Ansonica grapes. Drinking temperature is 6–10°C (42.8–50°F) according to preference.

The Trebbiano (Procanico) and Malvasia Bianca are also used to make an excellent, full-bodied, rounded, and velvet smooth Vin Santo. Drinking temperature is 6–10°C (42.8–50°F) according to preference (the sweeter the wine the more it is chilled).

The fresh Elba Rosato is chiefly made from Sangiovese grapes (known here as Sangioveto). Drinking temperature is 10–12°C (50–53.6°F). A very authentic and exciting Vin Santo Occhio di Pernice is made from 50–70% Sangiovese (50–70%) and 10–50% Malvasia Nera. This rosé Vin Santo is very warm, fulsome, intensely flavoured, and smooth as velvet. Drinking temperature is 8–12°C (46.4–53.6°F) as preferred (the sweeter the colder). Elba Rosso is made from 75–100% Sangiovese (Sangioveto, 75–100%) and is a very fruity, full, and rounded wine. Drinking temperature is 14–16°C

(57.2–60.8°F). The most interesting wine of Elba is undoubtedly the Aleatico, wholly made with grapes of this name. This old native variety produces a wonderful wine that is a deep ruby red, very aromatic, and full of character. The taste is powerful, rounded, warm, and light-footed. The minimum alcohol content is 16%. This wine can readily be kept for quite some time. The slight sweetness of this wine is not cloying in combination with its high level of alcohol but it does makes it difficult to serve with food. Drinking temperature is 12–16°C (53.6–60.8°F).

Umbria

Umbria is bounded in the east by the Apennines and, in the north-west by Tuscany, and in the south-west by Lazio. Umbria is one of only five regions in Italy that does not have any coast, being a fairly small region in the interior. Umbria's history of wine-making goes back some time but the area has not always been associated with quality wines. The climate here is difficult to cope with (very cold winters and extremely hot summers). This demands considerable patience and know-how in order to make fine wines. Hence really good wines have only been made in Umbria again during the past thirty years. The best known of them is the white Orvieto, but since Giorgio Lungarotti became involved in the family business, it has been mainly the red wines of Umbria that have been carrying off the prizes. Thanks in part to Lungarotti, two red wines from here have been added to the elite of DOCG wines.

TORGIANO DOC

Several excellent white, rosé, red, and even sparkling wines are made in the neighbourhood of Perugia. The white wine may be sold as Bianco (usually Trebbiano and Grechetto) or under the name of the specific grape such as Chardonnay, Pinot Grigio, or Riesling Italico. The single grape varietal wines must contain not less than 85% grape variety indicated on the label. Each of these wines is elegant, fresh, fruity, and fulsome in flavour. Drinking temperature is 10–12°C (50–53.6°F). The Rosato di Torgiano is chiefly made from Sangiovese and Canaiolo grapes that are vinified with the white Trebbiano Toscano grape. This produces a deeply coloured wine that is very fruity in both bouquet and taste. This is a dry wine that is extremely pleasant. Drinking temperature is 10–12°C (50–53.6°F). The Rosso di Torgiano is also made from Sangiovese and Canaiolo grapes, to which a little Trebbiano Toscano may have been added. Drinking temperature is 14–16°C (57.2–60.8°F). The other red wines of Torgiano are made from Pinot Nero or Cabernet Sauvignon. Both are excellent wines and quite typical for their grapes. Drinking temperature is 14–16°C (57.2–60.8°F) for Pinot Nero and 16°C (60.8°F) for Cabernet Sauvignon. The Torgiano Spumante is made from Chardonnay and Pinot Nero. This wine has fine bubbles, is an

attractive pale golden colour, possesses a very fruity nose of green apples and may blossom, and has a fine, elegant, dry and well-balanced taste. Drinking temperature is 8–10°C (46.4–50°F).

TORGIANO ROSSO RISERVA DOCG

This is another famous great name of Italian wine. The history of this wine is of quite recent origins but its quality is timeless. The vineyards of Torgiano Rosso Riserva lie in the hills above the small Medieval town of Torgiano, near Perugia. The wine is made from Sangiovese and Canaiolo, to which some Trebbiano Toscano, Ciliegiolo, and Montepulciano may have been added. To conform with the DOCG standards, this wine must be aged for at least three years (in cask and bottle) before it may be sold.

Torgiano Rosso Riserva is an astonishing wine with a wonderful ruby red colouring and an elegant but subtle bouquet of red and black fruit, herbs, spices, and a hint of tobacco.

It has a fulsome and rounded taste. Drinking temperature is 16–17°C (60.8–62.6°F).

MONTEFALCO SAGRANTINO DOCG

This wine originates in the sun drenched hills surrounding the little village of Montefalco, just to the south of Perugia. This noble Montefalco Sagrantino has only recently gained the distinction of DOCG status. There are two versions of this wine:

the dry secco is made wholly from Sagrantino grapes and then undergoes a compulsory ageing period of twelve months in wooden casks and eighteen months following bottling before it may be sold. This wine is dark ruby with purple glints when young. Once mature the colour tends towards mauve. The bouquet is intense and fruity and reminiscent of ripe blackberries. The taste is fulsome and warm (minimum alcohol 13%), dry and tannic. Drinking temperature is 16–18°C (60.8–64.4°F). The Passito is also made wholly from Sagrantino grapes but these are first partially sun-dried. Fermentation is a slow process, following centuries old methods. The resulting wine is ruby coloured with a characteristic blackberry bouquet and fulsome but slightly tannic taste that is warm and sweet (minimum 14.5% alcohol). Drinking temperature is 16–18°C (60.8–64.4°F) with meat or 14–16°C (57.2–60.8°F) with pastries. If you wish to chill this wine do so rather than ignore this wine.

ORVIETO DOC

The fame of this wine goes back to Etruscan times. Orvieto was originally famous solely as a sweet white wine and the dry version is of quite recent origins. If you look hard you may still find a superb old-fashioned sweet (abboccato/amabile/dolce) Orvieto. The dry wines dominate though, especially for export. To make Orvieto wine the grapes used are Trebbiano (known locally as Procanico),

Verdello, Canaiolo Bianco (Drupeggio), and Malvasia.

The secret of Orvieto lies in the underlying tufa rock and the micro-climate which causes the Botrytis cinerea. The grapes affected by the 'noble rot' are the ones used for the sweet wine. The intensity of the bouquet is dependant on the percentage of sugars in the wine but they all possess a subtle, elegant, and fruity bouquet and taste as smooth as velvet. The Secco is certainly extremely dry, but it remains mellow with a discernible slight bitter note in the finish.

Drinking temperature is 10–12°C(50–53.6°F) and 8–10°C (46.4–50°F) for Abbocato and Amabile wines. The Dolce is only made from late harvested grapes that are affected by the noble rot. This is a superlative wine that is sultry, astoundingly sensual, fulsome, and rich.

The very best of these wines is known as Muffa Nobile but they are exceedingly rare. This is a very full-bodied wine that is pure liquid gold, fatty, smooth, and almost liquorous, with a never-ending aftertaste. Drink at 6–8°C (42.8–46.4°F).

The Marche

The Marche is bounded to the west by the Apennines, Umbria, and a corner of Tuscany, in the north by Emilia, to the south by Abruzzo, and in the east by the Adriatic. The best-known towns along

Verdicchio dei Castelli di Jesi.   Superb Spumante.

the coast are Pesaro and Ancona, the best know inland places are Macerata and Ascoli Piceno. The entire area is crossed by countless rivers which flow from the Apennines to the Adriatic. The vineyards mainly thrive in these river valleys (the Conca, Foglia, Metauro, Cesano, and Tronto). There are three centres of wine-growing outside these valleys near Castelli di Jesi, Ascoli Piceno, and Ancona.

VERDICCHIO DEI CASTELLI DI JESI DOC
For centuries this was the only known wine from The Marche. It is produced between Pesaro and Ancona in the area surrounding Jesi. The name indicates this classic white is made from not less than 85% Verdicchio grapes. The result is light and pale gold. The nose of apple, hazelnut, other nuts, and peach is subtle, the taste is fresh, dry and well-balanced with slight bitter undertone. Those seeking the best choose Verdicchio dei Castelli di Jesi Riserva for a higher price. This wine is aged for an extra two years and it contains not less than 12.5% alcohol. Drink at 10–12°C (50–53.6°F).

VERNACCIA DI SERRAPETRONA DOC
This is an outstanding wine from partially dried Vernaccia Nera grapes (known locally as Vernaccia di Serrapetrona), supplemented if required with Sangiovese, Montepulciano, and Ciliegiolo. This Vernaccia is a rare natural sparkling wine. It is ruby red with intense bouquet of freshly-picked grapes. The taste is slightly sweet (amabile) to sweet (dolce) with a pleasant bitter undertone. Drink at 6–8°C (42.8–46.4°F) for the dolce and 8–10°C (46.4–50°F) for the amabile.

ROSSO CONERO DOC
In terms of the quality for its price, this is probably the best value red wine from Italy. This is not a great wine but it is extremely delicious and quite inexpensive.

It is produced just inland from the coast between Ancona and Macerata. Montepulciano grapes which may be supplemented with Sangiovese ensure a clear ruby red wine with pleasant fruity bouquet of blackberry and blackcurrant with a full, rounded,

Orvieto Classico.

Rosso Conero red.

Superieure version from the south of the area, contains slightly higher alcohol and is more full-bodied. Drink at 14–16°C (57.2–60.8°F) for young wines and 16–17°C (60.8–62.6°F) for older ones.

Excellent everyday vini da tavola wines are also produced in The Marche. One of the best of the houses is Colonnara in Cupramontana, who make a little gem of a wine every time.

Lazio

The region of Lazio extends from the Apennines, where it borders Umbria, Abruzzi, and Molise, to the Mediterranean. It is bounded to the north by Tuscany and to the south by Campania. The river Tiber plays an important role in the local wine-growing and the capital city of Rome is the region's largest market. The majority of the vineyards of Lazio are close to Rome. The other wine areas are found near Montefiascone in the north of Lazio, between Rieti and the border with Abruzzi, and north of Frosinone in the south of the region.

Lazio is mainly known for its white wines but some of the red wines are well worth discovering.

The entire region has volcanic geology and all the lakes such as those of Bolsena, Vico, Bracciano, Albano, and Nemi are actually formed in the caldera of extinct volcanoes. The climate is fairly benign, hot, and moist, so that the noble rot is stimulated.

Est! Est! Est! di Montefiascone.

and fleshy taste that is dry. Drink at 14–16°C (57.2–60.8°F) or 16–17°C (60.8–62.6°F) for a Riserva.

ROSSO PICENO DOC
The vineyards of Rosso Piceno are south of those of Rosso Conero, between Macerata and Ascoli Piceno. The vineyards run lateral to the coast. This red wine is made from Sangiovese and Montepulciano, to which Trebbiano or Passerina grapes may be added. The colour is ruby and the modest bouquet is reminiscent of black fruit. The taste is mellow, remarkably fulsome, and dry. The

Rosso Piceno red.

Fine Vini da Tavola.

The mountains, volcanic soil, the river Tiber, many lakes, climate, and rolling hills around Rome make this an ideal area for growing vines.

EST! EST!! EST!!! DI MONTEFASCIONE DOC

This wine has a richer past than the present-day quality might suggest. According to stories originating in the fourteenth century this was once an excellent wine. On one of his journeys, the bishop Giovanni Defuk sent his page Martino on ahead in search of the best wine with instructions to write 'Est!' (here it is) on the door of the inn that served the best wine. When he arrived in Montefiascone, the page was so taken with the local wine that he wrote 'Est! Est!! Est!!!' on the door of the inn. This name stuck and since that time and the wine has been known as Est! Est!! Est!!! di Montefascione. The quality is not what it was once reputed to be. The wine is produced from Trebbiano Toscano, Trebbiano Giallo (Rossetto), and Malvasia Bianca. The colour is a clear pale gold and the nose is very fruity and vinous, while the fulsome taste is rounded, mellow, and harmonious but may be either dry or slightly sweet. Drinking temperature is 10–12°C (50–53.6°F) for the Secco and 6–10°C (42.8–50°F) for an Amabile (the sweeter the colder).

COLLI ALBANI DOC

These white wines (Secco, Abboccato, Amabile, or Dolce) are made from Malvasia and Trebbiano to

Frascati.

which other white grapes may have been added. The colour is pale to dark gold and the nose is refined and pleasing. The taste is astonishingly fruity and delightful. Drinking temperature is 8–10°C (46.4–50°F) for Secco and Abboccato), or 6–8°C (42.8–46.4°F) for Amabile and Dolce. There is also an entirely acceptable Spumante dei Colli Albani.

FRASCATI DOC

Like the previous wine, Frascati hails from the southern side of Rome. This white wine from the Castelli Romani is probably Lazio's best-known wine. It is made from Malvasia and Trebbiano, perhaps supplemented with Greco. The colour is pale to darker gold and the bouquet is fruity and delicate, while the taste is velvet smooth. juicy, playful, seductive, and approachable. This is not a difficult wine. It is made of average quality as a dry Secco (Asciutto) and also as Amabile, but also in outstanding and extremely rare Canellino quality. This is a sweet wine produced from grapes that have the noble rot. This is a superlative wine that is rarely exported. Drinking temperature is 8–10°C (46.4–50°F) for the Secco and Amabile but 6–8°C for a Canellino. It may be drunk warmer if that is preferred. Excellent Frascati Spumante is also made from the same grapes.

MARINO DOC

This is a mellow, fruity white wine made from grapes that are varieties of Malvasia and Trebbiano. These Marino wines are available as dry (secco/asciutto), medium dry (abboccato), slightly sweet (amabile). or sweet (dolce) versions. Drink at 8–10°C (46.4–50°F) but 6–8°C (42.8–46.4°F) for the sweet wines. A first-class Marino Spumante is made using the same grapes.

Abruzzi

The region of Abruzzi (Abruzzi is the plural of Abruzzo) is bounded in the north by The Marche, to the west by Lazio, and to the south by Molise. The eastern boundary is formed by the Adriatic. Except for a small strip of land along the coast, the rest of Abruzzi consists of hills, mountains, and valleys. The climate varies from Mediterranean on the coast to continental in the mountains. The best place for cultivating vines has to be chosen with the utmost care. These lie to the north and south of the only true town of Abruzzi, which is Pescara, situated in the valley of the river Pescara. The vineyards sit at the foot of the imposing mountains known as Gran Sasso and Montagna della Maiella. Only two DOC wines originate from this region.

MONTEPULCIANO D' ABRUZZO DOC

The Montepulciano grapevines were introduced to of Abruzzi almost 200 years ago. They produce a smooth dry red wine that is slightly tannic, juicy, and amenable. Depending on its maker a Montepulciano d' Abruzzo can vary from a superb

Montepulciano, Cerasuolo and Trebbiano d'Abruzzo.

Biferno.

everyday wine to a more serious one. The minimum two years old Riservas are always recommended. Drink at 12–14°C (53.6–57.2°F) for young wines and 14–16°C (57.2–60.8°F) for older ones and Riservas. Montepulciano d' Abruzzo Cerasuolo is delightful cherry red rosé made from Montepulciano grapes. This is a pleasant fruity rosé. Drink at 10–12°C (50–53.6°F). The best Abruzzi reds originate from the Colli Teramane hills. In addition to the mandatory Montepulciano the makers are permitted to 10% Sangiovese. These wines are fuller and more robust than the ordinary Montepulciano d' Abruzzo, especially the fine Riservas, which must be at least three years old and contain no less than 12.5% alcohol. Drink at 14–16°C (57.2–60.8°F) but 16–17°C (60.8–62.6°F) for Riserva wines.

TREBBIANO D' ABRUZZO DOC
A first class white wine made with Trebbiano grapes with a mellow and delicate nose, juicy, approachable, and dry taste. Most is of reasonable quality but with truly excellent examples of Trebbiano d' Abruzzo. Drink at 8–10°C (46.4–50°F).

Molise

For many years Molise was linked with its northern neighbours of Abruzzi. Many books still give the wine area as Abruzzo e Molise. This is because the

quality of Molise wines was too low for a DOC nomination. The quality has improved so much in recent times that Molise now has DOC.

BIFERNO DOC
The only wine from these parts to have established a name is the Biferno Rosso. This is made from Montepulciano, Trebbiano, and Aglianico grapes around Campobasso. The colour is ruby red towards granite red with age. There is a subtle and pleasing nose reminiscent of blackberry and blackcurrant, while the slightly tannic taste is muted and dry. The Riservas are more full-bodied and mature (not less than three years), and clearly contain more alcohol (minimum 13%). Drink at 14–16°C (57.2–60.8°F) but 16–17°C (60.8–62.6°F) for Riservas.

Campania

Campania is an elongated area on the Tyrrhenian Sea in south-western Italy. The fortunate country-side of Campania felix was much appreciated by the Romans. Naples, the capital of Campania, is one of the liveliest cities in Italy. The cultivation of vineyards in Campania is yet another proof of how skilled the ancient Greek and Roman wine-growers were. Despite all the modern technology, the best wines of Campania are still produced from the same places as 2000–4000 years ago. The grapes

Greci di Tufo.

introduced by the Greeks way back then have survived to modern times. The Aglianico and Greco vines of today both originate from the original vines planted by the ancient Greeks.

GRECO DI TUFO DOC

This is a famous dry and fresh white wine that is elegant and full-bodied, made from Greco grapes. This Greco di Tufo is produced around Avellino, from where the red Taurasi also comes. The ordinary Greco di Tufo is a pleasant white wine but the top ones are little gems of finesse. Drink at 10–12°C (50–53.6°F). An excellent Greco Spumante is also made.

TAURASI DOCG

This is the only top flight wine from Campania. It is made around Avellino, south of Benevento, in common with the white Greco di Tufo. The centre-point of the denominated area is the small town of Taurasi. This fine red wine is made with Aglianico grapes. Its colour is ruby to granite red and there is a very aromatic and sensual bouquet with fulsome and well-balanced taste that is rounded and harmonious. The prolonged nose of the aftertaste is quite astonishing. A sublime Taurasi Riserva is also made with at least 12.5% alcohol and no less than four years ageing. Drinking temperature is 14–16°C (57.2–60.8°F) but 16–18°C (60.8–64.4°F) for the older and Riserva wines.

FALERNO DEL MASSICO DOC

This is a relatively unknown small wine area in the neighbourhood of Caserta. Excellent red wines are made here from Aglianico and Piedirosso grapes perhaps augmented with Primitivo and Barbera. This red is powerful, full-bodied, rounded, and remarkably warm (minimum alcohol 12.5%). The taste is velvet smooth, making it popular with wine drinkers. Drink at 14–16°C (57.2–60.8°F) but 16–17°C (60.8–62.6°F) for a Riserva. An authentic wine is produced from the Primitivo grape. The main grape is augmented with Aglianico, Piedirosso, or Barbera. The colour is a deep ruby red and both the nose and taste are reminiscent of freshly picked and overripe grapes. The taste is fulsome, powerful, and warm (minimum 13% alcohol). Primitivo may be either dry or slightly sweet. The best wines are aged for longer and sold as Riserva or Vecchio. Drinking temperature is 16–18°C (60.8–64.4°F).

Puglia

Puglia is one of the largest wine producing regions of Italy. It is found in the extreme south east of Italy, forming the 'heel' to the boot shape of Italy. The coastline of Puglia with both the Adriatic and the Ionian Seas is extensive. To the west Puglia borders Campania and Basilicata and to the north with Molise. Puglia's landscape is entirely different to the bordering regions. There are no mountains, though a couple of high plateaux. The climate is distinctly Mediterranean, hence hot and dry. Fortunately wine-growing and making has improved enormously in recent years throughout Puglia and work is well under way to further improve both the quality and individual identity of the local wines.

MOSCATO DI TRANI DOC

This sultry and velvet smooth Moscato is probably a relic of the ancient Greeks. The very aromatic Moscato (minimum 14.5% alcohol) and the Moscato Liquoroso (minimum 18% alcohol) are delicious after a meal. Drinking temperature is 6–8°C (42.8–46.4°F).

ALEATICO DI PUGLIA DOC

This is a fairly old-fashioned type of sweet red wine made from Aleatico, often supplemented with Negroamaro, Malvasia Nera, and Primitivo. This dark red dolce naturale is made by allowing part of the harvested grapes to dry out. The bouquet is big and very aromatic and the taste is warm (minimum 15% alcohol), characteristic for the wine and velvet smooth. The

Moscato di Trani.

Locorotondo.

Alessano, usually supplemented with Fiano, Bombino, and Malvasia. Locorotondo is a very pleasant, fresh and elegant dry white wine. A quite reasonable Locorotondo Spumante is also produced. Drinking temperature is 8–10°C (46.4–50°F).

MARTINA FRANCA DOC
North of Taranto a white wine that is similar to Locorotondo is made. This Martina Franca is pale golden coloured with a hint of green. It is dry, fresh, and elegant. Just like the Locorotondo, a reasonable Spumante versions of this wine is also made. Drinking temperature is 8–10°C (46.4–50°F).

PRIMITIVO DI MANDURIA DOC
Four types of heavy and sultry red wines are made here from Primitivo grapes that probably arrived from ancient Greece. The ordinary Primitivo has low residual sugars and 14% alcohol. The Dolce Naturale is clearly sweeter and contains at least 16% alcohol. Drinking temperature is 10–16°C (50–60.8°F) for the Secco and ordinary Primitivo but 6–12°C (42.8–53.6°F) for the Dolce and Liquoroso Dolce.

SQUINZANO DOC
These rosato and rosso wines are made in the area between Brindisi and Lecce. The basis grapes used are Malvasia Nera and Sangiovese. The Rosato is a delicious and fulsome warm wine (minimum alcohol 12.5%) with a juicy and very modest taste. Drinking temperature is 10–12°C (50–53.6°F). The Rosso is a full-bodied and robust wine with at least 12.5% alcohol. The best Riserva wines are aged for two years and contain at least 13% alcohol. Drinking temperature is 14–17°C (57.2–62.6°F).

SALICE SALENTINO DOC
Although only the Rosso and Rosato Salice Salentino are known outside of Italy, there are also a number of very pleasing white and superb sweet red wines made here. The Bianco (Chardonnay) and Pinot Bianco (may be augmented with Chardonnay and Sauvignon Blanc) are fruity, fresh, and lively.

degree of the sweetness is quite acceptable. The Liquoroso is much fuller in body, sweeter, and warmer (18.5% alcohol). The best wine gets an additional three years ageing before sale (Riserva). Drinking temperature is 8–14°C (46.4–57.2°F) for the ordinary wine and 6–16°C (42.8–60.8°F) according to preference for the Liquoroso.

LOCOROTONDO DOC
This wine area is located between Bari and Brindisi, in the southern part of Puglia. Very acceptable white wines are made here using Verdeca and Bianco d'

Primitivo di Manduria.

Primitivo di Manduria Dolce Naturale.

Salice Salentini Rosso.

Copertino Rosso.

Some young wines possess an unruly tingle to the tongue before they age. The taste is otherwise mild and approachable. Drinking temperature is 10–12°C (50–53.6°F). A reasonable Pinot Bianco Spumante is also produced. The Rosato is fruity and fresh, dry and mellow, sometimes with a slight tingle on the tongue when young. There is also a Rosato Spumante. Drinking temperature is 10–12°C (50–53.6°F). The Rosso is quite characteristic, robust, mellow, warm, full-bodied, and rounded. The best wines enjoy at least two years ageing and contain slightly more alcohol. Drinking temperature is 14–16°C (57.2–60.8°F).

COPERTINO DOC
This is a superb Rosato from Primitivo, Montepulciano, Sangiovese, Negroamaro, and Malvasia grapes. It is mellow, fulsome, and dry but certainly not harsh. Nose and taste are characteristic containing fruit and certain vegetal notes with a pleasing undertone of bitterness. Drink at 10–12°C (50–53.6°F). The Rosso is ruby red, dry, full-bodied, rounded, juicy, and velvet smooth. The Riservas are aged for a least two years and contain at least 12.5% alcohol. Drink at 14–16°C (57.2–60.8°F) but 16–17°C (60.8–62.6°F) for a Riserva.

Basilicata

After leaving Italy's 'boot' you enter Basilicata before reaching the toe of the boot, which is Calabria. The region is named Basilicata (for a long time it was known as Lucania). Basilicata has a fascinating landscape, that is rugged and unspoiled and dominated by a mountainous interior and short stretch of superb coast. Basilicata lies on both the Tyrrhenian and Ionian Sea and bounds Campania in the west and Puglia in the east. The regional capital of Potenza is certainly no tourist hot spot.. Those who search can find indications of former civilisations in both Potenza and the second town of Montera. The ancient Greeks and Romans have left a considerable monument to their presence behind and this is equally true in wine-growing. For

instance the only DOC wine bears the name of the ancient Grecian Hellenico grape, known in Italian as Aglianico.

AGLIANICO DEL VULTURE DOC
The name of Vulture is derived from an extinct volcano near Potenza. The soil on the slopes of the extinct volcano are extremely suitable for growing vines which face the sun and therefore soak up the maximum sunshine. If this wine was produced anywhere else in Italy it would almost certainly be granted the top status for Italian wines. Despite this Aglianico del Vulture is still a superlative wine.

The colour varies from ruby red to granite red with hints of orange with age. The bouquet is fairly subtle and characteristic of the wine. The taste is a full one and fresh, and powerful when the wine is young. With age the taste mellows into more juice. This wine is dry to slightly sweet. The better wines are aged in casks for longer and possess more body and alcohol. The Vecchio must be at least three years old and a Riserva not less than five. Drinking temperature is 14–16°C (57.2–60.8°F) but 16–17°C (60.8–62.6°F) for a Riserva. A somewhat strange Aglianico Spumante Naturale is also made.

Calabria

Calabria lies in the toe of the Italian boot. This is very rugged but wonderful land that is almost surrounded by sea on three sides: the Tyrrhenian Sea, The Straits of Messina, and the Gulf of Squillace. The Greeks once regarded Calabria as the Garden of Eden. The cultural inheritance can be found in towns such as Cosenza and above all Reggio di Calabria. The ancient Greeks founded the wine-growing in Calabria but all the old and famous wines have more or less disappeared and are forgotten, but something of the Greek civilisation can still be touched on with an old and matured Cirò. Superb white and rosé wines are made here but the area is most famous for its red wines.

CIRÒ D.O.C.
Note the stress on the second syllable in the name. The famous ancient temple of Cremista stood where the present settlement of Cirò now stands. That temple was dedicated to Dionysos, the Greek God of wine, indicating how important the area was for the ancient Greeks. The wines of Cremista, that were the direct predecessors of today's Cirò, were famous in their day.

Cirò Bianco is made from Greco Bianco and Trebbiano but it always remains in the shadows of the local Rosato and Rosso wines. There has been considerable success in recent years in producing very acceptable white Cirò wines that are fresh and lively. Drinking temperature is 8–10°C (46.4–50°F). Cirò Rosato is made from Gaglioppo, augmented if required with no more than 5% Trebbiano and Greco. This dry rosé wine is deep in colour, fairly subtle in bouquet, full-bodied and warm (minimum

Aglianco del Vulture.

Aglianco del Vulture Riserva.

191

Cirò.

go skiing in the early morning on the highest mountains and swim in the afternoon in the warm sea and enjoy the many beaches. While life on the island is much as throughout southern Italy, the landscape and weather have more in common with the coast of North Africa. Sicily is one of the largest wine producing regions of Italy but the inhabitants here drink less than elsewhere in Italy so that the Sicilian wine industry is heavily dependant on export. No effort or money has been spared in recent years to expand these exports and the wine industry on the island has undergone a major revolution in the past twenty years. The full-bodied and sultry sweet Muscat and Marsala wines which were once the island's pride have been improved where possible, while new modern-style wines have been increasingly marketed. In addition to the famous DOC wines huge quantities are also made here of

Indicazione Geografica Tipica white.

Indicazione Geografica Tipica red.

12.5% alcohol), with an inviting taste. Drink at 10–12°C (50–53.6°F). The Cirò Rosso undoubtedly the best of the three and also Calabria's best wine. It is made from the same grape as the Rosato. The basic Cirò wines must contain at least 12.5% alcohol and are dry, juicy, refined, fulsome and warm in taste. The wines from the centre of the region around the villages of Cirò and Cirò Marina bear the Classico name. Whether Classico or not, Cirò Rosso wines that contain at least 13.5% alcohol are called Superiore. Wines aged for at least two years are known as Riserva. The best wine should be the Cirò Rosso Classico Superiore Riserva. Drink at 16°C (60.8°F) for the basic wine and 16–18°C (60.8–64.4°F) for the better and older Classico Superiore and Riserva.

Sicily

The triangular island of Sicily is not just the largest island of Italy but also of the entire Mediterranean. Virtually ever race of people that was linked in the past to the Mediterranean has left its traces behind on Sicily. The landscape and the lives of the Sicilians and of the surrounding islands is influenced by the volcanoes and the sea. More than 80% of the area consists of mountains, mostly of volcanic origins. Certain of the volcanoes such as Mount Etna and Stromboli are still active. Sicily is a land of great contrasts. Hence the pampered holidaymaker can

excellent Indicazione Geografica Tipica (IDG) and Vini da Tavola.

FARO DOC

This is a small wine area near Messina, in the north east of the island, that makes good red wine from Nerello, Nocera, and where necessary also Calabrese, Gaglioppo, and Sangiovese grapes. Drinking temperature is 14–16°C (57.2–60.8°F).

MALVASIA DELLE LIPARI DOC

This is one of many Malvasia wines to be found that are made on the main island and smaller Aeolian islands. This Malvasia originates from the island of Le Lipari that lies off the coast near Messina. This golden yellow wine is very aromatic. It can be made in a number of ways but only using fresh Malvasia grapes with some partially dried Passito grapes for Liquoroso types or even pressed with a small quantity of currants.

The ordinary Malvasia contains at least 15% alcohol, Passito 18%, and Liquoroso 20%. Drinking temperature is according to taste 10–12°C (50–53.6°F) for the less sweet versions and either 16–18°C (60.8–64.4°F) or 6–8°C (42.8–46.4°F) for the sweeter and heavier types.

ETNA DOC

Reasonable white, rosé, and red wines are made from vines on the fertile slopes of Mount Etna near Catania. The Bianco and Bianco Superiore are made from Carricante and Cataratto Bianco grapes, possibly augmented with Trebbiano and Minella Bianca. Serve this fresh, dry, mild, and light wine as an aperitif or with fish. Drink at 8–10°C (46.4–50°F). The Rosato and Rosso wines are made from Nerello (Mascalese and Mantellato/Cappuccio). Both wines are dry, fulsome, warm (minimum 12.5% alcohol), sturdy in structure and quite strong in taste. Drink at 12°C (53.6°F) for the Rosato and 16°C (60.8°F) for the Rosso.

MOSCATO DI NOTO DOC

This wine was highly regarded by the ancient Romans who called it Pollio. It is made near Siracusa. The Moscato Naturale (minimum 11.5% alcohol) smells intensely of freshly-picked Muscat grapes and this is reflected in the taste. Drink at 8–10°C (46.4–50°F). The Moscato Spumante (minimum 13% alcohol) is a full and sultry sparkling wine of stuporific aromatic strength. Such a wine does not fail to evoke the emotions. Drink at 8–10°C (46.4–50°F). The Moscato Liquoroso (minimum 22% alcohol) is a fortified wine. This wine combines the sweet and fruity strength of the Muscat grapes

Etna Rosso (red).

with the warmth and roundness provided by the alcohol. Drink at 6–8°C (42.8–46.4°F).

MOSCATO DI SIRACUSA DOC

This another cousin from the Moscato family. It is a seductive and very aromatic wine that is fulsome, elegant, and extremely pleasant. It is a treacherous wine though with its minimum alcohol of 16.5%. Drinking temperature is 6–8°C (42.8–46.4°F).

MOSCATO DI PANTELLERIA DOC

Pantelleria is one of the many islands that lie off the coast of Sicily near Trapani. Two quite surprising wines are made here which seem to hark straight back to the time of the ancient Greeks. Both use the native Zibibbo Muscat grape as the basic material. The Moscato Naturale (minimum 12.5% alcohol) both tastes and smells of Muscat grapes. The Moscato Vino Naturalmente Dolce uses partially dried grapes in its making, which increases the alcoholic content to a minimum of 17.5%.

There are also gorgeous Spumante and Liquoroso type wines. Serve all these Muscat wines with desserts that are in themselves not too sweet or as an after dinner liqueur. Drink at 6–12°C/42.8–53.6°F (the sweeter the colder). The Passito is only made from partially dried grapes. This is an extremely sensual Moscato that has much strength, sultry fruitiness, and warmth (minimum alcohol 14%).

There is also a sweeter Liquoroso with not less than 21.5% alcohol. The very best wines have 'Extra' added to their names. These must be of outstanding quality and finesse and contain not less than 23.9% alcohol. Drink at 8–10°C (46.4–50°F) for the Passito and 6–8°C (42.8–46.4°F) for the Liquoroso.

ALCAMO/BIANCO ALCAMO DOC

This is certainly the island's best known wine. Alcamo originates from the area between Trapani and Palermo in the north western part of Sicily. This wine is made from Cataratto Bianco (Commune/Lucido) to which Damaschino, Grecanico, and Trebbiano

Alcamo.

may have been added. The colour is pale yellow with a hint of green and the bouquet is barely discernible. By contrast, the taste is fresh, juicy, pronouncedly fruity, and mellow. Drink at 10–12°C (50–53.6°F).

MARSALA DOC

Without doubt this is he oldest and best known fortified wine from Sicily, and perhaps the most English in style. The man behind the success of this famous wine is the Englishman John Woodhouse who first brought this liqueur wine to Britain. Another Englishman, Benjamin Ingham, first

Marsala Fine.

adapted the solera system (used for sherry) for use with Marsala. The must from pressing grapes such as Grillo, Catarratto, Pignatello, Calabrese, Nerello, Damaschino, Inzolia, and Nero d' Avola is distilled with pure wine alcohol to make Marsala. The following types are recognised.

– Marsala Fine: at least one year old and 17% alcohol
– Marsala Superiore: at least two years old and 18% alcohol.
– Marsala Superiore Riserva: at least two years old and 18% alcohol.
– Marsala Vergine/Solera: at least five years old and 18% alcohol.
– Marsala Vergine/Solera Stravecchio/Solera Riserva: at least ten years old and 18% alcohol.

Each type has its own character, colour, nose, and taste, depending on the grapes used, sugar content of the must, the amount of wine alcohol added, and duration of the ageing process. Drink at 8–18°C (46.4–64.4°F) depending on personal preference, the type of wine, and the dish with which it is served.

Sardinia

Sardinia is an island of much contrast. There is a gentle coastal strip, rugged and precipitous

mountains, lots of tourist attractions, and unspoiled places where nature flourishes. Sardinia is second only to Sicily in terms of the sizes of Mediterranean islands. Much of the land is mountainous. Vines are concentrated at the foot of these mountains, in the valleys, and on the flatter areas along the coast, where most also people live.

CANONAU DI SARDEGNA DOC

Canonau (Alicante) vines were brought to the island by the Spanish. Canonau di Sardegna is produced in the south-east of the island. You may find of local place names on the label such as Oliena, Nepente di Oliena (around Nuoro), Capo Ferrato (around Cagliari) and Jerzu (between Nuoro and Cagliari). This ruby red wine may be dry or slightly sweet Rosato or Rosso. It has an original taste that is pleasant, juicy, and warm (minimum 12.5% alcohol). The Riserva has at least 13% alcohol and is aged for at least two years. There is also a Liquoroso Secco with 18% alcohol and a Liquoroso Dolce Naturale with 16% alcohol. Drink at 10–12°C for the dry Liquoroso Secco, 6–8°C (42.8–46.4°F) or 14–18°C (57.2–64.4°F) for the Liquoroso Dolce Naturale, 10–12°C (50–53.6°F) for the Rosato, 16°C (60.8°F) for the ordinary Rosso, and 17°C (62.6°F) for the Rosso Riserva.

MOSCATO DI SARDEGNA DOC

This fine pale golden Muscat is aromatic, refined, and sensual. The taste is sweet, elegant, and fruity. Local place names may be added to label in the north of the island such as Tempio Pausania, Tempio, or Gallura. Drink at 10–12°C (50–53.6°F).

VERMENTINO DI SARDEGNA DOC

This is a pale golden wine with a green tinge. Its bouquet is subtle, more elegant than fulsome. The taste is fresh, juicy, and dry to slightly sweet with a slight touch of bitterness in the finish. There is also an elegant Vermentino di Sardegna Spumante. Drinking temperature is 10–12°C (50–53.6°F).

VERMENTINO DI GALLURA DOC

This Vermentino is made in the north. It has greater subtlety and finesse than ordinary Vermentino di Sardegna and is always dry and fresh tasting. This Vermentino generally contains higher alcohol and certainly the Superiore which must contain at least 14%. Drinking temperature is 10–12°C (50–53.6°F).

MALVASIA DI CAGLIARI DOC

This is actually a collection of wines made from Malvasia grapes. They are all produced in the area around Cagliari. The dry Malvasia Secco and sweet Malvasia Dolce Naturale are full-bodied and alcoholic wines (minimum alcohol 14%).

They are aromatic and refined with some bitter undertones including a suggestion of burnt almond. Drink at 10–12°C (50–53.6°F) for the Secco and 8–10°C (46.4–50°F) for the Dolce. The dry Malvasia Liquoroso Secco and sweet Malvasia Liquoroso Dolce Naturale are fortified wines of great quality, especially the Riserva examples, which must be aged for more than two years. These aromatic wines contain at least 175% alcohol. Drink at 10–12°C (50–53.6°F) for the Secco and 8–10°C (46.4–50°F) for the Dulce.

MONICA DI CAGLIARI DOC

These wines from Monica grapes are produced as dry Monica Secco and a sweet Monica Dolce Naturale. Both are ruby red wines that are aromatic and sultry with fulsome, mellow, but seductive tastes. The Secco contains at least 14% alcohol while the Dolce is not less than 14.5%. Drink at 14–18°C (57.2–64.4°F) for the Secco and 10–12°C (50–53.6°F) for the Dolce. A dry Monica Liquoroso Secco and sweet Monica Liquoroso Dolce Naturale are stronger and fuller in taste than ordinary Monica. Both wines contain at least 17.5% alcohol. Where possible choose a superlative Riserva of these (aged for at least two years). Drinking temperature is 14–18°C (57.2–64.4°F) for a Secco and 6–12°C (42.8–53.6°F) for a Dolce.

MOSCATO DI CAGLIARI DOC

This is an outstanding Muscat wine that is very aromatic and powerful. It is available as a Dolce Naturale or heavier Liquoroso Dolce Naturale. Drinking temperature is 6–12°C (42.8–53.6°F) according to personal tastes.

NASCO DI CAGLIARI DOC

These are dry (Secco), sweet (Dolce Naturale), or even fortified dry or sweet white wines (Liquoroso Secco or Liquoroso Dolce Naturale) from Nasco grapes. These are of outstanding quality, especially the Riserva. Drink at 10–12°C (50–53.6°F) for a Secco and 6–10°C (42.8–50°F) for a Dolce.

NURAGUS DI CAGLIARI DOC

The Nuragus is an ancient variety of Sardinian grape that was quite probably brought to the island by the Phoenicians. The grape once grew throughout Sardinia but today Nuragus wine is only produced in the south of the island, between Cagliari and Nuoro. This is a pale golden wine with green glints that has a subtle but inviting bouquet. The taste is pleasingly fresh, making this dry to slightly sweet wine very palatable. There is also a Nuragus Frizzante Naturale. Drink at 10–12°C (50–53.6°F) for the dry wines and 8–10°C (46.4–50°F) for the slightly sweet ones.

GIRO DI CAGLIARI DOC

This robust red from Giro grapes is made in a variety of styles. The dry Secco contains at least 14% alcohol while the sweet Dolce Naturale is not less than 14.5%. Both are sultry and extremely aromatic with the nose of freshly-picked grapes, and are fulsome, velvet smooth, and warm in taste. Drink at 16°C (60.8°F) for a Secco and 10–12°C (50–53.6°F) for a Dolce Naturale.
There is also a much fuller Liquoroso version of both in Secco or Dolce Naturale (with not less than

17.5% alcohol). Drink at 16–18°C (60.8–64.4°F) for a Secco and 10–12°C (50–53.6°F) for the Dolce.

CARIGNANO DEL SULCIS DOC

The Carignano grape was introduced by the Spanish. Today the grape is almost restricted to the area around Cagliari.
The Rosato is a dry, fresh, and mellow and there is a Frizzante version. Drink at 10–12°C (50–53.6°F). The Rosso is ruby red, without any pronounced nose but it is deliciously dry and juicy with a mellow taste. Choose a Riserva (minimum 12.5% alcohol and at least three years old). Drink at 16–18°C (60.8–64.4°F).

VERNACCIA DI ORISTANO DOC

This Vernaccia is golden yellow with an intense aromatic bouquet of almond and white blossom with a warm (minimum 15% alcohol), fulsome, sultry, and seductive taste with a hint of bitter almond.
The Superiore and Riserva are fuller, slightly stronger in alcohol (15.5%) and have longer to mature (three and five years). There are also sweet Liquoroso Dolce and dry Liquoroso Secco versions. Both are made with must distilled with wine alcohol.
The Dolce contains at least 16.5% alcohol and the Secco 18%. Drink at 10–12°C (50–53.6°F) for the Secco and 8–12°C (46.4–53.6°F) for a Dolce according to taste.

ARBOREA DOC

Three types of wine are made around Oristano. The Trebbiano is a greenish yellow wine with fairly modest nose but superlative fresh and fulsome taste. Drink at 10–12°C (50–53.6°F) for the Secco and 8–10°C for the Abboccato. There is also a delicious Trebbiano Frizzante Naturale that is available as either Secco or Abboccato. The Sangiovese Rosato is a wonderful cherry red and it has an inviting yet modest bouquet while its dry taste is juicy and fresh. Drinking temperature is 10–12°C (50–53.6°F). The Sangiovese Rosso is an amenable dry wine that is mellow, rounded, and fresh tasting. Drink at 14–16°C (57.2–60.8°F).

ALGHERO DOC

Countless different wines are made in the north west of Sardinia. The Frizzante Bianco Secco, Spumante Bianco Secco, Torbato Spumante Secco, Chardonnay Spumante Secco, and Vermentino Frizzante are outstanding aperitif wines but they are also great with sea food. Drink at 8–10°C (46.4–50°F). The still Bianco, Chardonnay, Sauvignon Blanc, and Torbato are ideal with seafood and also with white meat. Drink at 10–12°C (50–53.6°F).
The light-bodied nature of the Rosato makes it a wine for lunch-time. The Rosso Novello, Rosso, and Sangiovese are amenable red wines. Drink at 12–14°C (53.6–57.2°F).

Greece

Greek wine growing

Greek wines fall into two market segments: the branded wines and those with the name of their place of origin. Large numbers of just about drinkable wines fall within the branded sector but also some very top quality wines. This is extremely confusing for the European consumer, particularly as some wines with place of origin also appear to be of poor quality. Many Greek wines are already past it by the time they reach European consumers due to either wrong storage or poor transport. The consumer is therefore best advised to only buy Greek wines from respected importers such as Tsantalis. Greek wine-growers have an ideal climate for cultivating vines and making wine, especially close to the sea. Many different microclimates, combined with varying local soil conditions such as chalk and rock, and the different varieties of grapes used ensure different characters for the various wines. At present some 300 different types of grape are grown in Greece. Many of these are of French origin such as Sauvignon Blanc, Chardonnay, Cabernet Sauvignon, Pinot Noir, and Merlot, but the majority are native and sometimes ancient varieties. The best known of them are Assyrtiko (Santorini, Sithonia, Athos), Vilana (Heraklion, Crete), Robola (Cephalonia), Savatiano (Attiki, Beotia, Euboea), Giorgitiko (Nemea), Xinomavro (Naoussa, Amynteon, Goumenissa, Rapsani), Mavrodaphne (Achaia, Cephalonia), Mandelaria (Paros, Rhodes, Heraklion Crete), Moschofilero (Mantinia), Muscat (Patras, Samos), and Rhoditis (Achaia, Anchialos, Macedonia, Thrace).

The Greek regions, from north to south, are Thrace, Macedonia, Ipeiros, Thessalia, Central Greece, The Ionian islands (Eptanesos), Eastern Aegean islands, The Peloponnese, Cyclades islands, Dodecanese islands and Crete. The following descriptions of the better Greek wines are made by region, travelling from north to south. The Greek landscape does not generally feature large mountains with a few exceptions but the country is naturally divided into smaller areas by small mountains and hills.

Thrace, Macedonia

Thrace is in the extreme north-east of Greece, bordering on Bulgaria and Turkey. Thrace, which was once a land of gorgeous, stunningly sweet wines such as those of Thasos, is now something of a bywater. The present vineyards that are mainly planted with vines such as the blue grape Mavroudi and Pamidi and white Zoumiatiko, are principally used for making bulk wine and indifferent table wines. The Greek Macedonia is situated to the west of Thrace and borders Bulgaria and the newly independent state of Macedonia. This area also has a long tradition of wine-growing and making.

Greek vineyard for quality wines.

Currently there are four wines with guaranteed origin made here and at least six oinos topikos (vins de pays or country wines) of excellent quality. Macedonia's vineyards are situated on sunny slopes on the hills inland, along the coast, and on the Chalkidiki peninsula.

Drama

Excellent country wines (oinos topikos or vins de pays) are made on the border between Thrace and Macedonia by the Lazaridi company, which only started operating in 1992. The winery is one of the most up-to-date in Greece and a perfect example of responsible and modern wine-making. Lazaridi make five dry wines under the Amethystos name (white, rosé, red, and fumé) and an excellent Château Julia white. The white wines are made from Sauvignon Blanc, Semillon , and Assyrtiko; the rosés are produced from Cabernet Sauvignon, and the reds from Cabernet Franc, Cabernet Sauvignon, Merlot, and Limnio.

In view of the high quality, the grape varieties used, and prices that the Greeks regard as on the high side, these wines are more likely to be found in Britain, The USA, or Japan than in Greece. Lazaridi has proved with these exceptional wines that it is possible to make wines with French grape varieties without producing imitations of French wines. Each of the Lazaridi wines has its own character, with an emphasis on the style of the bouquet.

Amynteon

Excellent wines from Drama.

This is the most northerly wine area of Greece. The climate here is wholly continental and the vineyards are sited at heights of around 650 metres (2,132 feet). The blue grape varieties of Xinomavro and Negoska thrive here. Drinking temperature is 14–16°C (57.2–60.8°F).

Goumenissa

The growers in Goumenissa, about 80 km (50 miles) north-west of Thessalia, also use the Xinomavro and Negoska grapes for their local red wines. The vineyards of Goumenissa are sited at about 250 metres (820 feet) high on chalky soil.

Goumenissa is a dark red wine with glints of purple. Its nose is reminiscent of ripe fruit such as fig, cherry, and gooseberry, and the well-balanced taste is elegant and smooth, almost caressing in the aftertaste.

Naoussa

Naoussa is Macedonia's best-known wine. The vineyards are sited on the slopes of the Vermio hills at a height of 150 to 650 metres (492–2,132 feet). Naoussa is wholly made from Xynomavro grapes. The young wine is aged for at least twelve months in small casks of French oak. The colour of the wine is dark red and the nose suggests small fruit like blackcurrant with a hint of spice such as cinnamon and vanilla from the oak. The taste is fulsome, rounded, warm, and rich. This wine is better left for at least two to three years before drinking. The harsh tannin of the young wine is then changed into velvet smooth luxuriance. Drinking temperature is 16°C (60.8°F).

There are also Reserve and Grand Reserve quality Naoussa wines. These wines are generally cask-aged in French oak for two years. These are deeply-coloured red wines with a hint of brown and the nose often exhibits associations with sweet and overripe fruits or even dried fruit such as fig and prune. Oak only plays a modest role in the bouquet and taste, subtle and in the background without dominating. These robust wines contain considerable tannin and

need to be laid down for several years. You will then eventually be rewarded with an excellent wine that reaches the level of top French wines. Choose a wine from the houses of either Tsantali or Boutari. Drinking temperature is 17–18°C (62.6–64.4°F).

Côtes de Meliton

This nominated origin wine comes from the Chalkidiki peninsula, that lies in the sea like Poseidon's trident. Only two of the 'forks' of the peninsula grow wine. These are Sithonia in the centre and Athos to the east.

Naoussa and Cava Tsantali.

The relatively recently planted vineyards of Porto-Carras are to be found on the Sithonia arm of the peninsula. These were established in the 1960s by a wealthy Greek shipowner. Many believe that the finest wines of Greece are produced here. Under the watchful eyes of French wine experts, including Prof. Emile Peynaud of Bordeaux, various French and Greek grape varieties were planted on slate and shale soils, such as Assyrtiko, Athiri, Rhoditis, and Sauvignon Blanc for white wines, and Limnio, Cabernet Sauvignon, Cabernet Franc, Syrah, and Cinsault for red wines. Now excellent white, rosé, and red wines are successfully made using a balanced assembly of Greek and French grapes. The greatest wines are made here from vineyards with exceptionally low yields of 40 hectolitres per hectare for white wines and as low as 30 hectolitres per

Côtes de Meliton and Malagousia.

hectare for reds. Grape picking is still entirely done by hand.

The white wines are not cask aged but the better reds are. The Côtes de Meliton Blanc de Blancs (Athiri, Assyrtiko, and Rhoditis) is smooth, light, and dry with a subtle floral bouquet. Drinking temperature is 10–12°C (50–53.6°F). Côtes de Meliton Melissanthi (Athiri, Assyrtiko, and Sauvignon Blanc) is more fruity with hints of melon and apricot than the Blanc de Blancs. Drinking temperature is 10–12°C (50–53.6°F). Côtes de Meliton Limnio (Limnio, Cabernet Sauvignon, and Cabernet Franc) is aged in small casks for twelve months. This wine is a delightful ruby red and it is elegant, lithe, and has a hint of spice. Drinking temperature is 14–16°C (57.2–60.8°F). Côtes de Meliton Château Carras (Cabernet Franc, Cabernet Sauvignon, Limnio) has a longer period of cask maturing in wood. It is a full-bodied and elegant red wine with hints of purple and a fine bouquet in which the time in the cask is reflected without dominating. There is a prolonged aftertaste. This wine can be happily left to mature for ten years. Drinking temperature is 16°C (60.8°F). Côtes de Meliton Domaine Carras Grande Reserve (Cabernet Franc, Cabernet Sauvignon, and Limnio) will have rested for at least three years in the cellars of their wine house. This wine too can be kept for ten years. The colour is somewhat more reddish brown than the Château Carras, with hints of terracotta. The bouquet is fulsome and exceedingly pleasant, suggesting soft red and black fruit. The taste is very elegant and velvet smooth with a very prolonged aftertaste. Drinking temperature is 16–17°C (60.8–62.6°F). Porto-Carras also make a superb rosé and two superlative modern wines, their white Malagousia and red Porphyrogenito.

Epanomi

The Gerovassiliou make very proper and modern-style topikos oinos or country wines from French and Greek grape varieties in Epanomi to the west of Chalkidiki. The white Ktima Gerovassiliou (Assyrtiko and Malagouzia) is fine and elegant with a surprising bouquet of freshly-sliced green peppers (paprika).

Their white Fumé (Chardonnay and Assyrtiko) is full-bodied, rounded, and very pleasant.

The red Ktima Gerovassiliou (Grenache Rouge and Petite Syrah) is exciting and fulsome in flavour and is also rounded and warm. The tannin in the wine means it can be kept for at least five years. Other good wines, though less impressive are those of Lazaridi (Drama).

The house of Tsantali makes several quite pleasing white and red topikos oinos or country wines in curious 'belly' bottles known as Makedonikos Topikos Oinos. Tsantali also produce a reasonable Athos Topikos Oinos and a subtle Agioritikos made from Assirtiko and Sauvignon Blanc. Finally, the Cava-style wines made by Tsantali and Boutaris are exceptionally good.

Zitsa

Zitsa's vineyards are found to the north of Ipeiros, against the Albanian border at a height of about 600 metres (1,968 feet). Delicious still and sparkling wines are made here from Debina grapes. These wines are characterised by their elegance, freshness, and exuberant fruitiness. The sparkling Zitsa is

Gerovassiliou Epanomi white.

Gerovassiliou Epanomi red.

Still, semi-sparkling Zitsa.   *Sparkling Zitsa.*

available as semi-sparkling or imiafrodis krasi and fully-sparkling or afrodis krasi versions. Drinking temperature is 8–10°C (46.4–50°F).

Metsovo

A Greek politician named Averoff dreamed of making the best wine of Greece. Although he never achieved this himself, his company has scaled unprecedented heights and may well make its founder's dreams come true. The vineyards are on south-easterly facing slopes of the Pindos mountains. Fine red wines have been produced here for centuries but unfortunately the ancient vines were entirely destroyed by phylloxera. The original vines were replaced by Cabernet Sauvignon. Excellent Katogi Averoff red wine is made from these grapes, which are related to the Greek Agiorgitiko. This great wine can certainly be kept for ten years because of the tannin it contains. This ruby red wine is characterised by its intense aromatic power and fulsome taste that is velvet smooth (after maturing). Katogi Averoff is now regarded as one of Greece's best wines and it is very expensive. Drinking temperature is 17–18°C (62.6–64.4°F).

Thessalia

Thessalia is situated to the south of Macedonia and it borders Ipeiros to the west, the Aegaen to the east, and Central Greece to the south. The area is dominated by the imposing Mount Olympus (2,917 metres/9,570 feet) and it is bisected by the Pineios river. Thessalia is clearly an agricultural region. The best vineyards are sited on slopes or close to the sea. The vines planted on flat countryside are for grapes sold to be eaten or for poor wines.

Rapsani

Rapsani's vineyards are planted on the slopes of Mount Olympus at heights of 300–500 metres (984-1,640 feet). The climate here is fairly moist and above

all cold in the winter. Yet the siting of the vineyards guarantees full sunshine and excellent red wines. The basic grapes used for Rapsani are Xinomavro, Krassato, and Stavroto, which combines to produce a fresh, rich, and elegant red wine. Drinking temperature is 14–16°C (57.2–60.8°F).

Nea Anchialos

The vineyards of Nea Anchialos are sited close to the sea near Volos. The Rhoditis vines grow at a height of 100–200 metres (328-656 feet) and their grapes make a fresh and elegant white wine. Drinking temperature is 8–10°C (46.4–50°F).

Central Greece

This area is the centre of the Greek mainland, bounded in the north by Ipeiros and Thessalia, in the west by the Ionian Sea, and in the east by the Aegean. Vast quantities of wine are produced here but the region only has one guaranteed source of origin wine. The other wines are all table wines or country wines. The three areas that together form Central Greece do produce an excellent Cava-style wine (Hatzi Michalis) and very good topikos oinos

Rapsani.

(Hatzi Michalis, Zarogikas, and Cambas). There are very fruity retsina (appellation traditionelle) wines from Thebe and Messoghia that are made from Rhoditis and Savatiano. There has been substantial investment in this region recently in French grape varieties and the better Greek ones. It is anticipated that fine wines will originate from here in the future.

KANTZA
This is a very subtle white wine made from Savatiano and Rhoditis, that is like a retsina without the resin. Drinking temperature is 8–10°C (46.4–50°F).

Ionian Islands

The Ionian Islands lie to the west of the Greek mainland on a latitude with Ipeiros, Central Greece, and parts of the Peloponnese. Vines arc cultivated on virtually all of these islands. The conquest by the Turks in this part of Greece – also known as Eptanessos or the seven islands – was of sufficiently short duration that the inhabitants were able to continue to cultivate vines and make wine. The wine industry in the most northerly island of Corfu (Kerkyra) has been somewhat depressed by the rise of tourism and the growing of olives. Here too though excellent white wines are made such as that from the house of Ktima Roppa. This is an old-fashioned and traditional wine with the culture of 'flor' (a film created by the fermentation) in the same way as sherry. The wine is a lot like dry sherry. The grapes used are Robola and Kakotrychi. New businesses are developing modern-style dry white wines of elegance using the native Kakotrychi grapes. Production of this new wine is very limited. Very little wine worth mentioning is produced at present on the islands of Paxi, Lefkas, and Ithaki (with the exception perhaps of Lefkas's Santa Mavra). Cephalonia (Kefallinia) does make good wine though.

KEFALLINIA ROBOLA
Robola, also known as Rombola, is one of the finest white grape varieties of Greece. This grapevine thrives extremely well on the seven Ionian islands, thanks to both the weather and soil structure. The summers are hot but there are light sea breezes to provide the necessary moisture and cooling. The vineyards are sited at 600 metres (1,968 feet) and sometimes as high as 900 metres (2,952 feet). Robola's colour is fairly pale yellow with a tinge of green. The bouquet, with hints of hazelnut and citrus fruit, is seductive and the taste is mellow, elegant, and extremely pleasant. Drinking temperature is 10–12°C (50–53.6°F).

KEFALLINIA MAVRODAPHNE
This is a first class sweet red wine made from Mavrodaphne grapes. At first glance it resembles a ruby port in looks. Drinking temperature is 8–12°C (46.6–53.6°F) or 14–16°C (57.2–60.8°F) according to preference.

Cephalonia Robola.

KEFALLINIA MUSCAT
This is a first class sweet Muscat wine that is very aromatic. Drinking temperature is 6–10°C (42.8–50°F). A number of reasonable white and red wines are also made on Cephalonia. The white wines, made from grapes such as Rhoditis, Sideritis, Tsaoussi, Zakinthino, Robola, or Sauvignon Blanc, are fresh and fruity. The reds, made from Agiorgitiko, Mavrodaphne, or Tymiathiko, are fresh, fruity, very aromatic, and not always equally dry.

VERDEA
On Zakynthos just as on Corfu, a fresh green white wine in the style of a Madeira is made that is known as Verdea. This is an excellent aperitif. Drinking temperature is 8–10°C (46.4–50°F).

Eastern Aegean Islands

The Aegean is spread out to the east of mainland of Greece and the coast of Turkey and is filled with countless islands. Vines have been cultivated on these islands and wine made for at least 6,000 years and the sweet, luxuriant wines of Limnos, Lesbos, Chios, and Samos are legendary. Each island has its own microclimate and soil structure which ensure wines of an individual character.

undulating hills rising to 450 metres (1,476 feet) and valleys in which the wine-growing and agriculture is concentrated. This white Limnos wine is yellow-green in colour with a very fruity nose of fresh Muscat grapes. The taste is fulsome and rounded. Drinking temperature is 10–12°C (50–53.6°F).

Several acceptable red wines are also made on the island of Limnio grapes.

LIMNOS MUSCAT

This is a superb sweet and luxuriant Muscat wine that is very aromatic with suggestions of roses and honey. The taste is fulsome, rounded, and velvet smooth. Drinking temperature is 6–12°C (42.8–53.6°F).

SAMOS

The island of Samos is much hillier than Limnos but it is ideal for growing vines. They are cultivated on terraces carved out of the sides of the two mountains on the island to a height of 800 metres (2,624 feet). The Muscat grapes thrive extraordinarily well here but the superb taste of this Samos Muscat is largely due to the great care taken with the grapes on the vines and in the winery.

The co-operatively organised growers have completely renewed their wine-making equipment in recent times with modern horizontally-operated pneumatic presses, computer-temperature control, stainless steel tanks, and new oak casks.

The quality of Samos wines was already excellent but not always uniform. Consumer tastes have also changed so that heavy and sticky wine without freshness is no longer popular. By controlling the temperature during fermentation, a much fresher and more balanced wine is now made.

The Samos Vin Doux Naturel and Samos Vin Doux Naturel Grand Cru are natural sweet wines with alcohol content of around 15%. These are golden yellow wines with a floral nose (roses in particular), and suggestion of ripe fruit and honey. The rich taste is rounded and fatty, and although sweet, remains reasonably fresh. Drinking temperature is 6–12°C (42.8–53.6°F) according to taste.

Samos Vin de Liqueur is modified with wine alcohol, making it both sweeter and more alcoholic than the ordinary Vin Doux Naturel. Drinking temperature is 6–8°C (42.8–46.4°F).

Samos Nectar is another natural sweet wine with alcohol of 14%. This wine is made with partially dried grapes and it is aged in wooden casks. This is a fuller and richer wine than the previous three Samos wines but is exceptional both in taste and class. Drinking temperature is 6–8°C (42.8–46.4°F).

Samos also produces a small amount of dry white wine from Muscat (Samena) grapes. Drinking temperature is 10–12°C (50–53.6°F).

Peloponnese

From the mainland of Attika the Peloponnese are reached across the Straights of Corinth

Samos Vin Doux.

(Korinthiakos Kolpos) and the Corinth Canal. The Peloponnese are a predominantly agricultural region of Greece, famous for their sultanas and Corinthian grapes that are better known as currants. The Peloponnese is a fairly hilly region, dominated by Mount Taygete (2,407 metres/7,896 feet). Most of the vineyards are in the north of the 'island', including the guaranteed origin wines of Patras, Mantineia, and Nemea. In addition to these three wines, the Peloponnese also produce a large quantity of reasonable to good table wine and topikos oinos. The increasingly common modern wines made with the well-known French grapes of Chardonnay, Sauvignon Blanc, Ugni Blanc, Cabernet Sauvignon, Cabernet Franc, Merlot, Grenache Rouge, and Carignan etc. are surprising but not exactly exciting. These grapes do produce outstanding results though when combined with Greek varieties such as Mavrodaphne or Agiorgitiko.

PATRAS

Patras is in Achaia, in the north west of the Peloponnese. The local vineyards are mainly sited on chalk-bearing soils on slopes around the town of Patra, at heights of between 200 and 450 metres (656 and 1,476 feet).

The basic grape used here is the Rhoditis, which produces superb white wines that are fresh, fruity,

very elegant, and dry. Drinking temperature 8–10°C (46.4–50°F).

PATRAS MAVRODAPHNE

The famous Patraiki Mavrodaphne red liqueur wine originates from the area around Patras.

This wine is made with Mavrodaphne grapes and is a full-bodied and sturdy wine that is spicy and very aromatic. The wine is aged in wooden casks for a number of years. Patras Mavrodaphne makes a good and inexpensive replacement for red port although it has its own character which resembles that of a port or oloroso sherry.

Drinking temperature is 6–14°C (42.8–57.2°F) according to taste.

PATRAS MUSCAT/ PATRAS RION MUSCAT

Both are exceptional fresh sweet but fresh Muscat wines. They are golden in colour, luxuriant and rather like honey. Drinking temperature is 6–10°C (42.8–50°F).

NEMEA

Nemea, or the blood of Hercules, is made from

Patras Mavrodaphne.

Agiorgitiko grapes picked from vineyards at heights of 250–800 metres (656–2,624 feet) that are close to Mount Kilini. after Naoussa, Nemea is the most popular of the Greek wines. Nemea is aged for at least twelve months in casks of French oak. The colour is intense purple to mauve and the very aromatic bouquet suggests prune, peach, cinnamon and other spices. The fulsome taste is complex, rounded, robust, warm, and well-balanced. Drinking temperature is 16–17°C (60.8–62.6°F).

MANTINIA

Mantinia is the most southerly of the three major designated wines of the Peloponnese. Fresh, light, dry white wines are produced here from the native Moschofilero grape. The vineyards are situated on a plateau at about 650 metres (2,132 feet) in the vicinity of the ruins of the ancient town of Mantinia. This is an elegant white wine. Drinking temperature is 10–12°C (50–53.6°F).

Cyclades Islands

The Cyclades Islands are stretched out in the Aegean Sea to the south-east of the Peloponnese. The best known of the islands is the astonishingly beautiful Santorini (Thira).

SANTORINI (THIRA)

Santorini (Thira) was once known as Kallistè, or 'the most beautiful', and this is certainly true of this island that is one of the most picturesque throughout the Mediterranean region. The island has steep cliffs that plunge over 300 metres (984 feet) to the sea on top of which the fairy tale town of Thira is perched. The island is of volcanic origins and this can be readily seen in the geology. There are varying layers of pumice stone, chalk, and shale. The array of colours in the ground here is quite extraordinary with black, grey, red, and brown through to purple. The charm and individual style of Santorini's wines are the result of a combination of the volcanic geology and a moist and hot climate. Santorini makes a range of different wines from dry to very sweet. The dry white Santorini is wholly made from Assyrtiko grapes and it is elegant, fruity (citrus fruit), lively, with a fulsome taste that includes a slightly fiery tingle. Drinking temperature is 10–12°C (50–53.6°F). The dry white Santorini Fumé wines are partially fermented in small oak casks and aged for about six months in their own sediment. This wine has definite traces of vanilla (from the wood) and hints of hazelnuts, toast, smoke, and white flowers in its nose and taste. Drinking temperature is 10–12°C (50–53.6°F). The most exciting wine from the island is probably that made from Assyrtiko, mixed with Aidani and Athiri. The wine known as Nycteri is either dry or sweet but always extremely fruity and aromatic with a fulsome rich taste. The Vin Santo made from Assyrtiko en

Rhodes Ilios and Chevalier de Rhodes.

Aidani is very exciting. This wine is made from overripe grapes and its colour is yellow with orange glints. The bouquet is reminiscent of citrus fruit while the taste is simultaneously fresh and luxuriant. Drinking temperature is 6–8°C (42.8–46.4°F).

PAROS
The vineyards on the island of Paros grow two types of grapes, white Monemvassia and red Mandilaria. The Paros wine is made from combining these two grape varieties. The vines are grown on terraces and their manner of pruning is relatively uncommon. The vines are pruned to keep them low in habit but their side shoots may be up to five metres (16 feet) long. The Paros wine is cherry-like in colour, which is characteristic of the Mandilaria grape. The bouquet is full of fruit and floral notes while the mellow taste is fulsome and rich with fairly substantial tannin. Drinking temperature is 16–17°C (60.8–62.6°F).

DODECANESE ISLANDS
These islands are in the eastern Aegaen to the south east of the Cyclades. The Greek 'Dodekanisos' means 'twelve islands' but only the islands of Rhodes and Kos are dealt with here. In the case of Kos it almost exclusively produces poor to reasonable quality table wine.

RHODES
Wines from the island of Rhodes are fairly well known in Europe due both to its good quality and the island's history. The Knights Templar used Rhodes as a staging post during the times of the

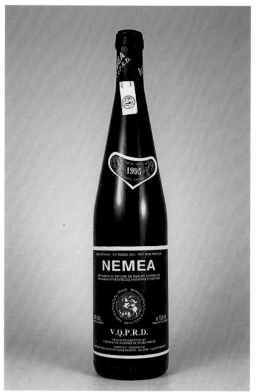

Nemea.

Crusades. The ruins of their famous fortifications (Krach) are still there to be seen. The vineyards of Rhodes in the north have underlying chalk or slate/shale while those of the south are sited on sandy soil. The climate is ideal for wine-growing with hot summers that are low in rainfall but with cooling from the northerly Meltem wind and yet again warming for the south of the island by southerly breezes. Rhodes makes two good still wines and a fine sparkling one.

The first is a white wine called Ilios (Greek for 'sun') made from Athiri grapes. It is an elegant, slightly aromatic wine that is lithe and pleasing. Drinking temperature is 8–10°C (46.4–50°F).

Chevalier de Rhodes, made from Mandilaria, is an excellent red wine with a purple to mauve colour, a soft aromatic nose but a sturdy yet elegant taste with the necessary tannin. Drinking temperature is 16°C (60.8°F). Rhodes Brut is made from Athiri grapes by the Compagnie Agricole Industrielle de Rhodes (CAIR) just like the previous two wines. Despite its designation as Brut, this sensual and naturally sparkling wine, made by the traditional method, is not absolutely dry. The power of this wine lies in its abundant fruitiness and mellow, almost caressing taste. For those who do not find this wine convivial enough, there is also a Demi-Sec version. Drinking temperature is 6–8°C (42.8–46.4°F).

RHODES MUSCAT

Rhodes Brut.

This is a sultry and seductive wine from Muscat Blanc and Muscat Trani grapes. The colour is golden yellow and the very aromatic bouquet has floral notes and hints of honey. The taste is sweet but remains elegant and fresh. The wine contains 15% alcohol. Drinking temperature is 6–8°C (42.8–46.4°F) but can be served less chilled depending on the occasion and the season.

Crete (Kriti)

In terms of size, Crete is the fifth largest island in the Mediterranean region. Many may recall the stories from their school days of Knossos and the palace of King Minos, where the Greek hero Theseus slew the Minotaur and fled with the beautiful Ariadne. Crete is a small and elongated island to the south of the Greek mainland. The 260 km (162 miles) long island is dominated by the mountains of Lefka Ori (2,453 metres/8,047 feet) and Idi (2,456 metres/8,353 feet). The vineyards are spread out in the central and eastern parts of the island. The mountains protect the vines from the hot and dry winds from Africa. There are four guaranteed origin wines that have been nominated on Crete and several outstanding topikos oinos. Very old-fashioned types of Rancio wines are still made in the west of the island near Chania, using grapes from ancient native Romeiko and Liatiko vines, which may be mixed with some Grenache.

ARCHANES
This is a full-bodied and spicy red wine that is easily drunk. It originates from the south of the island around Heraklion. Wines have been made here for at least 4,000 years as proven by the ancient wine press at Vathipetro, which originates from Minoan times. Archanes is a red wine made from Kotsifali and Mandilaria grapes. This is normally a ruby red wine that is lithe, rounded, and elegant with a very pleasing taste but quality in recent times has been extremely variable. Drinking temperature is 14–16°C (57.2–60.8°F).

DAPHNES
This is a red liqueur wine of good quality that is made from Liatiko grapes. It is full-bodied, pleasant, and very aromatic. This wine is a relic from ancient Cretan civilisations and almost as old as the Liatikos grape vines, which were cultivated during Minoan times. Drinking temperature is according to taste either 6–8°C (42.8–46.4°F) or slightly below room temperature (12–14°C/53.6–57.2°F).

PEZA
This ancient Cretan red wine is made from Kotsifali and Mandilari grapes. It is a dark mauve wine with a slightly unusual vegetal and fruity taste but it is pleasing and supple. Both alcohol, of not less than 12.5%, and body are normally in good balance with each other but in recent years the quality of this wine has not been consistent from every producer.

Drinking temperature is 16°C (60.8°F).

Peza also produces a white wine made from the ancient and native Vilana grape variety. This is greenish yellow and fairly aromatic and fruity with reasonable freshness and suppleness of taste. Drinking temperature is 10–12°C (50–53.6°F).

SITIA

This wine too is available as either a red or white. The vineyards of Sitia are situated at the eastern tip of the island at a height of about 600 metres (1,968 feet). The ancient grape varieties that thrive here are Liatiko used for red wines and Vilana from which the white wines are made. Sitia white is fairly green in colour with a fresh taste that is supple and pleasing rather than exciting. Drinking temperature is 8–10°C (46.4–50°F).

Dry red Sitia is fairly dark in colour with a mild nose and fulsome, supple, and comforting taste. Drinking temperature is 14–16°C (57.2–60.8°F).

RETSINA

Retsina is a traditional appellation rather than a guaranteed origin wine. This wine has a long history and character all of its own. Because Retsina is produced in more than fifteen different wine areas of both the Greek mainland and the islands it is impossible to place this wine within a region. Retsina's origins go back a very long way to the time when it was difficult to ship and transport wine so

Peza white and Tsantali red.

Patras Retsina.

that solutions were sought for this problem. Wine was shipped in amphoras that were covered with jute cloths that has been soaked in resin.

The resin from species of pine trees dripped into the wine before it hardened which imparted the characteristic resinous taste. Resin proved to be good as an antiseptic as well as for sealing the amphoras. No-one was made sick by this wine which was certainly not true of all other wines at that time.

Modern technology makes the use of resin's antiseptic properties unnecessary but the Greeks in their taverns were so attached to the taste that pine resin was intentionally added to the wine's must prior to fermentation.

The resin is removed from the wine during clarification but the taste and above all the smell remain in the wine. Most Retsinas are made from Savatiano and Rhoditis grapes in central Greece.

There are a variety of types and tastes, ranging from very light to extremely heavy. Drinking temperature is 8–10°C (46.4–50°F).

Former Yugoslavia

Slovenia

The north of the country is mountainous while inland is either flat or gently undulating. The farthest south-east has a beautiful stretch of coastline. The climate is central European and continental with mountain influences in the north and Mediterranean one in the south. The summers are generally quite hot and the winters cold, though not normally extremely so.

Wine areas

The small country of Slovenia has no fewer than fourteen different wine areas. These are grouped together in this book into three main areas.

Primorje (Primorski vinorodni region)

Primorje in the Slovenian language means 'by the sea'. This area does have a small stretch of coastline but most of the area is cut off a mere 10 km (6 miles) or so from the sea behind the Italian enclave of Trieste. The northern part of Primorje borders the

Quality Vrhusko Vino of Primorje.

Primorje red.

Fruili region of northern Italy and is more than 50 km (31 miles) from the sea. However the name is not inappropriate for the denominated wine area for the sea influences the climate of this wine-growing region. Primorje has both a continental and a Mediterranean climate. This combination of weather influences helps to produce countless strongly alcoholic and dry red wines, especially from the area around Koper. Primorje is the only Slovenian region that makes more red wines than others. The white and rosé wines here are also full-bodied, powerful, warm, and with little acidity.

Brisko (Brda)

Excellent sparkling wines are among the wines from here, made from Chardonnay, Beli Pinot, Rebula, and Prosecco. There are also fresh white wines made from Rebula, Beli Pinot, Sauvignon Blanc, Sivi Pinot, Chardonnay, Furlanski Tokay, and Malvasia (Malvasija) but with the exception of some Rebulas, these are not really very convincing. Drinking at 8–12°C (46.4–53.6°F). There are also reasonable but somewhat rustic and unbalanced red wines made from grapes such as Merlot, Cabernet Franc, Cabernet Sauvignon, Modri Pinot, and Prosecco. Drinking at 14–16°C (57.2–60.8°F).

VIPAVA

This is an excellent dry white wine and most are usually modern in style and taste. Grapes used are Rebula, Sauvignon Blanc, Beli Pinot, Chardonnay, Furlanski Tokay, Laski Riesling (Welsch Riesling), Malvasia (Malvazija), Zelen, and Pinela, with the last two frequently underestimated. These grapes represent the authenticity and strength of this region better than the other imported varieties. Drinking at 8–12°C (46.4–53.6°F). There is a surprisingly delicious, fresh, and mellow rosé made from Barbera and Merlot. Drinking at 10–12°C (50–53.6°F).
The ordinary red wines (Modri Pinot, Prosecco, Refosc) are very acceptable. Some wines, such as the Merlot Biljenski Grici, Barbera, and Cabernet, are of excellent quality, particularly in view of

Quality white wine from Brda, Primorje.

their prices. Drinking at 12–14°C (53.6–57.2°F). The best are aged in small oak casks, although often from inferior Slovenian oak which imparts a strong, almost resinous taste that stifles finesse in most whites. This is a shame for behind the strong taste of the oak there is a fresh, pleasing wine of great potential. The Chardonnay Barrique of Vipava is closer to a ponderous Australian Semillon than an elegant Burgundian Chardonnay. This is not a poor wine but better choice of wood would yield greater freshness and elegance. Drinking at 10–12°C (50–53.6°F). The Merlot Barrique of Vipava has a disturbing over-pronounced wood taste suggesting

this Slovenian timber. Despite this the Merlot is not at all bad. It is fresh and fruity with hints of plum, fruit stone, and schnapps, with a mellow taste. Drinking at 14–16°C (57.2–60.8°F).

Kraški/Karst

Ancient and famous Kraški Teran wine originates from Karst. This is made from Refošč grapes which are related to the Italian variety of Refosco and the wine is said according to popular belief to work as a tonic for health because of its high concentration of lactic and amino acids in the wine and the presence of iron. The colour is ruby red with glints of purple and the wine is very fruity with hints of redcurrant in both the bouquet and taste. This is a wine with a velvet smooth texture that is not excessively alcoholic. Drinking at 16°C (60.8°F).

Other wines made here include fairly uninteresting sparkling wines (Frizzante, Chardonnay, and Rosé), charming white wines made from Malvasia (Malvazija), Beli Pinot, Chardonnay, Laski Riesling (Welsch Riesling), Rebula, Sauvignon Blanc, and Sivi Pinot, and excellent reds from Refošc, Cabernet Sauvignon, Merlot, Modri Pinot, and Prosecco.

KOPER

More than 70% of the production here consists of red wines that are chiefly made from Refošc. This is a wine area with a future, although the winery

Fine Sauvignon from Vipava, Primorje.

Chardonnay Barrique from Vipava, Primorje.

installations are far from ideal owing to shortage of money. Most wines are too lacking in freshness to be able to compete in foreign markets, yet there is considerable potential here in the combination of soil and ideal weather conditions.

The dry white wines such as Sauvignon Blanc, Chardonnay, and Beli Pinot are not recommended due to their lack of freshness. Much wine is fairly coarse and devoid of either character or style.

If however you should choose an old-fashioned syrupy white wine such as Malvazija, Sivi Pinot, Sladki Muskat, or Rumeni Muskat, then you will get value for money. Drinking temperature is 10–12°C (50–53.6°F). The wine made from overripe grapes selected by hand and picked late is excellent, whether or not the grapes have been visited by botrytis (the noble rot). Extremely interesting wines include the Chardonnay Izbor (Auslese), Malvazija Pozna Trgatev (Spätlese), the sweet Sladki Refošc, and an extremely rare Passito made from Cabernet Sauvignon (Sušeno Grozdje). The red wines like most of the local rosés are of reasonable quality but these red wines could also benefit from more modern vinification methodology. Many of the wines give a somewhat overblown appearance (too much wood, too much tannin, lots of alcohol, but otherwise little individual character). Choose from the better crus where possible from the Cabernet Sauvignon, Cabernet Franc, Refošc, Malocrn, Merlot, Modri Pinot, and Prosecco. Drinking temperature is 16°C (60.8°F).

Chardonnay from Koper, Primorje.

Podravje (Podravski Vinorodni Region)

Podravje means the valley of the Drava, which is one of the two important rivers in this region. The climate here in the extreme north-east of Slovenia is continental of a Central European nature. This helps the area to produce fine, fresh, elegant, and aromatic white wines. Podravje is also renowned for its delightful sweet wines (Pozna Trgatev, Izbor, Jagodni Izbor, Suhi Jagodni Izbor, and Ledeno Vino). Podravje borders on Hungary and Austria in the north, and Croatia to the east.

Prekmurske Gorice

This area has been fairly inaccessible for a long time with vineyards that are scattered, presenting a problem for the production of high quality wines. Despite this they have succeeded in making first class and fresh white wines such as those from the two varieties of Riesling which are very fine. Reasonable to good white wines are made here from grapes such as Laški Riesling (Welsch Riesling), Sipon, Zeleni Silvanec, Beli Pinot, Sivi Pinot, Renski Riesling (Rhine Riesling), Rizvanec, Ranina, Zlahtnine, and some very acceptable Chardonnays.

Most red wines here (from Modri Pinot and Modra Frankinja) are fresh and fruity but lack depth.

Radgona-Kapelske Gorice

This is a very promising are best known for its individual style Traminer and superb Zlata Radgonska Penina.

This is the first Slovenian sparkling wine made by the traditional method.

There are also excellent wines such as Pozne Trgatve (Spätlese), Arhivska Vina (Riserva), and Jagodni Izbor (Beerenauslese) from Radgona-Kapelske Gorice. Choose the most sultry wines such as Rumeni Muskat, Muskat Ottonel, Sivi Pinot, or Traminer, and for the best crus such as Perko, Kobilšcak, Radenski Vrh, Hraÿsenski Vrh, Muršcak or Rožicki, which produce the very best Traminer. There are first class fresh and dry white wines made from grapes such as Laški Riesling (Welsch Riesling), Renski Riesling (Rhine Riesling), Beli Pinot, Sivi Pinot, Sipon, Ranina, Rizvanec, Zeleni Silvanec, and Zlahtnine.

There are also pleasant fresh and fruity wines made from Modri Pinot.

Central Slovenske Gorice

The influence of Austria on the wine-making here is noticeable. The local white wines are fresh and elegant and some of them are very delicious. The best dry white wines are made from Renski Riesling (Rhine Riesling) en Laški Riesling (Welsch Riesling), Beli Pinot, and Traminer. There are outstanding

Pozne Trgatve (Spätlese), Izbori (Auslese), Suhi Jagodni Izbor (Trocken Beerenauslese) and Ledeno Vino (Eiswein). The red wines of Slovenske Gorice (Portugalka, Modra Frankrinja, Modri Pinot en Gamay) are fresh, light, and fruity. Drinking temperature is 12–14°C (53.6–57.2°F). A few very acceptable sparkling wines made by the traditional method are also produced here.

Ljutomer Ormoske Gorice

The white wines from this area are certainly among the best in Europe. Unfortunately the means are not to hand to make their wines better known. The wines from the local cooperative Jeruzalem Ormoz should have a large market potential in Europe. You are unlikely to encounter such fine Pinot Blanc (Beli Pinot) anywhere else than from Ljutomer Ormoške Gorice. The bouquet is redolent of may blossom and other white flowers, perhaps with a hint of broom, and even fruit stone liquor (Slibowitz). The taste is very fresh with elegant and refined acidity, the relationship between alcohol, body, and fruit is perfect, and the price is a gift. Drinking temperature is 10–12°C (50–53.6°F). Wines are made from Sauvignon Blanc throughout Slovenia and these sell well and quickly yet few of them are worthwhile. The exception to this is the Sauvignon Blanc of Ljutomersko-Ormoške, especially from the prev-

Excellent Pinot Blanc from Lutjomersko-Ormöske.

Fine Sauvignon from Lutjomersko-Ormöske.

iously mentioned cooperative. Gooseberry, hay and grass, asparagus, citrus fruit, and a hint of smoke in the background can all be discerned in this wine that resembles a very good Sancerre. This wine is so smooth it is almost like salve yet it remains extremely fresh and aromatic. Drinking temperature is 8–10°C (46.4–50°F). Further excellent dry white wines are also made from varieties such as Renski Riesling (Rhine Riesling), Laški Riesling (Welsch Riesling), and Sipon. You may find fine medium dry to semi-sweet whites like those of Sivi Pinot, Rulandec, Chardonnay, Zeleni Silvanec, Traminer, and Muskat Otonel. Tasting a medium dry Chardonnay takes some getting used to but the sunny, very aromatic, fulsome, and warm taste even convinces died-in-the-wool Chardonnay enthusiasts. Wines made from late harvested grapes of excellent quality include Pozna Trgatev made from Chardonnay, Laški Riesling (Welsch Riesling), Renski Riesling (Rhine Riesling), and Sauvignon Blanc, the Jagodni Izbor (Beerenauslese) made from Sipon, and Ledeno Vino (Eiswein) using Laški Riesling (Welsch Riesling). Despite their very sweet nature, these wines are unbelievably fresh due to the fine acidity which is characteristic of this area.

Maribor

The oldest vines in the world may well be those of Maribor, if we are to believe the Slovenians. Some 35 litres of wine are still made each year from vines that are 450 years old. The variety is Kölner Blauer or Zametna Crnina in the local language, meaning 'black velvet'. This very special wine is bottled in miniatures that are sold with a certificate of authenticity. This is a highly desirable item for collectors of wine curios. In addition to this rarity there are also excellent fresh and elegant white wines made here from grapes such as Laski Riesling (Welsch Riesling), Renski Riesling (Rhine Riesling), Sivi Pinot, Zeleni Silvanec, Traminer, and Rumeni Muskat. The local Sauvignon Blanc is perhaps less pronounced than that of Ljutomersko-Ormoske, but it is certainly of high quality. Maribor also produces excellent wines made from late picked grapes such as their Izbor (Auslese), Jagodni Izbor (Beerenauslese), Suhi Jagodni Izbor (Trocken Beerenauslese), and Ledeno Vino (Eiswein). A number of fresh and light red wines are made here as well from varieties like Portugalka, Kraljevina, Modra Frankinja and Zametovka. Drinking temperature is 12–14°C (53.6–57.2°F).

Haloze

Almost exclusively white wines are made from the hills of Haloze, on the border with Croatia. The chalk soil imparts great beauty and elegance to these wines. These are further examples of wines that are totally underestimated by the European wine buyers. The prices for the quality is extraordinarily low for wines that are so completely western European in character. The best of the whites are made from Laški Riesling (Welsch Riesling), Sipon, Beli Pinot, Sauvignon Blanc, Chardonnay, Sivi Pinot, Renski Riesling (Rhine Riesling), Rumeni Muskat, and Traminer. Haloze also produces some light reds from Modri Pinot and Modra Frankinja that are pleasing but not truly spectacular. The wines made from late picked grapes such as Pozne Trgatve, Izbori, Jagodni Izbori, Suhi Jagodni Izbori, and Ledeno Vino are very good.

Posavje (Posavski Vinorodni Region)

Posavje means the valley of the Sava, which is the river that together with its tributaries, the Sotla, Savinja, and Krka provides the necessary moisture to this region. Posavje is situated south of Podravje, against the Croatian border. The area has a climate that is principally central European and continental but with moderating Mediterranean influences from the south, especially in Bela Krajina. Every type of wine is produced here from fresh to sweet, from light to moderately full-bodied, and white, rosé, and red, still or sparkling. Posavje is renowned for its excellent late harvest sweet wines such as (Pozna Trgatev) and for Eiswein (Ledeno Vino), and others produced from grapes carefully selected such as Izbor, Jagodni Izbor, and Suhi Jagodni Izbor.

Šmarje-Viṙštanj

This is another area where a great deal of white wine is made such as excellent Laski Riesling (Welsch Riesling), Beli Pinot, Chardonnay, Sivi Pinot, Renski Riesling (Rhine Riesling), Zeleni Silvaniec, Traminer, Ranina, Rizvanec, Sauvignon Blanc, and Zlahtnina. The reds here are fairly light, fresh and fruity and chiefly made from Frankinja, Modri Pinot, Portugalka, Sentlovrenka, Kraljevina, Gamay, Zweigelt, and Zametovka.

Bizeljsko-Sremic

This is a first class white wine area using Sipon, Beli Pinot, Laški Riesling (Welsch Riesling), Zeleni Silvanec, Sauvignon Blanc, and Chardonnay. There are reasonable to good red wines from Modri Pinot and Modra Frankinja, and full-bodied, warm and strong Pozne Trgatve (Spätlese), Suhi Jagodni Izbori (Trockenbeerenauslese), and Ledeno Vino (Eiswein). The last of these is an elegant sparkling wine made by the traditional method. There is also a rare and amusing port-type wine.

Dolensjka

Well-known Cviček comes from Dolensjka. This is a light wine with relatively low alcohol that is elegant and fresh with subtle body and a dry but certainly not hard taste. This surprising rosé is made from blue grapes, including Frankinja, Zametovka, Kraljevina, and Sentlovrenka together with white grapes such as Laški Riesling, Zeleni Silvanec, Rumeni Plavec. This wine is widely served at local festivities because of its tremendous freshness coupled with low alcohol. Slovenians believe that Cviček is beneficial for the digestion (acidity versus fat) and with its low sugar and alcohol it is suitable for diabetics.

Other good wines from this area are whites such as Laški Riesling (Welsch Riesling), Zeleni Silvanec, Sauvignon Blanc, and Chardonnay, and the red Modra Frankrinja.

Bela Krajina

This southernmost wine area of Slovenia produces excellent red wines from varieties such as Modra Frankinja, Zametovka, Portugalka, Sentlovrenka, Gamay, and Modri Pinot.

One of the best red wines from Slovenia is probably the locally made Metliška Črnina. They have also been making white wines from Laški Riesling (Welsch Riesling), Belin Pinot, Renski Riesling (Rhine Riesling), Zeleni Silvanec, Sivin Pinot, Rumeni Muskat, Chardonnay, and Sauvignon Blanc since the 1980s. These wines tend more towards full-bodied, heavy, and ponderous than elegance and balance. By contrast the Pozne Trgatve, Jagodni Izbori, and Ledeno Vino wines of Bela Krajina are excellent.

Croatia

Wine-growing

Croatian wine-growing with 650 square kilometres in cultivation mainly consists of a fairly large number of small areas. It is not worthwhile during this period when the Croatian industry is re-building itself to describe each of these areas individually. One of the attractive aspects of Croatian wine-growers is their determination to improve their native varieties of grapes.

This makes it more difficult for them to sell their very specific wines of local character but increasing numbers of consumers are discovering that the native grapes guarantee greater authenticity of the terroir.

Wine areas

Croatia can be loosely divided into two large zones: the interior on the one hand and the coastal area and islands on the other.

The interior

Most wine gowing areas are close to Zagreb. There are seven areas within the interior zone: Plesivica, Zagrorje-Medjimurje, Prigorje-Bilogora, Moslavina, Pokuplje, Slavonija, and Podunavlje, which in their turn are subdivided into about districts.

The best wine areas are Sveta Jana-Slavetic in Plesivica, Moslavina in the area of the same name, Virovitica-Podravina-Slatina and Kutjevo in Slavonija, and Erdut-Dalj-Aljmas in Podunavlje.

The best wines

Many vineyards in this part of Croatia have been destroyed so that judgement is a relative one.

Graševina

Graševina is the local name for Welsch Riesling that is known in Slovenia as Laški Riesling. Some very special white wines are made here from Graševina, especially in the district of Kutjevo in Slavonija. This is a fine dry white wine that is elegant and fresh. Drinking temperature is 10–12°C (50–53.6°F). Other good whites include those made from Rhine Riesling, Gewürztraminer, Chardonnay, and Sauvignon Blanc. None of these wines though has the same finesse as the Graševina from Kutjevo. Small amounts of red wine are now also being made in the interior of Croatia, principally from Frankovka grapes.

The coast

This is the most important area for Croatian wine. Most of the vineyards here are sited along the coast and on countless islands close to the coast. The position is ideal with steep rocks above the Adriatic and a Mediterranean climate that is hot and dry. Unfortunately the Balkan wars have had a tremendously bad effect on the wine industry, directly through destruction and indirectly through loss of manpower.

Although the coastal area was more directly affected than the islands, the economic consequences are clearly apparent on the islands of Krk (Vrbnicka Zlahtina), Hvar (Ivan Dolac), Korčula (Posip), and above all on Pelješac (Dingač, Postup). The coastal region officially consists of four areas (Istra and the coast, Northern Dalmatia, the interior of Dalmatia, and Central/Southern Dalmatia. These are in turn subdivided into some 50 districts. The best wine-growing areas are Porec and Rovinj in Istra/the coastal strip, Primosten in Northern Dalmatia, Cara-Smokvica, Dingač-Postup, Neretva-Opuzen, and Ston in Central/Southern Dalmatia.

Malvazija Istarska

Excellent wine is made in Porec and Rovinj in the region of Istra from Malvasia (Malvazija) grapes. This is a fresh and fruity dry white. Drinking temperature is 10–12°C (50–53.6°F).

There are also several interesting red wines from Istra of which the first choice should be the Teran. The Merlot from Istra is well made but lacks identity.

Vrbnicka Zlahtina

The island of Krk (to the south-east of Rijeka) is the home of Vrbnicka Zlahtina. This is a delightful white wine made from white Zlahtina grapes (Zlahtina Bijela), which is a native speciality of Krk.

Vrbnicka Zlahtina in common with most Croatian whites is fulsome and rounded but also oustandingly fruity in both the bouquet and taste. Drinking temperature is 10–12°C (50–53.6°F).

Kaštelet

Two very acceptable wines originate from the chalky surrounds of Kaštel, slightly north of Split. These are the white and red Kaštelet wines.

The white is an approachable and fresh dry wine. Drinking temperature is 8–10°C. The red is made from Plavac Mali and Vranac grapes and is a very pleasing wine that is full-bodied and amenable. Drinking temperature is 14–16°C (57.2°–60.8F).

Plavac

The island of Brac lies off the coast from Split. Plavac made here is a very nice red wine. The best Plavec comes from the small town of Bol to the south of the island. Bolski Plavac is a very special red wine that is full-bodied, powerful, and fleshy. Drinking at 14–16°C (57.2–60.8°F).

Ivan Dolač

The island of Hvar to the south of Split is renowned for its hot sun and red Ivan Dolac. This wine is solely made from grapes in a small enclave of just 8 hectares from which the Plavac Mali grapes are hand picked. Ivan Dolac is one of the better Croatian reds and it is full-bodied, powerful, warm, and rounded. Drinking at 16°C (60.8°F).

Faros

Another good red from the island of Hvar is the Faros made from Plavac Mali. The name of this wine is derived from the settlement of Pharos in ancient Greece. Drinking at 14–16°C (57.2–60.8°F).

Kaštelet.

Ivan Dolăc.

Pošip

The island of Korčula is south of Hvar and at a similar latitude to Pelješac. The superb Pošip white wine made here is probably the best known Croatian wine made from the native variety of grape of that name and has been made from these grapes for centuries. The grapes are entirely hand picked. Pošip is a delightful full-bodied, rounded, and powerful white elevated from others by superb fruitiness in both inose and taste. Drinking at 10–12°C (50–53.6°F).

Dingač en Postup

The elongated island of Pelješac is about 50 km (31 miles) north of Dubrovnik. The vineyards are difficult to reach and growers once carried their grapes on donkeys along dangerous narrow tracks but since a 400 metres (1,312 feet) long tunnel was built through the mountains about 25 years ago they have been able to bring the grape harvest in quickly to the wineries in Potomje. Cultivating vines in this terrain with slopes of 70% and more requires considerable effort even with this improvement. Two wines with world reputations emerge from this environment: Dingač and Postup, both made with Plavac Mali grapes. These grapes do not thrive anywhere else as well as on these Dalmatian islands. In addition to the geology and climate, the position of the vineyards is also favourable. The grapes benefit from the sun in three ways: directly through radiation, and by reflection from the stony ground and from the sea. These are ideal circumstances for this native variety. Dingač is made from vines on the steepest hills in the centre of the island where the position is most favourable in respect of sea and the sun. These wines are full-bodied and warm with alcohol of 13–15%, powerful, fleshy, unforgettable, and exceptionally delicious.

The better vintages of Dingač can be kept for five years and sometimes ten, with the very best years keeping for fifteen years or more. Postup comes from the north of the island where the slopes are less steep. Postup is clearly related to Dingač, with similar quality but less bite, body, and flesh. Despite this, Postup is an excellent warm, full-bodied and powerful wine that generally possesses greater finesse and elegance than a Dingač. Drinking at 14–16°C (57.2–60.8°F) for a Postup and 16–17°C (60.8–62.6°F) for a Dingač.

Prošek

This liqueur wine is notorious with holidaymakers to the Dalmatian coast resorts. It smells and tastes deliciously of overripe grapes and slips down very readily, especially if served chilled on a sunny terrace. Yet with its alcohol of 15% this wine is more

Dingăc.

Postup.

Wines from Mostar, Bosnia-Herzegovina.

treacherous than people think. Drinking at 10–12°C (50–53.6°F).

Bosnia-Herzegovina

Bosnia-Herzegovina is less well known by wine connoisseurs than Slovenia and Croatia, yet the local wine industry has been under way here for more than 2,000 years. The excellent wine from the once picturesque town of Mostar was highly regarded by the Austrian emperors. Zilavka Mostar from Zilavka grapes is an outstanding dry white wine which acquires its strength and finesse from gravel soil and hot sun. Drinking at 10–12°C (50–53.6°F). The acceptable dry red Blatina Mostar comes from the same locality. Drinking temperature is 14–16°C (57.2–60.8°F). Wines from Bosnia-Herzegovina use the same classification and language on the label as Croatian wines.

Serbia/Montenegro

It is perhaps already apparent that the best wines from the former Yugoslavia do not come from Serbia or Montenegro but these two countries do make some reasonable to good wines. At present the status and future of wine-growing and making in Serbia and Montenegro is entirely unclear. Serbia was known for good white wines from Graševina (Welsch Riesling), both mixed with native Smederevka grapes and on its own. The best area of Serbia was probably Fruska-Gora, which with Graševina made fine wines from Sauvignon Blanc. Excellent rosé and red wines were made in Zupa province from Prokupač grapes, sometimes with Plovdina grapes. Some acceptable full-bodied and powerful wines were also made in Montenegro from Vranac grapes with some of bitterness in their taste.

Prokupăc.

Vranac.

Krater.

Macedonia

The landscape of the independent state of Macedonia is dominated by mountains, valleys, and wonderful lakes in the south of the country.

The climate has influences from the Mediterranean, Central European (continental), and the mountains. The present state of the wine industry in Macedonia is still relatively unknown.

Many of the sweeter wines disappear into the German market to satisfy that country's demand for 'liebliche' wine. Only a few dry red wines are worth

the effort to discover at present but this will probably change soon.

The dry red wines from the area of Tikves are classic examples of old-fashioned Balkan wines, which could find a European market if a little more care was taken in their making.

The best wines are made from Kratošja and Teran grapes (which united become Krater). The loose chalk soil imparts its own character on the wine. Drinking temperature is 15–16°C (59–60.8°F).

The old-style Macedonian wine made from Kratošja is of reasonable quality. It is a mellow and amenable red wine that is easily drunk. Drinking temperature is 13–15°C (55.4–59°F).

Connoisseurs consider the best Prošek (Prošek Dionisos) comes from Macedonia. Just as in Croatia this wine has a sweet and superb bouquet and taste of overripe grapes. It is just as easily consumed and equally strong at 15% alcohol. Drinking temperature is 10–12°C (50–53.6°F).

Macedonian red wine.

Macedonian.

Bulgaria

Statistics show that Bulgaria has achieved great success through the modernisation and adaptation of its wine industry. New grape varieties that are successful have been planted with great haste, such as Cabernet Sauvignon, Merlot, Sauvignon Blanc, and Chardonnay and inexpensive wines that are easily drunk when young are made in great volume which have conquered the European market through intelligent marketing. Yet Bulgaria has had a rich history of wine-making, producing good wines from native grapes such as the red wine varieties Pamid, Mavrud, Melnik, Gamza, and Rkatziteli, Misket, and Dimiat for white wines. The climate in Bulgaria is a combination of a maritime one from the Black Sea, a Mediterranean climate in the south, and Central European climate in the centre and north of the country. The geology permits the production of high quality wines on a large scale. The ultra modern wineries are extremely efficient and the vinification methods are well managed.

Wine areas

Bulgaria is divided into a number of large regions which in turn are divided into smaller wine areas.

Dolinata na Struma Region (south-west region)

This area is distinguished by its Mediterranean type climate and underlying chalk and sand which are ideal for producing red wine. First class Cabernet Sauvignon is produced in Melnik, which is slightly spicy and mellow. Cabernet Sauvignon/Melnik of Petrich somewhat more powerful and has a fuller taste. The best wines are undoubtedly the Reserves made from the native Elnik grape. These are powerful, full-bodied and rounded wines with some bite to them.

Gamza from Suhindol.

Ljubimec Merlot.

Plovdiv Cabernet Sauvignon.

Trakiiska Nizina Region (southern region)

This is the land of the ancient Thracians who were active wine-makers as long ago as 700 BC. It is also the largest wine area of Bulgaria. Because of the favourable climate the majority of the wines here are reds. The superb full-bodied and rounded wine that was characteristic of the area, made from native Mavrud grapes, is still produced in Assenovgrad. Mavrud wines are relatively speaking rare by comparison with other Bulgarian wines but they are of excellent quality.

Delicious mellow Merlots originate from Haskovo that are well-rounded and cask aged for a number of years. These are very acceptable but have little Bulgarian character. The Merlot from neighbouring Stambolovo is better. This wine receives a long period (in Bulgarian terms) ageing in wooden casks and it tastes wonderful. The best Cabernet Sauvignons and Merlots originate around Mount Sakar in the Strandja region, such as Lyubimets.

Rozova Dolina Region (the southern Balkans)

This is the domain of Cabernet Sauvignon. High quality Cabernet Sauvignon and Merlots of European style come from Oriachovitza in the Controliran region. Cabernet Sauvignon from Plovdiv is fairly powerful and at first acquaintance resembles a French wine. Perhaps the finest

Chardonnay from Bulgaria originates from Sliven but here too the juicy Merlots and Pinot Noirs dominate.

Dunavska Ravina Region (northern region)

Similar volumes of red and white wines are produced here, mainly of good quality. Palinevki make reasonable mellow fruity wines from Cabernet Sauvignon and Merlot. Suhindol in the Controliran region make fine Gamza, sometimes on its own but also in combination with French grapes such as Merlot. True Gamza wines are superb, spicy, aromatic, full-bodied, rounded, and powerful. Young Gamza is often very high in tannin, and this is equally true of Melnik and other native Bulgarian blue grapes. Merlot grapes make the wines more mellow and enable it to be drunk sooner. In addition to this Gamza/Merlot there are also reasonable Cabernet Sauvignon wines made in this area which are light, fresh, and elegant. These wines also have a creamy texture and discernible blackcurrant bouquet.

Ruse

Ruse is situated right against the Romanian border. Many of the whites here produced are slightly sweet The combination for example of Welsch Riesling and native Misket produces surprising results. These sultry sweet white wines manage to stay fresh with light spicy undertones thanks to the Welsch Riesling. Excellent Welsch Riesling wines are also made which are generally high in residual sugars. This wine is fresh, fruity, and floral with a mellow and pleasing taste. There are also acceptable French-style Cabernet Sauvignon, Merlot, and Cinsault. Svischtov of the Controliran Region forms part of the Ruse area. Powerful full-bodied and aromatic red wines are made around Svischtov from grapes such as Cabernet Sauvignon. The northern position here makes these Cabernet wines less heavy than similar wines from Melnik or Plovdiv. It is more elegant and fresh with characteristic aromas of mint, spices,

Preslav rosé.

Khan Krum Riesling and Dimiat.

vanilla, redcurrant, and blackcurrant. Despite its powerful nose and taste this wine remains smooth+.

Chernomorski Region (eastern region)

This region is bounded by the Black Sea and has a moderate maritime climate which is beneficial for white wines. Burgas lies close to the Black Sea coast and reasonable white wines are made here. Ugni Blanc grapes provide the bulk and Muscat the sweetness and aromatic properties. Many of these wines are not particularly dry and plenty of them are quite sweet. Preslav is a little further inland but still influenced by the Black Sea. First class dry and fruity Chardonnays are produced here on chalky soil and simple, tasty rosé wines. Schumen produces several ponderous Sauvignon Blanc wines that lack the freshness and charm of a good Sauvignon. Despite fruitiness, alcohol, and the name, these wines have little to offer. Even the Muscat grapes unusually offer little nose or taste. There are also fresh and mellow sparkling wines made from Chardonnay in Schumen that are mentioned for the sake of completeness.

The Chardonnay Reserve wines from Khan Krum, near Schumen are of far better quality. This is a first class fruity wine with wood in its nose and an excellent taste. The country wines made from Riesling and Dimiat are surprisingly pleasant and distinguish themselves by their fruity bouquets of peach and apricot. Novi Pazar in the Controliran region also forms part of the Schumen area. First class Chardonnays are made here that are full, fruity, powerful, and elegant.

Russe Cabernet Sauvignon and Cinsault.

Chernomorski Chardonnay.

Sauvignon

Romania

Romania has an impressive wine-making past. Archaeological finds have shown that primitive wine-making was in existence some 6,000 years ago. The ancient Greeks and the Romans made Romanian wine more widely known.

Today Romania has 275,000 hectares in cultivation for wine-making and produces about 8 million hectolitres per annum (approx. 10% of French production) which places it in the European top ten of wine-producing countries. The climate and the geology in Romania is very beneficial for wine growing.

Although French origin grape varieties are grown in Romania there is still considerable effort directed towards their native varieties with support from their government. The only obstacle in the way of well deserved success is perhaps lack of infrastructure and good means of distribution. Much still needs to be done too to improve the image of Romanian wine. Some Romanian wines of course do not achieve much in the way of heights but the best wines are true gems of craftmanship.

Southern Carpathians

This wine area, which is renowned for the vineyards of Muntenia, Oltenia, Dealu Mare, Pietroasele, Arges, Valea Mare, Stefanesti, and Dragasci, lies at the foot of these mountains, on the hills between the mountains, and on the southern-facing flat areas.

Dealu Mare in particular is quite well known and gains grudging respect from connoisseurs. Excellent wines are made here from Cabernet Sauvignon, Merlot, and Pinot Noir from vines grown in ferruginous soil.

Well-known districts of Dealu Mare are Valea Calugareasca, Tohani, Urlati, Ceptura, and Pietroasele. The superlative Tamaioasa Romaneasca and Grasa dessert wines are made from native grapes bearing these names that are grown in the gently undulating hills of Pietrosele.

Excellent but light dry whites are made from native Feteasca Regal and Tamaioasa Romaneasca grown on terraces on the Arges hills, perhaps with addition of some 'borrowed' Sauvignon Blanc, Welsch Riesling, and Muscat Ottonel. The enormous vineyards of Dragasani that extend to more than 10,000 hectares produce dry light whites of low alcohol and several Muscat Ottonel and Tamaioasa Romaneasca dessert wines. A number of reasonable reds are made from the terraces of Drubeta-Turnu Severin-Corcova, alongside the banks of the Danube – here known as the Dunãrca.

The vineyards of Segarcea are situated to the south of the town of Craiova, from where mainly Cabernet Sauvignon reds emerge.

Fine old-style Riesling from Dealu Mare.

Romanian wines from the Southern Carpathians.

Life is enjoyed in the wine-growing areas.

Eastern-Carpathians (Romanian Moldova)

This area with is renowned vineyards of Cotnari, Odobesti, Panciu, Nicoresti, Husi, and Dealurile Moldovei, borders the Ukraine (Russian Federation). The soil chiefly consists of a mixture of humus and chalk.

Many wines here are made from the native grapes of Feteasca Alba, Feteasca Regala, Feteasca Negra, and Galbena, possibly supplemented with or even supplanted by imported grapes such as Rhine Riesling, Welsch Riesling, Pinot Gris, Traminer, or Sauvignon Blanc. Cotnary, which is one of the best known vineyards of Romania, is in this area. Cotnary produces two great dessert wines, Grasa and a Tamaioasa Romaneasca which has an unusual nose of roasted coffee.

The Babeasca Neagra red wines from the Nicoresti area are also of interest and also the fine dry whites made from Husi in the Dealurile Moldovei region. Considerable amounts of cheap whites and reds are made around the area of Tecuci Galati close to the Ukrainian border.

Transylvania/Bana

To many European ears Transylvania conjures up bloodthirsty horror stories of Count Dracula. In reality the area has wonderful natural landscape with great tracts of woodland, castles, and some well-known scattered vineyards such as those of Tarnave, Alba Iulia, and Bistrita.

Fine sweet white wines are made here and a few excellent dry whites, in particular those from the Tarnave vineyards. The basic grapes used are Feteasca Regala, Feteasca Alba, Welsch Riesling, Muscat Ottonel, and Sauvignon Blanc. Recently they have also begun to make very acceptable sparkling dry wines by the traditional method.

Alba Iulia produces full-bodied dry or sweet whites that are filled with extract from fully ripened Feteasca Alba, Feteasca Regala, Welsch Riesling, and Pinot Gris. Several interesting dry whites are made from the same native grapes in Bistrita. A great deal of everyday local Romanian wine originates from Banat that is made from Kadarka grapes. There are also a few reasonable wines made from the ferruginous soils around Minis (Kadarka and Cabernet Sauvignon) and from the area around Recas by the river Bega (Cabernet Sauvignon).

Dobrogea

This area is in the south-east, between Bucharest and the Black Sea. Dobrogea is mainly known for the vineyards of Murfatlar.

The climate here is very hot and the soil is much the same as in Champagne in France: light, brittle, and chalky. Medium dry and sweet whites of great class originate from the Murfatlar vineyards made from Feteasca Regala, Chardonnay, Welsch Riesling, and Pinot Gris.

There are also excellent dry to medium dry reds and whites made from Babeasca Neagra, Cabernet Sauvignon, Merlot, Pinot Noir, Muscat Ottonel, and Tamaioasa Romaneasca. The Chardonnays that have been visited by botrytis (noble rot) are of world class.

Former Soviet Union

Policies regarding the wine industry in the former Soviet Union countries used to be determined by the Comecon in Moscow.

The wine plants that were required to produce quantity before quality have generally been dismantled throughout the former Soviet Union. Increasing numbers of smaller companies have been established, each of which has to fight to achieve any renewal and modernisation.

Moldova

Moldova is a relatively small state wedged in between the big neighbours of the Ukraine and Romania. In terms of culture and language, Moldova forms an entity with Romania.

Moldova's wine-making goes back to the times of the ancient Romans. In the times of the Czars, Moldova's wine industry flourished greatly. When phylloxera decimated the vineyards of Western Europe, certain French growers set up in Moldova in order to survive the crisis. These brought French varieties of grapevine with them.

Moldova's climate is ideal for growing grapes and making wine from them: it is cold in winter and hot in summer, which is particularly beneficial for white wine. Despite this it is difficult to find any good wines in Moldova.

The taste of Moldovan wine is not really very western. These are very acidic wines with little bouquet that are heavily oxidised. Efforts to change this are underway with support from The United Kingdom, The Netherlands, and France.

The basic grapes used are the native Feteasca Alba, Rkatsiteli, and Saperavi. Feteasca provides a very fruity white with a nose of peach and apricot though without the required freshness. Rkatsiteli stands out because of its spicy and floral bouquet combined with a pleasing freshness. Saperavi are blue grapes

Dry sparkling Crimean wines, the Ukraine.

Medium-dry sparkling Crimean, the Ukraine.

that provide red wine with backbone and a greater potential for ageing. In addition to the native grapes mentioned, Moldova also makes wide use of French grapes such as the white Sauvignon, Riesling, and Aligoté. Aligoté is a grape from Burgundy that is only occasionally used in quality wines such as Aligoté de Bouzeron.

In Moldova though Aligoté plays a major role because of the high acidity. Moldovans are crazy about ten year-old fully oxidised Aligoté wine. There are also excellent sherry-type wines made from Aligoté, Sauvignon Blanc, Riesling, and Rkatsiteli. An unusual wine that is certainly not inferior to sherry is sold in Moldova under the old name for Jerez of Xérés (which is strictly forbidden outside of Moldova).

The best whites are made by the Englishman Hugh Ryman, working with the cooperative of Hincesti. These are an excellent full and powerful Chardonnay that is rich and fruity, and a Rkatsiteli which is very fruity and exceptionally pleasant. The same Hincesti-Ryman also make very acceptable Merlots and Cabernets. Very good reds are made either wholly of Cabernet Sauvignon or with the addition of Saperavi, such as the Rochu and Negru which are very similar in style to an excellent Bordeaux red. Several sparkling wines are also produced here though most are so highly oxidised that little pleasure is to be derived from them. The rare undamaged and still fresh examples though are of very good quality. Most observers consider it obvious that Moldova has a great future.

Ukraine

Recently much effort has been invested in the area around Odessa and Nikolajev, close to the Black Sea, and around Dnjeprpetrovsk on the Dnjepr, to replace the old but highly productive varieties of grapes with better quality new ones such as Riesling and Cabernet Sauvignon. The sparkling wines from the Crimea, of which in reality most come from Moldova, were a household name. The current economic uncertainty of the Ukraine leaves little positive that can be said at the moment.

Russia

During the time of Perestroika the Russian government carried out a policy of dissuading people from their wide-scale problem of vodka drinking. The wine industry was subsidised and consumption of wine (instead of vodka) was encouraged. Enormous wine plants or Kombinats produced an never-ending flow of syrupy, full-bodied, and often heavily oxidised white and red wines, ranging from somewhat on the dry side to extremely sweet. These wines were produced in the Black Sea region, around the Sea of Azov (Krasnodar), the Don basin, Stavropol, and the Crimea, and also utilised imported bulk wine from Bulgaria, Moldova,

Medium-dry red sparkling Crimean, the Ukraine. *Georgian wines.*

Hungary, and Algeria. These foreign bulk wines were blended with wines from native grapes which lost their own identity.

Given the current uncertain economic situation in Russia and the significant lack of funds, it is impossible to give a clear picture of the current state of the Russian wine industry.

Georgia

Georgia, which is sandwiched between Russia and Turkey, produces a tremendous volume of good white, rosé, red, and sparkling wines but these are rarely seen outside of the country.

Some Georgian wines are unlikely to charm Western consumers because of their earthy tones and somewhat tart acidity. This results from the old-fashioned wine-making methods that are still in regular use in which entire bunches of grapes are left and more or less 'forgotten' for a time in earthenware pitchers to ferment. Georgian wines can easily be recognised by the decorative labels with at least six or seven gold medals on them on somewhat ungainly bottles.

White wines are dominated by the two native grapes varieties of Rkatsiteli and Mtsvane. Several strange but high quality dry wines are made from these two types of grape. These are Tsinandali, Gurdzhaani, and Vazisubani.

The equally excellent Napareuli wine is made solely from Rkatsiteli, and Manavi uses just Mtsvane. Tsitska, Tsolikauri, and Bakhtrioni are all made from native grape varieties of the same name. These wines and the Manavi and Vazisubani previously mentioned are all firm, fruity, and harmonious wines. Tsinandali, Gurdzhaani, Napareuli, and Manavi are all aged in wooden casks for at least three years. These wines are not truly fresh but they have marvellous fruitiness and a very elegant nose with a light and mellow fruity taste (by Georgian standards). Those who truly wish to try the authentic and very localised taste of old-fashioned Georgian wines (from earthenware pitchers) should try the Rkatsiteli, Sameba, or Tibaani. The colour of these dry white

wines – made from pure Rkatsiteli in the case of the first and from Rkatsiteli and Mtsvani in the case of the others – is between dark yellow and amber. The bouquet is somewhat fruity, suggesting perhaps currants with clear sherry-like undertones. All these three wines are more alcoholic at 12–13% than the other white wines mentioned.

Full-bodied red wines are made here from Saperavi (Kvareli, Napareuli and Mukuzani) and Cabernet Sauvignon (Teliani). All these wines are cask aged for at least three years. These are not only full-bodied wines, they are also strong in tannin and have moderate levels of alcohol (12–12.5%) and fairly fruity with suggestions of overripe fruit and currants. Georgia also produces countless dry and sweet white, rosé, and red sparkling wines.

There are also reasonable to good fortified wines that are naturally sweet, made from grapes such as Rkatsiteli and Mtsvane. The Georgians themselves are not very fussy when it comes to the right wine for the dish being eaten. By Western standards the dry wines should be served at 10–12°C (50–53.6°F), the dry reds at 16–17°C (60.8–62.6°F), sweet reds at 10–12°C (50–53.6°F), and sparkling wines between 6 (42.8F) and 8°C (46.4°F).

Armenia

Armenia might be the birthplace of the grapevine, with the stories of Noah's Ark that is thought to have been set in the region of Turkey, Iran, Azerbaijan, and Georgia, between the Black and Caspian Seas. Armenia is best known for its excellent brandies produced close to Mount Arafat but the country also makes a number of very acceptable quality red wines, such as those in the south-west of the country in the area around Yeghegnadzor. These are sturdy wines that are high in tannin and high levels of acidity. Drinking temperature is 14–16°C (57.2–60.8°F).

The southern states of the former Soviet Union

Grape vines are now cultivated in some strange places thanks to gigantic irrigation projects. Some of the southern states of the former Soviet Union such as Azerbaijan, Kazakhstan, Kyrgyzstan, Tajikistan, Turkmenistan, and Uzbekistan were making reasonable table wines and good dessert wines (Muscatel, Port. and Madeira type wines) until recently. The unsettled economic situation in these countries has had a negative effect on the local wine industries.

Hungary

Both Hungary and the former Czechoslovakia were able to adapt their political, social, and economic positions following the revolution. Hungary has even managed within ten years to undo the neglect of thirty years. The Czech and Slovak Republics are also well on course to achieve similar results although at a slower pace, perhaps because beer is more popular than wine.

Hungary is a relatively small Central European state with the greatest distance from east to west being 530 km (331 miles) and 270 km (168 miles) from north to south. The climate is determined by changing fronts from three different climate systems: the severe Russian continental climate, the pleasant Mediterranean climate, and remnants of a moderate maritime climate. Winters are moderately cold and the summers are hot.

Hungarian wine-growing

Hungarian wine-growing dates back to the time of the Roman emperor Probus who had vineyards planted on slopes along the Danube in about 276 AD. These vineyards were significantly extended during the period that the Austro-Hungarian Empire flourished. During the period of Soviet domination Hungary was 'permitted' to produce large amounts of steel so that the wine industry was to a large extent

neglected. The Hungarian wines of that era were produced in huge agricultural plants and disappeared to the USSR. Most of them were heavy, acidic, very alcoholic, and heavily oxidised. With the exception of the Tokay wines, Hungarian wines at this time had little honour left. After 1989 the state industries were hopelessly in decline and it was not known how the damage that had been done could be put right.

Hárslevelü.

The removal of the Soviet Union as an export market was not immediately replaced by the markets of Western European. European standards were far higher and the Hungarian wine industry desperately needed renovation and modernisation. While the monolithic former state concerns found it extremely difficult to attract investment because they were too large, lacked agility, and were too old-fashioned, a few dynamic wine-makers were saved by foreign investors. The terroir is good, the prospects very promising, and by Western standards the investments were not huge. New vineyards were planted, old vines replaced, completely new wineries were built, and others were renovated to meet modern demands. Only businesses which could offer the highest quality stood any chance in the markets of Western Europe.

Cabernet Sauvignon.

That the Hungarian wine industry is heading in the right direction is due to people like Zoltan Zilai of the Hungarian wine foundation and the many dynamic growers such as Attila Gere, Zoltan Polgár, Tibor Kovács (Hétszölö), János Arvay (Disnókö), András Bacsó (Oremus), Attila Domokos (Bátaapáti), Akos Kamocsai (Hilltop), Vilmos Tummerer, Ede Tiffán, Sándor Tóth, Jószef Bock, and many others.

Tradition versus high-technology

Hungary's great diversity in wine has its origins in the curiosity of three different climate types (maritime, continental, and Mediterranean). Furthermore Hungary also possesses some unique varieties of grapes.

The north is best known for its firm, fresh, and aromatic white wines and fresh, fruity, and fairly light red wines, while the south is mainly famous for sturdy, alcoholic, full-bodied, and well-rounded reds. The Hungarians generally have great respect for both tradition and character. For the former state industries tradition seemed to stretch back no further than the past forty years but many of the newer companies are seeking the soul of the more traditional Hungarian wines of before World War II.

Hungarian grapes

It is a shame that most Europeans are only aware (in addition to the famous Tokay or Tokaj wines) of the

Oremus.

none-too-dry and ponderous Bull's Blood reds from Eger (Egri Bikavér) that are often oxidised and Nemes Kadarka.

Hungary has so much more to offer. One factor behind the great diversity of Hungarian wines is the considerable variety of grapes permitted. At least 35 different types form the basis of Hungarian wines. The country grows many native varieties in addition to the well-known European (French and Austrian) types. The most important of these are described below together with their characteristics.

Wine houses

It is possible to try all the good Hungarian wines without the need to travel widely by visiting a Budapest wine house.

These trading companies have many years of experience of the Hungarian wine trade and know the best years and wines to choose. The houses of Vinárium, Corvinum, Hungarovin, and Zwack are highly recommended. Each of these four offers a very broad range of high quality wines.

Hungarian wine areas

It is impossible in short to describe all the wine areas of Hungary so the emphasis is placed on the best of them.

In 1998 there were at least 22 different wine areas in Hungary of which the best are Sopron, Ászár-Nesmzmély, and Etyek (north west), Matraalja, Eger, and Tokajhegyalja (north east), Villány Siklós, Szekszárd, and Tolna (south west), with to a lesser extent Badacsony (north east), Balatonfüred-Csopak, Balatonmellék, and Dél-Balaton (Lake Balaton).

Sopron

Sopron is a perfect example of a restored and cared for old historic town. The old town centre is one of the most attractive in Europe. The area surrounding the town is also beautiful with green undulating hills and enormous fields of oilseed rape.

The Sopron wine area borders Austria and is greatly influenced by that country. Sopron's main tour de force is its Kékfrankos red wine. This is masculine and powerful wine that is high in tannin, full-bodied, and acidic with discernible bouquet of morello cherry, bilberry, and peppers (paprika). Drinking temperature is 14–16°C (57.2–60.8°F).

Ignore the area's cheaper wines and choose instead the better wines from companies like Vinex (Soproni Cabernet Sauvignon), Hungarovin (Soproni Cabernet Sauvignon 'Kavar'), Gangl (Soproni Cabernet Sauvignon), Interconsult (Soproni Sauvignon Blanc 'Kamocsay Borok' – among the top two Hungarian Sauvignon Blancs – or Weninger (the famous Austrian wine house that works with Attila Gere in Villány-Siklós. The Soproni Kékfrankos is a 'must have'.

Somló

This tiny area between Sopron and Lake Balaton surrounds the town of this name. Very alcoholic and oxidised white wines are made here on underlying clay, basalt, and sandstone that are very acidic and high in minerals. The principal grapes are Juhfark, Furmint, Olaszrizling, and Hárslevelü. Somloi Jurfark is certainly not a western-style wine but many Hungarians, including professional tasters, continue to find this wine superb. This is inexplicable for many because even the best wines act like a rasp on the tongue. The bouquet has notes of hot butter, nuts including chestnuts, or even of beans that succeed in slightly diminishing this effect.

Pannonhalma-Sokoróaja

This is one of the smaller wine areas of Hungary to the south of Györ. The soil consists mainly of loess and ancient forest humus. Several very acceptable full-bodied and sturdy white wines with a rich taste are made here from grapes such as Tramini and Olaszrizling. Drinking temperature is 10–12°C (50–53.6°F).

Aszár-Nesmély

These are two small wine areas to the north-west of

Superb quality Törley Brut.

Budapest where mainly white wines are made from Olaszrizling (Riesling Aromatico, Italian Riesling, Welsch Riesling), Rajnai Riesling (Rhine Riesling), Rizlilngszilváni (Müller-Thurgau), and Leányka (Mädschentraube). Each of these wines is very fresh, intensely fruity, and exceptionally pleasing. Drinking temperature is 10–12°C (50–53.6°F).

François President sparkling wine.

Mór

This is an elongated area to the north of the town of this name where Ezerjó grapes produce white wine that is fairly acidic that has a remote resemblance with Gros Plant du Pays Nantais. The wines from this area have strong grapefruit bouquets. Drinking temperature is 14–16°C (57.2–60.8°F).

Etyek

Etyek to the west of Budapest is the closest wine area to the capital. Those who like their wine harsh will certainly find it here. Chardonnays here are greener than anywhere else and rarely convincing. Some wines even smell strongly of sulphur but these are best ignored.
The Sauvignon Blancs of Etyek Vinum and Hungarovin (György Villa Selection) are much better. The best wines are perhaps the less commercial ones such as Etyeki Királyléanyka of Etyekvinum and Olaszrizling György Villa of Hungarovin. Drinking temperature is 8–12°C (46.4–53.6°F).
Etyek produces an outstanding sparkling wine (Pezgö) by the traditional method. These are wines than can readily compete with most Champagnes except the top cuvées. Two that are recommended are François Président and Törley Brut, which both come from Hungarovin, which cooperates with the German sparkling wine house of Henkell.

Mátraalja (Mátra mountains)

En route between Budapest and Eger you pass through Gyóngós and the beautiful 50 km (31 miles) long Mátra range of mountains.
The entire area is covered in dense woodland and is an ideal wine-growing and walking area. The soil is of volcanic origin and hence ideal for cultivating vines for wine. The wines from here are mainly whites that are dry to sweet. The Hárslevelü and Szürkebarat here are good. Some recommended wines include Abasári Olaszrizling of Sándor Kiss, the seductive sweet Muscat Ottonel of Mátyás Szöke

and most of the Tramini wines. The much rarer red wines are surprisingly good, such as the Zweigelt and Cabernet Sauvignon of Mátyás Szöke and the Kékfrankos Vinitor of Szölökert Coöperative of Nagyréde.

Some of the rosés are also worth while considering. The most surprising wines are probably the superb Sauvignon Blancs and Chardonnays. Not only are these wines of great style and quality (like the Mátra Hill Sauvignon Blanc and Chardonnay of Szölöskert or the Mátraaljai Chardonnay of Mátyás Szöke) but they cost much less than the average Hungarian Sauvignon or Chardonnay. Drinking temperature is 8–12°C (46.4–53.6°F).

Eger

The town of Eger is situated in a hilly area about 130 km (81 miles) east of Budapest. The volcanic soil here also seems highly beneficial for wine-growing. The Eger Bull's Blood or Egri Bikavér is world famous but of variable quality. The Egervin company is typical of the wine tradition in this area. They make several fine wines such as their slightly sweet Debröi Hárslevelü, which is like a glass filled with floral honey.

Much has changed since Egervin have used a 'flying wine-maker' from Australia. All the oxygen is now removed from the bottles and replaced with nitrogen so that the white wines become less easily 'tired'. The quality of the red wines is also heading upwards. The lesser quality Kadarka is being replaced with Kékfrankos, Cabernet Sauvignon, and Merlot. The testing laboratory in Eger is also doing development work with Blauweburger grapes. Egri Cabernet Sauvignon 1996 and Egri Merlot 1996 are superb and the 1995 Egri Bikavér (Bull's Blood) is exceptionally fine.

The best Bull's Blood (Egri Bikavér) though comes from Vilmos Thummerer, who is probably one of Hungary's best winemakers, and certainly the best from Eger. Although excellent white wines from grapes such as Leányka, Királyleányka, Pinot Blanc, and Olaszrizling are worth tasting, the finest wines from Eger are the perfect Egri Cabernet Sauvignon and Egri Bikavér. Those made by Thummerer have

The entrance to the Egervin cellars.

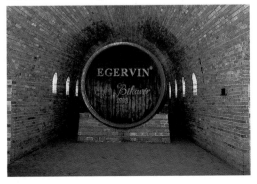

Wine tasting in Egervin's cellars.

great potential to age well. Drinking temperature is 14–18°C (57.2–64.4°F) depending on the quality. Warmer is better with the best quality wines.

Bükkalja

This area between Eger and Miskolc has been somewhat neglected. This is a great shame for in the past fine wines were made that were intended to be used in production of sparkling wines. This area has great potential but has been poorly managed. The soil consists of loess and chalk yet unfortunately only produces very simple white wines that are very acidic. Drinking temperature is 8–10°C (46.4–50°F).

Tokajhegyalja

The gently undulating hills, cool valleys, winding rivers that are teeming with fish, rustic villages in pastel colours and storks all conspire to make the area around Tokaj extremely picturesque.

The Tokaj area is best known for its Tokay (Tokaji), which is like liquid gold. It is not surprising that the bidding in Latin 'Oremus!' (Let us pray!) is above the entrance to the town's cellars. Tokay is no ordinary wine.

Probably no other wine region in Hungary has seen such major changes as Tokajhegyalja since the ending of Soviet domination. The arrival of foreign investors quickened the pace of the renewal process but this also caused an enormous identity crisis in the region. Before the break up of the Communist Bloc the wineries' equipment had not been well maintained and the wines contained substantial amounts of iron oxide (rust). Fortunately now that most equipment has been replaced this problem will soon be consigned to the past.

There are countless old bottles still awaiting customers in the intriguing cellars of the old Tokay houses that are covered in black cellar mould. Those who want to try the traditional-style Tokay are best directed to the former state company Tokaj Kereskedöház (Tokay Trading House).

An impressive array of vintages are available from them. For those who prefer the modern Tokay they

Disznókö cellars, Tokaj.

will find it with the French-Hungarian firm of Disznókö (AXA Millésimes), Château Pajzos & Megyer (GAN) and Hétszölö (Grand Millésimes de France-Suntory), or the Spanish-Hungarian Oremus (Vega Sicilia).

The involvement of foreign investors has meant that substantial time and money has been invested here in soil improvement, new planting, new equipment, better hygiene and quality control of the grapes and wines. This has resulted in a significant improvement in quality.

The modern wine-making techniques vary greatly with those of the traditional makers. The emphasis is on retaining the freshness and fruitiness in the wine and great efforts are made to try to prevent contact with oxygen (the reductive method) as opposed to the older slow oxidisation process still used by Tokaj

Kereskedöház. Wines made by the reductive process not only taste better and have a more pleasing bouquet (without that heavy sherry-like aroma typical of the oxidisation process), they also become clear very much more quickly. This means that the consumer does not have to wait so long for the wines to become drinkable so that they can be relatively less expensive. After initial scorn, the traditional wine-makers now accept the results of the more modern wine-makers.

TOKAJI FURMINT

In addition to the superior Tokay wines, Tokay also produces white wines from Furmint grapes which have a traditional oxidised taste similar to those of the Jura and Jerez. Drinking temperature is 8–12°C (46.4–53.6°F) according to taste.

The Tokaji mountain.

Ultra modern cellars of Disnókö, Tokaj.

Tokay Museum.

Onset of botrytis.

TOKAJI EDES SZAMORODNI

In those years when too few aszú grapes with noble rot (botrytis) can be harvested to make a sweet Tokay, the Edes (slightly sweet) Tokaji Edes Szamorodni ('as it comes') is produced instead.

For those who do not wish to wait so long for a pleasant and delightful wine, that is also less expensive, then a good Tokaji Edes Szamorodni is a solution. This wine is comparable with a three puttonyos wine (puttonyos relates to the amount of aszú added to the base wine) that is similar to a German Auslese, which has a wonderful bouquet of overripe fruit in which the upper notes are peach, apricot, raisin, almond, vanilla, and various floral

Tokay Furmint.

Tokay Szamorodny Edes.   *Botrytis's full effect.*

notes such as lily-of-the-valley and may blossom. Szamorodni Edes is often served in Hungary as an aperitif or with goose liver. Drinking temperature is 8–10°C/46.4–50°F (but cooler is also possible).

TOKAJI SZÁRAZ SZAMORODNI

The dry (száraz) Tokaji Száraz Szamorodni has much in common with a Fino Jerez (sherry). Drinking temperature is 10–12°C (50–53.6°F).

TOKAJI ASZÚ

The secret of Tokay wine is the microclimate which causes autumnal mists in the morning which are driven away later in the day by the heat of the sun. These are ideal environmental conditions for Botrytis cinerea (the noble rot) which eviscerates almost all the moisture from the grapes, leaving a very high concentration of sugars, aromatic, and flavour substances in the grapes.

The withered grapes (known locally as aszú) are picked by hand and collected in containers known as puttonyos which hold about 20 kg aszú grapes. Wine is naturally created under the pressure of the grape's own weight (eszencia) that has intense flavour. This eszencia is added to the 'base' white wine. The higher the number of puttonyos that are added, the greater is the quality of the wine. Wines can be found that are two, three, four, and five puttonyos, with six puttonyos wines more difficult to

Rare six puttonyos Aszú.

find. The wine is then aged in wooden casks. Tokaji Aszú is then usually bottled in half litre 'belly' bottles and left for some years in the impressive cellars of Tokaj. Rare Tokaji Aszú Eszencia wine is made in exceptional years with more than six puttonyos, and then left for decades before being sold. Such outstanding vintages are years such as 1947 and 1963. Take care not to become confused with the ordinary Eszencia, which is also sold separately. The ordinary Eszencia is just nectar with sugar of 400 grams per litre but also high acidity of 17 grams or more that this wine seems less sweet than it actually is. Tasting a traditional Tokay (Tokaji) is a real experience, that is not quickly forgotten. You will be captured by an overwhelming bouquet with aromas of cedarwood, leather, preserved fruit, honey, tobacco, hazelnuts and other nuts, gingerbread, and exotic spices. Modern-style Tokaji Aszú (such as Disnókö) have a deep amber colour, very elegant bouquet of sun-dried apricots, quince, tobacco, leather, almonds, coffee, toast, and acacia honey for

Casks of Aszú and Eszencia.

a five putt, and of sun-dried apricots, white truffles, botrytis, tobacco, cedarwood (cigar box), honey, dates, prunes, and toast for a six putt. These wines have power, finesse, a superb acidity which balances the extreme caressing nature of the wine. Drinking temperature is 6–10°C (42.8–50°F).

TOKAJ, TOKAJI OR TOKAY?

Tokaj is a town in the north east of Hungary. The Hungarians name their wines with the name of the grape or type of wine, preceded with the place of origin in the genitive form. Hence a Cabernet France from Sopron becomes a Soproni Cabernet Franc. Hajósi comes from Hajós, Villanyi from Villány etc. Therefore wine from Tokaj becomes Tokaji Aszú or Tokaji Furmint but is still known as a Tokay in English. Finally to confuse matters further, the French came in contact with this liquid gold and decided to name their Pinot Gris wines Tokay. The labels of Alsatian wines may bear Tokay Pinot Gris instead of Pinot Gris d' Alsace. It is to be hoped this etymological confusion will soon be ended.

Kunság

The area of Kunság (known as Kiskunság up to 1998) is on the Great Plain (Alföld) of Hungary to the south of the town of Kecskemet and extends to the small town of Hajós. This region does not have a real history of wine making, dating back to the end of the nineteenth century when it was found that phylloxera less readily affected vines grown on sandy soils such as those in the south of Hungary. The climate is also not ideal for wine-growing with very hot and totally dry summers and extremely cold winters. The wines from this area are mainly intended for sale as bulk wine and they have little to offer except the high alcohol of both reds and whites, and the syrupy nature of the whites. Drinking temperature is 8–10°C (46.4–50°F) for white wines and 12–16°C (53.6–60.8°F) for reds.

Csongrád

This wine region is also situated on the Hungarian

Tokay wine tasting.

Great Plain (Alföld) to the west of the town of Szeged. The sandy soil is interspersed with some loess and the extremes of weather here produce heavy alcoholic red and white wines of very modest quality. Drinking temperature is 8–10°C (46.4–50°F) for whites and 12–16°C (53.6–60°F) for reds.

Hajós-Baja

The south of Hungary is blessed with a Mediterranean-type climate moderated by maritime influences. This makes the area a paradise for birds. Great flocks of exotic birds such as bee-eaters return each spring to nest in the soft sand dunes.

Although most wines from the south to the west of Csongrád and Kunság are generally of modest quality, an exception to this are the wines from the company of Brilliant Holding of Hajós.

Wines are made here that are steeped in Hungarian tradition but under extremely hygienic conditions and with the use of modern technology (no chaptalization, cask maturing in oak, use of nitrogen during bottling, extra long Portuguese corks). Both rosé wines from Brilliant are fresh and fruity, one being made from Pinot Noir, the other from Kékfrankos.

The rest of the wines are all reds and all of them are real beauties: Hajosi Kékfrankos, Cabernet Sauvignon, and Zweigelt. These are wines of great class that have an ability to age well. Drinking temperature is 10–12°C (50–53.6°F) for the rosés and 14–17°C (57.2–62.6°F) for the reds.

Tasting of young, modern Tokay.

Szeksárd

This area is regarded as one of the oldest wine regions of Hungary. The local microclimate is perfect and there is a fertile sedimentary soil of loess. Szeksárdi Bikavér (Bull's Blood) has an excellent reputation and an older history than that from Eger. This wine is dark red and its bouquet is reminiscent of redcurrants with suggestions of toast. The taste is dry, fresh, very tannic, fulsome, and rounded. Drinking temperature is 15–17°C (59–62.6°F).

In addition to outstanding red wines such as Merlot, Cabernet Sauvignon, Cabernet Franc, Kadarka, and Kékfrankos, Szeksárd also produces excellent Kadarka rosé and whites from Chardonnay, Sauvignon Blanc, and Olaszrizling.

One wine that deserves a special mention is the

Wines from Hajós and Szeksard.

making skills, everything is possible. The wines from this company are the fruit of bringing together the Hungarian wine traditions with the latest technology, combined with ideal climate and geological conditions.

Hajósi Kékfrankos

Hajósi Cabernet Sauvignon

Hajósi Zweigelt

TOLNAI MÖCSÉNYI ZÖLD VELTELINI
This wine is fresh and fruity and should be drunk at 8–10°C (46.4–50°F).

TOLNAI MÖCSÉNYI TRAMINI
This is a subtle, elegant, and very fine wine to be drunk at 10–12°C (50–53.6°F).

sublime Bátaszéki Sauvignon Blanc of the winemaker Akos Kamocsay of Hilltop Neszmély. Their 1997 Sauvignon Blanc was undoubtedly one of the best Hungarian whites of its vintage. It possesses a bouquet in which newly mown grass, wild chervil, stinging nettles, and suggestions of elderflower can be discerned. Drinking temperature is 9–10°C (48.2–50°F).

TOLNAI MÖCSÉNYI SAUVIGNON BLANC
The new member of the family produced from Sauvignon Blanc is delightful. It has vegetal notes in its nose such as green peppers (paprika), asparagus, and mange-tout (*Pisum sativum*). Drinking temperature is 9–10°C (48.2–50°F).

Tolna

Tolna is a new wine area that was part of Szekszárd until recently. Although the name of Tolna is little known outside of Hungary, the area produces wines of exceptional quality. The wines were better known for a long time under the name Bátaapáti, but these days the better wines bear the Möscényi Kastélyborok name on the label. The company of Európai Bortermelök, which is a joint venture between Piero Antinori and Peter Zwack set up in 1991, is a typical example of what can happen elsewhere in Hungary. Hungary has the capability to become a top wine-producing country. With good insight, plenty of foreign investment, government help, and good wine-

TOLNAI MÖCSÉNYI CHARDONNAY
This cask-aged wine is generally very characteristic of the grape with an immediate and rich bouquet and excellent balance between fresh acidity and rounded body. Drinking temperature is 10–12°C (50–53.6°F).

Szeksárdi Kadarka Siller

Szeksárdi Cabernet Sauvignon

Szeksárdi Cabernet Franc

TOLNAI MÖCSÉNYI KÉKFRANKOS

These are a fresh and elegant crystal-clear rosé and a classic deep red wine with a mellow but full-bodied texture.

TOLNAI MÖCSÉNYI SPECIAL RESERVE

The top cuvée is a blend of Cabernet Sauvignon and Cabernet Franc. This Special Reserve is very rich and complex, filling the mouth with flavour, with a good balance between spice and body. The finish is prolonged and superb. This wine needs to be kept for at least two to three years before drinking. Drinking temperature is 17–18°C (62.6–64.4°F).

Villány-Siklós

This is the most southerly of Hungary's wine areas and it consists of two parts. Both sections are sited at the foot of the Villányi mountain. Siklós is better known for its predominantly white wines and Villány for its fine reds. There are six top wine producers in Villány. It is surely no coincidence that the six best wine-makers of Hungary originated from Villány. They are Attila and Támas Gere, Zoltan Polgár, Ede Tiffan, Joszef Bock, Vylyan. Villány wines are quite likely to develop into some of the best in Europe in the coming years. Each wine-maker has an individual style but the power and depth of the red wines is apparent, which is the result of the great care with which the grapes are selected, the volcanic soil, and the very beneficial climate.

VILLÁNYI ROSÉ

Some wine-makers produce a light rosé that is fairly unconvincing but Vylyan makes an excellent Cabernet Sauvignon based rosé. The best rosés from here though are those made from Kékfrankos Kékoportó, which may perhaps contain a little Pinot Noir, Zweigelt, or Kadarka. These are very fresh wines that are elegant, fruity and full-bodied. The Joszef Bock is particularly recommended. Drinking temperature is 10–12°C (50–53.6°F).

VILLÁNYI KÉKOPORTÓ

The better Kékoportó wines (Tiffan, Polgar, or Bock)

Grape harvest in Villany (Bock).

Villányi rosé.

are intensely coloured, fresh, concentrated, fruity, velvet smooth, fruity, mellow, and slightly tannic. There are also excellent cask-aged Kékoportó Barriques (e.g. Vylyan). Drinking temperature is 14–16°C (57.2–60.8°F) or 16–17°C (60.8–62.6°F) for the Barrique.

VILLÁNYI KÉKFRANKOS

This is an authentic full-bodied and rounded fresh red wine that is full of tannin. (Tamás Gere, Bock, or Polgar).
Drinking temperature is 14–16°C (57.2–60.8°F).

VILLÁNYI PINOT NOIR

The Pinot Noir grape thrives on the volcanic soil. Támas Gere is a Pinot Noir specialist and he vinifies the wine separately. It is a full-bodied, fiery, and powerful wine with delicate acidity and distinctive taste of terroir.
Drinking temperature is 14–16°C (57.2–60.8°F).

VILLÁNYI MERLOT

These are good wines with definite bouquet of cedarwood, blackcurrant, and hint of roses. They possess a fulsome and rounded taste and are velvet smooth in structure.

Villányi Kékoportó.

VILLÁNYI
PINOT NOIR
1996

VILLÁNY - SIKLÓSI BORVIDÉK

Pinot Noir szőlőből készült,
ászokhordós érlelésű, rubinvörös,
finom aromájú, elegáns vörösbor.

Fogyasztása 16-18 °C-on ajánlott.
Kitűnően harmonizál a vörös
és a vadhúsokból készített ételek ízeivel.

Palackozás dátuma: 1998. június
PRODUCE OF HUNGARY

12,3 % Vol.   75 cl e

5 995971 956461

Villányi Pinot Noir.

These wines are superbly made but never either exciting or typically Hungarian.
Drinking temperature is 14–16°C (57.2–60.8°F).

VILLÁNYI CABERNET FRANC

This is certainly not a native grape variety and in the rest of Hungary this wine would be inconsequential but here in Villány it develops a character of its own, possibly as a result of the volcanic soil. It is dark in colour while the nose is reminiscent of ripe plum or even prune, and blueberry, while the taste is fulsome, firm, and rich, with the required tannin. Drinking temperature is 16°C (60.8°F).

VILLÁNYI CABERNET SAUVIGNON

Villány's volcanic soils and favourable climate helps to produce Cabernet Sauvignon wines of great style.

Villányi Cabernet Franc.

Villányi Cabernet Sauvignon.

Villányi Cabernet Sauvignon.

Although not native, the grapes here produce a wine that is characteristic of this southern region, filled with colour, very aromatic with suggestions of berries and peppers, with a fulsome and powerfully fiery taste with considerable tannin. These wines of superb class have great potential for ageing well, especially those that are cask aged (such as those of Vylyan, Bock, and Tiffan). Drinking temperature is 16–17°C (60.8–62.6°F).

CUVÉES

A cuvée is generally a better class of wine. These are made from various combinations such as the classic

Villányi Cabernet Sauvignon Barrique

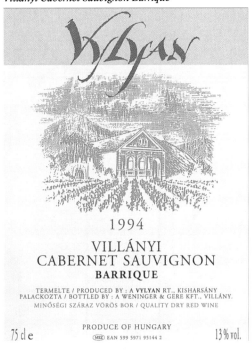

Cabernet Sauvignon, Cabernet Franc, and Merlot, or Franco-Hungarian Cabernet Sauvignon and Cabernet Franc with Kékfrankós or Kékoportó), pure Hungarian Kékfrankos and Kékofrankós, Austro-Hungarian Blauburger, Zweigelt, Kékfrankos, Kékofrankós, or French in style Cabernet Sauvignon and Pinot Noir with an impossible accent .

There are countless excellent cuvées that each has its own character and taste. The best classical ones come from Polgar, Bock, Támas and Attila Gere, and Tiffan.
Tiffan and Vylyan make the best Hungarian and Austro-Hungarian style cuvées, while Bock and Vylyan specialise in unusual cuvées of Pinot Noir and Cabernet Sauvignon.

VILLÁNY WHITE WINES
Although Villány is best known for its reds and Siklós for its whites, there are some Villány whites. Pince Polgár offers a very wide range of wines, perhaps slightly too broad in scope, evidenced by the combinations of Olaszrizling, Sauvignon Blanc, and somewhat green Chardonnay.

The 100% Olaszrizling, Tramini, Chardonnay Barrique are excellent, and the Hárslevelü and Muskotály (Muscat) are superb.

Villányi Cuvée Jammertal.

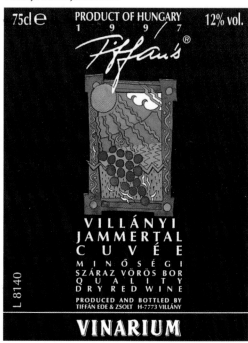

Villányi Cabernet Sauvignon and Franc Cuvée.

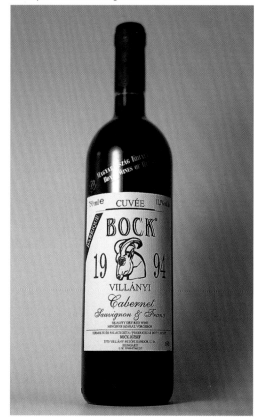

Villányi Cabernet Sauvignon Cuvée.

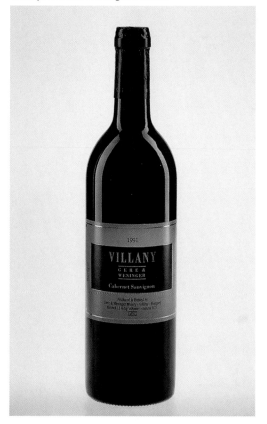

Villányi Olaszrizling.

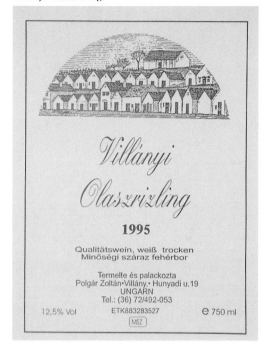

Villányi Chardonnay.

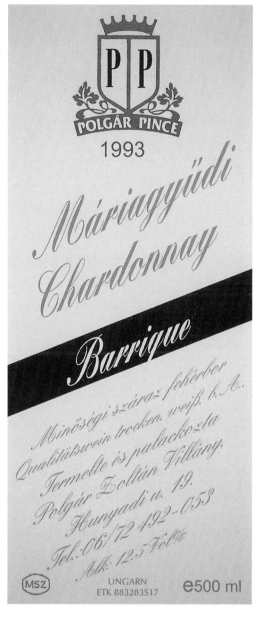

SIKLÓSI OLASZRIZLING
A delicious dry and characteristic white is made here by Bock. Drinking temperature is 10–12°C (50–53.6°F).

SIKLÓSI HÁRSLEVELÜ
Although these grapes often yield semi-sweet wines, Bock produces a freshly vinified dry wine with superb bouquet with hints of lime blossom and mild fruity notes in both nose and taste. Drinking temperature is 10–12°C (50–53.6°F).

SIKLÓSI CHARDONNAY
This southern Chardonnay is not comparable with the often green wine of northern countries. The Chardonnay of Siklós (from Bock) is fulsome, aromatic and seductive. It is both fresh and rounded and also well balanced. Drinking temperature is 10–12°C (50–53.6°F).

MECSEK
This wine region is split into two areas: one surrounding Pécs and the other around Mohács. Both areas are in undulating hills and are blessed with a warm Mediterranean-style climate. The underlying strata here is a mixture of rock, sand, soft slate, and much chalk.
The blue Cirfandli, white Chardonnay and Olaszrizling thrive here best with also some Muskotály (Muscat).

CIRFANDLI
This variety of grapes was introduced to Hungary from Northern Italy by way of Austria. The wine from these grapes is of very variable quality. In poor years it is barely drinkable but in good vintages a superb wine is produced that is full-bodied, fresh, very spicy, and generally with sugar residues. Drinking temperature is 14–16°C (57.2–60.8°F).

CHARDONNAY
The local Chardonnay here is of good quality and surprisingly fresh and aromatic for such a southern wine with hints of butter, chalk, and citrus fruit. It is rounded and full-bodied. Some of the wines containing sugar residues are not so dry. Drinking temperature is 10–12°C (50–53.6°F).

Villányi Muskotály.

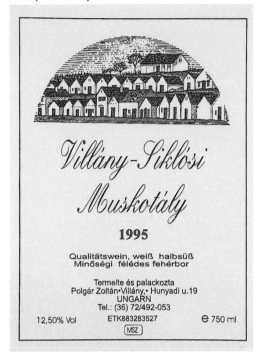

Villány-Siklósi

Muskotály

1995

Qualitätswein, weiß halbsüß
Minőségi félédes fehérbor

Termelte és palackozta
Polgár Zoltán•Villány,• Hunyadi u.19
UNGARN
Tel.: (36) 72/492-053
12,50% Vol   ETK883283527   ℮ 750 ml
[MSZ]

Villányi Hárslevelü.

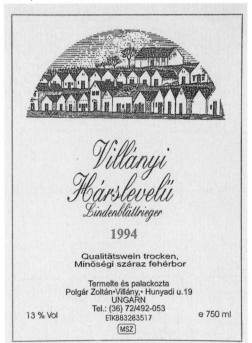

Villányi

Hárslevelü

Lindenblättrieger

1994

Qualitätswein trocken,
Minőségi száraz fehérbor

Termelte és palackozta
Polgár Zoltán•Villány,• Hunyadi u.19
UNGARN
Tel.: (36) 72/492-053
13 % Vol   ETK883283517   ℮ 750 ml
[MSZ]

The Balaton

The area surrounding Lake Balaton is ideal for

Villányi-Siklósi Borvidék.

SIKLÓSI CHARDONNAY
BARRIQUE 1996

VILLÁNY - SIKLÓSI BORVIDÉK

Ezen a történelmi borvidéken
a Chardonnay szőlő rendkívül szép
bort ad. Csodálatos illat és zamatvilága
új tölgyfa hordóban érlelve
bontakozik ki legteljesebben.

Ajánlható aperitifként, de kitűnő
borjúsültekhez, fehér húsú házi
szárnyasokhoz és halakhoz.

Fogyasztása 8-10 °C-on ajánlott.

Palackozás dátuma: 1998. június
PRODUCE OF HUNGARY

12,5 % Vol.   75 cl ℮

summer holidays. The lake itself is a watersports
paradise. The lake is 77 km (48 miles) long and 14
km (9 miles) wide as its broadest point. The water is
only some 3–4 metres (10–13 feet) deep except
around the Bay of Tihany where the lake can be 12
metres (39 feet) deep.
The climate is mild in winter and hot in summer
(above 25°C).

The water temperature varies in the summer between
20 and 26°C (68–78.8°F). In addition to still wines,
the wine areas around Lake Balaton also produce
several very acceptable sparkling wines.

DÉL-BALATON

The soil of the most southerly of the three wine areas around Lake Balaton is a mixture of sand and clay. Most of the wine-makers no longer produce ponderous, heavy, and oxidised wines as was once the case. The young wines are fresh, mild, light, and fruity and are chiefly made from Irsai Olivér, Tramini, Olaszrizling, Chardonnay, and Muskotály (Muscat). There are also a few reds made from Merlot, Cabernet Sauvignon, Cabernet Franc, and Kékfrankos. The local reds and whites here are generally very simple affairs but the exception is the superb, taut wines of Chapel Hill in Balatonboglár which are full of character. These wines originate from small areas of land on volcanic soil. The Chapel Hill Sauvignon Blanc and those of Ottó Légli are two of the surprising exceptions.

BALATONMELLÉK

The soil of this most western of the Lake Balaton wine areas on the northern shore consists of chalk, marl, and some tufa, interspersed with volcanic outcrops. This makes the area ideal for white wines and hence it is planted with Olaszrizling, Rajnai Rizling, Rizling Szilváni, Szrkebarát, Sauvignon Blanc, Chardonnay, and some other white grape varieties.

The outstanding wine-maker Sander Tóth makes excellent aromatic, full-bodied, and classic-style Chardonnay, but also exceptionally sensual wines such as the Aldozói Zöldveltelini and Enit.

Badacsony

This fairly small wine area is sited around the town of this name on the northern shores of Lake Balaton. The soil chiefly consists of basalt and other volcanic types. This imparts high acidity, a rich bouquet, and fulsome but fiery taste to the local wines. The area's speciality is an exceptionally sultry, slightly sweet to sweet wine that is made from late harvested Kéknyelü, Szrkebarát, Tramini, Rajnai Rizling, and Muskotály (Muscat) grapes.

But there are also many fresh and scented dry white wines that are made from Olaszrizling, Zöld Veltelini, and Sauvignon Blanc, plus full-bodied, rich Chardonnays.

Balatonfüred-Csopak

This is the most north-westerly of the areas around Lake Balaton, situated around the town of Csopak. The soil is mainly underlying strata of volcanic origin with shale, ferruginous sandstone, rock, and chalk. White wines are produced here from Olaszrizling, Rajnai Rizling, Rizling Szilvány, Tramini, Muskotály, Sauvignon Blanc, and Chardonnay), reds from Cabernet Franc, Merlot, Pinot Noir, and Zweigelt, plus rosés from Merlot, Zweigelt, and Kékfrankos). Balatonfüred wines are full-bodied, powerful, and rounded, while those of Csopak possess greater finesse, acidity, and elegance.

Lake Balaton.

The Czech and Slovak Republics

The Czech and Slovak Republics separated from each other quite recently. Both countries have a very turbulent history behind them.

The economic position in both countries is far from ideal, although the Czech Republic is developing rapidly. Slovakia is of greater interest as a wine producer while the Czech Republic is more of a place of pilgrimage for true beer lovers as the home of Pilsener Urquell and the true Budweiser. The Czech Republic is the origin in the town of Plzen (Pilsen) of all Pilsener type beers. Despite this, vines are also cultivated in the Czech Republic as well as in Slovakia.

Czech Republic

The Czech Republic is the most western of the two countries in both geography and culture. The roughly rectangular country borders Germany, Austria, Slovakia, and Poland.

Unlike Slovakia, the Czech Republic does not have a centuries old tradition of wine-making. Bohemia and Moravia that form today's Czech Republic have always been beer drinking territory, perhaps influenced by Germany. The Czechs are the world's biggest beer drinkers, consuming 160 litres per inhabitant per annum, and for this reason the importance of wine is unlikely to gain much headway

Rulandské Bílé.

Popular tourist wine.

at present, although the growth in tourism is creating a market for wine.

The Czech vineyards (34,000 hectares in 1996) are divided between the two halves of the country, with Bohemia to the north west and Moravia to the south. When compared with beer consumption the amount of wine consumed is quite low at just 12 litres per head of population per annum. Despite this almost five times as much wine is imported into the country

Müller-Thurgau.

Ryzlink Rynsky Bohemia.

as is exported. Most Czech wines (two-thirds) are whites, followed by red, and sparkling wines.

The varieties of grapes are modern: Grüner-Veltliner, Gewürztraminer, Müller-Thurgau, Pinot Blanc, Pinot Gris, Sauvignon Blanc, Sylvaner, Traminer, Vlassky Ryzlink (Welsch Riesling), Rynsky Ryzlink (Rhine Riesling), and Zluty Muskat for the whites with Frankovka (Blau Fränkisch, Kékfrankos), Zweigelt, Cabernet Sauvignon, the native Vavrinec, and the old-fashioned St. Laurent for reds.

Bohemia

The Czech Republic is split into Bohemia and Moravia.

Wine-growing in Bohemia covers a relatively small area. There are about 650 hectares of vines that are mainly planted alongside the Elbe river. These are the remnants of vineyards planted by Emperor Rudolf II (1552-1612).

There are six areas of wine-growing within Bohemia but the area around Prague (Praha) and Cáslav are little more than symbolic with less than 10 hectares of vineyards. Bohemia hardly enjoys a good climate for wine-growing with an average annual temperature of a mere 8°C (46.4°F) and an average of only 14.5°C (58°F) during the growth period. There are only 1,600–1,800 hours of sunshine per annum, and precipitation is 500–550 mm per annum. The soil is mainly chalk-bearing but also incorporates weathered basalt.

The Melník area, near the town of Melník on the delta of the Moldau (Vltava) and Elbe (Labe) rivers, is Bohemia's largest wine-growing region. Various branded wines are produced here of which the best known is Ludmila, which is sold in squat cylindrical bottles known as 'ink pots'. The base wine for Ludmila is Modrý Portugal (or Blue Portugal). This wine is clearly acidic with a taste of hazelnut. White Ludmila mainly consists of Müller-Thurgau grapes and has a mild floral bouquet and tastes of fresh fruit. Both wines are drunk when young. The first Bohemian sekt is also made in Melník, known as

Chateau Melník Brut, which is popular in the Czech Republic for its fresh taste and high acidity.

The next wine region to Melník has the town of Roudnice as its centre. Here the vineyards are planted on fairly steep hills alongside the Elbe (Labe). The dry white wines here are mainly made from Sylván Zelený (green Sylvaner), producing a mildly bitter and spicy taste. The red Svatovavrinecké (St. Laurens) is an intense dark red wine with fulsome taste and mild nose redolent of fruit stones. The young wine is fairly unruly but the taste becomes more rounded with age.

In the Zernoseky area the vineyards are sited on south-facing slopes overlooking the river Elbe (Labe) and the central mountains of Bohemia. The best-known mountain is Radobýl and one of the most important places within this area is Litomerice.

The most widely main wines here are from Müller-Thurgau, Ryzlink Rýnský (Rhine Riesling), Rulandské Bílé (White Rulander), and Tramín Cervený (Red Traminer). These are dry wines characterised by their pronounced bouquets. The Tramín Cervený (Red Traminer) is golden yellow and possesses a distinctive bouquet and spicy taste.

The most widely drunk of the reds from here is the Svatovavrinecké. This is a dark red wine with a piquant taste that is dominated by tannin. The area of Most was the largest of the Medieval wine areas but wine-growing and making fell into decay here in recent times. It was not until late in the twentieth century that new vineyards were planted on areas such as the spoil tips from the lignite (brown coal) mines. The vineyards here regularly suffer from frosts but the wine from this area is of reasonable quality in good years.

The whites include Müller-Thurgau, Ryzlink Rýnský (Rhine Riesling), and Rulandské Bílé, while the reds include Svatovavrinecké (St. Laurens) and Zweigeltrebe. These are typical grape varieties for northern latitudes. The white wines have a pronounced aroma and tart taste.

The red wines are intensely coloured and have a definite taste of tannin. The wine-making centre of this area is Chrámce. Kosher wine is also made here from grapes cultivated and picked under supervision of a Prague rabbi. This wine is made under very strict conditions of hygiene. The entire process from the pressing of the grapes to filling the bottles is carried out by Jews.

The wine is pasteurised because no other preservative than sulphur dioxide is permitted.

Moravia

Conditions for wine-growing are better in Moravia than Bohemia. There is a tradition here of wine-making that goes back at least a thousand years. The start of wine-making coincides with the occupation by the Roman legions in third century BC.

At present there are about 12,000 hectares of productive vines in Moravia. The climate is relatively favourable. The average annual temperature is

Vinum Frankovka.   *Moravsky Muskát.*

between 10°C (50°F) and 15°C (59°F) during the growing seasons. Average precipitation is 500–700 mm per annum. The consistency of the soil is extremely varied, ranging through slate-like strata and chalk-bearing layers to gravel, and predominantly clay soils. The vineyards are cultivated on both slopes and level ground with a preference for frost-free locations.

The branded wines are with the odd exception of second rank and some of them are sweetened. The best quality wines are those indicated as Kabinett, Spätlese, and Auslese. These wines are produced under strict control of the Czech state's agriculture and food inspectors. During production no sugar may be added and wines must achieve set levels for residual sugars to achieve one of the predicates. The label must not only indicate the wine-growing area but also the place of origin. Some growers also name the specific vineyard from which the grapes were picked. The entire region is subdivided into ten wine-growing areas.

The Brno wine area lies to the south and south-east of Brno where the vineyards are sited on gentle slopes.

The wines here have a characteristic bouquet and the best-known examples are from Rajhrad and Dolní Kounice. One of the wines from the area is a Moravian Muscat (Moravský Muýkát) made from a Moravian grape variety. The wine is yellow and has a marked Muscat nose and fairly full but tart flavour.

The relatively small Bzenec wine area is situated on the right bank of the Morava river between Kyjov and Veselí. The vineyards here are planted on higher slopes in hot and dry locations. The town of Bzenec is the heart of this area.

The best-known wines are the Rýnský Ryzlink characterised by a pale greenish yellow colour and marked nose with a hint of lime blossom and a fulsome tart taste. The wine can be drunk young but shows more quality when allowed to age. Rýnský Ryzlink is also the basis for the famous Bzenecká Lipka (Bzenec lime tree). This wine has a very muted nose and fulsome taste with balanced acidity. Other grapes grown here are Rulandské Bílé, Neuburské

(Neuburger), and Ryzlink Vlaýský. Few red wine grapes are grown in this area.

The Mikulov wine area is one of the largest that extends from Novomlýnské Nádrze to the border with Austria.

The best-known towns are Valtice, Mikulov, and Lednice. This is an area of mainly white wines that are fulsome in taste with pleasing acidity and striking character. A number of wines are produced here with quality predicates, mainly made from Ryzlink Vlaýký, Veltlínské Zelené, Muýkát Moravský, Ryzlink Rýnský, Chardonnay, and Aurelius. There is also a plant improvement station at Perná where frost and disease resistant grape varieties are developed. The Aurelius and Pálava grapes were developed here. Trials are currently being run with Malverina, Hybia, Savilon, Kaberon, and other varieties.

Müller-Thurgau is highly regarded here for its yellow-green colour, characteristic taste of spice and intense nose that is reminiscent of ripe peaches. Pálava is also green-yellow with a spicy and fairly fulsome taste.

The most interesting of the red wines is the Frankovka from Valtice, which has a fulsome taste with sharp acidity and tannin. The colour is a bright red and the taste is characteristically of cinnamon.

The Mutenice area extends between Hustopece and Hodonín. The best vineyards here are centrally located within the area on slopes. The best-known places are Cejkovice, Mutenice, and Ratíýkovice. Both reds and whites are made in this area. The Tramín Cervený from Mutenice has a golden yellow colour and spicy taste and nose. The Rulandskéýedé (Grey Rulander) of Ratíýkovice is a rare wine with a characteristic bouquet and taste. The Frankovka from Cejkovice is bright red with a fulsome taste and excellent acidity and tannin.

The wine area of Velké Pavlovice is situated to the south-east of Brno, on the left bank of the Svratka river. The best-known towns are Velké Pavlovice, Kobylí, and Velké Bílovice. This is mainly a red wine producing area.

The Frankovka here is dry with striking acidity and pleasing bitterness. The Svatovavrinecké is an intense red with a fulsome and velvet-smooth taste and well-balanced acidity and tannin. The nose suggests stone fruit. The Rulandské Modré is a dry ruby red wine with floral nose that after sufficient ageing is reminiscent of stone fruit. There is mild bitterness but the whole is fulsome and harmonious. The Modrý Portugal is a dark red and fresh wine with a coarse taste.

The Znojmo area is in the Dyjsko-Svratecký valley on the Dyje river, bordering Austria in thc south of the area. This area has countless wine centres of which Znojmo, Yatov and NovýYaldorf are the best known. It is a predominantly white wine area and its proximity to Austria manifests itself in similar types and quality of wine.

The finest Moravian vineyard of Yobes is on the Austrian border. The ideal climate here ripens the Rulandské ýedé, Ryzlink Rýnský, and Ryzlink Vlaský fully. The wines from the Yobes vineyard are

Ryzlink Rynsky Pozdní Sběr   *Dry Slovakian Tokay.*

characterised by their fullness and pronounced bouquet. The Sauvignon Blanc from Znojmo is pale yellow-green and has a wonderful nose that in lesser years is reminiscent of nettles and in good years of ripe peaches. The Irsai Oliver from Yatov has a bewitching Muscat bouquet and fulsome and harmonious taste. The Neuburské is a dry wine that is green-yellow with a gentle nose and fulsome taste with mild bitterness. In good years this wine is capable of maturing well and develops into a fine rounded wine after five years. The Ryzlink Vlaský is a mildly aromatic dry wine with higher acidity, green-yellow colour, and spicy aroma. It is drunk when young.

The Stráznice area is situated to the east of Hodonín on the left bank of the Morava, close to the border with Slovakia. The best known wine places are Blatnice, Blatnicka, and Stráznice.

The Rulandské Bílé from Stráznice is a green-yellow dry wine which by Czech standards is a top class wine of great character. It is full-bodied and slightly spicy, leaving a prolonged and pleasing aftertaste. This wine has good potential for maturing and certainly acquires greater character with age. The branded Blatnický Rohác is made from Ryzlink Rýnský grapes. This wine is pale green-yellow and it has a strikingly fresh bouquet and fulsome taste.

The Kyjov area is situated to the east of Brno between the Livava and Kyjovka rivers, to the west of the Bzenec area.

The best known places are Borýov and Kyjov. The vineyards are mainly sited on south facing slopes. Pleasant white and red wines are produced here from grapes such as Müller-Thurgau and Rulandské Bílé. A new variety of red-wine grape, André, is grown here that is a cross between Frankovka and Svatovavrinecké. This produces high acidity and levels of tannin.

The Uherské-Hradiyte area is spread out on the right bank of the Morava, near Chriby in Moravské Slovácko (Moravian Slovakia). The best known places are Bílovice, Uherské, Hradiyte, and Velehrad. These wines have pronounced acidity and a full-bodied character that is typical of the grapes used. The reds are deeply coloured with a harmonious balance of tannin and acidity. The wines from Velehrad have good potential for ageing. The Müller-Thurgau wines from Velehrad are yellowish in colour with a pronounced spicy bouquet and rounded taste. The Zweigeltrebe wines are pale ruby with a mild, not oppressive bouquet and pleasing taste that is characteristic.

The Podluzí area is close to Hodonín, and bounded to the east by the Stráznice area and to the west by Mikulov area. The central places here are Hodonín and Dolní Bojanovice. The Veltlín Zelený (Green Veltliner) from the Nechory vineyards is pale green-yellow, with mildly spicy taste and bouquet, and slightly tart finish.

Slovakia

Slovakia is much smaller than the Czech Republic and this is made more telling by the fact that about one third of the country consists of the Tatra mountains (Nízke Tatry). Slovakia borders Poland, Hungary, Austria, and the Czech Republic. The climate is continental with mountain influences, with hot dry summers and very cold winters.

The vineyards are concentrated in two areas, in the south west near Bratislava, close to the Czech, Austrian, and Hungarian borders, and to the east of Kosice against the border with Hungary and the Ukraine. Both areas are characterised by many rivers, the Danube (Donau) and its tributaries the Váh, Nitra, and Hron in the west and Hronád, Topla, and Ondava in the east. These two large areas are subdivided into eight sub areas. From west to east these are: Skalika-Zahorie, The Lesser Carpathians, Hlohovec-Trnava, Nitra, The Danube Valley, and Mody Kamen for the western section and East Slovakia and Tokay for the eastern zone. The best vineyards are sited in the Lesser Carpathians and close to the towns of Nitra, Hlohovec, and Trnava. The soil in these places consists of a mixture of clay and sand. Modra and Pezinok also make reasonable wines. The best known Slovakian wine though is however Tokay (written here in the same manner as in English).

When the boundaries of Tokay (Tokaji) were established in 1908 both countries were still part of the Austro-Hungarian empire.

The strictly defined Tokay wine area includes Sátoraljaúhely, Sárospatak, Szerencs, and en Tokaj (all in present-day Hungary) and Kiss Tronja (Trna), Vinicky (Szolske), and Slovenské Nové Mesto (all in present-day Slovakia).

This started to become confused once the Hungarians and Czechoslovakians gained their independence in 1918.

There was a long drawn-out legal dispute over the right to use the Tokaji name. The Hungarians demanded its exclusive use because most of the Tokay vineyards were in Hungary, together with the town of Tokaj, which is at the epicentre of the designated area.

Because no agreement was possible the Hungarians bought up virtually all the wine from what is now the Slovakian Tokay area before the fall of the Communist Bloc. This wine was then treated as Hungarian Tokay. After the fall of communism in Hungary, the monolithic state Tokay company was gradually privatised. The emphasis there now is on quality and authenticity, so the Slovakian Tokay was totally ignored.

When Slovakia separated from the former Czechoslovakia in 1989, the local growers went on the offensive and started to market Slovakian Tokay, to the great dismay of the Hungarian government.

The damaging litigation is not yet concluded but this is good news for the consumer.

Slovakian Tokay is made from the same grapes as its Hungarian namesake, on similar soil, and according to the same vinification practice with oxidisation of the wine. The colour, bouquet, and taste closely resemble an Hungarian Tokay but the price is much lower.

Austria

Austrian wines have re-established themselves after the great disaster of the anti-freeze scandal of fifteen years ago.

Austria can satisfy the true wine lover like no other country with its countless different types and tastes of wine. Austrian wines are convivial, informal, and inviting, reflecting the culture and picturesque landscape of the country.

St Laurent grapes are less well-known.

Neuberger Eiswein (Neusiedler See).

Wine regions

The Austrian wine industry is concentrated in the east and south-east of the country.

The Alps in the west make wine-growing virtually impossible. The country has borders with Germany in the west, Italy to the south, but the vineyards are along the borders with the Czech Republic, Slovakia, Hungary, and Slovenia.

The 55,000 hectares of vines in cultivation in Austria are in four main wine-producing regions. From north to south, these are Lower Austria (Niederöster-reich), Vienna (Wien), Burgenland, and Styria (Steiermark).

This four main regions are further subdivided into sixteen wine regions.

Lower Austria (Niederösterreich)

There are about 32,000 hectares of vineyards in a fairly large area running from the Czech-Hungarian border to the south of Vienna.

Austria's most popular wine: Grüner-Veltliner.

Federspiel, Wachau.

Smaragd, Wachau.

Weinviertel

This is the biggest of the sixteen Austrian wine regions and about one third of all Austrian wine is produced here.

This region is well-known from wine books for the long narrow streets in the villages with their rows of wine cellars (known as kellergassen), where the local wines can be tasted and purchased.

The wines made from the Grüner Veltliner grapes are also well known, accounting for at least 50% of the production here. In addition to Grüner Veltliner the grapes grown include Welsch Riesling, Rhine Riesling, Weiss Burgunder, and Morillon (Chardonnay) for the whites, and Blauer Portugieser and Zweigelt for the reds. The soil of the Weinviertel (or wine quarter) is chiefly black loam and chalk.

Kamptal

Kamptal is best known for its very good Grüner Veltliner wines with typically peppery nose and fresh acidity.

Other good to excellent wines include Riesling and Chardonnay whites and excellent red Zweigelt, Pinot Noir, and Cabernet Sauvignon, mainly from

Trockenbeerenauslese ñ pure nectar.

Steinfeder, Wachau.

Renowned Ruster
Ausbruch, Neusiedler
See-Hügelland.

Langelois dry wine,
Kamptal.

Langelois Grau and
Weissburgunder, Kamptal.

Several top Wachau
wines.

the village of Langenlois. Kamptal sets the pace in Europe for its biological approach to wine-making. The soil here is clay with some chalk and although still mainly a white wine area, red wine production is on the increase.

Kremstal

First class Grüner Veltliner, Riesling, and Chardonnay wines are made in this wine region around the town of Krems. The underlying rock is granite in the west and there is clay with loess in the east and south east that yield elegant, fruity, and very aromatic whites.

Wachau

This region in the picturesque valley of the Danube makes quality wines, including excellent Grüner Veltliner, Neuburger, Chardonnay, and Weiss Burgunder.

The vineyards are arranged in terraces on steep slopes above the Danube. The underlying geology is mainly of basalt and other igneous rock. This region produces the finest wines of Austria although the competition with Styria is becoming more intense.

Traisental

This area surrounds the town of St Polten and stretches as far as the Danube. Extremely fruity Grüner Veltliner, Welsch Riesling, Rhine Riesling, and Morillon (Chardonnay) are produced here on soil of loam and sand.

Donauland

Donauland is a transitional area on both sides of the river Danube (Donau), between Krems and Vienna. The soil of loam and clay with interspersed chalk

produces first class Grüner Veltliner, Riesling, and Weiss Burgunder.

Carnuntum

The style of vine cultivation here is known as 'gemischter Satz', or mixed vines, in which different varieties are planted together in the same vineyard. The vines benefit from the influences of both the Danube and Neusiedler See or lake.

The soil consists mainly of clay, sand, gravel, and chalk. The characteristic grapes are Grüner Veltliner, Welsch Riesling, Weiss Burgunder, and Morillon (Chardonnay) for whites and Zweigelt and St. Laurent for red wines.

Thermenregion

This is the most southerly of the Lower Austrian wine regions, south of Vienna and west of the Neusiedler See.

The name of this region is derived from the many hot springs of volcanic origin in this area. The

Weninger is a top
Burgenland wine house.

underlying ground is hard rock with an upper layer of clay and chalk.

The historical and commercial centre of this region is Gumpold-kirschen. The white wines from here are full-bodied and very aromatic while the reds are full-bodied and powerful.

Burgenland

Burgenland comprises two parts that are both next to the Hungarian border.

The northern part is formed by Neusiedlersee and Neusiedler See-Hügelland is directly influenced by the Neusiedler See or lake, while the southern part of Mittelburgenland and Südburgenland is less influenced by the lake.

Neusiedlersee

Fine Zweigelt wine from Neusiedler See.

The Central European climate is hot and dry but is combined here with humidity from the waters of the Neusiedler See which is the basis for the region's success.

Botrytis or the noble rot thrives here to produce exceptionally fine Prädikat wines. The area's strength lies in its Edelfäule wines (noble rot wines), straw wines, Eiswein (ice wines), and other sweet wines made from Welsch Riesling, Weiss Bur4gunder Bouvier, and Muskat Ottonel grapes. But the reds here are also excellent, such as those from St. Laurent, Blau Fränkisch, Cabernet Sauvignon, and Pinot Noir.

Neusiedler See-Hügelland

This area is located on the other – western – side of the Neusiedler See lake, between the lakes of the plains and the Thermen-region. It is best known for its seductive sweet wines such as the famous Ruster Ausbruch.

The whites are made from Welsch Riesling, Weiss Burgunder, Neuburger, Sauvignon, and Morillon (Chardonnay).

Excellent red wines are made in the area around the picturesque village of Rust from Fränkisch, Zweigelt, and Cabernet Sauvignon. Most of the vineyards are sited on soils of clay, sand, chalk, and black loam.

Neusiedler See-Hügelland Ruster W‰lsch Riesling

Mittelburgenland

The soil here is heavier clay and a greater proportion of red wine is made. The excellent dry reds are full-bodied, powerful, tannic, and made from Fränkisch and Zweigelt.

Very successful efforts to age the wine in small wooden casks (barriques) have been made. Beside the reds there are also reasonable Welsch Rieslings and Weiss Burgunders made here.

Südburgenland

Südburgenland is Austria's smallest wine region. The wines here reflect the outstanding beauty of the idyllic landscape.

Very powerful reds are made from Fränkisch and Zweigelt grapes grown on hills of loam, clay, and sand, and a few good whites are produced from Welsch Riesling and Muskat Ottonel.

Süd-Oststeiermark (South Styria)

This fairly large area lies to the east of Graz. The soil is a mixture of clay and volcanic rock and the climate conditions are very beneficial (hot and wet). Very acceptable white wines are made here from Welsch Riesling, Weiss Burgunder, Traminer, Ruländer, Rhine Riesling, and Morillon (Chardonnay).

West-Steiermark (West Styria)

The western part of Styria is smaller than Süd-Oststeiermark and lies to the west of Graz. The region's speciality is very fresh and fruity rosé wines with blackcurrant bouquet and taste called Schilcher, made from Blauer Wildbacher. The best wines hail from vineyards planted on gneis and slate.

Südsteiermark (Southern Styria)

The pretty undulating green landscape of southern Styria is reminiscent of Tuscany in Italy. The wines from Welsch Riesling, Sauvignon Blanc, Morillon (Chardonnay), and Muskateller are of great class and compete with the best wines from Wachau. Because of the small scale of the local wine industry, the emphasis is wholly on making wines of quality and authenticity. The mainly young growers have great plans for the future. A breakthrough into international markets must soon be a possibility.

Beerenauslese for a quiet night in.

Switzerland

Switzerland is unbelievably beautiful with breathtaking mountains, deep valleys, lakes, picturesque towns and villages, and so much besides. However if anyone starts to discuss Swiss wine then conversation becomes animated. The opponents consider Swiss wines to be ridiculously expensive and of very modest quality. They declare that no good wine can be made from such poor grapes as Chasselas. The Swiss wine enthusiast on the other hand maintains that the authenticity of the Swiss terroir and very successful combination of soil, siting, and grape makes Swiss wine special. Furthermore, they add the Swiss do not just make white wines and their prices are a reflection of the difficult conditions under which the grapes are cultivated. Those who taste the wines objectively will find them exciting and of great class. There are even outstanding Swiss white wines, certainly in the case of wines made close to the great lakes. Some Merlots from Ticino are better than the best French wines. It is however true that the prices of some wines are kept artificially high by the protectionist stance of the Swiss government and the fact that Swiss wine consumption is about the same as the production. Yet anyone who visits the terraces of Dezaley, Epesses, or Sion will realise that it costs as much to maintain one terrace as an entire vineyard elsewhere. It is possible that the Swiss government will soon help with subsidies to maintain the famous Swiss wine terraces. The Swiss open their borders to the import of wines in 2002. Swiss wine prices will clearly have to be revised but the businesses that specialise in quality and authenticity will be rewarded in the longer term.

Wine-growing

Despite the presence of the mountains, conditions

Valais from the air.

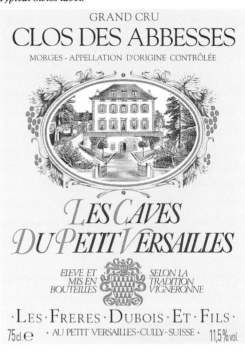

Typical Swiss label.

are highly beneficial for the Swiss wine-grower. Most of the vineyards are situated in valleys or close to the lakes. The vineyards in the valleys are warmed by the föhn, a warm airstream across the Alps, especially around Valais (Wallis), Grisons

Merlot del Ticino AC.

Epesses AC.

La Braise d'Enfer

Epesses

Appellation d'origine contrôlée
Les mille reflets de la grappe sont empreints des
mille feux de la braise qui couva longtemps sous
ce coteau donnant à ce vin une saveur ardente
exprimée pour vous par

LES FRERES DUBOIS ET FILS
AU PETIT VERSAILLES-CULLY-SUISSE

(Graubünderland), and north-east Switzerland. Near the lakes the light and heat from the sun is reflected by the surface of the water (Neuchâtel, Geneva, and Vaud). The vines in many vineyards close to lakes are heated in three different ways because their soil consists of basalt and pebbles. The local growers describe it as having 'three suns', the direct sun, the reflected sun from the pebbles, and from the water. It does not get better than this. The sunniest parts of Switzerland are Ticino (which has a trace of Mediterranean climate, Valais (Wallis), and Vaud. It is not surprising that the best Swiss reds come from here. The Swiss wine-growing regions are dealt with individually because their soils vary widely.

Wine regions

Our tour of the Swiss wine regions starts in Italian-speaking Ticino, then to Francophone Suisse Romande and finally to German speaking Ostschweiz.

Ticino, Mesolcina, and Poschiavo

It is not correct to speak of just Ticino as part of Italian-speaking Switzerland for parts of Grisons (Graubünderland) i.e Mesolcina and Poschiavo are also Italian speaking. Grisons is therefore also included here.

MESOLCINA AND POSCHIAVO

These two southern areas of Grisons (Graubünderland), Mesolcina (also known as

Misox) and Poschiavo, solely produce red wine from Merlot and several hybrid blue grape varieties. Almost the entire production is sold locally.

TICINO

Ticino is ranked fourth in scale of the wine-producing cantons of Switzerland. Prior to the invasion of phylloxera Ticino had some 7000 hectares of vineyards but only about 1,200 hectares remain. Ticino is divided into the southern Sottoceneri and northern Sopraceneri. The border between the two areas is formed by the Monte Ceneri. The underlying ground of Sottoceneri consists mainly of a mixture of chalk, minerals, clay, and sand.

The vineyards lie on both sides of Lake Lugano, between Chiasso and Mendrisio in the south and Lugano and Rivera in the north. Sopraceneri has a different geology which is more typical of the Alps, but with less chalk and more granite and sand. The great lakes of Lago Lugano, Lago Maggiore, and to a lesser extent Lago di Como, play an important role. The hot Mediterranean climate is somewhat tempered by them.

MERLOT DEL TICINO

One of the wines of Ticino of course is the Merlot del Ticino Denominazione di Origine. Merlot grapes were planted in Ticino following destruction of the vineyards by phylloxera. The results are surprising.

One of the world's top Merlots.

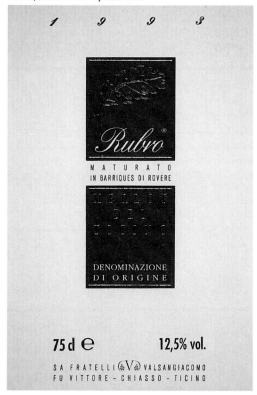

Rubro

MATURATO
IN BARRIQUES DI ROVERE

DENOMINAZIONE
DI ORIGINE

75 d ℮   12,5% vol.

SA FRATELLI V VALSANGIACOMO
FU VITTORE - CHIASSO - TICINO

Two of the best from here can even hold par with the famous Pétrus.

Not all Merlot del Ticino wines have the same quality as the top representatives of course. Most are seductive, light, lithe, and with little acidity or tannin. The colour is generally granite red and the nose is reminiscent of wild black cherry with hints too of other red fruit. Only the better wines are cask aged in wood, possessing strong tannin that becomes velvet smooth with age. These wines are sturdier and more powerful. The best wines carry the strongly coveted VITI quality mark with its indication Controlo Ufficiale di Qualita (official quality control). Drinking temperature is 12–14°C (53.6–57.2°F).

The better, more sturdy Merlot that is cask aged in wood is best served with roast meat. Drinking temperature is 14–17°C (57.2–62.6°F).

There is also a white wine and a superb light rosé wine, both made from Merlot. Drinking temperature is 8–10°C (46.4–50°F) for the Merlot Bianco and Merlot Rosato.

NOSTRANO

Nostrano is certainly the oldest and most traditional wine of Ticino. It is made from the native Bondola, perhaps supplemented with Freisa, Bonarda, or Malbec.

This wine is somewhat rustic yet very enjoyable. Drinking temperature is 14°C (57.2°F). There is also

Merlot from a small wine area.

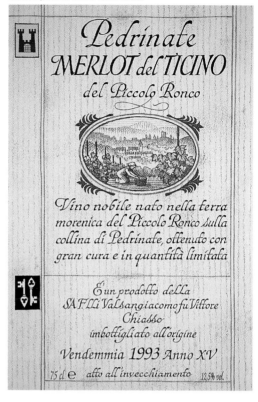

Excellent Merlot from Ticino.

Merlot del Ticino Rosato (rose).

Merlot del Ticino Spumante.

a white Nostrano Bianco. Drinking temperature is 8–10°C (46.4–50°F).

BONDOLA
Just like Nostrano this typical Ticino red wine is wholly made from Bondola grapes. Drinking temperature is 14°C (57.2°F).

OTHER WINES OF TICINO
Occasionally you may come across a Ticino Spumante (drinking temperature 5–6°C/41–42.8°F), Ticino Pinot Nero (14°C/57.2°F), and various whites of Chasselas (8–10°C/46.4–50°F), Chardonnay (10–12°C/50–53.6°F), Sauvignon (8–10°C/46.4–50°F), Semillon (10–11°C/50–51.8°F), and Riesling x Sylvaner (10–11°C/50–51.8°F). There are also white wines made from blends of Chasselas, Sauvignon, and Semillon which are delicious with fish (8–10°C/46.4–50°F).

Bianco del Mendrisiotto (white), Ticino.

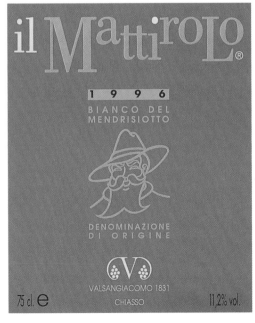

Dézaley-Marsens Grand Cru, Vaud.

Suisse Romande (French speaking Switzerland)

The Francophone wine regions are situated in the south-east of the country, and this is where most of the country's wines are grown and made. Although Berne, Fribourg, Neuchâtel, and Vaud play a role that certainly is not to be underestimated, it is principally Valais that is responsible for the best quality and greatest volume. Suisse Romande is virtually synonymous with white wine from the Chasselas grape which fails to achieve such quality and diversity of taste and styles anywhere else in the world. You will find Chasselas wines bearing the name of the grape and their place of origin but also many such as Neuchâtel without the grape variety, and even some with traditional names such as Fendant and Perlan. Chasselas also possesses a number of famous crus, some of which are no greater than the vineyards of a single village or even a hamlet such as Dézaley, Epesses, Yvorne, and Aigle.

Such diversity is possible because the Chasselas grapes are fairly neutral in themselves and therefore take on the character of their terroir. The better the terroir, the better the wine. Alongside the dominant role of Chasselas, Pinot Noir and Gamay are playing an increasingly important role for red wines. While the area cultivated for white wines grows slowly, there has been explosive growth in planting of vines for red wines in recent years. This may be related to the increasing demand for red wines and the lifting of imports of red wine that has already occurred (whites in 2002) which has seen Swiss Francs flooding abroad. At present a great deal of French

Côtes du Rhône, Beaujolais, and Burgundy is imported. It is therefore not so surprising that increasing amounts of Syrah, Pinot Noir, and Gamay are being planted. It is worth noting that Valais is actually situated high in the Rhône valley and that its climate varies little with that of the French Rhône region.

Valais

The vineyards of Valais produce about 40% of all Swiss wine. Although Valais is world-renowned for its Fendant and Dôle, the true wine connoisseur is attracted by the native grape varieties. Anyone who takes the time to discover the unique wines of Valais will fall in love for the rest of their life with this rugged but superbly beautiful area. Valais is at the foot of the Alps, spread along the high Rhône valley to either side of the town of Sion. The area is protected against excessive precipitation by the Alps to the north and south. Most vineyards are sited on terraces that jut out from the steep hills above the Rhône valley. Ingenious irrigation systems were established long ago to bring the necessary water to the terraces.

Today this is carried out by better regulated spray installations. The valley and especially the steep slopes get the full sun which aids development of the grapes. The warm föhn mountain wind keeps temperatures pleasant until well into autumn so that the grapes are able to ripen. The ground chiefly consists of loose poor soil but it retains water and

warmth well. In common with elsewhere in Switzerland the geology in Valais is just as varied with scree from glaciers, chalk, gravel, and shale. Chasselas accounts for 45% of the total production followed by Sylvaner (known here as Gros Rhin) and countless 'specialities', such as the native Amigne, Arvine, or Petite Arvine, Humagne Blanche and Rèze, and imported varieties like Muscat, Païen (Savagnin Blanc), Marsanne Blanche, or Ermitage, Chardonnay, Riesling x Sylvaner (Müller-Thurgau), Pinot Blanc, Malvoisie (Pinot Gris), and Gewürztraminer. Many of these types of grape are used to make wines from grapes that are harvested, and sometimes also partially sun dried (flétri).

Three ancient native grape varieties have also recently been give new life. These are Gwäss or Gouais, Lafnetscha, and Himbertschna but their role is still quite limited. Of red wine grapes, Pinot Noir thrives well on chalky Valais soil while Gamay prefers a less chalky footing. Other red wine grapes that do well here include Humagne Rouge, Cornalin, Syrah, Diolinoir, and Durize.

AMIGNE

Amigne is a rare sweet wine that is elegant, rich, and seductive with a stout character from the slate and chalk soils of Vétroz. If you come across an Amigne do not ask the price, just buy it! Drinking temperature is 8–10°C (46.4–50°F).

ARVINE (PETITE ARVINE)

While the previous two white wines need to be drunk within three or at most four years after they are made,

Typical Valais vineyard.

the wines of the Arvine and Petite Arvine grapes aged well. These are wines with a strong personality that are seductive, possessing a fruity bouquet, and are often high in alcohol (13% or more) and sometimes sugar residues. These unusual grapes thrive on very steep rocky ground.

The yield is quite low but the price of these gems is not untoward. Arvine and Petite Arvine Sêche (dry) has a characteristic salty taste and nose of citrus fruit. Arvine and Petite Arvine Flétri (partially dried grapes) is sweet and superb. Drinking temperature is 8–10°C (46.4–50°F) for the dry wines and 6–9°C (42.8–48.2°F) for the sweet ones.

DÔLE BLANCHE
This is a very interesting wine that is made from the same blue Pinot Noir minimum 80%) and Gamay grapes used for the Dôle. Drinking temperature is 8–12°C (46.4–53.6°F).

ERMITAGE
Ermitage or Marsanne Blanche is a grape that originates from the French Rhône valley. Here it delivers a first class white Ermitage Sec but even more importantly the excellent sweet Ermitage Flétri. The second of these wines originates from vineyards on the steep slopes of Sion, Fully, and Sierre. Few wines develop such an impressive series of aromas as a top-class Ermitage Flétri. Drinking temperature is 8–12°C (46.4–53.6°F) for dry wines and 6–9°C (42.8–48.2°F) for the sweet ones.

Home of the Petite Arvine.

Renowned Sion Fendant, Valais.

FENDANT
Fendant is undoubtedly the best advertisement for Valais and it is living proof that a soft grape such as Chasselas can make fine wines from the roughest of soils.

Fendant is certainly not a philosophical wine, more a matter of straightforward pleasure. Every Fendant is an ambassador for Valais and its individual terroir. Hence a Fendant from Sion tastes different from one from Sierre.

In general it can be said that the best Fendant is a dry, lively wine which is high on juice, with definite flinty undertones.

Drinking temperature is 8–10°C (46.4–50°F) for light and fruity Fendant but 10–12°C (50–53.6°F) for sturdier examples.

HUMAGNE BLANCHE
This wine from Valais is claimed to have 'magical' properties as a tonic. Whether or not this is true, it is an excellent wine that is difficult to find. Drinking temperature is 8–12°C (46.4–53.6°F).

JOHANNISBERG
This is another well-known white wine from Valais. Johannisberg is the local Valais name for the Sylvaner grapes which thrive well here.

The wine is mellow and soft yet rounded and sometimes even fulsome with discernible nose and taste of Muscat. It is the unexpected taste of Muscat that makes this wine such a good aperitif. Drinking temperature is 8–12°C/46.4–53.6°F (the colder the better).

MALVOISIE
Malvoisie (Pinot Gris) also produces a dry wine or a sweet from partially dried grapes. The dry Malvoisie is excellent with mushrooms and other fungi. Malvoisie Flétri is superb with pate de foie gras. Drinking temperature is 8–12°C (46.4–53.6°F) for dry wines and 6–9°C (42.8–48.2°F) for sweet ones.

PAIEN
The wines made from Paien or Heida, as it is also known (meaning heaths), are quite unusual. Grapes grow on this very ancient native variety at altitudes of more than 1,000 metres (3,280 feet).
In the Jura and Savoie in France its is known as Savagnin, Traminer in Alsace and certain German vineyards, and Tramini in Italy. The wine is fresh and quite dry with recognisable fresh nose of green apples. Drinking temperature is 8–10°C (46.4–50°F).

RÈZE
The rare Rèze grape is still used piecemeal in Anniviers to make wine. This Vin des Glaciers ('glacier' wine) is remarkably tart and green if drunk young. Allow it to age though and it develops a quite unusual but exciting nose. Drinking temperature is 6–9°C (42.8–48.2°F).

OTHER WHITE WINES
Valais also makes a number of other first class white wines (but in small volume) from Chardonnay (on the increase), Gewürztraminer, Gouais, Himbertscha, Lafnetscha, Muscat, Pinot Blanc, Riesling, Riesling x Sylvaner (Müller Thurgau), and Sauvignon.

GAMAY ROSÉ
A light and amenable rosé that is quite convivial for informal drinking is made from Gamay grapes. Drinking temperature is 8–10°C (46.4–50°F).

OEIL DE PERDRIX
This is a light and cheerful rosé that is 100% Pinot Noir.
Drinking temperature is 8–10°C (46.4–50°F).

CORNALIN
A fruity and comforting red wine from grapes of the same name that is fairly high in tannin when young but amenable and smooth with age.
Drinking temperature is 12–14°C (53.6–57.2°F).

DÔLE
This famous Valais red wine must contain at least 80% Pinot Noir, which may be supplemented with other blue grapes grown in Valais such as Humagne, Syrah, or Cornalin.
Dôle is typical of Pinot Noir. It is comforting, fruity, velvet smooth, rounded, and harmonious. Drinking temperature is 14°C (57.2°F).

Superb Oeil-de-Perdrix rosé, Valais

Best-known Swiss red: Dôle du Valais.

GORON

Goron is the lesser brother of Dôle with less alcohol and less body. This pleasing light and comforting wine is often served with cold meats and snacks. Drinking temperature is 12–14°C (53.6–57.2°F).

HUMAGNE ROUGE

Despite its name, the red Humagne has nothing whatever in common with the white grapes and wine. Humagne Rouge wine is very aromatic and a bit rustic but it improves a little with age. Drinking temperature is 14–16°C (57.2–60.8°F).

PINOT NOIR

The 100% Pinot Noir wine is fuller than the Dôle and also has a richer nose and flavour with more body and character. Drinking temperature is 14–16°C (53.6–57.2°F).

SYRAH

This variety of grapes, which originally came from the Shiraz valley in Iran, was introduced by the French to the Rhône valley. Here too in Valais, these sturdy grapes produce firm and powerful wines full of extract and with a rich bouquet. Drinking temperature is 14–16°C (57.2–60.8°F).

Vaud

Vaud is one of the most attractive vineyard landscapes in Switzerland. It combines the ruggedness of Valais with the more gentle landscape of Geneva and Neuchâtel. There are superb views of the mountains, lakes, marvellous wine domains, and castles. Vaud is also a paradise for both lovers of nature and gastronomy.

There are two parts to the area: to the south it extends along the northern shore of Lake Geneva or Lac Léman and to the north along the southern part of Lac de Neuchâtel. These two areas are subdivided into six districts of Chablais (Aigle), Lavaux (between Montreux and Lausanne), and La Côte (between Lausanne and Nyon) by Lake Geneva and Côtes de l' Orbe, Bonvillars, and Vully around Lac de Neuchâtel. Most of the vineyards enjoy a microclimate influenced by the lakes. The two lakes ensure additional cooling and humidity when it is very hot and additional sunlight and warmth during autumn when the sun shines. The western area of La Côte gets less rain that Lavaux and Chablais in the east, while the latter benefits more from the warming föhn mountain wind. Although some vineyards reach heights of 600 and even 700 metres (1,968 and 2,296 feet), most are sited between 400 to 500 metres (1,312–1,640 feet). The geology in Vaud also comprises chalk, glacial scree, calciferous sandstone, clay, and rock.

About 99% of all wine from Vaud is made from Chasselas grapes. A little Riesling x Sylvaner (Müller-Thurgau) is produced in Côte de l'Orbe and a little Chardonnay, Gewürztraminer, Muscat, Pinot Gris, Pinot Blanc, Riesling, and Sylvaner is made for the local catering trade. With the red wines (that account for less than 20% of the total production) Gamay dominates with two-thirds of the reds and Pinot Noir accounts for about one third. Small amounts of Syrah and Mondeuse are also made for the local catering trade. Vaud wines are identified by their place of origin and not the variety of grape from which they are made.

Chablais

This wine area comprises five places of origin: Bex, Ollon, Aigle, Yvorne, and Villeneuve. The Chasselas whites are fresh and lively while remaining elegant and rich. They can be recognised by the relatively high mineral content (magnesium in Aigle and Villeneuve, other minerals in Ollon, lots of flint in Bex, and gypsum in Ollon and Bex). Chablais whites also reflects their terroir in the bouquet. If you take the wine route you will be confronted with a tremendous assortment of different aromatic nuances. Floral notes and aniseed in Bex, wet stone, resin, and roses in Ollon, floral scents with fruit, flint, burnt earth or caramel with age in Aigle, hazelnut, peach, and apricot in Yvorne, and slate, flint, and fruit in Villeneuve. Drinking temperature is 10–12°C (50–53.6°F).

Lavaux

There are six places of origin in Lavaux: Montreux-Vevey, Chardonne, St. Saphorin, Epesses, Villette, and Lutry, together with two Grand Crus of Dézaley and Calamin. Nowhere in Switzerland has more beautiful landscape than here, especially around Dézaley and Calamin. Thousands of terraces are arranged in rows above Lake Geneva to form an indescribable scene, particularly in autumn.

Chasselas here produces a wine with more body that is fuller and sturdier than in the west. The taste of terroir is also more pronounced. Discover lemon balm and mint (Montreux-Vevey), pear and blackcurrant (Chardonne), pineapple, truffle, and white pepper (Epesses), or grapefruit and roses (Lutry). Some of the best wines, such as those of

Dézaley-Marsens Grand Cru vineyards.

Dézaley-Marsens Grand Cru.

Villette red wine from Lavaux, Vaud.

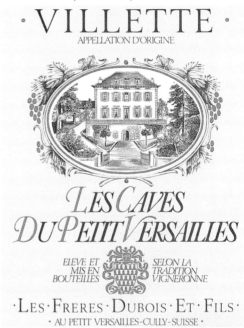

Little gems from Lavaux, Vaud.

Dézaley, contain surprising aromas of almond, toast, tea, and honey, tending when older towards hazelnut, beeswax, and preserved fruit (Dézaley-Marsens, Dubois). Drinking temperature for a Lavaux is 8–10°C (53.6–50°F) and 10–12°C (50–53.6°F) for a Dézaley and Calamin.

Lavaux reds are also well worth while, such as St. Saphorin (cherry, kirsch, slight bitter note, full and rounded) and Villette (red fruit, wild strawberry, bilberry, raspberry, blackberry, mellow and comforting). Drinking temperature is 12–14°C (53.6–57.2°F).

La Côte

About half of the wines of Vaud come from the area between Geneva and Lausanne. This is gently undulating countryside with picturesque villages, large villas of the wealthy, and castles. The first thing that strikes one about the local wine is the slight natural sparkle that tingles and its elegance. This is much lighter wine than those of Lavaux and Chablais, but it has much to offer in terms of a floral and fruity nose. La Côte has no Grand Cru, only twelve places of origin: Morges, Aubonne, Perroy, Féchy, Mont-sur-Rolle, Tartegnin, Côteau de Vincy, Bursinel, Vinzel, Luins, Begnins, and Nyon. Drinking temperature is 8–10°C (46.4–50°F).

Bonvillars, Côtes de l'Orbe, Vully

Although these three wine areas lie on the shores of the Lac de Neuchâtel, they form part of Vaud. The

wine on the other hand is far closer in style to its northern neighbours of Neuchâtel. They are fresh, light, elegant, and often slightly sparkling. The wine is made from Chasselas grapes. Drinking temperature is 8–10°C (46.4–50°F).

In addition to white wines, the following reds are also produced in Vaud.

SALVAGNIN

This Vaud red made from Gamay and/or Pinot Noir is fresh, fruity, and lithe. Drinking temperature is 12°C (53.6°F) with fish or 12–14°C (53.6–57.2°F) with meat.

OEIL DE PERDRIX

This light-on-its-feet, cheerful, and comforting rosé mainly originates from Vully and Bonvillars. The colour is known as 'partridge eye' – a colour between pale pink and orange. Drinking temperature is 10–12°C (50–53.6°F).

Geneva

Geneva is the third largest wine-producing canton of Switzerland after Valais and Vaud. The landscape around Geneva is much more gentle and less hilly than the other two main wine regions. The vineyards can therefore be larger and mechanisation is possible. This has no effect on quality but certainly on the price of the wine. The growers in the Geneva region have also been busy rationalising the processes and searching for the most suitable grape varieties for quality wines. The area is fairly flat with just the odd undulation but it is encircled by mountains which protect the vineyards against too much precipitation. The proximity of Lake Geneva (Lac Léman) also protects the vineyards against night frost during the growing and blossoming periods. Here too the underlying geology is fairly diverse. The soil beneath most of the area is about one third clay, except in Jura where there tends to be more clay. Lully and Peney have higher levels of chalk in their soil and the more highly sited vineyards of Dardagny and surrounding areas have calciferous sandstone and loess. The vineyards right beside the lake are predominantly gravel.

The universally present Chasselas grape is losing ground to aromatic types of grape such as Chardonnay, Gewürztraminer, Pinot Gris, Pinot Blanc, Riesling x Sylvaner (Müller-Thurgau), and some Sauvignon, Sylvaner, and Aligoté, which is a speciality of Lully. The dominant blue grape is Gamay, followed by Pinot Noir, and Merlot.

New grape varieties that have recently arrived on the scene are Gamaret, Gamay x Eeichensteiner B 28, Cabernet Franc, and Cabernet Sauvignon. Geneva is in the throes of development and the coming decades may prove to be quite surprising. The wine-growing region of Geneva is subdivided into three areas: Entre Arve et Lac (east of Geneva and between the Arve and the lake), Entre Arve et Rhône (west of Geneva and between the rivers Arve and Rhône), and Mandement (north of Geneva, the Rhône, and the lake).

Mandement is the largest of the three areas and accounts for about two thirds of the region's production. The most interesting wines though come from the area between the Arve and Rhône, where the ground is gravel and chalk, giving a greater stamp of terroir with hints of flint in the bouquet. These wines originate mainly for the hills around Bernex, Confignon, Lully, and Sévenoze.

CHASSELAS DE GENÈVE/PERLAN

These wines will be found with the name of the canton or community in which they were produced, such as Jussy, Choulex, Lully, Dardagny, Russin, Peissy, Satigny, or Chouilly. Because of strict rules which limit the yield, the quality of Geneva Chasselas wines have improved immeasurably in recent decades. The bouquet is fresh and floral, the taste is lively, fresh, and dry with the not uncommon presence of a slight tingle. Drinking temperature is 8–10°C (46.4–50°F).

OTHER WHITE WINES

Chardonnay, Pinot Blanc, and Pinot Gris from here are excellent. The Muscat and Gewürztraminer wines are very aromatic and of good quality. The Sauvignon is nice but not exactly exciting. Finally the Aligoté of Lully makes a very special aperitif.

GAMAY DE GENÈVE

Here too the wine is either given this generic name of Gamay de Genève or bears the name of the producing community. This Gamay is a true-to-type and typical Gamay. It is fresh, fruity, fulsome, comforting, approachable, and juicy. Drinking temperature is 10–12°C (50–53.6°F).

PINOT NOIR DE GENÈVE

This is a very fine red wine that is fruity and very comforting. Drinking temperature is 14°C (57.2°F).

OTHER RED WINES

The first results from Cabernet Franc and Cabernet Sauvignon are very promising. The still rare Merlot has thrived well in the higher located vineyards for some time. Drinking temperature is 14°C (57.2°F).

OEIL-DE-PERDRIX/GAMAY ROSÉ

These two different rosé wines are simple, fresh, fruity, and amenable. Drinking temperature is 8–10°C (46.4–50°F).

Neuchâtel

The wine region of Neuchâtel is situated on the north-west shore of the Lac de Neuchâtel and is separated from France by the Jura. The climate is fairly mild, sunny, and dry. The presence of the lake keeps winters mild but autumns can be misty which can be harmful for the grape harvest. The underlying ground here at the foot of the Jura mountains is mainly chalk rock with other rock outcrops, loam, and loess. There are lots of mineral salts in the soil which can usually be detected in the taste of the wine. What strikes the visitor most is how small each plot of land is. Only the bigger wine houses possess larger vineyards.

It is fairly obvious that mainly white wines will be made here on this chalk. Chasselas accounts for about 75% of these but there are also Pinot Gris, Riesling x Sylvaner (Müller-Thurgau), and Chardonnay grapes here which are increasingly successful. There are also some traces of Sylvaner, Riesling, and Gewürztraminer. The unique Pinot Noir is used to make red wines and the extremely pleasant Oeil-de-Perdrix rosé.

NEUCHÂTEL

Wines bearing this name are Chasselas. The best of them come from the villages of Cressier, Auvernier, Cortaillod, Boudry, and La Béroche.

The surprise of these Chasselas wines, which are lighter than those of Valais and Vaud, is their elegant tingle and salty undertones. The local wines houses pour the wine from a height which creates a slight sparkle that is often accompanied by a star of carbonic acid gas bubbles (*le vin fait l' étoile*). Drinking temperature is 8–12°C (46.4–53.6°F) depending on the quality: the better the less it needs chilling.

NEUCHÂTEL PINOT NOIR

Pinot Noir from Neuchâtel is often fairly unyielding and high in tannin when young but becomes more mellow and amenable with age. The taste is fresh, elegant, complex, and fairly classical. Drinking temperature is 14°C (57.2°F).

NEUCHÂTEL OEIL-DE-PERDRIX

The colour of this rosé is said to resemble the colour of the eyes of a partridge that has been shot. The brownish colour slowly disappears to become the pinkish orange that is characteristic of this rosé. Fortunately the taste of this wine is much more cheering than its name might suggest. It is an elegant and fresh wine from Pinot Noir. Drinking temperature is 8–10°C (46.4–50°F).

Other wines

Chardonnay from Neuchâtel is exceptionally good and at first glance resembles a good Burgundy. It is a first class aperitif. The other specialities are rather rare. Gewürztraminer wines are aromatic but not powerful, Pinot Blanc is light and elegant, Pinot Gris is superb, while the Riesling x Sylvaner (Müller-Thurgau) and Sylvaner are not always convincing. For the sake of completeness there is also a small amount of reasonable quality sparkling wine.

Fribourg

While Neuchâtel wines originate from the north-western shores of the eponymous lake, those of Fribourg are made to the east of Lac de Neuchâtel, from around Broye in the south and Vully in the north. Vully's vineyards stretch to between the lakes of Neuchâtel and Morat. The ground here is clay, sand, and calciferous sandstone. The climate is clearly moderated by the lake. The Chasselas grape holds sway here too but there are a number of interesting specialities such as the wines of Chardonnay, Gewürztraminer, Pinot Blanc, Pinot Gris, Riesling x Sylvaner (Müller-Thurgau), and Freisammer, which is a cross between Sylvaner and Pinot Gris. There is also an excellent Oeil-de-Perdrix and superb Pinot Noir.

CHASSELAS FRIBOURGEOIS

The wines of Vully, Faverges, and Cheyres are fresh, elegant, fruity, and quite light. They clearly portray their terroir. Drinking temperature is 8–12°C (46.4–53.6°F) with a preference for not overcooling.

PINOT NOIR FRIBOURGEOIS

This exceptionally fruity wine is redolent of raspberry and has plenty of body and juice. Drinking temperature is 14°C (57.2°F).

Other wines

Of all the other rare Fribourg wines, the best are the fresh and elegant Oeil-de-Perdrix, fulsome Chardonnay, sultry Pinot Gris, and the Gewürztraminer.

Jura

This is a relatively new wine region. The first vineyards were planted only in 1986 and the first grape harvest was in 1990. This is quite strange since the position has a beneficial mild microclimate and equally useful rocky ground. At present the Pinot Noir reds, with their hints of cherry and other red fruit, are more convincing than the Riesling x Sylvaner (Müller-Thurgau) whites. When the vines of the Pinot Noir come to maturity in a few years from now the expectations are quite exciting. There have also been excellent results from Pinot Gris with notes of honey, preserved, and exotic fruit.

Berne (Bern)

The canton of Berne forms the boundary between the French and Germany speaking parts of Switzerland. Most of the vineyards are in the area around the Lac de Bienne (Bielersee), to the north of Lac de Neuchâtel. The remainder of the vineyards are situated much further to the south east of the Thoune and Brienz lakes, in the area around Interlaken. The vineyards of Lac de Bienne are planted on chalk on the left bank and chalk-bearing sandstone on the right bank. The Thoune lake vineyards have underlying rock with a thin covering of soil. The vineyards also derive benefit from the föhn winds.

CHASSELAS

Chasselas dominates here too where – on chalk-bearing soil – it produces fresh and elegant wines that are slightly sparkling. The wines from the south-east shore are slightly more full and heavy but also less elegant. Drinking temperature is 8–10°C (46.4–50°F).

PINOT NOIR

These are full-bodied and fruity wines that are rounded and comforting, though never ponderous. Drinking temperature is 12°C (53.6°F) with fish and 14°C (57.2°F) with meat.

Ostschweiz

Eastern Switzerland is the name given by the German speaking Swiss but in fact the region is in the north east. The region covers more than a third of the entire country, east of a line drawn through Thun, Berne, Solothurn, Basle (Basel), and north of a line through Thun and Chur. The German-speaking wine region consists of sixteen cantons and half of the French language canton of Berne that was dealt with under Suisse Romande, which in wine terms belongs to Ostschweiz. This is the tiny area around Lac de Thoune (Thunersee).

Wine-growing is quite widely dispersed throughout the large Ostschweiz region, and relatively small scale. There is a mosaic of tiny vineyards. The largest north-eastern wine cantons are those of Zürich, Schaffhausen, Aargau, Graubünden (without Misox and Mesolcina, see Ticino), Thurgau, St. Gallen, and Basle (Basel). The remaining cantons of Schwyz, Berne (Thunersee), Lucerne, Appenzell, Solothurn, Glarus, Zug, and Unterwalden between them only account for 2.5% of the total production of Ostschweiz. In order to understand the relative size of the area of vines under cultivation in Ostschweiz, it is worth bearing in mind that its total of 2,300 hectares in one third of the country is less than that of either Valais or Vaud. Prior to the visit of phylloxera much more wine was made in Ostschweiz.

The combination of phylloxera and the increasing demands of quality between them have decimated the vineyards of Ostschweiz. This is most noticeable around Basle, partly due to the expansion of the city, and in Thurgau and Solothurn. The climate in Ostschweiz is also not particularly beneficial for wine-growing, being too cold and too wet. Better conditions though can be found in the immediate surrounds of the many lakes (Thunersee, Brienzersee, Zurichsee, Zuger See, Vierwaldstätter See, Walensee, Bodensee), the rivers (Rhine, Aar, Reuss, and Thur), and in the valleys through which

Fine assortment of Neuchâtel wines, Montmollin.

the föhn blows (St. Gallen, Grisons). The lowest vineyards are at 300 metres (984 feet) near Basle and the highest at 600 metres (1,968 feet) in the Herrschaft of Grisons (Graubünderland). The greatest risk for wine growers in Ostschweiz is prolonged winter frost or deadly night frosts in spring during blossoming. Over the centuries the creative Swiss have come up with all manner of ways of protecting their vines against the cold. In addition to the widely used spraying and heating methods, the local growers have developed their own method. The vines are covered with straw or even with what resembles an eiderdown. The soil in Ostschweiz varies from west to east. In the western part, close to the Jura mountains, chalk is more prevalent; in the centre it is mainly calciferous sandstone, while in the east glacial scree and shale dominate. Because autumns are quite cold in Ostschweiz, only early ripening varieties of grapes thrive.

The leading type here for white wines is Riesling x Sylvaner (Müller-Thurgau), and the lead blue grape is Pinot Noir. Blue grapes account for at least 70% of all the vines planted. Other varieties can be found here and there in small amounts. The Räuschling is a speciality white of Zürich and the Limmat valley, which is beginning to attract more attention. You may also encounter some Gewürztraminer, Pinot Blanc, Pinot Gris (often named Tokayer here), Freisamer, Ebling, Chardonnay, Chasselas, Completer (in Grisons). The choice with blue grapes is more limited. You may find some new varieties such as Gamaret and B 28 (both Gamay x Reichensteiner). Ostschweiz can be subdivided for

ease into three areas of the west (Berne (Thunersee), Unterwalden, Uri, Lucerne, Zug, Aargau, Solothurn, and Basle), the centre (Schwyz, Glarus, Zürich, Thurgau, and Schaffhausen), and the east (Grisons, St. Gallen, and Appenzell).

RIESLING X SYLVANER (MÜLLER THURGAU)

The label bears the name of the canton or the commune of the wine's origin. There are countless and varied local types of these wines with their individual tastes and style but they are generally fresh, fruity (somewhat like Muscat), and elegant. Drinking temperature is 8–12°C/46.4–53.6°F (the lighter the wine the cooler it is drunk).

BLAUBURGUNDER/CLEVNER

This wine is made from Pinot Noir grapes throughout Ostschweiz. They vary widely from very light and fruity to firm and full of tannin. The best Pinot Noir generally come from the Rhine valley in Grisons and St. Gallen, where the wine is often cask aged in oak barriques. Drinking temperature is 12–14°C (53.6–57.2°F) for 'ordinary' Blauburgunder/Clevner), and 14–16°C (57.2–60.8°F) for cask aged examples from St. Gallen and Grisons.

FEDERWEISSER/SCHILLER/SÜSSDRUCK

The various Pinot Noir (Blauburgunder, Clevner) rosé wines of Ostschweiz are given these poetic names. These are generally extremely fruity, mellow, and elegant wines that are amenable and comforting. Drinking temperature is 8–12°C/46.4–53.6°F (the fuller the wine the less it is chilled).

Germany

Germany takes sixth place among the wine-producing nations of the world. Much of the production is intended for export, while Germany itself imports huge volumes of wine. This demonstrates the complexity of the German position. It seems as though the best German wines – but unfortunately also some of the worst – disappear into export markets while the Germans themselves tend to prefer beer or imported wines.

Compared with a country like France, the consumption of wine in Germany is quite low. Changes are also apparent though in Germany. Although the German government has always maintained that the German system of wine control was watertight and the best in Europe, in reality things were sometimes not right with the cheaper German wines.
Some wine traders were clearly more interested in quick profits than being ambassadors for the German wine industry. Creations with names such as 'Alte Wein Tradition' and 'Kellergeister' have done much to damage the reputation of German wines. On the other hand with the absurd prices of Bordeaux wines, in particular those of Sauternes, increasing numbers of people have been looking for cheaper

Modern German quality wine: Bernkasteler Doctor, Mosel-Saar-Ruwer.

Beerenauslese (BA).

alternatives. These can be found in Germany at prices that are quite attractive.
The demand for good quality but affordable German wine has increased in the past decade or so. The demand for dry German wines has also grown explosively. Most of the growers were quickly able to adapt themselves to the market situation. Growers constantly seek to find ways to guarantee the wine's quality while keeping the prices acceptable for everyone.

Wine-growing

Although a few wine-makers succeed in making excellent red wines, German is white wine country, because of its climate. Although the quality of red wines has improved, the price charged for the level of quality available is somewhat on the high side. Slightly more than 85% of the area cultivated by vines in Germany is planted with white grape varieties.
Before the reunification of Germany the proportion of red wine grapes had risen sharply from 13% in 1984 to almost 19% in 1994. Because the wine-growing areas of the former East Germany mainly grew white varieties, the proportion has now decreased slightly.
The choice of grapes grown has also shifted in favour of better quality. Hence the very productive Müller-Thurgau is losing ground in favour of Riesling. Besides these two most important types of grape you can also find Kerner, Silvaner (Sylvaner), Scheurebe, Bacchus, Ruländer (or Grauburgunder/Pinot Gris), Morio-Muskat, Huxelrebe, Faberrebe, Gutedel

(Chasselas), Weissburgunder (Pinot Blanc), Ortega, Elbling, Roter Traminer, Ehrenfelser, Optima, Reichensteiner, and Perle. The dominant blue grape is Spätburgunder (Pinot Noir), followed by Blauer Portugieser, Blauer Trollinger, Müllerebe (Pinot Meunier), Dornfelder, Lemberger, and Heroldrebe. German wines are characteristically fruity in a refined way with relatively low alcohol, even with dry wines.

Wine regions

Germany's wine regions are mainly situated to the north of the Bodensee (on the Swiss border) to the Ahr, north of Koblenz on the one hand and also with two small regions around Dresden and south of Halle on the other. There are thirteen wine regions in all, eleven in the south west and two in the east. Each wine region produces several different types of wine, with the taste and style being related to the soil, microclimate, capabilities, wine maker's preferences, and also of course the demands of the market.

To deal with every type of German wine is an impossible task. Instead this book provides general guidance about the taste and styles of the majority of wines from the different regions. In general one can deem that the more northern and eastern wines are mainly light, mildly fruity, with subtle bouquets and taste, and sharper acidity. The wines of the south are generally fuller and have more powerful tastes and bouquets but milder acidity. The most important characteristics of the regions is listed below, running from south to north.

Baden

The wine region of Baden is in the south-east of Germany, forming a fairly long strip from the northern shore of the Bodensee by way of the famous Black Forest (Schwarzwald), Freiburg, and Baden-Baden, to Karlsruhe and Heidelberg, slightly south of the point where the Neckar and Rhine meet. Baden is the second largest wine region of Germany and it has a great diversity of wines to offer. Baden's soil

Modern-style wine from Baden.

Top German wine.

German Sekt (sparkling).

chiefly consists of loess, loam, gravel, some chalk, and volcanic rocks.

The full-bodied and rounded white wines are made from Müller-Thurgau, Ruländer, Gutedel, Gewürztraminer, and Riesling grapes. These wines often possess spicy and powerful bouquets. Spätburgunder is used to make velvet smooth red wines that are lively and rounded, and also the gloriously refreshing Weissherbst.

Württemberg

The vineyards of Württemberg are situated on hills above the Neckar and its tributaries. The area starts near Tübingen and continues past the provincial capital of Stuttgart to Heilbronn and Bad Mergentheim. Württemberg is Germany's largest wine-growing region as far as red wine is concerned. About half the vineyards are planted with blue grape varieties.

The soil here consists of sedimentary layers, chalk rock with fossilised shells, marl, and loess. Unfortunately the fine wines from this area almost never leave their area of production. Very fruity reds are made from Müllerebe, Spätburgunder, Portugieser, and Lemberger, while sturdy, powerful, and often slightly rustic whites are made from Riesling, Müller-Thurgau, Kerner, and Silvaner (Sylvaner).

Hessische Bergstrasse

This region is relatively small and comprises a tongue of land between Heidelberg and Bensheim. The area is bounded by the Rhine in the west and the superb Odenwald in the east. The soil is almost exclusively loess, which is good for white wines. Here too little of the local production leaves the area. Riesling dominates here followed by the fragrant Müller-Thurgau and subtle Silvaner (Sylvaner). Most wines are elegant and fruity with fine acidity. They are also very refreshing.

Franconia (Franken)

The vineyards of Franconia are on the hills overlooking the river Main as it runs through Würzburg and Aschaffenburg.

The soil mainly consists of loess, sandstone, and chalk rock. Franconia has been renowned for centuries for two things: the Steinwein from Würzburg, which is so popular that all the wines from the region bear the Stein name, and the idiosyncratic but awkward green Bocksbeutel flagon-shaped bottles. The shape makes them awkward to stack in wine racks intended for round bottles. Franconian wines are mainly produced from Müller-Thurgau and Silvaner (Sylvaner) which yield very dry and sturdy wines with good acidity and full-bodied structure.

Rheinpfalz

Rheinpfalz is the most French of all the German wine regions. The distance to the French border is minimal and the older growers of Rheinpfalz can recall times when many French bought wine in Rheinpfalz. In some areas the locals still speak fluent French, especially south of the town of Landau, which was once a French garrison town. In fact the most southerly vineyard of Rheinpfalz, the Schweigener

Traditional Franconian Bocksbeutel.

Outstanding Riesling from Rheinpfalz.

Spätlese from Rheinpfalz.

Superb Niersteiner, Rheinhessen.

Modern dry Riesling from Rheinhessen.

Sonnenberg, is actually in France but its German wine growers were permitted to take their harvest to Germany to be turned into German wine. Rheinpfalz soil is chiefly loam, clay, and weathered chalk rock. This region is the second largest in Germany in terms of area and the most productive.

The best vineyards are in the north of the region, mainly around Wachenheim, Forst, Deidesheim, and Ruppertsberg, which is renowned for its superlative Riesling.

In addition to powerful, full-bodied, aromatic, and elegant Rieslings, Rheinpfalz also produces a number of good whites made from Müller-Thurgau, Kerner, Silvaner (Sylvaner), and Morio-Muskat. The rarer red wines from grapes such as Portugieser are mellow, mild, and fruity. Dornfelder grapes also yield excellent results.

Rheinhessen

This region, between Worms in the south and Mainz in the north is wedged between a loop of the Rhine and its tributary the Nahe. This is easily the largest wine area of Germany in terms of area of vineyards but second to Rheinpfalz in terms of production. The wines of Rheinhessen once enjoyed great fame, especially during the time of Charlemagne. Rheinhessen became famous at a stroke because of the excellent quality of the local wine from the vineyards surrounding the Liebfrau church of Worms. The wine, known as Liebfraumilch, used to be of extremely high quality but it is now permitted to be made in four areas: Rheinhessen, Rheinpfalz, Rheingau, and Nahe. Today's Liebfraumilch – of which the quality swings between reasonable and revoltingly sweet and shallow – unfortunately no longer has anything in common with the legendary wine. Rheinhessen soil consists of loess, chalk rock, and sand, offering great potential for inventive wine-makers. The very best Rheinhessen wines undoubtedly come from the area around Nierstein, where the Riesling in particular delivers excellent results from the sunny terraces overlooking the Rhine. Riesling grapes here yield mild and fruity

wines with a rounded and fulsome taste. Besides Riesling, there are also Müller-Thurgau and Silvaner (Sylvaner) for white wines and Portugieser and Spätburgunder for reds. One of the finest German reds is the full and fruity classic Spätburgunder from the little village of Ingelheim, in the Grosslage Kaiserpfalz.

Nahe

Nahe lies to the west of Rheinhessen on either side of the river of that name.

The soil in the north around Bad Kreuznach consists of loam and sand, while in the south it tends towards quartzite and porphyry. Nahe bridges the gap in wine terms between the fragrant wines of the Mosel, the elegant ones from the Rheingau, and the milder ones of Rheinhessen. Müller-Thurgau, Riesling, and Silvaner (Sylvaner) here deliver subtle and fragrant wines.

Rheingau

The Rheingau is not only the geographical centre of the German wine industry, but also its historic centre.

The relatively small region lies on the northern bank of the Rhine between Hocheim and Lorch. With the

Trocken (dry) Grauburgunder from Nahe.

exception of the small Grosslagen of Daubhaus (north of Hocheim), Steil (near Assmannshausen), and Burgweg (near Lorch) the Rheingau forms one continuous area on the hills of the Taunus.

The Rheingau is renowned for its wonderful landscape, its superlative wines, and its important role in Germany's history of wine. All the basis-concepts and terminology of present-day German wine law originated here. The first wines to be made from late harvested grapes were made here and also the first Trockenbeerenauslesen. Riesling thrives nowhere else as well as it does here on soil consisting of loess, loam, and weathered slate.

Rheingau's celebrated Riesling is elegant, fruity, fresh, and of great class. The best wines often possess a firm, almost spicy character, and enough acidity to enable them to be kept for several years. In addition to the Riesling, the Rheingau is also world renowned for Spätburgunder wines from Assenhausen that are outstanding for a German red wine.

Mittelrhein

Four wine regions come together where the Nahe joins the Rhine: Nahe, Rheinhessen, Rheingau, and Mittelrhein. The last of these is an extended area from Bingen by way of Bacharach and Koblenz to the mouth of the Ahr, in the north of the region. The vineyards are sited on terraces on either side of the Rhine. The landscape is quite literally breathtaking. Wines from Mittelrhein need to be discovered locally.

These wines are characteristic of their terroir, slate on the hills but more clay near the river. Riesling here is responsible for the best wines, which are elegant, fruity, and well structured, sometimes with quite high acidity. The Müller-Thurgau and Kerner are more mellow but are also quite strongly acidic.

Mosel-Saar-Ruwer

This widely known wine region stretches itself out along the Saar, Ruwer, and the Mosel rivers, from Saarburg by way of Trier to Koblenz. The vineyards are sited on steep slopes above the gently curving river Mosel, emanating a scene of timeless tranquillity.

The slopes chiefly consist of slate that is high in minerals, which is good for the wine's finesse. Admittedly not all the wines from this region are worthy of superlatives as unfortunately there are some very modest to almost undrinkable 'sugar' wines or lesser Mosels.

The true Mosel wines are sensational with their rich nose, elegant character, and great class. Mosels come in a wide variety of styles from mellow, fruity, and amenable to more challenging, rich, and extremely aromatic. The best of them are undoubtedly the Rieslings, especially those from the famous wine villages of Bernkastel, Piesport, Wehlen, Brauneberg, Graach, Zeltingen, and Erden. Besides Riesling,

Müller-Thurgau and the old-fashioned Elbling thrive here too.

Ahr

The Ahr is one of Germany's smallest wine regions. It is situated south of Bonn near Bad Neuenahr-Ahrweiler.

The rugged and impressive Ahr valley is a popular place for both nature lovers and walkers. Once the top of the Eifel has been reached, nothing tastes better than a cool glass of Portugieser red wine. The Ahr is after all a red wine area , although the volcanic origin of the soil, together with lots of slate makes it suitable for making first class whites too. The decision to make red wine though was rather more for economic than viticultural reasons.

So many good white wines are made in Germany that the Ahr region, with a rather limited area available, decided there was more money to be made from planting blue grape varieties. Two blue grape varieties, the Spätburgunder and Portugieser, yield velvet smooth, elegant, and fruity red wines here. These are complemented by Riesling and Müller-Thurgau, which produce elegant, fresh, lively, and very aromatic wines.

Classic German label for an otherwise superb Mosel.

Saxony (Sachsen)

This is one of the 'new' wine regions of Germany in the former East Germany. Together with the other 'new' region of Saale/Unstruut they form the most northerly of the German wine areas. Sachsen is the furthest east along the banks of the Elbe, on either side of Dresden.

It is a very small area with several scattered vineyards sited between Pillnitz and Diesbar Seusslitz, with the towns of Meissen and Radebeul at its centre. The soil of these vineyards is extremely varied (including sand, porphyry, and loam). Müller-Thurgau, Weissburgunder, and Traminer produce dry and fruity wines here with a refreshing degree of acidity. The rare local wines are light and mellow and the Elbtal-Sekt is of very acceptable quality.

Saale/Unstrut

This small area to the south of Halle is the most northerly wine area of Germany and with the United Kingdom, the most northerly of Europe. The severe continental climate forces the growers to harvest their grapes as early and quickly as possible. Few sweet wines are therefore likely to be encountered, certainly no late harvested types. Most of them are dry and often pretty tart.

White grapes particularly thrive on a soil of sandstone with plenty of fossilised shells, but the rare reds prove the potential of the area. Müller-Thurgau is undemanding and productive and here it successfully produces fresh vegetal wines with a pleasing fragrance of grapefruit. The Silvaner (Sylvaner) are better though, producing mellow and fresh wines with milder acidity and nose of citrus fruit.

The best places are reserved for Riesling, which yield especially good results on chalk soils. The Riesling is fresh, powerful, full-bodied, with a characteristic nose of pear.

Other grapes such as Weissburgunder (green apple) and Traminer (mellow and rounded), yield reasonable wines for easy and early drinking. Portugieser reds have a seductive scent of raspberry but are often a bit too rigid.

Top quality Riesling Spätlese Trocken (dry) goes well with poultry and white meat.

Drinking temperature

German wines need to be served at the correct temperature. Whites that are too cold and reds that are too warm are the most common mistakes. People are often accustomed to drink their wines in this way which is a great pity for every wine has a message to deliver, provided the taster is receptive and judges the wine for its true value.

Type of wine	Drinking temperature	
Very sweet (Trockenbeerenauslese, Eiswein)	6–8°C	(42.8–46.4°F)
Light young white wine (to Kabinett)	8–10°C	(46.4–50°F)
Full, rich white wine (e.g. Halbtrocken, Spätlese, Auslese)	10–12°C	(50–53.6°F)
Rosé, new autumn white, Schiller, Rotling, Badisch Rotgold	8–10°C	(46.4–50°F)
Light young red wine (e.g. Portugieser, Trollinger)	11–13°C	(51.8–55.4°F)
Rich red wine (e.g. Spätburgunder, Spätlese)	13–14°C	(55.4–57.2°F)
Rich red wine (cask matured)	14–16°C	(57.2–60.8°F)

Luxembourg, Belgium, The Netherlands and United Kingdom

England, Wales, Luxembourg, Belgium, the Netherlands, and the former East Germany form the northern boundary of the European wine-growing area.

Of the first four of these countries, only Luxembourg has a centuries-old tradition of making wine.

Thanks however to the advances in technology and knowledge in recent decades, the other three countries are developing rapidly. The local wine-making in both England and Belgium has become a really serious matter in recent years. The climate changes that are happening, with the average temperature increases further north of the past fifteen years may well mean that these relative newcomers to wine-making like Belgium, The Netherlands, England, and Wales may come to play a greater role in the history of Europe's wine industry.

Luxembourg

Poets and writers have waxed lyrical about the unspoiled beauty of the Luxembourgeois Moselle since the times of the ancient Roman empire, as evidenced by the delightful verse of Ausonius about the 'Mosella'. Julius Caesar's words in praise of the magnificent landscape and superb wines of the Luxembourgeois Moselle may have been less poetic but were equally important.

Yet the valley of the 'Mousel' (as it is known locally) forms only a small part of the Grand Duchy of Luxembourg. There is much more to see in the relatively small European country that is wedged between France, Germany, and Belgium. The country has a character all of its own and three cultures have been melded together to form the true 'Letzeburger'.

Wormeldange Riesling.

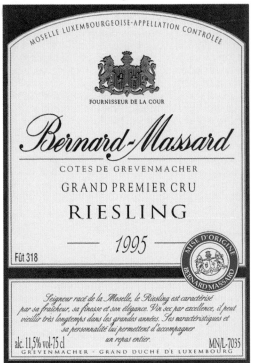

Grand Premier Cru Riesling.

The wine-growing

Luxembourg's vineyards are all situated on the west bank of the Moselle. The wine area starts at Schenen on the French border and finishes at Wasserbillig on the German border. The Moselle valley is between 300 and 400 metres (984 and 1,312 feet) wide and is flanked by softly undulating hills. The vineyards lie at heights of 150–250 metres (492–820 feet) above sea level.

The soil varies from marl in the southern canton of Reumich to chalk rock in the Grevenmacher canton in the north.

The landscape also varies from soft featured and gently undulating at Reumich (known for its mellow and almost caressing wines) to hard and rugged at Grevenmacher (known for its elegant but pithy wines with clear indication of terroir). The grapes can be happily left to grow and ripen here because it is never either too hot or too cold because the river moderates extremes of temperature.

Wines

One remark before we start: many find Luxembourgeois wines delicious, light, and amenable thirst quenchers for drinking young.

The best Luxembourgeois wines though really need to be laid down for a time before they are drunk. These wines are quite markedly acidic because of the northern position of the vineyards.

A period of rest makes them more tasty and balanced. This is certainly true of the best of the Riesling, Gewürztraminer, and Pinot Gris.

MOUSSEUX DU LUXEMBOURG
The ordinary sparkling wine of Luxembourg is pleasant and fresh. It is a typical summer wine. Drinking temperature is 6–8°C (42.8–46.4°F).

CRÉMANT DE LUXEMBOURG
Crémant de Luxembourg can impart any moment of the day with extra cachet by its elegant character, very fine bubbles, and subtle bouquet. Drinking temperature is 6–8°C (42.8–46.4°F).

ELBLING
This dry wine is extremely acidic. Drinking temperature is 8–10°C (46.4–50°F).

RIVANER
This is a very fruity wine that is mellow – sometimes almost caressingly so – that suits any occasion. Drinking temperature is 8–10°C (46.4–50°F).

PINOT BLANC
This white wine is fresh and delicate. It can be served with almost any dish. Drinking temperature is 8–10°C (46.4–50°F).

AUXERROIS
This is a full and more rounded white than the Pinot Blanc. Drinking temperature is 10–12°C (50–53.6°F).

PINOT GRIS
Most Pinot Gris is rounded and full-bodied with a light and comforting undertone and hints of spice. It is a very seductive wine. Drinking temperature is 10–12°C (50–53.6°F).

RIESLING
This is the king of Luxembourgeois wines. It is fruity, elegant, firm, and complex. Drinking temperature is 10–12°C (50–53.6°F).

GEWÜRZTRAMINER
The Gewürztraminer combines its power and sultriness here with the retention of a modest elegance. Drinking temperature is 10–12°C (50–53.6°F).

PINOT NOIR
Luxembourgeois Pinot Noir is less full-bodied than those of Bourgogne and even less than those of Alsace.
The strong points are the pleasing fruitiness, playful freshness, and seductive nature. Drinking temperature is 12–14°C (53.6–57.2°F) for the lighter

Crémant de Luxembourg.

First class Grevenmacher Riesling.

Probably Luxembourg's finest Riesling.

examples and 14–16°C (57.2–60.8°F) for the more full-bodied ones from sunnier vintage years.

Belgium

Belgium already had a wine industry about a hundred years or so ago. After a long period of neglect Belgium has seen a significant re-emergence of wine-making in recent years. A wine culture has re-established a place of honour once more in a nation of beer drinkers. Only the cultivation of grapes in the open air is dealt with in this book, not the growing of grapes under glass.

Hageland Appellation Contrôlée

The Belgians have succeeded in gaining their own appellation d'origine contrôlée (AC) for Hageland, which is an area within the triangle formed by Louvain-Diest-Tienen in the Belgian province of Brabant. Vines were being cultivated here in the twelfth century, and possibly earlier. The area flourished in its heydays during the fourteenth and fifteenth centuries and there was still an active trade with neighbouring Flanders and Holland in the sixteenth century.

The success of the Hageland growers in such a northern position is partly due to the position of the vineyards on the hills. The soil mainly consists of sand and ferruginous underlying layers. Hageland would not have achieved success though without the persistence of a handful of 'wine freaks' who decided to blow new life into the area. Their dream was realised 28 years later when Hageland's AC status

was recognised in 1997 by the European Court. Unfortunately Hageland AC will never become more than a small scale hobby that has got out of control. Most of the domains are too small and unable to cope with the increasing demand from the local catering establishments and individual customers. There were nine recognised growers in Hageland at the end of 1997.

These are Hageling of Tienen, Wijnhoeve Boschberg of Scherpenheuvel, Wijnhoeve Elzenbosch and Wijnkelder Kluisberg of Assent, Hagelander of Rillaar, Dox Wijn of Halen, Domein Sire Pynnock (perhaps the best) of Louvain, and Wijngoed St. Denis of Tielt-Winge.

Other wine areas

Wine is also made in other parts of the Belgian province of Brabant in addition to Hageland at De Wijngaerd and Wijngaard Kartuizerhof at Borgloon, Soniënwijn Cellars in Overijse), and elsewhere in Limburg at Wijnkasteel Genoels-Elderen at Riemst (who make a surprisingly good Chardonnay), and in Wallonia (French speaking Belgium) on a tip of a former coal mine at Château de Trazégnies at the town of Trazégnies under the smoke clouds of Charleroi.

These vineyards are all of recent origin and no more than 20 years old, some not yet 10 years old. It will

Maastricht Müller-Thurgau and Riesling.

Wine from Made (Dutch Brabant).

hectare. A guild of vineyard proprietors has been in existence in The Netherlands for at least seven years. This fulfils a mainly advisory rather than controlling function. The best-known of these vineyards are understandably those in the south on the delightful hills of Limburg such as Cadier and Keer, Cuyk, Guttecoven, Meijel, Mesch-Eijden, Oirsbeek, Schin op Geul, Ubachsberg, Velden, Venlo, Vijlen, Wahlwiller, and Wittem.

There are also vineyards elsewhere such as the province of Brabant at Bavel, Eindhoven, Etten-Leur, Lexmond, Luyksgestel, Made, Nederweert, Someren, and Veldhoven), province of Drenthe at Donderen, Flevoland near Lelystad, province of Gelderland at Angeren, Arnhem, Barneveld, Beesd, Ermelo, and Wageningen), province of North Holland near Amsterdam, Middenbeemster, province of South Holland at Goudriaan, Vlaardingen, Voorschoten, and Zuidland, province of Overijssel at Deventer, Kampen, Markelo, Nijverdal, and Zwolle, province of Utrecht at Maarssen, and province of Zeeland at Nieuw Haamstede and 's-Heer Arenskerke.

A wide variety of grape varieties has been tried and are still being tested. Some of these trials were doomed to failure from the start such as Cabernet Sauvignon and Cabernet Franc, while others may be considered dubious choices such as Muscat, Chardonnay, or Gewürztraminer. More logical choices for trials include Sauvignon, Sylvaner, Pinot Blanc, and Chasselas.

In addition to these known varieties new varieties such as Triomphe d' Alsace, Regent, Léon Millot, Seyval Blanc, and Phoenix are widely grown because they are more suited to the Dutch climate. These varieties are renowned for their productivity under the most difficult conditions. Better results in terms of quality are achieved with Kerner, Auxerrois, Riesling, Pinot Blanc, and Müller-Thurgau for white wines and Dornfelder, Zweigelt, Trollinger, Portugieser, and Pinot Noir/Spätburgunder for red wines. Wines are made at each of these vineyards and from all of the varieties of grapes mentioned. Honesty requires me to admit that only a small proportion of this manages to rise above the quality of a German 'Landwein' – the equivalent of a country wine or vins de pays. Some of these wines are barely drinkable with the best will in the world. This is due to the newness of the vineyards and amateur nature of the wine-makers. The quality of the top domains however can be termed reasonable.

Since the yields are low due to both natural and human circumstances, the costs of production are somewhat high.

not be possible to pass judgement on Belgian wines for a few more years yet.

Most growers use fairly logical choices of grapes for such northerly latitudes in Müller-Thurgau , Pinot Blanc, Pinot Gris, Auxerrois, Kerner, Riesling, and Sieger for white wines and Pinot Noir, Gamay, and Dornfelder for reds. Experiments with Chardonnay that is accustomed to warmer climes have been encouraging in places. A drinkable sparkling wine is also made at the Soniënwijn cellars.

The Netherlands

Quite a few small-scale Dutch growers in The Netherlands also make their own 'wine' just as the Belgian growers but much of that originates from grape extract or grapes grown under glass which falls outside the scope of this book.

The wine that interests us is that made from grapes picked from genuine vineyards. The Netherlands has at least 100 small vineyards plus some ten larger professional scale vineyards of more than one

Dutch wines are worth discovering if only as curiosities. Certain recommended white wines made from grapes such as Müller-Thurgau, Auxerrois, and Riesling) are:

- Apostelhoeve, the Hulst family, Maastricht (Limburg)
- Hoeve Nekum, Bollen family, Maastricht (Limburg)

- Wijngaard De Goltenhof, Theo v.d. Linden, Venlo (Limburg)
- De Linie, Marius van Stokkum, Made (Brabant)

Recommended red wines from grapes such as Regent and Pinot Noir) are:

- Wijngaard Wageningse Berg, Jan Oude Voshaar, Wageningen (Gelderland), certified organic
- Domaine des Blaireaux, Dassen and Dullaart, Maastricht (Limburg)
- Château Forét Verte, Groenewoud, Raamsdonkveer (Brabant)
- Château Neercanne, Peter Harkema, Maastricht (Limburg)

The United Kingdom

English wine-growing and making was regarded as a bit of a joke until not so long ago but no-one is laughing any more at the fanatical English and Welsh wine growers.

English and Welsh wine growers have achieved tremendous results during the past fifteen years and by the end of the second millennium wine-making in the United Kingdom had become serious business.

Wine-growing conditions

At present there are 450 genuine small vineyards in the British Isles, spread throughout southern England, including Cornwall and the Isle of Wight, Wales, and even Ireland.

It is very difficult for would-be wine growers to find a good position for a vineyard since the positioning of the vineyard in terms of its elevation, soil, position in respect of the sun, prevailing wind, and water etc. is of utmost importance in the moist and cool climate. It is only possible to make wine when these circumstances are ideal.

It is important that a vineyard in the British Isles is on a south-facing slope where it will catch the maximum sun and warmth. The soil also needs to be free draining, and the hill must not be susceptible to cold or in a frost pocket. Wind must be able to circulate freely throughout the vines but not to such an extent as to cause damage. The slope must not be

Lamberhurst Vineyards, Kent.

Biddenden Schönburger, Kent.

too wet because of the risk of fungal infection. Finally the vineyard must not be too close to the sea to prevent the vines from absorbing excessive salt. The more the vineyard fulfils these demands the greater is the chance that good wine can be made from its grapes. The geology also plays a role of course and the British Isles has a tremendously diverse geology. Clay dominates in East Anglia though this is interspersed with flint or coarse gravel almost everywhere. Along the banks of the Thames loams and sand dominate with gravel here and there.

Chalk, sandstone, and clay are common in Kent but in Canterbury (Elham Valley and Nicholas at Ash) there is chalk rock, Tenterden and Biddenden have loam and sand, and Lamberhurst is sited on loam, sand, clay, and sandstone (all these vineyards are in Kent). The famous Carr Taylor vineyards in Sussex grow their vines in soil that is sandy but rich in ironstone and other metallic minerals, with underlying soft slate.

Clay and or sand dominates elsewhere in Sussex. Chalk is found again in Hampshire at Winchester but at Wellow it is gravel-bearing loam. Further to the south-west the geology is dominated by sand and rocks. Some of the northern vineyards on the Isle of Wight are sited on heavy clay (Barton Manor), while the southern ones of Adgestone are on hard chalk. Wiltshire soil is chiefly sand and chalk, that of Dorset is mainly chalk.

The south-westerly vineyards of Cornwall are on soft loam with granite here and there. Devon is well-known for its attractive sandstone and slates that ensure excellent drainage. Wales and the Welsh Borders mainly have sand and clay soils with localised red sandstone as at Three Choirs.

Wine regions

England and Wales do not have geographically defined official places of origin for their wines. Of the

Assortment of English wines from Lamberhurst, Kent.

Assortment of English wines from Lamberhurst, Kent.

approximately 450 vineyards (1,035 hectares), about 95% are sited in England and the rest in Wales. Those 1,035 hectares of vineyards are run by 115 wineries, chiefly in South East and South West England, Wessex (the west), and East Anglia (the east). More than 90% of English and Welsh wines are white. The most northerly vineyard is Withworth Hell, not far from the Scottish border. The northern wineries are often provided with grapes from more southerly vineyards. Northern England and the Midlands or Mercia forms a triangle in which Whitworth Hall, Wroxeter, and Windmill are situated. Most of the vineyards are not truly commercial. Wine can only be made seriously in the most sheltered and

Thorncroft, Surrey.

White wine from Devon.

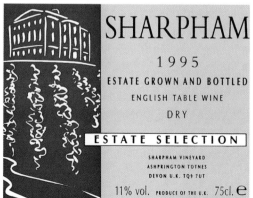

SHARPHAM

1995

ESTATE GROWN AND BOTTLED

ENGLISH TABLE WINE

DRY

ESTATE SELECTION

SHARPHAM VINEYARD
ASHPRINGTON TOTNES
DEVON U.K. TQ9 7UT

11% vol. PRODUCE OF THE U.K. 75cl. e

Hidden Spring, East Sussex.

HIDDEN SPRING
VINEYARD
1995

ENGLISH
TABLE
WINE

Produce of UK

11.5% VOL
75 cl.e

Grown by
and bottled for
Hidden Spring
Vines Cross Road
Horam, E. Sussex, UK
Tel/Fax: 01435 812640

Fine Huxelrebe from Biddenden, Kent.

Müller-Thurgau does well in England.

perhaps the best-known English vineyards of Kent and The Sussex Weald (East Sussex). This is a very productive area and new vineyards are being established or extended all the time. Excellent wines are made at Biddenden, Elham, Tenterden, and Lamberhurst. The vineyards of Surrey and West Sussex lie to the west of Kent and East Sussex and further west are those of Hampshire, the Isle of Wight, Wiltshire, and Dorset. Finally the vineyards of Devon and Cornwall are the most southerly British wine areas. The largest wine production comes from the South-East of England (includes Kent, East and West Sussex, Hampshire, the Isle of Wight, Oxfordshire, and Surrey), East Anglia (includes Essex and Suffolk), Wessex (Somerset and Dorset), the South-West (Devon and Cornwall), and South Mercia (Gloucestershire and the border counties).

Ortega grapes also produce good wine.

warmest places. Wales has fewer wineries and vineyards but the quality of some of the Welsh wines is quite outstanding. The Welsh Borders (between Wroxeter and Tintern) supply superb grapes for the best Welsh wineries, such as Three Choirs in Newent. The local Bacchus, Reichensteiner, and Schönburger. Travelling east from Wales one comes to the Thames Valley and Chiltern wine areas where the vineyards are mainly established between Oxford and Wantage, in area around Reading and Slough, and between Aylesbury and Hemel Hempstead. Further to the east is East Anglia, where there are vineyards between Norwich, Cambridge, Chelmsford, and Ipswich. To the south of this are

First class Bacchus from Lamberhurst.

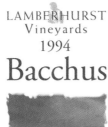

It's not Champagne but its delicious.

Permitted grape varieties

The grapes used are excellent and it is generally agreed that the choice of grapes will play a major role in the future of English wine-making, though perhaps not everywhere. From a list of more than 35 varieties we identify the most popular types. These are Bacchus, Chardonnay, Dornfelder, Kerner, Kernling, Ortega, Pinot Noir, Regner, Siegerrebe, Triomphe d' Alsace, Wrotham Pinot, and Wurzer. Bacchus is the most widely grown of these, accounting for more than 9% of the vines planted. Bacchus is a hybrid of Sylvaner, Riesling, and Müller-Thurgau that produces better wine than ordinary Müller-Thurgau. The best Bacchus wines stand out with their Muscat-like nose. Pinot Noir virtually never achieves full ripening here and is used mainly to produce lighter wines that are virtually rosés.

Experimental grape varieties

These are varieties which are only permitted to be grown on trial under control and supervision of the authorities. A typical example of these is Phoenix.

English and Welsh quality wines

It is important to make a clear distinction between the barely drinkable 'British wines', that are made from imported grape juice and the properly regulated English and Welsh Wines.
English wines originate from England and Welsh wines from Wales. The harvested grapes often have too little natural sugar and too much acid to make well-balanced wine. In common with other northern vineyards, it is permitted in Britain – according to strict EC standards – to add 3.5–4.5% of the alcohol through chaptalisation by the addition of sugar. In other words 7–9 kilograms of sugar is added to the unfermented must. This enriching process is known in Britain as amelioration. It is also permitted to add a little concentrated grape juice (the process known in German as Sussreserve) to the fermented wine to give it more roundness and a fuller taste. This is done with wines that are otherwise too sharply acidic. English and Welsh wines are mainly fresh and aromatic whites that are generally dry, 'off dry' (very slightly sweet), or medium dry. The bouquet usually has subtle floral notes. The greatest strength of these wines is their fresh and refreshing character. In addition to still whites there are also a few pink (rosé), red, and sparkling wines made. The sparkling wines in particular are becoming increasingly popular. This is not at all surprising since a good

English table wine.

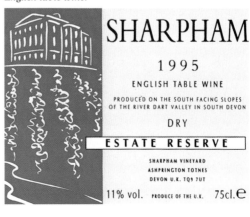

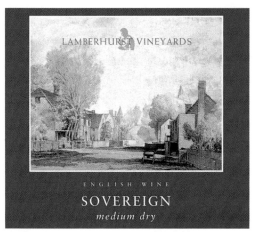

ENGLISH WINE

SOVEREIGN
medium dry

Lamberhurst wines are highly recommended.

Champagne is made from fresh white wine that is almost acidic, with subtle aromas. It was after all the English who made Champagne famous, even if it was invented by a French monk

Recommended wineries, wine-makers, and wines
- Biddenden Vineyards, Biddenden (Kent)
- Lamberhurst Vineyards, Lamberhurst (Kent)
- Hidden Spring Vineyards, Horam (East Sussex)
- Carr Taylor Vineyards, Westfield, Hastings (East Sussex)
- Three Choirs Vineyards, Newent (Welsh Borders)
- Sharpham Vineyards, Totnes (Devon)
- Chiltern Valley, Old Luxters, Hambleden, Henley on Thames (Oxfordshire)

According to those in the know, Martin Fowke, the wine maker of Three Choirs, is a rising star in the firmament of not just English and Welsh wine but

Sharpham is an established name, also for reds

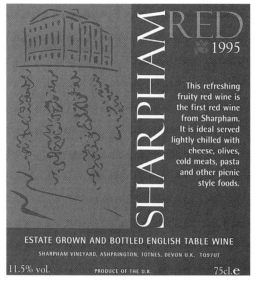

also of European wine. Three Choirs has risen sharply in recent years to join the established order of Lamberhurst, Carr Taylor, Biddenden, and Sharpham among others. The Late Harvest in particular (unique for the British Isles), Bacchus, and Siegerrebe look likely to be very successful. The same Martin Fowke also makes an excellent red wine at the Welsh Glyndwr.

Mark Sharpham of Sharpham Vineyards has created much ado in recent years with his cask aged whites and reds. This is certainly a name to remember.

Excellent but only EC table wine.

First class estate owned by Sharpham.

1994

Beenleigh

CABERNET SAUVIGNON/MERLOT

English Table Wine

Estate Grown and Bottled by
BEENLEIGH MANOR VINEYARDS, DEVON, UK.

12.5%vol   PRODUCE OF THE UK   75cl

Hidden Spring is first class.

Africa

Anyone who thinks of Africa in terms of wine will almost certainly immediately thing of South Africa and rightly so for it is the largest producer although wine is also made these days in Zimbabwe.

Zimbabwe

Few people will have heard of wine-growing in Zimbabwe and for those who have it will not be very positive. This fairly young wine industry is concentrated in the north-east of the country between the capital, Harare, and the border town of Mutare, in the wine areas of Marodera and Odzi, and the southern wine areas of Gweru and Bulawayo. Zimbabwe produces white, rosé, and red wines.

The white wines are made from grapes such as Clairette, Colombard, Chenin Blanc, and Riesling for dry wines and Muscatel and Hanenpoot for sweet ones. The white wines are certainly not for keeping. The first attempts have delivered reasonably full-bodied wines with fairly harsh acidity. Rosés from Pinotage and Cinsault are fairly dry but less full-bodied. These too should be drunk young. The reds come from Cabernet Sauvignon, Merlot, Pinotage, and Cinsault. They are fairly full-bodied, quite dry, but lack backbone. It is not a wine to keep. It is to be seen if Zimbabwe can make pleasing and drinkable wines in the future.

South Africa

South Africa has undergone drastic political, social, and ethnological changes in the past ten to twenty years. Present day South Africa, in which the development of the economy is problematical could be given a big impulse by its wine industry. Ten years ago the wine was boycotted throughout most of the world but now South African wine seems set to conquer Europe, having made good starts in the United Kingdom and the Netherlands because of the historical links of both these countries with South Africa.

Proud wine-growers will tell you that South Africa is the oldest of the 'New World' wine countries. The reality is that vines were not introduced into South Africa until 1655 while the first vines were planted in Mexico and Japan in 1530 and in Argentina and Peru around 1560. South Africa certainly started cultivating vines before California (1697) and New Zealand (1813).

Wine-growing conditions

South Africa is in the Southern Hemisphere within the latitudes that are most favoured for cultivating vines and making wine. The South African climate can be likened to that of the Mediterranean. The best wine-growing areas are at the foot of the mountains and in the valleys. The grapes have no shortage of sunshine here. The temperature in winter drops to no lower than 0–10°C (32–50°F). Cooling sea breezes bring the necessary moisture to the vineyards. Most rain falls between May to August.

The geology underfoot varies from granite in the foothills of the mountains to sandstone at Table Mountain, soft slate at Malmesbury, and slate and loess along the rivers. There are great differences from one vineyard to another. This makes the estate wines from the smaller domains additionally interesting. The production of wine is mainly in the hands of cooperative wineries (85% of the total) of

Chardonnay from the Coastal Region.

which the most important is the KWV. South Africa is at present the eighth largest wine-producing country with 3% of the world production compared with France at 22%, Italy with 20 %, and Spain with almost 14%.

All wine that is exported is provided with a quality seal. Samples are taken of these wines and the wine must meet organoleptic standards, or put in other words must fulfil certain criteria in terms of our senses: colour, scent, taste, character, etc., but also in terms of the veracity of the declared place of origin, grape varieties, and year of the vintage. The wine also undergoes extensive chemical analysis.

Wine regions

South Africa has had a clear system of naming the places of origin of its wines since 1973, based on the geographical and climatological properties of the wine.

Most of the wine-growing areas are in the south west of the country, between Cape Town and the coast. Wine is also made in the north and east of the country at Olifantsrivier, Orange River, and Klein Karoo.

Wines can originate from a specific local area such as these or from larger regions such as Coastal Region (Swartland, Tulbagh, Paarl, and Stellenbosch). and Breede River Region (Worcester and Robertson). Excellent examples of this type of wine

Swartland Pinotage.

are the successful Fleur du Cap range and Stellenrijck from the Coastal Region.

In our visit to these wine regions we start in the north, travel via the west to the south and then east.

Orange River

This is a relatively unknown area alongside the border with Namibia. The wine is acceptable at a reasonable price but little is exported.

Olifantsrivier

This area is slightly south of Orange River, running more or less parallel to the coast. The climate here between Koekenaap and Citrusdal is somewhat drier with less rain and higher temperatures than near Cape Town. Extremely pleasant wine at very acceptable prices originates from here but virtually only for the domestic market.

Piketberg

The area around Piketberg has extremely hot summers making irrigation essential, particularly as there is so little rainfall throughout the year. The wine is first class and quite reasonably priced.

Swartland

This area is further south, between Piketberg, Darling, Malmesbury, and Tulbagh. The quality of the wines start to improve now. The area used to be renowned for its sweet port-type wines. Nowadays two types of wine are produced here: light, tasty, convivial, and inexpensive modern wines such as Swartland, but also top quality wines from noble grapes such as Alles Verloren.

Tulbagh

This is a very small place of origin in the south east of Swartland. Reasonable to good cooperative wines are made alongside excellent classic wines here depending on the microclimate. We know the area in Europe chiefly from Drostdy-Hof and Twee Jonge Gezellen.

Paarl-Wellington

We have come closer now to Cape Town – about 50 km (31 miles) away. This is the home of the KWV and is undoubtedly the most famous of the South African wine areas (in part because of the annual Nederburg wine auctions and tasting sessions). Plenty of simple and inexpensive wine is produced here but Paarl-Wellington is best known for its

Steen from Tulbagh.

L'Ormarins from Franschhoek.

outstanding top wines from houses known in Europe such as KWV, Laborie, Landskroon, Nederburg, and Simonsvlei. The climate here is truly comparable with the Mediterranean, with long hot summers and just enough rain to not be dependent on irrigation. The best known wines from this area are the Sauvignon Blanc, Steen (Chenin Blanc), and Chardonnay whites, and Pinotage and Cabernet Sauvignon reds.

The descendants of French Huguenots have turned their area into a place of pilgrimage. There is a Huguenot monument at Franschhoek (which translates literally as 'French corner') but also superb wines. In addition to the other well-known varieties, the French Huguenots had a preference for Semillon. A number of very good wine houses of South Africa are situated in Franschhoek: Bellingham, Chamonix, Haute Provence, L'Ormarins, La Motte, and Plaisir de Merle. The white wines of Franschhoek of today are often more traditionally 'French' than some French wines!

Durbanville

This wine area is somewhat troubled by the encroaching suburbs of Cape Town but manages to survive.

Durbanville is best known for its good quality red wines but also makes outstanding whites.

A rising star in the firmament.

Rust en Vrede is a top estate.

Neighbouring Paarl enjoys much greater fame which is not entirely just but Durbanville is busily working hard to overtake its rival. Names that are known in Europe include Altijdgedacht, Diemersdal, Meerendal, and Theuniskraal.

Constantia

This wine area is south of Cape Town and by far the wettest of all the South African wine areas.

This is also where the first Dutch settlers or boers planted their first vineyards. Constantia was famous for many years for its superb sweet Muscat wines but now produces wines of every type of good to outstanding quality. The best-known wine houses of Constantia are Buitenverwachting, Groot Constantia, and Klein Constantia.

Stellenbosch

Stellenbosch is not only the area that makes the highest quality wines, it is also the research and study centre for the wine industry.

Renowned wines such as Alto, Bergkelder, Jacobsdal, Kanonkop, Le Bonheur, Meerlust, Middelvlei, Neil Ellis, Rust en Vrede, Simonsig, Thelema, and Uitkijk originate from this area close to Cape Town.

Stellenbosch is also famous for the quality of its blended red wines and also for superlative white and varietal wines. Kanonkop probably produces the finest Pinotage of South Africa.

Single grape Chardonnay.

Worcester

This is a fairly large wine area that is responsible for about a quarter of the South African production. There are at least nineteen cooperative ventures in this area, although none of them is known in Europe. The many different soil types and varied microclimates between the Breede River valley and its tributaries means that there are widely differing wines ranging from reasonable to good.

A great deal of wine is also distilled here to make a very acceptable local brandy by KWV among others.

Overberg (Walker Bay, Hermanus, Elgin)

This tiny and virtually unknown area lies on the south coast about half-way between Cape Town and Bredasdorp.

It is a relative newcomer that promises much for the future. The soil is broken slate and the cool, moist climate guarantees the finest Chardonnay of the country but also excellent Pinot Noir.
Two absolutely outstanding wines are Hamilton-Russel and Wildekrans.

Robertson

This is a fairly large wine area between Worcester and Klein Karoo. It was once famed for its fortified sweet wine. Today it produces superb whites and reds of which the Chardonnay and Shiraz are truly outstanding.
You can also find several sublime pure Shiraz wines in contrast with other areas where Shiraz is almost systematically blended with other grapes such as Cabernet Sauvignon. There are plenty of good wine houses such as Rietvallei, Robertson, Rooiberg, Van Loveren, Weltevrede, and Zandvliet.

Klein Karoo

Finally the largest wine region of South Africa is Klein Karoo, which is also the most easterly area. It is very hot in summer here and irrigation is essential. Klein Karoo is famous for its sweet fortified wine but also for the surprisingly fresh and fruity Steen (Chenin Blanc).

CAPE RIESLING/KAAPSE RIESLING
In spite of the name this is not Riesling as we know it in Europe but a different grape, the Crouchen Blanc, of which the origins are unclear. It is often used to make very acceptable table wines but also produces some good firm wines with interesting

Excellent Chardonnay from Robertson.

vegetal aromas such as straw and grass. Drinking temperature is 8–10°C (46.4–50°F).

COLOMBARD

This grape variety hails originally from the French south-west, origins of most of the Huguenots. Its yields fresh and fruity wines that are excellent as an aperitif or to served with grilled fish. Drinking temperature is 8–10°C (46.4–50°F).

STEEN (CHENIN BLANC)

These grapes originate from the Loire. The grape is particularly used for its fine acidity. In South Africa though it delivers surprisingly mellow wines that are almost sweet as well as dry as chalk examples that are fresh and fruity. Drinking temperature is 8–10°C (46.4–50°F).

SAUVIGNON BLANC

Also known on occasion as Fumé Blanc as in the United States. South African Sauvignon Blanc wines are very herbal with definite notes of grass, with peppery undertones. The taste is fresh, dry, aromatic, and beautifully rounded. Drinking temperature is 8–10°C (46.4–50°F).

CHARDONNAY

This Burgundian grape also thrives in South Africa. The special cuvées in particular, that are aged in oak barrels, are extremely exciting. Chardonnay is fruity, rich, and rounded with a robust taste Drinking temperature is 10–12°C (50–53.6°F).

PINOTAGE

This grape is the true South African speciality. It was formed from a cross based on old root stock with Pinot Noir, and Cinsault (known locally as Hermitage) about which little is known. The variety was created by Prof. Abraham Perold in 1925 and it combines the reliability of Cinsault in terms of volume and quality, even in poor years, with the finesse of Pinot Noir.

Most of the wines are drunk still too young but there are certain top quality Pinotage wines such as Kanonskop which aged well (five to ten years). Pinotage smells and tastes of dark ripe fruit with hints of spices. Some of the best Pinotage wines contain quite substantial tannin when they are young. A local speciality is 'Beesvleis Pinotage', which is a beef stew cooked in Pinotage. Drinking temperature is 16°C (60.8°F).

CABERNET SAUVIGNON

This is the ubiquitous Bordeaux grape variety. Here in South Africa, Cabernet Sauvignon produces sturdy, highly tannic wines with herbal aromas and hints of red fruit and blackcurrant. There is a good balance between fruit and ripe woody notes. It is

Sauvignon Blanc.

Franschhoek Chardonnay.

Pinotage.

Cabernet Sauvignon.

superb with red meat and mature hard cheeses. Drinking temperature is 16–17°C (60.8–62.6°F).

MERLOT

This Bordeaux grape appears to be gaining ground in South Africa, especially in the Stellenbosch and Paarl regions. Merlot is a full-bodied and velvet smooth wine with rich and warm nuances that include cherry. Drinking temperature is 16°C (60.8°F).

PINOT NOIR

This grape, like Chardonnay originates in Burgundy. It is a fairly temperamental variety which only produces excellent results in good hands and in good years. A good Pinot Noir is characteristically light in colour and quite aromatic with herbal notes and those of red fruit in its nose. Drinking temperature is 14–16°C (57.2–60.8°F).

SHIRAZ

The Shiraz here is often an amenable if not slightly exotic wine with sensual nose and taste. This wine is often excellent with plenty of warmth and spicy undertones and is ideal with grilled lamb or game. Drinking temperature is 16°C (60.8°F).

TINTA BAROCCA

Tinta Barocca is a surprising wine that is full-bodied,

One of the best South African Shiraz wines.

The renowned blended Bordeaux-type Rubicon from Meerlust.

Pongráz is a fine sparkling wine.

Superb blend from Rust en Vrede.

warm, exciting, but also fruity, elegant, and refined. Drinking temperature is 16°C (60.8°F).

BLENDS

The Bordeaux type blends of Cabernet Sauvignon/Cabernet Franc/Merlot (Meerlust Rubicon) are often excellent, especially where the process of cask maturing in oak is well done. These are superb, full-bodied, rich, and complex wines with blackcurrant and bilberry in their bouquet, mixed with spices and vanilla.

Cabernet-Shiraz are very exciting wines which often age extremely well. Serve this full-bodied, warm, powerful, and complex wine with roast or grilled meat or mature hard cheese.

The fairly new Pinotage-Merlots are quite promising. This is a wine filled with taste that combines spice and fruit. Drinking temperature is 16–17°C (60.8–62.6°F).

Sparkling wines

South Africa makes a number of very good sparkling wines. The best are made by the méthode traditionnelle which is known here as méthode cap classique.

Only a few of these wines, such as the Pongrácz, could compete with top quality Champagnes The other sparkling wines that are not made by the

Robertson Muscatel.

Port-type wine from Swartland.

Krone Borealis from Twee Jonge Gezellen.

traditional method are also known as sparkling wine, and they can also be very tasty. Drinking temperature is 6–8°C (42.8–46.4°F).

Fortified wines

The sweet South African wines such as Muscadel and Hanenpoot (Muscat of Alexandria) can be readily recommended.

The heavy and sultry wines that used to be have become somewhat fresher and more interesting. The port and sherry type wines of South Africa can withstand judgement alongside the top European originals. They miss some of the finer freshness of the true ports and sherries but compensate for this with their sunny character.

North America

The American continent contains a relatively small number of wine-producing countries. The Spanish introduced vines into Peru (no longer a true wine-producing country), Argentina, Chile, Mexico, and California, the Portuguese to Brazil, the British to the United States and Canada, the French to Quebec, Uruguay (French Basques), and some parts of the United States. The American continent together with Australia and New Zealand, and South Africa form the 'New World' wine regions. Our tour through the Americas begins in Canada and we then visit the USA and finish in Mexico.

Canada

Three different wine-growing areas can be distinguished in Canada. Quebec is the oldest but not the best, the high quality Ontario (near Niagara Falls), and British Columbia in the west of the country.

Wine-growing regions

The three wine-growing regions from east to west are:

Quebec

Quebec is the French-speaking province of Canada. The weather circumstances are everything but ideal for cultivating vines and making wine. Temperatures can drop to minus 40°C/°F or even lower in winter which is fatal for vines. A handful of enthusiasts tried a surprising way to protect the vines against the cold of winter. The vines are kept pruned low and before the first frosts they are covered with a layer of earth which is then removed in spring. Apart from this interesting cultivation technique and the hard

working nature of the local growers, there is little else positive to say about this wine region. The wines that we tasted were extremely dubious and their prices far too high.

Ontario

Ontario is the wine region in Canada with the longest continuous activity. The vineyards are in three districts: the Niagara Peninsula, Lake Erie North Shore, and Pelee Island. These three districts are all close to the Great Lakes. The epicentre of the wine industry is the town of Niagara-on-Lake, where the present-day generation of wine growers and makers have their origins in Germany, France, Italy, and even The Netherlands. Although Ontario shares the same latitude as the Côtes du Rhône, its climate is much harsher. The summers are hot and winters extremely cold. Wine-growing is only possible close to the most southerly of the five Great Lakes, Lake Erie. The soil here consists of a mixture of clay, gravel, and loam which is rich in minerals and trace elements. The underlying geology consists of hard rock which gives additional complexity to the wines. Various hybrid grape varieties are grown here such as Seyval Blanc and Vidal for white wines and Maréchal Foch and Baco Noir for reds. Although Seyval, Vidal, and Baco Noir deliver good to excellent results the Ontario growers are increasingly choosing to plant more *vinifera* varieties such as Pinot Auxerrois, Chardonnay, Gewürztraminer, Pinot Blanc, and Riesling on the one hand and Pinot Noir, Gamay, Cabernet Sauvignon, Cabernet Franc, and Merlot on the other.

British Columbia

Although wine has been made here for some considerable time which left much to be desired, the

Ontario Cabernet Franc.

Vidal Dry.

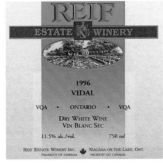

Dry Riesling.

past decade has seen this region striving for the best quality. The old hybrid or even worse native America *Vitis labrusca* vines have increasingly been replaced with *Vitis vinifera* varieties. Wine is made in two districts: the western Fraser Valley and Vancouver Island, and the eastern Okanagan and Similkameen valleys.

The first two areas and the Similkameen Valley are recent additions that are busily in the process of development. The historical heart of British Columbia lies in the Okanagan Valley where the weather conditions are more suited to growing grapes and making wines. The summers are hot and dry, with little rainfall.

The soil consists of rock, fine sand, clay, and alluvial deposits in the south. The more northerly vineyards that are cooler and more humid are mainly planted with French and German grape varieties of Auxerrois, Bacchus, Chardonnay, Erenfelser, Gewürztraminer, Pinot Blanc, Pinot Gris, and Riesling, while the more southerly ones have the traditional red varieties of Pinot Noir and Merlot. British Columbia has three types of winery.

The Majors are the large wine industries which get their grapes from far and wide, the Estates use only those grown in British Columbia, of which at least 50% is from their own vineyards. They are required to conduct all viticultural and wine-making activities within their own winery. The Farms are mainly smaller in scale and must meet the same requirements as the Estates except that 75% of the grapes must come from their own vineyards.

The wines

It is best advised to buy only wines that have a VQA neck seal (Vintner's Quality Alliance). These wines are not only strictly controlled in respect of their guaranteed origin but are also quality tested for taste, colour, bouquet etc. This gives assurance that you have bought one of the better Canadian wines. Canada also has two levels of guarantee of origin: the broad Provincial Designation Wines category i.e. British Columbia or Ontario, and the more precise Viticultural Areas Wines which originate from one of the recognised wine districts such as Okanagan Valley, Similkameen Valley, Fraser Valley, or Vancouver Island for British Columbia, and Niagara Peninsula, Lake Erie North Shore, or Pelee Island for Ontario.

The strength of Canadian wines is their firm and fresh white wines and the sultry, overripe sweet wines. Some wine-makers and growers though, mainly in Ontario, can also make excellent rounded and full-bodied reds. Most of the Canadian red wines though are very light in structure and a bit shallow. The same goes for Canadian wines as elsewhere: do not choose the very cheapest wines for a little more money will yield far better quality. The following types of white wine are generally recommended.

VIDAL DRY

This is a fresh and firm dry wine with a bouquet of

Choose VQA wines.

green apple and sometimes, with the better ones, hints of citrus fruit. Drinking temperature is 10–12°C (50–53.6°F).

SEYVAL DRY

This wine is less severely dry than the Vidal and it has a nose containing grapefruit and the occasional hint of flowers and spices. It has a good balance between acidity, alcohol, fruit, and sweetness. Drinking temperature is 10–12°C (50–53.6°F).

RIESLING DRY

This is a very elegant wine that is quite fresh but not harsh and it possesses interesting floral notes in its nose. Most of these wines are of the 'off-dry' sort with some sugar residues which enhance the delicious taste.

The best of these wines are drier but they have seductive bouquets in which pear, apple, and spring blossom appear. Late harvest wines have a touch of botrytis, which makes them more complex and attractive. Drinking temperature is 10–12°C (50–53.6°F).

Chardonnay.

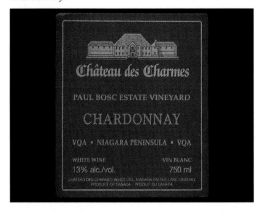

Ice Wine.

CHARDONNAY DRY

Most Canadian Chardonnays are fresh and a touch green (unripe apples), partially full-bodied, with a subtle bouquet of butter, wood, and citrus fruit.

The best Chardonnays (bottled sur lie, reserve, and barrel fermented) are more complex, full-bodied, and creamier.

These wines also possess the elegant hints of toast and croissants of the better Burgundies.

There are also typically hints of butterscotch, toffee, or caramel which are more Californian and Chilean in nature.

Drinking temperature is 10–12°C (50–53.6°F) for the simpler wines and 12–14°C (53.6–57.2°F) for the better examples.

GEWÜRZTRAMINER

This wine that is generally vinified as 'off-dry' with sugar residues, is full bodied and slightly spicy. It has a seductive bouquet in which lychee, melon, peach, and spices can be detected. Drinking temperature is 10–12°C (50–53.6°F).

GEWÜRZTRAMINER MEDIUM DRY/ LATE HARVEST

This one is fuller and more seductive than the 'off-dry' version.

It has a good balance between sweetness, alcohol, fruit, and acidity. Drinking temperature is 8–10°C (46.4–50°F).

VIDAL MEDIUM DRY/LATE HARVEST

This grape achieves its best I believe in sweeter wines. The bouquet of citrus and tropical fruits keeps the sultry, comforting ripeness of banana and honey · in balance. The relatively high acidity also moderates the otherwise very sweet taste of the wine.

RIESLING MEDIUM DRY/LATE HARVEST

Fine medium dry to sweet wines are made from the noble Riesling here just as they are in Germany. The fresh and refined acidity of Riesling keeps the wine well balanced in spite of its cosseting sweetness. There are very attractive floral aromas and also apple, peach, and honey with the sweeter Late Harvest, and the occasional mineral undertones. Drinking temperature is 8–10°C (46.4–50°F).

ICE-WINE

Ice-wine is probably the best-known Canadian speciality. The best of these wines walk off with major prizes at the majority of the international exhibitions. Ice-wine can in principle be made from any type of grape including red varieties like Cabernet Sauvignon or Franc, but with a few exceptions the most interesting of them are produced from Vidal and Riesling. The method of making Ice-wines is the same as that for making German or

Chardonnay Reserve.

Gewürztraminer.

Gamay Rosé.

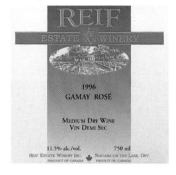

Cabernet Sauvignon.

become more rustic notes of leather, animal, and humus. Drinking temperature is 14–16°C (57,2–60.8°F).

CABERNET
Bear in mind that many Canadian Cabernet wines are a blend of Cabernet Sauvignon and Cabernet Franc but may also contain Merlot. These are generally well-made wines but the best of them are simply fantastic. They have constantly caused great surprise in blind tastings with their power, complexity, seductive fruitiness, and elegant tannin. Drinking temperature is 16–17°C (60–62.6°F).

Other wines

The best wine houses also make excellent Sauvignon Blancs, Aligotés, Gamay Blancs and Rouges. These wines are not very abundant though.

Recommended wines

The following wines from the best Canadian wineries are well worth trying.
– *Ontario:* Château des Charmes, Hildebrand Estates Winery, Inniskillin, Marijnissen Estates, Reif Estate Winery (all Niagara-on-the-Lake); D'Angelo (Amherstburg); Henry of Pelham (St. Catharines); Stoney Ridge Cellars (Winona); Lakeview Cellars (Vineland); Cave Spring Cellars (Jordan); Colio Estate (Harrow); and Pelee Island Winery (Kingsville).
– *British Columbia:* Calona Vineyards, Quails' Gate, Summerhill, Mission Hill, Cedar Creek, St. Humbertus (all Kelowna); Hawthorne Mountains, Inniskillin Okanoga, Jackson Triggs, Peller Estate (Okanoga); Domaine Combret, Tinhorn Creek (Oliver); and Langley's Estate Winery (Langley).

Austrian Eiswein and French Vins de Glace from the south-west of France.

The grapes are allowed to hang until frozen by the frost. They are then quickly pressed and the tasteless frozen liquid remains behind with the seeds and skins, with only the honey sweet juices emerging from the press.

These juices are so concentrated that the yeast cells which can normally live up to a level of alcohol of 15% are finished by 8 or 9%. Ice-wines are very complex, powerful, extremely aromatic wines with notes such as apricot, peach, sweet melon, and honey with Vidal grapes and tropical flowers, apricot, citrus fruit, toffee, and vegetal nuances with Riesling. To gain double the pleasure serve it cold at 8–10°C (46.4–50°F) but then allow it to warm up slowly.

ROSÉ
Most Canadian rosés are very lightly structured and not terribly interesting. They are certainly fruity but despite good acidity and reasonable complexity most are knocked back like soft drinks. Drinking temperature is 10–12°C (50–53.6°F).

BACO NOIR
This is an extremely surprising French-Canadian hybrid which produces quite exciting results in Canada with full-bodied wines with lots of juice and taste that are very scented with suggestions of blackcurrant, blueberries, tobacco, and animal undertones. Some top Baco Noirs slightly resemble better Rhône Syrah wines. Drinking temperature is 16–17°C (60.8–62.6°F).

PINOT NOIR
The typical bouquet is of woodland fruits, cherry, and a hint of wild strawberry which when older

Henry of Pelham is a rising star in Ontario.

283

United States

Anyone who couples the United States with wine will automatically think first of California, the biggest producer of North American wines. But just as there is more to California than the Napa Valley, the United States has other wine-producing areas besides California.

In fact there are four large wine zones across the United States. They are the North East (New York: Finger Lakes, Lake Erie, Hudson River, and Long Island), the South and Mid-West (Texas, Carolina, New Mexico, Georgia, Missouri, Arkansas, and Iowa); California (Napa, Sonoma, and Carneros); and the North West (Washington State, Oregon, and Idaho).

The wine industry has grown up in the past decades and more and more Americans have come to envy the success of the Californian wine-growers. Many European wine companies too which feel restricted in the European market have also decided to take an active part in the US industry. The wine industry is still 'big business' in the USA but a new generation of growers and makers has emerged with a tremendous passion for making good wine. There are increasing numbers of small-scale growers who dare to take on the gigantic Californian wine producers.

North-East

While the vineyards of Ontario in Canada are on the northern shore of Lake Erie, the majority of the North-East's vineyards in the United States are on the southern shore between Detroit and Buffalo. The Finger Lakes area is slightly further east and to the south of Lake Ontario.

There are also vineyards towards the coast on the banks of the Hudson River, on Long Island near New York, and further away near Boston. The remaining vineyards of the North-East can be found in the valley of the Ohio river and south of Washington DC, in the Shenandoah Valley.

The local wine industry dates back to the first pioneering settlers of the sixteenth century. For many years hybrids and native species that were not varieties of *Vitis vinifera* were used like Alexander, Catawba, Delaware, and Concord. The results from these were not really satisfactory because of the 'foxy' aroma these vines give to the wines that is characteristic of varieties and sub species of *Vitis labrusca*. The 'foxy' aroma is best described as the smell of a dirty old pelt on which old-fashioned home-made fruit jam has been smeared.

More suitable French hybrids were introduced during the early 1940s such as Baco Noir and Seyval. From the early 1950s and particularly in the 1970s large scale plantings were made of *Vitis vinifera*

Californian Chardonnay.

Napa County Chardonnay.

vines. Thirty years later this helped to cause a major breakthrough.

New York's climate is marginal for cultivating vines and making wines. The summers are generally very warm and dry but the winters are often exceptionally raw. Wine-growing is only possible where the climate is moderated by the big rivers, lakes, or the Atlantic Ocean. It is extremely important to plant the vines in subsoil that is free draining. The North-East region contains the following officially recognised places of origin known as AVA (American Viticultural Areas): New York (includes Finger Lakes, Lake Erie, Hudson River, The Hamptons (Long Island), New England (Western Connecticut Highlands, South-eastern New England), Ohio, Michigan, and Virginia (including the Shenandoah Valley).

Despite government campaigns promoting the planting of *Vitis vinifera* varieties, some still persist with the old-fashioned and inferior Concord, Catawba, Delaware, and Niagara. The very best wines though are made with Chardonnay, Riesling, Cabernet Sauvignon, Cabernet Franc (Hudson River), Merlot, and Pinot Noir.

The wines from such as the Concord are really nothing special. Considerable amounts of sugar are often added to the must to mask the high acidity and strong taste, which certainly do nothing to aid the wine's finesse. The *Vitis vinifera* wines are very taut which is understandable give the climate but they

Oregon AVA Pinot Noir.

are also extremely aromatic and particularly fruity. These are not high flight wines but the quality is steadily improving.

South and Middle-East

The south west of the United States is not really suited to wine-growing with the exception of certain parts of Texas. But American determination can overcome much and the odd place has been found here and there to grow vines after a long search. The South and Middle-East region is enormous and the vineyards are spread widely. They lie between Denver in the centre of the United States, Columbia on the eastern seaboard, south to a line formed by Austin, New Orleans, and Orlando, and finally Florida.

The first pioneers, but more particularly the first monks, planted the first vineyards in New Mexico. The territory now known as New Mexico and Texas was then part of the Spanish Empire. German immigrants introduced wine-growing to Missouri, Georgia, and Carolina in the nineteenth century. Other immigrants did the same in Arkansas. These vineyards, which combined European *Vitis vinifera* with many native and hybrid varieties, have never become well-known and their wines were all intended for local consumption.

When wine-growing and making started to catch on in America in the 1960s and 1970s, the growers of Texas, New Mexico, Georgia, and both North and South Carolina saw their opportunity. The area of vines in cultivation in Missouri, Arkansas, Iowa, Arizona, Colorado, Tennessee, Mississippi, Louisiana, and Florida has also been substantially extended and the cultivation and varieties improved during the past twenty years.

The climate is not really favourable, for the summers are extremely hot and the winters severe. It is too dry in the north of the region but irrigation can work wonders. In the south on the other hand it is too wet but here growers seek out places that are sighted at higher levels, where it is more windy and drier. The extensive area has a number of official places of origin or AVAs. These include Texas Hill Country, Bell Mountain, Fredericksburg, and Escondido in Texas; New Mexico, Missouri, and Virginia. Although there are still many native and hybrid varieties grown in these areas the houses that are really serious about wine are increasingly switching to *Vitis vinifera* varieties.

There is one native grape though that springs a surprise: the Scuppernong, which makes a pleasing and very aromatic Muscat-like sweet wine in some of the southern states. All the other native and hybrid varieties are really only intended for local consumption.

The most widely used varieties of grape now are Chardonnay, Sauvignon Blanc, Riesling, Trebbiano, Chenin Blanc, and Colombard for white wines and Cabernet Sauvignon, Cabernet Franc, Merlot, and Zinfandel for reds. Although you will rarely encounter these wines in Europe, the wines from Texas are worth discovering.

North-West

The North-West region is better known as Washington State and Oregon. The Columbia and Snake rivers are vital for the wine industry. The area lies to the south-east of Seattle, on both sides of Portland. Wine-making in this region is a fairly recent phenomenon. There were trials in the nineteenth century with native and hybrid grapes but the first *Vitis vinifera* varieties were not introduced until the end of that century. Wine-growing started to become larger in scale during the twentieth century thanks to a major irrigation project. The final real breakthrough for areas such as Oregon occurred in the 1970s, when serious-minded growers planted leading European varieties. Oregon's Pinot Noir is now known world-wide thanks to investment by several leading French companies like Drouhin of Beaune.

The climate in the north-west of the United States is moderate in Oregon but almost desert-like in Washington State where the dependence on irrigation is total.

The winters are also colder and drier in Washington State than Oregon. The soil varies widely, from loam in Oregon to layers of volcanic origin in Washington. The choice of grape variety is therefore extremely important.

Various varieties are grown in the two large AVAs of Washington State (Columbia Valley, Yakima Valley, and Walla Walla Valley), and West Pacific (including Oregon, Willamette Valley, and Umpqua Valley). Pinot Noir with some Chardonnay dominates in Oregon, Cabernet Sauvignon and Merlot in Washington State. The picture is completed in Washington State with Chenin Blanc, Semillon, and Sauvignon Blanc, while Oregon also produces reasonable to good Pinot Gris.

It goes without saying that there is much chaff among the corn in both areas and results vary from years to years through changing weather, especially in Oregon. But by choosing from the better wines you will find that there are truly some great ones.

Washington State Sauvignon Blanc.

OREGON PINOT NOIR

Some Pinot Noir wines from Oregon can hold their own against the best French wines. They are superb in colour, have seductive bouquets of red and black fruits such as blackberry, blackcurrant, redcurrant, and cherry, and touches of herbs and spices, including sweetwood, and a complex and harmonious texture.

They are also elegant with a refined taste. There may also be suggestions of truffle, exotic woods, and a good balance between acidity, alcohol, fruit, and tannin, with a prolonged aftertaste. These wines can be kept for at least five to ten years when they

Drouhin family Pinot Noir.

Top Oregon Pinot Noir.

286

develop a nose of plum, fungi, humus, leather, and herbs. Drinking temperature is 12–14°C (53.6–57.2°F) when young and 14–16°C (57.2–60.8°F) when mature.

California

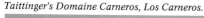

California is the best-known wine region of America. The region is subdivided into six main areas. From north to south these are the North Coast (north of San Francisco, home of Napa Valley, Sonoma, Carneros wines), Humboldt (on the banks of the Sacramento River), Sierra Foothills (at the foot of the Sierra Mountains east of Sacramento), Central Coast (south of San Francisco to slightly north of Los Angeles), Central Valley (a huge area on the banks of the San Joaquin River), and South Coast (between Los Angeles and San Diego).

Franciscan monks from Spain were the first to risk an attempt to plant vines here in the eighteenth century. The wine produced was for their own use. A Frenchman from Bordeaux with the rather appropriate name of Jean Louis Vignes saw the possibilities here in 1830 and he imported countless European varieties of grapes.

Things really took off though after the Gold Rush. The growers left the south alone and concentrated their efforts in the central and northern areas where there was a ready market with the large city of San Francisco. The quality of those wines was from modest to poor. In those days California made ponderous syrupy wines of little character and freshness. This was the start of the huge American bulk wine industry. Prohibition from 1919 to 1933, which banned the production of alcoholic drink on a commercial scale, was a major blow for the Californian wine trade.

It seemed for a long time as though the growers would not survive this crisis. It was not until the 1970s that changes started to take place. Winemaking became a recognised profession and people from California went to study at first hand in Europe with the best wine-makers. The result is nothing less than spectacular.

There are still many 'wimpy wines' (plonk) in California, but quality is becoming more important than quantity with both the big business and small wineries.

Yet many still regard California as a massive industrialised wine region with its enormous vineyards, wineries like palaces, batteries of high towering stainless steel storage tanks etc. Despite this the numbers of smaller producers is growing in places like the Sonoma Valley, and Carneros. These growers and makers not only know what they are talking about, they also bring much verve and passion to their wine-making.

Hence the massive rows of readily saleable Chardonnay and Cabernet Sauvignon are becoming smaller in scale and some even dare to replace them with specialist varieties such as Viognier for white wines and Barbera, Sangiovese, Syrah, and Grenache for reds.

Taittinger's Domaine Carneros, Los Carneros.

Increasingly common Viognier.

Mendocino County Chardonnay.

It is surprising to see how increasingly European in style the Americas are becoming while some European companies exceed the previously reviled Californian monoliths with their futuristic 'high-tech' wineries in Languedoc Roussillon or Penedés.

Wine-growing conditions

California's climate is quite varied, which is not surprising given the large area of the state. In rough terms the climate on the coast is similar to the Mediterranean with warm summers and mild winters. Summer in the Central Valley is exceptionally hot and dry, while summer in the area immediately behind the coast is much moister and can be misty.

The highest temperatures are in the Central Valley and the mildest are on the coast. The North Coast vineyards get the most rainfall. The soil is also varied as a result of the many earthquakes that have occurred throughout the area. The soil varies from alluvial and sedimentary deposits to strata of volcanic origin.

The notion of terroir that is so strong in Europe is not given much credence in California. The variety of grape is far more likely to be chosen as suitable for the climate than the soil. In the past when grapes were just regarded as yet another crop, the vines were planted in the most fertile soil, where the highest yield could be expected. This, when combined with the high wine yield from the grapes, explains why the wines used to be so ponderous and characterless. Fortunately the best growers have put an end to that policy.

Wine areas

California is a very large wine region in which the following guaranteed places of origin are the best known:

Mendocino County, Lake County, Sonoma County (includes the famous Russian River Valley and Sonoma Valley), Napa Valley, Los Carneros, Central Valley, Sierra Foothills, Livermore Valley, Santa Cruz Mountains, Monterey County, San Joaquin Valley, San Luis Obispo Valley, and Santa Barbara County.

Irrigation is permitted throughout California but not necessary everywhere.

The most popular grape varieties are Chardonnay, Colombard, Chenin Blanc, Fumé Blanc (Sauvignon Blanc), Riesling, Gewürztraminer, Pinot Blanc, and Viognier for white wines and Cabernet Sauvignon, Pinot Noir, Merlot, Barbera, Sangiovese, Syrah, and Grenache for reds. The classic Californian grape variety of Zinfandel is starting to play an increasingly important role.

Taittinger's Domaine Carneros sparkler.

Chardonnay.

Wines

You may encounter thousands of different types of Californian wine because of the great differences in climate, soil, wine-making method, yield, and target group for marketing.

CALIFORNIAN CHAMPAGNE (CHAMPAIGN)

The powerful houses of Champagne forbid everyone from using their name outside the designated area of Champagne in France yet you will find the term 'Champagne' used in the USA on other wines. To avoid long drawn out and costly law suits in the American courts, the Champagne houses have had to accept that names such as 'Californian Champagne' are legally permitted here.

They are however restricted to the domestic markets so that the so-called Californian Champagne must be sold in Europe merely as 'sparkling wine'. American sparkling wines are made in both pink (rosé) and white and from quite dry to sweet. The driest is the Brut, followed by Extra Dry, Dry/Sec, and Demi-Sec, which is the sweetest.

Only the highest quality sparklers are made in the United States by the traditional method with second fermentation in the bottle. Most are produced by the charmat or bulk method. This shows that some people still think of wine as a product to be made down to a price. A third method is the transfer method which combines aspects of both the other methods. The results are of better quality than with the ordinary bulk method but remain cheaper than the traditional way.

Whether white or rosé, some of these wines are well worth discovering. Two of the leading Champagne houses make good 'Champagne' style wines in America. Those of Mumm are good while the Taittinger product is excellent. The Mumm wines from the Napa Valley are livelier and more unruly than those of Taittinger, which come from Carneros, and are more grown-up and full-bodied. Drinking temperature is 6–8°C (42.8–46.4°F).

CHARDONNAY

Chardonnay is regarded as the best variety of white wine grape in the world and the best Chardonnay some declare comes from the Sonoma Valley. Certainly there are remarkably good Chardonnays made in California, especially in Sonoma County. Californian Chardonnay is full-bodied, broad, rich, and very aromatic with hints of fig, pineapple, ripe apple, melon, citrus fruit, and honey.

The wine is further improved by cask maturing in oak with notes of toast, nuts, vanilla, butter, toffee, and butterscotch etc. These Chardonnays are not cheap but if you choose a good one you will find it is sumptuous. Drinking temperature is 10–12°C (50–53.6°F).

Sauvignon Blanc.

White Grenache blush wine.

FUMÉ BLANC (SAUVIGNON BLANC)

Sauvignon Blanc is generally known as Fumé Blanc here, which is a trend started by Robert Mondavi in the 1960s.

Californian Sauvignon Blanc often possesses light smoky aromas and is notably vegetal too with hints of green olives, freshly-mown grass, dill, and fennel, but generally is also very fruity with fresh fig, melon, and citrus fruit etc. to be discovered. The wine is fresh but not firm like a white Bordeaux. Although most Sauvignon Blancs are dry, you may also encounter some sweeter examples. Drinking temperature is 8–10°C (46.4–50°F).

CHENIN BLANC

This grape is highly popular in California, especially in the Central Valley, where it is used to make fresh, fruity, and inexpensive wines. A more delicious, light, and fruity version that is ideal for a 'happy hour' is made in Sonoma. Drinking temperature is 8–10°C (46.4–50°F).

JOHANNISBERG RIESLING/WHITE RIESLING

Do not expect elegance and refinement here but a firm white wine. This noble grape delivers fresh and melon fruity wine for everyday drinking, say with fish or poultry, here in California.

Only a handful of wine-makers succeed in creating very elegant Rieslings, which have a passing resemblance at great distance with the wines of Alsace and Germany. There are also several very good Late Harvest Rieslings. Drinking temperature is 8–10°C (46.4–50°F).

GEWÜRZTRAMINER

Although the Americans have great difficulty with the name this wine is certainly no joke. Most of the local Gewürztraminer is made as sweet wine with floral notes, suggestions of Muscat, a hint of spice, and sultry, but Gewürztraminer Dry is becoming increasingly popular.

Many Americans drink the sweet or slightly sweet 'off-dry' Gewürztraminer as an aperitif. The dry Gewürztraminer is excellent with chicken and Oriental dishes. Drinking temperature is 10–12°C/50–53.6°F (dry), 8–10°C/46.4–50°F (off-dry) and 6–8°C/42.8–46.4°F (sweet).

WHITE ZINFANDEL/BLUSH WINES/WHITE GRENACHE

Zinfandel and Grenache are famous blue grapes but there are also white wines made with them. The wine is of course not truly white but a light pink. These are quite recent creations which are mainly aimed at the younger market.

Most wines are not wholly dry and some of them are even slightly sweet. They have a nose in which vanilla ice cream with strawberries can be found in

the White Zin or red fruit in the White Grenache. Drinking temperature is 10–12°C (50–53.6°F).

MUSCAT

These are sultry, sweet wines that in addition to the recognisable Muscat grape nose have apricot, peach, and ripe pear in their bouquet. The wine is often served with goose liver in California but it is better suited to serve with a fruit dessert. Drinking temperature is 6–8°C (42.8–46.4°F).

CABERNET SAUVIGNON

The name is often unceremoniously shorted to 'Cab'. This classic is one of the better wines of California. It is dark coloured and very aromatic with grassy and vegetal hints here, plus suggestions of green tea and leaves.

The wine is quite full-bodied. The wine can be undrinkable when young through an over-exposure to new oak. After a few years it develops its full beauty with a nose in which cherry, berries, herbs, currant, cedarwood, tobacco, vanilla, mint, pepper, and chocolate can be discerned. It is very much a wine to serve with haute cuisine. Drinking temperature is 16–17°C (60.8–62.6°F).

MERLOT

Somewhat similar to a Cabernet Sauvignon but much softer and more rounded. The Merlot is approachable much sooner than the Cabernet Sauvignon. It is a real seducer with nose of black cherry, plum, toffee, chocolate, orange, mint, cedarwood, green tea, and violets. The structure is full-bodied and rich while the taste is velvet smooth. Drinking temperature is 14–16°C (57.2–60.8°F).

PINOT NOIR

The Pinot Noir is able to combine complexity and elegance like no other grape. It requires some courage to plant Pinot Noir in California but perhaps not in Los Carneros.

The desired results will not be achieved every year but when the weather permits, the results are overwhelming. Californian Pinot Noirs are quick seducers that are fresh and fruity (cherry) with a hint of herbs and mushrooms, but also a sensual nose containing coffee and cedarwood. The texture is full-bodied, elegant, complex, and velvet smooth. Drinking temperature is 14–16°C (57.2–60.8°F).

ZINFANDEL

This is the Californian grape. It probably originated from the Italian Primitivo and certainly not from the Hungarian Zirfandli.

Zinfandel remains recognisable for the suggestions of vanilla ice cream with strawberries or raspberries in its bouquet, whether made as white, rosé, or red wine. The wine is fairly full-bodied, rich and tannic,

with a peppery undertone. The whole of America loves its 'Zin' and Europe is also now starting to enjoy it too. Drinking temperature is 14–16°C (57.2–60.8°F).

PETITE SYRAH/SYRAH

These are two different grape varieties which both originate from the French Rhône. Both produce substantial and firm wines that are deeply coloured and very aromatic with hints of blueberry, raspberry, fruit jam, pepper, and herbs. Drinking temperature is 16–17°C (60.8–62.6°F).

GAMAY/GAMAY BEAUJOLAIS

These are very fruity wines that are very fresh and mellow with little acidity or tannin. They are a perfect introduction for a newcomer to wine drinking, with chicken or turkey for instance. Drinking temperature is 12–14°C (53.6–57.2°F).

Mexico

Mexico is probably the oldest wine-producing country of the New World.
Vines were introduced by the Spanish conquistadors under the command of the famous Hernando Cortez

Cask-aged Zinfandel.

Mexican Fumé Blanc of L.A. Cetto.

in the sixteenth century. The results were very disappointing though because of the tremendous heat and arid conditions. The Spanish searched for better places to plant the vines further north in California but the results here were also less than satisfactory. It was only in the eighteenth century that Franciscan monks improved the Spanish vineyards and extended those in the former greater California. After California was separated from Mexico, wine-growing in Baja California (the Mexican part of California) fell into total neglect. Several large American and European wine and drinks companies saw an opportunity in the later twentieth century to establish a wine industry in Mexico in the best locations.

Of these companies the firm of Domecq achieved short-term success with Mexican wine. Because of the very hot and dry conditions it is essential for wine-growing to find cooler places so sites were sought on the high plateaux. Hence some vineyards are sited at 1,000 to 1,500 metres (3,280–4,921 feet). Although there are others companies engaged in the industry, only three are well-known internationally. These are L.A. Cetto, Mission Santo Thomas, and Domecq to a lesser extent in terms of the wine than the name

L.A. Cetto and Domecq have vineyards in Baja California, about 80 km (50 miles) south of the bode with the United States, in the Guadaloupe Valley, and Mission Santo Thomas has them in the Santo Thomas Valley. There are also vineyards in the Baja California of the smaller scale but high quality wine producer of Monte Xanic. Monte Xanic offers a small range of wines, with a sultry and unforgettable Chardonnay and excellent Cabernet Sauvignon. Both wines are very expensive and difficult to get hold of. Domecq sold its best vineyards to L.A. Cetto and appears to be less interested in wine. Mission Santo Thomas has entered into a joint venture with the famous Californian company of Wente and is extremely busy. Their Sauvignon Blanc, Chenin Blanc, and Cabernet Sauvignon are absolute gems.

L.A. Cetto makes a wide range of different types of wine from very acceptable cheap ones for local consumption to excellent Cabernet Sauvignon, Nebbiolo, Zinfandel, and Petite Syrah that are mainly intended for export.

Mexican wines, as the taster will soon discover, are long on sensuality and short on finesse. The success of Mexican wine is due to the soft acidity and fulsome, rounded, and warm taste. In addition the wines from producers such as L.A. Cetto are really quite cheap for the quality they offer. Drinking temperature is 14–16°C (57.2–60.8°F) for the Cabernet Sauvignon and 16–17°C (60.8–62.6°F) for the other red wines.

Cabernet Sauvignon of L.A. Cetto.

Petite Syrah of L.A. Cetto.

South America

In the previous chapter we saw that the Spanish Conquistadors of Hernando Cortéz and the like introduced vines into Mexico in the sixteenth century. Wine-growing was introduced to other parts of South America soon afterwards. In addition to the Spaniards in Peru, Argentina, and Chile, great roles in the wine-growing history of South America have been played by the Portuguese in Brazil and the Basques in Uruguay. This chapter looks in turn at the wines of Brazil, Uruguay, Argentina, and Chile.

Brazil

Brazil is still a relatively unknown wine-growing area and Brazilian wines are seldom encountered, yet despite this Brazil does produce good wines.

Brazilian wine-growing dates back to the sixteenth century when Don Martin Afonso de Souza, envoy of the Portuguese king, Don Juan III, planted the first vines at Santos El Baballero Brás Cubas. These vines had been brought from the island of Madeira. The Portuguese also took vines to the north-east of Brazil and sold the wine to the Dutch who controlled that territory at the time.

The arrival of Portuguese wine-growers from the Azores in the eighteenth century briefly created a new impetus in the Brazilian wine industry. Because the European varieties were too susceptible to disease, the Brazilians chose North American grapes such as Alexander, Isabella, Catawba, Concord, and Delaware which are all varieties of *Vitis labrus*. The results of these experiments were not uniformly successful and the arrival of German, Italian, and French immigrants in Brazil brought both better knowledge and vines.

Brazil has three large wine-growing regions: Rio Grande del Sur, Nordeste, and Vale de São Francisco. Many of the grapes are still grown as dessert grapes that can be harvested three times each year because of the favourable climate. Slightly less than half of the grapes are destined for wine production.

Only about 20 percent of Brazil's vines are of the better *Vitis vinifera* varieties, while the others are hybrids and North American varieties, which are used for industrial wine. Acceptable to very good wines are made from *Vitis vinifera* varieties such as Merlot, Cabernet Franc, Cabernet Sauvignon, Gamay, Pinot Noir, Barbera, Riesling Italico, Chardonnay, Moscato, Semillon, Trebbiano, and Sauvignon Blanc. Brazil's potential as a wine-producing country can be shown by the many foreign companies investing in the industry like Moët et Chandon, Mumm, Remy Martin, Martini & Rosso, Domecq, and Seagram. Increasing numbers of Japanese companies are also entering the fray. It is clear that Brazil will soon become one of the major South American wine producers.

Wine quality is getting better year by year. The control of hygiene and grape quality has been increased and the present wines are remarkably pleasing. A new era is just beginning for Brazilian wine. For those who wish to try Brazilian wine for themselves the Vinicola Miolo of Vale dos Vinhedos at Porto Alegre can certainly be recommended. It is probably Brazil's best wine at the present time.

Uruguay

While Chile and Argentina have been known as wine producers for some time, Uruguay has been busy in recent years in a spectacular effort to overtake them. Uruguay is relatively small as a country in comparison with its two giant neighbours Brazil and Argentina. Despite this the country has a rich history of wine production.

Vines were introduced by the Conquistadors in the sixteenth century and wine-making was in the hands of the Monks for a considerable period of time. Uruguay wine production got a major boost when thousands of immigrants settled from France, Algeria, Germany, Italy, and Switzerland. These brought the noble grapevine *Vitis vinifera* with them. A leading role was played by the French Basque Pascal Harriague who introduced Tannat and Folle Noire to Uruguay in 1870. Tannat is well-known from South-West France, especially in Madiran where it makes superb wines for laying down from people like Alain Brumon. Meanwhile Tannat has become the flagship of the Uruguayan wine industry.

Other *Vitis vinifera* varieties such as Cabernet Sauvignon, Merlot, Malbec, and Gamay, Spanish varieties such as Bobal, and Garnacha and Italian vines like Barbera and Nebbiolo were planted in the late nineteenth and early twentieth centuries. None of these grapes though managed to achieve the popularity or quality of Tannat.

There are nine producing zones in Uruguay: Norte, Litoral Norte, Noreste, Literal Sur, Centro, Centro Oriental, Suroeste, Sur, and Sureste but most wine is produced in the south of the country around the capital Montevideo.

The climate is moderate with sufficient rain to make irrigation unnecessary. The difference between day and night time temperatures is considerable in the

Average Uruguay white wine.

Tannat RPF of Pisano.

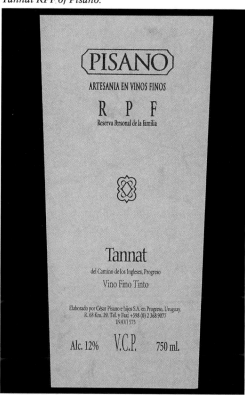

north of the country. The soil varies between loose clay in the south through loose and fertile sediments in the south-east, sand and gravel in the centre, firm clay in the north-east, and gravel in the north.

White wines are overwhelmingly in the majority in Uruguay and they are not of the best quality. The best of them come from Sauvignon Blanc, Chardonnay, Pinot Blanc, Riesling, Gewürtztraminer, and Viognier and are fresh, powerful, and very aromatic.

The reds from Cabernet Sauvignon, Cabernet Franc, Merlot, Nebbiolo, and Barbara are carefully made and concentrated with bouquets of ripe fruit.

Despite this Tannat is the more convincing wine. It is full-bodied and deep, very concentrated with firm but not harsh tannin and possesses heady aromas of ripe fruit and spices with a rich, powerful, and rounded masculine taste. It is certainly a wine that can be kept and is ideal with roasted and grilled meat. Drinking temperature is 16–18°C (60–64°F).

Bear in mind that good Uruguayan wine is not cheap and avoid doubtful cheap examples in supermarkets, seeking out instead better wines such as Tannat RPF of Bodega Pisano, Castel Pujol Tannat of Juan Carrau, Tannat Viejo of Bodega Stagnari, or Don Pascual Tannat Barrels.

Reasonable Tannat-Merlot.

First class Uruguay red wine.

Argentina

The Conquistadors also introduced vines into Argentina in the sixteenth century. The resulting wines were used by Spanish Jesuits for both religious and medicinal purposes.

The industry only acquired its present form in the nineteenth century as a result of a flood of European immigrants who brought better vines with them such as Cabernet, Pinot Noir, Malbec, Syrah, Barbera, and Sangiovese for red wines and Chenin, Riesling, and Torrontés for whites.

The first independent wine houses were established by German, Italian, Spanish, and French immigrants. Argentina's vineyards lie at the foot of the Andes, far removed from the pollution of industrial cities. The climate is continental, being very dry and very hot, verging on desert.

Irrigation with water from pure mountain streams has created the ideal conditions for wine-growing.

The French brought Syrah grapes

Wine areas

Wine-growing is possible along almost half the length of the Andes (between the 25th and 40th parallels). The vineyards arise like cooling oases in otherwise desert-like terrain.

It is possible to grow a wide range of varieties of grape here because of the big difference in day and night time temperatures. Argentina has five large wine areas. From north to south, these are:

– Salta/Cafayate that lies just below latitude 25 degrees south, along the banks of the Rio Sali, between the towns of these names. Wines such as Cafayate and those of the renowned Etchart Bodega come from here.

– La Rioja/Chilecito which lies just below 30 degrees south. This area is known for its Bodega La Riojana wines.

– Mendoza is undoubtedly the best-known wine area of Argentina. It lies above the latitude 35 degrees south, on the banks of the Rio Mendoza and Rio Tunuyan, and is known for numerous good bodegas such as Etchart, Nieto y Senetiner, Trapiche, Norton, and Flichman.

Cafayate Cabernet Sauvignon.

Malbec is Argentina's flagship.

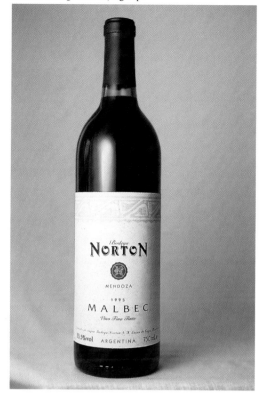

Norton's sublime Colleccion Privada.

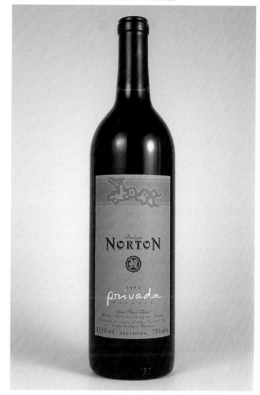

An area within Mendoza is regarded by insiders as the area with the greatest potential for the twenty-first century.

This is Lujan de Cuyo to the south-west of the town of Mendoza, which produces outstanding Malbec wines with its own denomination of Lujan de Cuyo. Given the significant levels of investment by the major wine producers and distillers it is apparent that something important in terms of quality is happening here.

– San Rafael, lies along a latitude of 35 degrees south, between the Rio Diamante and Rio Atuel. Only the wines of Bodega Goyenechea are known to some extent outside of Argentina.

– Rio Negro, the most southerly area, lies just north 40 degrees south on the banks of the Rio Negro. Wines from this area are hardly known outside Argentina.

Wines

Argentina has been climbing steadily up into the ranks of the top five wine producing countries and in terms of total production has challenged Spain's third position. It is only the past decade or so that Argentine wine has been discovered in Europe and much of their wine does certainly not deserve to be called 'quality wine'. But the quality winery of Trapiche Bodega (which is famous for its Fond de Cave Chardonnay and Cabernet Sauvignon) has

Flichman's Aberdeen Angus Centenario.

Nieto y Senetiner Chardonnay.

show the way to other top class Argentine wines. Now wines such as Torrontés and Cafayate Cabernet Sauvignon from the Etchart Bodega have become known along with a number of red wines from Norton such as Syrah, Cabernet Sauvignon, Barbera, and Malbec and Finca Flinchman's tasty Syrah and

Cabernet Sauvignon and their superb Aberdeen Angus Malbec and Cabernet Sauvignon.

Nieto y Senetiner is less well-known in Europe but is certainly one of the Argentine's best houses with the outstanding Syrah, Malbec, Cabernet Sauvignon, Merlot, Barbera, Sauvignon Blanc, and Torrontés. Tupungato Valley is also becoming known for its whites and Barbera reds.

SAUVIGNON BLANC

Argentina's Sauvignon Blanc (except the cheaper versions) have a pleasing aroma of citrus fruits, peach, apricot, kiwi, and grapefruit with slight vegetative undertones. It is fresh and quite dry, making it a perfect aperitif served at 9–10°C (48–50°F).

TORRONTÉS

Torrontés is Argentina's white wine speciality. The better ones are greenish-yellow with hints of gold. The bouquet is never truly exuberant, tending towards subtle floral aromas and a hint of exotic fruit. The taste is fresh but never sharply so and is well

Torrontés is the white grape of Argentina.

Trapiche Chardonnay.

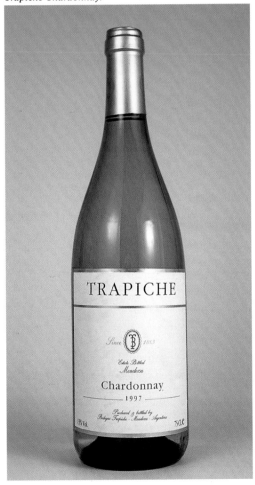

Nieto y Senetiner Barbera.

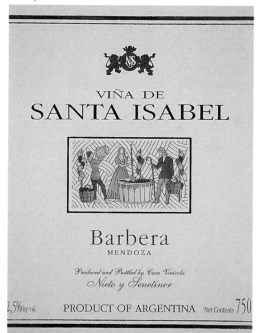

Nieto y Senetiner Syrah.

balanced and harmonious. Drink at 8–10°C (46–50°F).

CHARDONNAY

Argentine Chardonnay is often pale golden with a green tinge.

The bouquet is seductive and reminiscent of ripe apples and hot creamery butter with a hint of wood and vanilla.

The texture is generally full and rounded, complex and broad. Drinking temperature is 10–12°C (50–53°F).

The finest Argentine Chardonnays such as Trapiche Fond de Cave retain their elegance despite a luxuriant and heady creaminess. The bouquet is of ripe apple, honey, butter, and spices such as cinnamon. Drinking temperature is 12–14°C (53.6–57.2°F).

BARBERA

This is a deeply coloured wine with wonderful aromas of young fruit such as cherries and raspberries. The taste if velvet smooth, harmonious, and elegant. This wine seduces one easily with its combination of fresh acidity and relative high alcohol content. Drinking temperature is 13–14°C (55.4–57.2°F).

MERLOT

This wine is particularly fruity, particularly suggesting plum and bilberry with a hint of blackberry. It harmonious taste a mild tannin make this a pleasant charmer. Drinking temperature is 14–15°C (57.2–59°F).

SYRAH

This is a very dark-coloured wine with intense aromatic power (spices, pepper, vanilla, toast, and red fruits). It is full-bodied, possesses great strength but is not strongly tannic to the tongue with a rounded and mild aftertaste. Drinking temperature is 16–17°C (60.8–62.6°F).

CABERNET SAUVIGNON

This a classic wine produced from the wonderful

Norton Cabernet Sauvignon.

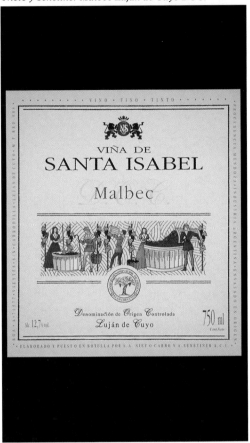

Bordeaux grape but it possesses less tannin than its French counterparts. The bouquet is reminiscent of red and blue woodland fruits with hints of wood and nuts. The taste is soft, full, and rounded with a long and pleasing aftertaste. Drinking temperature is 16°C (60.8°F).

The best Cabernet Sauvignon wines are aged in wood for a long period as in France. These top wines such as Fond de Cave Cabernet Sauvignon of Trapiche possess greater aromatic power than their younger counterparts. They have a bouquet of cedarwood, tobacco, vanilla, chocolate, and lots of ripe fruit (such as blackcurrant). Drinking temperature is 16–17°C (60.8–62.6°F).

MALBEC

Malbec and Torrontés form the flagship of Argentine wine. These grapes from south-western France thrive here, especially in Lujan de Cuyo. The colour is dark red tinged with purple and the bouquet is reminiscent of blackcurrants, raspberries, cherries, and plums.

The structure and tannin are both strong but mellow with age to form a superb full-bodied and rounded wine of great complexity. Drinking temperature is 16–17°C (60.8–62.6°F).

MALBEC LUJAN DE CUYO DENOMINACION DE ORIGEN CONTROLADA

This is the apotheosis of Argentine wines. Only the very best wines are permitted to carry this fiercely sought denomination of origin and they must contain at least 80 percent Malbec, all of which must come from the Luca de Cuyo area. The finest of these is probably the Viña de Santa Isabel Malbec Lujan de Cuyo DOC from the Casa Vinícola Nieto y Senetiner. It possesses an intense ruby red colouring with purple tinges and has a very fresh and fruity bouquet of red fruit, honey, and vanilla with suggestions of chocolate and sweet wood. It is an extremely complex wine that is both refined and powerful, full-bodied and rounded, with great potential for keeping.

If this wine is a foretaste of what can be expected from Lujan de Cayo in this new century then let there be more. Drinking temperature is 17–18°C (62.6–64.4°F).

Chile

Chile is a very elongated but relatively narrow country of 5,000 km long and 90 to 400 km wide (3125 miles long and 56 to 250 miles wide), nestling at the foot of the Andes mountains. Grapes are grown here over some 1400 km (875 miles) between the 27th and 39th parallels.

An assortment of different soil types and micro-climates ensure quite a degree of diversity in the types of wine.

Chile's climate is similar to the Mediterranean with damp winters and spring and a dry summer. Chile is blessed with perfect conditions for quality wines with a fairly marked difference between day and night time temperatures, lots of hours of sunshine, and fairly high humidity from the nearby ocean.

Chilean wine was in a state of almost medieval lethargy until some years ago, following a surge in quality in the nineteenth century as a result of the arrival of European immigrants.

Wine-growing was started by the Conquistadors. The same out-dated methods to make and keep wine had been used for centuries and these were far from hygienic. This changed radically in the late 1970s when the Spanish firm of Torres were the first to

establish themselves in Chile. The vineyards were cleaned out and new vines planted while the wine-making equipment was either extensively renovated or totally replaced by ultra modern equipment. The old and often dirty wine vats were replaced with small barriques of new wood. Despite this it was surprisingly long before modern Chilean wines reached Europe.

Names such as Villard, Santa Rita, Torres, Errazuriz, and Santa Carolina were the first to do so. Exports only got going in a big way in the 1990s. Big companies like Torres and Concha y Toro (Spain), Lafite Rothschild, Marnier Lapostelle, Pernod Ricard, Larose Trintaudon, Bruno Prats of Cos d'Estournel, and Mouton Rothschild (France) and Mondavi of California are still investing millions of dollars in the Chilean wine industry.

Wine-growing areas

Chile has four large wine regions of which Aconcagua, the Valle Central, and the Region Sur o Meridional are the best. These four are split into sub regions and where necessary also into zones. The most productive areas are Maule, Curicó, Rapel, and Maipo, all located within the Valle Central between Santiago and Cauquenes.

Chile makes excellent wine.

Los Vascos of Lafite Rothschild.

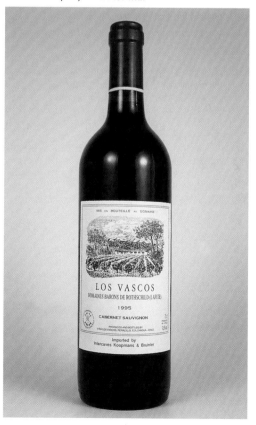

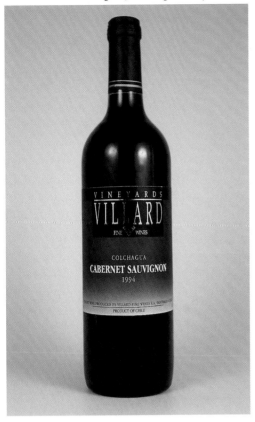

Villard Cabernet Sauvignon, Aconcagua valley.

Erazuriz Chardonnay, Casablanca valley.

Aconcagua

The Aconcagua region is the furthest north Chilean wine-growing area and it comprises two sub regions of the Valle del Aconcagua and the Valle de Casablanca.

The Aconcagua valley is fairly flat and extends from the Andes to the sea. This long valley is 4 kilometres (2¹/₂ miles) across at its widest point and is enclosed by mountains of 1,500–1,800 metres (4,921–5,905 feet) high. The climate is of the Mediterranean type: moderately hot.

The Casablanca valley is smaller but more densely planted than the Aconcagua valley. It lies closer to the sea and therefore benefits from the cooling and moist sea breezes which are always apparent here. There are also not mountains but undulating hills of no more than 400 metres (1,300 feet).

Valle Central

Running from north to south you first encounter the Maipo valley then the Rappel valley, followed by the Curicó valley, and then the Maule valley.

The Maipo valley, called Maipo for short, runs on either side of the river of the same name. This valley stretches from the foot of the Andes to the sea and varies in height from 1,000 metres (3,280 feet) in the east to 500 metres (1,640 feet) in the west. This height difference and oceanic influence from the west lead to a big difference in planting from east to west.

The Valle de Rapel or just Rapel is much larger than the Maipo valley and is watered by the rivers Cachapoal and Tinguirrica, which run into the Rapel river. The average height is quite low, less than 500 metres (1,640 feet) but some vineyards are sited at up to 1,000 metres (3,280 feet) at the foot of the mountains. It is more than twice as humid here as in the Maipo valley because of the moist sea winds which easily enter the valley.

The Valle de Curicó or just Curicó is much smaller than the Rapel valley but is more efficiently and densely planted so that the vineyards useful area is slightly greater than that of the Rapel. This valley does not get its name from the river of the same name but from the town of Curicó. The vineyards are situated mainly in the central plain but a few are located on the steeper ground at the foot of the mountains. The climate here is quite moist as a result of the nearby ocean.

The Valle del Maul or Maule is the most southerly valley of this central part of the Chilean wine industry. It is an enormous area but not necessarily efficiently planted everywhere. Irrigation comes from the Maule and its tributaries. The quiet elongated

Rapel valley Chardonnay.

Cabernet Sauvignon is most widely planted.

valley is surround by the Andes in the east and the hills behind the coast to the west. Despite this it is a fairly moist area, particularly in winter.

Other wine areas

A further two wine areas are situated in the extreme north and south of Chile. Coquimbo region in the north has sub zones of the Elqui, Limari, and Choapa valleys and in the south there are the Iata and Bio valleys. These areas produce a great deal of base wine for the famous Pisco wine distillery. Changes have been taking place here in recent years such as the introduction of better grapes.

The wines

Chile produces a great deal of Cabernet Sauvignon (about 47 percent of the total production) followed by Sauvignon Blanc, Chardonnay, and Merlot. Small amounts of Riesling, Pinot Noir, Chenin Blanc, Semillon, and Gewürtztraminer are also produced. Chardonnay was originally not so widely planted but has seen explosive growth, with a seventeen fold increase between 1985 and 1996.

SAUVIGNON BLANC
This classic Bordeaux grape is also known as Fumé

Blanc here. Chilean Sauvignon Blanc varies in intensity and quality from area to area and also from maker to maker. The colour of ordinary Sauvignon Blanc is mainly pale yellow tinged with green. The bouquet is very seductive with fresh aromas of tropical fruit and freshly mowed grass. Some wines have a hint of citrus fruits, gooseberry (Santa Carolina), or flowers (Santa Digna, Torres). The taste is always fresh without being firm as can be the case in Bordeaux. Drinking temperature is 8–10°C (46.4–50°F).

SAUVIGNON BLANC RESERVA ESPECIAL
This wine is cask aged in wood and possesses a characteristic bouquet of wood and vanilla without losing its fruitiness. Drinking temperature is 10°C (50°F).

SAUVIGNON BLANC LATE HARVEST
This is a rare wine from Concha y Toro that has heady aromas of white fruits (such as peach and apricot), melon and honey. It is a luxuriant and sweet yet fresh white wine with a broad taste and long aftertaste. Drinking temperature is 8–10°C (46.4–50°F).

CHARDONNAY
The taste of Chilean Chardonnay is largely a matter

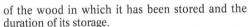

of the wood in which it has been stored and the duration of its storage.

The humidity of its place of origin also plays a role. Chardonnay here is generally pale straw yellow with a green tinge. Most wines have a fresh and fruity bouquet with aromas of apple, citrus fruits such as grapefruit, and pineapple and passion fruit. Those Chardonnays made from riper grapes exude heady aromas more distinctly of honey, butter, mango, cinnamon, apricot, peach, and occasional note of tropical flowers. Those cask aged in good quality wood also acquire a fresh bouquet of oak, hazelnut, toast, and vanilla. These wines are distinguished as in Spain by the additions of the names Reserva and Gran Reserva.

All Chardonnays are fresh and mild, creamy, dry but not harsh, rounded, and full in taste. The taste (and price) varies from simplicity to good, broad, complex, and superb. Drinking temperature is 10–12°C (50–53.6°F) for young wines and 12–14°C (53.6–57.2°F) for Reserva and Gran Reserva.

SEMILLON

The ordinary wine of this noble Bordeaux grape here is fresh and intensely aromatic (citrus fruits including grapefruit with occasional hint of vanilla). This dry wine is balanced, rich, full-bodied and strongly alcoholic (13–14%). Its alcoholic strength makes it difficult to combine with food. Drinking temperature is 10–12°C (50–53.6°F).

SEMILLON LATE HARVEST

The colour tends to golden yellow and has a bouquet reminiscent of honey and overripe fruits (peach and apricot). The taste is velvet smooth, luxuriant, sweet, and rich with high alcohol and a prolonged aftertaste.

Drinking temperature is 8–9°C (46.4–48.2°F).

RIESLING

This wine is green-yellow, fresh, elegant rather than complex with distinctive aromas of green spices with a hint of honey. The fruitiness comes to the surface in the taste. Drinking temperature is 10–12°C (50–53.6°F).

GEWÜRTZTRAMINER

Most Chilean Gewürtztraminers are meant to be drunk as young and fruity.

The colour tends to straw yellow and the bouquet has a suggestion of lychee, apricot, and kiwi with a slight spicy undertone.

There are both dry and slightly sweet versions. These wines are tasty and fruity thirst quenchers but can also be served at table. Drinking temperature is 10–12°C (50–53.6°F).

Erazuriz Cabernet Sauvignon.

Caliterra Chardonnay, Mondavi.

Sparkling wines

Chile produces a number of sparkling wines varying from moderate to excellent.

Choose one of the better ones such as Viña Miguel Torres Brut Nature which has a fresh spring-like aroma of meadow flowers combined with luxuriant white tropical fruits and a fresh but delicate taste of Chardonnay with the full, rich, and rounded taste of Pinot Noir. Drinking temperature is 6–8°C (42.8–46.4°F).

CABERNET SAUVIGNON

This noble Bordeaux grape also produces classic, elegant, and complex wines in Chile.

The ordinary Cabernet Sauvignon is fresh and fruity but it is worth while buying the better wines such as Reserva and Gran Reserva. These offer much richer bouquets and greater complexity for very little extra. The colour is dark ruby red with the occasional tinge of brown.

The aroma is reminiscent of plum, blackcurrant, strawberry, mint, and pepper with undertones of vanilla, chocolate, nuts, cedarwood, tobacco, and toast.

When young this wine is very tannic but the tannin is more muted after two to three years. Drinking temperature is 16–17°C (60.8–62.6°F).

MERLOT

This is another classic Bordeaux grape that thrives here. The wine is dark ruby, cherry, or granite red with some purple tinges here and there. Plum, blackcurrant, blueberry, black cherry, morello cherry, and strawberries can be detected in the bouquet with undertones of pepper, mint, green herbs, wood, and vanilla.

The tannin is mainly mellow and the taste full and rounded. These Chilean Merlots readily charm and are suited for drinking with lighter meat dishes. Drinking temperature is 14–16°C (57.2–60.8°F).

PINOT NOIR

This fairly rare wine is certainly worth trying to find. The colour is a fairly pale ruby red with purple tinges. The bouquet is fresh and fruity (including rose hip) and the taste is generous, approachable, and specially pleasing. Hints of herbs and spices can be detected in the prolonged aftertaste. Drinking temperature is 14–16°C (57.2–60.8°F).

Australia and New Zealand

Although both countries have made wine for many years the real breakthrough for Australia and New Zealand has really only occurred within the past twenty or so years. Australian wines in the meantime have become a by-word throughout the world while those from New Zealand are unfortunately still reserved for connoisseurs but that will soon change.

Australia

No New World wine-producing country has had such an influence on the entire philosophy of wine as Australia. The wine industry was also established here by European immigrants. Australia set about a radical change in wine-making techniques so that good wines could be made for a few Australian dollars.

The European industry tried for years to protect themselves against these Australian wines but the public proved en masse to prefer the tasty Australian wines that were ready to drink, amenable, comforting, rounded, full-bodied, and warm. What is more they were much cheaper. It seems as though after years of battle Australia has not only won market for itself but also much more. Countless 'flying wine-makers' from Australia now fly from one European company to another to teach them how to achieve the same kind of results.

More and more Australians are also establishing themselves in the South of France in order to make Franco-Australian wines. No other New World country has similar achievements.

History

Australia's wine history is certainly not as old as the land itself. Southern Australia was first discovered by the Dutchman Abel Tasman and then eastern Australia was discovered much later by the Briton James Cook. The Aboriginal people certainly drank no wine.

The first vines arrived in the late eighteenth century, intended for a botanical garden. The first official wine-growers arrived in the early nineteenth century. The Scot James Busby, with some experience of winegrowing and making acquired in France, successfully planted the first vineyards in the Hunter Valley. Vines were soon growing elsewhere in Australia. Apart from Hunter Valley on the east coast, they were planted in the south, around Adelaide, Southern Vale, and Barossa.

The initial wines tasted somewhat like the present day Rhône wines through the excess of sun and too little water, although they were sold somewhat cheekily in London as 'Australian Burgundy' or even 'Burgundy'.

The wine industry was given a sudden and unexpected impulse after World War I when thousands of soldiers were suddenly discharged with no work for them. The government encouraged soldiers to make a new life for themselves in growing and making wine. This proved to be a success, indeed perhaps too successful given the hefty over production of wine that arose. The growers directed their efforts increasingly towards the production of port and sherry type fortified wines. This gave the growers two ways of getting rid of their surplus. The demand for fortified wines was huge and wine spirit was needed in order to make them.

Up to the 1960s most Australians preferred to drink beer or gin to wine. The Australian wines were mainly intended for the local Greek and Italian immigrants and for export. When the Australian government took measures to reduce drinking and driving, the pattern of alcohol consumption began to change.

Consumption of wine gradually increased in Australia, both at home and in restaurants, bars, and such places. Better wines started to be drunk but the bulk wine market remained very active. Wine in a can, bag, or box is still widespread here. With a consumption of 19 litres of wine per capita per annum the population of Australia still lags well behind that of most European countries, but a new style of life is clearly to be seen.

The drinking habits of the world consumers changed in the 1970s. Far less sweet wine was drunk, with dry wines becoming far more popular. Australian producers reacted well by seeking out cooler places to grow their grapes such as the Eden Valley and Coonawarra which are more suitable for grapes like Sauvignon Blanc, Colombard, Riesling, Chenin Blanc, and Chardonnay.

A similar change also occurred with red wine. Because Australian wines have now been discovered throughout the world, the Australian wine industry has seen explosive growth which continues into the new millennium. The Australian government has developed far-reaching plans to make Australia, one of the world's largest producing nations, after Italy, France, and Spain.

Wine-growing conditions

Australian wine-growing is quite typical of the New World scene with huge vineyards spread across enormous territories between South Australia (Barossa and Coonawarra), Victoria (Yarra), and New South Wales (Hunter), plus hi-tech equipment and methodology and staggering yields. Despite all this Australia is not anywhere near the output of wine-producing countries like Italy, France, and Spain. A large proportion of the potential harvest is destroyed by natural hazards such as hail, rain, extreme heat, fire, kangaroos, foxes, crows, and grey-backed silvereyes.

Considerable government support has been invested developing and extending the local wine industry. Up to the 1970s the most popular wines were mainly sweet Rieslings.

The plantings of Riesling have been decimated since the arrival of Chardonnay vines, because the wines from these are more successful in the export market. Chardonnay is now the most widely planted grape variety but Shiraz is also gaining ground too. Besides these there are also a number of other varieties which are new to Australia that are gaining popularity. Hence in addition to new plantings of Shiraz, Cabernet Sauvignon, Cabernet Franc, Malbec, Merlot, Pinot Noir, and Ruby Cabernet (Cabernet and Cinsaut), increasing numbers of Sangiovese and

Two top Australian wines.

Barbera vines are also being planted. The white grape that surprises everyone and is gaining popularity at the expense of Chardonnay, Semillon, Riesling, Sauvignon Blanc, Chenin Blanc, Colombard, Muscadelle, and Traminer is the Verdelho.

Australian wine-makers are often accused of putting more emphasis on the variety of grape than on the aspects related to terroir.

The criticism is not entirely justified because each wine is a combination of factors: the grape variety, soil, climate, and of course the underground water. Australian winemakers can guarantee their customers constant quality by blending together wines from different areas. This can compensate year in year out for the vagaries of the Australian climate. The result is a superb wine with a distinctive character. Australian wines are almost always produced from a number of vineyards. It is possible for 'single vineyard' wines to be made in Australia, but given the enormous size of many of them, this would lack credibility while also adding unnecessary costs and uncertainty. This would also be contrary to the 'flavour for dollar' policy that has made Australian wines world famous. A 'single vineyard' wine would vary in quality from year to year and this is not what today's consumers want.

It is often essential in Australia to irrigate the vines. This is strictly forbidden in most European countries, even during the most extreme periods of dry weather. New World wine countries though regard irrigation as a perfectly natural occurrence. Their systems are so well refined that the vines can be drip fed at whatever height is required. Spray equipment is installed on both sides of the vines but it is also possible to spray from just one side. This gives the vine a contrasting signal so that the leaves absorb water rather than the grapes in order to maintain a good balance between sun and moisture.

The technique by which the skins are left in contact to extract the maximum possible aromatic and flavour substances in the juice (macération pelliculaire), is only used in poor years in Australia. The grapes normally have more than adequate aromatic and flavour substances in them as a result of the good sun/moisture balance.

The malolactic fermentation with lactic acids that is used in Europe is only partially used here. Australian wines do not by nature have high levels of acidity, so that it makes no sense, nor is it desirable for a complete malolactic fermentation to take place. The sun also has a beneficial effect on the growth of the vines. Australian winemakers rarely need to add fertilizer to the soil. Those in favour of organic wine-making do not need to ring any alarm bells here as they do in Europe.

Australian wine-makers ideas about cask maturing in wood are also different. In order to provide plenty of flavour at a price they have used wood chips to give cheaper wines a characteristic 'oaked' taste. This is a thing of the past though for today the best Australian companies use huge tanks in which a sort of giant wheel constantly agitates the young wine. This gives the wine regular contact with large oak planks that can be pushed into the tank through special apertures. The length of time that the wine spends in these tanks is determined by the desired strength of the taste of oak required. The eventual result has much greater finesse than the use of oak chips. High-technology therefore can also have its good sides. In this way the top wines are still matured in oak casks, while cheaper ones acquire their oak taste more quickly and efficiently. This system is also more environmentally friendly and considerably reduces the number of oak trees that need to be felled.

Wine regions

Vines are grown in almost every part of Australia but wines are only produced in the cooler southern parts. Australia can be roughly split into seven large regions.
From west to east these are Western Australia, Northern Territory, South Australia, Queensland, New South Wales, Victoria, and the island of Tasmania. The only ones of much importance to us are Western Australia (Margaret River), South Australia (Barossa Valley, Padthaway, and Coonawarra), Victoria (Yarra Valley), and New

Wines from the 'Terra Rossa' soil.

South Wales (Hunter Valley). Each of these regions has its own climate and soil conditions.

Western Australia

The only good wine area of Western Australia lies far to the south of Perth, just inland from the south-western coastal strip.

Margaret River

Margaret river is an extremely interesting area that is less well-known outside Australia, but this is likely to change. The climate is strongly influenced by the ocean.
The soil is mainly a mixture of gravel and gravel-bearing loam and sand on underlying granite. Margaret River is mainly known for its good Cabernet Sauvignon, but other grapes do well here too.

South Australia

South Australia is known for the following wine areas.

Clare Valley

This is one of Australia's oldest wine-producing areas which has existed since the second half of the nineteenth century. High quality wines, and in particular very aromatic reds and superb floral Rieslings come from the Clare Valley. The climate is predominantly a moderate continental one with big differences between day and night temperatures, especially in summer. There is enough rainfall, mainly in the spring, to make irrigation unnecessary. The soil is mainly open calciferous red or brown clay.

Adelaide Hills

The vineyards in this area are sited at heights of 400–500 metres (1,312–1,640 feet) and are becoming better known thanks to the production of very acceptable sparkling and quality wines. The altitude of the vineyards somewhat mitigates the heat and leads to increased rainfall. Since most of the rain falls in winter though irrigation is still necessary. The soil around Adelaide consists of a fairly infertile mixture of loam and sand.

McLaren Vale

McLaren Vale is one of Australia's best wine-producing areas and certainly the best in terms of the varied grapes and types of wine. The area is best known for the powerful dark and very aromatic reds and mighty whites. Despite the cooling effect of the ocean too little rain falls here and irrigation is necessary. McLaren Vale has many different soil types which explains the diversity of the wine. It is mainly sand and loam on underlying clay and chalk, or sand, or red or black weathered loam.

Barossa Valley

The Barossa Valley is probably the best-known wine area of Australia, both because of its wines and its rich history. The valley was the first territory of the early German settlers who started the wine industry here. German is still spoken here. The climate is hot, sunny, and with little moisture. Despite this there is little irrigation. The vines are trained low, almost like creepers, and the yield is intentionally kept low. This produces excellent wine which is very concentrated, full of colour and structure. The soil chiefly consists of brown sandy soil or clay to dark sand.

Padthaway

This is a lesser known wine region on fairly level terrain that largely consists of loam or terra rossa with good underlying drainage. The shortage of rainfall here makes irrigation during summer necessary. The area mainly produces commercial wine but is switching over to quality wines such as those of Hardy.

Coonawarra

This is an extremely well-known area within South Australia where wine-growing started way back in the late nineteenth century. The finest Australian Cabernet Sauvignons originate from here these days. The area is situated immediately behind the coastal strip and is favourably influenced by the ocean. The climate here is a moderate maritime one with fairly cool summers (by Australian standards). The loose red terra rossa soil has become a by-word throughout the world. If there is anywhere in Australia where it is possible to speak of the character of the terroir then it is Coonawarra.

South Australia wines.

Red wine from Victoria.

Victoria

Apart from the Yarra Valley, the wine areas in the state of Victoria are little known outside Australia. It consists of three areas.

Great Western

This area is likely to become better known for its sparkling wines, which are Australia's first. Great Western resembles an Australian desert-like version of Tuscany, with many gently undulating hills. The climate is dry but fairly cool by Australian standards. The difference between day and night temperatures can be quite high in summer. There is low rainfall and irrigation is therefore usually necessary. The soil consists principally of layers of poor, highly acidic soil with salty undertones which does not simplify the making of the wines from here.

Drumborg

This is a fairly unknown area within the hinterland of Portland. The three well-known grapes of Pinot Noir, Chardonnay, and Pinot Meunier provide the basis for sparkling wines. The area is ideally suited for making sparkling wines because it gets relatively less hours of sun than the rest of southern Australia.

Yarra Valley

The Yarra Valley, which is better known than the other two areas of Victoria, is situated on the outskirts of Melbourne. The soil is a mixture of loam, clay, and sand that is extremely acidic. Some of the better land also has gravel and broken rock. Here too there is insufficient rainfall, making irrigation essential. The climate though is fairly cool, so that the Yarra Valley is able to produce some truly elegant wines.

New South Wales

New South Wales is a large wine-growing area of which the only well-known part is the Hunter Valley. The area lies to the south of Canberra and stretches to the north of Sydney and Newcastle.

Tumbarumba

Tumbarumba is best known for its sparkling wines. The area is a difficult one for wine-growing with severe winters, excessive rainfall, and cool summers. Despite this the locals manage to produce reasonable to good whites and reds from Sauvignon Blanc, Chardonnay, and Pinot Noir on pretty acid soil.

Griffith/Riverina

This area lies further inland than the previous one.

The hot and humid climate in summer makes it ideal here to produce late harvest and noble rot wines, that are mainly made from Semillon. The soil is level layers of sand and loam, interspersed with some clay.

Young

The Young area lies inland and to the north west of Canberra. The vineyards are sited fairly high on hills. Although there is fairly substantial rainfall here during the otherwise moderately hot summer, irrigation remains necessary. Despite this the Young area produces reasonable to good wines.

Cowra

Cowra is situated in the hinterland of Sydney. This is a fairly recent newcomer that is barely more than 25 years old. The vineyards are sited on slopes along the local river. The soil is a mixture of clay, loam, and sand that is fairly highly acidic. The climate tends towards continental with hot dry summers. Despite this there is fairly considerable rainfall during the growing period so that irrigation is not always required. Cowra's wines are mainly whites and they are characterised by plenty of taste for little money.

Lower Hunter Valley

This is one of Australia's oldest wine-growing areas, and it is mainly known for its superb Semillon and Syrah. The climate is hot but there is sufficient moisture. The soil on the slopes where the vineyards are situated is mainly sand, which is ideal for white wines.

Upper Hunter Valley

This too is a white wine area, mainly producing Chardonnay and Semillon. It is somewhat hotter and drier here than in the Lower Hunter Valley. The soil chiefly consists of a mixture of salty and acidic loam and sand. The Upper Hunter Valley is perhaps the most picturesque wine area in Australia.

Wines

Australia produces and sells many different types of wine. Those that come from one area are characterised by the combination of terroir and grape variety. The blends on the other hand are derived from more than one areas or region and their style owes much more to the particular wine-maker. The type of oak (French, American, or German) used for the casks is also very important. Finally, the price of the wine also has a great bearing on the eventual complexity of the wine but in general every bottle of Australian wine offers value for money or even better.

The following descriptions are intended to stimulate you to do your own research.

SPARKLING WINES

In view of the remarkably low price it is best to choose a true traditional method sparkler that has undergone a second fermentation in the bottle. The white Brut sparkling wines are usually fresh and fruity with sometimes vegetal undertones. Drinking temperature is 8°C (46.4°F). The Rosé Brut sparkling wines are generally somewhat less dry than the whites. The nose is very fruity with a slight hint of acid drops, strawberry, cherry, and raspberry. Drinking temperature is 6–8°C (42.8–46.4°F).

CHARDONNAY

This is the success of the Australian wine industry in the past twenty years. The simple, young, Chardonnay that is not cask aged is a nice wine that can be very pleasant but the best ones are cask aged. The wine is fully ripened with an intense colour, very complex structure, and wonderful nose containing exotic and citrus fruit with earthy undertones and suggestions of toast and nuts. Drinking temperature is 10–12°C/50–53.6°F (unoaked) or 12–14°C/53.6–57.2°F (barrel select).

SEMILLON

As strange as it may seem this typical Bordeaux grape used in e.g. Sauternes, produces a surprising wine in Australia that closely resembles a white Burgundy. This is why it is often blended with Chardonnay. Semillon is a somewhat strange term in Australia though for some areas call it Chenin Blanc, Crouchen, or even Riesling, such as in the Hunter Valley. The true Australian Semillon though is superb. The bouquet is reminiscent of ripe and sweet fruit with suggestions of citrus fruit and flowers. Drinking temperature is 10–12°C (50–53.6°F).

SEMILLON/CHARDONNAY

This is a popular blend in Australia. This aromatic wine smells of fresh citrus fruit, peach, apricot, and tropical fruit. The Chardonnay imparts a buttery character and the complexity while Semillon and oak provide smoothness and the rounded taste. A little Colombard is also often added to this blend to make the wine slightly fresher. Drinking temperature is 10–12°C (50–53.6°F).

SAUVIGNON BLANC

Australian Sauvignon Blanc resembles a good Sancerre rather than a white Bordeaux. Both these French areas grow Sauvignon as their basic variety. The wines are very aromatic with characteristic vegetal undertones such as freshly sliced green peppers (paprika).
The taste is fresh and lively and less taut than that of a white Bordeaux. Drinking temperature is 8–10°C (46.4–50°F).

CHENIN BLANC

This variety of grape originates from the Loire Valley

in France. Here in Australia it produces an entirely different wine than in Vouvray or Montlouis. These are sultry, full-bodied, rich wines, with a good balance between sweet and sour. Drinking temperature is 10–12°C (50–53.6°F).

RHINE RIESLING
This is the true Riesling grape, originating from Germany (see remark at Semillon). Various types of wine are made with Riesling, which can be dry, off-dry (slightly sweet), or sweet, either affected by botrytis or not. The latter type of wine is given the name 'Noble', which refers to the noble rot. Riesling here produces fresh wines with a nose reminiscent of lemons.
Drinking temperature is 8–10°C/46.4–50°F (young), 10–12°C/50–53.6°F (aged) and 6–10°C/42.8–50°F according to taste for the Noble Riesling.

GEWÜRZTRAMINER
This is a very popular grape and wine with the Australians, although they have great problems with the name. Australian Gewürztraminers are interesting, exotic wines with fruity and spicy aromas, a full and prolonged taste and long finish. Drinking temperature is 10–12°C (50–53.6°F).

RIESLING/GEWÜRZTRAMINER
This is an interesting blend which combines the freshness and citrus fruit nose of Riesling with the roundness and fresh spiciness of the Gewürztraminer.
Most wines are off-dry or even medium-dry. Drinking temperature is 8–10°C (46.4–50°F).

VERDELHO
This is a very surprising grape that originates in Portugal which here produces good fresh wines with sensual and powerful aromas of tropical fruit. Drinking temperature is 10–12°C (50–53.6°F).

ORANGE MUSCAT
This is the local and attractive name for the Muscat of Alexandria, widely known from the area around the Mediterranean. This grape produces extremely aromatic and tasty late harvest dessert wines here.

FLORA
This grape is used to produce late harvest dessert wines with characteristic aromas of ripe fruit and a full and powerful taste. Flora is a hybrid resulting from crossing Gewürztraminer and Semillon. Orange Muscat and Flora are separately vinified by the famous Brown Brothers winery as a Late Harvest wine and then blended. This results in a marvellously rich and complex wine with much power. Drinking temperature is 6–8°C (42.8–46.4°F).

GRENACHE/SHIRAZ
Rosé wines are not at all common in Australia. This blend usually results in very fruity wines with a bouquet of fresh strawberry. Drinking temperature is 10–12°C (50–53.6°F).

CABERNET SAUVIGNON
Australia too makes wines that are wholly Cabernet Sauvignon. Most wines though are blends of Cabernet Sauvignon and Shiraz, or Cabernet Sauvignon, Merlot, and Shiraz. The pure Cabernet Sauvignon wines are full-bodied, rich, powerful, and complex. These wines need to be laid down for at least five years to mellow because they are remarkably full of tannin. These are outstanding wines with a nose of plum, blackcurrant, blueberry, and the occasional hints of chocolate, vanilla, tobacco, or cedarwood. Drinking temperature is 16–17°C (60.8–62.6°F).

CABERNET FRANC
Cabernet Franc grapes are mainly grown in northeast Victoria and blended with grapes such as Merlot. This rather rare red wine is unfortunately somewhat underestimated in Australia. Drinking temperature is 14–16°C (57.2–60.8°F).

MERLOT/CABERNET FRANC
Merlot is also little used on its own and mainly vinified or blended with the Cabernets or even with

Chardonnay-Semillon-Colombard.

Late harvest Muscat.

Late harvest Muscat Orange & Flora.

Cabernet and Chardonnay: two great successes.

Shiraz . The combination of 65% Merlot and 35% Cabernet Franc that is then cask aged for twelve months is quite common in Australia. This produces a fruity wine with fresh acidity and mellow taste. Drinking temperature is 14–16°C (57.2–60.8°F).

PINOT NOIR

This Burgundian grape will be encountered here less widely than in the Bordeaux or Rhône types. Despite this, Australian Pinot Noir is proof of the skill of the successful Australian wine-makers. Anybody can make wine from the idiosyncratic Pinot Noir but to make good wine requires considerable know-how and plenty of passion. Various styles of Pinot Noir are to be found in Australia, from light, fruity and generous, to full-bodied, sultry, with animal undertones and sometimes a little on the heavy side. The best of them are somewhere in between these two extremes and simultaneously elegant and full-bodied with a seductive nose containing plum and cherry with a rich, almost caressing taste. Drinking temperature is 14–16°C (57.2–60.8°F).

SHIRAZ

The Australians use the original name for this grape and not its bastardisation into French as Syrah. The Shiraz grape originally came from the Shiraz valley in Iran and was brought to Europe by the Crusaders. Australian Shiraz is a sensual tour-de-force with plenty of colour, tannin, and acidity but also a wonderful bouquet containing overripe dark fruit such as plum, and spices (e.g. white pepper). Mature Shiraz develops animal undertones with a nose of leather and Russian fur, plus sometimes the smell of freshly-roasted Mocca coffee. Drinking temperature is 16–17°C (60.8–62.6°F).

SHIRAZ/CABERNET

This is very common blend that produces a wine of intense colour with plenty of fruit and a mellow and rounded but fulsome taste. The bouquet mainly evokes thoughts of cherry and blackcurrant with a hint of pepper. Drinking temperature is 16–17°C (60.8–62.6°F).

TARRANGO

This is an interesting hybrid resulting from crossing the Portuguese Touriga and extremely productive Sultana, which is better known in its dried form. This fairly recent Australian development is causing a major revolution. People who are not accustomed to drinking wine fall for the fruity charm of the Tarrango, which can be served at almost any time if chilled. Tarrango wines have been deliberately inserted into international blind wine-tastings to cause confusion because it so closely resembles a French Beaujolais. Drinking temperature is 12–14°C (53.6–57.2°F).

Classic Cabernet-Merlot.

Superb Shiraz.

Cabernet Sauvignon-Shiraz.

Tarrango is Australia's Beaujolais.

New Zealand

Many have made their first acquaintance with New Zealand wines during the past decade. These exceptional wines with their natural elegance and considerable aromatic properties have managed to win everyone over.

New Zealand growers have remained sober and modest despite all the praise from both the media and professionals. They put their success down to the richness of their beautiful green country, which they happily call 'God's own country'. The link between man and nature in New Zealand is quite remarkable and it is as if man feels at one with nature.

This passion for the land is also to be found in the New Zealand wines where the essence of the land and the fruit are overwhelming united.

The country

New Zealand is in the south western Pacific Ocean and consists of two main islands and countless smaller ones. North Island and South Island that form the bulk of the country are between them about 1,500 km (937 miles) long and 200 km (125 miles) wide at the broadest point.

The majority of the 3,500,000 inhabitants live on North Island, in towns and cities such as Auckland, Hamilton, and Wellington. The main towns of medium size on South Island are Christchurch and Dunedin.

North Island has tempestuous volcanic origins and some volcanoes are still active, especially around Lake Taupo, where there are many geysers and hot water springs. Much of the island is mountainous with several summits above 2,500 metres (8,202 feet). The extreme north of the island has gently undulating hills. South Island is dominated by the Southern Alps, crowned by the 3,764 metre high Mount Cook. The centre of these Alps are covered with enormous glaciers and ice fields. The south-western coast is

characterised by its countless fjord-like sea inlets which were formed by glaciers. The south and east of the island is somewhat flatter and covered with thick layers of fertile alluvial soil.

The climate

The climate is fairly mild and moist with rainfall distributed across the year fairly evenly. The differences in temperature between day and night and between the seasons is insignificant, especially on North Island. Both islands suffer from wet westerly winds but the north-south alignment of the islands and the central mountain ridges means that these only affect the west. Hence twenty times as much rain falls in the west of South Island as in the east. Fortunately the average sun hours here is more than 2,000 hours per year, which is ideal for wine-growing.

History

New Zealand is a multicultural society. The original inhabitants are the Polynesian Maoris who make up 10% of the population today. They have an important place in New Zealand society. The other 90% of population that is mainly white are British, French, Greek, Yugoslav, Dutch, Indonesian, or Chinese immigrants or their descendants. The Anglican church missionaries were the first to engage themselves in growing and making wine. They were of the opinion that the Maoris must first adapt to the good aspects of civilisation before becoming Christians. They were put to work in the vineyards but it was more then twenty years before the first glass of New Zealand could be drunk. French missionaries improved the cultivation of the vines and extended them. This was taken over by English and Spanish immigrants between 1860 and 1870. The conditions at that time with fungus, plagues of insects, and earthquakes were so severe that the market for the wines was limited. Most English immigrants ignored the wine in favour of imported port and sherry.

The wine industry came under severe strain around 1900 because of social and church movements which attempted to get a prohibition on alcohol introduced. The movement towards prohibition receded after World War II and the wine industry got fresh impetus from Dalmatian immigrants among others. The demand for local wine grew because of the large influx of wine-drinking immigrants such as those from Greece, Italy, and Yugoslavia. The English immigrants now too began to value New Zealand wines. Australian wine houses such as Penfolds injected the necessary investment to create a real breakthrough. Light, mild, and fruity Müller-Thurgau wines were remarkably popular in the 1970s and during the 1980s these German vines were replaced with French varieties. The results were astonishing. New Zealand Chardonnay, Sauvignon Blanc, Gewürztraminer, Pinot Noir, Cabernet Sauvignon, and Merlot are of excellent quality and the demand

New Zealand Chardonnay.

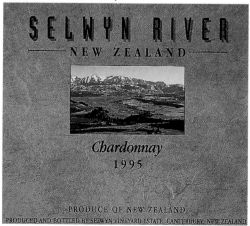

SELWYN RIVER

—— NEW ZEALAND ——

Chardonnay
1995

PRODUCE OF NEW ZEALAND
PRODUCED AND BOTTLED BY SELWYN VINEYARD ESTATE, CANTERBURY, NEW ZEALAND

for them has grown at record pace, especially in Britain. Within fifteen years New Zealand managed to become one of the great wine countries and today its wines are valued everywhere.

Wine regions

There are nine major wine regions. These are (from north to south): Northland/Auckland (the historical heart of New Zealand wine), Waikato/Bay of Plenty, Gisborne, Hawke's Bay, Wairrapa on North Island, and Nelson, Marlborough, Canterbury, en Otago on South Island. The best wines mainly originate from three main areas.

Gisborne

Gisborne is probably the best area for Chardonnay in New Zealand. The Chardonnays here are very full-bodied and rounded because of the mild climate and fertile alluvial soil.

Hawke's Bay

The oldest wineries of the country are here. The climate is very mild and the soil extremely varied, ranging from fertile alluvial soil to gravel. This explains the tremendous diversity in styles of the local wines. Hawke's Bay is mainly known for its Cabernet Sauvignon and Chardonnay wines.

Marlborough

This area is situated in the north of South Island. The finest Sauvignon Blanc wines in the world are made here but the local sparkling wine is also getting much better.

The climate is more definite here than on North Island, with plenty of sun, little rain, and fairly low temperatures. The soil is characteristically rocky with boulders, pebbles, and gravel. In addition to the wonderful Sauvignon Blanc, excellent Riesling and Chardonnay wines are also made here and very

One of New Zealand's best Chardonnays.

acceptable Pinot Noir, Cabernet Sauvignon, and Merlot reds.

The wines

New Zealand wines stand out not just because of their quality, but also their fairly high prices. The New Zealanders believe the superb quality of their wines will give them the edge and they trust in the healthy understanding of the wine world. Fortunately for them increasing numbers of wine experts have decided that the price of the best New Zealand wines is in proportion to their quality.

What is it that makes New Zealand wines so good? It is a combination of their climate but also their techniques. The traditional know-how of European wine-makers has been combined with the most modern vinification methods. But New Zealanders would not be the people they are if their wines did not reflect the same respect for nature as the people themselves. Disease and pests are dealt with by natural biological means and no industrial sugar is added. Any stabilising or preserving substances that are allowed to be added to the wine (such as sulphur and citric acid) are prescribed in law.

CHARDONNAY

New Zealand Chardonnay is made in a variety of styles, with and without cask maturing in oak, with and without additional contact with the grape skins during vinification (macération pelliculaire), and they are clearly characteristic of the area from which they come. The best Chardonnays are full-bodied and very aromatic (peach, apricot, and apple) and recognised by their fine and elegant acidity. Drinking temperature 11–14°C (51.8–57.2°F).

SAUVIGNON BLANC

The Sauvignons Blancs are among the best of the world. Nowhere else derives so much power and expressive bouquet from Sauvignon grapes. This is not a mellow Bordeaux type Sauvignon, rather closer to a top-level Sancerre with overwhelming aromas of gooseberry, flint, green pepper (paprika), asparagus,

Hawke's Bay Chardonnay.   *Marlborough Chardonnay.*

melon, or passion fruit. A New Zealand Sauvignon grabs hold of you and does not let go. Everyone who tastes it is won over by the great strength and fruitiness. Drinking temperature 10–12°C (50–53.6°F).

RIESLING

The Rieslings, especially those of the South Island, are very elegant and aromatic. Some still possess slight residual sugar (off-dry) which is very pleasing. When the Riesling grapes have been affected by botrytis, the wines are of a very rare quality that is fulsome, rich and sensual, with hints of dried fruit like apricot and also honey in the bouquet. Drinking temperature 8–10°C (46.4–50°F).

GEWÜRZTRAMINER

Although less well-known than the previously mentioned white wines, New Zealand Gewürz-

New Zealand Sauvignon Blanc.

Merlot.   *Cabernet Sauvignon.*

traminer wines are remarkably superb. They are powerful, fulsome and exotically spicy. Drinking temperature 10–12°C (50–53.6°F).

CABERNET SAUVIGNON/MERLOT/ CABERNET FRANC/MALBEC

The red wines have improved in quality immeasurably in recent years. The best of them are the Cabernet Sauvignon, Merlot, and Cabernet Franc wines, which may have been blended with a little Malbec and aged in oak casks. Although these top wines have much in common with a classic Bordeaux wine, they manage to retain a character of their own. Drinking temperature 16–17°C (60.8–62.6°F).

PINOT NOIR

Increasingly more and better Pinot Noir wines are being made, which here deliver full-bodied and rich wines that are filled with aromas.
These wines benefit from ageing for a few years in the bottle before being drunk. Drinking temperature 14–16°C (57.2–60.8°F).

SYRAH AND PINOTAGE

Finally wines have been made more recently from Syrah and Pinotage grapes. The Syrah still has some problems of adaptation but the initial results of the Pinotage are encouraging.

Fortified wines

To complete the story there are also New Zealand sherry and port type wines but these do not attain the level of the true article.

Index

Acknowledgements

It would not be possible to write such a book as this without help. I would like to thank the following organizations and people for their help with both information and illustrations for this book. In particular I would like to thank those who gave their support, understanding, and patience.

France: The French Embassy, The Hague; Sopexa (Michel, Vincent, Mathieu, Thera, Colette), The Hague; Cordier Wine and Oud & Hustinx, Haarlem, The Netherlands; Château Manos, Cadillac; CIVR Bergerac; Comte de Bosredon, Château de Bélingard, Pomport; Château Pique-Sègue, Montravel, Port-Ste Foy; Alain Brumont, Château Bouscassé, Château Montus, Maumusson; Etienne Brana, Irouléguy, St. Jean Pied de Port; Domaine Nigri, Monein; Vignerons de Tursan, Geaune; Comte de Négret, Fronton; Vignerons de Beaupuy, Marmande; Les Vins du Sud Ouest, Castanet Tolosan; Vignerons Catalans, Perpignan; La Cave de L' Abbé Rous, Banyuls; Gérard Bertran, St. André de Roquelongue; C.I. Vins du Languedoc, Narbonne; Caves Languedoc Roussillon, Montpellier; Skalli, Séte; Comte Péraldi, Corsica; Domaine d' Alzipratu, Corsica; Domaine Leccia, Corsica; Château de Fontcreuse, Cassis; Château Revelette, Côteaux d' Aix en Provence, Jouques; Guy Negrel, Mas de Cadenet, Trets; Domaine de l' Escarelle, La Celle; Cave Coopérative Clairette de Die et Crus de la Vallée du Rhône, Die; CI Vins d' AOC Côtes du Rhône et Vallée du Rhône, Avignon; Château Mont-Redon, Châteauneuf du Pape; Chapoutier, Tain l' Hermitage; J.P. & J.F. Quénard, Chignin; Vignerons Foreziens, Trelins; Rougeyron, Châteaugay; Vignerons de St-Pourçain; Georges Duboeuf, Romanèche Thorins; Joseph Drouhin, Beaune; Henri Maire, Arbois; CI Vins d' Alsace, Colmar; Georges Lorentz, Bergheim; Laroppe Côtes de Toul, Bruley; Lamé Delisle Boucard, Vins de Bourgueil, Ingrandes; Jacques Bailly, Vins de Sancerre, Bué; Château de Villeneuve, Souzay-Champigny; François Chidaine, Montlouis; Lisa Heidemanns, Vignobles Germain/Château de Fesles, Thouarce; Gérard Bigonneau, Reuilly/Quincy, Brinay; Philippe Portier, Quincy, Brinay; Veuve Amiot, Saumur; Cave du Haut-Poitou, Neuville de Poitou; Champagne De Venoge, Epernay; Champagne Taittinger, Reims.

Spain: ICEX Amsterdam/Madrid (Pilar); Vinos de España, Amsterdam; Sherry Institute of Spain (Woudine), Amsterdam; ICEX Seville (Isabel); Asociacion Exportadores de Vinos de Navarra (Conchi), Pamplona; Excal, Valladolid; Yolanda Piñero Chacón, Ribeira del Guadiana, Gijón; Jean Arnaud, Gastrovino, Tilburg; Intercaves-Koopmans & Bruinier, Zwolle; Oud & Hustinx, Haarlem; Castillo de Perelada, Amsterdam; Bodegas Antaño, Rueda; Hijos de Antonio Barcelo, Viña Mayor, Madrid; Marqués de Cáceres, Cenicero; Vinos de los Herederos del Marques de Riscal, Elciego; Bodega Julián Chivite, Cintruénigo; Señorio de Sarria, Pamplona; Bodegas Virgen Blanca, Lerin; Bodegas Guelbenzu, Cascante; Bodegas Ochoa, Olite; Bodega Ntra. Sra. del Romero, Cascante; Bodegas Fariña, Casaseca de las Chanas; Bodegas Frutos Villar, Cigales; Torremilanos, Bodegas Peñalba Lopez, Aranda de Duero; Barbadillo, Sanlœcar de Barrameda.

Portugal: Van Heijst wine importers, Hilversum; Adega Cooperativa Torres Vedras, Torres Vedras.

Italy: ICE Amsterdam; ICE Rome; Paul Blom, Schermer, Hoorn; Intercaves/Koopmans & Bruinier, Zwolle.

The Balkans: Du Frêne, Babberich; W & L Logic Sales (Slovenia), Eemnes; Koninklijke Cooijmans (Romania), Tilburg.

Greece: Aridjis, De Griekse Wijnhandel, Utrecht.

Hungary: The Hungarian Embassy, The Hague; Egervin, Eger; Euróbor, Bátaapáti; Briljant Holding, Budapest; Pince Polgár, Pince Bock, Attila Gere, and Tiffans of Villány; Hétszölö, Diznókö, and Tokaji Kereskedöhaz, Tokaj; Vylyan Winery, Szeged; Henkell & Söhnlein Hungaria, Budapest; Imperial Wijnkoperij, Regina Meij, Den Dolder.

Austria: Wines from Austria, Vienna; Regina Meij, Imperial wine merchants, Den Dolder; Spiegel Wine Importers, Amsterdam.

Switzerland: SWEA Lausanne; Marcel Dubois, Cully; André Darbellay, Bonvin, Sion; Valsangiacomo, Chiasso; Montmollin, Auvernier.

Germany: German Embassy, The Hague; The German Wine Promotion Bureau, The Hague; Deinhard, Koblenz; Oud & Hustinx, Haarlem.

Luxembourg: Bernard Massard, Grevenmacher.

United Kingdom: British Embassy, The Hague; Chiltern Valley, Henley-on-Thames; Hidden Spring, Horam; Sharpharm Vineyard, Devon.

319

South Africa: South African Embassy, The Hague; Kaapkelder, Teuge; Guy Hickling, Johannesberg

Canada: Canadian Embassy, The Hague; Fema Trading, Grave; Château des Charmes, Niagara-on-the-Lake; Klaus Reif, Niagara-on-the-Lake.

USA: American Embassy, The Hague; Wine Institute of California, Alphen a/d Rijn; Oud & Hustinx, Haarlem.

Brazil: Brazilian Trade Bureau, Den Haag; Adriano Miolo, Cidade Alta.

Uruguay: Daniel Pisano, Progreso; Ing. Javier Carrau, Castel Pujol, Gutiérrez.

Argentina: Intercaves/Koopmans & Bruinier (Trapiche), Zwolle; Ricardo Puebla, Nieto y Senetiner, Mendoza.

Chile: Pro Chile, Den Haag; Pro Chile, Milano; Intercaves/Koopmans & Bruinier, Zwolle; Jacobus Boelen, Amsterdam; Jean Arnaud, Tilburg.

Australia: The Australian Wine Bureau, London; Phil Laffer, Orlando Wyndham, Barossa Valley; Brown Brothers, Milawa/London; Intercaves/Koopmans & Bruinier, Zwolle.

New Zealand: New Zealand Embassy, The Hague; Quality Wines, Naarden.

Others: Wine Information Centre, The Hague; André Kerstens, Tilburg (and many others).

Photographs: Bert de Leeuw, Drent Fotografie, Steenstraat 56, Arnhem; Foto Willemz, Steenstraat 5, Arnhem; Foto Combi Kramer, Looierstraat 43, Arnhem.

And others who I have probably overlooked.

I also wish to personally thank the following for their tremendous inspiration and support.
Marianne & Philip Mallard (Pique-Sègue/Dauzan Lavergne), Laurent de Bosredon, Thierry Dauilhiac (Saussignac), Marie Laurence Prince Doutreloux (CIVR Bergerac), Marie Casanave (CIVR Bergerac), Georges Lorentz, Marc Chapoutier, Ben Weerdmeester, Claude & Pierre Emmanuel Taittinger, Véronique & Frédéric Drouhin, Bernard Georges (Duboeuf), Christian Duport (Val Joanis), Jean Abeille (Mont-Redon), Peter Fischer (Revelette), Guy Négrel (Mas Cadenet), Gerard Mulder (Listel, The Netherlands), Piet Rutten (Jean Arnaud), Robert Handjes (Kerstens), Dick van Baren (Oud & Hustinx), Bart Pol (Intercaves/Koopmans & Bruinier), Robbers & v/d Hoogen, Arnhem, Michel Leroux (Sopexa NL), Paul Molleman (Wine Institute of California NL), Zoltán Zilai (Magyar Szölö- és Borkultúra Alapitvány, Budapest), Peter Mosoni (Agricultural University, Gödöllö), Attila Domokos (Bátaapáti), János Arvay (Disnókö), Jószef Kurunczi (Wotan Panzió, Tórókbálint), Attila Máhr (Aranysárkány Etterem, Szentendre), Marianne Nuberg (Vinos de España NL), José Maria Fernández, ICEX Brussels, Fernando & Mercedes Chivite, Ricardo Guelbenzu Morte, Hervé Lalau, Gondola, Belgium, Robert Leenaers, Hubrecht Duijker, René van Heusden, Karel Koolhoven, Ronald de Groot, and John van de Ven (Ven Verscentrum).

Finally my thanks are due to my dear wife Jantine and to Ronan and Yannick, without whom this book would never have been completed.